Building Online Communities with Drupal, phpBB, and WordPress

Robert T. Douglass, Mike Little,
and Jared W. Smith

Apress®

Building Online Communities with Drupal, phpBB, and WordPress

ISBN-13 (pbk): 978-1-59059-562-6
ISBN-10 (pbk): 1-59059-562-9

Printed and bound in the United States of America 9 8 7 6 5 4 3 2

Lead Editor: Matt Wade
Technical Reviewers: Steve Potts, James Walker
Editorial Board: Steve Anglin, Dan Appleman, Ewan Buckingham, Gary Cornell, Tony Davis, Jason Gilmore, Jonathan Hassell, Chris Mills, Dominic Shakeshaft, Jim Sumser
Project Manager: Sofia Marchant
Copy Edit Manager: Nicole LeClerc
Copy Editor: Marilyn Smith
Assistant Production Director: Kari Brooks-Copony
Production Editor: Lori Bring
Compositor: Linda Weidemann
Proofreader: Linda Seifert
Indexer: Rebecca Plunkett
Artist: Kinetic Publishing Services, LLC
Cover Designer: Kurt Krames
Manufacturing Director: Tom Debolski

Distributed to the book trade worldwide by Springer-Verlag New York, Inc., 233 Spring Street, 6th Floor, New York, NY 10013. Phone 1-800-SPRINGER, fax 201-348-4505, e-mail `orders-ny@springer-sbm.com`, or visit `http://www.springeronline.com`.

For information on translations, please contact Apress directly at 2560 Ninth Street, Suite 219, Berkeley, CA 94710. Phone 510-549-5930, fax 510-549-5939, e-mail `info@apress.com`, or visit `http://www.apress.com`.

The source code for this book is available to readers at `http://www.apress.com` in the Source Code section.

I'm dedicating my portion of this book to my Aunt Sobeida Linder, whose inspiring spirit in the face of nearly impossible odds sets an example we can all admire and try to live up to. She personified the phrase "live life to the fullest," as she did exactly that with every day she had, good days and bad. We miss you tremendously.

Jared Smith

Contents at a Glance

Contents

PART 3 ■■■ WordPress

About the Authors

ROBERT T. DOUGLASS is a core developer and member of the security team for the Drupal project. As a leading voice in the Drupal community, he works hard to introduce new programmers and webmasters to the joys of building web sites with Drupal. To this end, Robert headed Drupal's involvement in the Google Summer of Code, 2005. Robert is a freelance Drupal consultant and programmer, working out of his home in Germany.

MIKE LITTLE is one of the founders of the WordPress project and is still an occasional contributing developer. He wrote his first computer program over 26 years ago. He has been programming professionally for more than 15 years in a variety of languages, including PHP, Java, JSP, Perl, C, and assembler. He first encountered the Web in 1993 and has been fiddling with it ever since.

When he is not tapping away at a keyboard, he likes to read—mostly science fiction, fantasy, biographies, and the odd technical book. He listens to music as much as possible.

JARED W. SMITH started his foray into message board communities at the increasingly less tender age of 15, when he first participated in various message boards on the Web. He particularly was amazed at the layout of the Ultimate Bulletin Board (UBB), Infopop's groundbreaking community solution, and he decided he must give a UBB-based community a shot on his own site. Of course, most 15-year-olds don't have $160 to shell out at a whim. It was at this time that Jared stumbled over phpBB 1.0.0, which, sure enough, was a free message board solution that looked—gasp!—just like UBB!

Immediately, Jared became intrigued with the product. The easy installation amazed him, and he loved the speed. There was a problem though: the first editions of the board weren't that great looking. The borders were too thick on the edges, the fonts were too small, no CSS was used, and so on, but no matter. He dove into the code and totally reworked the design for his now-defunct Windows support site, WindowsLaunchpad.com. Jared learned a lot from that experience and proceeded to begin writing and releasing modifications such as the Anchor Hack, which returned users to the last post in a thread after they posted, and an enhanced version of another Who's Online hack, which he optimized for performance and redesigned to present the information in a clearer format. His work, including work with the phpBB 2.0.*x* series, earned him multiple accolades such as "phpBB of the Month" at phpBBHacks.com, where he was one of the original support team members and now serves as an advisor to the webmaster.

Presently, Jared blogs about a variety of topics at `www.jaredwsmith.com` (using WordPress, no less), and in the very near future, he will be maintaining a phpBB board there as well. In his scarce spare time, Jared has fun being lousy at first-person shooter-style games, goes canoeing with his friends in the summer, and is the most unlikely sports buff you may ever meet. He presently resides in beautiful downtown Charleston, South Carolina, with a friend and the best kitty ever, Penelope.

About the Technical Reviewers

STEVE POTTS graduated from Manchester University with a Bachelor's degree in Applied Computing, and then went on to pursue a Master's degree at the Open University in Computing for Commerce and Industry.

Even before his start in higher education, he was working hard in the defense industry to squeeze an immense amount of failure-resistant software into what was such a remarkably small footprint that digital watches would find it miniature now.

Given his obvious disposition for being meticulous (his friends have other words to describe this), he is an accomplished technical editor who has worked on Java, XHTML, PHP, and Wireless publications, including the award-winning "Son of Web Pages That Suck."

His work to date has involved hundreds of applications in defense, handheld devices, smartphones, mobile Internet, and the Web.

Steve is founder of his technical consultancy outfit Free Balloon, and he holds the rewarding position of CTO at Hawdale Associates, an invigorating usability and design customer experience company operating out of Manchester, England.

JAMES WALKER is a founder and lead developer at Bryght, a Vancouver-based company offering Drupal hosting and services. He is also an active member of the Drupal community, having made several core contributions over the past three years. He also maintains nine contributed modules and advises on the security team. When not promoting Drupal world domination, he enjoys spending time with his wife and two children.

Acknowledgments

I have many people to thank for the keen insight and thoughtful support that was given to me while writing about Drupal. First, the fantastic Apress team, for great support at all stages of writing. Then, James Walker, my technical editor, not only for making sure that what I was writing was true, but also for deepening my understanding of Drupal and for always knowing the best way to present any idea or concept. Then, to the Drupal community, including Dries Buytaert, Steven Wittens, Morbus Iff, and so many others who suffered through early drafts and helped me focus my ideas and writing. Finally, to my wife Kimiko, who helped me get to a place where I could undertake this project and stood by me throughout the entire process.

Robert Douglass

I would like to thank Matt Mullenweg for his passion and dedication to all things WordPress. Without Matt, WordPress would not be the fantastic product it is. Thanks also go to Michel for starting b2, to Ryan and all the developers for continually improving a great product, to Podz and the fantastic support team, and to Lorelle and the great documentation team. WordPress is enriched by its community; I cannot name you all, but you know who you are. Thanks to Chris (c3ro) for allowing me to use his theme as a starting point in Chapter 16. Thanks to all the great developers and designers who have released plug-ins and themes for WordPress. Without those, I would have had a lot less to write about. Special thanks to Steve Potts for moral as well as technical support.

Mike Little

The cast of characters that drive me to do what I love to do is immense, and could take up a book in and of itself. First off, I must thank the phpBB Group members, who are responsible for writing the phpBB software. Without them, I might not have gotten into so many technologies that have advanced my primary hobby, not to mention I wouldn't be writing this right now. Patrick O'Keefe of phpBBHacks.com continues to be instrumental in giving me a stage to show the world what I can do, and I directly credit him for helping me be successful in the phpBB arena. I must also thank my parents, who for years put up with me running into the room screaming "Check out this hack I just wrote!" or "Look at my rounded post entries!" I must especially thank my dad, Jerry, for telling my mom it's perfectly fine for me to be working on my projects instead of being out on the streets doing God-knows-what. Matt Owen, formerly of the *Post and Courier* in Charleston, SC, brought me my 15 minutes of fame and dramatically increased my traffic, and helped solidify my position as a proud Internet geek long before it was cool. I also must thank CR4CK1NT0SH for breaking into WindowsLaunchpad.com one night, as he taught me just how important it is to be on the ball with security updates. Additional thanks go to Brad, who has always been there as my Number Two man (and vice versa!) in my myriad of community ventures; Chris, for ultimately being right about the importance of learning HTML and ditching FrontPage; Sam, Nick, Derick, Phillip C., Philip K., *et. al.* for providing such lively discussion, past and present, on my communities no matter how much I move them around or tweak them; and all the girls I crushed on in high school. For some reason, I thought my phpBB skills would impress you. ☺

Jared Smith

Introduction

Building an online community can be a daunting task. Countless different applications are available for you to use as the foundation of your community. When I first envisioned this book, I saw that online communities were primarily based on three different types of applications: content management systems, bulletin boards, and blogs. I then found three open-source applications that fit into these categories that I believe are at the top of their class. Let's take a closer look at each of the categories and the selected application.

A content management system, or CMS, is an application that can be used to deal with various methods of web publishing. A CMS can generally be customized by adding or removing specific features, so that the end result is only those features that you want for your community. Features included with a CMS can include file management, photo galleries, private messaging, discussion forums, articles, polls, and much more. Many online newspapers, magazines, and other news sources use a CMS for their web presence. You've probably been a user of a CMS without even realizing it. An extremely popular web site built around a CMS is `http://slashdot.org/`. In the first portion of this book, Robert Douglass will teach you about the CMS named Drupal. You can find the official web site for Drupal at `http://www.drupal.org/`.

Bulletin boards, also known as forums, are a medium in which users can post messages and reply to those already posted. Bulletin boards are a great medium for creating a community where users interact to help each other out with a particular subject, or just to discuss common interests. Bulletin boards exist across the Internet, discussing everything from automobile repair to web hosting. Today's bulletin boards allow you to have customizable user profiles, embed images in your posts, generate polls, and host private and public forums, just to name a few features. In the second section of the book, Jared Smith will cover everything you need to know to get started with the phpBB bulletin board package. You can find the official web site for the phpBB project at `http://www.phpbb.com/`.

Blogs have emerged in the last few years to become a very strong player in the online community arena. Blogs are generally sites that express a single person's views about life, politics, a particular hobby, or anything in between. Companies have been hiring professional bloggers to do nothing but blog about things happening at their company and help generate a "buzz" around the company. The user interaction in blogs comes from comments, which users can leave on each blog post, and TrackBacks, which enable other blog owners to link their blog posts to yours. In the final section of the book, Mike Little will explain how to set up your own blog using WordPress. The official site for WordPress can be found at `http://www.wordpress.org/`.

I know that you will find this book to be a valuable resource in choosing and using the application that is right for your community. If you create a great community based on the information in this book, I'd love to hear about it!

Matt Wade, Editor (`matt@apress.com`)

PART 1

Drupal

CHAPTER 1

Introducing Drupal

This chapter will introduce you to Drupal, walk you through the installation process, and provide a shotgun tour of the basic functionality. By the end of this chapter, you will be well on your way to making a dynamic web site to be the center of your online community. Let's begin with a couple basic questions, which have multiple answers.

What Is Drupal?

Drupal is a set of scripts written in PHP that provide the framework and basic functionality for building feature-rich and dynamic web sites. It is a content management system (CMS), because it greatly simplifies the process of authoring, managing, and publishing content—such as text, images, files, and audio—to the Web. It is a forum, a blogging tool, and an organizer of information. It is an extensible platform on which you can build custom modules, and it is a set of programming APIs that allows web developers to create custom web applications very rapidly and efficiently.

Drupal is also a vibrant online community with thousands of enthusiastic people from around the world. This community spans the `Drupal.org` site, several mailing lists, user groups in various countries, a number of nonprofit organizations, some small companies, and a growing army of freelancers who earn their living partially or completely from using or developing Drupal. The community has events, often coinciding with major conferences, and is an excellent example of massively distributed cooperation.

Who Should Use Drupal?

Drupal is for anyone who wants to have a web site that is well suited for (but not limited to) multiuser communities. Drupal is for bloggers who want more than just a blog, groups who need to cooperate online, activists who want to spread a message, educators who want to provide online learning tools, artists who want to share media online, businesses or individuals who want to sell goods online, and programmers who want to work with a platform that is extensible, clean, efficient, and well architected.

Developers find Drupal very easy to customize and extend. Drupal departs from some of the conventions and techniques of the past, and is therefore for anyone who is eager to learn or who is investigating modern best practices for web application building. Drupal is for anyone who is investing their efforts for the long-term payoff and has the patience to cope with a system that is sometimes admittedly complex.

Drupal is not for those who want a blog, want it now, and don't need any other features. Those people should choose a free online service like Blogger.

Installing Drupal

This section will walk you through the steps of installing Drupal, including evaluating the requirements, downloading the correct files, creating the database, and importing the database definition. Here is an overview of the steps:

1. Get the Drupal download from `Drupal.org`.
2. Create a database for your Drupal site. Supported database management systems are MySQL, MySQLi, and PostgreSQL.
3. Import the database definition from the `database/database.xxsql` file that comes with the Drupal download.
4. Move the Drupal files to the web server.
5. Adjust the values for `$db_url` and `$base_url` in the appropriate `settings.php` file.
6. Access your Drupal site with the value given for `$base_url`.

I'll explain each of these steps in detail in the following sections. But before you can install Drupal, you need to make sure that your system meets its requirements.

Meeting Drupal Requirements

The most common configuration for running Drupal is on an Apache web server with PHP 4 and a MySQL database. Drupal can run on other web servers, with other versions of PHP (PHP 5), and with other databases, but the Apache/PHP/MySQL combination is still the most tested and trustworthy. Here are the specific requirements.

Web Server

You need a web server that can execute PHP scripts. The Apache server is the overwhelming first choice for most of the people currently running Drupal. Drupal's core distribution is always tested with the latest 1.3.*x* version of Apache, but Drupal is known to work with the 2.0.*x* versions as well. Less common, but also supported, is the use of the Microsoft Internet Information Services (IIS) server. (For more information about running Drupal with the Windows IIS server, see `http://drupal.org/node/3854` and `http://drupal.org/node/940`.)

PHP

Drupal requires the 4.3.3 or greater version of PHP. Drupal is PHP 5-compatible.

PHP Extensions

When configuring PHP or choosing hosting, you need to make sure that the following PHP extensions are available:

- The PHP extension for the database you wish to use (MySQL, MySQLi, or PostgreSQL) is required.
- The PHP XML extension. It is enabled by default in a standard PHP installation. The Windows version of PHP has built-in support for this extension.

- The PHP `mbstring` extension is required to support Drupal in handling text in the UTF-8 character encoding format (Unicode).
- In order for Drupal to be able to manipulate images (such as for making thumbnails), you need to have a PHP extension to support it. You can use either the GD library (included with PHP `http://www.php.net/gd/`) or ImageMagick (`http://www.imagemagick.org/`).

PHP Directives

Drupal requires PHP to be configured with the following specific directives in order to function correctly:

- `session.save_handler`: `user`
- `session.cache_limiter`: `none`
- `memory_limit`: `24M` (recommended)

The `24M` memory limit is the upper limit of what will ever be used; the average usage is much lower. However, PHP's default limit of `8M` is too low for some Drupal operations and will cause problems.

You can configure these directives directly in the `php.ini` file, or if you are using an Apache web server, through the `.htaccess` file (included with the Drupal installation). Setting the directives using an `.htaccess` file also requires that the Apache web server be configured to allow this (see the `AllowOverride` directive for Apache at `http://apache-server.com/tutorials/ATusing-htaccess.html`). PHP will also need to be installed as an Apache module for `.htaccess` support.

Database Server

Drupal requires a SQL database server that is supported by PHP. The recommended server is MySQL, version 3.23.17 or later, including MySQL 4.*x*. Drupal now supports the PHP MySQLi extension (`http://php.net/mysqli`), as well.

PostgreSQL 7.4 and higher is officially supported and maintained for the core Drupal installation. The level of support that is given to PostgreSQL among the contributed modules is less consistent. If you choose to run Drupal on PostgreSQL, you may find yourself in the position of tweaking the SQL scripts used to create database schemas for contributed modules in order to make them compatible with your database server.

Mail Server

Many of Drupal's features, including user registration, depend on the server's ability to send e-mail. Your web server needs to have a mail server available for these functions to work. Drupal uses PHP's `mail()` function to send e-mail (see `http://php.net/mail`). These two `php.ini` directives are needed to support mail:

```
SMTP = localhost
smtp_port = 25
```

Fortunately, this is par for the course for professional LAMP (Linux, Apache, MySQL, and PHP) hosting services, and you will rarely need to worry about this when installing Drupal.

Obtaining Drupal

You can download the latest Drupal releases from `http://drupal.org/project`. Place the files in the download package somewhere in the document root of the web server. They can be either at the top level or in a subdirectory. If you are running other web applications on the same server in the same document root, putting Drupal in a subdirectory is the better choice.

For GNU/Linux users, the quickest way to get Drupal onto your server is to open a shell and use the `wget` tool to download the Drupal archive directly from `Drupal.org`. You can then unpack the archive using the `tar` command:

```
wget http://drupal.org/files/projects/drupal-x.x.x.tar.gz
tar -zxvf drupal-x.x.x.tar.gz
```

Alternatively, use a File Transfer Protocol (FTP) or Secure Copy Protocol (SCP) client to move the archive from your local machine to the web server and unpack it into the web directory.

Setting Up the Database

Drupal does not create the database for you. For this, you will need to become familiar with the tools provided by the database management system that you have chosen to use. For MySQL, the PHP-based web application phpMyAdmin (`http://sourceforge.net/projects/phpmyadmin/`) is popular. For PostgreSQL, phpPgAdmin (`http://sourceforge.net/projects/phppgadmin/`) is a common choice. Both are often included as standard fare by web hosting companies selling hosting packages.

■ **Note** All of the examples for working with the database server in this chapter are MySQL-specific.

No matter which database manager you choose, you need to take the following steps to prepare the database for use by Drupal.

Create the database: It is not particularly important what you name the database. It is important that you know what the name is. Some hosts will prefix the name you provide. Similarly, some web hosts will truncate the name to fit into a certain number of characters. So, make sure to double-check what the database is actually called, because you will need to know this when you're configuring Drupal.

Create the database user and assign rights: Access to any database is granted on a database-user basis. Do not use the root user or the database admin user to access your database, as this presents a security risk. Instead, you need to create a user who has permissions to access the Drupal database. This can usually be done with the same tools that you used to create the database. Create the user account and grant it `SELECT`, `INSERT`, `UPDATE`, `DELETE`, `CREATE`, and `LOCK TABLES` privileges. If you're using a command-line tool, don't forget to use `FLUSH PRIVILEGES` as well.

Import the schema: Once the database is created and a user is assigned, with the appropriate privileges, it is time to import the schema for the core Drupal database. The SQL instructions to do this are found in the database/database.mysql and database.pgsql files that come with your Drupal distribution. In order to import the schema, execute the instructions in the file appropriate to your database. There are command-line methods for doing this, and the database management tools mentioned earlier can help you do this as well.

As an example, let's go through the GNU/Linux command-line versions of these steps for a MySQL database. First, create the database:

```
$ mysqladmin -u db_user -p create db_name
```

db_user is an existing MySQL user who has the rights to create databases. This will often be root. The db_name is the name of the database you wish to create.

You also need a database user who is allowed to connect to the database you just created. This might be the db_user from the previous command, in which case you can skip this step. Otherwise, to create a new database user, connect to the MySQL server as root and use GRANT to create a new user:

```
$ mysql -u root -p
mysql> GRANT SELECT,INSERT,UPDATE,DELETE,CREATE,LOCK TABLES➥
ON db_name.* ➥
TO 'db_user'@'localhost' ➥
IDENTIFIED BY 'password';
```

db_name is the database name, db_user is the name this new user will have, and password is the password that will be used when making a database connection. This example assumes that the user will be accessing the database only from the current machine, or localhost. Replace localhost with the appropriate domain or IP address if the connection will be made to a different machine.

Finally, import the database schema from the database/database.mysql file that came with the Drupal distribution:

```
$ mysql -u db_user -p db_name < database/database.mysql
```

Setting the Database and Base URLs

Now you must edit the sites/default/settings.php file that is part of the Drupal installation you downloaded from Drupal.org. You must give values to the database URL ($db_url) and the base URL ($base_url) variables. The database URL is the single most important configuration setting that you are asked to make while installing Drupal. You need four pieces of information to do it correctly:

- The database management system you are using; MySQL, MySQLi, or PostgreSQL
- The name of the database
- The name of the database user
- The database user's password

Once you have these four pieces of information, you can begin to set the database URL. Find the section in settings.php where the database URL is set:

```
 * Database URL format:
 * $db_url = 'mysql://username:password@localhost/database';
 * $db_url = 'mysqli://username:password@localhost/database';
 * $db_url = 'pgsql://username:password@localhost/database';
 */
$db_url = 'mysql://username:password@localhost/database';
```

Pick the variant that applies to your database. By default, MySQL is given as the suggested example, and all the supported systems are given as examples in the comments. Next, replace username in the URL with the name of the database user, replace password with the database user's password, and replace database with the name of your database. In some cases, if the web server and the database server are running on different machines or have different domains or IP addresses, you will need to replace localhost with the name of the host on which the database is running.

With the database URL set, the second task in settings.php is to set the $base_url variable. The $base_url variable is used to make all of the relative paths on your Drupal site into absolute URLs. As such, it is essential for the site to work. The $base_url variable is composed of the domain of your site (http://your.domain.com) plus the path to the subdirectory where you installed Drupal, (/sub/directory). Here is the section of settings.php where $base_url is set:

```
/**
 * Base URL:
 *
 * The URL of your website's main page. It is not allowed to have
 * a trailing slash; Drupal will add it for you.
 */
$base_url = 'http://localhost';
```

The following are some examples of valid $base_url settings:

```
$base_url = 'http://www.somesite.com';
$base_url = 'http://subdomain.othersite.net';
```

These examples are fine if you installed Drupal directly at the top of the document root. If you installed Drupal in a subdirectory, the $base_url setting will look like this:

```
$base_url= 'http://your.domain.com/sub/directory';
```

Never add a forward slash at the end. These $base_url values are wrong:

```
$base_url = 'http://your.domain.com/';                 // Wrong!
$base_url = 'http://your.domain.com/sub/directory/';   // Wrong!
```

Accessing the Drupal Site

To access the Drupal site, open your browser and navigate to the value that you set for the $base_url. If you've done everything correctly, you'll see the screen shown in Figure 1-1.

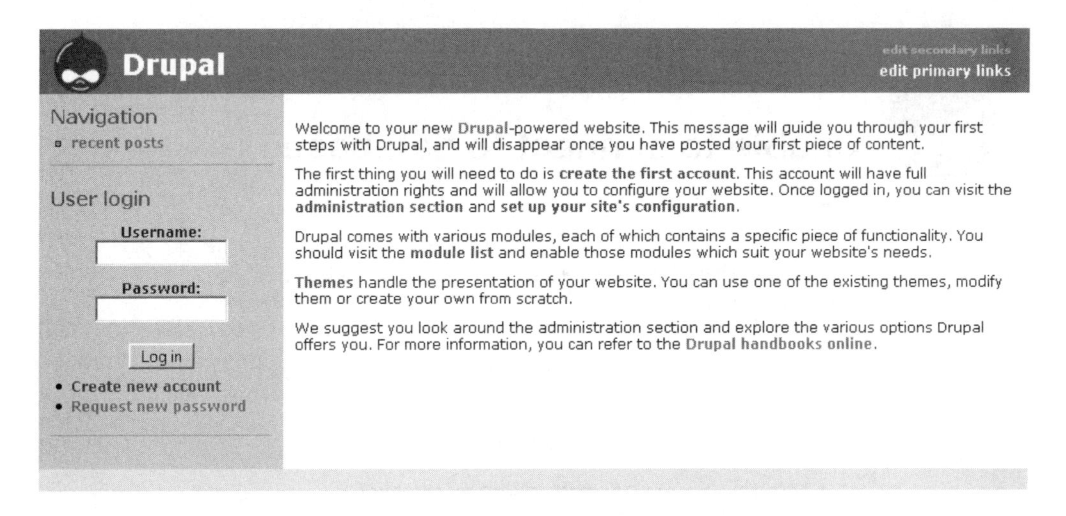

Figure 1-1. *Drupal, freshly installed*

Troubleshooting Installation Problems

The most common problems that people have when installing Drupal include not being able to connect to the database server and an incorrect base URL.

Unable to Connect to the Database Server

If you see the message shown in Figure 1-2, you need to review your database configuration and the value that you entered for the database URL. As the message indicates, Drupal is not able to connect to the database server.

Here is a list of things to check to solve this problem:

- Is the database server running?
- Did you create a database for your Drupal site?
- Did you create a database user for the Drupal database?
- Are the username, password, and database name correctly entered for the `$db_url` variable in the `settings.php` file?
- If the database server is running on a server other than `localhost`, is the host entered correctly in the `$db_url` variable in `settings.php`?
- Are you using the correct database connection type for your database server? MySQL should use `mysql://`, MySQLi should use `mysqli://`, and PostgreSQL should use `pgsql://`.

Unable to connect to database server
This either means that the username and password information in your settings.php file is incorrect or we can't contact the MySQL database server. This could mean your hosting provider's database server is down.
The MySQL error was: Access denied for user 'xxxx'@'localhost' (using password: YES).
Currently, the username is xxxx and the database server is localhost.
Are you sure you have the correct username and password?
Are you sure that you have typed the correct hostname?
Are you sure that the database server is running?
For more help, see the Installation and upgrading handbook. If you are unsure what these terms mean you should probably contact your hosting provider.

Figure 1-2. *Drupal cannot connect to your database server.*

An alternate cause of Drupal not being able to connect to the database is that the version of PHP being used doesn't have the requisite database extension activated. PHP needs special libraries to connect to different database servers from different vendors. To diagnose whether this is preventing the database connection from being made, consult the details of a `phpinfo();` page and look for the section corresponding to your database.

■ **Tip** `phpinfo()` is a PHP function that "Outputs lots of PHP information" (`http://php.net/phpinfo`). It is very useful for assessing whether PHP is installed correctly and whether the appropriate directives and settings to support Drupal are in place. To execute `phpinfo()`, place a file in your document root named `phpinfo.php` with the following line: <?php phpinfo(); ?>. Request the file from the server with your browser to see the information.

Incorrect $base_url

If your site appears as shown in Figure 1-3, without the Drupal icon and the pretty shades of blue, and if all of the links lead to Page Not Found errors, the culprit is likely the `$base_url` variable in `settings.php`. Correct that setting, and your site should work.

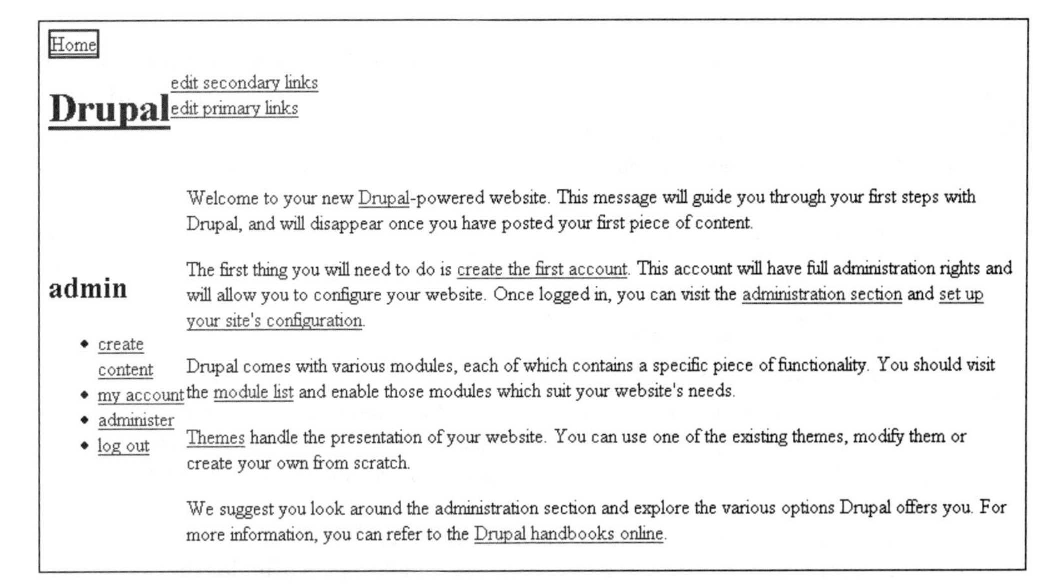

Figure 1-3. *Setting the $base_url incorrectly results in this display.*

Creating the First User

The very first step once you arrive intact at the initial screen is to make the administer (admin) user. The admin user is the user whose ID number is 1, and who has "superuser" rights to administer the entire site.

■ Note Creating the first Drupal user is a critical step in the installation. The first user has superuser privileges and is the account that will be used to configure and administer the site. Make sure to complete this step immediately, and keep track of the username and password details.

To create the admin user, click the *create first account* link. You will be asked for the username and e-mail address of this user. When you provide this information and click Submit, Drupal will attempt to send a message to the e-mail address you provided. The e-mail will contain the randomly generated password for your admin user account. This password will also be displayed on the screen. Write down (or copy) this password, in case something goes wrong in the following steps (if you close your browser at an untimely moment, for example).

Drupal will also display a button that says Log in. Click this button now to log in as the administrator. You will be taken to the admin user's details page, where you can set some user preferences for the account. The important step you should take now is to change your password. Then you can ignore the e-mail that Drupal sent to you with the random password.

■ **Note** If you are setting up a site on your local Windows machine, it is likely that an error will be displayed at the point when Drupal tried to send an e-mail to the administrator's account. The error results from the fact that PHP isn't able to find an installed and configured mail server on your machine. This will be the common experience for people who are installing Drupal on their local machine running Windows, since it is somewhat unusual to run mail servers on your workstation.

Creating the files Directory

Drupal needs a place to store uploaded files. These files range from user pictures, to files attached to postings, to images and music files. These are all typically stored in a folder in the root Drupal installation called `files` and a subdirectory therein called `pictures`. If these directories don't exist, Drupal will create them for you. If you are installing Drupal on Windows, all is fine, and you can skip this section.

If you are installing Drupal on a flavor of *nix (a UNIX or Linux system), you will want to take an extra moment now to create the directories manually. The reason for this is that the `files` directory is the one place where web site users will be able to interact directly with the file system on your server; this is where their uploaded files will be stored. You therefore want to pay special attention to the permissions of this directory. Letting Drupal create the directory for you may not result in the best configuration, and may not even be possible, depending on how your system is configured.

The first step to creating the `files` directory with the optimal permissions is to determine the username of the web server process. To find out what user the Apache web server is running as, look in the `httpd.conf` file, which is responsible for the Apache configuration. There you will find an entry like this (from Debian 3.1):

```
User www-data
```

The actual name of the user depends on the operating system and distribution. Other common names for the user include `wwwrun`, `www`, `apache`, and `wwwuser`.

■ **Note** Some Apache servers run using suPHP (`http://www.suphp.org/`), and others are run as a CGI module. In both of these cases, the name of the process running the web server will be different. If you are unsure, contact your hosting service.

Once you know the username of the web server, you can create the `files` directory:

```
$ mkdir files
$ mkdir files/pictures
```

Change the permissions so that the user is the web server and the group is a user group to which any of the developers working on your site will belong. I'll call the web server `www-data` and the users' group `developers`:

```
$ chown -R www-data:developers files
```

Finally, make sure that these directories have the proper permissions:

```
$chmod -R 755 files
```

Using Other Installation Methods

It isn't always necessary to install Drupal by hand. Depending on your hosting company, the operating system of your server, and the Drupal distribution that you have chosen, many tools are available to aid in the installation process or eliminate it altogether.

CivicSpace

An alternative to installing Drupal completely manually is to download and use CivicSpace (available from CivicSpace Labs, at `http://civicspacelabs.org`). CivicSpace is a distribution of Drupal that packs many useful modules together and helps you to install and configure them. Almost everything distributed with CivicSpace can be found at `Drupal.org`, so the information in this book applies to CivicSpace as well as Drupal.

The CivicSpace installation script takes care of some of the initial user creation, database connection, and configuration tasks, as shown in Figure 1-4. You will still need to manually create the database and database user, as well as assign the user rights.

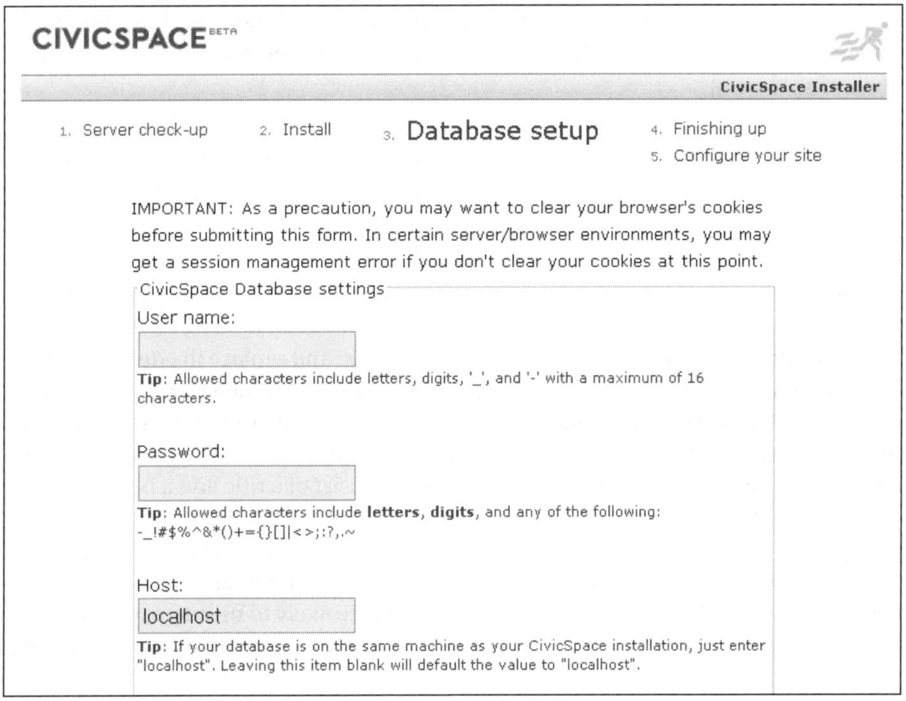

Figure 1-4. *The CivicSpace installer*

Fantastico and Debian

Two options for completely automated installations of Drupal include Fantastico (offered by many web hosts) and the Debian operating system. Fantastico is a set of scripts to install web applications (such as Drupal) on a server, and Debian is a GNU/Linux distribution that allows you to install Drupal using the `apt-get` tool, which installs and updates Debian packages. If you're using one of these tools, make sure to check that they are installing the latest stable version of Drupal, or you risk missing out on features and security measures.

Managed Drupal Services

If you don't want to mess with the hosting and installation aspects of Drupal, Bryght (`http://www.bryght.com/`) is a company that offers turnkey managed Drupal hosting. You sign up for this service and get access to a completely installed Drupal site. The service takes responsibility for upgrades, compatibility of modules, security issues, and stability of the servers, leaving you with the task of creating your online community using Drupal. You can even use your account as a reseller platform, selling further Drupal installations to your clients.

Creating Drupal Content

In Drupal, there is a concept of a front page, which will be the page shown whenever your site is accessed with the value that you gave as the `$base_url`, with no further path information. At the moment, with your freshly installed Drupal site that has no content, this front page will show the following message:

> *Welcome to your new Drupal-powered website. This message will guide you through your first steps with Drupal, and will disappear once you have posted your first piece of content.*

As it states, this message will no longer appear as soon as you add some content to your site. So let's do that now!

The content you create will be promoted to the front page and replace the default message. This is Drupal's default behavior (you will see how to modify this behavior in Chapter 2).

Drupal has two types of content enabled by default, and several other types that can easily be turned on. The two default content types are *pages* and *stories*. These two content types represent the most basic form of content in Drupal. Both consist of a title and a body used for the main content. Pages have an extra Log message field, which is intended to be used by the author to keep notes or comments about the content being created. Pages are the Drupal equivalent of static pages for brochure sites. Stories can be used for content on news sites or for journals where content is created regularly, and visitors are likely to be interested in the latest news. You might also create stories if you want to use Drupal as a single-user blogging site.

Adding a News Story

To add a news story to your new site, click the *create content* link in the main navigation menu. This will bring you to a page that lists all of the various content types that can be created. By default, the choices are page and story types.

Click the *story* link to create a new story. Give the story a title, write some text in the Body field, and click Preview to see what it will look like when published. Keep editing the text and previewing it until you are satisfied, and then click Submit.

When you click Submit, the story is saved to the database and published. In Chapter 2, you will see how to change the workflow so that content isn't published immediately. By default, Drupal allows you to use only a restricted set of HTML tags in the text. This is a function of the filter system, which is also covered in Chapter 2.

Congratulations, you've just created content with Drupal! Figure 1-5 shows an example of a test story.

Notice the two tabs on the story page: View and Edit. These appear only to people who have permission to edit the story, which by default is the superuser (user 1) or the person who created it. If you click the Edit tab, you can edit the story, or even delete it. If you log out and view the story as an anonymous user, the View and Edit tabs will no longer appear.

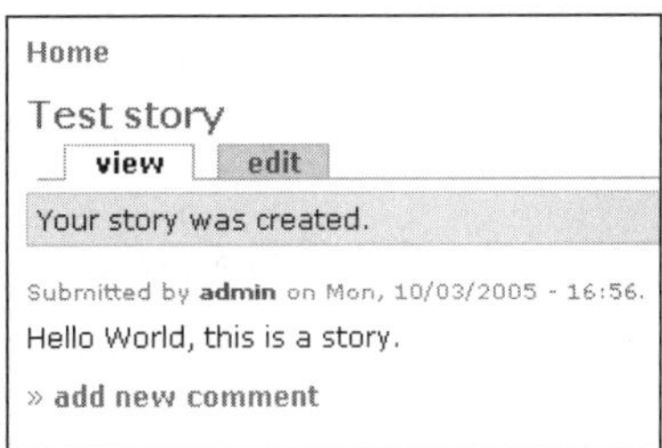

Figure 1-5. *Viewing a new story*

You will also notice that you can add comments to this story. Once again, this is the default configuration. Chapter 2 describes how to turn off the comments for either a single post or for an entire comment type.

Changing the Front Page

Now let's look at the site's front page again. Click the Drupal icon or the *Home* link to return to the front page. Instead of the default message introducing you to your new site, you see a view of the story you just created. If you entered longer text for the body of the story, it will have been shortened on the front page. The shortened view of a post in Drupal is called a *teaser*.

The front page is a listing of recent content that has been added to your site. If you add several more stories or pages, they will all be listed on the front page in reverse chronological order, from newest to oldest.

With Drupal, you can control what content should be used as the front page. While the default system of showing a list of recent content will work for some sites, others will want to have a "Welcome" type front page. You can make a page like this by clicking *create content* and creating a page that you intend to be used as the front page. Alternatively, click the link to one of the stories that you've already created if you would like it to be the front page. Once you have completed the page and are looking at the final product, note the URL for the page. It will look something like this:

```
http://www.yoursite.com/?q=node/7
```

You might have noticed already that all the individual postings have URLs that are similar to this. The first one you made is `node/1`, the second is `node/2`, and so forth. Determine which `node` number you just created—the one you intend to be the new front page. Perhaps it is `node/7`, as in the example here. If so, Drupal considers the path to that page to be `node/7`. This is the part that you will need to know, so make a note of it.

Now navigate to *administer ➤ settings*. This is the site settings page (covered in depth in Chapter 2). Here, you can tell Drupal which path to use as the front page. In the General Settings group, find the Default Front Page field. It has the value node, which to Drupal means a list of recent content. Change that to whatever posting number you created to be the front page (node/7 in the previous example), and then click the Submit button at the bottom of the site settings page. If you visit the front page now, it will show the page that you made.

Touring Drupal's Features

This section will guide you through some of Drupal's features, just to get your feet wet. All of these items will be revisited and discussed in detail in the following chapters.

Introducing Themes

Drupal takes great care to keep the elements of content and its presentation of a site separate. This allows you to come up with multiple designs for the same content. These designs are called *themes*. Each theme can consist of one or more files that work together to present the content of your site in a unique way. Drupal has four themes available as part of the core download, and many more available in the contributions repository on Drupal.org.

To see themes in action, navigate to *administer ➤ themes*. This page presents a list of all the installed themes. You can enable them individually by checking the Enabled check box, and you can choose one to be the default theme. Drupal allows registered users to choose which theme to use from among the enabled themes. That user will then experience the site in the theme of their choice. If you want your site to be viewed in only one theme at all times, leave only one theme enabled.

Try enabling the Pushbutton theme and setting it as the default, and then click Save Configuration. Your front page should now look something like Figure 1-6.

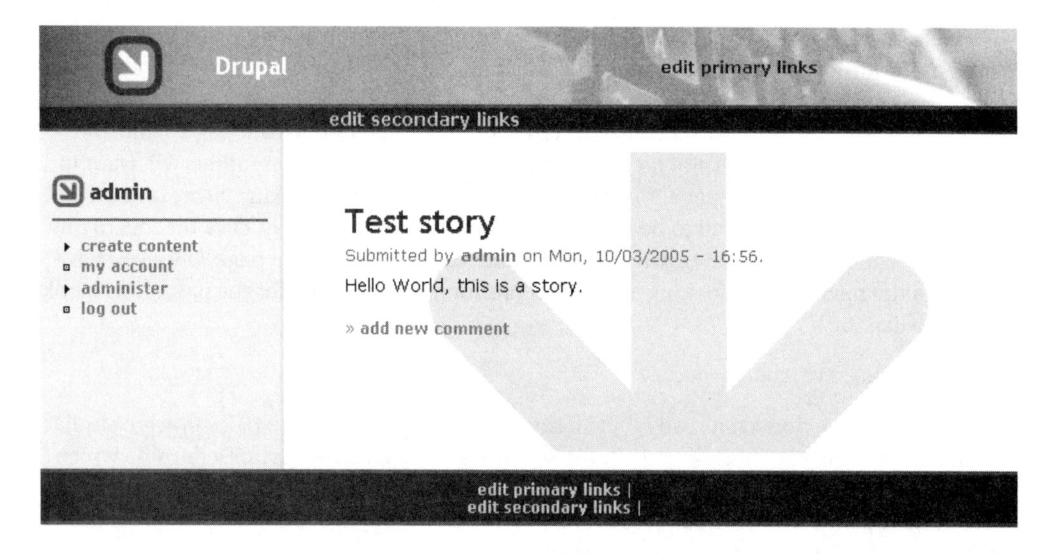

Figure 1-6. *The Pushbutton theme*

Introducing Blocks

A *block* is a unit of content that you can place in the various regions of the layout. Blocks can do many different things. The login fields and the main navigation menu are each blocks, for example.

To see the list of available blocks, navigate to *administer* ➤ *blocks*. The table on the blocks page lists all of the available blocks by region, or under Disabled for those blocks that are not yet turned on. You can enable any of the disabled blocks by checking the Enabled check box and clicking Save Blocks. You can also change the region of the screen where they appear. You have the choice of right or left sidebar, header, footer, or content. Feel free to try moving blocks around and turning them on or off.

Tip If you disable the user login block and get logged out, you will need to use the following URL to get to the login screen: `http://www.yoursite.com/?q=user`. If you disable the navigation block and are left wondering how you'll ever get back to the block administration page to turn it back on, don't despair—here's the URL: `http://www.yoursite.com/?q=admin/block`.

Blocks are generally provided by modules, which means that as you enable or install more modules, more blocks will be available. Make sure to visit the block administration page whenever you enable a new module to see what it has to offer.

Introducing Modules

A fresh installation of Drupal has only a small fraction of the available functionality enabled. The most common way to enhance Drupal and add functionality is through *modules*. Drupal comes with more than 30 modules installed, but most of them are disabled by default.

To see a list of available modules, navigate to *administer* ➤ *modules*. All of the modules listed on this page correspond to individual files in the `/modules` directory in your Drupal installation. You can enable them simply by checking the Enable check box and clicking Save Configuration. I describe each of these core modules in detail in Chapter 3. I highly recommend trying them all out, one by one! To get you started, Exercise 1-1 demonstrates how to use the Menu module.

Exercise 1-1. Build a Custom Menu

A common question for people unaccustomed to working with Drupal is, "How do I make a custom navigation menu that links to pages I choose?" This exercise shows you how to do just that.

1. Select *administer* ➤ *modules*. On the module administration page, enable the Menu module.
2. Select *administer* ➤ *menus* and click the Add Menu tab.
3. On the Add Menu page, give your menu a name (for example, **Custom Menu**), and then click Submit.

4. Select *administer* ➤ *blocks*. On the block administration page, enable the block for the menu you just added (for example, the Custom Menu block), and pick the region where it is to appear. Click Save Blocks.

5. Click *create content*. Choose a content type to create as a test; page is a good choice. Choose a title for the new content and write some text in the Body field.

6. At the bottom of the content-creation form, click the Menu Item Settings link to expand the options. These settings will create a link in your custom menu to the page currently being created.

7. The Title field in the Menu Item Settings options will be the text of the hyperlink in your custom menu. Enter some text, such as **Test page**.

8. The Parent Item drop-down selection box is used to place the link to the page you are creating in the menu. All of the items at the top of the list belong to the navigation menu. Scroll past all of those to the very bottom until you find the Custom Menu option. Choose this, as the goal is to place the link to the current page in your newly created custom menu. Figure 1-7 shows what the form will look like at this point.

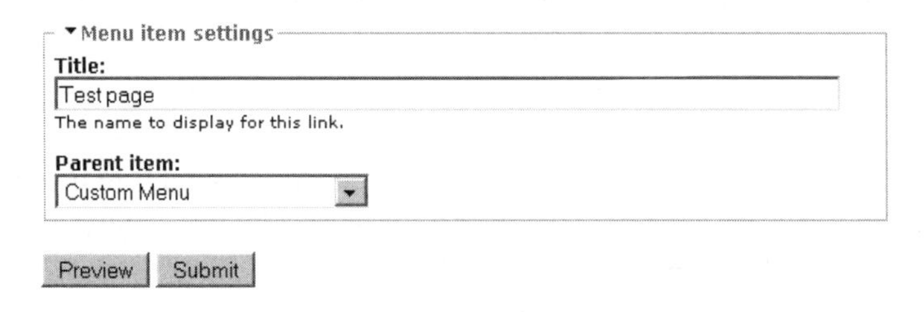

Figure 1-7. *Adding a custom menu item.*

9. Submit the form to create your new page, The result will be a link called *Test page* in the new custom menu. Clicking the *Test page* link will take you to the page you just created.

10. Create more content, or edit existing content, repeating steps 6 through 9 to fill out your custom menu.

Introducing Nodes

For Drupal, every posting that you make has a content type. You choose the content type from the list of available types from the *create content* page. The content types that come with the core Drupal download include pages, stories, books, polls, forum posts, and blogs.

While each of the content types is different from the others in some way, they all share certain characteristics. They all have a title, an author, and a creation date, and they can track revisions. They also share certain features: they can have comments, categories, file uploads as attachments, and more. In fact, all of the content types in Drupal can have these and other services. For Drupal to offer these services to all content types, even when the content types are inherently different from each other, it needs some general way of dealing with content—some abstract idea of content that allows Drupal to deal with forums and blogs in the same manner when it comes to comments or categories. To this end, all of the main content types in Drupal are called *nodes*.

When Drupal builds pages for display, it first deals with the content at the general, or node, level. This is convenient for providing services like comments and categories. Then Drupal deals with the content at the specific content-type level, which is what makes a forum different from a blog, and so forth.

For anyone who has dealt with XML or other hierarchical data structures, the use of the term *node* will make sense, though hierarchy isn't inherently implied here. For those of you who have a background in object-oriented programming, you can think of *node* as the generic superclass, and all of the specific content types as subclasses that inherit from it. Otherwise, it is safe to think of *node* as a synonym for *content*, or *posting*.

The strategy of handling all content first as a generalized node, and then as a specific content type is extremely powerful and helps programmers extend Drupal with surprisingly little effort. The abstract handling of nodes is one of the features that make Drupal a stellar platform for building all sorts of web applications.

Introducing Comments

One of the services that Drupal extends to all content (node) types is the option of enabling comments. Comments give visitors to your site the chance to participate in the dialogue started by the original post in the form of comments that are typically displayed below the post itself. This is how Drupal forums are built.

In the default Drupal installation, comments are enabled for every content type, so no further configuration is needed to use this feature.

Introducing Taxonomy

Drupal has an excellent tool for helping you name and organize the content you create on your web site: the Taxonomy module. In fact, it is one of Drupal's killer features because of the numerous ways in which it is used and the value it adds to your site.

Note The definition of *taxonomy*, according to the Cambridge dictionary (`http://dictionary.➥cambridge.org/define.asp?key=81540&dict=CALD`) is "a system for naming and organizing things, especially plants and animals, into groups which share similar qualities." Drupal taxonomies use vocabularies, which are the "groups which share similar qualities." The words that actually describe things are called *terms*, and are added to vocabularies. In other words, all of the terms that you would use to describe one aspect of something go into the same vocabulary. For example, black, green, gray, and orange would go into a Color vocabulary.

The easiest way to understand what the Taxonomy module can do for you is to consider the tags that are used on sites like Flickr and del.icio.us. Tags let people describe content—such as bookmarks, blogs, and pictures—with keywords. Drupal can do this, too, using the Taxonomy module. Exercise 1-2 demonstrates how to use the Taxonomy module to set up free tagging. Chapter 3 discusses this module in detail.

Exercise 1-2. Set Up Free Tagging for Pages

This exercise will show you how to add free tagging to the Page content type.

1. Select *administer* ➤ *modules*. Enable the Page module, if necessary, and the Taxonomy module.
2. Select *administer* ➤ *categories*. This is the control panel for the Taxonomy module (*categories* is more readily understandable to most people than *taxonomy*).
3. From the category administration page, click the Add Vocabulary tab.
4. Give this vocabulary the name **Tags**. Skip the Description and Help text for now. The Types field lists all of the various content types that you have enabled. Check the box next to Page. Find the Free Tagging check box and check it. Then click Submit.
5. Create a new page by clicking *create content* and choosing Page.
6. On the content-creation form, underneath the Title field, is a new field called Tags. Here is where you enter your tags. Tags are separated by commas, allowing you to make multiple-word tags. For example, "City, New York, Travel" would create three tags for the page: City, New York, and Travel. Enter some tags for the page, finish creating the body text for the page, and click Submit.
7. The newly created page will show each of the tags you entered as a link. These links lead to a list of all content on your site that has been tagged with that particular tag. Figure 1-8 shows an example of a page with free tagging categories.

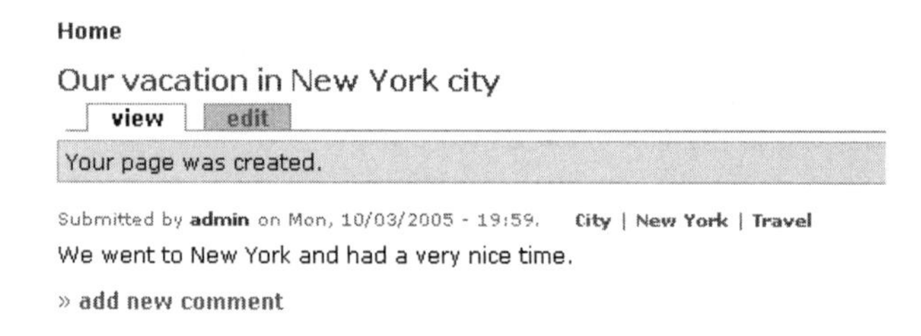

Figure 1-8. *A page with free-tagging categories*

Summary

This chapter introduced Drupal, the PHP content management system/web portal available from `Drupal.org`. You worked through the steps for installing Drupal, and then created some content. Next, you got a brief tour of Drupal's core capabilities and some basic concepts. You learned that you can change the way your site is presented by changing the theme and extend the functionality of your site by enabling blocks and modules. Finally, you were introduced to the concepts of nodes and taxonomy, two of the fundamental ideas behind the Drupal architecture.

In Chapter 2, I will show you all of the basic configuration options available for your Drupal site.

CHAPTER 2

Configuring Drupal

Now that you have Drupal installed and have posted some content, it's time to configure your site. This chapter will guide you through the many configuration settings that you have available as a Drupal administrator.

Here, you will learn how to configure general settings, such as your site's name, whether to cache content, and how the site's URLs should look. You will see what choices you have for controlling whether other users can acquire accounts to use your site, and how to enable and disable modules so that you can tailor your site's functionality to fit your needs. A discussion of Drupal's publishing workflow for content will show you the various publishing options that are available, and the section on comments will help you decide which guidelines your site will have for governing comments to postings. A brief discussion of themes will allow you to select the initial look and feel for your site (themes are covered in more detail in Chapter 5). The final section introduces categories, one of Drupal's most useful and flexible features.

This chapter addresses many common questions that people have when looking at a fresh Drupal installation for the first time. It covers issues such as what content appears on the front page, how to make sure that your site can accept uploaded files, and how to turn on the many modules that come with Drupal. These are the essential skills that you will need to ensure that your site is fully functional and ready to build your online community.

Configuring Site Settings

To begin configuring Drupal, make sure that you are logged in as the administrator (the account that you created in Chapter 1), and then select *administer* ➤ *settings* in the navigation block to get to the site settings page (the URL to the page is `http://localhost/?q=admin/settings`).

When you access the site settings page, Drupal takes the opportunity to check some aspects of your installation in order to help you avoid problems. Because of this, you may be confronted with one or more messages when you access this page for the first time.

One thing that Drupal checks is whether a directory exists for uploaded files. If you followed the instructions in Chapter 1, that directory should exist and be ready for action. If it isn't there yet, Drupal will try to create it. If Drupal succeeds in creating the `files` directory, you will see this message:

```
The directory files has been created.
```

If Drupal tells you that it was unable to create the `files` directory, the most likely problem is that the web server doesn't have permission to write to the `files` directory. For Linux servers, you can solve this problem by changing the group ownership of the folder to the same user that runs the web server, often `apache` or `www`.

Another message that you may see, especially if you are running Drupal on Windows, is this:

```
The built-in GD image toolkit requires that the GD module for PHP be installed and
configured properly. For more information see http://php.net/image.
```

If you see this message, you are encouraged to follow the link to `http://php.net/image` and follow the instructions there.

The rest of the page is divided into eight main sections: General Settings, Error Handling, Cache Settings, File System Settings, Image Handling Settings, RSS Feed Settings, Date Settings, and String Handling. You can expand or collapse each section by clicking the section heading.

General Settings

The General Settings section contains settings that help define the site, including its purpose, how to contact the administrator, the front page, and so on. The following settings are available:

Name: The name of your site has several important functions. First, it appears in the HTML `<title>` element and thus in the title bar of the browser. Second, it can be toggled on or off to be displayed on the site itself (some themes don't support this option). Finally, if you enable RSS syndication for your site, the name of your site will show up in the RSS feed for your site as well.

■ **Note** RSS stands for Really Simple Syndication. See `http://en.wikipedia.org/wiki/Really_Simple_Syndication` for more information about RSS.

E-mail address: This e-mail address should belong to the administrator of the site. Be prepared to receive all site-related mail traffic to this address. For example, it is used in the welcome e-mail that is sent to newly registered users.

Slogan: The optional slogan summarizes the purpose of your site in a couple words or sentences. If you enter a slogan, it will be used in the `<title>` element of your front page in conjunction with the site name. For example, a site named `CoolWidgets.biz` with the slogan "You can't live widgout it!" will display `CoolWidgets.biz | You can't live widgout it!` in the title bar of the browser. The slogan can be displayed on your site and can be toggled on or off from the theme settings pages (see the "Choosing Theme Settings" section later in this chapter). The slogan is used in your site's RSS feeds as well.

Mission: The mission is another, generally longer, blurb of text, which is usually displayed on the front page. It, too, can be toggled on or off from the theme settings pages.

Footer message: The footer message is text that will appear in the site's footer. Some people use this as a space for banner ads or links to their terms of service, legal, or contact pages.

Tip The name, slogan, mission, and footer message all play a significant role in defining your site in the eyes of search engines, so it is worthwhile to make sure that they accurately reflect the purpose and content of your site.

Anonymous user: This determines the name that will be given to site visitors in logs and posts if they are not logged in. For example, if someone visits your site and leaves a comment without first creating an account and signing in, the post will be attributed to whatever name you set here. The default is Anonymous.

Note In Drupal, the anonymous user is represented by the user id (uid) 0.

Default front page: This is the Drupal path that will act as your front page. You can use any valid path. The following are some examples of paths:

- `node`: A listing of all content that has been promoted to the front page. This is the default setting.
- `node/`*`nid`*: Where *`nid`* is a specific node (content) ID, such as `node/302`. Use this syntax to make a specific node (page, blog, story, and so on) function as the front page.
- `blog`: A listing of all published blogs (requires the Blog module to be enabled).
- `user`: The current user's homepage or a page where visitors can log in, register, or request a new password.

Clean URLs: Enabling "clean" URLs is a means of hiding the `GET` parameter `q`. The result is that the characters `?q=` no longer appear in the URL. What is this worth? It is more human-readable, first of all. Furthermore, it is more search engine-friendly, as the URL doesn't immediately announce to the spidering engine that the page is being built dynamically. Clean URLs are dependent on Apache `mod_rewrite` support. (See `http://httpd.apache.org/docs/1.3/mod/mod_rewrite.html` for more information about `mod_rewrite`.)

Figure 2-1 shows an example of a front page with its name, mission, slogan, and footer visible.

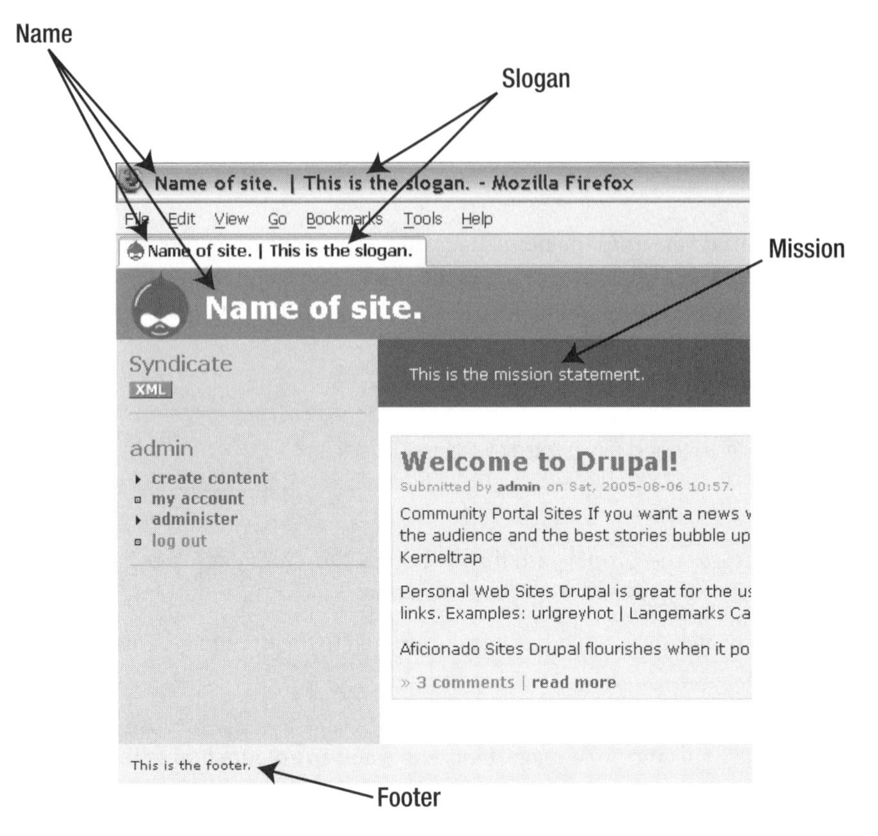

Figure 2-1. *Front page with name, mission, slogan, and footer*

HOW DRUPAL BUILDS URLS

Drupal gets all of its information about which page to display from the URL in the address bar. Because Drupal is database-driven, and each page is dynamically created by PHP scripts, these URLs do not point to physical files on the server, but rather convey information to Drupal about what is being requested.

In Drupal, all requests are directed to `index.php`. This happens by virtue of the request rewriting that is defined in the `.htaccess` file. Both of these files can be found in the root of your Drupal installation. (See the `.htaccess` file for more details about request rewriting.) If the URL has `GET` parameters in the form `?q=admin/user`, the final URL that is given to `index.php` will be `http://www.yoursite.com/`**`index.php`**`?q=admin/user` (you don't see this happening, though). If you have clean URLs enabled and the original URL is `http://www.yoursite.com/node/1`, it will get rewritten to `http://www.yoursite.com/`**`index.php?q=`**`node/1`. In every case, the request will have the parameter `q` with some sort of path information behind it, and the entire request is directed to `index.php`. It is this path information, represented by the `q` parameter, that Drupal uses to decide which page to serve.

One of the first things done during a page request is the building of a menu map. The menu map is a hierarchical list of all the types of pages Drupal has available and the path to each type. Drupal builds this menu map by asking the modules which paths they support and by polling the database to see which paths have been defined by the administrator. (For performance reasons, paths that do not change are cached to reduce the work that needs to be done for building the menu map.) Drupal takes the `q` parameter from the HTTP request and splits it on the forward slash (`/`). Then, using these pieces of path information, Drupal starts searching the menu map for the entry that matches it, finally settling for the map entry that matches the most parts from left to right. After finding the most complete match, Drupal can decide which page to serve , and any additional unmatched parts of the `q` parameter are passed along as separate parameters.

The following are four paths that exist in your Drupal system, which you can access if you are logged in as the administrator.

Default Drupal URL	Clean URL	Path
`http://www.mysite.com/?q=admin`	`http://www.mysite.com/admin`	`admin`
`http://www.mysite.com/?q=admin/access`	`http://www.mysite.com/admin/access`	`admin/access`
`http://www.mysite.com/?q=admin/access/roles`	`http://www.mysite.com/admin/access/roles`	`admin/access/roles`
`http://www.mysite.com/?q=admin/access/rules`	`http://www.mysite.com/admin/access/rules`	`admin/access/rules`

For example, Drupal will handle the URL `http://www.mysite.com/?q=admin/access/value1/value2` as follows:

1. Extract the `q` value (`admin/access/value1/value2`).
2. Split the value into separate values on the `/`. This results in an array `{admin, access, value1, value2}`.
3. Find the entry in the menu map that exactly matches the most values from left to right. In this case, it will match `admin/access`.
4. Call the function associated with `admin/access` and make `value1` and `value2` available to the function.

Error Handling

Whenever your Drupal site receives an HTTP request that it either cannot handle (because it is asking for a page or resource that doesn't exist) or will not handle because of access restrictions, it will return an error page instead. Drupal provides built-in default pages for each of these cases, but you can define alternate pages to be used instead. Other errors that can occur include PHP errors, which arise when Drupal can't perform the requested operations. You can configure how these errors are handled and recorded through the Error Handling section of the site settings page. The settings here include those for Default 403 and Default 404 pages, error reporting, and discarding logs.

Default 403 (Access Denied) and Default 404 (Not Found) Pages

Drupal has an access system that determines what content a site visitor is allowed to see and which actions that visitor is allowed to execute. When visitors attempt so see content that they are not entitled to see or execute an action for which they do not have the necessary permissions, Drupal returns a page with the HTTP header `403 Access denied`. The default behavior is to print a page that says "Access denied – You are not authorized to access this page." If you want to elaborate on this or present a different message, you can do so by creating a Drupal page and entering the Drupal path to that page in the Default 403 (Access Denied) Page field.

■ **Note** *Drupal path* refers to the part of the URL that comes after the `?q=` in the URL, such as `admin/access` or `node/4/edit`.

Similarly, when Drupal receives a URL that cannot be mapped to an existing page or resource, it prints the message "Page not found." If you wish to expound on this, perhaps by offering some suggestions of popular content on your site, you can create a Drupal page and enter its path in the Default 404 (Not Found) Page field.

For example, you might want to create a different page to handle the 404 Not Found errors if you had pages or resources on your site that no longer exist but still get requested. Perhaps you used a dedicated blogging tool or a specialized bulletin board system on your site before deciding to switch to Drupal, and you notice from your server logs that people are still requesting URLs that point to the old, nonexistent system. You would want to make a Drupal page explaining that the resources have moved, with instructions on how to find them, and use that page's Drupal path as the value for the Default 404 (Not Found) Page setting.

Error Reporting

Sometimes, even high-quality code like Drupal runs into situations at the PHP level that cause errors. For example, when no mail server is configured and you attempt to create a new user, a process that involves sending mail, a PHP error will occur. By default, these errors will appear at the top of the page before any of the Drupal-generated HTML. A typical error might look like this:

```
warning: mail(): Failed to connect to mailserver at "localhost" port 25,
verify your "SMTP" and "smtp_port" setting in php.ini or use ini_set()
in C:\Apache2\htdocs\drupal\modules\user.module on line 374.
```

This is important and useful while setting up your site, as it helps you find the places where things are going wrong. On a live production site, however, this is not exactly the type of information you want to serve to your audience. Fortunately, Drupal offers the choice of reporting this error information to either both the screen and logs or to just the logs. Clearly, you'll want to have this set to the first option during development and the second after the site goes live. You can see all of the error information in the Watchdog logs (Drupal's logging system is called Watchdog) from the Administer page (`admin/logs`) at any time.

Discard Logs

The Discard Logs option lets you decide how long you want your log messages to be kept. The setting you choose depends on how much site traffic you get and whether there are size limits on your database imposed by your hosting company. You will want to be aware of how large the Watchdog table is and adjust this setting accordingly, so that you keep only as much log information as is useful to you.

Cache Settings

Drupal does everything its developers can think of to be efficient and fast. This is important for sites that receive high traffic. It saves on server costs by allowing a server to handle more requests and allows smaller servers to handle bigger sites.

One of the crucial elements in making Drupal efficient and fast is the cache system. By default, Drupal automatically caches the variables, menus, and filters that it uses internally to build pages. These elements are cached automatically and require no configuration or action on the part of the administrator. The main decisions left to the administrator are whether to cache pages and the minimum time that a cached page should be kept. These decisions are made with the Cache Settings options on the site settings page (`admin/settings`).

Page caching takes the final HTML output of each page, including the headers, exactly as it is sent to your browser and saves it into the cache database. Then, the next time that page is requested, the server only needs to look into its cache to see how that page should be built. This saves immense amounts of work for the server in terms of executing PHP code and making database queries, as the entire cached page can be served with a single query.

Cached pages are served only to anonymous users, never to registered users who are logged in. A crucial question arises, however, concerning how and when to rebuild the cached pages. In terms of performance, keeping cached pages as long as possible should be the goal, because they generate the least overhead. The problem with this becomes apparent on sites where the content is updated often, as the cache might prevent anonymous visitors from seeing changed or new content immediately. This problem is addressed with the Minimum Cache Lifetime setting, which specifies an amount of time that a cached page *must* stay in the cache before it can be replaced with new or updated content. When choosing this setting, try to balance the need for speedy page delivery with the inconvenience of having a lag time before new or updated content appears for anonymous users. Authenticated users will always see the newest version of content, no matter how the cache is configured.

File System Settings

Drupal offers two types of file downloading methods:

Public downloading: This means that the job of serving uploaded files to the browser falls on the underlying web server, which will serve them directly. Web servers are carefully optimized to be able to serve static resources like files in a very efficient way. This will always be the fastest method for offering downloads. The ramification is that the files must reside in a directory that is visible from the Web. Putting files in a Web-visible directory prevents you from having any control over who can download the file. Hotlinking—the practice of offering the URL to images or files on another server—will be possible, and depending on your goals, may not be desired. While some of these problems are addressable at the server administration level, it will never be possible for Drupal to control on a file-by-file basis whether or not a particular registered user can download something. To get that level of control, you will need to enable the private downloading method.

Private downloading: For the private downloading method to be effective, the files must reside in a directory that is not visible from the Web. The directory needs to be readable and writable by scripts, however, as PHP code will be responsible for putting the files into it and reading them out of it. In this scenario, the web server is never asked to serve the file directly. Instead, through use of a special URL, a PHP script is engaged to read the file in chunks and send the stream to the browser. Since the download is happening at the PHP level, code can be written to check if the current user actually has the permissions necessary to access the file. With greater control comes the cost of more server processing overhead and slower downloads.

The Download Method field in the File System Settings section determines which downloading method is to be used. Currently, you cannot combine these two methods, and changing methods on a live web site that already has uploaded content will break the existing links and is therefore strongly discouraged.

The File System Path setting is the path to the directory where uploaded files and images will be saved. How to address this directory depends on what setting you choose for Download Method. If you decide to use public downloads, you can use the standard `files` directory in the root of your Drupal installation. In this case, the value that you provide for the File System Path field is simply `files`. If you choose to use private downloads, you must provide a directory somewhere on your server that isn't visible to the Web, set the appropriate ownership and permissions on the directory so that it can be accessed via scripts, and provide the absolute or relative path to this directory.

The Temporary Directory setting is the path where uploaded files will be stored before they are handled by PHP scripts. This is typically `/tmp` on Linux machines.

Image Handling Settings

Drupal needs to know which image handling library it should use to deal with images that are uploaded to the system. The most common operations that are needed are resizing large images to make thumbnails and other, smaller versions of the original. The Image Handling group of settings will display all of the available options. This will typically include the GD2 library (`http://php.net/imagegd2`), which is included in all versions of PHP starting with 4.1.0. Drupal will issue a warning message if the GD2 library is unavailable; at which point, you need to check your PHP version and find out whether the library can be enabled.

Drupal also supports the ImageMagick library (`http://www.imagemagick.org/script/index.php`). For that library, you will need to install the `image.imagemagick.inc` file, which is part of the Image module. Refer to Chapter 4 for details on installing modules.

RSS Feed Settings

The settings for your site's RSS feeds are straightforward, enabling you to determine the maximum number of items that will be listed in your feeds, as well as to choose the format for the individual feed items. The format choices include Title Only, Titles Plus Teaser, and Full Text. These settings will apply to all of the RSS feeds that your site is capable of generating.

Date Settings

Drupal's date and time settings allow you to customize your site to best fit your audience's geographical profile. The two issues at hand are how your site will deal with time zones and the formatting of dates and times.

Time Zones

First, set the default time zone for your server. This is not necessarily straightforward and requires a decision on your part. Should the default time zone for the server be the time zone where the server is physically located, the time zone where the site administrator resides, or the time zone of the site's target audience, if this can be determined? Whichever time zone you choose will be used by default to display times and dates on your server. The different time zones appear in the Default Time Zone selection box and are represented by the number of hours offset from Greenwich Mean Time (GMT). For example, +0000 is GMT, +0100 is Central European Time, and –0500 is Eastern Standard Time.

If you want your site's users to be able to set their own time zone and view the dates and times adjusted accordingly, enable the Configurable Time Zones option. This will allow users to adjust their time zone on their user profile page. If they don't do this, all dates and times will be shown localized to the default time zone.

While it is true that Internet sites are by nature international, as anyone across the globe can access them, some sites do cater to an audience or a topic of interest for which a single time zone makes sense. For example, if your site covers news and events for a city or a region, you will probably want everything to be displayed in terms of local time, so you should therefore disable the Configurable Time Zones option. This would also be a common choice when you're using Drupal to power a site on an intranet.

Date and Time Formatting

Next, set the short, medium, and long date formats. Some date formats, like 2/28/2006 - 9:18 PM, are geared toward an American audience, and some formats, such as 28/02/2006 - 14:45 (day/month/year, 24-hour clock), are more familiar to a European audience. Choose the format that best reflects the preferences of your largest user group and also prevents any possible confusion. One suggestion is to use the following:

- Short date format: Feb 28, 2006 - 10:50am
- Medium date format: February 28, 2006 - 10:50am
- Long date format: Monday, February 28, 2006 - 10:50am

This leaves no room for confusion about which comes first, day or month, or whether 9:00 means AM or PM.

The First Day of Week setting mostly influences calendar views. The only module in the core modules that offers a calendar view is the Archive module. The first day of the week shows up on the far left in the calendar.

String Handling

Drupal handles and stores its textual data in the UTF-8 character encoding format in order to support the many written languages of the world. (See `http://www.unicode.org/` for more information about Unicode encoding.) Not all versions of PHP support this encoding fully without added extensions. To address this problem, the preferred solution is to install the `mbstring` extension to PHP, available from `http://www.php.net/manual/en/ref.mbstring.php`. If the `mbstring` extension is not available, `iconv` (`http://php.net/iconv`) or GNU `recode` (`http://www.gnu.org/software/recode/recode.html`) must be installed.

The String Handling group exists to show you the status of Drupal's string handling on your server. If Drupal is able to use UTF-8 encoding using an available library, this will be indicated. Otherwise, you will be prompted to install one of the three libraries mentioned in the previous paragraph, preferably `mbstring`.

Setting Up and Maintaining User Accounts

Nothing is more important to a community-driven site than users! As a site administrator, you want to make the process of obtaining a user account as easy and straightforward as possible, and make the communications that originate from your site friendly and informative.

Configuring User Accounts

Drupal offers three different ways to handle the creation of new user accounts, as well as complete control over the e-mail messages that are sent to people when they obtain a new account or when they forget their password.

User Registration Settings

To administer users, select *administer* ➤ *settings* ➤ *users* (`admin/settings/user`). On this page, the first group of radio buttons, labeled Public Registrations, determines how new users are added to the site. You have three choices:

Visitors can create accounts and no administrator approval is required: This is the default and the most suitable setting for a site where the goal is to make registration as open and easy as possible.

Visitors can create accounts but administrator approval is required: If you would like to have some control over who can have a user account, but you still want the process to be initiated by users visiting your site, you can choose this option. With this scheme, users are shown the same registration form as with the preceding option, and they are sent essentially the same welcome mail containing a password and links, with an additional message indicating that their account is currently pending approval. If they attempt to log in before approval has been granted, they are simply given the message "Sorry. Unrecognized username or password." Meanwhile, the site administrator has been sent an e-mail message indicating that a user has applied for an account with a link to that user's page. The administrator then has the chance to review the user's information and change the status from blocked to active. At the time of this writing, no further e-mail is sent to inform the new user of whether the account has been approved. A feature request (`http://drupal.org/node/19587`) has been submitted at `Drupal.org` to address this shortcoming.

Only site administrators can create new user accounts: With this option, anonymous visitors are not shown the Create New Account link in the login block. The path `user/register` becomes off limits to everyone, including administrators, and returns a 403 error ("Access denied – You are not authorized to access this page") when accessed.

The administrator can create new users under the Drupal path `admin/user/create`. The form requires the administrator to enter a username, e-mail address, and password for the new user. No e-mail is sent to users created this way, so it is up to the administrator to initiate communication with the person who will be using the newly created account. New users can either be told the password chosen for them, or they can request a new password using their username and e-mail (under the path `user/password`).

If you would like to provide more information, instructions, or a greeting to people as a part of the user registration form, enter that text in the User Registration Guidelines field. The text that you add here will be shown at the time a visitor chooses to create a new site account.

User E-Mail Settings

In the two registration variants where users initiate the process of creating a new user account, Drupal will send a welcome e-mail message with account details and welcome text. Drupal also sends an e-mail message when users forget their password and request a new one. The User E-Mail Settings section of the `admin/settings/user` page allows you to customize the text and templates for these three messages. The site administrator can edit the text and subjects for all of these messages. Also, you can use a number of placeholder variables to represent dynamic information, as shown in Table 2-1. These variables will be replaced with the appropriate values at the time the e-mail is sent.

Table 2-1. *Placeholders for User Welcome E-Mail*

Placeholder	Description
`%edit_uri`	The absolute URL to the screen where users can edit their account information. Equals `%site` plus the path `user/{uid}/edit`, where `{uid}` is the user's unique ID.
`%login_uri`	An absolute URL to the screen where users can log in. Equals the base URL of the site, plus the path `user/login`.
`%mailto`	The site's e-mail address.
`%password`	The user's password. New passwords are generated randomly by Drupal.
`%site`	The site name. Corresponds to the Name field of the General Settings section on the `admin/settings` page.
`%uri`	The URL to your site.
`%uri_brief`	A truncated version of the full URL to the site. It takes the form `www.sitename.com`, or `subdomain.sitename.net`. It is used in the welcome mail to illustrate how the new user's distributed authentication username looks. Distributed authentication is covered in Chapter 3.
`%username`	The username that was assigned by the administrator or chosen by the user.

User Pictures

The final section on the `admin/settings/user` page allows administrators to decide whether users can upload a small picture to become their online identity, or avatar, on the site. If you enable the Picture Support option, you must enter a value in the Picture Image Path field that points to the folder that will store the uploaded user pictures. This can be the `pictures` folder that Drupal created for you when you visited the `admin/settings/user` page for the first time, which is also the default value. You can also specify a path to a default picture, which will be shown in the case a user hasn't yet uploaded one.

Set the Picture Maximum Dimensions option in the form *height* × *width* to control the size of the avatars. Set the Picture Maximum File Size option to make sure the size of these files isn't too large.

Finally, you can write a message from the administrator in the Picture Guidelines field. This message will be shown to users along with the picture upload form. You can use this message to explain the purpose of the avatar picture, give instructions and guidance on how to prepare the image files, or detail restrictions that should be observed.

Once avatar picture support has been enabled, a Picture section will be added to the user account edit page (`user/`*`uid`*`/edit`). The picture itself will appear on the user account page (`user/`*`uid`*) and, depending on what theme is being used and how it is configured, on the content postings made by that user. Theme configuration is discussed in the "Configuring Themes" section later in this chapter.

Managing User Accounts

You have now chosen a user creation scheme that fits your needs. If you've allowed it, site visitors will begin setting up user accounts when they visit your site. Otherwise, you, as the administrator, will create the user accounts. Either way, several tasks are associated with maintaining user accounts. These tasks include password recovery, blocking users who abuse your site, and deleting defunct accounts.

User Account Creation

Any user with the Administer Users permission (see the "Controlling Access" section later in this chapter for more about permissions) can create new user accounts. The process of adding a new user is as simple as selecting *administer* ➤ *users* ➤ *add user* (`admin/user/create`) and providing a username, e-mail address, and password. As noted earlier, no mail is sent to the newly created user.

■ **Note** Form elements with asterisks are required fields and cannot be left blank.

The Drupal path to the user registration page is `user/register`. The typical way for an anonymous visitor to come to the registration page is via the user login block (see the "Using Blocks" section later in this chapter for details on enabling and configuring blocks). The user login block is activated by default and appears for any visitor who does not currently have an open session. It displays the links Create New Account and Request New Password. Clicking the Create New Account link takes you to the `user/register` page with text fields for Username and E-Mail Address. An invalid or duplicated e-mail address or a duplicated or forbidden username will prevent the creation of a new user.

Successful completion of the form will trigger an e-mail message to be sent from the Drupal server to the e-mail address that the user entered in the form. The e-mail will contain a welcome message, a randomly generated password, and links to various important pages back on the site. The user will need to log in using the password that was sent; at which point, it is advisable to immediately change the password to something easier to remember. This can be done on the `user/`*`uid`* page, where *`uid`* is the user's unique identification number.

Password Recovery

If a user forgets her password, she can use the Request New Password link (`user/password`) to have a recovery mail sent to her e-mail address. The mail will contain a one-time-only link to a page that allows her to enter a new password. The password will be set only if the page is accessed via the URL in the mail, as it will contain a unique hashed code that can be used by only that user and only one time.

■ **Note** Drupal does not store clear-text passwords in the database. Rather, every password is encrypted using the MD5 algorithm (`http://www.php.net/md5`) and the encrypted version of the password is stored. Every time a user attempts authentication, the password he enters is encrypted using the same algorithm, and the product of encryption is compared with the encrypted version in the database. This means that passwords are unrecoverable. As the site administrator, you do not know users' passwords, not even by looking in the database. This is intended to offer a level of security and privacy for Drupal site users. The users' only recourse for lost, stolen, or forgotten passwords is to request a new password, via the Request New Password link, or to have the administrator manually create a new one by visiting the user's page and updating the password to something new.

User Status

Administrators (anyone with the Administer Users permission, in this case) are able to access and configure individual user accounts. You can see a list of users by selecting *administer* ➤ *users* (`admin/user`). Clicking the Edit link for any of the users listed brings up the same form that the user herself uses to configure her account, with the addition of a couple administrative fields. The administrator is privy to all of the information and can even enter a new password. Note that the administrator cannot, under any circumstances, see the current password for a user.

In addition to the fields to which the user has access, administrators have access to two important user management tools: Status and Roles. Setting a user's Status to Blocked prevents the user from logging in to the site using that account. This should be used to deactivate accounts when users misbehave, fail to observe the site's guidelines, or use their account to introduce spam. A blocked user cannot log in and has no user account page (`user/`*`uid`*). The message given when a blocked user attempts to log in is "Sorry. Unrecognized username or password." No message is sent to alert a user that he has been blocked. If the user attempts to create a new user with the blocked name or password, the following messages are displayed:

```
The name blocked_name is already taken.
The e-mail address blocked_e-mail is already taken.
```

Note that the blocked user's posts on the site remain visible and intact. If the impetus for blocking the user was inappropriate content, the administrator will need to deal with the content separately. In general, it is advisable to block users and unpublish content rather than deleting it. This blocks the user from signing up with the same name or e-mail address and keeps the evidence of wrongdoing or bad behavior intact.

■ **Note** If you want to delete a user account, you must block it first. If you try to delete an account that hasn't been blocked, you will see an error message. Deleting users is irreversible.

Using the Roles field, you can determine which roles a particular user is allowed to play on your site. Each role is attached to different permissions, which govern what content can be viewed or created, as well as what actions a user can take. User roles and the Roles field are covered in the following section on access control.

Controlling Access

Drupal has a role-based permissions system, which enables you to create different groups of users with different permissions. This section explores how to create roles and assign permissions to them. Also covered in this section are the access rules that can be set to restrict which usernames, e-mail addresses, or hosts are allowed to create accounts on your site.

Roles and Permissions

Drupal strives to offer fine-grained control over the access of content and the execution of actions. It is important that you, the site administrator, can decide exactly what each user is able to see and do on the site. To support this, all users are assigned roles and permissions. A role describes a profile or use case for a user or group of users. For example, you may have roles named Moderator, Editor, and Admin.

Two roles are defined by Drupal by default:

- The Anonymous User role is assigned to any visitor to the site who either does not have an account or is not logged in.
- The Authenticated User role is assigned to logged-in users. Newly registered users are automatically assigned to this role.

You can see a list of roles by selecting *administer* ➤ *access control* ➤ *roles* (`admin/access/roles`). To create a new role, type the name of the role into the text field and click Add Role. The new role will appear in the list. You can edit your new role as well, which allows you to change its name. Once you have defined a new role, it will be visible to administrators as a check box field in the list of roles on each user's account details page (`user/uid/edit`), as well as on the permissions page.

A role is not useful unless it has permissions assigned to it. To view the table of permissions and roles, navigate to *administer* ➤ *access control* (`admin/access`). This page lists all of the available permissions (rows) and the roles to which they are assigned (columns). Permissions are typically formulated as actions describing what they allow. For example, the Post Comments Without Approval permission, if granted, allows the comments posted by a user to appear immediately on the site, without further moderation. Otherwise, the comments need to be approved by someone who has the Moderate Comments permission.

Since the Anonymous User role includes anyone who does not have an account or is not logged in, it should be given the fewest permissions. In the default Drupal installation, the Anonymous User role is granted only the Access Content permission. This guarantees that visitors to the site can read published blogs, stories, pages, and so on. The Anonymous User is not granted the Access Comments permission by default. If you would like anonymous visitors to read forum threads and other comments, you must explicitly grant them this right.

A user may have more than one role. A user's permissions are the set of all permissions from all roles he is in, so the administrator has the opportunity to define layers of access (and responsibility) in the form of many roles, each with a small but targeted set of permissions. You might decide that your forums, for example, should be visible to anyone who visits the site. You would then grant the Anonymous User role the Access Comments permission, as forums are made up of many comments. If you decide that normal registered users should be allowed to post comments and you don't want to bother with reading each comment and approving it, you would grant the Authenticated User role the Post Comments Without Approval permission.

■ **Note** When you grant the Post Comments Without Approval permission, Drupal automatically grants the Post Comments permission as well. This is logical, since the former includes the latter.

Now let's say that you want to have a group of trusted users who have the ability to moderate comments by marking them with flags like "inappropriate content," which, depending on how moderation is configured, might lead to the comment being unpublished. To set this up, you could define a role named Moderator. The Moderator role would receive the Moderate Comments permission, and users who are moderators would be given both the Authenticated User and the Moderator roles. Since the permissions from both roles are added together, these users would have a total of four permissions pertaining to comments: Access Comments, Post Comments, Post Comments Without Approval, and Moderate Comments.

Note that in Figure 2-2 the Access Comments permission is assigned to both the Anonymous User role and the Authenticated User role. This is because the Anonymous User role is unique among roles. It cannot be assigned to users as can all other roles. Users who are assigned the Anonymous User role cannot have any other roles and vice versa.

In general, the permissions are self-explanatory. For example, the Upload Files and View Uploaded Files permissions are straightforward. Only users in a role that has the Upload Files permission will ever be shown a file upload form. Users who do not have the View Uploaded Files permission will not be shown links to uploaded files.

Permission	anonymous user	authenticated user	moderator
comment module			
access comments	☑	☑	☐
administer comments	☐	☐	☐
administer moderation	☐	☐	☐
moderate comments	☐	☐	☑
post comments	☑	☑	☐
post comments without approval	☑	☑	☐

Figure 2-2. *Sample permissions for a Moderator role*

You've already been introduced to the Access Content permission. Users who do not have this permission will not be able to see anything on the site, so it is normally granted to every user.

A couple of the permissions are very powerful—perhaps more powerful than their names reveal—and therefore merit closer attention. The Administer Nodes permission grants nearly complete control over all the content on the site. Users possessing this permission can access all content on the site and execute any action on it, including changing the content, changing the author of the content, unpublishing the content, and even deleting it. Furthermore, the Administer Nodes permission allows a user to access the configuration pages where each content type is customized. Clearly, this permission should not be granted lightly.

Another important permission is Bypass Input Data Check. Drupal normally prevents users from creating posts that contain anything that might be a malicious attempt to inject computer code or scripting elements into a site. Entering a `<script>` tag in a Drupal blog, for example, will normally result in the message "Terminated request because of suspicious input data." Roles possessing the Bypass Input Data Check permission are exempt from this check. Grant this permission only to users who have legitimate reasons for creating content with code and scripts embedded.

■ **Tip** If you want to have a site that discusses computer code, check out the Codefilter module (`http://drupal.org/project/codefilter`). It helps overcome the problem of terminated requests due to suspicious input data by escaping code into HTML entities such as `<` or `>`.

Access Rules

Chances are that not all visitors to your site will behave themselves. Some will have an agenda that runs counter to your site's goals. This group of shady users includes spammers and a wide variety of people who will use their power to post content to deface, defame, defile, and defraud. Furthermore, your site on the open Internet is likely to come under a number of automated attacks, which attempt to do anything from take over your server to fill your logs with links to dubious sites. Some people may use scripts to attempt to post large numbers of comments or automatically register thousands of new users. The limit to what can happen is only in the imagination and intention of the bad guys. As a site administrator, you need to be equipped to mitigate their efforts, and Drupal gives you a set of tools to help you survive these attacks.

Select *administer* ➤ *access control* ➤ *access rules* (admin/access/rules) to access tools to block or allow specific usernames, e-mail addresses, or hosts (IP addresses). By building specific or general rules, you can block access from known problem sources.

The access rules consist of an access type (allow|deny), a rule type (username|e-mail|host), and a mask. The masks use pattern matching, where the percent sign (%) matches any number of characters, even zero characters, and the underscore (_) matches exactly one character. Exercise 2-1 demonstrates adding an access rule.

Exercise 2-1. Block Offensive Usernames

Suppose you want to block all usernames that contain the text *bad word*.

1. Create a new rule by selecting *access control* ➤ *account rules* ➤ *add rule* (admin/access/rules/add).
2. Select Deny and Username, and then enter the mask %bad word%, as shown in Figure 2-3.

Figure 2-3. *Blocking a username*

3. Click the Add Rule button. Your rule is now in effect.
4. To test it and make sure it behaves as you expected, go to the Check Rules subtab (admin/access/rules/check). Here, you can enter any username in the Username field, and then click the Check Username button see if the name would be allowed or denied. For this example, try usernames like real bad word, bad words, and not a bad word. They should all be denied. Then try badword and ad word. They should be allowed.

Perhaps you have a user who creates multiple versions of himself with different e-mail addresses from the same domain—mike@domain.com, bob@domain.com, jim@domain.com, and so on. You don't want to kick the user off the site, but you do want to limit him to one account. To do this, you make a rule that denies all e-mail accounts from domain.com, as shown in Figure 2-4. At this point, all of the e-mail addresses from domain.com are blocked. Now you add another rule allowing one particular address, bob@domain.com. The result, which you can confirm using the Check Rules subtab, is that only bob@domain.com is allowed to create a user account and other e-mail from domain.com is blocked. Allowing rules trump denying rules.

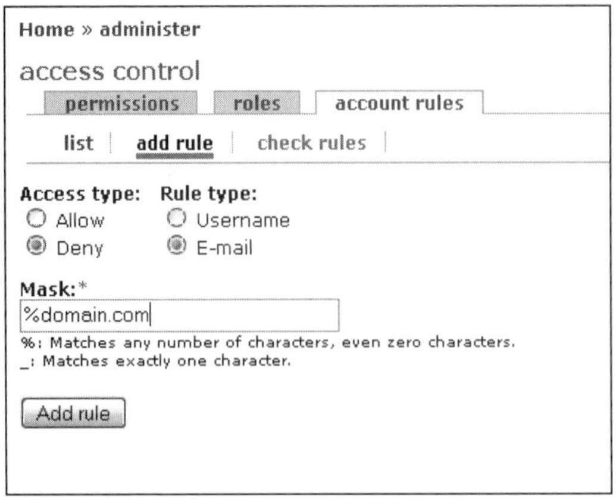

Home » administer

access control

permissions roles account rules

list add rule check rules

Access type: Rule type:
Allow Username
Deny E-mail

Mask:*
%domain.com
%: Matches any number of characters, even zero characters.
_: Matches exactly one character.

Add rule

Figure 2-4. *Blocking users from a particular domain*

Tip Hosts, or IP addresses, identify the computer from which a visitor has accessed your site. If an attacker is using a computer to launch an attack on your server, you can help protect yourself by banning the IP address of the attacking computer. While it is possible to do this from the Rules tab of the Access Control screen, there is an easier way. The Statistics module, described in Chapter 3, keeps a record of who accesses your site and their IP addresses. Using the Top Visitors log (`admin/logs/visitors`), it is possible to identify possible cases of abuse and ban IP addresses directly with the click of a link. Of course, if you know that thugs in some dark and distant country are after you, and you know their IP address, you should block it preemptively, but this is rarely the case.

Using Modules

The Drupal codebase consists of a four entry point files in the root directory (`cron.php`, `index.php`, `update.php`, and `xmlrpc.php`), a core API mostly stored in the `includes` folder, themes in the `themes` folder, and modules in the `modules` directory. The chief mechanism for extending and modifying the functionality of Drupal lies in its modules.

A *module* is a file with the extension `.module` and can be either in the `modules` directory or in a subfolder of that directory. For example, the `blog.module` file be kept either at `modules/blog.module` or at `modules/blog/blog.module`.

Drupal scans the `modules` directory to build a list of available modules. You can see this list by selecting *administer* ➤ *modules* (`admin/modules`). A module must be enabled before its code is included and its functionality is available. The check boxes on the right indicate each module's status.

The default Drupal installation comes with a number of modules, not all of which are enabled. You'll find a complete description of all core modules and their configurations in Chapter 3. None of the core modules require any further steps such as downloading extra files, modifying the database, or applying patches to Drupal code before they can be used. Many of them require some sort of configuration, which can usually be done via a link in the *administer* ➤ *settings* menu. If you have the Help module enabled, you can read a description of each activated module by clicking the *administer* ➤ *help* link (`admin/help`).

You can add functionality to Drupal through the installation of contributed modules. In fact, all except the most basic Drupal sites will rely heavily on contributed modules. More than 180 contributed modules for the current release are listed at `http://drupal.org/project/releases`. The number of contributed modules is a testament to the extensibility of the Drupal platform and the ease with which new developers are able to learn the Drupal APIs and begin contributing.

The steps for installing a module can vary from simply copying the module into the `modules` directory and enabling it from the *administer* ➤ *modules* pages to modifying the database, patching code, or running upgrade scripts. Chapter 4 covers installing and using contributed modules.

Using Blocks

Blocks are pieces or units of content that are positioned in any of the defined regions of your Drupal site. They contain content ranging from core functions, such as the user login box and the navigation menu, to extras, such as Who's New and Who's Online boxes. Modules are responsible for generating most blocks, so enabling more modules generally leads to more blocks being available for display.

A new feature in Drupal 4.7 is the ability to place blocks in regions other than the left or right sidebars. The predefined regions include the sidebars, the header, the footer, and the main content area. Site administrators can also create their own blocks, which can contain normal HTML as well as PHP code. As the administrator, you have complete control over where and when a block is shown. This makes blocks a serious option for enhancing your Drupal site. In Chapter 5, I will show you how to define your own regions.

Administering Blocks

To administer blocks, select *administer* ➤ *blocks* (`admin/block`). If you are using either the Bluemarine or Pushbutton theme, you will see five yellow stripes that highlight the various regions on your site. This is to aid you in deciding where a certain block should appear. You will also see that there is a separate block configuration page for every theme that you have enabled. This allows you to have different block configurations for each theme.

All available blocks are grouped by region. The controls for enabling blocks and moving them to the various regions are self-explanatory. The Weight selection box for each block controls the order of the blocks within a sidebar. As with all Drupal weights, smaller numbers float to the top of lists, while larger numbers sink to the bottom of lists. Negative numbers are allowed and, as they are smaller than positive numbers, will cause a block to appear nearer to the top. If you have the Throttle module enabled, each block also displays a check box indicating whether its display should be dependent on throttle conditions. (For a discussion of the Throttle module, see Chapter 3.)

Clicking the *configure* link for any of the blocks listed reveals the true power administrators have over where blocks appear.

Custom Visibility Settings

The first field on the block configuration page, Custom Visibility Settings, deals with the question of whether authenticated users should be able to customize which blocks are visible to them when they visit the site. The first option, "Users cannot control whether or not they see this block," means essentially that the administrator-defined visibility settings are to be honored, and the user will not be given the choice to enable/disable this block. The other two options, "Show this block by default, but let individual users hide it" and "Hide this block by default but let individual users show it," both allow users to enable/disable the block for themselves, but differ in whether the block is initially shown or not shown. (Users can enable or disable custom blocks from their user account editing page, `user/`*`uid`*`/edit`.)

Page-Specific Visibility Settings

The Page Specific Visibility Settings options allow the administrator to define exactly on which pages a block should appear. Two approaches are available for doing this. The first leverages the Drupal menu system to build a list of pages where a block should or shouldn't appear, and the second allows the administrator to write a segment of PHP code that determines whether or not a block is to appear.

The first two options of the Show Block on Specific Pages field, "Show on every page except the listed pages" and "Show on only the listed pages," expect a list of Drupal paths, possibly including wildcards. You can use any Drupal path or path fragment as a mask, as well as the asterisk wildcard (*) to cover whole sections of the site. If you have the Path module activated, you can also use the custom paths, or aliases, that you have created. The special variable `<front>` exists to represent the front page of your site, which is difficult to address otherwise, as it has no path. Exercise 2-2 demonstrates controlling block visibility with the "Show on only the listed pages" option.

Exercise 2-2. Make a Block Visible to Only Administrators

Suppose you would like to know who is currently visiting your site, but this is not information that you want your visitors themselves to be able to see. The solution is to activate the Who's Online block and use a path fragment to limit the visibility of the block to an area that only you (or other administrators) can access. One such area is the User Administration section on the `admin/user` page. The Administer Users permission is required to access this path, and since you will probably not want to extend this permission to normal site visitors, it is a perfect candidate for showing information that only you or other administrators are supposed to see.

1. Navigate to *administer* ➤ *blocks* and find the Who's Online block. Click its Configure link. In the Page Specific Visibility Settings section, set the "Show block on specific pages" option to "Show on only the listed pages." Now you can specify a path, and the block will appear only on pages that match the path you specify.

2. The path to the user administration section of the site is `admin/user`. Since you want the block to appear on that and all related pages, use the wildcard character to match the entire section: `admin/user/*`. Enter this value in the Pages field and click Save Block.

3. You are returned to the block listing page. Now that you have specified the access to the block, you can turn it on. Click Enabled, decide whether the block should appear on the left or right, optionally set a weight to control where it appears in relation to the other blocks in the same sidebar, and then click Save Blocks. The block is now enabled and should appear only on the desired pages.

4. To test whether the block appears where you expect it to, and nowhere else, select *administer ➤ users*. The block should appear there, as well as on the pages for adding users and configuration. The block should not appear on any other pages.

5. To test that users who are not administrators cannot view the block, you need to create a test account with a different username, log in as that user, and attempt to access the `admin/user` path. Not only should you not be able to access the page where the block is visible, it should not appear on any other pages and should not be presented as an option to be enabled on the user page for this user.

Most cases for determining block visibility can be handled using Drupal paths. For the rest of the cases, the administrator has complete flexibility and control in the form of the third option for the Show Block on Specific Pages field, "Show if the following PHP code returns TRUE." This option takes a segment of PHP code, runs it, and uses the result (a value of `TRUE` or `FALSE`) to decide whether or not to display the block. See Exercise 2-3 for an example.

Adding Blocks

Block administration offers not only flexibility to determine where existing blocks appear, but also the ability to create completely new blocks.

To create a new block, click the Add Block tab on the block administration page (`admin/block/add`). The Name field will appear as the heading of your block on the page. The field is not mandatory and does not need to be unique. To make sure you can identify your new block on the administration pages, give it a unique description. This field is also not mandatory, but if you add a description, it must be unique.

Next, choose an input format and write the body of your block. Since you can elect to write PHP code in the block, the possibilities for what you can do are endless. In fact, writing PHP in blocks is one of the easiest and most accessible ways to extend your Drupal site. Exercise 2-3 demonstrates how to create a new block using PHP code.

Tip You can find ready-to-use code for many different custom blocks at `http://drupal.org/node/17170`.

Exercise 2-3. Play Block Lottery!

Imagine how many visitors your site would get if every time they viewed a page, they had a chance to win the lottery. It doesn't matter which page is viewed—if the lucky number is drawn, a winner has been chosen. Here's how to make a random You Win! block for your site.

1. Create a new block (`admin/block/add`) named Block Lottery. Use the following message for the body (or create your own):

```
<p><strong>You win!</strong></p>
<p>You have won block lottery. Congratulations, and enjoy the site.</p>
```

2. Enter a description and save the block.

3. Select *administer* ➤ *block* (`admin/block`), and then click Configure for the Block Lottery block. For the Show Block on Specific Pages field, choose the third option, "Show if the following PHP code returns TRUE."

4. In the Pages field, enter the following code:

```
<?php
if (rand(1, 10) === 10) return TRUE;
?>
```

5. Save the block configuration. This returns you to the block administration page. Activate the block and start playing Block Lottery.

The code you entered in step 4 chooses a random number between 1 and 10, and if it is equal to 10, returns the value `TRUE` (the return value `FALSE` is implicit). If `TRUE` is returned, the block is shown; otherwise, it is not shown.

Now on every page view, there is a 10% chance that the block will be shown. If you have bad luck with lotteries in general, you may need to visit more than ten pages before you see the block appear.

Managing Content

Drupal is more than a tool for getting your content online. In addition, it offers rich tools for controlling where content is shown on your site, what types of text can be allowed inside of content, and a revision history to track the changes that you make to existing content. Many of these controls can be applied differently to different types of content, allowing you to tailor your site to meet your specific needs.

Configuring Content

You can set options that apply to site-wide content, as well as just to specific content types.

Site-Wide Content

To configure settings that apply to all of your site's content, select *administer* ➤ *settings* ➤ *posts* (`admin/settings/node`). This page has the following settings:

Number of posts on main page: This sets the number of posts that will be displayed whenever your front page is a list of posts, such as the default front page, `node`. All such listing pages have an automatic pagination feature for accessing the rest of the posts beyond whatever number you set for this field.

Length of trimmed posts: For every node, Drupal prepares a shortened teaser view and a full view. The teaser view uses an algorithm to find a logical place in the content text to break off. The text is truncated and followed by a Read More link, which takes you to the full view. The Length of Trimmed Posts setting sets the maximum number of characters that will be shown in the teaser view. If Drupal finds a more logical place to break that has fewer characters than this setting, such as after an HTML block level element, it will. Note that this has only a limited influence on the actual displayed size of the teaser, since it doesn't take into account factors such as images or different font sizes that may be in the text. If you always want your posts to be viewed in full, set this to Unlimited.

■ **Tip** If you want to control where Drupal breaks the text for the teaser view, use `<!--break-->` at the desired location in the text.

Preview post: This controls whether users can submit new nodes or comments directly, without seeing a preview version first. In addition to its very useful function in reducing human error, the preview has a secondary benefit as well. If your site allows anonymous users to post nodes or comments of any type, I recommend that you require this preview. It makes it somewhat harder to post to the site via an automated script and can help reduce spam.

Publishing Status

Drupal defines four different attributes content can have to determine its publishing status:

Published: Published content is generally visible. Unpublished nodes cannot be seen by anyone who does not have the Administer Nodes permission.

In moderation queue: The moderation queue is all of the content on your site that needs approval from an administrator or moderator before being published.

Promoted to front page: This is a somewhat misleading name. It should read "Promoted to the list of all promoted content." This flag ensures that a node will appear in the list of content generated by the Drupal path `node`, which is the default front page in any Drupal installation. The content will be promoted to the front page only if the path to the front page remains `node`.

Sticky at top of lists: The default front page lists content in reverse chronological order, from newest to oldest. Marking content as sticky makes it appear at the top of the list instead of taking its place in the historical order, and it will stay there, along with any other sticky content, for as long as it is marked sticky.

Create new revision: This causes a new revision of the content to be created every time the user executes an update. When revisions are present, an extra tab appears on the content page alongside View and Edit. On this tab, revisions can be viewed or deleted and rollbacks to earlier versions can be executed. This is a powerful feature when combined with moderation, as normal users can submit an updated version of a published node. The revision then goes into the moderation queue, and the previously published version stays visible to the general public. An administrator or a moderator can then review the revision and decide whether to publish or delete it. This is how documentation in the Drupal handbook is maintained on `Drupal.org`, and is similar to the functionality found in wikis (`http://en.wikipedia.org/wiki/Wiki`).

You can set these states individually (if you have the Administer Nodes permission) when you create content, as shown in Figure 2-5, or configure them for each content type, as described in the next section.

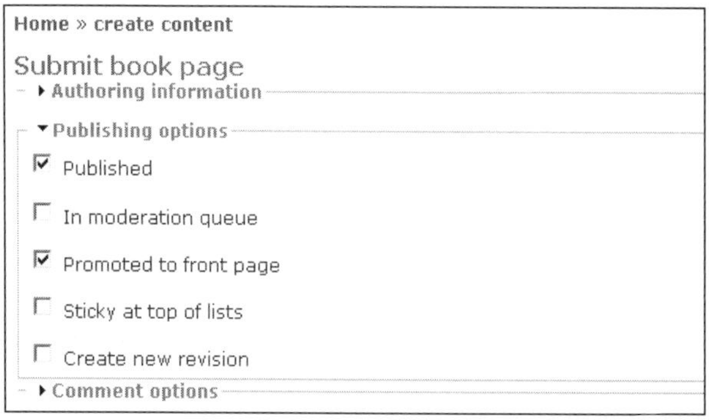

Home » create content
Submit book page
▸ Authoring information
▾ Publishing options
☑ Published
☐ In moderation queue
☑ Promoted to front page
☐ Sticky at top of lists
☐ Create new revision
▸ Comment options

Figure 2-5. *Publishing options for a page*

Type-Specific Configuration

You can configure individual content types separately, so that not every post made to your site behaves the same way. For example, it is unlikely that you will want everything to be automatically promoted to the front page of your site. Perhaps only really interesting content should make it to the front page, and all the rest should be visible only in the other sections, such as the forums or in individuals' blogs. These are the types of decisions you can make from the content types page, accessed by selecting *administer* ➤ *settings* ➤ *content types* (`admin/settings/content-types`).

All of the active content types, such as stories or pages, will be listed. Clicking the *configure* link for one of the content types listed will show you a page with at least two sections: Submission Form and Workflow. The Explanation or Submission Guidelines field is your chance to instruct users on how this particular content type is to be used on your site and provide any other guidelines or tips you may want to convey to them. The instructions appear above the form for this content type when it is being created.

If you want to enforce a minimum length policy for a content type, the Minimum Number of Words setting is the right tool. If you specify a minimum number of words, a validation error will occur if the post is shorter.

With the Workflow and Revisions of the Workflow Group settings, you can decide for every node type what the initial publishing state should be when the node is created. Individual modules can also inject their own workflow settings forms into the workflow group. If the Comment module is enabled, for each node type, you can decide whether comments should be read/write, read only, or disabled. If the Upload module is enabled, you can decide whether a node type should support file attachments. If so, users will be shown a file upload form on that node's create/edit page.

■ **Tip** Whenever you enable new modules, check the content types pages (`admin/settings/content-types`) for extra options that the enabled module may have added.

Filtering Content

A key aspect of all Drupal sites is that they gather text-based input from users and display it in web pages. Whenever user-provided text is included in an HTML document, there is risk that the text might interfere with the HTML in some way, or even worse, allow attackers to damage a site or render it useless. This could happen in many ways, from malformed or inappropriate HTML tags breaking the carefully designed layout of a site to a single line of JavaScript code that redirects the page to a different site selling questionable merchandise. Thankfully, Drupal has a sophisticated tool for handling this threat: content filtering.

The content filtering system allows administrators to decide what type of content each user role is allowed to contribute. This can range from restrictive (no HTML tags and no scripts) to complete freedom (anything goes, even PHP code, which will be executed). Each different profile is called an *input format* and can consist of as many or as few *filters* as you choose. The filters are applied at the time content is served, which means that the same input can be represented in different ways depending on which filters are applied. To configure input formats, select *administer* ➤ *input formats* (`admin/filters`).

The `admin/filters` page lists all input formats and which user roles are allowed to use them. There are also radio buttons to indicate which input format should be the default for all new content that is created. When a user's role has more than one input format available, he will be able to decide which one to use whenever he creates new content. If you feel that this places too much burden on your users to make decisions, enable only one input format for that particular role, and the choice will be removed.

An input format consists of zero or more filters, which are applied to content in an order that you specify. To see which filters are involved in any input format, click Configure for one of the input types from the `admin/filters` page. The resulting page lists all of the available filters. Check off each filter that should apply to this input format.

In the default Drupal installation, the available filters include HTML filter, line break converter, and PHP evaluator. Various modules can add their own filters, which then show up in the list. Module-contributed filters range from fun gimmicks (for example, the Smileys module replaces certain combinations of symbols like :-) with a small graphic smiley) to useful additions (for example, the Wiki module handles a full wiki syntax and functionality, all built into a content filter).

■ Tip Many contributed modules, such as the Glossary (http://drupal.org/project/glossary), Textile (http://drupal.org/project/textile), and Markdown with Smartypants (http://drupal.org/node/9838) modules, leverage content filtering. They work to give the people creating content more flexibility or to enhance the quality of their input. For example, some filters simplify the process of generating HTML, and others scan what is written for important vocabulary words or technical terms that have been defined elsewhere.

HTML Filter

The HTML filter strips or escapes any tags that are not explicitly allowed. The administrator controls the list of allowed tags for the content. To see exactly how this filter behaves, click the Configure tab for one of the filter formats for which the HTML filter is enabled (*administer ➤ input formats ➤ configure ➤ configure*). The first option, Filter HTML Tags, specifies whether HTML tags are removed from the output completely or escaped so that the tag itself is visible in the output. Escaping involves replacing the following characters with their HTML entities:

- & (ampersand) becomes &
- " (double quote) becomes "
- ' (single quote) becomes '
- < (less than) becomes <
- > (greater than) becomes >

Escaping has the advantage that if a user enters a tag that isn't allowed, she sees the tag in the output and can conclude that using that tag won't work. The disadvantage is that she might leave the escaped tags there, detracting from the quality of the content.

■ Tip The Codefilter module (http://drupal.org/project/codefilter) is ideal for sites that want to discuss PHP code.

The next field for configuring the HTML filter is Allowed HTML Tags. This is a space-separated list of HTML tags that you allow for this input format. The HTML Style Attributes field decides whether tags can possess an HTML style attribute. Since it is legal for almost any HTML tag to have this attribute, the HTML filter strips it by default to prevent users from writing things like this:

```
<a href="path to my site" style="font-size: 50em">check this out</a>
```

While you might not mind someone linking to his site from within a post, you will probably object if the text appears in gigantic sizes on the screen. Worse than destroying your layout, however, are the various security risks involved with allowing anyone with a user account (potentially anyone) to enter content on your site without some level of control. The family of attacks that one could perpetrate against your site in this case are referred to as *cross-site scripting* (XSS, defined at http://en.wikipedia.org/wiki/XSS), and the HTML filter is your first line of defense against these types of attacks.

If the Display HTML Help check box is checked, each content creation form will display a link to the Compose Tips page (filter/tips), where users can read more instructions on using the particular filters that are enabled for them. This might be helpful if your target audience doesn't know any HTML and you want to encourage them to apply markup to their posts for linking or formatting purposes. Note that there are several contributed modules available that address this need; most users will balk at having to write HTML.

Tip The TinyMCE module (http://drupal.org/project/tinymce) allows WYSIWYG HTML editing and integrates nicely with the Image module (http://drupal.org/project/image). Both modules are discussed in Chapter 4.

The final field on the HTML filter's configuration page is Spam Link Deterrent. In early 2005, Google announced (http://en.wikipedia.org/wiki/Blog_spam#nofollow) that it would no longer award any page rank credit to sites based on links with the rel="nofollow" attribute in them. This was done in response to the increasing phenomenon of spammers posting comments on blogs with links to their own sites just to increase their page ranking with Google and other search engines. Drupal quickly responded, and by checking the Spam Link Deterrent option, you ensure that any links posted by your site's users will have the rel="nofollow" attribute, and Google will not follow them when spidering. Let's hope that the incentive for comment spam will dwindle as spammers realize that they are wasting their time.

Line Break Converter and PHP Evaluator Filters

The line break converter filter is less complicated than the HTML filter. Its sole purpose is to detect hard (carriage return) and soft (Shift plus carriage return) line breaks in users' posts and replace them with <p> or <br> elements accordingly, so that the post retains its paragraphs without the user needing to use any HTML. No extra configuration is necessary for the line break converter.

The PHP evaluator is also straightforward. Anything that falls between <?php and ?> in the post will be evaluated as PHP code. This is great for creating custom pages or including third-party scripts into your Drupal site. However, you should be very careful to whom you grant permission to use this filter! Someone could literally write a post that reads all the information from your database, changes your password, sends mail on your behalf, or whatever else one can think of and achieve using PHP code. If you do not intend to use this filter yourself, I recommend turning it off for all input types.

Caution If you don't need the PHP evaluator filter on your site, turn it off. Because it allows running PHP code, it presents a serious security risk.

Ordering of Filters

Sometimes, the order in which filters are applied is important. For example, if you were to install the Smileys module so that users could decorate their posts with happy or sad faces, the Smileys module filter would look for various character sequences and replace them with HTML image tags. If the input format also included the HTML filter and it was configured to strip HTML tags, and it was applied after the smileys, the smileys would simply disappear. To avoid conflicts like this, Drupal allows you to set the order in which filters are applied.

The Rearrange tab shows a list of enabled filters for an input format and their weight. Filters with smaller weights are executed earlier than filters with larger weights. If you are having any problems with your filters not generating the output that you expect, take a look at the order and try to determine where the conflict arises.

Viewing, Searching, and Updating Content

The content administration page (`admin/node`), accessed by selecting *administer* ➤ *content*, shows an overview of the content on your site and offers a search function to assist you in executing bulk operations on multiple nodes (content) at once.

Search Filters

The search function has a fine-grained filter, so that you can select nodes with exactly the status, type, or category that you are interested in seeing. You can successively refine your search. Clicking the Filter button replaces it with three new buttons. These let you refine your search by adding another filter, undo the most recent search, or reset the filter altogether.

The search criteria are saved in your session, so they will still be applied when you return to the content administration page (`admin/node`). The search filters become especially helpful when your site has a lot of content.

Update Options

As explained earlier in this chapter, Drupal defines four different attributes that content can have to determine its publishing status. Now let's look at the different transitions between these states that a node can take. These are represented on the content administration page (`admin/node`) as Update Options. The administrator can select nodes from the list on this page by clicking the check box, and whatever update option is executed will be applied to all of the selected nodes.

Approve the selected posts: Executing this action on a node will take the node out of the moderation queue and publish it.

Promote the selected posts: This guarantees that a node is published and promoted. It does not influence whether the node remains in the moderation queue.

Make the selected posts sticky: Sets sticky to true *and* published to true, so executing this action on unpublished nodes will have the undocumented side effect of publishing them.

Demote the selected posts: Sets promoted to false, but leaves status unchanged.

Unpublish the selected posts: Sets published to false.

Delete the selected posts: Deletes all selected nodes.

Managing Comments

Any content can support user comments. Comments are also the principal building blocks of user forums. As a result, comments can become a defining characteristic of your site and a great source of user-supplied content.

Configuring Comments

To configure comments, select *administer* ➤ *comments* ➤ *configure* (`admin/comment/configure`). From the comment configuration page, you can control how comments are displayed and the fields for posting comments.

Comment Viewing Options

The first group of fields on the comment configuration page, Comment Viewing Options, controls how comments are presented on your site.

Default display mode: This determines how comments appear on the page. Comments can be flat or threaded, expanded or collapsed. The comments on `Drupal.org` are threaded and expanded.

Default display order: This determines whether comments are displayed in chronological or reverse chronological order. While this is mostly a matter of personal preference, you should consider that threaded comment listings work better in chronological order.

Default comments per page: This is the number of comments that will be displayed before pagination kicks in.

Comment controls: If you want your users to choose for themselves how comments should be displayed, this field should be set to display the comment controls above and/or below the comments. If you feel that this clutters the page and presents the user with too many options, you can disable the personalized comment controls.

Comment Posting Settings

The second group of fields on the comment configuration page, Comment Posting Settings, details comment workflow and the fields that are presented to users when they create comments.

Anonymous poster settings: This determines whether anonymous users may or may not enter contact information, and if so, whether the information is required.

Name, e-mail, and homepage: These are the contact information fields that are requested. If the information is required, the name and e-mail fields become mandatory fields. Names matching the usernames of registered users are not allowed. When comments from anonymous users are displayed, the name they supply will be wrapped in a hyperlink pointing to the site they entered as their homepage.

Comment subject field: This determines whether the subject field should be enabled for comments. Once again, this is a matter of taste. One could argue that anyone commenting on a posting is going to talk about the posting and therefore shares the subject of the posting. On the other hand, maybe the commenter wants to address only one specific point relating to the posting, so it might make sense to allow subject fields.

Preview comment: Requiring that users preview their comments before posting helps avoid errors (the users see what they're about to post) and also to filter out script-generated comments (spam), as the posting process is made more complicated by the added step. On the other hand, it is one more click that you are expecting your users to make before they can add content to your site. I'm sure many well-thought-out comments have evaporated into the ether because the author thought that she was finished with the process after clicking Preview.

Location of comment submission form: Would you rather have the comment submission form appear below the post or on a separate page? Having it appear on a separate page clutters the content page less but puts one more click between your users and the comment they want to post.

Managing the Comment Approval Queue

The user permissions page (`admin/access`) contains two permissions concerning a user's ability to post comments: Post Comments and Post Comments Without Approval. When a user in a role that allows Post Comments but not Post Comments Without Approval creates a comment, it is not immediately visible on the web site. Instead, it has been placed in the comment approval queue.

To view the comment approval queue, select *administer* ➤ *comments* ➤ *approval queue* (`admin/comment/list/approval`). From the list, you can decide to delete comments (if they are inappropriate or otherwise unwanted) or edit them to set their publishing status to Published.

■ **Note** When a user submits a comment that is destined for the comment approval queue, she is shown this message: "Your comment has been queued for moderation by site administrators and will be published after approval."

Configuring Themes

What your site can do and how it does it is only half the story. Of equal importance and interest is how the site looks. This, in Drupal, is the domain of themes. A *theme* is a set of files that works together to present your site's content. Drupal, being flexible and modular in its architecture, typically breaks down themes into three layers: engines, templates, and styles. However, you should be aware that Drupal doesn't need any themes to make web sites. All of the functions that generate HTML are defined in the core Drupal files and contributed modules, and are called *themable functions*. The job of any theme is to apply styles to the HTML and selectively override themable functions if you need to change that HTML.

Themes are also responsible for several site features such as the site logo, primary and secondary links, the footer, the mission statement, and so forth. These features can be turned on or off and configured as a part of configuring your theme. Chapter 5 explains how to install, customize, and create themes. Here, you'll learn how to configure themes.

Enabling Themes

Drupal includes four themes in its core distribution. As the administrator, you can decide which theme to use as a default for the site.

Select *administer* ➤ *themes* (`admin/themes`) to see a list of all the available themes. Changing the theme selected as the default and saving the configuration will change the look of your site. Try it out! You can test each of the available themes and decide which theme suits your needs best.

If more than one theme is enabled, registered users will have the choice of which theme they would like to use when visiting your site. They can make this choice from their user account page. A possible application of this feature might include making different versions of your site available for different needs: low-bandwidth version, text-only version, Flash version, and so on. It is also quite handy if you are a web designer and want to show your client how a site might look with different designs and styles.

Choosing Theme Settings

To set various configuration settings for all of your themes at the global level, select *administer* ➤ *themes* and click the Configure tab (`admin/themes/settings`). This page also lists links to the theme-specific settings pages for the individual themes. In general, settings at the individual theme level will override those at the global level.

Logo

The first group of options on any theme configuration page is labeled Logo Image Settings. You can either use the custom logo, if you are particularly thrilled with Drupal's little blue alien in a drop of water, or you can make and use your own logo. You can add your logo to a site in two ways. The first way is to upload your logo to the server using the File Transfer Protocol (FTP) or Secure Copy Protocol (SCP) and enter its path into the Path field for the Custom Logo option. In this case, make sure to uncheck the Use the Default Logo option. The second option is to use the Upload Logo Image field and the Save Configuration button to send a logo to the server via HTTP upload.

■ **Note** You will be able to upload a logo image using the Upload Logo Image field only if you have correctly configured the file system path where the image is to be stored. See the "File System Settings" section earlier in this chapter for details.

Shortcut Icon Settings

A shortcut (`favicon.ico`) icon (`http://en.wikipedia.org/wiki/Favicon`) is a 16×16 image that is sent to the browser for use in the address bar and tabs to help identify the site. Drupal aids you in customizing this often-overlooked detail for your site, even for each theme. You have the same options as with the custom logo: you can either place the icon on your server and then enter the path to the custom icon, or you can use the Upload Icon Image field to upload the file via HTTP. As with the custom logo, the upload doesn't occur until you click the Save Configuration button.

Primary and Secondary Links

Under the Global Settings heading are two fields, Primary Links and Secondary Links, which you can use to create a set of links that can then be displayed on your site. While this isn't the only way to create navigation links, it is a practical and quick way to get the job done. Primary and secondary links can be set only at the global level, not for individual themes.

A primary or secondary link consists of three pieces of information that you enter in the three columns of the table provided: Link Text, URL, and Description. The link text is the part of the link that is visible. The URL can be either an absolute URL (beginning with `http://`) or a Drupal path. Absolute URLs are used to link to other sites or resources on your server outside Drupal, whereas any resource inside Drupal (such as your blogs, forums, pages, or recent posts) are represented by a Drupal path. The description will be used for the `title` parameter of the resulting `<a>` tag, or hyperlink, which will be created. Here are some examples of primary and secondary links:

Link Text	URL (Type)	Description	Resulting HTML
Forums	`forum` (Drupal path)	Discussion forums	`<a href="http://www.yoursite.com/?q=forum" title="Discussion forums">Forums</a>`
Recent posts	`tracker` (Drupal path)	The most recent posts	`<a href="http://www.yoursite.com/?q=tracker" title="The most recent posts">Recent posts</a>`
Yahoo!	`http://www.yahoo.com` (absolute)	A portal to everything	`<a href="http://www.yahoo.com" title="A portal to everything">Yahoo!</a>`

Display Post Information

Post information includes the username and date of publication for any given node. By checking the various node types listed, you decide whether this information is displayed. You would probably opt to show post information on a site where many users are submitting content. You would likely want to hide the post information on a homepage or corporate site where there is either a single author or all the information is speaking for a single entity. This can be configured only at the global level, not for individual themes.

Toggle Display

Other settings that you can turn on or off include Site Name, Site Slogan, and Mission Statement. These are all text that you configured on the general site settings page (`admin/settings`).

Then there are the primary and secondary links that you created on the theme configuration global settings page (`admin/themes/settings`). Enabling the User Pictures in Posts option or the User Pictures in Comments option controls whether user pictures or avatars are displayed in posts or comments. These fields will be disabled unless you first enable picture support from the `admin/settings/user` page.

Finally, if you have the Search module enabled, you can toggle the search box with the Search Box setting. You can set the toggle display settings globally or individually for each installed theme.

Using Categories

One of Drupal's hottest features is its outstanding support for classification of content through the application of categories. Categories are sometimes referred to as *taxonomies*, a slightly more technical term that means basically the same thing. You need to have the Taxonomy module enabled in order to use categories.

Note Categories require the Taxonomy module to be enabled.

Understanding Vocabularies and Terms

Drupal divides the task of categorization into two general concepts: vocabularies and terms. A *vocabulary* represents a general concept and is collection of words or phrases that are all different ways of describing the same thing. A *term* is a word or phrase providing a concrete example of the vocabulary's general concept.

For example, if *Animals* were a vocabulary, *dog, bird, fish,* and *cow* would all be terms in it. If you were trying to categorize the news, you might use terms like *International, State,* and *Local* to describe the different types of news. In Drupal, that structure would be represented with a vocabulary *News* that has three terms:

```
News
    International
    State
    Local
```

Vocabularies can be assigned to different content types. This allows you to categorize every post of that type using the terms in the vocabulary. If you were to assign the News vocabulary to story types, every time you created a new story, you would have the choice of categorizing it as International, State, or Local. When the content is viewed, Drupal displays category links indicating how the content has been categorized and leading to pages that show other content in the same category.

These features alone make categories a great tool for organizing the content on your web site. They allow visitors to get to all of the posts that have been made within a certain category and give content creators an opportunity to classify the content they are creating.

The category system is capable of much more, however. The hierarchy of a vocabulary is not limited to a simple list of terms. For example, you could expand the International term of the News taxonomy to have subcategories as well:

```
News
    International
        Politics
        Business
        Travel
```

Here, the International term has three subterms: Politics, Business, and Travel. In this case, those three terms have International as a parent. If each term can have only one parent,

Drupal calls it a single hierarchy. A multiple hierarchy exists when terms can have multiple parents, as illustrated in Figure 2-6.

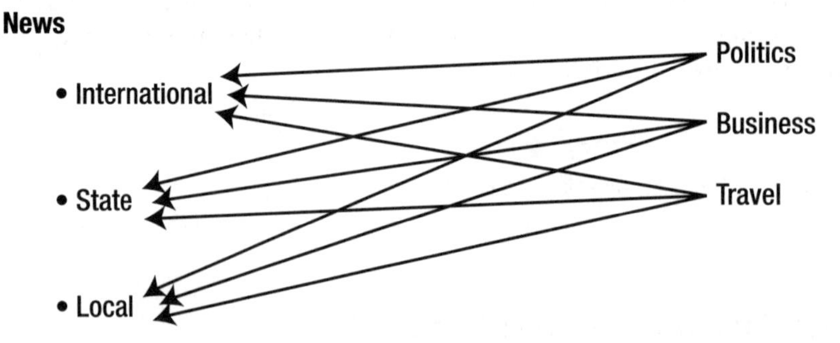

Figure 2-6. *Multiple hierarchy example*

This flexibility allows you to model very complex relationships within a vocabulary. To add to the possibilities, you can create many different vocabularies, and each content type can have more than one vocabulary assigned to it. This allows you to not only categorize your content, but to categorize it in different ways or realms. The hierarchy in Figure 2-7 could be replaced, for example, with two vocabularies: News Area and News Topic.

News area	News topic
• International	• Politics
• State	• Business
• Local	• Travel

Figure 2-7. *Multiple vocabularies example*

Using these two vocabularies, you could provide very detailed information about every story (or any other content) that you write. Your site could then easily be organized into sections like International News, Regional News, and Local News, each with the subsections Politics, Business, and Travel.

Drupal is also capable of listing the content in different categories or combinations of categories based on the information it receives in the URL. This means you can easily make custom sections that display local news about politics simply by entering the correct URL. Category listings—even complex listings built from two or more terms—have their own RSS feeds, so visitors to your site can easily subscribe to the various categories or channels with their feed reader, without requiring you to program anything. Finally, there are many Drupal modules that use the category system for a wide variety of tasks, such as creating the structure of forums or image galleries, making site navigation menus, providing access control to content, and changing the theme to style different sections of your site differently. As you can see, the category system adds whole new dimensions to what your site can achieve.

Configuring Categories

You configure categories by selecting *administer* ➤ *categories* (`admin/taxonomy`). This involves adding vocabularies, and you also may add terms.

Adding a Vocabulary

The first step to configuring categories is to add a vocabulary, from the `admin/taxonomy/add/vocabulary` page. The following settings appear on this page:

Vocabulary name: This name will be used to identify the vocabulary on the administration page and will also show up as the label for categories form on content creation pages.

Description: This text is used by only a few modules and plays no role in the normal use case for categories. You can safely leave this field blank unless instructed otherwise by a particular module.

Help text: This will be shown to users when they categorize their posts. Use it to clarify how you expect the categories to be applied.

Types: This is a list of content types. Check each one that should be categorized with this vocabulary.

Related terms: Checking this turns on functionality that allows you to specify weak relationships between terms that are somehow related. It adds another form to the term-editing form. The new form allows you to specify one or more existing terms, which are then considered to be related. This would be helpful if you were using taxonomy to build a glossary, for example. There you could have a term *Website* and indicate that *Homepage* is a related term. Then the glossary entry for *Website* would have the annotation "See also: Homepage." Related terms are useful only if a module, such as the Glossary module, makes specific use of them. For the most typical case, node categorization, you will not need them.

■ **Tip** The Glossary module (`http://drupal.org/project/glossary`) builds a category-based glossary on your web site to help visitors quickly find the definitions for technical terms or jargon that might appear in your content. It makes use of the related terms functionality of the category system.

Free tagging: Sites like del.icio.us (`http://del.icio.us/`) and Flickr (`http://www.flickr.com/`) have championed the use of free tagging for categorizing content. Instead of the site administrator creating a set of terms and expecting the users to choose one or more of them as they apply, the users themselves can create the terms as a list of words that apply, thus the name *free tagging*. Drupal offers free tagging as an option as well. By checking the Free Tagging check box on the edit vocabulary page, you give the users of the site control over the terms in the vocabulary; they will create the terms every time they create content. Instead of being presented with a drop-down selection box for the categories, as is the case with normal vocabularies, the users will have a text field into which they can type a list of their tags, separated by commas.

■ **Tip** The Tagadelic module (`http://drupal.org/project/tagadelic`) shows free tagging tags in the style made famous by Flickr (`http://www.flickr.com/photos/tags/`), with each tag's size adjusted to the number of posts associated with it.

Hierarchy: If your terms are to appear in a flat list, then the Hierarchy field should be Disabled. If child terms should have only one parent, choose Single. Single represents a one-to-many relationship between a parent and its children. If terms should be able to have multiple parents, choose Multiple. This represents a *many-to-many* relationship between parents and children (child terms can have many parents).

Multiple select: This allows you to assign more than one term to content. This is useful if you want the content to appear in more than one category list. Free tagging categories are always multiple select and will take care of this detail for you.

Required: If the vocabulary is set as Required, users will be forced to select at least one term from it when they create content. The `<none>` option will disappear from vocabulary selection boxes on the content creation forms.

Weight: This determines the order in which vocabularies are listed on the `admin/taxonomy` page, as well as the order in which they are presented in the content creation forms. As is customary, larger numbers move toward the bottom and smaller numbers go toward the top.

Now your vocabulary has been created and configured. If it is a free tagging vocabulary, your work is finished, as users and content creators will provide the actual terms, or tags. For other vocabularies, the next step is to make the list of terms and, if appropriate, determine the hierarchy.

Adding Terms

To see an overview of a vocabulary's terms, select *administer* ➤ *categories* ➤ *edit terms* for the appropriate vocabulary. Alongside the list of existing terms is an Add Term tab, which brings you to the page for adding terms. The important fields here are Name and Parents. The name is what the user will be presented with in the selection box when choosing categories, and the Parents setting determines the hierarchy of the terms within the vocabulary.

The Description and Synonyms fields are virtually unused by core modules and can be left blank most of the time. The Weight setting controls the placement of the term in the list of terms belonging to that vocabulary.

When you click Submit to create a new term, you will be returned to the page for adding terms, to facilitate adding many terms quickly and easily.

Leveraging Categories with Custom URLs

Drupal offers a very special tool for querying content based on categories using the URL or Drupal path. It enables you to construct a path to get a list of content in one or more categories and display the list either as a normal page or as an RSS feed. It allows for Boolean AND or OR operators to combine terms, and it allows you to specify a depth so that you can obtain an entire hierarchy of terms.

■Note A URL is a complete address that includes the protocol (HTTP), your domain, and depending on whether you have clean URLs enabled, the ?q= parameter. The path, on the other hand, is the value for the q parameter. So if the URL is http://www.yoursite.com/?q=taxonomy/term/2, the path is taxonomy/term/2. With clean URLs enabled, the URL would be http://www.yoursite.com/taxonomy/term/2, and the path would be the same.

Finding Term IDs

The first thing that you need in order to query the taxonomy (category) system is the ID number of the term(s) you are interested in. You'll need to do some sleuthing to find this, but it is not hard to do. Select *administer* ➤ *categories* ➤ *edit terms* to go to the edit page of a vocabulary. There you will see a list of terms as well as an Edit link for each one. The Edit link provides the important clue that you are seeking. Hover your cursor over the link, and the URL to the link will appear in the status bar at the bottom of your browser window (if it doesn't, click the link and it will appear in the navigation bar at the top of your browser window). It should look something like this:

```
http://www.yoursite.com/admin/taxonomy/edit/term/4?destination=admin%2Ftaxonomy%2F2
```

The pertinent part of this URL is the term/4 segment in the middle. That tells you that you are looking at term number 4.

■Note The technical term for category in Drupal-speak is *taxonomy*. The Taxonomy module is responsible for Drupal's category functionality, and the Drupal paths that you will be building to query your site will all start with the word *taxonomy*. Therefore, this section refers to categories using the technical term, taxonomies.

The term ID (tid) is essential information when building URL-based taxonomy queries, so having an easy way to find them is essential. If you are able to look into your database, you can open the term_data table and use it as a reference. The tid column contains the number you are looking for, and you can see the term's name in the name column.

Once you have a term number in hand, you can build a simple path to view all of the content that is tagged or categorized with that term. The form of the path is taxonomy/term/*tid*, where *tid* is the term ID number. Here is an example using the tid 4 with clean URLs:

```
http://www.yoursite.com/taxonomy/term/4
```

And here is an example without clean URLs:

```
http://www.yoursite.com/?q=taxonomy/term/4
```

Using the AND and OR Operators

The simple syntax used in the previous example can be enhanced by asking for more than one term. If you want to see a list of all the content that is classified with both tids 4 and 5, here is what the path would look like:

```
taxonomy/term/4,5
```

Notice that the comma (,) is used to separate the two tids. The comma functions as the AND operator; only content with classified with tid 4 AND tid 5 will be shown. If you would like to see content with tid 4 OR tid 5, use the plus (+) operator instead:

```
taxonomy/term/4+5
```

The list of terms can be arbitrarily long, but only one of the two operators should be used; don't mix the AND operator with the OR operator:

```
taxonomy/term/4,6,7,14,33
taxonomy/term/5+3+2+56+122
```

Indicating Depth

If your taxonomy vocabulary represents a hierarchy, you can construct paths to return just a segment of the hierarchy. Consider the following hierarchy:

```
term 1
    term 2
        term 3
        term 4
            term 5
    term 6
```

You already know what the path should look like to get a list of content for tid 1:

```
taxonomy/term/1
```

This is a shorthand for the longer syntax that follows this form:

```
taxonomy/term/tid/depth
```

Depth is the number of levels in the hierarchy below the tid that should be returned, and it defaults to zero (0). So these two paths are equivalent:

```
taxonomy/term/1
taxonomy/term/1/0
```

Now watch what happens when you ask for a depth of 1:

```
taxonomy/term/1/1
```

You now get a list that includes content categorized with tids 1, 2, and 6, as these are the direct children of tid 1. Increase the depth to 2, and the list will grow to include tids 3 and 4. A depth of 3 or greater will produce the entire hierarchy. Can you predict which terms this path will produce?

```
taxonomy/term/4+6/1
```

It will list all content that is classified with either tid 4 or 6 or any of their direct children, which includes tid 5.

Returning a Page or a Feed

Each of the resulting lists in the previous examples can be returned as a page, which is the default and what you've seen so far, or returned as an RSS feed. All that is needed is an extra segment on the end of the path that specifies feed or page. Here is the full syntax for taxonomy queries:

```
taxonomy/term/tids/depth/{page | feed}

taxonomy/term/1/0/page
taxonomy/term/1/0/feed

taxonomy/term/4+6/1/page
taxonomy/term/4+6/1/feed
```

Note that you need to use the full syntax, including the depth segment, if you're asking for an RSS feed.

Clearly there is much power to be unleashed by using Drupal's categories in creative ways. There are few, if any, comparable systems available, and this feature alone sets Drupal apart from most projects working in the PHP/CMS space.

Summary

This chapter covered the basic configuration possibilities for a new Drupal installation. You have seen how to enable modules, control the placement of blocks, administer user permissions, and set up categories. You have been introduced to Drupal themes and some of the configuration options you have for customizing them. Many of these tasks will be revisited as more modules and content types are enabled. Modules can define their own blocks, user permissions, and settings, so every module that you enable will usually require some adjustment to some or all of these areas.

Here's a review of how to access each of the areas described in this chapter:

Area	Path
Site settings	admin/settings
User registration and e-mail settings	admin/settings/user
User creation	admin/user/create
Account rules	admin/access/rules
Enabling and disabling modules	admin/modules
Block administration	admin/block
Comment configuration	admin/comment/configure
Input formats	admin/filters
Content overview	admin/node
Theme selection	admin/themes
Category configuration	admin/taxonomy

The next chapter presents the core Drupal modules. It shows you what modules can do and how you can use them together to further customize your site. This will include various content types like stories, polls, and blogs, as well as modules that add general functionality to your site like uploading files or doing full text searches. You will see how your Drupal site can get itself listed in the directory of Drupal sites and how you can define forms to collect profile information from your user base.

Contributed modules offer some of the most interesting and significant ways to extend Drupal's capabilities, and they are discussed in Chapter 4.

CHAPTER 3

Using the Drupal Core Modules

Drupal comes with 31 core modules, which address everything from basic functions such as user management (the User module), logging (the Watchdog module), and analysis of access to the site (the Statistics module) to advanced features such as managing a hierarchical series of collaborative pages that can be versioned and moderated (the Book module). Becoming familiar with these modules and mastering their usage will help you get the most out of Drupal and create powerful web sites. This chapter explores each of the core modules, which are presented in alphabetical order for easy reference.

The modules covered in this chapter are included when you download Drupal. The core modules have been well tested, adhere to strict standards of coding, and provide basic functionality and services that are useful to a wide spectrum of types of sites. To use them, you simply need to make sure that they are enabled. As explained in Chapter 2, to see the available modules, select *administer* ➤ *modules* (`admin/modules`). On this page, the modules are listed with check boxes to set their status. Any additional configuration tasks for a specific module are described in the section about that module in this chapter.

Aggregator Module

RSS has been a revolutionary force in finding and distributing content on the Web. The ability of a site or program to query other sites about what content is available has led to the advent of aggregator sites such as Weblogs (`http://weblogs.com/`), Feedster (`http://feedster.com/`), Bloglines (`http://www.bloglines.com/`), and Technorati (`http://www.technorati.com/`). These sites regularly access RSS feeds from around the Web and catalog the results. RSS also allows visitors to your site to subscribe to your content using popular feed readers like FeedDemon (`http://www.bradsoft.com/feeddemon/`), SharpReader (`http://www.sharpreader.net/`), NetNewsWire (`http://www.apple.com/downloads/macosx/internet_utilities/netnewswire.html`), and iPodder (`http://www.ipodder.org/`).

The widespread use of syndication and subscription has led to a vast improvement in the delivery of targeted information on the Web. Not only do individuals have more tools to filter and collect information of interest, but the entire cycle of publishing and discovery has been shortened dramatically. Your feed reader will tell you whenever it detects new content on sites to which you have subscribed. Drupal 4.7 includes support for aggregating content for the various syndication specifications, including all versions of RSS and Atom.

Drupal's Aggregator module reads syndicated feeds from other sites, in essence allowing your Drupal site to act as a feed reader. It will publish the titles, headlines, and teasers from articles and posts in the feeds, as well as provide links to the original content. Thus, your site becomes a hub for the latest news from around the Internet, focused on whichever topics you choose.

The feeds are updated regularly using Drupal's scheduled task functionality (`cron.php`) on a schedule you set. (Refer to Chapter 6 for instructions on configuring scheduled tasks using `cron.php`, which is necessary for having Aggregator feed items updated automatically.) You also have the ability to update the feeds manually from the administration interface.

■ **Note** A *feed* is a collection of the latest articles from a site. This collection will change in time as the feed's site is updated. Drupal will purge all of the feed items that are no longer current from your database, so that those displayed reflect the items that are current on the source site. Keep this idea of impermanence in mind when considering some of the more advanced features of the Aggregator module, such as categorizing feed items. Is it worth the work when they will all eventually be replaced by newer items?

Identifying Feeds

The process of configuring your site to act as an aggregator of syndicated content starts with finding the URLs of feeds to which you wish to subscribe. Fortunately, for many sites on the Web, this is as easy as locating the RSS link or icon, right-clicking it, and choosing Copy Link Location. For other sites, including most blogs hosted by Blogger (`http://blogger.com`), the feed URL is embedded in the page source header, and no link or icon is provided. Modern browsers such as Firefox recognize this and will indicate that a feed is available for subscription, but if you want to extract the feed from the page, you will usually need to look at the page source and locate the feed link in the header. It will look something like the following:

```
<link rel="alternate" type="application/rss+xml" title="RSS"
href="http://ihatetobacco.blogspot.com/atom.xml" />
```

or

```
<link rel="EditURI" type="application/rsd+xml" title="RSD"
href="http://www.blogger.com/rsd.g?blogID=6180553" />
```

The type parameter `"application/rss+xml"` or `"application/rsd+xml"` is the indication that this is a syndication feed. The part you're interested in for instructing Drupal to subscribe to the feed is the value for the `href` parameter:

```
http://ihatetobacco.blogspot.com/atom.xml
```

or

```
http://www.blogger.com/rsd.g?blogID=6180553
```

■ **Note** The proper MIME type for Atom feeds is `application/atom+xml`. See `http://atompub.org/2004/10/20/draft-ietf-atompub-format-03.html#rfc.section.2` for more information about the Atom format.

Configuring Feeds

Now that you have found interesting feeds, you are ready to use the Aggregator module to subscribe to them. To configure feeds, you add them, optionally categorize them, and set permissions for them.

Adding Feeds

Make sure that the Aggregator module is enabled (`admin/modules`), and navigate to the Aggregator's main administration screen, `admin/aggregator`. From there, use the Add Feed tab (`aggregator/add/feed`) to add your first feed. Fill in the fields on this tab:

- The Title field is the title you wish to give the feed. It will be used when displaying the feed items.
- The URL field is where you should enter the feed's URL. Examples of URLs are `http://drupal.org/rss.xml` and `http://civicspacelabs.org/home/node/feed`.
- The Update Interval field determines the minimum amount of time that should elapse before your site checks the remote site for updates.

In deciding on an update interval, keep in mind that you shouldn't have your site check for updates more often than is necessary. Importing feeds is a relatively time-consuming operation for your web site, not to mention the extra Internet traffic and load that is generated for the remote sites. If a site is likely to be updated only once a day, you don't need to check every hour. On the other hand, if a site is constantly updated, as is `Drupal.org`, you'll want to schedule the updates more often.

■ **Note** Web etiquette suggests that you should not update your aggregator feeds any more frequently than every 30 minutes. This is out of courtesy to the site providing the feed, as feed readers can generate abundant amounts of traffic and server overhead if not held in check. It is also worth noting that since feed updates are managed by the `cron.php`-based automated tasks (see Chapter 6), the actual frequency of updates is inherently dependent on the cron schedule.

After adding your feed information, click Submit. You will return to the main Aggregator administration page, where you should see your feed listed. At this point, the feed has not yet been updated and no items have been imported. Click the *update items* link for your new feed to test it and to import the latest items from the remote site. If the update is successful, you will be able to see the items by clicking the *news aggregator* menu item (Drupal path `aggregator`).

■ **Tip** The RSS feed for `Drupal.org` is `http://drupal.org/rss.xml`. It is a listing of the most recent content that has been promoted to the front page.

Categorizing Feeds

The Aggregator module also allows you to categorize your feeds so that they can be grouped by topic or area of interest. To add a feed category, return to the Aggregator's main administration page and click the Add Category tab (`admin/aggregator/add/category`). Add as many categories as you want. Now, whenever you create a new feed or edit an existing feed, you will be given the chance to categorize the feed based on the categories you just created. Furthermore, the various categories have their own listing pages. Click the *news aggregator* menu item (Drupal path `aggregator`), and you will see that the categories now appear as menu items below the *news aggregator* item.

Sometimes, categorizing an entire feed isn't really accurate enough. Perhaps your favorite blog author who usually writes about politics suddenly decides to include a blog post about cooking. Fortunately, Drupal offers a mechanism for categorizing the individual feed items as well: the Categorize tab from any individual feed's page (`aggregator/sources/`*`feed_id`*`/categorize`). This gives you fine-grained control over which items appear in which categories.

Setting Permissions

The Aggregator module defines two permissions: Access News Feeds and Administer News Feed. The final step in configuring your news feeds is assigning the appropriate permissions to user roles. As explained in Chapter 2, you set permissions by navigating to *administer* ➤ `access control` page (`admin/access`).

Viewing Feeds

The Aggregator module provides many different options for viewing the feeds. If you navigate to the block administration page (`admin/block`), you'll see that every feed and feed category can be shown in a block. Blocks showing feeds offer an additional convenience feature in conjunction with the Blog module. When the Blog module is enabled, feed items in blocks appear with a *b:* icon next to them. Clicking this icon is a convenient way to create a new blog entry that cites the feed item and provides a link to the original source. This is a very user-friendly feature that encourages your site's bloggers to write about the things they read in the feed items.

Once you have configured news sources (feeds), the *news aggregator* link in the main menu will show a submenu labeled *sources* (`aggregator/sources`), which leads to a page where the feed items are grouped by source. If you have categorized your feeds, you'll also see the submenu item *categories* (`aggregator/categories`), with the feed items grouped by category.

Archive Module

The Archive module presents a calendar view of your site's content and a searching mechanism. Days on which content was submitted show as a link to those entries. After you enable the Archive module, you'll see a Calendar to Browse Archives block, which you can configure to show the calendar.

The path to any given day in the archive takes the form `archive/`*`year/month/day`*. To see the content from April 23, 2005, for example, use the path `archive/2005/4/23`.

Block Module

The Block module is responsible for managing blocks, which are units of content provided by the various modules or added by the administrator. Blocks added by the administrator are called custom blocks, and they can contain HTML or PHP code.

Details on using blocks and configuring the Block module were presented in Chapter 2. There, you learned that blocks can appear in any of the default regions of the screen (left and right sidebars, the header, the footer, and the main content area) or in administrator-defined regions, which will be covered in Chapter 5. You can also configure blocks to appear on some pages but not others.

The Block module defines one permission, Administer Blocks, which allows a user role to create, position, and configure blocks.

Blog Module

Drupal is a pioneer in the area of multiuser blogging. With your Drupal site, each registered user can have a blog. Bloggers receive their own blog URL, which displays all of their blog posts, yet the content created by the individual users can appear elsewhere on the site as well. This feature makes Drupal an excellent choice for bridging the gap between individual blogs and an online community.

Configuring Blogs

To get started with the Blog module, you need to assign the Edit Own Blog permission to the user roles that should be able to maintain individual blogs. Users with the proper permissions can then create new blog entries using the *create content* ➤ *personal blog* entry link.

As with all other Drupal content, you can categorize blogs (with the Taxonomy module). Additionally, blogs can have file uploads (thanks to the Upload module), store revision history, be promoted to the front page, and have comments. Chapter 2 details these configuration settings.

The blogging experience can be enhanced further with the help of a number of contributed modules and external tools. The BlogAPI module, described in the next section, allows users to post to their blogs using popular desktop tools such as ecto (`http://ecto.kung-foo.tv/`), w.bloggar (`http://www.wbloggar.com/`), and iBlog (`http://www.iblog.com/home.php`). In addition, the following contributed modules enhance the blog module's functionality:

- TrackBack support (a method of notification about the citation or referencing of blog posts between web sites) can be added by installing the TrackBack module: `http://drupal.org/project/trackback`.
- Every blog can have a different theme with the Blog Theme module: `http://drupal.org/node/19248`.
- Blogroll functionality (for managing lists of links to other blogs and sites) is added with the Blogroll module: `http://drupal.org/project/blogroll`.

Accessing Blogs

Each blogger has a path that lists all of her personal blog entries. This path always follows the pattern `blog/uid` where *uid* is that user's ID number. The Drupal path `blog` will display a page with all blog entries from all users, providing a useful overview of all blogging activity.

RSS 2.0 feeds are provided for each individual's blog, as well as for the blog page that lists all blog entries. A user's blog feed can be accessed using the path `blog/uid/feed`, and the feed for all blogs is `blog/feed`. Blog posts that are promoted to the front page will appear in the site's main feed as well.

BlogAPI Module

Publishing to a web site by using a web browser has its limitations. Despite the progress that has been made in developing WYSIWYG editors such as TinyMCE, it is still not as comfortable to type and format large portions of text as it is using a word processing program such as OpenOffice. Furthermore, it is impossible to use a browser to compose to a web site when not connected to the Internet, so working on your blogs offline isn't an option. Finally, if you maintain blogs on many different web sites, the interface may be different for each one, making the whole process take much more time and effort than necessary. The BlogAPI module, in conjunction with desktop blogging tools such as ecto, w.bloggar, or iBlog, addresses these weaknesses and opens up the possibility of editing your blog posts offline using comfortable text editing programs.

■ **Note** You could, of course, use a program like OpenOffice (`http://www.openoffice.org`) to edit your blog posts offline, which may be more comfortable than using a program like ecto, even though you would need to copy and paste your work into the browser.

Configuring BlogAPI

Enable the BlogAPI module and configure it from the `admin/settings/blogapi` page, which has only one field to configure.

The Blog Types field allows you to select the blog content types to publish. The BlogAPI module allows you to create virtually any content type from your desktop publishing client. If you select more than one type of content in the Blog Types field, your blogging client will later give you the choice of which "blog" to publish to. This refers to which content type you wish to create.

Publishing to Your Site Using BlogAPI

Table 3-1 lists some of the programs that you can use to publish to your Drupal site using the BlogAPI module.

Table 3-1. *Some XML-RPC Publishing Tools*

Program	Operating System	Web Site
w.bloggar	Windows	`http://www.wbloggar.com/`
ecto	Windows, Mac OS X	`http://ecto.kung-foo.tv/`
iBlog	MacOSX	`http://www.iblog.com/home.php`
BlogApp	Mac OS X	`http://www.objectivelabs.com/blogapp.php`
MarsEdit	Mac OS X	`http://www.ranchero.com/marsedit`
BloGTK	GNU/Linux	`http://blogtk.sourceforge.net/`
BlogniX	GNU/Linux	`http://blognix.sourceforge.net/`

Book Module

The Book module is one of the most useful of all Drupal modules due to its ability to add a high level of structure and organization to the content on your site. Its main function is to maintain a hierarchy of content and to offer a means of ordered navigation between them. These are the familiar *previous*, *next*, and *up* links that you can see at `Drupal.org` in the handbook (for example, at `http://drupal.org/node/22963`). Furthermore, the Book module has a content type of its own, called *book pages*.

Using Book Pages

The book page was created for use on `Drupal.org` to facilitate the collaborative creation and editing of documentation. In order to give everyone the chance to contribute to the Drupal handbooks (`http://drupal.org/handbooks`), it was necessary to let all site users make new book pages and edit existing pages. The danger, of course, is that not everyone writes good documentation, and some people might even do malicious things like delete or deface the existing documentation, so some level of moderation was needed. The solution was that any new book pages and any revisions of existing book pages would be subject to approval by a moderator. When an existing book page gets edited, the changes are saved as a revision, and the original version of the page continues to be displayed on the site.

The book page content type differs from other content types in a number of subtle yet important ways. In addition to the Title and Body fields, which are common to other types such as blogs, pages, and stories, the page for creating book type content has the following fields:

- The Parent field controls the page's position within the overall hierarchy. A book is defined as a content node that lives at the top level of the book hierarchy (has no parent) and all of its children. This is achieved by choosing <top-level> as the value for the Parent field.

- The Weight field controls the order of pages within a particular level of the hierarchy. As usual, content with lighter weights (smaller numbers) will appear before content with heavier weights (larger numbers).

- The Log Message field is intended to be used as part of a collaborative editing workflow that makes book pages unique among content types. Someone making an edit can use this field to indicate to the moderators or other editors what was changed and why.

The Book module introduces three permissions: Create Book Pages, Edit Own Book Pages, and Maintain Books. The Create Book Pages and Edit Own Book Pages permissions are self-explanatory and deal with only the book page content type. Users with the Maintain Books permission can edit book pages that are not their own, and they can put posts of any content type (and from any author) into the book outline hierarchy.

Working with the Book Outline

Select *administer* ➤ *content* ➤ *books* (admin/node/book) to see an overview of all the books. Clicking the *outline* link for any of the books will bring you to a page that details the hierarchical structure of that book, including all of the book pages and other content types that have been added to the outline, as shown in Figure 3-1.

Book: top-level

list | books

list | orphan pages

Title	Weight	Operations
Book: top-level	0	view edit delete
Page 1	1	view edit delete
Sub page 1	1	view edit delete
Sub page 2	2	view edit delete
Page 2	2	view edit delete
Page 3	3	view edit delete
Page 4	4	view edit delete

Save book pages

Figure 3-1. *The book outline*

Besides providing an overview of the book hierarchy, the outline view offers a convenient way to adjust the weights for the various content nodes so that they are in the desired order. The additional link *orphan pages* (admin/node/book/orphan) will identify any nodes that were once children in the book outline but now have no parent because the parent node was deleted.

Where the Book module really starts to display its power is with content node types other than book pages. With the Book module enabled, you can add any content type to the book outline. For users who have the Create Book Pages permission, all content nodes will have a new Outline tab, which they can use to add that node to a book outline. Furthermore, any node that is in the book outline will have an *add child page* link, which makes a book page a descendent from the current page in the book hierarchy. These tools can be used to organize all of the content on your site into logical groups and hierarchies that can be navigated sequentially using the *previous* and *next* links.

Viewing Book Pages

The book page content type has a number of alternative views, including the following:

- The print-friendly version strips out design elements from your web site and presents the content in a way that is more efficient for printing pages on paper.
- The export DocBook XML view produces an XML document from your content, which can be used by other tools that read DocBook XML documents.
- The export OPML view presents the content in the book outline in Outline Processor Markup Language (OPML) format for viewing and editing with OPML-compatible tools.

The DocBook XML and OPML export views are a step toward being able to create and edit structured web site content offline, which is useful if you intend to create flyers, brochures, or treeware books.

■ **Note** See `http://www.oasis-open.org/docbook/` for more information about DocBook XML and `http://www.opml.org/` for details on OPML. Note that the Drupal 4.7 core functionality does not support importing content via OPML or DocBook XML.

The Book module generates a new block, which you can enable from the block administration page (`admin/block`). The book navigation block, shown in Figure 3-2, appears on the page with any node that is in a book outline. It displays a fragment of the book outline relative to the current node, including the parent's lineage up to the top-level node and all of the current node's children. This makes navigating in the book hierarchy especially easy.

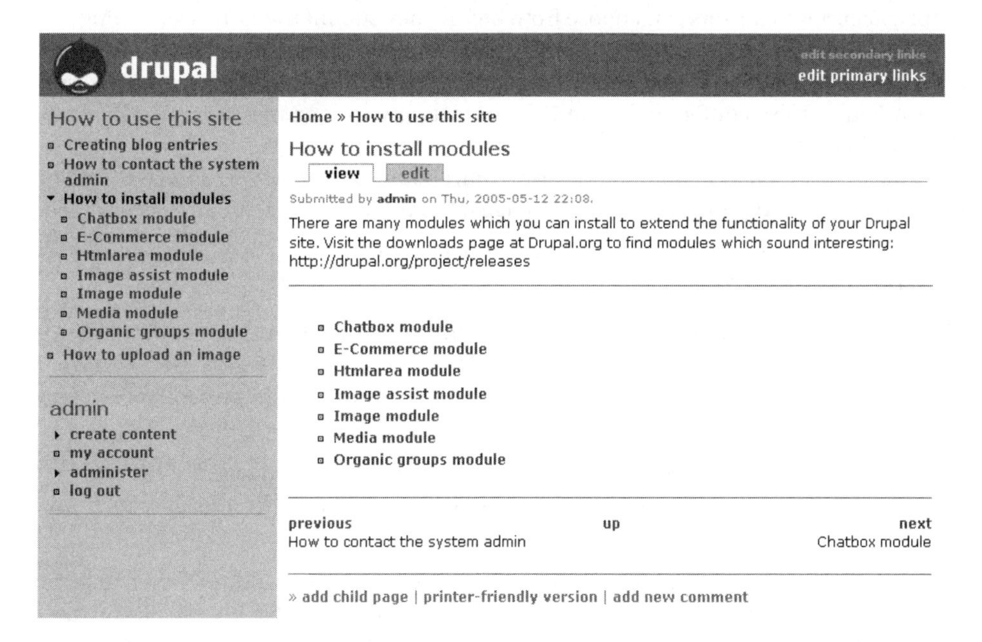

Figure 3-2. *The book navigation block in the left sidebar displays a fragment of the book outline relative to the current node.*

Comment Module

The Comment module adds the ability to allow users to comment on any content node type. With options for the display format, as well as the publishing workflow, the Comment module gives your site a large amount of flexibility in configuring user comments. Comments and configuring the Comment module were covered in Chapter 2.

Contact Module

The Contact module provides a personal contact form for every registered user. This form lets people send e-mail messages to each other without publishing their e-mail addresses on the web site. Each user can decide whether he wants to enable his contact form. The Contact module also provides a form for contacting the site administrator, the sitewide contact form, which serves as a simple and effective way to gather feedback.

Using the Personal Contact Form

When the Contact module is enabled, a Contact tab (`user/`*`uid`*`/contact`) will be visible on each user's profile screen. Users can enable their personal contact form from their user account editing page by checking the Personal Contact Form field in the Contact Settings section. When a user has allowed it, other registered users can send him messages via the Contact tab. There is a limit on the number of messages users can send per hour, to prevent abuse.

Using the Sitewide Contact Form

The sitewide contact form (Drupal path `contact`) is quite useful because you can set up a number of categories that users can choose from before they submit the form. Depending on which category they choose, the contact e-mail can be sent to different addresses, allowing support questions to go to `support@yoursite.com`, suggestions to `suggestions@yoursite.com`, and so forth. You can also configure the sitewide contact form to send these e-mail messages to multiple recipients.

To set up categories that people can choose from, choose *administer* ➤ *contact* (`admin/contact`). The Add Category tab on this page takes you to a form with three fields:

- The Category field identifies the purpose of the mail that the user is sending, as well as determines who will receive it.
- The Recipients field is for the contact e-mail address. If more than one e-mail address is to receive the mail, enter them here separated by commas. Every time a user submits the sitewide contact form for this category, all of these e-mail addresses will receive the message.
- The Auto-reply field is for an optional message that will be mailed to the user's e-mail address, possibly thanking him for his submission or relaying other information. If you leave this field empty, no auto-reply e-mail will be sent.

If you would like to have a *contact us* link in your navigation menu, and you have the Menu module enabled, select *administer* ➤ *menus* (`admin/menu`) to access the list of enabled and disabled menu items. One of the disabled items is *contact us*. Enable this menu item, and the link will appear in your navigation menu.

Drupal Module

Drupal offers a system of distributed authentication that allows people to use the same username and password at multiple sites. The sites communicate with each other to check authentication credentials and to decide whether a username and password combination should be allowed or denied. This is called *distributed authentication.* If you want your site to have this feature, you need to enable the Drupal module. The Drupal module also lets you run Drupal as a directory server that receives ping notification from other Drupal sites, creating a listing of sites.

■ **Note** At the time this was written, a lively debate was unfolding on `Drupal.org` about the future of the Drupal module (`http://drupal.org/node/31716`). It is worth checking up on this thread to see where the issue stands.

Using Distributed Authentication

Drupal distributed authentication is a way to save site users the extra steps of creating redundant accounts on multiple sites. With distributed authentication, users can register on one site, and then use an extended version of their login information to log in to any site that supports Drupal distributed authentication. This is not only convenient for users, but it's also useful in situations where sites want to maintain a shared user base but not a shared database.

When logging in to a Drupal site using distributed authentication, your username takes on an extended form that includes the site that is expected to do the actual authenticating. The extended username takes the form *`username`*`@www.`*`domain`*`.com`. For example, if Bob is a registered user at `www.bobs-site.org` with the username `bob`, his extended username is `bob@www.bobs-site.org`, and his password remains unchanged. When Bob uses this extended username to log in to another Drupal-powered site, that site will send a request to Bob's original site, `www.bobs-site.com`, and ask it if a user `bob` with the password that he entered should be authenticated.

You should be aware that the current implementation of distributed authentication raises some security concerns. Someone could alter the code of her site to save a record of the passwords of users who log in. This is true of any web site you visit, not just Drupal. As long as the username and password only buys access to just that site, there is little incentive to do this. If, however, it would allow the malicious person to log in to other sites as well—in this case, any Drupal site that has the Drupal module enabled—the incentive is greater, and so is the potential loss or damage. The attacker would be able to masquerade on those sites using your user identity and execute actions on your behalf.

■ **Caution** Drupal's distributed authentication is inherently insecure. If you do not know that you can trust the owner(s) of a particular site, never use your distributed authentication (Drupal ID) to log in to it.

Running a Directory Server

The Drupal module offers a simple service by which other Drupal sites can announce their existence or ping a central server on a regular basis. While there are many possible applications of such a service, the most common use is along the lines of the now defunct Drupal Sites page on Drupal.org, which was simply a long list of sites that run Drupal.

■ **Note** CivicSpaceLabs.org uses the directory server to generate a list of sites running CivicSpace (which is based on Drupal): http://civicspacelabs.org/home/directory.

In practice, any site that has the Drupal module enabled can function as a directory server. When another site pings the site, the remote site's name, slogan, and mission are added to the list of sites.

For example, you might use a directory server on a college or university where individual labs or departments are setting up many different Drupal sites. Each one could ping a central server at the university to compile a list of all the various sites as they come online.

In its current state, the directory server service lacks some basic features: the administrator cannot block a certain site from pinging and being added to the list, and the administrator cannot limit the incoming pings to a certain set of domains or IP addresses.

■ **Note** The promise of truly secure and flexible distributed authentication is very attractive. If you are interested in helping the Drupal team fix the current shortcomings of the Drupal module and develop a top-notch solution, please join us at Drupal.org. Your help is welcome.

Configuring the Drupal Module

After you enable the Drupal module, you can access its settings at admin/settings/drupal. This page contains the following fields:

- The Drupal XML-RPC Server field is the path to the XML-RPC endpoint for the directory server. This is typically http://*site_url*/xmlrpc.php.
- The Drupal Directory field determines whether the site will ping the directory server every time scheduled tasks are run with cron.php. Distributed authentication does not depend on this being enabled; it is fully functional as soon as the Drupal module is turned on.

In order for your site to be listed in the remote Drupal directory, the Name, Slogan, and Mission field on the admin/settings page of your site must be set.

Filter Module

The Filter module manages the filters and input formats that it and other modules define. As explained in Chapter 2, filters process all content before it is displayed in the browser. They can do interesting things such as prevent unwanted or dangerous code or scripts from being executed, parse wiki syntax or other forms of markup, convert line breaks to HTML `<br>` tags, and detect e-mail addresses or URLs in the text and convert them into hyperlinks.

The Filter module is a required module and is enabled automatically. You can configure it by selecting *administer* ➤ *input formats* (`admin/filters`). Configuring this module was covered in Chapter 2.

Forum Module

Forums are one of the most popular formats for group discussion on the Internet and often form an online community of their own. Most Web users are accustomed to some flavor of discussion forum. Drupal is equipped with a flexible Forum module, which you can configure to suit a number of different approaches to forums, leveraging the entire range of standard Drupal features such as categories, file uploads, and content filtering.

After you enable the Forum module, you must define some forums and optionally, some containers. Additionally, since a forum topic consists of a content node and comments, the configuration of the Comment module plays a large role in how your forums look and behave. The configuration page for comments is `admin/comment/configure`. See Chapter 2 for details on configuring comments.

Configuring Containers and Forums

To access the forum configuration page, select *administer* ➤ *forums* (`admin/forum`). This page has three tabs: Add Container, Add Forum, and Configure.

Containers are groups of forums and, though they aren't necessary, they lend a nice bit of organization or overview to your forums, especially if you have more than a couple forums. Containers are a means of organizing your forums by topic. Topics cannot be posted to containers; containers are merely for organizing forums.

■ Note On `Drupal.org`, you can see the application of containers on the forums page (`http://www.drupal.org/forum`). The containers are General, Support, and Development, and they are visually set apart from the individual forum topics. The actual topics, or threads, can be posted to the forums.

Select the Add Container tab to view the form to add a new container. The contents of the Container Name and Description fields will be visible to users in the forum overview. Use the Parent and Weight fields to place the container in the hierarchy. Containers are best left at the top level. Once you have defined your containers (or decided you don't need any), you can define your forums. Select the Add Forum tab to add forums. This page is identical to the one for adding containers. Although it is possible to add a forum with another forum as its parent, it is more logical to have all of your forums be either top-level or the child of a container. Users will be given the choice of which forum to post to whenever they create a new forum topic.

The Configure tab on the forum configuration page (`admin/forum/configure`) has several settings that apply to the way forums are displayed. The first setting, Forum Icon Path, determines whether forum icons are applied and where they come from. Entering a path in this field will simultaneously activate the forum icons and instruct Drupal where to look for them. To test this, enter **misc** in this field and save the configuration. You should notice various icons appearing in your forums to designate their status. Six icons are available:

- `forum-closed.png` is displayed when comments are disabled on a forum.
- `forum-default.png` is displayed on any forum when no other icon is displayed.
- `forum-hot.png` is shown when the number of comments and replies exceeds the Hot Topic Threshold setting, as set on the forum configuration page (`admin/forum/configure`).
- `forum-hot-new.png` is shown when the forum is both hot and it is the first time a user has viewed it.
- `forum-new.png` is shown on forums or comments the first time a user views them.
- `forum-sticky.png` is shown whenever a forum is designated as sticky.

If you provide a set of icons with the same names and point Drupal to their location via the Forum Icon Path field, your custom icons will be used instead of the default ones.

Setting Up Forum Categories

When you've finished defining your forums and containers, it is worth revisiting the category administration page (`admin/taxonomy`), which was covered in detail in Chapter 2, along with using categories and the Taxonomy module.

All that work you just did to configure your containers and forums did little more than create a special taxonomy vocabulary called *Forums*, which, at its core, is no different from any other taxonomy vocabulary. If you look into the details for your *Forums* vocabulary, you will see some of the decisions that were made for you by the Forum module. For example, in the Types field, only Forum Topic is checked. If you want to, you can check more content types, which would then show the *Forums* vocabulary on the content-creation form for that type.

You could also categorize your blog entries with the same hierarchy that your forums have. Don't expect your blogs to show up in the forums, however. Both blogs and forums would appear on taxonomy listing pages of the form (`taxonomy/term/`*`tid`*).

The other fields listed for the *Forums* vocabulary are also fair game. By changing the Hierarchy setting from Single to Multiple, you can make it possible for a forum to have multiple parents. This could be useful if one theme or topic applies to all of your containers. Make this forum topic have multiple containers as parents, and it will show up in each one (but note that this would probably get abused by users eager to grab people's attention, so I don't recommend this option).

Help Module

Every module is responsible for providing some text that explains how to use it. This is referred to as the *help text*. The Help module's main responsibility is gathering this text from each activated module and displaying it on a page, `admin/help`, along with a simple glossary of some common Drupal terms.

■ Tip The Help module may not provide exactly the help text you wish to offer your site visitors. If you wish to create more help text for your site's audience, consider using the Help Edit module (`http://drupal.org/node/18031`).

Legacy Module

Over time, the way Drupal builds various paths has changed. If you are upgrading from an older version of Drupal, you will still receive requests from the Internet for these old paths. The Legacy module's job is to recognize these paths and redirect them to the correct version. The following mappings are taken into consideration:

- `taxonomy/page/or/52,97` to `taxonomy/term/52+97`
- `taxonomy/feed/or/52,97` to `taxonomy/term/52+97/0/feed`
- `blog/feed/52` to `blog/52/feed`
- `node/view/52` to `node/52`
- `book/view/52` to `node/52`
- `user/view/52` to `user/52`

If you started out using a recent version of Drupal (4.6 or later), you don't need to use the Legacy module, and you can leave it disabled.

Locale Module

The Locale module allows you to switch the Drupal interface to another language. A Drupal site can have its interface in an unlimited number of languages, with one specified as the default. Visitors to your site will be presented with the default language, but authenticated users can switch the language by editing their account from the *my account* page.

The Locale module not only translates the interface text to another language, but it also lets you change the wording of any text without needing to alter the source code. Leaving the Drupal code unchanged is always advantageous when it comes time to upgrade your site, so using the Locale module is the preferred way to manage all Drupal text.

The text on your site can be divided into two groups: built-in text and text created as content by you or another site user. Content added to the site (blogs, stories, and so on) does not fall under the scope of the Locale module. However, you have access to all of the built-in text via this module. For example, the following are some translatable strings on the administration page (`admin`):

```
Home
administer
Welcome to the administration section. Below are the most recent system events
```

■ **Tip** You can create multilingual sites with Drupal through a combination of the core Locale module and the Internationalization module (`http://drupal.org/project/i18n`) from the contributed module repository.

The Drupal community includes a number of active translators who have, at the time of this writing, translated the interface into 30 languages. This includes languages with non-Western (ISO-8859-1) characters such as Japanese and Arabic. You can find a list of the available translations at `http://drupal.org/project/Translations`.

Enabling and Importing Translations

After enabling the Locale module from the `admin/modules` window, browse to *`administer` ➤ `localization` ➤ `add language`* (`admin/locale/language/add`), and choose the language you would like to add from the Language Name list. Then click the Add Language button immediately below the list. You will be taken to the list of activated languages (`admin/locale`), where you can confirm your selection. If the language you are looking for does not appear in the Language Name list, or if you wish to add a country-specific variation of a language such as en-US, use the Custom Language fields on the `admin/locale/language/add` page.

You can import and export Drupal translations from Portable Object (PO) files. A PO file contains many entries, each describing the relation between an original untranslated text and its corresponding translated version. (See `http://www.gnu.org/software/gettext/manual/html_node/gettext_9.html` for a good description of PO files.) The files are text-based and editable using a number of programs designed for the purpose (see `http://drupal.org/node/11131` for a list of such programs).

Once you have downloaded the appropriate PO file from `Drupal.org`, you can import it directly into your web site from the import page (`admin/locale/language/import`). Select the file using the Language File field, and make sure to select the appropriate language (activated or not) from the list of languages in the Import Into field.

After Drupal has processed the file, you will see a report indicating how much of the base language was covered by the translation (the different translations are at different stages of completion). This information appears in the Translated column of the report, shown as a percentage of the total number of strings in the Drupal codebase. Importing a language that hasn't yet been activated adds the language, but it will still need to be activated. Any strings that were left untranslated after importing the PO file will be displayed in English. Figure 3-3 shows the Drupal interface after being translated into Japanese.

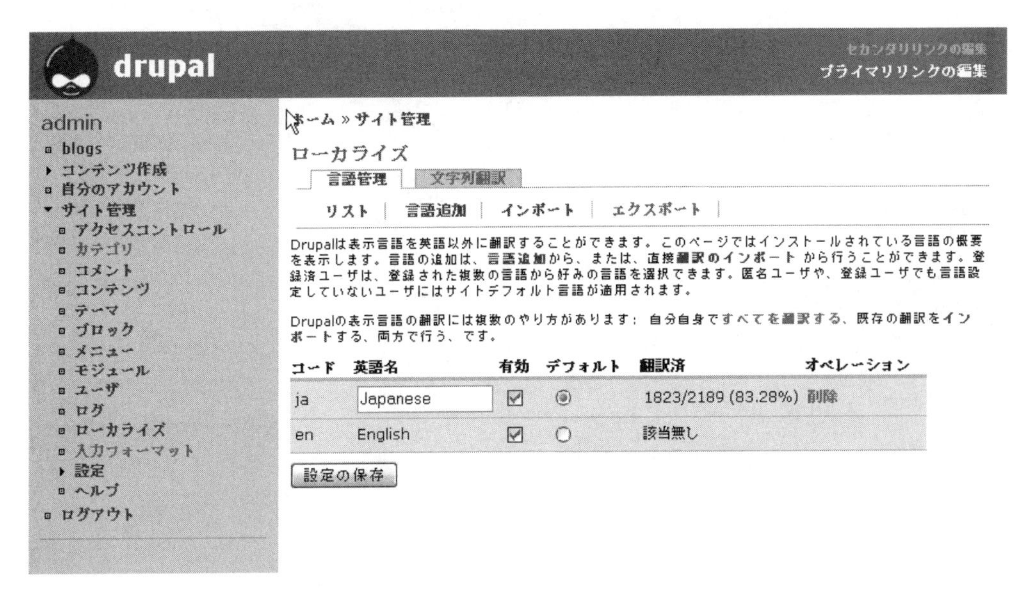

Figure 3-3. *The Drupal interface translated into Japanese*

Translating Strings

Drupal provides you with the tools to translate any of the strings in its interface directly from the web browser. Perhaps the PO file that you imported didn't cover 100% of the interface, or perhaps you would like to customize the translations.

You start this process by searching for strings, using the Manage Strings tab of the `admin/locale` page (`admin/locale/string/search`). String searches are case-sensitive. Wildcards are unnecessary, since string fragments will be matched. Using the Language and Search In controls, you can refine your search to strings in a specific language that are translated, untranslated, or both. Leaving the Strings to Search For field blank will return all of the strings matching the other selected criteria. To search for all of the strings in a target language that still need translating, leave the search form blank, choose the target language, and select Only Untranslated Strings. Drupal will return all of the strings that exist in English but not the target language.

Figure 3-4 shows an example of the results of searching for strings that are not yet translated into Japanese. The fact that these strings don't exist in Japanese can be recognized by the language code in strike-through (~~ja~~) in the Locales column. Locales that have translations are listed normally. Use the *edit* link for any of these strings to provide a translation.

In many cases, the original string is one or more words that can be translated directly. Often, however, either HTML or placeholders for dynamic strings are involved. The translator needs to be able to recognize both of these in order not to change the placeholder or the HTML, but rather to use the placeholder in the appropriate place within the translated string. Here is an example of a string that contains both:

```
<a href="%link">more help. . .</a>
```

String	Locales	Operations
%count comments modules/comment.module:195 ;283 modules/node.module:82	ja	edit delete
%count days includes/common.inc:0	ja	edit delete
%count guests modules/user.module:553 ;556	ja	edit delete
%count hours includes/common.inc:0	ja	edit delete
%count items modules/aggregator.module:86 ;708;719	ja	edit delete
%count min includes/common.inc:0	ja	edit delete
%count new comments modules/comment.module:198	ja	edit delete
%count posts modules/archive.module:136	ja	edit delete
%count reads modules/statistics.module:101	ja	edit delete
%count sec includes/common.inc:0	ja	edit delete
%count users modules/user.module:553 ;556	ja	edit delete

Figure 3-4. *Managing untranslated strings*

In this example, the text to be translated is `more help. . . .` It is surrounded by an anchor tag whose `href` element is dynamically added at runtime. Placeholder variables are always of the form `%variable`. The placeholder variable in this example is `%link`, and it will be replaced by Drupal with the appropriate URL when the string is shown on a page.

Phrases or sentences that might occur in singular or plural forms are split into two separate strings, like this:

```
%count weeks
1 week
```

The translator would then provide a translation for *weeks* in the first string, taking care to put the `%count` placeholder in the correct position for that language, and a translation for *1 week* in the second string.

Exercise 3-1 demonstrates using the Locale module to translate strings.

Exercise 3-1. Use Translations to Rephrase English Text

One very useful application of translations is to rephrase or tweak English text in the Drupal interface. You do this, in effect, by translating English into English. For example, consider the Syndication block, which displays the icon linking to your site's RSS feed. Maybe you feel that "Syndication" doesn't speak to your user base, and you would rather have the block say "Using RSS? Subscribe here!" The steps to achieve this, using the Locale module, are as follows:

1. Select *administer ➤ localization ➤ add language* (`admin/locale/language/add`).
2. Add an appropriate variant of English (such as en-US or en-CA) in the Language Code field, and a name for this variant in the Language Name in English field. This could be Customized English, for example.

3. From the locale administration page (`admin/locale`), set the newly created language to be the default language. This new language doesn't yet contain any translations, so the default text will still be used for the site's interface, as it was before.

4. Navigate to the page on the site where the text you wish to translate can be found. This is an important step, and the following steps will not work if you skip it. You need to do this because your new language is still unaware of all of the text that exist on your site, and only becomes aware of the text after it has appeared in the browser one time. Only after the text you wish to translate has been loaded once will you be able to locate it using the string manager search function.

5. Select *administer* ➤ *localization* ➤ *manage strings* (`admin/locale/string/search`) and search for the word(s) that you would like to rephrase. For this example, search for **Syndicate** (case-sensitive).

6. When you have located the text that you wish to rephrase or change, click its *edit* link. You will then be able to provide a translation of the original text, which will appear in its stead. For this example, enter **Using RSS? Subscribe here!**, which will subsequently appear anywhere that "Syndicate" previously appeared.

Exporting Translations

You can export either your custom translations or a template of the untranslated strings. Exporting the translations or the template allows you to use an external editor to do the translating, which is significantly more efficient than using the web interface. You can also use the resulting file to load a translation into another site or share with others (on `Drupal.org`, for example).

Start an export by clicking the Export tab on the localization page (`admin/locale/language/export`). You have the choice of exporting a translation (if you've made any) or the base template. Either choice will result in the creation of a PO file on your local hard drive.

■ **Caution** At the point when you've created and activated the first alternate language, the database table that tracks the source strings is empty. It gets populated with the source strings as they are used in the Drupal code. This means your first search will return only a small fraction of the total number of untranslated strings. Solve this problem by having a program such as Wget (`http://www.gnu.org/software/wget/wget.html`) access all of the pages on your site, so that all the text is displayed. If you are interested in only a couple of strings, navigating to the page where they appear will have the same effect.

Menu Module

One of the most important aspects of any web site is its navigation menus. Furthermore, one of the first questions many people have about using Drupal is, "How do I make my own navigation menu?" The Menu module is the tool that allows you to customize and create navigation menus.

Drupal comes with a default navigation menu that serves as the main control panel for your Drupal site. By now, you are probably very familiar with this menu and its *create content*, *my account*, and *administer* links. The Menu module allows you to modify this menu, as well as create your own custom menus. You can then place your custom menus in blocks and administer them with the tools for configuring and positioning of blocks (discussed in Chapter 2). The Menu module also adds an item to content-creation forms that allows you to place a link to the item being created directly into a menu. This allows for a very comfortable workflow of creating content and then linking to it within a menu hierarchy, all from the same form.

Modifying Menus

After activating the Menu module, you can access the menu administration page (`admin/menu`). On this page, you will see a table representing the navigation menu, which is the same navigation menu that you are accustomed to dealing with so far. All of the individual items and subitems are listed in the table as rows. Figure 3-5 shows the navigation menu in its initial state, before undertaking any changes.

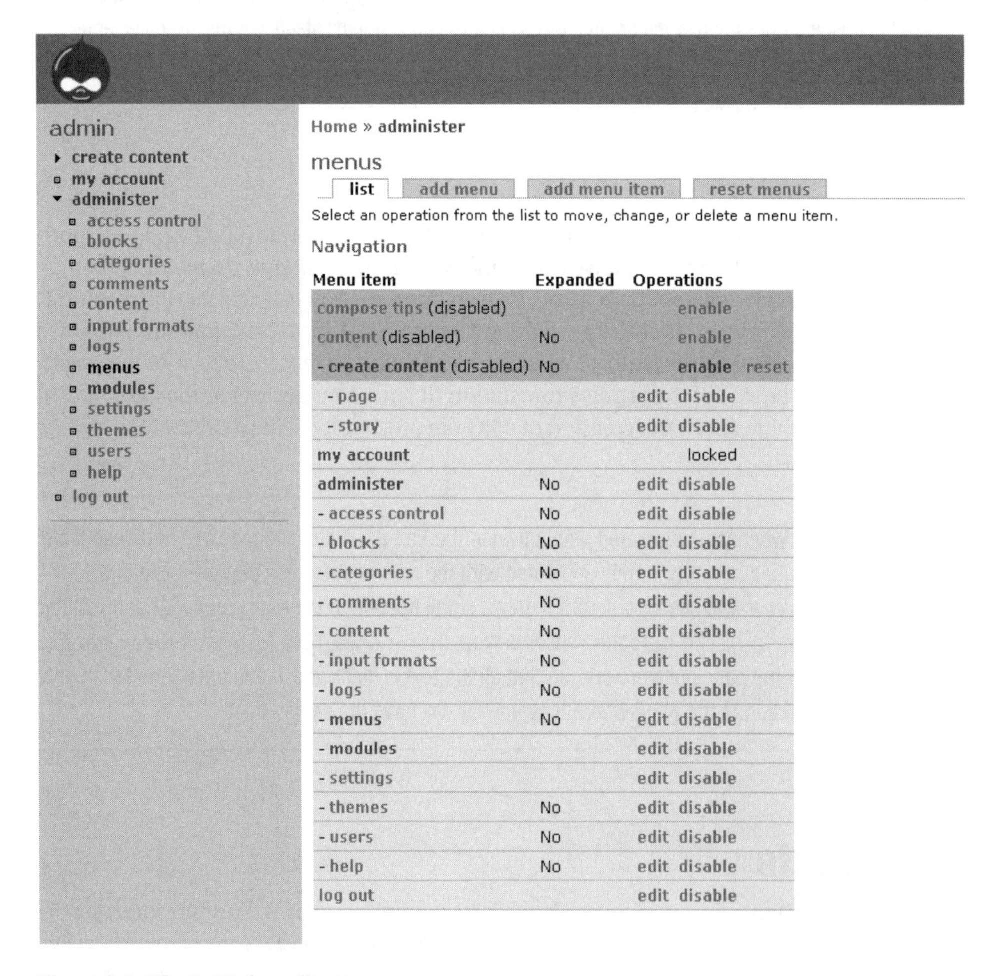

Figure 3-5. *The initial navigation menu*

Not all of the items in the table are visible in the navigation menu. For example, *compose tips* and *content* are disabled in the table, and therefore don't show up in the menu. All of the menu items except for *my account* have a status of either enabled or disabled, which you can change. The *my account* item has a status of locked, meaning that item is essential for the system to operate and must never be disabled.

You can disable any of the currently enabled items by clicking the *disable* link. Try this with the *help* link, for example, and it will disappear from the navigation menu and show up in the table as disabled. You will notice that the menu item now has two links in its row: *enable* and *reset*. The *enable* link will cause the *help* link to reappear, but the *reset* link will remain. This is because every menu item tracks whether it has been modified by the administrator. Any links that you modify will have a *reset* link, which will restore them to their original state.

The menu system is hierarchical, meaning that menu items can have children. The *administer* link is an example of an item that has children. This expresses itself visually in either an unexpanded or an expanded state, as shown in Figure 3-6.

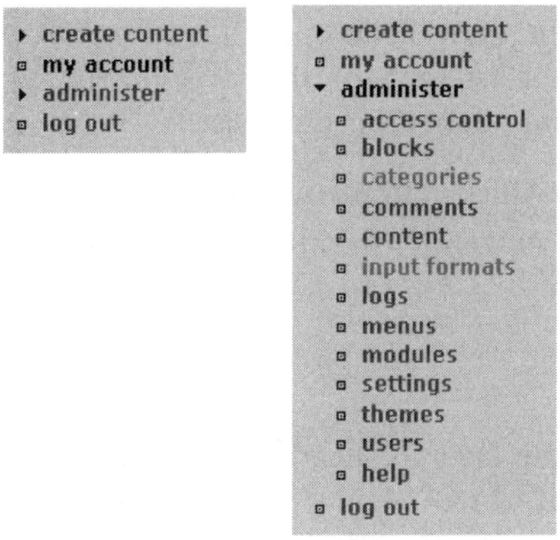

Figure 3-6. *Unexpanded and expanded menu items*

If you disable the *administer* link, all of its children will move up one level in the hierarchy but will themselves stay activated. Note that this works differently for the *create content* link for internal reasons. In that case, the *create content* link stays visible as long as any of its children are enabled.

Adding Custom Menus

To add a new custom menu, click *add menu* (`admin/menu/menu/add`). The next page asks for the title of your new menu. Choose a title and submit it, and Drupal will create it.

Now you will want to add some menu items to the new menu. Click *add menu item* to do this (`admin/menu/item/add`). This page has the following fields:

- The Title field on this form contains the visible text, which the user will see in the menu hyperlink.
- The Description field is used to set the HTML `title` attribute of the hyperlinks in the menu so that the description is displayed as a tool tip when the user hovers the mouse over it.

- The Path field is the target of the link, synonymous with the `href` attribute of an anchor element. It can be either an absolute URL to some resource on the Web or a Drupal path (see Chapter 2 for a description of the different types of paths). You could, for example, create a content node such as a book page named Terms of Service. You would then be able to make a menu item called Terms of Service. In this case, the value in the Path field would look something like `node/7`.

■ **Tip** Enable the Path module, described later in this chapter, to create custom paths for nodes.

- The Expanded field applies to items that have subitems. It controls whether the menu is expanded by default. If the menu should always show the subitems, check Expanded. The default is for a menu item with subitems to expand when you click it.
- The Parent Item field is important because it determines in which menu the item is to appear and where on the menu it is located. Forgetting to explicitly set this will result in the item landing in whatever menu is at the top of the list, probably the navigation menu. Every menu that you've created appears in the Parent Item drop-down list.
- The Weight field allows you to control the order in which your menu items appear. Smaller, lighter numbers appear nearer to the top, and larger, heavier numbers sink toward the bottom.

Showing Menus

After you have created a menu using the administrative interface, you need to tell Drupal where to show it. Navigate to the block administration page (`admin/block`), and you will see your new custom menu listed as a block. Enable the block and customize it to your liking (as discussed in Chapter 2). Then it will then appear on your site.

Adding Menu Links the Easy Way

When the Menu module is enabled, all content-creation forms will have an extra section titled Menu Item Settings. These settings enable you to place a link to the content being created in any of the existing menus. The Title field contains the text that will be displayed for the link, and the Parent Item field determines in which menu and in which order the menu item will appear. Pay careful attention to the Parent Item setting, as all of the available menus are listed.

■ **Tip** The Menu module lets you put links to any content pages into navigation menus directly from the content-creation form itself.

Resetting Menus

The Reset Menus tab on the menu administration page (`admin/menu/reset`) allows you to reset the menus to their original state. Resetting the menus not only restores the built-in navigation menu to its original state, but it also deletes any custom menus you may have made. Do not reset the menus if you have made custom menus that you wish to keep.

■ **Caution** The Reset Menus tab on the menu administration page (`admin/menu/reset`) will delete your custom menus!

Node Module

Almost all of the content on your Drupal site belongs to some variety of node type. Blog posts, stories, book pages, and forum topics are all *nodes*, and any module that has its own type of content usually defines a new type of node as well. The Node module provides a common set of services to all of these content types.

The Node module keeps track of content information such as who created the content, what type of content it is, and whether revisions have been made. It also provides a framework that allows other modules to extend virtually any content type. Comments, file uploads, and categories are all examples of services to node types that are offered by other modules, but coordinated by the Node module.

The configuration of the Node module includes settings on the content overview page (`admin/node`), the content types administration page (`admin/settings/content-types`), and the posts settings page (`admin/settings/node`). These settings were covered in Chapter 2.

Page and Story Modules

The Page and Story modules are nearly indistinguishable, even at the code level. Neither module offers any special configuration options beyond setting permissions and the content types configuration page (`admin/node/configure/types`). Both modules offer very plain content node types with a title and body. You can choose to use either one—they do the same thing.

One reason you might decide to enable both modules is to use them with different configurations. For example, you might want anonymous users to be able to submit stories, and these stories should have the In Moderation status on creation. On the other hand, authenticated users may be able to submit pages that not only have the Published status by default, but also have file attachments (see the section on the Upload module later in this chapter for details on file uploads).

Path Module

We live in the time of search engines, and optimizing your site to work well with the crawling and indexing programs that are used to build search engines is vital. Your site's ranking in the results of search engines such as Google or Yahoo! will greatly influence how many visitors it gets. One very important factor in facilitating this is the nature of the URLs that are used by your site to link to all of the content. If the URLs are meaningful and contain keywords pertinent to the content they link to, your site will fare better in the search results. Drupal offers several tools to help you with this goal. The first tool, clean URLs, can be turned on from the admin/settings page, as explained in Chapter 2. The second, and arguably more important, tool is the Path module.

The Path module allows you to create custom paths for any Drupal content node or alternate aliases for existing paths. This module allows you to replace URLs like node/5 with more meaningful names like instructions_for_use or info/instructions. Also, if you're migrating an existing site to Drupal, you can use the Path module to make sure the old URLs do not get broken. You can make an alias for node (the default front page) called index.html. Then, when you switch from your old system to Drupal, the users who have bookmarked index.html won't be left in the cold.

Creating Path Aliases

After you have enabled the Path module, users with the Create URL Aliases permission will have a Path Alias field available to them on all content-creation forms. The Path Alias value must be unique and not contain characters unsuitable for URLs; the & and ? characters in particular should be avoided (the slash, /, is fine). When a path has been assigned an alias, users will be able to access the content using that path alias instead of the normal path. For example, creating a blog post may generate a path like node/5. If this blog post is given a path alias of tech-news, users can access it with either of the following URLs:

```
http://www.yoursite.com/node/5
http://www.yoursite.com/tech-news
```

The second URL is clearly more meaningful both to humans and to search engines.

■ **Note** The Path module cannot handle absolute URLs or links to external sites.

Users who have the Administer URL Aliases permission can create aliases by selecting *administer* ➤ *url aliases* (admin/path). This page offers a list of existing aliases that can be modified or deleted, as well as the opportunity to create new aliases. Each alias has an Existing System Path field and a New Path Alias field.

Creating Aliases to Drupal Paths

In addition to making aliases to content nodes, you can also make aliases to other Drupal paths. Perhaps you're interested in an easier path to get to the configuration page for the Bluemarine theme. The Existing System Path field entry is admin/themes/settings/bluemarine. In the New Path Alias field, you might enter something like configure/bluemarine. Now the following two URLs take you to the same screen (the Bluemarine theme must be enabled):

```
http://www.yoursite.com/admin/themes/settings/bluemarine
http://www.yoursite.com/configure/bluemarine
```

■ **Tip** The Pathauto module (`http://drupal.org/node/17345`) automatically generates path aliases for various kinds of content (nodes, categories, and users) when no explicit alias is provided by the user. The patterns used for generating the aliases is fully configurable, making the Pathauto module an indispensable tool for search engine optimization.

Ping Module

The Ping module has one important function: to ping Ping-O-Matic (`http://pingomatic.com`) whenever your site has new content. This happens every time scheduled tasks are executed with `cron.php`, so you must have scheduled tasks configured in order for it to work. The `pingomatic.com` site, in turn, notifies a slew of sites, like `technorati.com`, which monitor activity on the Web. The Ping module offers a great way to make sure that your web site is visible on the Web and to help people interested in your content find where it is.

No configuration is necessary for the Ping module. Once you've enabled it and configured scheduled `cron.php` tasks, it will do its job in the background. See Chapter 6 for information about configuring `cron.php` tasks.

Poll Module

A *poll* is a multiple-choice question that each user is allowed to answer once. All votes are counted, and the running results can be seen represented as a bar graph. Polls can be either active or closed. After a poll is closed, it is no longer possible to vote on it.

Creating Polls

To create a poll, activate the Poll module and go to `node/add/poll`. Give your poll a title that explains it, and then enter a number of choices. You can set the initial votes to something other than zero, if you have a reason to do so. If you need more than five choices, check the Need More Choices box and then click Preview. You will be given five more choice fields. The Poll Duration field lets you set a time frame for the poll to be open to voting, after which the poll will be closed and voting will no longer be possible.

Figure 3-7 shows an example of a poll in action.

Figure 3-7. *A sample poll*

Administering Polls

The following items apply to administering polls:

- Polls are normal content nodes and as such can have comments, uploaded files, categories, and so on.
- You can publish or unpublish polls, subject them to moderation, and promote them to the front page.

- The Drupal path poll will show a listing of all polls on the site.
- You can activate the Most Recent Poll block the block administration page (admin/block).
- By granting the Vote on Polls permission, you can allow anonymous users to vote on polls.

The Poll module tries to limit each user to one vote. It does this by recording the user ID of registered users and the IP address of nonregistered users. This has a couple of side effects worth noting. People whose Internet service providers share IP addresses or people accessing the Internet via a shared router will have bad luck as anonymous users. Only the first one accessing the poll will get to vote. If both anonymous users and authenticated users can vote, there is nothing to stop people from voting, logging in, and voting again. The best solution is to allow only authenticated users to vote.

Profile Module

Collecting information from your users about themselves is a common and important function for many types of web sites. The Profile module exists to facilitate this. It allows you to define what information you care to collect from each authenticated user. You can decide whether to collect information via the registration form or from extra tabs added to the user's profile page. You can specify whether the information is required and whether the information is public or private. You are also able to define multiple categories of profile information to collect and show the information collected from all users on special pages you define.

As an example, imagine that you have a site that discusses music. You are interested in knowing which users play musical instruments. To achieve this goal, you might create a list of instruments (a drop-down <select> box) and have it visible on the registration form as an optional field. You would then be able to generate a list of users who play each of the instruments on separate pages, one for each instrument.

Now suppose that you also want to list those musicians on your site who offer lessons for their instrument. You will need to collect more information to maintain this list, such as teaching qualifications, what levels they can teach (beginner, student, and/or advanced), and where they are located. All of this is possible with the Profile module.

Creating Custom Profile Fields

Once you have enabled the Profile module, you can begin defining custom profile fields by selecting *administer* ➤ *settings* ➤ *profiles* (admin/settings/profile). On this page, you choose a form element to add from the listed elements: a single-line text field, a multiple-line text field, a check box, two types of lists, a URL, and a date. In the example of creating a form to collect information about which instrument someone plays, the best type of form element is a list selection (admin/settings/profile/add/selection), which will allow you to define a list of instruments from which the users can choose. Alternatively, if you want the users to type in the name of their instrument, you could use a single-line text field. Let's assume a list selection element for this example.

Complete the list selection form as follows:

Category: This field is used to name and organize groups of profile fields. Each group will have its own tab added to users' account pages. Each tab will show all of the like-categorized profile fields.

Title: This field is the label for the form element that you are creating. For the instrument-selection example, this should be something like *Your instrument.*

Form name: This field contains a unique name that Drupal will use to track this information for each user. It must be unique, not only among all of the profile fields you create, but also among the fields internal to Drupal (which you can't possibly be aware of without reading the code). To avoid namespace conflicts with other possible values, the form is prepopulated with `profile_`. This is intended to be used as a prefix to the name that you give it. While it is not mandatory that you keep to this convention, it is recommended. Add the name of this field after the underscore, without any blank spaces, making sure it is unique. For the instrument example, this could be `profile_instrument`.

Explanation: Use this field to offer instructions to your users regarding what this particular field is for and what type of information they should be giving you. This is optional and can be omitted if the field name makes it obvious. In the case of a field with the name *Your instrument,* it is probably safe to say that no additional instructions are needed, so you could leave the Explanation field blank.

Selection options: This field is unique to the list selection type of profile field. The entries correspond to the various options (`<option>`) that will appear in the selection box (`<select>`). Enter each option that you wish to offer on its own line. Figure 3-8 shows the values entered in the Selection Options field, as well as the drop-down selection box that is generated from them.

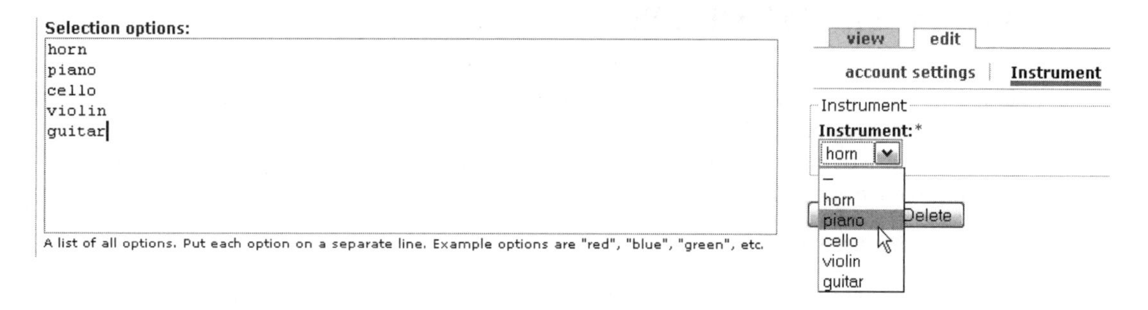

Figure 3-8. *Selection options and the generated selection box*

Weight: This field determines the order in which the custom fields appear.

Visibility: This field deals with the question of whether the field should be publicly visible or private. Private fields are visible only to users with the Administer Users permission. Each user can, of course, see the values in his own profile fields. The Visibility setting also determines whether the information should be listed on pages that list members. The Visibility options include the following:

- Hidden profile field, only accessible by administrators, modules, and themes
- Private field, content only available to privileged users
- Public field, content shown on profile page but not used on member list pages
- Public field, content shown on profile page and on member list pages

Page title: For fields where Visibility is set to "Public field, content shown on profile page and on member list pages," you have the option of specifying a page title. Doing so will instruct Drupal to create a special page that lists the users who have entered the same value for this field. This could be useful to list all of the violin players or all of the tuba players on your site, for example. This field can use the placeholder variable `%value`, which will be replaced with the value that the user chooses for this field. For the `profile_instrument`, you could set the page title to `Plays the %value`. For every instrument that you entered for the selection options, there will be a page titled *Plays the piano, Plays the guitar, Plays the accordion,* and so forth.

The user must enter a value: When checked, this will make the current profile field (`profile_instrument`, for example) required. The user must enter it in order to submit the profile form. In reality, this makes sense only if the next field is checked as well.

Visible in user registration form: As you can guess, this field determines whether the field appears on the user registration form.

After you complete the form, submit your profile field and try it out! If you checked "Visible in user registration form," you can try creating a new user account by logging out and clicking *Create new account* (`user/register`). There, you should see a drop-down selection list of instruments. If you then navigate to the *my account* page and click *edit*, you will see a link to the new profile group next to the *account settings* link.

Viewing Profile Listing Pages

The Profile module exposes a Drupal path `profile`, which generates a list of all users in your system along with their public profile information. If you have the Menu module enabled, you can activate the menu item in the main navigation menu called *user list*, which is a link to the `profile` page. For every field that you have given a page title, there is a special listing page for users who have entered like values:

```
profile/form_name/value
```

For example, users who answered guitar for the Instrument field would be listed on a page with this path:

```
profile/profile_instrument/guitar
```

Search Module

With the aid of the Search module, Drupal will index all of the content on your site and make it available through keyword searches. As with any search engine, ranking the search results is an important consideration, as eventually, more results than anyone cares to sort through will be returned. Ideally, the most relevant results will appear highest on the list.

Drupal uses an advanced algorithm for searching, which considers both the relative importance of the text based on the HTML in which it is found and whether there are site-internal links pointing to the node in which the text is found. For example, text inside an `<h1>` element will be given a higher search ranking than text in a `<p>` element. If a content node has been linked to by other content nodes on the site, that will also work to boost the relevance of the keywords found inside it.

Enabling the Search Box

You can display a search box on your site in three ways:

- Most themes have a global search form built in, which you can toggle on or off from the global theme settings page (`admin/themes/settings`) or from your theme's specific configuration page.
- You can show the search form within a block by enabling and configuring the Search Form block. You do this in the normal fashion from the block administration page (`admin/block`).
- You can access a dedicated search page by using the Drupal path `search`. This page corresponds to a menu item in the main navigation menu. The menu item is disabled by default, so you will need to use the Menu module to turn it on.

You can search on either content or users. Searching for content is done from the path `search/node` and returns a page of links to content that contains the search term(s). The search box displayed by the theme and the search box in the block both search for content by default. Searching for users is done from the path `search/user` and returns a result set of links to users whose profiles or usernames contain the search strings.

Building the Search Index

Indexing the content on your site in a way that facilitates effective, fast, and intelligent searching is a computationally expensive operation. Therefore, Drupal performs indexing in batches during scheduled `cron.php` tasks. This means that the search index will not be built, and the search functions will not work, unless you have configured scheduled `cron.php` tasks.

The second ramification of this fact is that new content will not be found by searching until a `cron.php` task has been run, so you will need to schedule these tasks frequently enough to keep the index up-to-date. If your site receives new content frequently, the scheduled tasks must also be run relatively frequently. Refer to Chapter 6 for instructions on configuring scheduled tasks.

Statistics Module

The Statistics module records and displays information about how your site is accessed. The information it collects includes a counter for every content node that records how many times it has been viewed, the referring URL of every page view, the host name (IP address), and the username (if a registered site user is doing the viewing).

Configuring Statistics

After enabling the Statistics module, you must configure it by selecting *administer* ➤ *settings* ➤ *statistics* (`admin/settings/statistics`). This page has the following settings:

- To record the referrer and IP address of visitors to your site, you must enable the Enable Access Log setting.
- If you enable the access log, set a sensible limit for storing the statistics in the Discard Access Logs Older Than field. On busy sites, the `accesslog` table in the database can grow quite large, as every visit results in a row being added to the database. The statistics that are older than the time limit you set will be discarded in the course of scheduled `cron.php` tasks. If you have not scheduled any `cron.php` tasks, older log entries will never be discarded. (See Chapter 6 for information about `cron.php` tasks.)
- If you are interested in tracking how many times each content node has been viewed, activate the Content Viewing Counter Settings. The number of content views is normally visible only to users with the Access Statistics permission.
- You are also given the option of displaying the view counter to everyone with the Display Counter Views option.

Banning Abusive Users

One of the most useful features of the Statistics module is that it allows you to identify visitors who are abusing your site. Usually, these are not human visitors, but rather search engine crawlers that are malfunctioning or machines automatically accessing your site in an abusive manner. Once you identify a user, usually represented by an IP address, that is abusing your site, you can ban access from that particular abuser. This is a fantastic tool if your site is buckling under an artificially high load that is being generated by attackers or corrupt automated programs generating excessive requests.

The Statistics module defines four views of the statistics it gathers: top referrers (`admin/logs/referers`), top pages (`admin/logs/pages`), top visitors (`admin/logs/users`), and recent hits (`admin/logs/hits`). On the top visitors page, you can inspect the usage patterns of specific host names and perhaps detect abuse. You can see the drain that a particular visitor is putting on your site by looking at either the number of hits or the total page generation time. Each unique visitor can be banned using the *ban* link.

■ **Caution** Be careful not to ban yourself!

System Module

The System module is required by Drupal. It is responsible for, among other things, knowing where the files in your Drupal installation are found and handling the settings of individual modules. It needs no special attention from you as a site administrator.

Taxonomy Module

The Taxonomy module is responsible for categories. The Taxonomy module is far more than a means for tagging blog posts. It is a full API for modules and programmers to leverage all types of relationships and classifications of content. On its own, it provides categories for content, including simple lists, hierarchical categories, and free tagging. The Taxonomy module is extended by numerous contributed modules and even some core modules. The Forum module, for example, requires the Taxonomy module. Chapter 2 covers the use and configuration of the Taxonomy module.

Throttle Module

Having a full-featured site with every possible bell and whistle is nice and makes life fun, but it is also important that the site be able to withstand sudden spikes of traffic. Every feature that you enable increases the cost of loading pages, in terms of CPU cycles and database queries. The more work your server has to do to load a page, the fewer pages it will be able to serve per second.

If you or one of your users happens to write a fantastic article that gets mentioned on a popular site like Boing Boing (`http://www.boingboing.net`) or Slashdot (`http://slashdot.org`), you will start getting enormous amounts of traffic. (Drupal administrators will tell you that they are thankful for the Throttle module when Slashdotting does occur.) Alternatively, if someone decides to launch a denial-of-service attack on your site, the server may be faced with hundreds or thousands of requests a second. The Throttle module exists solely to prepare for such situations. You can use it to decide, in times of exceptionally high traffic, which blocks or modules should be automatically shut off or throttled in order to be able to serve more pages per second and better keep up with the load.

Two statistics can be used as a trigger for the Throttle module: the number of anonymous users and the number of authenticated users. The Throttle module monitors these two types of users by periodically looking in the `sessions` table and counting each type of user. If either count exceeds the limit you set, Drupal turns on the throttle, and throttled blocks and modules are no longer loaded. As soon as the number of users falls below the specified limits, Drupal turns off the throttle.

Throttling Modules and Blocks

Once you have enabled the Throttle module, two familiar administration pages will look somewhat different. These are the module administration page (`admin/modules`) and the block administration page (`admin/block`).

On the module administration page (`admin/modules`), the table listing all of the modules and their status will have an extra column, named Throttle. All but the essential modules (such as System, Block, and User) have a check box that, when checked, means that the module and all of its functionality will be turned off in times of heavy load. Here, you must decide which modules perform site-critical functions and which do not. For example, in the case of the popular article that is attracting loads of traffic to your site, disabling the Node module in throttle conditions will prevent the article (and all other content) from being viewed. While this will probably solve your traffic problem, it will also make a very bad impression on those who came to read the article. So, the Node module is not a good target for throttle controls. The following are core modules that can safely be throttled without denying your site use of its most critical functions: Aggregator, Archive, Ping, Poll, Queue, Search, Statistics, and Tracker.

On the block administration page (`admin/block`), each block also has a check box that controls whether it should be displayed in throttle conditions. This is probably an easier decision to make, as many of the blocks are not critical to the functioning of the site (Who's Online, for example).

Configuring Throttle Thresholds

To configure the thresholds for triggering the throttle, select *administer* ➤ *settings* ➤ *throttle* (`admin/settings/throttle`). The values you choose for the Auto-throttle on Anonymous Users setting and the Auto-throttle on Authenticated Users setting depend on how your site is used and the type of server equipment on which it runs. Setting the values too low could lead to aspects of the site being throttled when that isn't even necessary. Setting the values too high could forsake all of the protections the throttling offers if the server is crippled before throttling kicks in. In the best circumstances, you will be able to monitor the number of authenticated users and guests and estimate how many of each your server can reasonably handle.

The final field on the throttle administration screen, Auto-throttle Probability Limiter, is the percentage of page views that will check to see if throttle conditions should be updated. A value of 10% means that one in ten page views will access the statistics table to evaluate whether to throttle. The lower this percentage, the lower the overhead the Throttle module itself costs. The lowest percentage, 0.1%, means only one in a thousand page views will incur the throttle overhead. Unless your site is very busy, this could lead to slow reaction times when conditions change. Since this is only the probability that a page view will trigger the throttle update code, several thousand page views might occur between updates. Depending on how fast the page views are coming in, that might be too late. On the other hand, there is incentive for keeping this percentage as low as possible to reduce overhead.

Tracker Module

The Tracker module is a nice utility for finding new content on a Drupal site. It adds a Track tab to each user's account page, as well as a *Recent posts* link (`tracker`) in the navigation menu. The tables show nodes that were created, edited, or commented upon recently. You only need to activate the module; no further configuration is necessary. Incidentally, the *Recent posts* link on `Drupal.org` is one of the most popular pages on the entire site.

Upload Module

The Upload module adds support for attaching an arbitrary number of uploaded files to any given content node. Other users can then download these attached files, and the first uploaded file on any given content node also appears in your RSS feed as an enclosure, making the Upload module a suitable tool for generating podcasts.

Configuring File Uploads

Some of the configuration for the Upload module has already been covered in Chapter 2, in the section on general settings. In particular, the Upload module requires values for the File

System Path setting on the general settings page (`admin/settings`). You can also specify a temporary directory where files will be saved first while Drupal is processing your upload.

The maximum size of the files that you will be able to upload is controlled by the PHP settings `post_max_size` and `upload_max_filesize`. You can adjust these values by explicitly setting them in your settings.php file, assuming your web server allows for this. Find the section of that file titled PHP Settings and add the following lines, adjusting the file size to suit your needs:

```
ini_set('post_max_size', '5M');
ini_set('upload_max_filesize', '5M');
```

Unfortunately, in some hosting environments, you are not allowed to override these settings. In such a case, the only recourse is to ask your host to change, or find another host. See `http://php.net/manual/en/ini.core.php#ini.post-max-size` and `http://php.net/manual/en/ini.core.php#ini.upload-max-filesize` for more information about these settings.

You can choose which content types can take attachments on the content type settings page (`admin/settings/content-types`). For each enabled node type, you can set the Attachments field to enabled or disabled.

The Upload module defines two permissions: Upload Files and View Uploaded Files. Every user role that is granted the Upload Files permission can also be individually configured by selecting *administer ➤ settings ➤ uploads* (`admin/settings/upload`). On this page, you can set the Permitted File Extensions, Maximum File Size Per Upload, and Total File Size Per User values. This gives you total control over what kind of files are uploaded to your system and how much space they should be allowed take.

Uploading Files

After you've configured the Upload module as described in the previous section, it's ready to use. Create or edit a node that can have attachments, and you will see an extra group of fields titled File Attachments at the bottom of the form.

To attach a file to the node, first locate the file on your local machine by either entering the path in the Attach New File field or by using the Browse button. Once you've selected the desired file, click the Attach button. The file will be uploaded to the server via HTTP and, if successful, you will be shown the same form with the attachment listed in a table, as shown in the example in Figure 3-9. You may repeat this process as often as you like, and thus attach multiple files to one node.

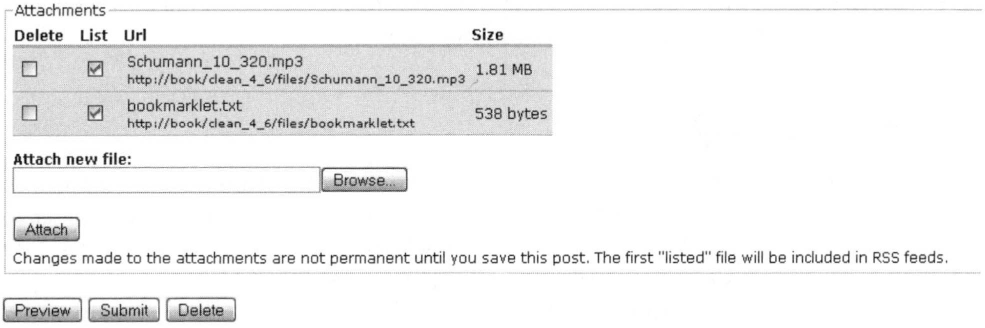

Attachments

Delete	List	Url	Size
☐	☑	Schumann_10_320.mp3 http://book/clean_4_6/files/Schumann_10_320.mp3	1.81 MB
☐	☑	bookmarklet.txt http://book/clean_4_6/files/bookmarklet.txt	538 bytes

Attach new file:

Browse...

Attach

Changes made to the attachments are not permanent until you save this post. The first "listed" file will be included in RSS feeds.

Preview Submit Delete

Figure 3-9. *Upload files attached to a node*

Caution The uploaded files are not permanently attached to a node until you click the Submit button.

After uploading files as attachments to a node, you must click the Submit button and save the node. Failing to do this will result in the attachments being lost.

To delete an attachment from a node, check the box in the Delete column next to the desired file and click Submit. The file will be removed from the node and deleted from the server.

The check boxes in the List column control whether a given uploaded file will be visible when the content is being displayed. Most of the time, you will want uploaded files to be visible, thus the box is checked by default. However, in some cases, you will not want the uploaded files to be visible. For example, if you are using the contributed Inline module (`http://drupal.org/project/inline`) to display links to the files within the text of your post, you may not want the link to show again below the post.

Tip Use the Img_assist module (`http://drupal.org/project/img_assist`) in conjunction with the Upload module to enable putting inline images in posts.

Podcasting

Drupal's built-in support for the RSS version 2.0 standard, including file enclosures, makes it an ideal platform for staging podcasts. The first file attachment of any node will show up in the RSS feed as an enclosure, meaning feed reader and podcasting software configured to do so will automatically download the file. Drupal supports podcasting out of the box!

Note Per Wikipedia.org (`http://en.wikipedia.org/wiki/Podcast`), "Podcasting is a method of publishing audio programs via the Internet, allowing users to subscribe to a feed of new files (usually MP3s)."

User Module

As I've said before, users are what make communities! The functionality of the User module was covered in Chapter 2 in the section concerning users.

Watchdog Module

Required by Drupal, the Watchdog module is always activated. It is responsible for the `admin/logs` page, which you can see by clicking *administer*. The main configuration option available for these logs is the Discard Log field on the general settings screen. As discussed in Chapter 2, you will want to be aware of how large the Watchdog table is and adjust this setting accordingly, so that you keep only as much log information as is useful to you.

■ **Caution** The size of the Watchdog table in the database can have a significant influence on the performance of your Drupal site. Do not keep logs any longer than is necessary.

Summary

The Drupal core modules cover a wide range of basic functionality, from advanced user profiles to statistics collection. Many types of web sites can be completely served with only the modules delivered with the standard Drupal download. Core modules can all be activated or deactivated without downloading other packages or adding extra database tables.

Drupal would be only a fraction as popular as it is, though, without the contributed modules. A quick look at the available module downloads (`http://drupal.org/project/Modules`) reveals the diverse range of contributed modules available. At the time of this writing, 120 contributed modules are available, with the number growing every week. The reason for the enormous number of modules is Drupal's highly extensible architecture and accessible programmer's API. In Chapter 4, you will look at a number of important contributed modules that can add diverse functionality and ease of use to your site.

CHAPTER 4

Adding Contributed Modules

One of Drupal's great strengths is the ease with which new functionality can be added in the form of contributed modules. The clear and well-defined hook system (http://drupaldocs.org/api/head/group/hooks) allows modules to interact with all of the Drupal subsystems, including the user, menu, taxonomy, filtering, and node-handling systems. As a result, more than 350 modules have been contributed to the Concurrent Versions System (CVS) repository (http://cvs.drupal.org/viewcvs/contributions/) at http://drupal.org/project/Modules.

The contributions repository is not only large, but it is also very diverse in its offerings. Some of the modules are for specific Drupal versions; some are well maintained, but some are not. Some are easy to install; some require patches to the core Drupal code. Many offer similar or duplicated functionality. This diversity is a great strength of Drupal, but it also means that you need to know which modules are best for any given situation and task.

This chapter will cover the installation, configuration, and use of a number of the best and most popular Drupal modules. The selection covered ranges from making input easier with WYSIWYG editors, to protecting your site from comment spam, to letting site users organize themselves into groups that share interests. These modules, in conjunction with the core modules delivered with Drupal, will provide you with a broad set of tools that you can apply to a diverse array of web sites.

Getting Drupal Modules

You can find a list of the available modules for the current release at Drupal.org:

```
http://drupal.org/project/Modules
```

Each module has a download link to an automatically generated archive file, which is updated with the latest changes from Drupal.org's CVS repository on a regular basis.

First, I'll give you an overview of the modules covered in this chapter, and then I'll explain the general installation process.

Introducing Some Useful Modules

Some of the most useful modules are those that help with creating content on your site. These include the TinyMCE module (WYSIWYG editor) and the Image and Image Assist modules (for image galleries and in-line images in posts).

The Flexinode module allows you to define your own data types (node types), complete with fields of varying types. The data collected with your defined node types can be shown in table form with sortable columns to facilitate searching.

The Event and Location modules can be used alone or in tandem to attach time and place information to any node type. Combined with the Flexinode module, the Event and Location modules allow you to create custom events calendars that not only track events, but also offer location information based on zip codes and geocoding, as well as deep linking to mapping services.

Organic groups are a way to encourage members of your site to organize into smaller working groups to share resources and have a space for online collaboration. The Organic Groups module introduces node-level permissions so that groups can have private content not visible to those who aren't members of the group. Group photo albums and RSS feeds for each group are among the other features available.

Protecting your site from abuse by spammers is the focus of the Spam module. Based on powerful Bayesian filters that continuously learn from the spam content that is submitted to your site, this module may be the only thing that keeps spammers from turning your site into an online billboard for drugs and sex products.

The Devel and Database Administration modules offer convenient tools for maintaining your database and developing Drupal code. They give you a window into the inner workings of Drupal, exposing not only the contents of your Drupal database, but also the actual SQL queries that are used to build each page. Turn to these modules to help solve database-related problems.

Installing Contributed Modules

The process for installing a contributed module typically consists of the following steps:

1. Make a backup of your site's database. This is especially important if the module requires that changes be made to your database. *Never neglect this step.*

2. Copy the entire module folder into the `modules` directory of your Drupal installation. Usually, the whole folder can be copied, but you may want to exclude some files that don't need to be on the server. The `.mysql` and `.pgsql` files, for example, can be omitted.

3. Update the database schema, if necessary. For a MySQL database, use the following GNU/Linux command:

   ```
   mysql -u user -p drupal < module.mysql
   ```

   Replace *`user`* with the MySQL username, *`drupal`* with the database being used, and *`module`*`.mysql` with the `.mysql` file distributed with the module. If your database is using table prefixes, you will need to update the database definition file directly to reflect this.

4. Apply any patches, if necessary.

5. Enable the module by navigating to *administer ➤ modules* (`admin/modules`) and checking its Enable box.

6. Configure the module, including setting new permissions defined by the module. As explained in Chapter 2, you administer permissions from *administer ➤ access control* (`admin/access`).

A module will typically consist of the following files contained in a folder of the same name as the module:

- README.txt: Always start here. The README file will explain what the module is for, what it can do, and any extra information you might need in deciding whether or not to install the module.
- INSTALL.txt: This file will provide directions for installing the module.
- CHANGELOG.txt: This file contains a running account of how the module has been altered or updated. This information is useful if you are upgrading a module and want to see how the newest version differs from the version you are currently using.
- .module: This file contains the PHP code that makes the module work. It typically consists of the module-specific implementations of the relevant Drupal hooks, as well as any other code needed for the module.

The following are some of the optional files sometimes included with a module:

- .mysql and .pgsql: These files contain the SQL to build the database schemas that will be used by the module. Not all modules require altering the database schemas, and not all modules support both MySQL and PostgreSQL. This should be explained in the INSTALL file for the individual modules.
- update.php: If present, this file can be used to change from one version of a module to a newer version. Make sure to consult the INSTALL file directions before applying the updates.
- .patch files: These files are present if any other Drupal files, core or otherwise, need to be patched in order for the module to work.
- MAINTAINERS.txt: This file lists the people who have write access to the CVS repository and who are willing to fix bugs and perhaps add features to the module.

The following sections include specific instructions for installing each of the modules described.

TinyMCE Module

All of the textual content submitted to a Drupal site is intended first and foremost for display as HTML in a web browser. Because of this, any formatting of the text—such as boldface, color, alignment, and so on—must be realized in HTML. In addition, the inclusion of images and hyperlinks within the text also must be achieved with HTML. This poses a problem to the end users who may have limited or no knowledge of HTML tags. Requiring these users to learn how to use tags is an invitation for badly formatted content and frustrated users. Fortunately, a number of solutions exist for this problem.

Drupal has at least three full WYSIWYG editors: TinyMCE (http://drupal.org/project/tinymce), Htmlarea (http://drupal.org/project/htmlarea), and FCKeditor (http://drupal.org/node/16118). The TinyMCE editor achieves a very nice balance between powerful features and ease of use, and it integrates well with the Image Assist contributed module and core Upload module for comfortable inclusion of images in posts. TinyMCE has the following features:

- Role-based profiles, which let you decide which user roles can use the editor, and how it looks for each of them
- More than 50 editor buttons that can be turned on or off for each profile
- A switch to easily turn the editor on or off when composing content

Installing the TinyMCE Module

The Drupal TinyMCE module has two parts: the Drupal module, which you can obtain from `Drupal.org`, and the TinyMCE project itself, which is hosted at SourceForge (`http://sourceforge.net/projects/tinymce/`). The `INSTALL.txt` file that is packaged with the Drupal module provides a link to the particular SourceForge download that is to be used. Both the Drupal module and the TinyMCE project are updated often, so you are encouraged to follow the installation instructions from both projects carefully to ensure compatibility.

Here are the steps for installing TinyMCE:

1. Download the TinyMCE module from `http://drupal.org/project/tinymce`.
2. Unpack the download and copy the `tinymce` folder into your Drupal `modules/` directory.
3. After making a backup of your site and database, update the database using the SQL in the `tinymce.mysql` or `tinymce.pgsql` file.
4. Follow the directions in the `tinymce/INSTALL.txt` file for obtaining the appropriate copy of the TinyMCE project.
5. The code from the TinyMCE project is also contained in a directory called `tinymce`. Place this directory inside the `modules/tinymce` directory so that the resulting structure is `modules/tinymce/tinymce/`, as shown in Figure 4-1.

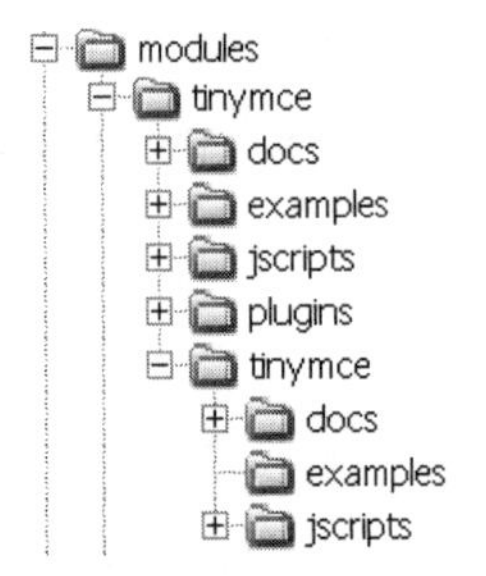

Figure 4-1. *The TinyMCE directory structure*

6. Navigate to *administer* ➤ *modules* (`admin/modules`) and enable the module.

After completing these steps, each text area on your entire site will have an additional link in the bottom-left corner. This link, *enable rich-text*, activates the default TinyMCE editor for that particular text area. The default configuration of the editor, as shown in Figure 4-2, is very minimal, with only nine basic buttons enabled.

Figure 4-2. *The default TinyMCE editor in action*

Configuring the TinyMCE Module

To configure TinyMCE, you need to set the appropriate Drupal permissions and input formats. Then you can configure whether TinyMCE appears as the editor by default and set up role-based profiles.

TinyMCE Permissions

Two permissions for the TinyMCE module are defined: Access TinyMCE and Administer TinyMCE. Any user role that should be able to use the editor needs the Access TinyMCE permission.

TinyMCE Input Formats

The TinyMCE module inserts HTML into posts. As the default input format filters many of the elements that TinyMCE uses to format text, you will need to create a new input format specifically for use with TinyMCE. You should set this input format to be the default for those user roles that use TinyMCE. As described in Chapter 2, to configure input formats, select *administer* ➤ *input formats* (`admin/filters`).

In order to be compatible with the full range of TinyMCE elements, the input format should allow the following set of elements:

```
<a> <blockquote> <br> <em> <hr> <img> <li> <ol> <p> <span> <strike>
<strong> <sub> <sup> <table> <tbody> <td> <tr> <u> <ul>
```

TinyMCE Default State

With the appropriate input format and permissions in place, you can begin configuring the TinyMCE module by navigating to *administer* ➤ *settings* ➤ *TinyMCE* (`admin/settings/tinymce`). This page will list all of the role-based configuration profiles that you have created, as well as the Default Tinymce State setting.

In all of the text areas where the TinyMCE editor can appear, there is a link that toggles between the editor and a plain text area. The Default Tinymce State setting determines whether the text area or the editor is loaded first by default. Users are able to override this setting in the TinyMCE Settings area of their user account page. What you choose as a default largely depends on who your users are and whether they will find the rich-text editor more of a convenience or a hassle.

Role-Based Profile Configuration

One of the TinyMCE's most attractive features is the vast control you have over how the editor looks, which buttons it displays, and what functionality is enabled. In order to make these decisions, you need to create one or more configuration profiles that can be assigned to your existing user roles.

From the TinyMCE settings page (`admin/settings/tinymce`), click *Create new profile* (`admin/settings/tinymce/add`). This leads to a new configuration screen with a wealth of options.

After naming your new profile, select the roles to which it will apply. The roles available will be those that have the Access TinyMCE permission. Each role can belong to only one profile, so the roles that you select here for this profile will not be available if you create another profile.

Editor Display and Formatting Options

You can set the following options for this profile's editor display and formatting options:

Make TinyMCE visible on: You can decide whether to show the editor on all text areas or only on those pages that you specify. For indicating specific pages, you can use any valid Drupal paths and use the asterisk (*) as a wildcard. You can also use `<front>` to indicate the front page (as you defined it on the `admin/settings` page).

Buttons: The Buttons group of options lets you decide exactly which buttons will be active in the editor for this particular profile. More than 50 buttons are available, ranging from basic formatting (boldface, italic, and so on) to scripts to check spelling and clean the HTML output.

Tip Try out the buttons before you activate them by visiting the TinyMCE web site: `http://tinymce.moxiecode.com/example_full.php?example=true`.

Editor appearance: The Editor appearance group of options lets you customize how the editor should appear.

- The Toolbar Location option lets you set whether the editor's toolbar appears above the text area (top) or below it (bottom).
- The Toolbar Alignment option sets the editor's toolbar to appear on the left or right, or in the center.
- The Path Location field refers to a context-sensitive display of the Document Object Model (DOM) hierarchy within the rich-text editor. Wherever the cursor is placed, the path will show you which HTML element it is dealing with, as well as that element's parents, all the way up the hierarchy within the editor. The example in Figure 4-3 shows the cursor in an `<li>` with an `<ol>` as its parent, which, in turn, is in a `<blockquote>` element, resulting in the path `blockquote » ol » li`. The main purpose of the path information is to help people with an understanding of HTML figure out why something in the editor works the way it does, which can be useful if achieving a particular format is proving to be a tricky task.

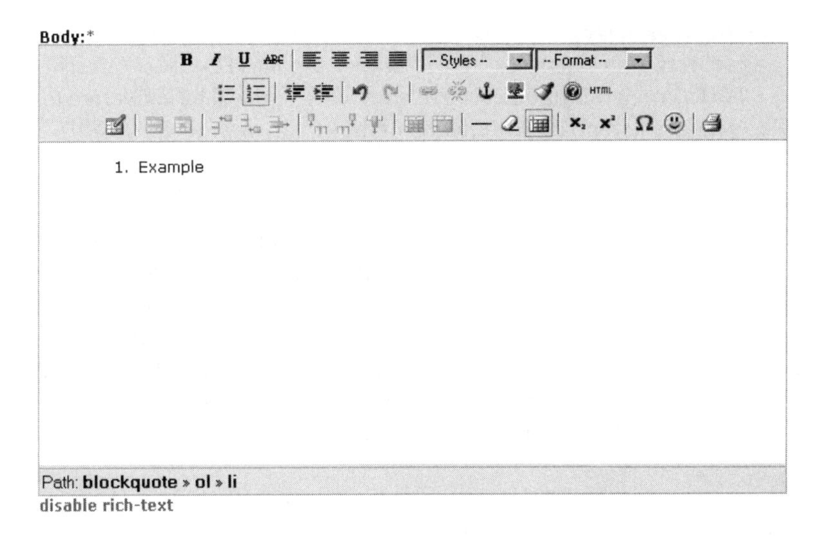

Figure 4-3. *Path information in the TinyMCE editor*

- The Enable Resizing Button option allows you to grab the bottom-right side of a text area and drag it to any size you need.

Block formats: The list of block formats allows you to remove options from the block element selector, which appears next to the styles selector in Drupal's Advanced theme. By default, the block format selector contains nine options, which correspond to the following HTML elements: `<p>`, `<address>`, `<pre>`, `<h1>`, `<h2>`, `<h3>`, `<h4>`, `<h5>`, and `<h6>`. These elements are all known as block-level elements because the default behavior for browsers is to place them on their own line. The rich-text editor allows any highlighted text to be promoted to block level using these controls. In reality, it is rather uncommon for all of them to have special meanings on any given web site. If this is the case on your web site, you can remove the irrelevant options from the list in the Block Formats field and avoid tempting your web users to add meaningless markup. Note that it is impossible to add elements other than these nine.

Cleanup and Output Options

TinyMCE can help guarantee the quality of the HTML that users enter into your web site. It does so by offering three different types of processing or cleanup of input.

Verify HTML: Setting Verify HTML to True will help eliminate HTML errors from user input. This includes detecting and closing unclosed elements, and stripping the <html>, <head>, and <body> tags. Occasionally, the editor may be used to make modifications to an entire HTML document, including the <html> and <head> tags. For this case, it is essential that you set Verify HTML to False, as the <head> tags will be stripped otherwise.

Preformatted: The Preformatted option, when set to True, will replace white space characters with their HTML entities, thus functioning like the <pre> tag. This might be a good idea if your site specializes in ASCII art, but in most other cases, it is probably a bad idea, as many web users will try to format their posts with the spacebar, a practice that should be discouraged.

Convert <font> tags to styles: This is a cleanup task that is highly recommended, as the `<font>` tag has been deprecated (see `http://www.w3.org/TR/REC-html40/present/graphics.html#edef-FONT`). When this option is enabled, `<font>` tags will be converted to `<span>` tags with style attributes to replace the function of the `<font>` tags.

CSS Settings

One of the most significant advances in modern web development is the widespread adoption of Cascading Style Sheets (CSS) as the preferred means for adding style elements to HTML. Gone are `<font>` tags, where size and color are embedded directly into the HTML. Most in-browser WYSIWYG editors, including TinyMCE, offer font, size, and color selectors that allow web users to apply their favorite shades of purple or pink to their postings, effectively marring the design and color scheme of your carefully designed web site. This is the reason why these elements are, by default, turned off in the Drupal TinyMCE module.

■ **Note** The styles selector is visible only in the Advanced theme.

Fortunately, there is a better way to offer these same features in a controlled and limited way that gives the web users the tools they want and eliminates the danger of them overstepping their bounds, stylistically. With TinyMCE, you can identify a style sheet that defines text attributes the user is encouraged to apply. TinyMCE will look at the style sheet and offer each defined style in a drop-down box, so it is easy for your users to apply style information.

The Editor CSS field gives you three options for where TinyMCE should look to find this style sheet:

Use theme CSS: This grabs the `style.css` file that is included in your Drupal theme. Figure 4-4 shows the list of style names available when using this option with the default Drupal Blumarine theme. While this option guarantees that the user won't be able to do anything that doesn't fit with the look and feel of your site, it is probably not the best choice. First, the style names are rather cryptic and theme-developer-oriented. Terms like *box*, *block*, and *node* don't really describe how the resulting style will look. Furthermore, some styles, like *error*, don't need to be accessible to web users.

Define CSS: This is the best option, and it also requires the most extra effort on your part. When you select this option, TinyMCE takes the value from the next field, CSS Path, and looks there for the style sheet to use.

CSS path: Here, you can enter any web-accessible URL. The variables `%h` and `%t` are available and are dynamically replaced with your host name and the path to the current theme, respectively. This allows a site that supports different themes for different users to have a fitting TinyMCE style sheet for each theme.

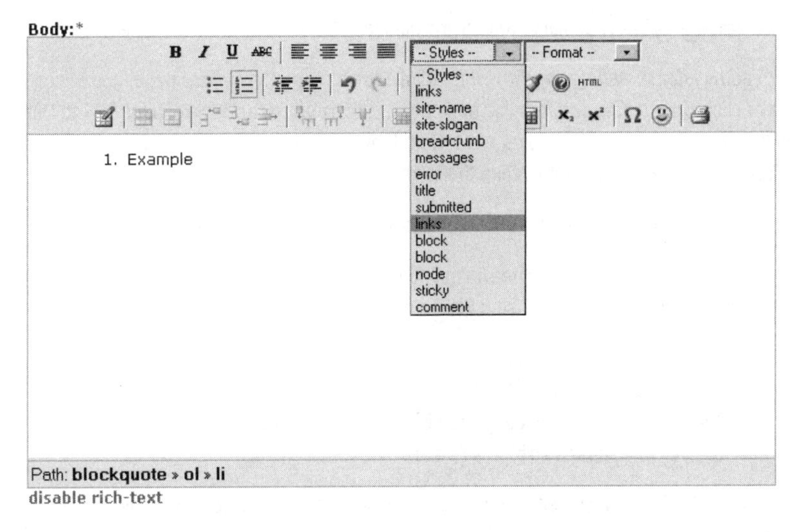

Figure 4-4. *Styles available with the Bluemarine theme*

■ **Caution** TinyMCE, which is visible only on editing screens, imports the style sheet you define in the CSS Path field itself. You will need to add the import for this style sheet to your theme as well. Otherwise, the style sheet will be loaded only when editing, and the styles visible in TinyMCE will not take effect when the content is being viewed normally.

Exercise 4-1 demonstrates how to add a custom style sheet for use with TinyMCE.

Exercise 4-1. Add a Custom Style Sheet for TinyMCE

Here are the steps for adding a custom style sheet containing the styles that should be available to your site's users:

1. Create a file named `tinymce_styles.css` with the following class rules. TinyMCE recognizes class rules and will ignore other selectors like element rules and ID rules.

```
.color-red {color: red;}
.color-blue {color: blue;}
.color-green {color: green;}

.font-sans { font-family: Arial, sans-serif; }
.font-serif { font-family: Roman, serif; }
.font-mono { font-family: Courier, monospace;}
.font-cursive { font-family: cursive; }
.font-fantasy { font-family: Palette, fantasy; }
.font-blackletter { font-family: serif; }
```

2. Place the `tinymce_styles.css` file in your theme directory; for example, *drupal*`/themes/bluemarine/`.

3. Navigate to *administer* ➤ *settings* ➤ *TinyMCE* (`admin/settings/tinymce`) page, and choose an existing profile or click *Create new profile* (`admin/settings/tinymce/add`). Set Editor CSS to Define CSS and CSS Path to `%h%ttinymce_styles.css`. Note that the variables `%h` and `%t` include trailing slashes already. This will evaluate to something like the following:

```
http://www.yourdomain.com/drupal/themes/bluemarine/tinymce_styles.css
```

4. Add the following bolded lines to the `<head>` section of your theme's `page.tpl.php` file, or the appropriate counterpart if you are not using PHPTemplate as a theme engine:

```
<?php print $styles ?>
<style type="text/css" media="all">
 @import "<?php print $directory ?>/tinymce_style.css ";</style>
<script type="text/javascript"> </script>
```

Now when you use the TinyMCE editor, you should have a styles selector that includes the class definitions you added, as shown in Figure 4-5.

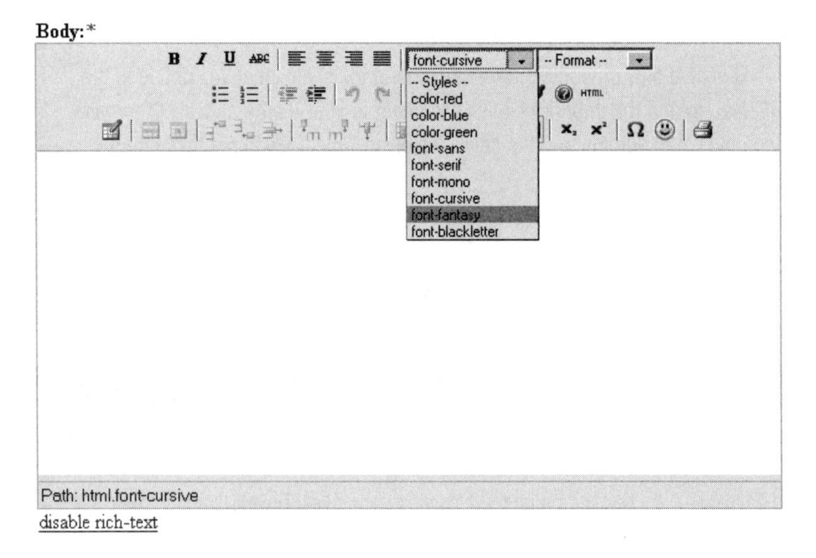

Figure 4-5. *TinyMCE with user-defined CSS classes*

If you apply a custom style to some text, click *disable rich-text*, and inspect the HTML, you will see that TinyMCE has surrounded portions of your text in `<span>` elements, like this:

```
<span class="font-serif">You can apply styles to your text.</span>
```

If you want to give the classes in your style sheet different names—perhaps to make them more descriptive than *box*, *block*, or *node*—or if you want to exclude some of the classes in the style sheet you are using, the CSS Classes field is the tool to use. It allows you to enter a list of `name=value;` pairs, which determine the name of the style shown to your users (*name*) and the class name that it corresponds to (`value`). For example, suppose that you want to offer the box and block styles with the names *introduction* and *summary*, and you don't want the node style to be available at all. You could achieve this by entering the following as the value for the CSS Classes field:

```
introduction=box;summary=block;
```

The names *introduction* and *summary* would appear in the list of available styles, and node would be inaccessible to the user.

Image Module

Images are one of the most popular forms of web content. Whole online communities can be built around the idea of sharing pictures, and with the popularity of digital cameras, almost everyone has photos ready to be uploaded. For the tasks of uploading photographs to the web site, generating thumbnails and standard sizes, and organizing them into galleries, the Image module is the tool to use.

Installing the Image Module

Installing the Image module is quite straightforward. Just download the module from `http://drupal.org/project/image`, place the entire `image` folder in the `modules` directory, and activate the module from the `admin/modules` page. If you wish to use the ImageMagick library (`http://www.imagemagick.org/script/index.php`) for converting and resizing images, you will also need to move the `/modules/image/ image.imagemagick.inc` file into the `/includes/` directory of your Drupal installation. If you wish to use the Image module's gallery-building functions, you need to make sure that the Taxonomy module is enabled.

Configuring the Image Module

To configure the Image module, you need to set the appropriate Drupal permissions and conversion library. Then you can configure file paths, file sizes, and galleries.

Image Module Permissions

The Image module defines two permissions: Administer Images and Create Images. Users with the Administer Images permission will be able to edit the gallery structure and define the various image sizes. Users need the Create Images permission in order to add images to the site.

Image Module Conversion Library

The most important issue in configuring the Image module is choosing and setting up the conversion library that you will use. The conversion library will be given the responsibility of taking the original images that are uploaded to the site and resizing them to standard sizes and thumbnails. Drupal automatically has support for the GD2 library (`http://www.php.net/image`), which has been bundled with PHP since version 4.3. The Image module adds support for the ImageMagick library as well. To choose which library should be used, navigate to *administer* ➤ *settings* (admin/settings), and in the Image Handling group, select an image processing toolkit.

If you choose a library other than GD2, you will need to save the changes and then fill in the additional field to specify a path to the binary library file that you have chosen. If you want to use ImageMagick, for example, you will first need to select ImageMagick Toolkit, save the changes, and then enter a value for the Location of the "Convert" Binary field. This is the absolute path to the convert (convert.exe on Windows) file.

Note The Image module needs either the GD2 or ImageMagick library to convert images.

Image Module File Paths

The Image module requires a directory inside the files directory for the storage of your images. When you select *administer* ➤ *settings* ➤ *image* (admin/settings/image) for the first time, Drupal will create two directories for you: files/images and files/images/temp. If you do not want to use the defaults set by Drupal, you have the opportunity to designate a different path and name in the Default Image Path field. Note that this path is relative to the files directory.

Image Module Derivative Sizes

When a new file is uploaded via the Image module, at least two (smaller) derivative sizes are created. The Image Sizes group on the Image module settings page (admin/settings/image) includes a table where these sizes can be determined. Each different derivative size has a name and dimensions. Two names, *thumbnail* and *preview*, are required by the Image module. You have the opportunity to define up to three additional names and the sizes for all five formats. The various forms of any given image file can then be accessed using the path node/*{nid}*&size=*name*, where *nid* is the node ID and *name* is one of the format names. If you want your web users to be able to access the uploaded photos in their original sizes as well as in the derivative sizes, you need to check the Allow Users to View Original Image option.

Image Module Galleries

The Image module has basic taxonomy-based image galleries. You configure galleries by selecting *administer* ➤ *image galleries* (admin/image). The form for adding galleries (admin/image/add) looks similar to the form for adding category terms, and with good reason. The Image module creates a vocabulary of categories to manage your galleries (see Chapter 2 for more on categories). You can build galleries hierarchically by assigning a parent in the Parent field and order them with the Weight field, just as with categories.

Note The gallery functions are dependent on the Taxonomy module. Make sure the Taxonomy module is enabled before trying to build galleries.

After you have configured the galleries, you can take a peek at what is going on behind the scenes by visiting the list of vocabularies: *administer* ➤ *categories* (admin/taxonomy). You will see the gallery structure you created is really a vocabulary managed by the Taxonomy module.

Uploading and Viewing Images

When you are ready to upload images to your site, select *content* ➤ *image* (node/add/image). The process for uploading images is straightforward, and the module will automatically make thumbnails and various derivative sizes on the server.

Since images are nodes, you make the same decisions about whether they should be promoted to the front page as with any other node type. In addition, you have the option of viewing your images in the context of the galleries you specified. If you have the Menu module activated, you can go to admin/menu and activate the navigation link for the galleries. Otherwise, you can add it to your primary or secondary links with the path image. (The Drupal path to your image galleries is image.)

■ **Tip** The Image module defines two blocks, named Latest Image and Random Image, which you can turn on from the block administration page (admin/blocks).

Image Assist Module

With the aid of the Image module, you can upload images to a Drupal web site and arrange them in galleries. In order for those images to be truly useful, however, you also need a means of incorporating them into your site's content. This is the job of the Image Assist (Img_assist) module. This module places an extra icon on content-creation forms. Clicking this icon launches a pop-up window for selecting and inserting images into the text of the node you are editing. This is the easiest way to incorporate in-line images into forums, blogs, pages, and so forth.

Installing the Image Assist Module

These are the steps for installing the Image Assist module:

1. Download the latest version of Img_assist from http://drupal.org/project/img_assist.
2. Place the entire img_assist folder in the /modules/ directory.
3. Make a backup of your database.
4. Load the database definition from the file appropriate to your database, either img_assist.mysql or imag_assist.pgsql.
5. Navigate to *administer* ➤ *modules* (admin/modules) and enable the module.

Configuring the Image Assist Module

To configure the Image Assist module, you need to set permissions and input formats. Then you can configure access, image output, and preview settings.

Image Assist HTML Use and Permissions

Image Assist can achieve the task of inserting images into posts in two ways:

- Insert special non-HTML tags called *macros* into the post. These macros are then replaced with HTML at page-load time by the content filter system.
- Insert finished HTML into the post, without any further filtering.

The macro tag approach has the advantage that you can change the template for inserted images on a live site, and the change will take place for all previously inserted images. This is helpful if you might be updating the look of your site sometime in the future. It also has the advantage that you can force your users into using Image Assist and only Image Assist, as opposed to typing the HTML for images directly into their posts. You could do this by using the input filters to disallow `<img>` tags in the posts.

On the other hand, using macro tags requires that you take the extra step of adding the Image Assist filter to your input format. Another disadvantage is that you cannot edit the HTML that is generated from within your post, so you cannot customize the appearance of your images on a per-node basis. Also, at page-load time, you might see a slight performance reduction compared with the pure HTML method, since Image Assist must run the regular expressions to find and replace the macro tags.

Here is a list of questions to answer when making the decision of whether to go with Image Assist macro tags or pure HTML:

- Do you need to restrict users from using the `<img>` tag directly?
- Do you need the HTML template for in-line images to remain consistent across your site over time, even if you decide to change it?
- Do you sometimes wish to change or customize the HTML for your in-line images for a particular post?

If you answered yes to either of the first two questions, the Image Assist macro tags are right for you. If you answered yes to third question, you probably want to use pure HTML.

The macro tags are used by default. There is no setting that makes pure HTML the default and only choice. The good news is that users with the Choose Format Type permission have the choice of whether to use the macro tags or pure HTML.

Regardless of which permission you set, however, you must tend to the input formats.

Image Assist Input Formats

Navigate to *administer* ➤ *input formats* (`admin/filters`) and look at your various formats. As an example, click *configure* for the Filtered HTML format. The two pertinent filters are the HTML filter and the Inline Images filter. If you want the macro tags to work, you need to include the Inline Images filter. If you want to be able to insert pure HTML using Image Assist, you need to configure the HTML filter to accept `<img>`, `<div>`, and `<a>` tags. Otherwise, your images will be filtered out. Finally, you need to check the order of the filters. Click *rearrange* and confirm that the Inline Images filter comes after (has a bigger number than) the HTML filter.

Note If you alter the Image Assist template to include tags other than `<img>`, `<div>`, and `<a>`, you may need to update your HTML filter to include the additional tags.

Image Assist Access Settings

Image Assist adds an icon below the text areas on your site. When you click this icon, you see a pop-up window that you can use to add images to the text area. The first configuration choice you make after navigating to *administer* ➤ *settings* ➤ *img_assist* (`admin/settings/img_assist`) is whether you want to allow these icons to appear with all text areas, even where it really makes no sense to add images, or if you want to make a list of paths to specify where the icons should appear.

The Display Img_assist On field gives you two choices: on all text areas (the default) or on specific pages. If you select on specific pages and save the settings, a Pages text box will appear. In the Pages text box, you can make a line-separated list of paths on which the Image Assist icon should appear below text areas.

Image Output Settings

The Image HTML Template field on the Image Assist settings page (`admin/settings/img_assist`) lets you edit the template for in-line images using eight placeholder variables to represent the dynamic parts.

- `%node-link`: URL to the image node.
- `%img-link`: URL to the (original) image file.
- `%src`, `%width`, `%height`, and `%alt`: Values to the common parameters in an `<img>` tag.
- `%caption`: Text to appear with the image. This can be configured to use the body portion of the image node.
- `%image-class`: A CSS class name that defaults to `image`. This can be overridden by editing the macro tag, so different image styles can be exposed from your style sheets.

Here is an example of an image HTML template:

```
<div class="%image-class">
  <a href="%node-link">
    <img src="%src" width="%width" height="%height" alt="%alt" /></a>
  <div class="caption">%caption</div>
</div>
```

When using the pop-up window to insert images, the Image Assist module performs a nice favor for you in that it loads the body text of the image nodes in case you want to use that as the image caption. The Preload Image Captions field, set to enabled by default, lets you turn this feature off.

Image Assist Preview Settings

The Default Derivative Selection field on the Image Assist settings page (`admin/settings/img_assist`) lets you decide which derivative size should be used as a default from the list of possible derivative sizes. It takes the list of derivatives from the Image module's settings.

The final two settings, Default Width of Image Thumbnail Previews and Max Number of Images to Preview, allow you to customize the size and number of thumbnail previews that appear in the pop-up window.

Using Image Assist

Now that you've configured the Image Assist module, you can use it to insert in-line images into posts. When you create a new story, blog, page, or similar node type that has one or more text areas for content, you will notice the Image Assist icon directly below the text areas. Click this icon, and the Image Assist pop-up window will appear (so make sure your browser allows pop-ups for your site), as shown in Figure 4-6.

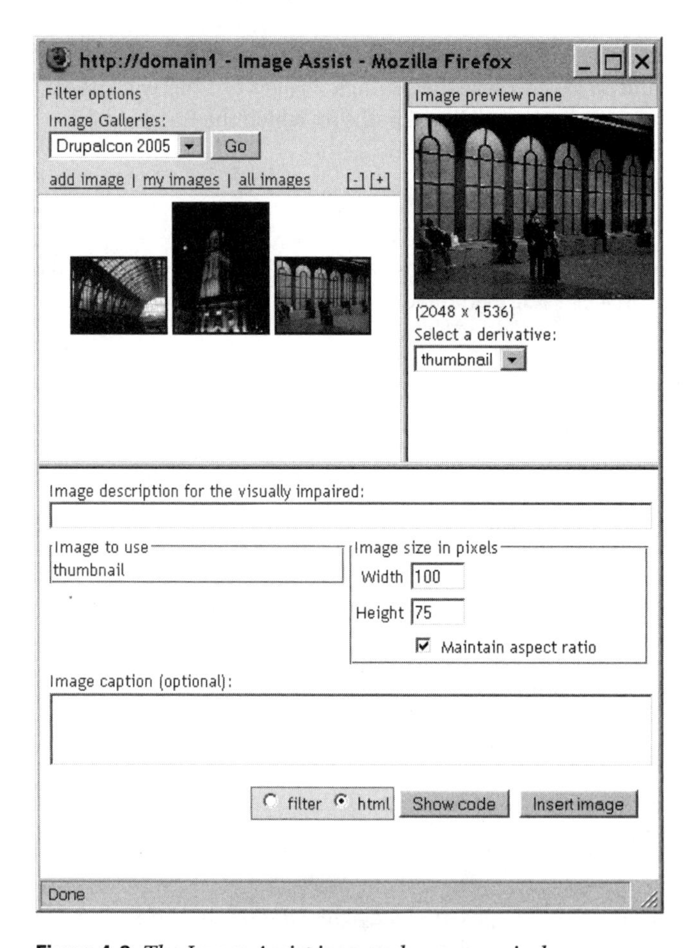

Figure 4-6. *The Image Assist icon and pop-up window*

Use this pop-up window as follows:

- If you set a value for Image Preview filter on the Image Assist settings page, you can use the Filter options to select the images you want to see by category. Each selection box represents a vocabulary. Click Go to update the selection.
- If the thumbnails are too small to see clearly or too large to fit nicely on the page, use the plus and minus links to change their size.
- You can upload an image by clicking the *add image* link. It works just like adding an image with the Image module.
- Click a thumbnail to see the preview version in this frame.
- You can enter some text in the Image Description for the Visually Impaired field. This will be the value of the `alt` parameter in your `<img>` tag.
- The Image to Use setting lets you choose between the available derivative sizes of the image for inclusion in your post.

■ **Caution** Before deciding to include the original image, make sure to refer to the Image Size in Pixels dimensions, to see if the image is appropriately sized to fit on the page without ruining your theme's layout.

- If the original is too big and the thumbnail is too small, you can adjust the size of the displayed image. Leave Maintain Aspect Ratio checked, and the height and width parameters will react to any changes by updating the other.

■ **Caution** The Width and Height fields set the `height` and `width` parameters of the `<img>` tag and do not actually resize the image. This is not the best practice, as it can result in more bandwidth use, slower page loading, and poor-quality images. Use these fields only when really necessary.

- You can edit the image caption, as represented by the `%caption` variable in the image HTML template. If you have enabled the Preload Image Captions setting on the Image Assist settings page, the body of the image node will appear here. You can edit it to fit your caption needs without changing the original node.
- The Filter and Html radio buttons are available to those users who have the Choose Format Type permission. Choosing Filter (the default) will result in a macro tag. Selecting Html will result in pure HTML.
- You can always preview the code by clicking the Show code button. The code that will be inserted into your post will appear in a second pop-up window for your review.

Finally, when you're ready, click the Insert image button, and the macro tag or HTML will be inserted into the text area where the cursor appeared before you opened the Image Assist window.

Here is an example of the macro tag that is generated:

```
[img_assist|fid=11|thumb=1|alt=Antwerp train station|caption=Antwerp train station]
```

You can remove images from posts simply by deleting the macro tag or HTML that Image Assist generated.

Flexinode Module

The very popular Flexinode module is designed to give you control over the information that your web site collects. It enables you to define your own data types, called *flexinodes*, with their own fields. These then function just like other content types (blogs, images, polls, and so on) in that web users can create them, edit them, delete them, and so on. The Flexinode content types can be promoted, moderated, and categorized, and they can participate in any other function Drupal provides for node types.

The examples of data types you can create are endless. How about an exercise log tracking what you've done at the gym, or a system to catalog all of the songs a composer has written? Virtually any information that you can imagine collecting through a web interface can be modeled with flexinodes.

Installing the Flexinode Module

Follow these steps to install the Flexinode module:

1. Download the latest version of Flexinode from `http://drupal.org/project/flexinode`.
2. Place the entire `flexinode` folder in the `/modules/` directory.
3. Load the database definition from the file appropriate to your database, either `flexinode.mysql` or `flexinode.pgsql`.
4. Move all of the files in `flexinode/contrib` into the `flexinode` directory.
5. Delete the empty `flexinode/contrib` directory.
6. After making a backup of your database, import the database definitions (`flexinode.mysql`) using the tool of your choice.
7. Navigate to *administer* ➤ *modules* (`admin/modules`) and enable the module.

Flexinode consists of the Drupal module (`flexinode.module`) and a number of included files representing the various field types that a flexinode can have. Seven of these field types were written by the module's original author (Jonathan Chaffer), and a number of contributed field types were written by various other people. When you put the entire `flexinode` folder into the `modules` directory, you moved all seven of the core field types there. In the archive file that you downloaded from `Drupal.org` is a folder named `flexinode/contrib`, which contains the various contributed field types. After perusing the README text, you can decide which of the contributed field types you would like to have available. These should also go into the modules/flexinode folder on the web server. In the end, an installation of Flexinode with all available field types will look like Figure 4-7.

Figure 4-7. *Flexinode directory structure*

Adding Custom Node Types

The first step in creating a custom flexinode type is naming and describing it. Then you can add your content type fields. As an example, let's say you want to create a type called Basketball Team and populate it with fields to track such things as a list of players, the team colors, and the team's motto.

Content Type Creation

To create a flexinode type, choose *administer* ➤ *content* ➤ *content types* ➤ *add content type* (admin/node/types/add_type). The content type name and description that you choose for your new type are analogous to the names and descriptions you can see for existing node types when you click create content (node/add). The help text will appear at the top of the form when you or other web users create new instances of the custom node. Use this field to give any special instructions that might be helpful to your users when creating new nodes of this type. Figure 4-8 shows an example of defining a new flexinode type named Basketball Team.

Home » administer » content » content types

edit content type

Content type name:*

basketball team

Description:

Everything you need to know about a little-league team

A one-line description of the content type.

Help text:

Make sure your team photo is smaller than 1MB in size before uploading.

Instructions to present to the user when adding new content of this type.

Submit Delete

Figures 4-8. *Defining a new flexinode type named Basketball Team*

The name and description you give your new content type appear with its choice on the content-creation form. Figure 4-9 shows the Basketball Team type added to the list of content choices.

admin
create content
basketball team
book page
story
my account
administer
log out
Home
create content
Choose the appropriate item from the list:
basketball team
Everything you need to know about a little-league team
book page
A book is a collaborative writing effort: users can collaborate
previously written. So when you have some information to s
written better, you can do something about it.
story
Stories are articles in their simplest form: they have a title,
used as a personal blog or for news articles.

Figure 4-9. *After creating the Basketball Team flexinode type, it appears in the list of content type choices. Notice its description shows up in this list.*

The help text you added for your new content type is displayed on the content-creation form for that type, as shown in Figure 4-10.

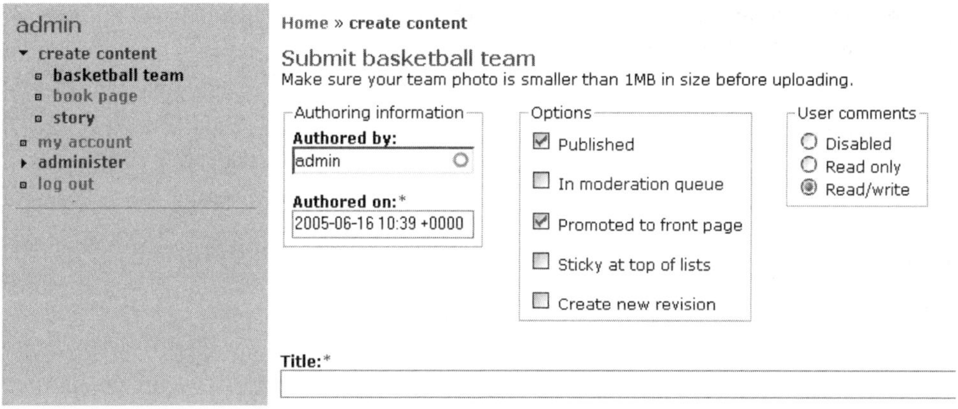

Figure 4-10. *When you select to use the Basketball Team flexinode type, its help text appears near the the top of the form.*

Content Type Fields

Next, you will want to add some fields to your new content type. In its empty state, it is nothing but a title. Your task is to determine what information you want to collect and how to best represent it.

To add a field, navigate to *administer* ➤ *content* ➤ *content types* ➤ *list* (`admin/node/types`). From this page, you can track all of your flexinode content types. The list of links on the right (*add checkbox*, *add file*, *add image*, and so on) correspond to the field type files that you included in the `modules/flexinode` folder during installation. Clicking one of these links will add a field of this type to the data model of your flexinode.

For the Basketball Team example, let's start with *add textfield* to add a field for the name of the team's contact person (the default Title field can be used for the team's name). The screen for adding a text field has seven fields:

- Field Label is the only required field on this form. The value entered here becomes the label on the text field you are adding to the Basketball Team type.
- The text you enter in the Description field will appear directly underneath the field and serves as a help text in case it isn't clear from the field label what this field is for.
- Entering a value in the Default Value field will prefill the field.
- If the field is to be required, so that it will be impossible to submit the form without filling in a value for it, check the Required Field check box.
- The teaser of a node is the summary version that is shown in lists. If this field is to appear as part of the teaser, check the Show in Teaser check box.
- Each flexinode type has a tabular view where all nodes of that type can be browsed, complete with sortable columns. If this field is to be one of the fields in that table, check the Show in Table check box.
- The Weight value orders the field among all other fields on the form.

Figure 4-11 shows an example of the edit field form for the text field and what it produces on the Baseball Team creation form.

Home » administer » content » content types

edit field

Field label:*

Contact person

Description:

The adult responsible for the team, usally the coach

A brief description of the field, to be displayed on the content submission form.

Default value:

☑ Required field

Whether the user must fill in the field when creating content.

☑ Show in teaser

Whether this field should be shown as part of the teaser.

☑ Show in table

Whether this field should be shown as part of this content type's **tabular view**.

Weight:

1

Optional. On the content editing form, the heavier fields will sink and the lighter fields will be positioned nearer the top.

Submit Delete

Home » create content

Submit basketball team

Make sure your team photo is smaller than 1MB in size before uploading.

Title:*

Contact person:*

The adult responsible for the team, usally the coach

Figure 4-11. *Adding a text field to the form*

These seven fields appear on all field type forms. A text field is the simplest field type and has only the standard seven configuration options. Others, such as drop-down menu and table, have extra configuration options in addition to the seven standard ones.

Adding a drop-down menu to the form, for determining which league a team plays in, is similar to adding the text field. Start by clicking *add dropdown menu* from the `admin/node/types` screen. In addition to the seven standard fields, the form for adding a drop-down menu has a group called Options. The values you enter here will become the various options in the content-creation form later. Clicking the More button provides additional fields in case you need more options.

In the same way, you will be able to add the other fields needed to complete the Basketball Team form. The example in Figure 4-12 uses various core and contributed field types, including the following:

- An e-mail address field for Contact email
- A table field for Players
- A text field for Motto
- An image field for Team photo
- Color pickers for the Team color fields

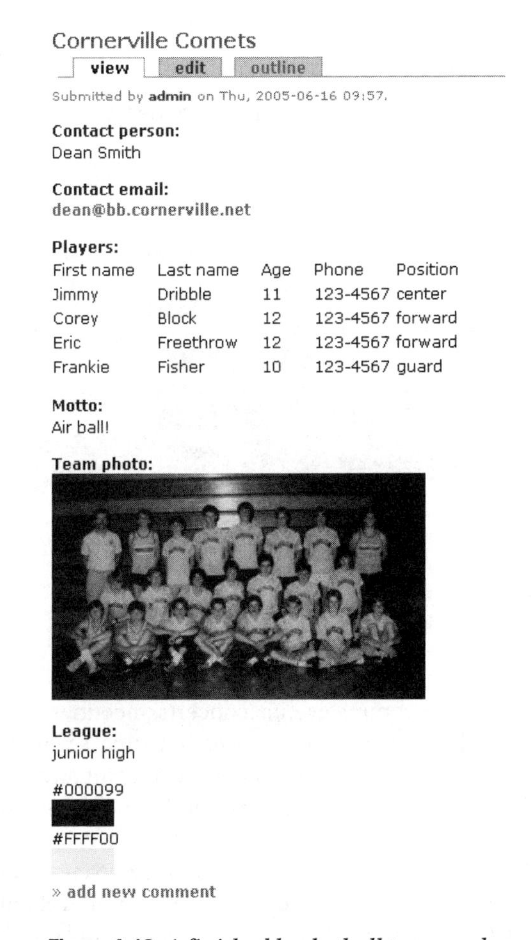

Figure 4-12. *A finished basketball team node*

Table View for the Content Type

Once you have finished designing your flexinode content type and have created a number of actual nodes—basketball teams, in this example—you can view the results in the tabular view that flexinode offers. There is no link offered to this tabular view, so you must create one yourself using the primary or secondary links, or perhaps with the Menu module.

The path to the table view takes the form `flexinode/table/type_id`, where *type_id* is the numerical ID assigned to the content type you wish to view. To find out exactly what this ID is, you will need to do a little sleuthing. Go to the content type editing screen for the type that you are interested in: *administer* ➤ *content* ➤ *content types* ➤ *edit content type*. The URL in your browser's address bar should look something like this:

```
http://localhost/drupal/?q=admin/node/types/edit_type/1
```

From this URL, you see that the type ID number is 1, thus the URL to the table view for this content type is as follows:

```
http://localhost/drupal/?q=flexinode/table/1
```

Figure 4-13 shows the table view for the sample Basketball Team flexinode type.

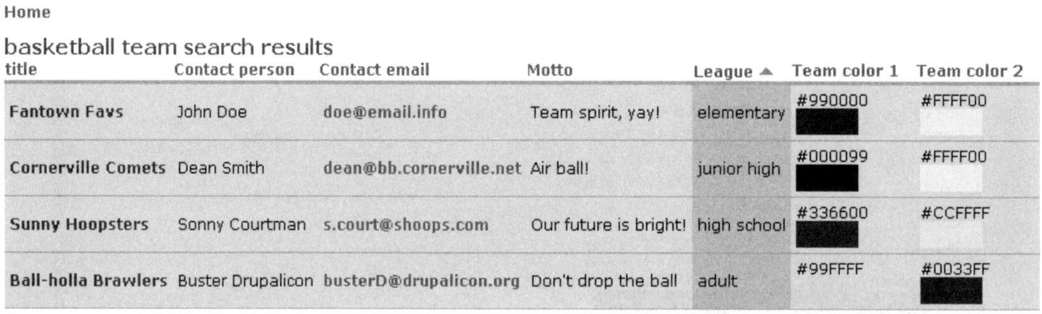

Home

basketball team search results

title	Contact person	Contact email	Motto	League ▲	Team color 1	Team color 2
Fantown Favs	John Doe	doe@email.info	Team spirit, yay!	elementary	#990000	#FFFF00
Cornerville Comets	Dean Smith	dean@bb.cornerville.net	Air ball!	junior high	#000099	#FFFF00
Sunny Hoopsters	Sonny Courtman	s.court@shoops.com	Our future is bright!	high school	#336600	#CCFFFF
Ball-holla Brawlers	Buster Drupalicon	busterD@drupalicon.org	Don't drop the ball	adult	#99FFFF	#0033FF

Figure 4-13. *The table view for basketball teams*

Event Module

Sites interested in publicizing information about upcoming events (concerts, meetings, deadlines, and so on) will find the Drupal Event module very useful. An *event*, in Drupal's view, is any node that has a start, and possibly an end, time. This flexibility opens the door for any node type to become an event. Events can be viewed in calendars, and the calendars can be filtered to show events based on node type and taxonomy categories.

As any node type can be "event-enabled," you can use the Flexinode module to create various event types. A site for a music school could create Concert, Rehearsal, Lecture, and Holiday (when the school is closed) event types. The Concert and Rehearsal event types could then use an ensemble taxonomy vocabulary to show when and where ensembles are rehearsing or playing concerts. It would then be possible to show calendars and schedules for queries such as "concerts and rehearsals for the symphony orchestra in May and June."

The Event module works particularly well for tracking the "when" aspect of events. Later in the chapter, I will show you how you can use the Location module to track the "where" part of events.

Installing the Event Module

Follow these steps to install the Event module:

1. Download the latest version of the Event module from `http://drupal.org/project/event`.

2. Perform the recommended backup of your database, and then import the database definitions (`event.mysql` or `event.pgsql`) using the tool of your choice.

3. Place the Event module with all its files under `modules/event`.

4. Navigate to *administer* ➤ *modules* (`admin/modules`) and enable the module.

Once the Event module has been installed, you need to configure it and also decide which node types are to become event-enabled. After you've configured the Event module and enabled at least one node type to be event-aware, you will be ready to create some events.

Configuring the Event Module

Select *administer* ➤ *settings* ➤ *event* (`admin/settings/event`) to see the configuration settings for the Event module. Depending on where your site's audience is located, you need to decide how to save and display time zones. You also have options for the display of events.

Time Zone Input

The first field, Event Time Zone Input, is a means of locating the event, answering the question, "In which time zone does this event take place?" You have three options:

Use the sitewide time zone: This setting uses the site-wide setting that you set from the site settings page (`admin/settings`). If the web site and your events are in the same place, such as for an office intranet or a web site about sports in Boston, this option is appropriate.

Use the time zone of the user editing or creating the event: This uses the user's time zone (as configured on the user's profile page). This assumes that users will create only events that are local to them and that they have correctly configured their personal profile to reflect their time zone. This seems like too many assumptions to be practical in most cases.

Allow users to set event time zones: This setting lets users set the time zone for each event. If your site is going to track events from a large geographical region, this option is probably the best choice.

Time Zone Display

The Event Time Zone Display field answers the question, "The time for this event should be displayed adjusted to which time zone?" Imagine that your site is configured to Eastern Standard Time (EST). Jim in Chicago uses your site to announce his upcoming concert. which starts at 18:00 (6:00 p.m.). Since he and his concert are in Central Standard Time (CST), he saves the event with CST. George in California, which is on Pacific Standard Time (PST), visits the site and sees the announcement for Jim's concert. What time should George see: 18:00 CST (the event's time zone), 16:00 PST (George's time zone), or 19:00 EST (the web site's time zone)? These are your three choices for the Event Time Zone Display field:

Use the event's time zone: If it is an event that you want to attend (in the place that it is happening), this is the most logical setting. Since you will attend the event in person, you will naturally be in the same time zone as the event.

Use the user's time zone: Let's say the concert is also being broadcast by radio or webcast. Now you will definitely want to see the time of the concert adjusted to the time zone you are in, thus making this setting the better choice.

Use the sitewide time zone: This is probably not the best setting for most cases.

The Time Notation Preference field determines whether times will be displayed in 12- or 24-hour notation.

Event Block

The Event module defines a block that shows upcoming events. You can enable this block from the block administration page (`admin/blocks`). On the Event module configuration page, the Upcoming Event Block Limit setting allows you to control how many events will be displayed in the block.

■ **Note** The Event module defines two blocks: Calendar to Browse Events and List of Upcoming Events. You can activate and configure these blocks by navigating to *administer* ➤ *blocks* (`admin/blocks`). See Chapter 2 for details about administering blocks.

Event Overview Options

The events calendar has five different views: day, week, month, table, and list. Use the Default Overview field to select which of these views should be the default calendar view. If you choose Table, you can also use the Table View Default Period setting to specify how many days are to be shown.

When looking at the overview of events on a calendar view, it is possible to filter the display based on node type and taxonomy category. The queries for these filters are built by constructing special URLs, as described next. The Taxonomy Filter Controls field sets the display of this filter:

Never show taxonomy filter control: This allows you to hide the taxonomy filter control.

Only show taxonomy filter control when taxonomy filter view is requested: This shows the filter control only when a taxonomy query is built into the URL query.

Show taxonomy filter control on calendar views: This shows the filter control by default.

The same three options can also be applied to the Content Type Filter Controls field, which lets you filter the calendar view by node type.

Event-Enabling Node Types

For each type that you wish to be an event type, the content-creation form will have two extra fields for the start date and end date. As I mentioned earlier, a convenient way to make event types is by using the Flexinode module to create node types specifically for the purpose. These flexinode types should answer the *what* part of the question "What type of event is this?" Building on the music school example, you could define a Concert flexinode type that included flexinode fields to describe the repertoire and ticket-buying information. The Event module would take care of the *when* part: "When does this concert take place?"

To make a particular node type event-enabled, go to *administer* ➤ *settings* ➤ *configure* (for the particular content type) and set the Show in Event Calendar field. The default setting for this field is Never, which means that a node is not event-enabled, will not have the start and end fields, and will not show up in the calendar. Change this to either of the following settings:

All views: This means that the content type is event-enabled, will have the start and end fields, and can appear in calendars with other event types.

Only in views for this type: This also means that the content type is event-enabled and will have start and end fields, but it will show up only in calendars specific to this type. In other words, it will have a completely separate calendar all to itself.

Viewing Events

As noted earlier, the content-creation forms for your event types (`node/add/`*`type`*) will now have fields for entering starting and ending dates and times. If the ending time is earlier than the starting time, it is ignored, which is convenient for events where no ending time is specified. If an event spans more than one day, it will show up on all of the intermediary days in the calendar.

When you're viewing an event-enabled node, the start and end times will be shown, and a link to the calendar view will appear at the bottom. Clicking the *calendar* link will show the calendar with the day of the event highlighted. (The Drupal path to the current events calendar is `event`.) Figure 4-14 shows an example of a calendar view.

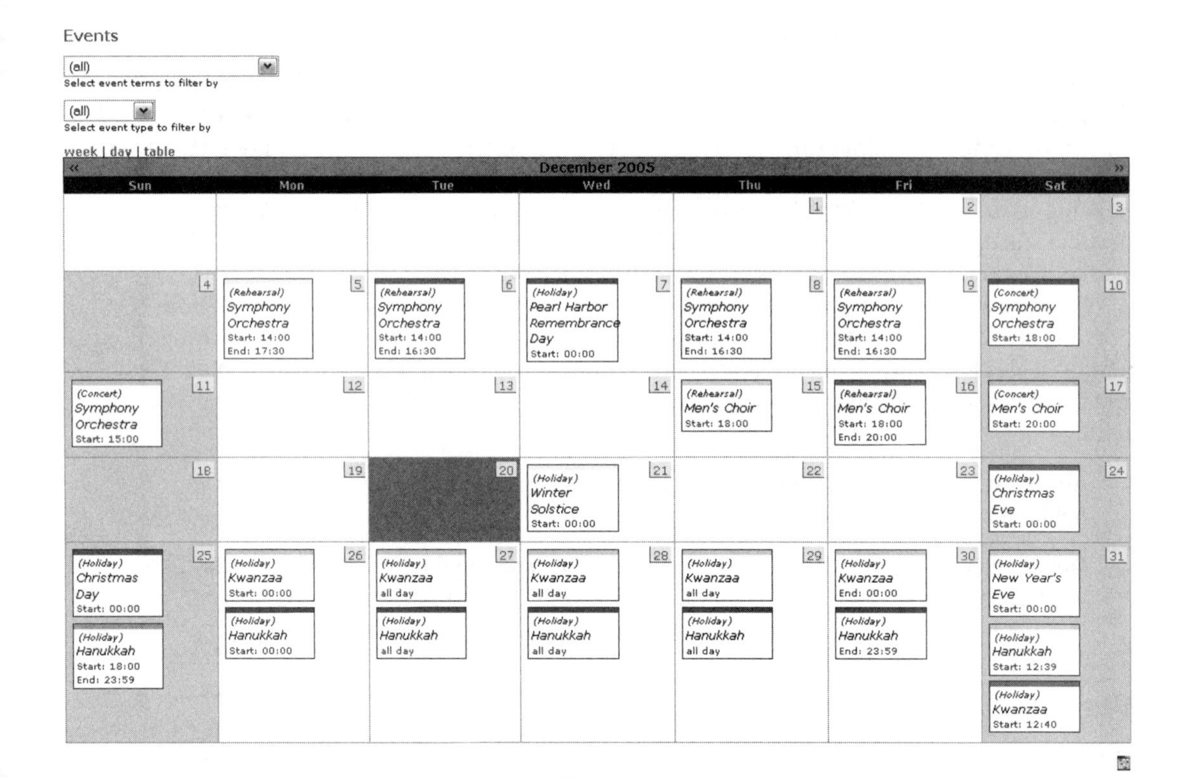

Figure 4-14. *The month of December showing rehearsals, concerts, and holidays*

The calendar view comes with selection boxes that you can use to filter the events being displayed. This is particularly useful when you're looking at a crowded calendar. The first selection box allows you to filter the calendar by taxonomy category, and the second filters by node type. Figure 4-15 shows an example of filtering by a taxonomy category.

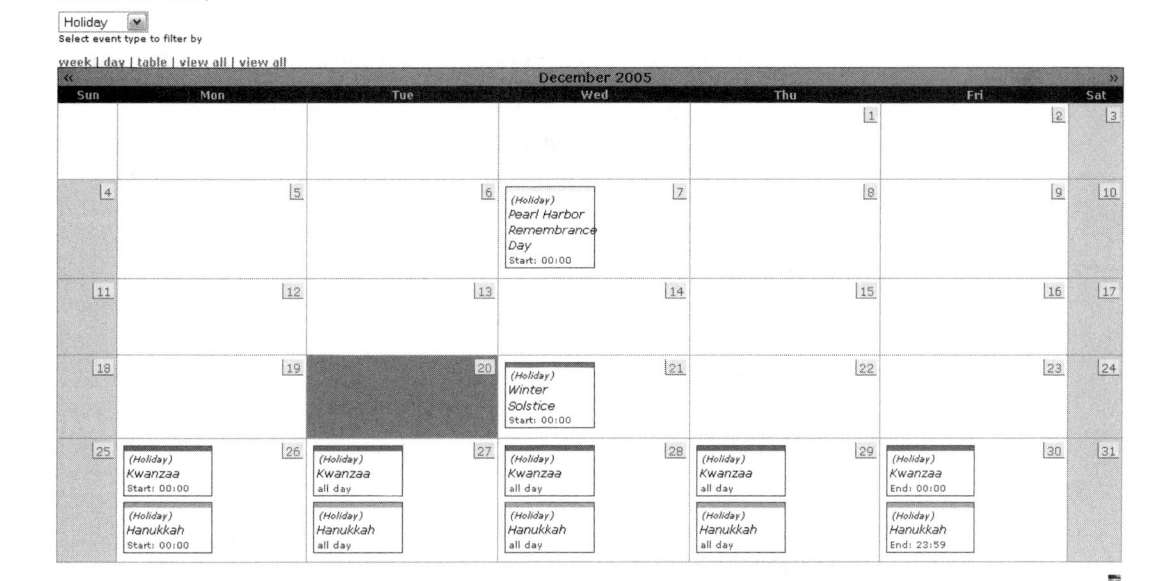

Figure 4-15. *The month of December showing only holidays when school is open (a taxonomy category)*

All of the parameters governing time range, category, and type of event can be built into the URL. This makes URL manipulation an effective tool for querying a Drupal site for its event information. Here is how event URLs are built:

```
?q=event/$year/$month/$day/$view_type/$content_type/$taxonomy_terms/$duration
```

The event URL variables are as follows:

- `$year`: A four-digit integer, such as 2005.
- `$month`: An integer from 1 to 12 representing the month.
- `$day`: A two-digit integer representing the day of the month to start from. Leading zeros are required, as in 03.
- `$view_type`: The type of calendar layout. Values include `month`, `week`, `day`, `table`, `ical` for an iCal export, and `feed` for an RSS feed.
- `$content_type`: A list of node types, separated by a plus sign (+). Flexinode types require only the integer value of the type. For example, to view story nodes and flexinode type 1, you would use `story+1`. The value `all` will show all types.

- `$taxonomy_terms`: A list of term IDs, separated by a plus sign (+). For example, to view entries assigned to the taxonomy terms with IDs 4 and 9, you would use `4+9`. The value `all` will show all terms.
- `$duration`: The number of days to display. Currently, only the table view observes this setting.

For example, suppose you wanted to see all of the Men's Choir concerts and rehearsals for the five-day period December 14 to 19. Here's what the URL would look like:

```
http://domain/?q=event/2005/12/14/table/1+2/10/5
```

This URL is built as follows:

- `$year`: `2005`
- `$month`: `12`, for December
- `$day`: `14`, the starting day
- `$view_type`: `table`
- `$content_type`: `1+2`, which means Concert and Rehearsal, since these are flexinode 1 and flexinode 2 types
- `$taxonomy_terms`: `10`, the taxonomy term for Men's Choir
- `$duration`: `5`, for five days

The result is a subset of the events shown in a tabular view, as illustrated in Figure 4-16.

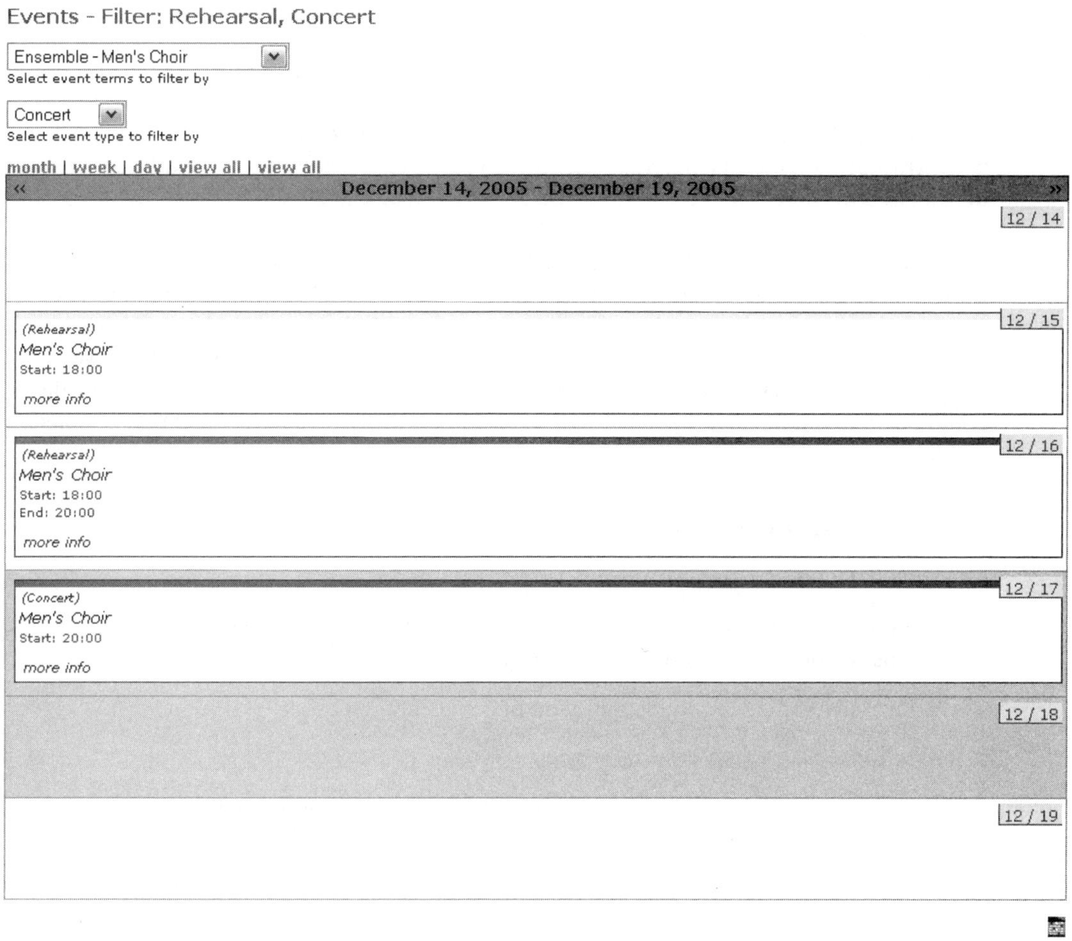

Events - Filter: Rehearsal, Concert

Ensemble - Men's Choir

Select event terms to filter by

Concert

Select event type to filter by

month | week | day | view all | view all

« December 14, 2005 - December 19, 2005 »

12 / 14

12 / 15

(Rehearsal)
Men's Choir
Start: 18:00
more info

12 / 16

(Rehearsal)
Men's Choir
Start: 18:00
End: 20:00
more info

12 / 17

(Concert)
Men's Choir
Start: 20:00
more info

12 / 18

12 / 19

Figure 4-16. *Men's Choir concerts and rehearsals from December 14 to 19*

Exporting Event Information

You can export your Drupal site's event information for external use by any program that supports the webcal protocol, such as iCal (`http://www.apple.com/macosx/features/ical/`) or as an RSS feed. The icon at the bottom right of the screen underneath the calendar will export the current display for iCal.

You can generate both RSS and iCal format using the URL manipulation techniques described in the preceding section, by substituting `ical` or `feed` for the `$view_type` variable. For example, for an RSS feed, the URL for displaying the Men's Choir rehearsals and concerts could be rewritten like this:

```
q=event/2005/12/1/feed/1+2/10
```

Location Module

Adding location information to content can be very useful. Whether it is a shipping address, a meeting place, or the place where a photograph was taken, location adds an interesting dimension and opens up new possibilities for how communities form and how web sites are used. The Location module provides a set of location services, including appending location information to content and users, doing proximity searches, and linking to external map providers.

Much like the Event module, the Location module lets you choose what content should have location information, and the concept of a location-enabled node type is analogous to the event-enabled node type, but with different information. Furthermore, the Location module complements the Event module in a very meaningful way in that it can be used to answer the question "Where does this event take place?" To draw on the examples in the Event module section of this chapter, the Concert and Rehearsal flexinode types could be location-enabled, making the events calendar even more useful.

Installing the Location Module

The Location module is made up of the following parts:

- A public API definition describing how to work with location information in Drupal. This can be found in the file `location_API.txt`.
- `location.module`, an implementation of the Location module
- `location.inc`, a set of common tools
- `earth.inc`, a set of tools for working with latitude and longitude values
- A set of 243 files found in `location/supported`, each representing a different country, providing location services that range from a list of states or provinces to proximity searches and geocoding of postal addresses
- `location/database/zipcodes.mysql`, the definition for an optional zip codes table, which is required for the advanced features like geocoding
- A growing number of `location/database/zipcodes.`*`country-code`*`.mysql` data dumps to provide zip code support for specific countries (the United States and Germany are currently available)

Follow these steps to install the Location module:

1. Download the latest version of the Location module from `http://drupal.org/project/location`.
2. Make a backup of your database.
3. Load the database definition from the file appropriate to your database, either `location.mysql` or `location.pgsql`.

4. Transfer the necessary files to the web server. As the `location` folder contains several very large data dumps and a couple hundred country-specific files, it is worth the effort to select only the files that you actually need. Figure 4-17 shows an example of a minimal directory structure for the Location module, which will be able to support locations in Mexico, the United States, and Canada.

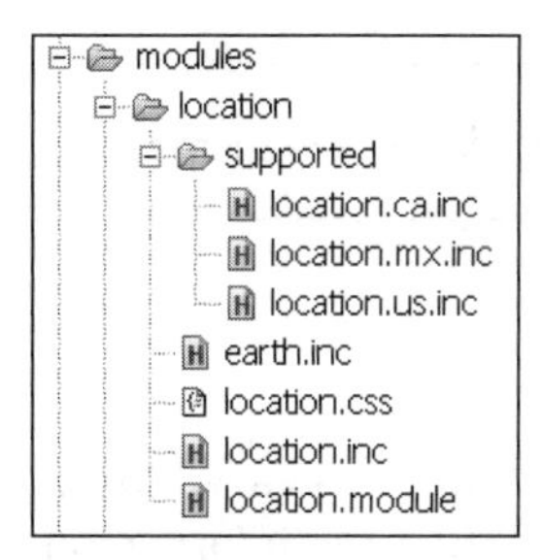

Figure 4-17. *Location module directory structure*

5. If you wish to work with the finer features of the Location module, create a table called `zipcodes` using the file `supported/zipcodes.mysql`. Then, depending on which data dumps are available, import zip code data into this table. The `supported/zipcodes.us.mysql` file, for example, provides the data dump for the United States. If you intend to run multiple location-enabled sites on the same database server, you might consider putting the `zipcodes` table in a separate database and sharing it among all the sites. Since it is used only for looking up zip code information and is never written to, this is a safe and efficient approach. See Chapter 6 for details on running multiple sites and database table prefixing.

6. Navigate to *administer* ➤ *modules* (`admin/modules`) and enable the module.

As with the Event module, your next steps are to configure the module and make some nodes location-enabled.

Configuring the Location Module

Select *administer* ➤ *settings* ➤ *location* (`admin/settings/location`) to see the configuration settings for the Location module.

Country Selection

As a convenience, the Location module lets you set a default country for your web site with the Default Country Selection field. This should be the country that generates the largest portion of your traffic. Whichever country you set here will be selected by default in all location forms.

If the locations your site tracks are all within one country, you can simplify matters even further by checking Hide Country Selection, which saves your users the step of selecting the country. The default country will be used instead.

Distance Units

Distances are an issue only when you're using the Location module to do proximity searches, which is possible only if you are working with one of the available zip code databases. In this case, you can set the Distance Unit field to select the units in which distances will be displayed for location-based searches.

Note The Drupal path to the location module's proximity search screen is `search/location`.

Location Display

The Location module handles the task of displaying location information (an address, basically) for those nodes that have it available. You might want to display this information some other way. The Toggle Location Display field allows you to turn off the default display of location information. The idea is that you would then write a themable function that would display the information in the form that you want. See Chapter 5 for instructions for writing custom themable functions.

User Location Information

You can collect location information for nodes and users. Knowing where your users are located can be very helpful, depending on the type of site you are building. For example, if your site is being used for a music school to track orchestra rehearsals and concerts, it might be very useful for your users to be able to add their address to their profile information for the sake of organizing carpools to rehearsals. The User Locations field turns this functionality on or off.

Country Location Features

The last section on the Location module settings page, entitled "Enable all *available* features for locations from the following countries," is a list of countries that have specific features available. It corresponds directly with the files found in the `modules/location/supported` folder.

The vast majority of the countries listed offer the feature of knowing their states or provinces and nothing else. Thus, the major practical implication of enabling ten or so countries from central Africa is that you will need to scroll through all these countries and their provinces when entering location information for specific nodes later. At the time of this writing, only three countries have significant features to offer: the United States, Canada, and Germany. The United States has the most full-featured set, including proximity searches and deep linking into map services such as Google or Yahoo! Maps for addresses. Germany and Canada have only partially implemented sets of features.

Tip If you would like to implement further location features for a country that does not have them, the `location_API.txt` file provides an excellent description of the programming API that needs to be used. The `supported/location.us.inc` file is a complete sample implementation of the API.

Location-Enabling Node Types

With the basic configuration options settled, the next step is to decide which node types should collect location information and exactly which information is desired or required. Node type configuration takes place from the `admin/node/configure/types` page, which lists all of the node types. Click *configure* for any of the listed node types, and you will see a section of the form titled Locative Information. The Enable for Locations field does just what it says. The rest of the fields allow you to customize the location form by making fields invisible, optional, or required, based on your specific needs.

Organic Groups Module

One of the hallmarks of vibrant online communities is the presence of a common interest or theme that unites those who are involved. Whether this common interest is relatively broad or narrow, there are likely to be smaller but related topics that are of interest only to a subset of the community. For instance, on a music school site, the brass players might want to organize their own rehearsals and brass ensemble concerts. The ability for these people to band together and form a group is the main offering of the Organic Groups (OG) module.

Groups have their own home page, can select their own theme (design template), can have content that is visible only to members of the group, and can have image galleries. Most important, they can be created and joined by users as the need arises, thus growing and thriving based on the current interests of the community. This is what makes them organic.

Until this point, none of the content on your Drupal site has had any sort of node-level access control. This means that if user A and user B have the same roles, they both are able to see the same content. The Organic Groups module is one of the modules that implement node-level permissions to decide who can see content. If user A is in a group and user B is not, and if that group's content is private, user B will not be able to see the same content that user A sees, despite the fact that they have the same roles.

Organic Groups isn't the only module in the contributions repository that implements node-level access controls. Other modules that provide access controls are Node Privacy by Role (`http://drupal.org/project/node_privacy_byrole`), Taxonomy Access Control (`http://drupal.org/project/taxonomy_access`), and Nodeperm Role (`http://drupal.org/project/nodeperm_role`). Unfortunately, these modules tend to interfere with each other. This is a basic weakness in the way Drupal's permissions are handled and is a topic of hot debate in the developer community. Be warned: do not try to mix multiple node-access modules!

■ **Caution** Do not try to use the Organic Groups module with other node-level access modules, as they are not designed to work together.

Installing the Organic Groups Module

Please take the time to back up your database before installing the Organic Groups module. While this is good advice for every module that has its own database definitions, it is especially important in this case, as the installation of the Organic Groups module will make fundamental changes in the database's data, and that will alter the way the database behaves. Specifically, there is a table, `node_access`, which controls whether a given user can view a given node. In the absence of a node-level access module such as Organic Groups, this table contains one row that grants access to all nodes to every user. Organic Groups will delete this row and instead manage node permissions on a per-node basis. While the Organic Groups module itself provides a mechanism for uninstalling itself, it is best to secure a backup before installing the module.

Download the latest version of the Organic Groups module from `http://drupal.org/project/og`. After making your backup, you can load the database definition from the `og.mysql` or `og.pgsql` file. Copy the `og` folder into your `modules` folder, and activate the Organic Groups, the Organic Groups Albums (og_album), and Taxonomy modules from the `admin/modules` page.

The Organic Groups module depends on the Image module and the Organic Groups Albums module to provide each group with its own photo gallery. Installing the Image module was covered earlier in this chapter.

■ **Note** In order for your groups to have their own image galleries, you will need the Image, Taxonomy, and Organic Groups modules. The Organic Groups module comes packaged with the Organic Groups download. The Image module is available from `http://drupal.org/project/image`. The Taxonomy module is a core module and is discussed in Chapter 3.

Activating Group Blocks

The Organic Groups module makes almost no sense without the Group Details block activated, so the logical place to start is on the block administration page (`admin/blocks`). Enable this block and decide where it should be located (right, left, weight, and so on). It is not necessary to specify paths where this block should or shouldn't appear, because the module takes care of this for you.

You can also decide whether you would like to activate the Group Subscribers and Group Albums blocks.

Configuring the Organic Groups Module

Select *administer* ➤ *settings* ➤ *og* (`admin/settings/og`) to see the configuration settings for the Organic Groups module.

Access Control Status

First, check the current status of the Organic Groups access permissions. In the Module Status section at the top of the page is a status message that should read "Organic groups access control is currently enabled" and a button that will should be labeled Disable when you first view this screen. Confirm that access control is enabled. If the status message tells you that the Organic Groups access control is disabled, use the button (which is labeled Enable) to enable access control before proceeding with further configuration.

You can use the Disable button to disable Organic Groups if you want to stop using it for whatever reason. The Organic Groups module can be enabled or disabled as many times as you like without negative side effects or loss of previous group-related information.

■ **Caution** Deactivating the Organic Groups module from the module administration page (`admin/modules`) without first disabling the module from the Organic Groups settings page (`admin/settings/og`) will lead to problems.

Submission Guidelines

The Explanation or Submission Guidelines provide you with a chance to offer guidance to anyone who is in the process of creating a new group. Depending on how you configure the Organic Groups module, there will be different options available in the form for creating new groups, so you are best advised to come back to this once you have made other fundamental decisions and experimented with the module a bit. Only then will you be able to judge which parts of the process might not be clear to your user base and thus what instructions they should be given.

Visibility of Posts

Someone must decide whether a given node should be visible only within a group or whether it also should be visible to others not in the group. There are cases for both usages. If groups are being used on your site to do private secretive work and the Organic Groups module is being used to provide this privacy, then the nodes that are created for that group should be visible only to the members of that group and no one else. On the other hand, if groups are being used to organize content that should otherwise be visible to nongroup members, nodes created for that group should remain accessible to the wider public. The Visibility of Posts field lets you decide who gets to make these decisions. It offers three choices:

- Visible only within the targeted groups
- Visible within the targeted groups and on other pages
- Visibility to be determined by the author/editor using a check box on the posting form

The first two options let you, the site administrator, make the visibility decision. The third option defers the decision to the user who creates content. The content-creation form will include a check box titled Public, and the node creator is left to make the choice.

Maximum Posts and User Pictures

The Maximum Posts on Group Home Page field determines how many content teasers will be shown on the group's home page before pagination begins. Checking the Show Member Pictures field will result in avatars being shown for content posts. However, this works only if user pictures have been configured (by selecting *administer* ➤ *settings* ➤ *users*).

Audience Required

Also found on the content-creation forms is a check box for each group to which a user belongs. The Audience Required setting controls whether this check box is a required field. Making the check box Required will disallow users from submitting content before assigning the content to at least one group. Set this to Required to make sure that the site's content exists only within the context of groups. Otherwise, choose Optional to give users the choice of whether their content should be posted to a group.

Omitted Content Types

The Omitted Content Types field allows you to exclude certain node types from the groups functionality altogether. This means that group-based visibility will not apply to nodes of this type. Excluded node types will simply have site-wide visibility. This is an effective way to help establish sections of the site that are for the community at large, while reserving other areas for groups that form around specific areas of interest.

Configuring Organic Groups Albums

In order to let your users' groups make photo albums, you need to have a free-tagging taxonomy vocabulary that can be used to manage the structure of the albums. An appropriate vocabulary will be created for you when you navigate to *administer* ➤ *settings* ➤ *og_album* (`admin/settings/og_album`). Visiting the page for the first time will prompt Drupal to create and configure a vocabulary called Group Albums. If you wish to use a different free-tagging vocabulary, you can update the Select Vocabulary field.

Creating Groups

Groups are another content type, just like blogs, pages, and stories. To create a group, you use the *group* link on the *Create content* page (`node/add`). In this case, the group node that you create serves as a container for all of the other content and activities of your group. You have the same general services that Drupal provides for other types of nodes, such as the ability to be categorized with the taxonomy system. Note that you must have the Create Groups permission to create a group.

When you create a new group, you will be faced with several decisions, among them the name and description of the group. You also get to decide how new group members will be admitted by setting the Selective field, which has the following options:

Open: This means that subscription requests are accepted immediately. Open is the easiest to maintain and the most organic.

Moderated: This means that subscription requests must be approved. If the group is moderated, the person who created the group is the manager. The manager will have the chance to approve or deny the request for subscription via the *subscribers* link in the Group Details block. This link shows not only how many current subscribers there are, but also how many requests for subscription have been made (in parentheses, as shown in Figure 4-18).

Invite only: With this setting, subscriptions must be created by an administrator. If the group is made to be invite only, the moderator should add users by clicking the *add subscribers* link that is visible as a tab on the page listing all of a group's subscribers. Users are added by entering a comma-separated list of usernames.

Closed: Subscriptions are managed fully by the administrator. Users cannot choose to join or invite others.

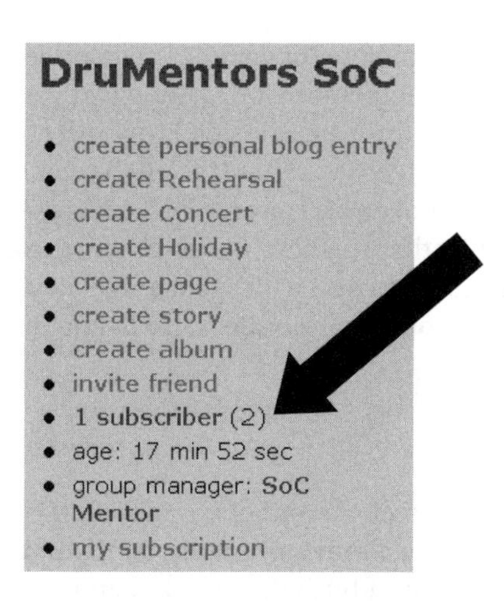

Figure 4-18. *The Group details block and the link to manage subscriptions*

■ **Note** The moderator of a group is the person who created the group. It is not currently possible to have more than one moderator. To change the moderator of a group, a user with the Administer Nodes permission must edit the group node and change the Authored By field to the username of the new moderator. Since the Administer Nodes permission is almost synonymous with being a site administrator, you should not grant this permission solely for the sake of changing group moderators. Until this facet of the Organic Groups module is better developed, it is advisable to either disallow the changing of moderators or to handle all requests to do so yourself. Be careful to whom you grant Administer Nodes permission!

Managing Groups

The Group Details block is the control panel for a group. It is visible on a group's homepage. You can add content, manage subscribers, create albums, manage e-mail subscriptions, and perform other group-related tasks from the Group Details block.

For example, you can arrange to receive e-mail notification whenever something gets posted to a group of which you are a member. In the Group Details block (see Figure 4-18), click the *my subscription* link to see and set the status of your e-mail subscription.

Spam Module

Recent years have seen an explosion in web site spam. *Spam* is any content posted to a web site that is unwanted or has an ulterior motive other than being part of the online community. The most common ulterior motive is getting links to third-party web sites published, in pursuit of the higher search engine rankings that come with the elevated page rank that their web sites enjoy when links from external sites point to them.

Some people are willing to do almost anything to get a link to their web site posted on your web site. They will sign up for accounts, and then post forums and make blog entries with blatant advertisements for their products. They will comment on other people's content, sometimes masking their intent in a thin veneer of compliments before getting to the business of self promotion. They will use scripts to find the holes in your site and flood you with postings.

Spammers show a lot of resourcefulness and absolutely no mercy. If given the chance, they will turn your web site into a wasteland of Viagra, poker, and payday loan advertisements. It is important to the health of your online community that you have a strong defense against this malicious activity. Just as people need to have means to deal with spam e-mail in their inbox, you need to have a way to deal with spam posts on your web site. You will find this defense in the Spam module.

Detecting Spam

The Spam module can be configured and trained to detect content of any kind that is considered spam, including comments and node types. The administrator has configuration options that allow the Spam module to automatically unpublish that content and/or notify the administrator.

Up to four different mechanisms can be used to identify content as spam: the Bayesian filter, custom filters, URL counting, and the Distributed Server Boycott List.

Bayesian Filter

The Bayesian filter learns to detect spam by being shown content that has been identified as spam by the site administrator. The best way to describe this method is to quote Jeremy Andrews, the author of the Spam module.

> *The Bayesian filter does statistical analysis on spam content, learning from spam and non-spam that it sees to determine the likelihood that new content is or is not spam. The filter starts out knowing nothing, and has to be trained every time it makes a mistake. This is done by marking spam content on your site as spam when you see it. Each word of the spam content will be remembered and assigned a probability. The more often a word shows up in spam content, the higher the probability that future content with the same word is also spam. As most comment spam contains links back to the spammer's websites (ie. to sell Prozac), the Bayesian filter provides a special option to quickly learn and block content that contains links to known spammer websites.*

For more information about Bayesian filtering, see `http://en.wikipedia.org/wiki/Bayesian_filtering`.

Custom Filters

As the site administrator, you can define custom filters that increase the probability of certain words and patterns to indicate spam. The filters will cause content to be marked as follows:

- Blacklisted content will be definitely marked as spam.
- Whitelisted content will definitely be marked as not spam.
- Graylisted content is marked as either usually spam or usually not spam, increasing or decreasing the likelihood of it being matched as such by the Bayesian filter.

URL Counting

Since the most common goal of spam content is to publish links back to the spammer's web site, a logical and effective method for identifying spam revolves around counting URLs in posts. The Spam module can be configured to mark content or comments as spam if they have more than a certain number of URLs in them, or alternatively, if the same URL appears more than a certain number of times.

Distributed Server Boycott List

The Distributed Server Boycott List is a set of lists of IP addresses of servers that are known to be open relays, open proxies, or to have other vulnerabilities that allow anyone to deliver e-mail to anywhere, through that server. The Spam module's fourth anti-spam mechanism uses these lists to check the IP addresses of users posting content and see if they are known e-mail spammers. Presumably, e-mail spammers are also content/comment spammers.

Installing the Spam Module

Follow these steps to install the Spam module:

1. Download the latest version of the Spam module from `http://drupal.org/project/spam`.

■ Note At the time of writing, this module was being rewritten. You are encouraged to follow developments on the Spam 2.0 module at `http://www.kerneltrap.org/jeremy/drupal/spam/`.

---

2. After backing up your data, import the file `spam.mysql` (or `spam.pgsql` if appropriate) into your database.
3. Although the Spam module comes delivered with many subfolders and extra files, the only one you need to get started is `spam.module`. Create a folder called `spam` in your `modules` directory and move `spam.module` into it.
4. Since the Spam module learns from experience and builds lists of words, URLs, and IP addresses associated with spam, the experience of other web site administrators can be very useful in avoiding spam. To this end, there are a number of database dumps of the spam filters from active sites that have dealt with large quantities of spam. These files are found in the `contributed/spam_tokens` folder that comes with the Spam module download. Optionally, you can load these files into your database.
5. Navigate to *administer* ➤ *modules* (`admin/modules`) and enable the module.

Configuring the Spam Module

To configure the Spam module, you need to set the appropriate Drupal permissions. You also need to visit the module's settings page and set up your filters and other spam prevention options.

Spam Module Permissions

The permissions structure of the Spam module is designed to let you divide your users into roughly three groups: those who can decide what content is or is not spam, those who are trustworthy and never create spam, and everyone else who cannot be trusted.

The Access Spam Rating and Administer Spam Rating permissions can be given to user roles who will help train the filter and identify spam. When looking at content, they will be able to mark it either as spam or not spam, thus assigning a new score (1 or 99) and biasing the spam filter's future handling of similar content. As this is an essential activity, if you are to have an effective filter, you will want to make sure that you have trustworthy people in your community who have these permissions, so that spam content will be quickly identified and marked as such. However, keep in mind that anyone with these permissions can unpublish anything on your site simply by marking it as spam, so trust is essential.

The Bypass Spam Filter permission can be granted to any user role who will never submit spam. This would certainly include user roles that receive the Access Spam Rating and Administer Spam Rating permissions. When users with the Bypass Spam Filter permission create content, it will not be passed through the Bayesian filter. The content can be marked as spam later, however. The only advantages to using this permission are a small performance gain, since less processing is done upon submitting content, and that no content will be falsely marked as spam for these users (a very small danger to begin with). It has the negative side effect that content from these users won't automatically train the filter. Thus, assigning this permission to too many users isn't a good idea.

Filters for Content Types

Select *administer* ➤ *settings* ➤ *spam* (`admin/settings/spam`) to see the configuration settings for the Spam module. The group of settings titled Filter gives you the chance to determine which content types will be eligible for spam filtering. As a rule of thumb, you should allow the Spam module to filter any content that can be created anonymously or by users whose trustworthiness cannot be guaranteed (that is, you don't know them personally). The options are as follows:

Filter comments: This should be checked in most cases. There are known scripts for attacking Drupal sites where the URLs for nodes are systematically probed and comments are posted. The scripts craftily hit low-numbered nodes (low-numbered nodes are usually older content on most sites) and stop before becoming very conspicuous, in a bid to create comment spam but not be detected. Since these scripts target comments, it is advisable to enable this option.

Filter open relays: This corresponds to the Distributed Server Boycott List method of spam filtering, described earlier. It uses the IP address of the user posting content and compares it to published lists of known spammers. Any content published from an IP address found on these lists will have a greatly increased chance of being marked as spam.

Filter spammer URLs: This instructs the Spam module to pay greater attention to the URLs in content and afford them special treatment. The URLs in posts marked as spam will be branded as positive identifiers for spam content, and any new content containing the same URLs will be marked as spam.

URL Limits

The Limits group on the Spam module's settings page deals with the number of URLs that can appear in either comments or normal content. For each, you can set the highest number of allowed URLs and the number of repeated URLs. Be careful when setting these that you don't preclude normal legitimate use of your web site. For example, if your site is supposed to have reviews of a certain type of web site, it is conceivable that someone would want to include several hyperlinks to reference the same page of the site being reviewed. On the other hand, setting these limits to something reasonable (between 3 to 5 in most cases) will catch and block the attempts of some spammers.

Actions for Identified Spam

What should happen when the spam filter identifies something as spam? That question is answered by the settings in the Actions group on the Spam module's settings page.

You can have the content or comment automatically unpublished by checking the Automatically Unpublish Spam field. This might be the best option if spam or potentially embarrassing content could hurt your business or reputation if allowed to persist on the site for any amount of time. Use this option if you are too busy to constantly police your site (better to be safe than sorry). On the other hand, it is possible (though rare) for the Spam module to identify false positives, and users whose content gets unpublished may get very irritated with your site.

The Notify Admin When Spam Detected field causes the administrator of the site to be notified whenever spam is identified. This should be checked as long as you leave possible spam published (Automatically Unpublish Spam is unchecked), or if you are worried about the chance of false positives. That way, you can closely monitor the Spam module's activities and see that it is doing its job correctly.

Advanced Spam Module Configuration

For everyone who wants to get the Spam module installed and running, the preceding configuration is all that needs to be done. If you're interested in playing around under the hood of the module and tweaking the Bayesian filter parameters, check the Advanced Configuration check box on the `admin/settings/spam` page and click Submit to see advanced options.

The following are two advanced options that you might find interesting (and that don't introduce any risks):

Display spam rating: This setting, under the Tools heading, will let you see the spam rating for any content or comments. This is a rating from 1 to 99, and the higher the rating, the more likely it is that it is spam.

Collect statistics: If you instruct the module to collect statistics, you will have access to interesting information, such as how many spam comments or content submissions have been posted and when the last occurrence was.

Managing URL Filters

Whenever content is identified as spam, the Bayesian filter takes the opportunity to extract all of the URLs contained within and pay special attention to them. The logic is that the spammers' golden eggs are the URLs, and therefore their most telling fingerprint.

Navigate to *administer* ➤ *spam* ➤ *URL filters* (`admin/spam/urls`), and you will see an overview of the URLs that the Spam module recognizes as spam URLs. This page also shows how many times each URL has been matched as spam, how many times it has been identified with content that is not spam, the spam probability that it carries (from 1 to 99), and the date of the last match.

This page can be useful for removing false positives from the filter in case a spammer does something nasty, like including a link to a legitimate site in her spam, thus tricking the spam filter into thinking that URL, too, is spam.

You can also use this page to take preventative measures and block URLs that you know are spammer sites from other sources. Your e-mail inbox could be a good source of these URLs. Every one of those free software and cheap drugs sites that are advertised in e-mail spam deserves to be fed to your site's spam filter. To do this, simply add the domain to the Add New URL Filter section and click Add New URL Filter. If the same witless spammer decides to expand and target your web site as well as your inbox, he will be out of luck.

Creating Custom Filters

Next to the URL Filters tab is a tab named Custom Filters (`admin/spam/custom`). Custom filters are a tool for you to help teach the filter by feeding it words, phrases, or regular expressions and telling it what to do with them when they are matched.

You create a new custom filter by entering a word, phrase, or Perl-compatible regular expression into the Custom Filter field. If it is a regular expression, you also need to check the Regular Expression check box, and your expression will be checked for validity when you submit the form. Then you need to determine what is to be done with the content that is found to match this filter by making a selection in the Match Effect field. The options are as follows:

- Always spam (blacklist)
- Usually spam (graylist)
- Usually not spam (graylist)
- Never spam (whitelist)

These various classifications affect the probability rating that the content is spam. Remember that the whole point of the Bayesian filter is to establish this rating, so your custom filter is simply taking part in all of the other calculations that will occur when any post or comment is being considered. Here are the technical details, taken from the help text for custom filters:

> *If your filter defines "always spam," this increases the chances the new content will be marked spam by 200%. If your filter defines "usually spam," this increases the chances the new content will be marked spam by 50%. If your filter defines "usually not spam," this decreases the chances the new content will be marked spam by 50%. And if your filter defines "never spam," this decreases the chances the new content will be marked spam by 200%.*

Since the same content can match several filters, they can play complementary or opposing roles. If a comment matches one Always Spam filter and five Usually Not Spam filters, the weight will be in favor of usually not spam, and the chances that the comment will be marked as spam will be reduced by 50%.

Whitelisting filters should be used sparingly and only in the context of training the filter not to repeat false positive identifications that it has made. The reason for this should be clear: if you open up the door for content to automatically be considered never spam, you can't be too surprised when spammers start walking through it.

If you are being bombarded with spam from a single source and you can block this source with one filter, and you are positive that the filter will not have any false positives, you might elect to check the Automatically Delete Spam check box. When checked, content matching this filter will be deleted from your site without any warning or notification. This is intended as an extreme defense when your site is suffering from the efforts of a concerted attack. Due to the extreme nature of this option, it is recommended only in last-resort cases. In most normal cases, you will want to have the option of browsing spam content to double-check that no false positives are being made.

Using Other Filters

In the `contributed/custom_filters` folder in the Spam module archive, you will find some SQL data dumps of custom filters that others have contributed based on experience from their sites. As noted earlier, you can choose to import these data dumps into your database and benefit from them as well. Here are some examples from the file `teledyn.mysql`:

```
/\b(mortgage|credit|kredit|casino|poker|debt)\S*\.\w{2,3}\b/i
/\b(texas-holdem|onlinegames|blackjack|bingo)\S*\.\w{2,3}\b/i
```

These expressions look for domains that contain any of the list of words *mortgage, credit, casino, bingo,* and so on. The domain `bingo123-use.la` would be matched, for example.

If you decide to use third-party filters, make sure to monitor the content that is being marked as spam to be on the lookout for false positives.

Database Administration Module

The Database Administration (dba) module allows you to view, edit, repair, and create backups for your Drupal database, all from within the administrator's web interface. It is a practical and convenient way to run SQL queries and view the results. It can also be used to import the database definitions for new modules, possibly saving you a trip to another application or command-line tool.

Installing the Database Administration Module

To install the dba module, download the latest version from `http://drupal.org/project/dba`. Then create a `modules/dba` folder and copy the `dba.module` file into it. If you are using PostgreSQL as your database, you need to take the extra steps found in the `README.pgsql` file. Finally, activate the module from the `admin/modules` page.

Configuring the Database Administration Module

The most important configuration decisions you need to make concerning the dba module have to do with user permissions. You can also set options for automatic backups and checking the database integrity.

Database Administration Module Permissions

To quote from the module's documentation:

> *If a user is granted (or manages to acquire) 'dba administer database' permissions, they are able to directly alter the database. At minimum, they are able to modify data, and possibly to drop tables. Depending on how you have defined your database permissions, the user may also be able to modify other databases unrelated to your Drupal installation. Use at your own risk!*

Clearly, the Dba Administer Database permission is not to be granted lightly.

The second permission that this module defines is Dba View Database, which allows users possessing it the chance to see the contents of the entire database. This includes user e-mail, the encrypted hash of user passwords, any private profile information, and so forth. Judicious use of this module and sparing grants of these two permissions are advised.

Automatic Database Backups

To configure the dba module, navigate to *administer* ➤ *settings* ➤ *dba* (`admin/settings/dba`). One of the useful features of this module is the ability to make backup SQL dumps of your database, and it can mail these backups to your e-mail address. Dumps can be made from individual tables, in which case, the backup filename will bear the name of the table, or of several tables or even the entire database. The following are settings that pertain to database backups:

Default backup filename: In the case of multiple tables, the name of the backup file is initially taken from this field, although this can be changed at the time you initiate the backup.

Automatically backup database every *(period of time)*: The automatic backups are disabled by default, but if you set this field to any of the given time periods, backups will be made as often as you have specified.

Automatic backup path: This is the path to the directory on your server where the backups will be saved. Backups are not automatically deleted, so this is a cleanup task that will be left to you.

Compress automatic backups: If compression libraries are available to PHP on your server, you can check this option, and backups will arrived in a compressed format, greatly reducing the size of the backup files.

Mail backup to administrator: Checking this option will result in the automatic database backups being mailed to the administrator's e-mail account (as defined on the site settings page, `admin/settings`).

Database Integrity Checks

The dba module, when used with the MySQL database, allows you to check the data integrity of your database. This is useful for routine maintenance as well as diagnosing problems. The Default Check Type field lets you tell MySQL which type of check to make. Here are the various options on the `admin/settings/dba` page, as described by the MySQL documentation (`http://dev.mysql.com/doc/mysql/en/check-table.html`):

- QUICK means don't scan the rows to check for incorrect links.
- FAST means to check only tables that haven't been closed properly.
- CHANGED means to check only tables that have been changed since the last check or haven't been closed properly.
- MEDIUM means to scan rows to verify that deleted links are okay. It also calculates a key checksum for the rows and verifies this with a calculated checksum for the keys.
- EXTENDED means to do a full key lookup for all keys for each row. This ensures that the table is 100% consistent, but takes a long time!

In the unlikely event that the data integrity of your database becomes compromised, there is a chance that it can be automatically repaired. The Repair Option field lets you determine when the repair link for a table is visible. The best setting is Automatic, as this not only hides superfluous links, but also serves to alert you (by the presence of the link) when the data integrity has been broken.

Using the Database Administration Module

To see an overview of the tables in your database, select *administer* ➤ *database*. For each table, you are shown the number of rows and have the following options:

- The View option shows the contents of the table.
- The Describe option shows the data structure of the table, as shown in Figure 4-19.

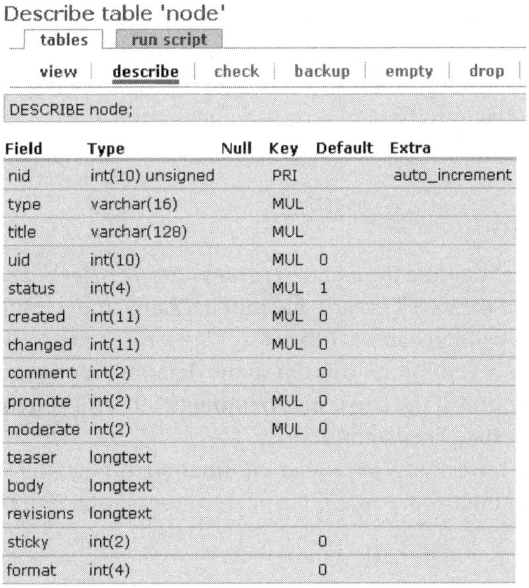

Describe table 'node'

tables | run script

view | describe | check | backup | empty | drop

DESCRIBE node;

Field	Type	Null	Key	Default	Extra
nid	int(10) unsigned		PRI		auto_increment
type	varchar(16)		MUL		
title	varchar(128)		MUL		
uid	int(10)		MUL	0	
status	int(4)		MUL	1	
created	int(11)		MUL	0	
changed	int(11)		MUL	0	
comment	int(2)			0	
promote	int(2)		MUL	0	
moderate	int(2)		MUL	0	
teaser	longtext				
body	longtext				
revisions	longtext				
sticky	int(2)			0	
format	int(4)			0	

Figure 4-19. *The node table described*

- The Check option checks the table (and its indexes) for errors and integrity.
- The Repair option attempts to fix errors found with check. See the MySQL documentation (http://dev.mysql.com/doc/mysql/en/repair-table.html) for details.
- The Backup option saves one or more tables in the form of a SQL dump to a file that you specify.
- The Empty option deletes all data from the table.
- The Drop option removes the table from the database.

Running Queries and Scripts

The dba module facilitates querying the database through SQL that you enter directly into the web browser or by using a file stored on your local machine. Using SQL that you type directly into the browser is a convenient way to run custom queries if you are familiar and comfortable with using SQL. To do this, select *administer* ➤ *database* and click the Query tab (admin/database/query).

You can also run scripts from files, which is an excellent tool for adding database definitions for modules that you are installing from files. To do this, select *administer* ➤ *database* and click the Script tab (admin/database/script).

Developer Tools (Devel) Module

The Devel module is an indispensable tool for programmers and system administrators who want to know how Drupal accesses the database. It collects all of the SQL queries that are made during the loading of a page and shows them as output at the bottom of the screen, along with the time they took and whether the same query was called more than once. This is an excellent way to start to understand what goes on behind the scenes in Drupal, as well as a means for spotting bottlenecks in performance. The Devel module also defines a couple of helper functions to be used for debugging while programming, integrates with Xdebug (http://www.xdebug.org/) to provide profiler information, and includes a number of scripts for generating dummy database data for the purposes of testing.

Installing the Devel Module

Download the latest version of the Devel module from http://drupal.org/project/devel. Create a modules/devel folder and move the devel.module file into it. Enable the module from the admin/modules page. The archive download comes with a devel/generated folder, which contains various scripts for automatically generating content in the database for the purpose of testing. Move these files to the server only if the site is a development site and you intend to use the scripts. Otherwise, you are best advised to omit them.

If you are using Xdebug and wish to have access to profiler information through the Devel module, you should add information to either your php.ini file or the .htaccess file. For php.ini, add the following:

```
xdebug.auto_profile=1
xdebug.auto_profile_mode=3
xdebug.output_dir='/php'
xdebug.default_enable=1
```

For .htaccess, add this:

```
php_value xdebug.auto_profile=1
php_value xdebug.auto_profile_mode=3
php_value xdebug.output_dir='/php'
php_value xdebug.default_enable=1
```

Configuring the Devel Module

To configure the Devel module, set its one permission and adjust its settings for the page timer and query log, if desired.

Devel Module Permissions

The Devel module defines one user permission, Access Devel Information, which should be enabled for any roles that are to be involved in development or optimization of the site. Only users with this permission will see the page timer and query log when they are turned on, as described next.

Page Timer and Query Log

To configure the Devel module, navigate to *administer* ➤ *settings* ➤ *devel* (admin/settings/devel). The settings page has options for enabling the page timer and the query log. The information they generate will be visible to users with the Access Devel Information permission.

The Query Execution Threshold field is the threshold in milliseconds for queries to be considered slow. Queries that exceed this threshold or execute more than once will be highlighted in the query log that appears at the bottom of each screen (when this log is turned on). You can adjust this threshold to give you the most meaningful data.

In many cases, Drupal will perform a set of queries and actions, only to redirect you to a screen or path other than the one you requested. A classic example of this is the 404 Not Found screen. For example, you request the page for node/4711, but there is no node with that ID, so Drupal tells you it can't find it. The problem this presents for debugging is that the SQL queries for the first part of the operation—the part where Drupal looks up 4711 and doesn't find anything—are not included in the query log because of the redirection that occurs thereafter. The Display Redirection Page field takes care of this problem by alerting you when a redirect is about to occur and waiting for your input before the redirect is carried out. This gives you the chance to inspect the queries that occur prior to the redirection as well as after.

Viewing Timer and Query Log Information

Using the page timer and query log is a simple matter of browsing your site with them enabled and enjoying the bounty of information that they produce. Figure 4-20 shows an excerpt from a timer and query log.

Executed 223 queries in 92.63 microseconds. Queries taking longer than 5 ms, and queries executed more than once, are highlighted.
Page execution time was 420.07 ms.

ms	#	query
0.46	1	SELECT COUNT(pid) FROM url_alias
0.21	1	SELECT src FROM url_alias WHERE dst = 'node'
0.64	1	SELECT name, filename, throttle, bootstrap FROM system WHERE type = 'module' AND status = 1
1.23	1	SELECT data, created, headers, expire FROM cache WHERE cid = 'menu:1:en'
0.54	1	SELECT dst FROM url_alias WHERE src = 'blogapi/rsd'
0.51	1	SELECT u.* FROM users u WHERE u.uid = 1 AND u.status < 3 LIMIT 0, 1
0.37	1	SELECT r.rid, r.name FROM role r INNER JOIN users_roles ur ON ur.rid = r.rid WHERE ur.uid = 1

Figure 4-20. *The page timer and query log*

Using Developer Functions

If you are writing code for Drupal, the following four functions can help you while you work:

- `dprint($str)`: Works like the PHP function `print( string arg )` function (`http://php.net/print`) but inside <pre> tags.
- `dprint_r($arr)`: Works like the PHP function `bool print_r ( mixed expression [, bool return] )` (`http://php.net/print_r`) but inside <pre> tags.
- `ddebug_backtrace()`: Works like the PHP function array `debug_backtrace ( void )` (`http://php.net/debug_backtrace`) but inside <pre> tags.
- `devel_variable()`: Outputs the global Drupal configuration variables array `$config`.

You can add these functions to the source code files or to text areas that are evaluated as PHP with the PHP filter as tools for debugging.

Emptying the Cache

Something that every new Drupal developer learns is that the cache table in the database can be emptied without ill effect to the integrity of the database or its data. In fact, when you're programming certain elements, such as the `hook_menu` function for a module, it is necessary to empty the cache from time to time. When developing Drupal, especially when making changes to the `hook_menu` function of a module or when dealing with filtered text, you usually need to clear the cache before your changes will become visible. Menus, variables, and other key elements are cached to improve the performance of the page-building process.

The Devel module offers a convenient link for developers so that they don't need to keep running database queries manually to clear the cache. With the Devel module enabled, an *Empty cache* link appears in the main navigation menu (`devel/cache/clear`).

Note There is almost no reason to clear the cache if you are not developing Drupal modules. But if you accidentally clear the cache, don't worry—you haven't hurt anything.

Summary

The repository of contributed Drupal modules is vast and diverse in scope. Installing and configuring Drupal modules tends to follow a common pattern that includes moving files into the `modules` folder on the web server, possibly updating the database schema, and enabling the module from the `admin/modules` screen. Modules usually have a settings page, which can be accessed via *administer* ➤ *settings*.

In this chapter, you learned how to install, configure, and use some useful modules: TinyMCE, Image, Image Assist, Flexinode, Event, Location, Organic Groups, Spam, Database Administration, and Devel.

In this and the previous chapters, you've learned how Drupal sites work and what you can do with them. In the next chapter, you will dive into the world of theming your Drupal site so that you can control how every element looks and make your site a visual masterpiece.

Based on an abstract theme layer, Drupal's theme system allows you to access and control the HTML that is created without needing to modify the source code for modules or core files. This is not only good software architecture, but it also opens the door for sophisticated usage such as running multiple sites (each with their own theme) off a common codebase. Running multiple Drupal sites is covered in Chapter 6.

CHAPTER 5

Adding and Customizing Themes

Drupal themes are the place where the worlds of graphic artists and programmers meet. A theme is a collection of files that defines the structure, style, and, to an extent, the behavior of your site. Themes use HTML code for the structure, CSS and images for the style, and PHP for determining behavior to give your site its look and feel.

Drupal has four themes as examples in the core distribution, and `Drupal.org` offers a number of contributed themes, ranging from completely finished solutions that are ready to be installed and used to those intended as clean starting points for your design efforts.

This chapter will show you how to download and install new themes. You will then see what components come together to be a theme, what template files look like and how they work, and how you can override themable functions to change the HTML that is being generated by your site. You will also learn how to create your own template files and how to make entire themes that are based on only CSS. Finally, I will recommend some modules that are helpful when theming a site.

Understanding Themes

Themes have two main responsibilities: providing the CSS and image files that are involved with your site's visual design and, if needed, overriding the default HTML output that is generated by Drupal's core files and modules. When customizing the look of your site, most of the work will be done at the CSS level, and this is therefore the theme's most important task.

You can get an overview of your installed themes by navigating to *administer ➤ themes* (`admin/themes`). The four themes that come with the Drupal core distribution are Bluemarine, Pushbutton, Chameleon, and Marvin.

The contributed themes repository on Drupal.org (`http://drupal.org/project/Themes`) is a great source for attractive and interesting themes. Figures 5-1 through 5-4 illustrate several different contributed themes showing the same content. At this level, the concept of a theme is clear. It is a look and feel for a site that the administrator can activate. Themes are a tool for keeping the separation between content and appearance clean. Content is stored in the database, and the theme decides how to present it.

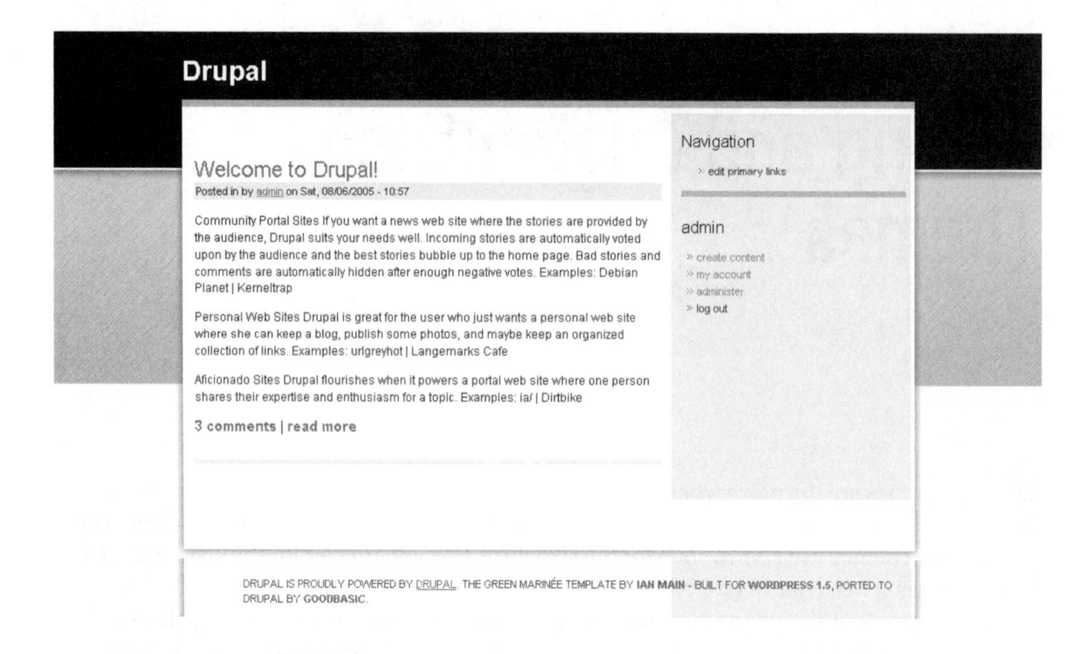

Figure 5-1. *Green Marinée theme*

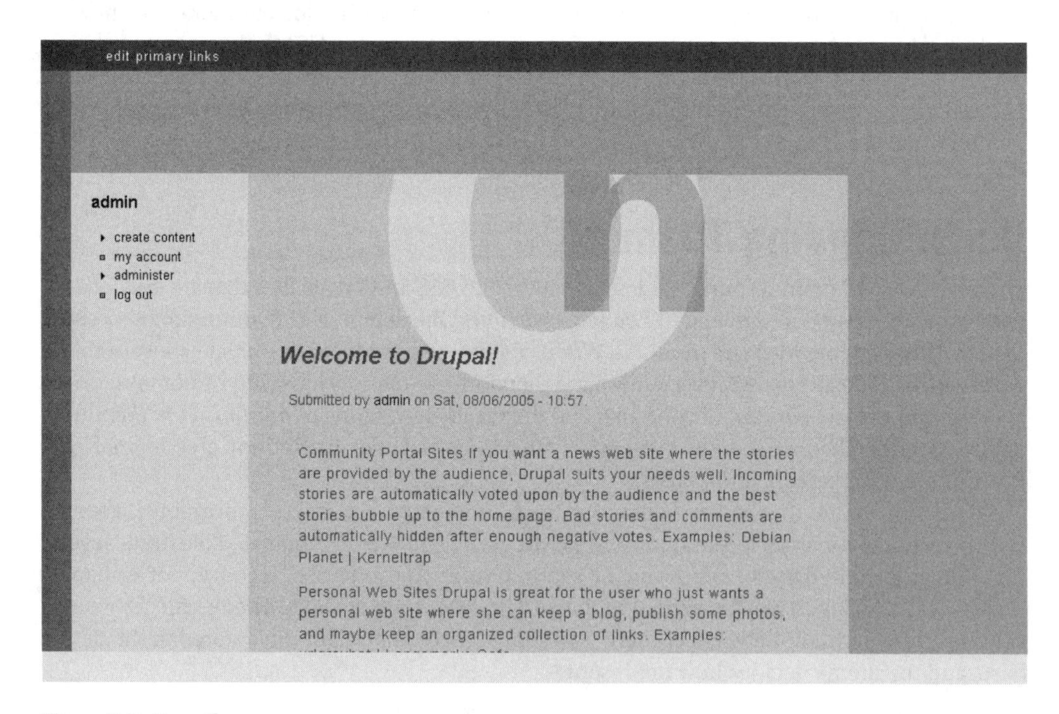

Figure 5-2. *Occy theme*

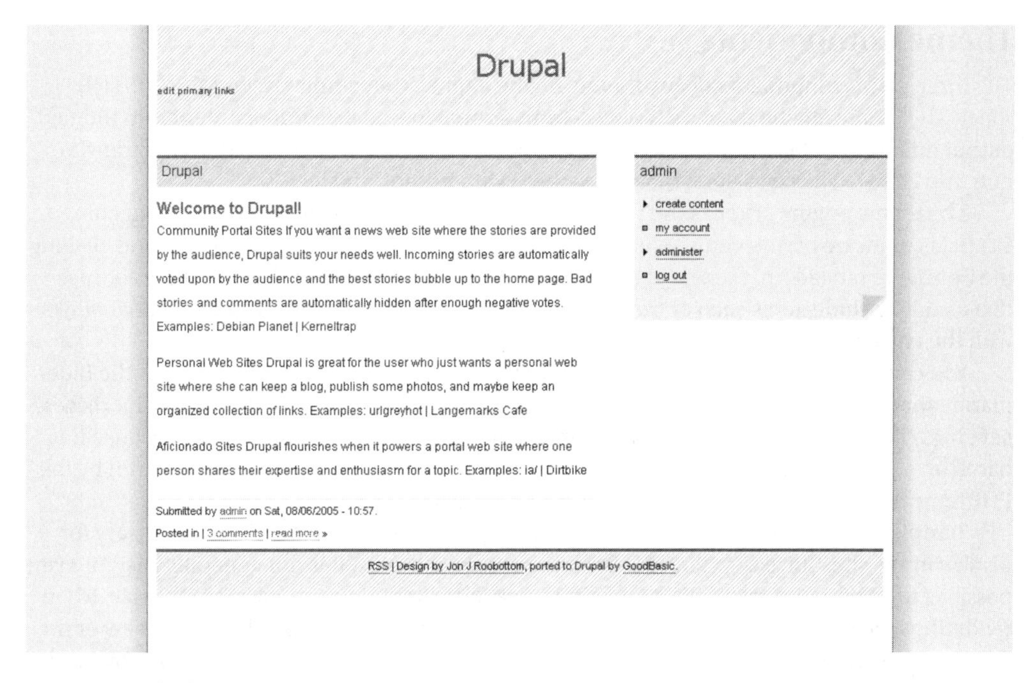

Figure 5-3. *Rdc theme*

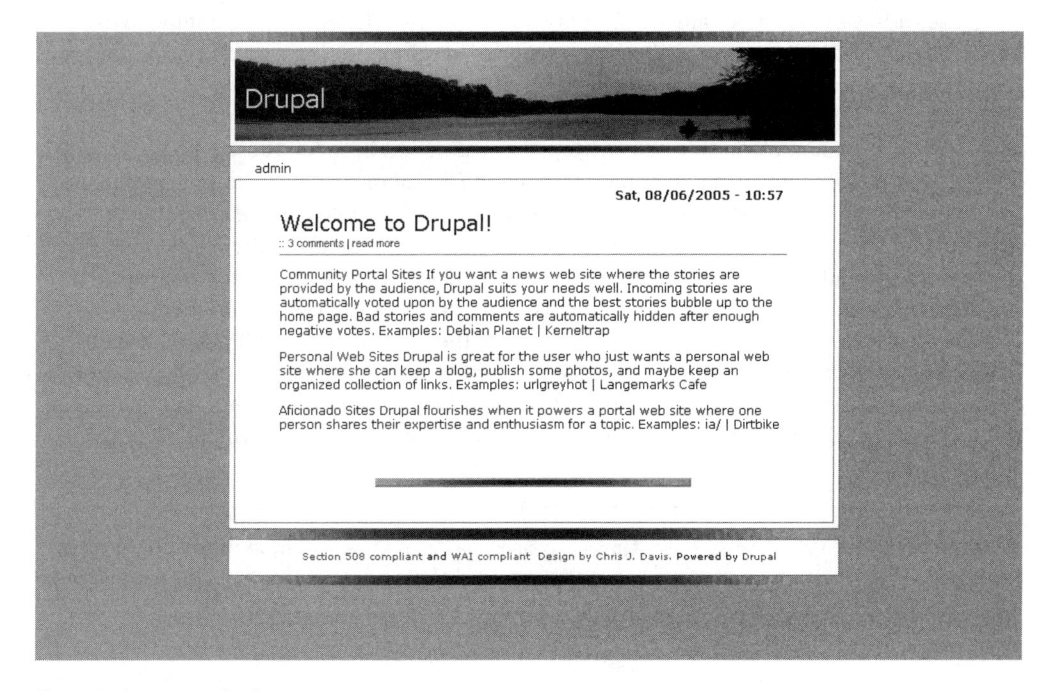

Figure 5-4. *Pastorale theme*

Theme Components

The three main components of any theme are the engine, the templates, and the CSS style sheet. The theme engine receives requests from Drupal to translate pure content into themed output and directs these requests to the appropriate template, which then does the translation into HTML. The style sheet then gives the HTML its look and feel.

The theme engine also has the role of managing any theme-specific settings that core Drupal is unaware of. You can see these settings by selecting *administer* ➤ *themes* and clicking the Configure tab (`admin/themes/settings`). In the Toggle Display section, you'll see settings that usually include items such as the site name, site slogan, primary links, and secondary links, with the choice of turning these settings on and off.

You can see the differences between themes by comparing the list of features for the Bluemarine theme (`admin/themes/settings/bluemarine`) and the Chameleon theme (`admin/themes/settings/chameleon`). Bluemarine has a larger set of features than Chameleon because it is based on a different theme engine, which is more fully implemented. Bluemarine is run by the PHPTemplate engine, and Chameleon has its own engine.

Templates take pure content from Drupal and decorate it with the HTML necessary for display in the site. Since a system like Drupal is rather complex, it is not generally easy, or even possible, to achieve this task without making some decisions along the way. For example, when rendering a blog post, the result will be different depending on whether the teaser view or the full view is requested. This type of decision is made in the template and is the reason why most templates require both HTML and PHP code (for the presentation logic).

Bluemarine is the name of a template that runs on the PHPTemplate engine. The files in the `themes/bluemarine` folder are the template files, and they depend on the engine to function. Without the files in `templates/engines/phptemplate`, Bluemarine would not even be recognized by Drupal as being a theme.

On the other hand, Chameleon is both a theme engine and a template at once. More accurately, when Chameleon was first written, the distinction between these two parts hadn't been as clearly delineated. Chameleon is included in Drupal mostly for historical and demonstration purposes and is known as a *pure* theme (meaning it handles theme calls directly in PHP without delegating them to a template or relying on an external engine). It demonstrates the essence of what a theme is and can be used and extended comfortably, but it lacks a certain flexibility, especially when it comes to reusing components across several themes.

The shortcomings of themes like Chameleon are the reason PHPTemplate was created. PHPTemplate, the theme engine, provides a comfortable and high-performance way to design theme elements that are easy to work with, modular, and reusable. It is now the standard method for theming Drupal sites, and this chapter will focus exclusively on theming with PHPTemplate.

■ Note The theme engine determines the templating language that is to be used by the theme. Engines can be written to support virtually any templating language. The standard theme engine for Drupal is PHPTemplate. Other common possibilities include Smarty, PHPTal, and XTemplate. To see which engines are available, visit `http://drupal.org/project/Theme%20engines`. For more information about the composition of themes, see `http://drupal.org/node/11774`.

How Drupal Finds Themes

Whenever you visit the theme administration page (admin/themes), Drupal looks to see which themes are available and lists them for you. This is a four-step process, which is important to be aware of if you are interested in modifying existing themes or making new themes:

1. Drupal looks for pure themes like Chameleon by searching for subdirectories of themes that contain a *name*.theme file. It expects that the name of the theme will match the directory in which it is found, so chameleon.theme should be found in the themes/chameleon folder, for example. Each pure theme is added to the list of themes.

2. Drupal determines which engines are available by looking for files with the .engine suffix in subdirectories of the themes/engines directory. These engines are given the responsibility of determining which templates fall under their control. A list of theme engines is made.

3. Drupal asks each engine to identify themes belonging to it. PHPTemplate accomplishes this by looking for subdirectories of themes that have a page.tpl.php file in them. The presence of this file is the only requirement of a PHPTemplate theme, and you could conceivably make a theme with nothing but page.tpl.php. Each theme engine then returns a list of themes under its control, and these are added to the list of themes.

4. Finally, there are CSS-only themes, called styles, which consist of nothing but a style sheet that is applied to an existing template or theme. For this, Drupal looks for files called style.css in subdirectories of known themes. Each style.css that is found behaves as an alternate style sheet that is applied to the HTML of the parent theme (in whose folder it resides). The list of styles is then added to the list of themes, which is now complete.

Table 5-1 shows the makeup of the default themes.

Table 5-1. *Components of the Core Themes*

Theme	Engine	Templates	CSS
Bluemarine Pushbutton	phptemplate.engine	*.tpl.php	themes/bluemarine/style.css themes/pushbutton/styles.css
Chameleon Marvin	chameleon.theme	chameleon.theme	themes/chameleon/style.css themes/chameleon/marvin/style.css

Figure 5-5 shows all of the theme-related files that are delivered with Drupal and their relationships based on Table 5-1. You will notice how the Marvin style exists as a subdirectory in the Chameleon theme and consists of only a style sheet. This figure also shows the default *.tpl.php template files in the phptemplate directory. These templates affect all PHPTemplate themes, unless they are specifically overridden within the themes themselves. Details on overriding templates and creating CSS-only themes (styles) are provided in the "Customizing Themes" section later in this chapter.

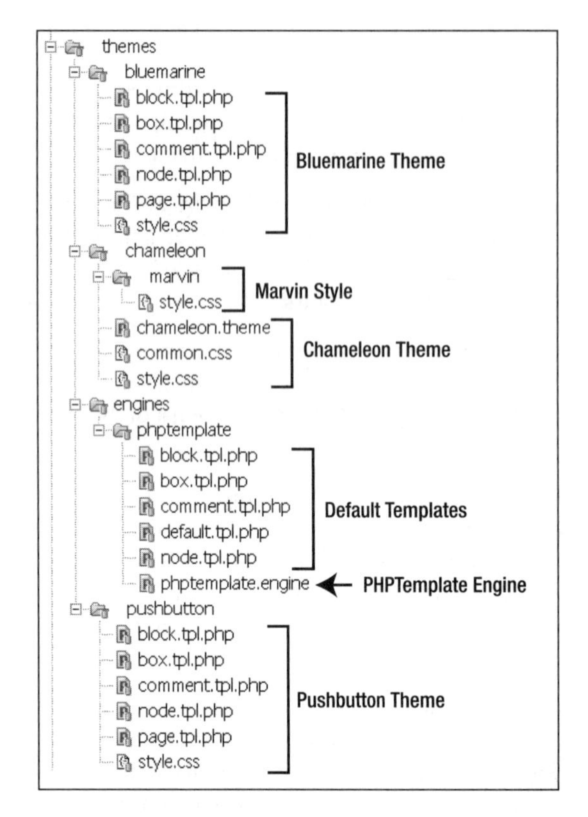

Figure 5-5. *Directory structure of the core themes*

Installing New Themes

You can find many themes available for download at `Drupal.org` (`http://drupal.org/project/Themes`). Installing them is a simple process, but you need to make sure that you have the necessary theme engine installed. This should always be clear from the theme's description on `Drupal.org`, but is often overlooked. If you do not have the proper theme engine (as determined by taking a peek in your `themes/engines` directory), locate and download the theme engine first (from `http://drupal.org/project/Theme%20engines`).

■ **Caution** Make sure that the version number of your theme, theme engine, and Drupal installation match. Version 4.7 themes are only guaranteed to work on Drupal 4.7 with a version 4.7 theme engine.

After downloading a theme, unpack it and move the unpacked folder to the `themes` directory. The name of the unpacked directory is the name of the theme. Navigate to *administer* ➤ *themes* (`admin/themes`), and you will see the theme listed. Activate the theme, and determine whether it is to be the main theme for the site. If not, you can activate it for your user account from your account page (*my account*).

Configure your theme by going to *administer* ➤ *themes* and clicking the Configure tab (`admin/themes/settings`). See Chapter 2 for a complete discussion on how to configure a theme, including setting the primary and secondary links, toggling post information, and so on. Your theme is now installed and configured.

To uninstall a theme, deactivate it from *administer* ➤ *themes* (`admin/themes`) and remove it from the `themes` directory.

Customizing Themes

It is very convenient that Drupal offers so many nice-looking themes. Having a functional site that looks nice without needing to do any work is a great luxury, especially if your site's appearance isn't your main focus. However, most people will want their sites to have a unique look to them—something that sets the site apart from others and contributes to the site's identity. Learning to customize existing themes or make new ones will greatly add to the quality of your Drupal experience.

The most common way to theme a Drupal site is to start with an existing theme and add your own elements. By testing several existing themes and choosing the one that brings you closest to your goals, you often save hours of work. You won't need to worry about the basics, such as deciding how many columns to use, whether the design should be fixed width or flexible, the size of the header, and so on. By modifying an existing theme, you can work incrementally, changing one element at a time, slowly morphing it into an original creation. Many of the trickier problems will have already been solved by the theme's original author.

On the other hand, a finished theme is often an intricate web of templates and style sheet information. If you find yourself spending a lot of time stripping away other people's ideas and longing for a clean slate, starting from scratch is not difficult and gives you the greatest control over your theme.

Whether you decide to modify an existing theme or make your own, a good understanding of how themable functions and templates work will be necessary, especially if you intend to modify the HTML that is being output.

Introducing Themable Functions

The HTML output that is generated by Drupal has been carefully crafted to be accessible, lightweight, and easily styled with CSS. Despite this, you may find yourself wanting to change the HTML output in some way. Drupal takes great care to make this possible without forcing you to change the source code of the core files and modules. Instead, all HTML that is output comes from *themable functions* that can be overwritten from within individual themes. The role of the theme is to provide alternate versions of themable functions for the cases where different output is desired.

Keeping these changes at the theme level, rather than needing to hack core files and modules, is a great advantage when it comes to upgrading Drupal to a new version, as it saves you from hunting down all the changes in the old version and reimplementing them in the new version. It is also necessary if you intend to host multiple sites from one codebase, a topic covered in Chapter 6.

You can identify themable functions in the core includes and modules by their name, which starts with `theme_`. This naming convention allows Drupal to identify the function's role and purpose, and also to override it by redirecting calls to an overriding function if one is available in the theme.

Table 5-2 lists some themable functions and what they do. It is far from complete but it will give you an idea of how themable functions are used in Drupal. Notice that all of the functions listed start with `theme_`.

Table 5-2. *Some Themable Functions*

Function	Location	Purpose
`theme_block`	`includes/theme.inc`	Handles blocks
`theme_box`	`includes/theme.inc`	Builds a container
`theme_breadcrumb`	`includes/theme.inc`	Generates a breadcrumb trail
`theme_comment`	`modules/comment.module`	Handles comments
`theme_form_element`	`includes/theme.inc`	Styles elements that are typically found in forms, such as text boxes and input tags
`theme_links`	`includes/theme.inc`	Takes a list of links such as primary and secondary links and styles them
`theme_book_navigation`	`modules/book.module`	Is responsible for the *previous*, *up*, and *next* links in book hierarchies
`theme_page`	`includes/theme.inc`	Generates Drupal pages
`theme_node`	`includes/theme.inc`	Handles nodes
`theme_profile_listing`	`modules/profile.module`	Takes one user and displays her profile fields (for use in lists of users)
`theme_submenu`	`includes/theme.inc`	Generates a submenu
`theme_user_profile`	`modules/user.module`	Generates the listing of a user's account information; the one seen by visiting `user/1`, for example
`theme_xml_icon`	`includes/theme.inc`	Generates an XML icon

Some of the themable functions listed in Table 5-2 are used often, as I'll explain next.

Main Themable Functions

A small number of themable functions are responsible for the overall layout and construction of a Drupal page, and they are most commonly implemented in custom themes. Here is a list of those functions and a short description of what they do:

- `theme_page($content)`: Places `$content` in a complete HTML page. Typically, `theme_page` will call further themable functions to get additional output such as the blocks, status messages, and HTML headers. All custom themes implement their own version of `theme_page`. In PHPTemplate, this is manifested in the form of a `page.tpl.php` file, which is the only required file a PHPTemplate theme must have.

- `theme_node($node, $teaser = FALSE, $page = FALSE)`: Provides the HTML wrapper for the content of a node. Based on the `$teaser` parameter, this function will return either the truncated preview version of a node or the full version. The `$page` variable determines whether the node is being displayed on its own page or in a list of nodes, and usually controls whether or not the title is printed as a heading. The function also handles calling `theme_links()` for any links that are to appear along with the node, such as taxonomy terms and whatever links have been added by modules, such as comment or subscription links.
- `theme_comment($comment, $links = 0)`: Handles the output of comments. This includes comments made to posts like blogs as well as comments in a threaded forum. Note that this does not handle the threading itself, just the HTML around the variable `$comment`. Whatever links are associated with the comment are expressed in the variable `$links`.
- `theme_block($block)`: Gets called for each block region and wraps the block content in HTML.
- `theme_box($title, $content, $region = 'main')`: Builds a generic container around content, usually with the use of `<div>` tags.

The `theme_page($content)` function is responsible for generating the actual page that gets sent to the browser. It is the last function that is called when building a page. To invoke this function correctly (without calling it directly), use the syntax `theme('page', $content)`. This tells Drupal that a themable function called `page` is to be called with the parameter `$content`. Drupal then starts looking for the appropriate function.

How Drupal Finds Themable Function Overrides

When a Drupal programmer wants to generate output by calling a themable function, he uses a special invocation that follows the pattern `theme($function_name, [$params, ...])` (see the `theme()` function in `includes/theme.inc`) to call the function dynamically instead of calling it directly. For example, to call the appropriate themable function `theme_foo`, you would use `theme('foo', $params...)`.

■ **Tip** The `theme()` function is used to call all `theme_foo` functions in Drupal. For example, to call `theme_foo($param1, $param2)`, use the syntax `theme('foo', $param1, $param2)`.

Drupal then looks in several places to see if a matching function is implemented and calls the first one that is found. It checks three areas, or *namespaces*, to find overrides to themable functions:

Theme's namespace: The first place Drupal checks is the active theme's namespace. If Bluemarine is the active theme, the namespace is `bluemarine`. Drupal will look for a function called `bluemarine_foo()` and call it with whatever extra parameters were passed to `theme()`. If `theme('foo', $bar)` is the original call, and a function named `bluemarine_foo` is found, the call will be `bluemarine_foo($bar)`.

Theme engine's namespace: If the `bluemarine` namespace doesn't provide a function to theme `foo`, then Drupal looks to the theme engine namespace next. Assuming that Bluemarine is the active theme, the engine's namespace is `phptemplate`, as Bluemarine is a PHPTemplate theme. The function that Drupal will look for is therefore called `phptemplate_foo($bar)`.

Default namespace: Finally, if the function is not found in the engine's namespace, Drupal will use the default namespace, which is `theme`. A function named `theme_foo($bar)` will be called, and this is the function provided by the core include file or module. Thus, you can see that the default implementation of any themable function must begin with the prefix `theme_`.

The active theme's own namespace is rarely used to override functions. You will not find many examples of `bluemarine_foo`, `bluemarine_breadcrumb`, and so on. Rather, you will see functions in the engine's namespace being written in the theme files. Anyone overriding a themable function is encouraged to take the engine's namespace to name the override functions. A strong and simple case can be made for this practice: if you want to move the function to a different theme or reuse it in some other way, you won't need to rename the function. Sticking with this policy will also allow you to copy whole theme directories and rename the directory, perhaps as the first step in creating a new theme. For the rest of the chapter, I will choose the option of naming themable functions after the theme engine and will not use the active theme's namespace.

■ **Note** Pure themes (Chameleon)—the themes that don't rely on an external theme engine—are the exception to the advice of not using the active theme's namespace. If you need to override a theme function and you are using the Chameleon theme, you must use the Chameleon namespace.

Table 5-3 shows some examples of common themable functions, what they would be named if overridden in the Bluemarine theme, and how they are evoked (parameters omitted).

Table 5-3. *Examples of Overriding Themable Functions in the Bluemarine Theme*

Default Version	Bluemarine Version	Invocation
`theme_links()`	`phptemplate_links()`	`theme('links')`
`theme_submenu()`	`phptemplate_submenu()`	`theme('submenu')`
`theme_xml_icon()`	`phptemplate_xml_icon()`	`theme('xml_icon')`

Exercise 5-1 demonstrates how to override a themable function.

Exercise 5-1. Theme Breadcrumb Links

Try your hand at overriding a themable function for the Bluemarine theme. Create a new file on your web server in the folder themes/bluemarine called template.php. Copy the following short code segment into the template.php file. Don't forget the <?php and ?>.

```
<?php
function phptemplate_breadcrumb($breadcrumb) {
  $output = '<h1>Hello World!</h1>';
  $output .= implode(' / ', $breadcrumb);
  return $output;
}
?>
```

In the unaltered Bluemarine theme, breadcrumb links are separated using the » character. This is the default HTML that is generated by Drupal. By including the phptemplate_breadcrumb function in the Bluemarine theme, the default HTML will no longer be used; instead, the HTML generated by the new function will be used. The phptemplate_breadcrumb function not only separates the breadcrumb links with a different character, but it also outputs a meaningful and original message directly above them.

Click through some pages on your site and you will see the result. You have successfully altered the default HTML for breadcrumbs from this:

```
<div class="breadcrumb">
  <a href="?q=" >Home</a> &raquo; <a href="?q=node/add" >create content</a>
</div>
```

to this:

```
<h1>Hello World!</h1>
<a href="?q=" >Home</a> / <a href="?q=node/add" >create content</a>
```

Using Template Files

In Exercise 5-1, you saw how a function could be written to override a themable function. As useful as this is, generating HTML from within functions can be very tiresome work. PHPTemplate makes the process of creating themable functions much easier and modular by introducing template files. The required file page.tpl.php is one such template file that will be used whenever theme('page') is called. This template must be provided by the theme itself.

Other template files are provided by the PHPTemplate engine. These include block.tpl.php, box.tpl.php, comment.tpl.php, and node.tpl.php (see Figure 5-5 earlier in the chapter). These files override the block, box, comment, and node themable functions, respectively. If any of these four files appear in your theme folder alongside page.tpl.php, they will override the version in themes/engines/phptemplate.

The template files are completely reusable; you could trade and mix the five standard tpl.php files between themes and expect, at a minimum, that they will be called at the appropriate time. Furthermore, since they are include files and not functions, you can write all the

HTML code without needing to worry about escaping quotation marks or concatenating strings—a fact that greatly improves the readability of template files over PHP functions that do the same thing.

PHP Code and Templates

If you are a web designer and you've been given the task of creating a Drupal theme, you need not be scared of the fact that the templates mix PHP and HTML code. Even if you've never programmed PHP before, the amount of skill and knowledge needed to work with the themes is small enough that you will be able to learn it quickly. Here are some examples of what you might see and explanations of what they do.

The first is a simple `print` construct:

```
<?php print $picture ?>
```

This construct prints the contents of a variable (sends the contents to the browser for display on the screen). In this case, the variable `$picture` is being printed. The `<?php` and `?>` tags identify the parts that are to be interpreted as PHP and keep the PHP separate from the rest of the template.

Here is a conditional `print` construct:

```
<?php print ($sticky) ? "sticky" : ""; ?>
```

This is a more elaborate version of the first example, which uses the `?` and `:` to make a decision. In this case, it can be read "if `$sticky` is set, print the text *sticky*; otherwise, print nothing (`""`)."

The following uses `if` to make a decision:

```
<?php if ($picture): ?>
  <br class='clear' />
<?php endif; ?>
```

In this example, the first line asks "is `$picture true`?" If so, the text `<br class='clear' />` will be printed. Note that the opening `if` statement must be closed by a corresponding `endif` statement.

Finally, this code creates a list:

```
<ul id="primary">
  <?php foreach ($primary_links as $link): ?>
    <li><?php print $link?></li>
  <?php endforeach; ?>
</ul>
```

This example shows how to build an unordered list `<ul>` with a variable number of list items `<li>`. It takes the variable `$primary_links`, which is an array, and uses the `foreach` operator to go over the array one item at a time, pointing the variable `$link` to the current item. For each primary link, an `<li>` element with the link's contents is printed. Notice the `endforeach` tag, which is needed to close the `foreach` tag.

The PHP code in template files rarely gets more complicated than this, and most of the time it will suffice if you can recognize which lines and bits belong together, so that you can copy and paste them without introducing errors.

Tip To learn more about PHP code, read *Beginning PHP5 and MySQL: From Novice to Professional*, by W. Jason Gilmore (Apress, 2004).

Template Variables

Template files are the meeting place of static content (HTML) and dynamic values (variables), as well as minimal logic, similar to the examples shown in the previous section, to account for the numerous variations that are possible in a dynamic site. While there are many approaches and philosophies for templating in general, PHPTemplate has evolved in a way that encourages simple and minimal logic. It uses variables that are pushed into the template from the theme engine.

Each template will have a number of variables available to it that are provided by the theme engine. In addition to the variables that are unique to each template, the variables `$id` and `$zebra` are always included by PHPTemplate, no matter which template is being called. These variables work as follows:

- `$id`: A sequential counter that is incremented every time the template is rendered. In the case of blocks, for example, it allows each block to have a unique ID on the page.
- `$zebra`: An alternating counter that has the value `odd` or `even`. This is useful for giving table rows alternating colors, for example.

Furthermore, the variable `$is_front` is also available. It is `true` whenever the front page is being displayed, so you can always write template code like this:

```
<?php if ($is_front) : ?> -- display when on front page -- <?php endif;?>
```

PHPTemplate Template Files

Here is an in depth look at the four `tpl.php` files included with PHPTemplate, as well as the `page.tpl.php` file that is included with the Bluemarine theme.

Block.tpl.php

The `block.tpl.php` file is included with the PHPTemplate engine and is therefore optional within individual themes. It is responsible for calls to `theme('block')` and generates the individual blocks within the various block regions. These are the blocks that you configure from the block administration page (`admin/blocks`). Table 5-4 lists the variables available in `block.tpl.php`.

Table 5-4. *Variables Available in block.tpl.php*

Variable	Description
`$block`	The block object (see `http://php.net/oop`). The following `$block->` variables are the standard fields of the `$block` object.
`$block->content`	The content of the block.
`$block->module`	The name of the module that is responsible for creating this block.
`$block->region`	Can be any of the regions defined in the `phptemplate_regions()` function: `left`, `right`, `header`, `footer`, `content`, as well as any custom regions that are defined in a *theme*`_regions()` function, if you have written one (see the "Adding Custom Regions for Blocks" section later in this chapter).
`$block->subject`	The title of the block.
`$block->delta`	A number given to the block by the module that produces it.
`$is_front`	A Boolean that will be `true` if the page being generated is the site's front page.
`$id`	An integer that uniquely identifies this block among all blocks on the page.
`$block_id`	An integer that uniquely identifies this block among all blocks of the same region.
`$zebra`	Alternates between the strings `even` and `odd`, in case you want to use alternating styles.
`$block_zebra`	Like `$zebra`, but is reset for each block region.

The default `block.tpl.php` template, shown in Listing 5-1, can be found at `themes/engines/phptemplate/block.tpl.php`.

Listing 5-1. *Default block.tpl.php*

```
<div class="<?php print "block block-$block->module" ?>"
    id="<?php print "block-$block->module-$block->delta"; ?>">
  <h2><?php print $block->subject ?></h2>
  <div class="content"><?php print $block->content ?></div>
</div>
```

As you can see, the two visual elements being used are the block's title, `$block->subject`, and the block's content, `$block->content`. The rest is the HTML that goes around the title and content. Notice that the outer `<div>` tag has two class attributes: `block` and `block-`*`module`* (*`module`* will be the name of the module that produced the block). This allows the style sheet to address the block generically as well as specifically according to the originating module.

Box.tpl.php

The `box.tpl.php` file overrides the `theme_box` function to enclose content in a generic box, usually a `<div>` tag, along with a title. The `box.tpl.php` template overrides the standard `theme_box` function, found in `includes/theme.inc`. Table 5-5 lists the variables available in `box.tpl.php`.

Table 5-5. *Variables Available in box.tpl.php*

Variable	Description
`$content`	The box's content.
`$region`	Specifies the region on the screen in which the box appears. Can be `main`, `left`, or `right`. Defaults to `main`.
`$title`	The title of the box.
`$id`	An integer that uniquely identifies this block among all blocks on the page.
`$zebra`	Alternates between the strings `even` and `odd`, in case you want to use alternating styles.
`$is_front`	A Boolean that will be `true` if the page being generated is the site's front page.

The default `box.tpl.php` template, shown in Listing 5-2, can be found at `themes/engines/phptemplate/box.tpl.php`.

Listing 5-2. *Default box.tpl.php*

```
<div class="box">
  <h2><?php print $title ?></h2>
  <div class="content"><?php print $content ?></div>
</div>
```

Comment.tpl.php

The `comment.tpl.php` file overrides the `theme_comment` function for the output of comments to posts, including forums. Table 5-6 lists the variables available in `comment.tpl.php`.

■ **Note** The `theme_comment` themable function is not responsible for controlling the threading of comments. See `theme_comment_thread_min()` and `theme_comment_thread_max()` in `modules/comment.module` for the functions responsible for threading.

Table 5-6. *Variables Available in comment.tpl.php*

Variable	Description
`$author`	Name of the comment's author as a link to his profile page.
`$comment`	The comment object as passed to the `theme_comment` function. The following `$comment->` variables are the standard fields in the `$comment` object.
`$comment->subject`	The comment's subject.
`$comment->comment`	The content of the comment (same as `$content`).
`$comment->name`	The name of the user who submitted the comment.
`$comment->timestamp`	The UNIX timestamp from when the comment was created.
`$comment->uid`	The user ID from the user who added the comment.
`$comment->new`	A Boolean value that is equal to `1` if the comment is being viewed for the first time by the current user, and `0` if the user has seen it before. This is used to add the red "new" text to new comments on `Drupal.org`.

Continued

Table 5-6. *Continued*

Variable	Description
`$content`	The comment itself.
`$date`	The comment's formatted submission date (same as `date` in `$submitted`).
`$links`	The contextual control links, like *reply*, *edit*, and *delete*, as a single string.
`$new`	If the user has not yet viewed this comment, `$new` will contain the translated text "new." Otherwise, it will be an empty string (use `$comment->new` to test if the comment is new).
`$picture`	If enabled and available, the comment author's picture in a hyperlink to the user's profile page.
`$submitted`	The translated text "Submitted by `user_link` on `date`."
`$title`	The subject of the title as a hyperlink to the comment itself using an anchor (#). This is like a permalink to the comment.
`$id`	An integer that uniquely identifies this comment among all comments on the page.
`$zebra`	Alternates between the strings `even` and `odd`, in case you want to use alternating styles.
`$is_front`	A Boolean that will be `true` if the page being generated is the site's front page.

The default `comment.tpl.php` template, shown in Listing 5-3, can be found at `themes/engines/phptemplate/comment.tpl.php`.

Listing 5-3. *Default comment.tpl.php*

```
<div class="comment <?php print ($comment->new) ? 'comment-new' : '' ?>">
<?php if ($comment->new) : ?>
  <a id="new"></a>
  <span class="new"><?php print $new ?></span>
<?php endif; ?>

<div class="title"><?php print $title ?></div>
  <?php print $picture ?>
  <div class="author"><?php print $submitted ?></div>
  <div class="content"><?php print $content ?></div>
  <?php if ($picture) : ?>
    <br class="clear" />
  <?php endif; ?>
  <div class="links"><?php print $links ?></div>
</div>
```

Notice that `$comment->new` plays a big role in templating the comments. If a user has not yet read a comment, the enclosing `<div>` gets an extra class `comment-new`, and an anchor `<a>` with the ID `new` is included in the output, as well as the translated text "new."

If the user's picture is printed, the line `<br class="clear" />` will also be printed at the end of the comment. This draws on the class `clear`, which is defined in the default Drupal style sheet (`misc/drupal.css`) and prevents floating images from breaking the layout. The `drupal.css` style sheet is discussed later in this chapter, in the "Using CSS for Themes" section.

Node.tpl.php

Any time a node (blog, page, event, image, and so on) is rendered, the `node.tpl.php` template is used. This template handles nodes that are displayed in full and nodes that are displayed as a teaser, such as they would appear in lists of nodes. You can also make a separate template for specific node types, as you'll see after the description of the default node template. Table 5-7 lists the variables available in `node.tpl.php`.

Table 5-7. *Variables Available in node.tpl.php*

Variable	Description
`$content`	Contains the node's teaser or the node's body, depending on the page context. This variable exists so that the logic of determining whether to show the full body or only the teaser can be left out of the template. The `$node` variable still has the `$node->teaser` and `$node->body` available, however. So, if you wish to use different logic for determining which to show, you can still do so.
`$date`	The formatted date of this node's creation.
`$links`	The HTML containing the node's contextual links, such as links to the comments or attachments.
`$teaser`	A Boolean that is `true` if the node is appearing in a context, like the front page, where only the teaser should be shown.
`$name`	The node author's username with a link to her profile page.
`$node`	The node object itself. This is very helpful to have available in the template, as modules can add their own fields to this object. Use this object to customize the node's theme based on these added fields. The following `$node->` variables are the standard fields of the `$node` object.
`$node->body`	The entire node contents.
`$node->changed`	The last modification date, as a UNIX timestamp.
`$node->created`	The creation date, as a UNIX timestamp.
`$node->nid`	The ID of the node.
`$node->teaser`	A shortened version of the node body.
`$node->title`	The title of the node.
`$node->type`	The content type (story, blog, forum, and so on).
`$node->uid`	The ID of the author.
`$node->username`	The username of the author.
`$node_url`	The node's permalink as a Drupal path.
`$picture`	The HTML to output the user's user picture.
`$submitted`	Information on who submitted the node and when: "Submitted by admin on Tue, 08/02/2005 - 18:29."
`$terms`	HTML code containing links to the taxonomy terms for this node.
`$title`	The node's title as a string.
`$sticky`	A Boolean that is `true` if the sticky flag is set (meaning it should stay at the top of lists).
`$taxonomy`	An array of links to the pages for the taxonomy terms associated with this node.

Continued

Table 5-7. *Continued*

Variable	Description
$page	A Boolean that indicates whether to display the node as a stand-alone page. If true, the theme does not need to display the title, because it will be provided by the menu system.
$id	An integer that uniquely identifies this node among all nodes on the page.
$is_front	A Boolean that is true if the page being generated is the site's front page.

The default node.tpl.php template, shown in Listing 5-4, can be found at themes/engines/phptemplate/node.tpl.php.

Listing 5-4. *Default node.tpl.php*

```
<div class="node<?php print ($sticky) ? " sticky" : ""; ?>">
  <?php if ($page == 0): ?>
    <h2><a href="<?php print $node_url ?>" title="<?php print $title ?>">
        <?php print $title ?></a></h2>
  <?php endif; ?>
  <?php print $picture ?>

  <div class="info">
    <?php print $submitted ?><span class="terms"><?php print $terms ?></span>
  </div>
  <div class="content">
    <?php print $content ?>
  </div>

  <?php if ($links): ?>
    <?php if ($picture): ?>
      <br class='clear' />
    <?php endif; ?>
    <div class="links"><?php print $links ?></div>
  <?php endif; ?>
</div>
```

As you can see from the template code, the default node template makes three important decisions (highlighted in Listing 5-4):

- The first is whether or not this node is being displayed in a list as opposed to on a page by itself. This is done with the test `<?php if ($page == 0): ?>`. If it is in a list, $page will be zero, and the template is responsible for printing the node's title. On pages where the node is being displayed solo (node/*nid*), the node's title will be printed by the menu system, and the theme doesn't need to worry about it.
- The second decision concerns the node's links (such as *add new comment*), if present.
- The third decision involves printing the line `<br class='clear' />` if there are not only links, but a user picture as well (the picture would have been printed earlier in the template). This is to prevent any float styles on the image above from breaking the layout.

The node.tpl.php file presents a special case, as it is responsible for handling many types of nodes. Clearly, there will be cases where a blog should use a different template than a image or a poll. To support this, PHPTemplate lets you create templates specific to one node type by using a naming convention: node-*type*.tpl.php. For example, you might have node-book.tpl.php and node-story.tpl.php for book and story nodes, respectively. Create one of these files in your theme's directory (in the same directory as page.tpl.php), and from then on, views of that particular node type will be passed on to the new template.

Occasionally, modules will provide their own node template for the particular node type in question. An example of this is provided by the Organic Groups module, which was discussed in Chapter 4. Listing 5-5 shows the template file for group nodes. Notice that it is greatly simplified and leaves out many things that are not relevant for a group's node.

Listing 5-5. *node-og.tpl.php*

```
<div class="node<?php print ($sticky) ? " sticky" : ""; ?>">
  <?php if ($page == 0): ?>
    <h2><a href="<?php print $node_url ?>" title="<?php print $title ?>">
      <?php print $title ?></a></h2>
  <?php endif; ?>

  <div class="content">
    <?php print $content ?>
  </div>
</div>
```

Page.tpl.php

The page.tpl.php file is the template that will handle calls to theme('page', $content). This call is the last thing that happens in the series of events leading up to a Drupal page being served. That places this template in the special position of defining the overall layout of the pages for your site. This is where you lay down the "big picture." It also has the special distinction of being the only file that a PHPTemplate theme is required to provide. It is easily the most important and most complex of all the standard tpl.php files, as can be seen by the number of variables and the amount of code it contains. Table 5-8 lists the variables available in page.tpl.php.

Table 5-8. *Variables Available in page.tpl.php*

Variable	Description
$breadcrumb	HTML that renders the breadcrumb links.
$closure	Normally contains client-side scripts that need to be included at the bottom of the page, thus is always the last thing to be printed before the closing </body> tag.
$content	HTML code of the central section of a page; the content that is unique to that particular page.
$footer_message	The text that was defined in the Footer Message field on the admin/settings page.
$head	HTML code generated by modules to be added to the <head> tag of the page. This typically includes tags for dynamically loading script files.

Continued

Table 5-8. *Continued*

Variable	Description
`$head_title`	The page's title, for display in the `<title>` tag. The `$head_title` variable is constructed either from `$title` and `$site_name` or `$site_name` and `$site_slogan`.
`$help`	Help text for the page, if it is available.
`$language`	The two-letter language code based on the locale in which the site is being displayed; for example, `en` for English or `de` for German.
`$layout`	A string (`'left'`, `'right'`, `'both'`, or *empty*) that indicates if and where blocks are found for this page. The idea is that the template can check which layout is being demanded and react accordingly.
`$logo`	The path to the image to be used as the site logo.
`$messages`	Status and error messages to the user.
`$mission`	The text of the mission statement as defined by the Mission field on the `admin/settings` page.
`$onload_attributes`	HTML code added inside the opening `<body>` tag of the page. Its main purpose is to expose the `onload` parameter of the `<body>` tag to modules so that they can trigger events when the page is loaded in the browser. This is the mechanism that allows the WYSIWYG editors like TinyMCE to function properly; the JavaScript that loads the editors will be embedded in `$onload_attributes`.
`$primary_links`	An array of links that are defined in the Primary Link Settings field of the `admin/themes/settings` page.
`$search_box`	The HTML to render the search box, if it is enabled.
`$secondary_links`	An array of links that are defined in the Secondary Link Settings field of the `admin/themes/settings` page.
`$sidebar_left`	HTML to render the left sidebar.
`$sidebar_right`	HTML to render the right sidebar.
`$site_name`	The name of the site, as specified by you from the `admin/settings` page.
`$site_slogan`	The text for the site slogan that is defined on the `admin/settings` page.
`$styles`	HTML for the `<head>` tag of the page that consists of style sheet imports in the correct order.
`$tabs`	HTML to render tabbed navigation for a page. An example of this is the view and edit tabs that are visible on node pages (when you're logged in and have the right privileges).
`$title`	The title of this page.

The PHPTemplate theme engine does not provide a `page.tpl.php` implementation; this is the realm of the individual themes. The `page.tpl.php` file provided by the Bluemarine theme is a good example of what needs to happen and what issues need to be addressed. As the file is relatively long, I'll discuss only excerpts here.

The first two lines are the `DOCTYPE` declaration and the opening `<html>` tag. Noteworthy is that the document is declared to be `XHTML 1.0 STRICT` and that the `lang` and `xml:lang` parameters of the `<html>` tag are both set dynamically using the `$language` variable provided to the template.

```
lang="<?php print $language ?>" xml:lang="<?php print $language ?>"
```

The document's <head> section looks like this:

```
<head>
  <title><?php print $head_title ?></title>
  <?php print $head ?>
  <?php print $styles ?>
  <script type="text/javascript"> </script>
</head>
```

You can see how the $head and $styles variables are used to inject scripts and style sheets into the head section. Both of these variables are built by the various modules involved in building the page. The empty <script> tag is there to avoid a rendering problem in Microsoft's Internet Explorer (discussed at http://www.bluerobot.com/web/css/fouc.asp).

Likewise, the <body> tag gains its parameters from the $onload_attributes variable, which is also built by the individual modules involved in serving any given page:

```
<body<?php print $onload_attributes ?>>
```

The following lines of code demonstrate how a themable function can be called from within a template:

```
<?php if ($secondary_links) { ?>
  <div id="secondary"><?php print theme('links', $secondary_links) ?></div>
<?php } ?>
      <?php if ($primary_links) { ?>
  <div id="primary"><?php print theme('links', $primary_links) ?></div>
<?php } ?>
```

In this case, the arrays containing primary and secondary links are themed for output. The default implementation is to separate the links using a pipe (|), but the theme can provide a different implementation of the function to change this behavior (the themable function also has an optional parameter $delimiter, which can be used to separate the links; see includes/theme.inc).

Bluemarine uses tables to determine the positioning of the sidebars, main content, and header. Depending on whether there is a left sidebar, a column in the table is included:

```
<?php if ($sidebar_left) { ?><td id="sidebar-left">
  <?php print $sidebar_left ?>
</td><?php } ?>
```

Tip For an example of a theme that doesn't use any tables for layout purposes, see the FriendsElectric theme by Steven Wittens, found at http://drupal.org/project/friendselectric.

The main content area is constructed using a number of variables:

```
<div id="main">
  <?php print $breadcrumb ?>
  <h1 class="title"><?php print $title ?></h1>
  <div class="tabs"><?php print $tabs ?></div>
```

```
  <?php print $help ?>
  <?php print $messages ?>
  <?php print $content; ?>
</div>
```

Most notable is the `$content` variable, which contains the main feature of the page—a node, a user, a list of taxonomy terms, or any other content.

The template ends by printing the `$closure` variable directly before the closing `<body>` tag:

```
<?php print $closure ?>
</body>
</html>
```

This is necessary to guarantee that modules have a chance to insert scripts at the bottom of the page. This is usually done in cases where the loading order of a script needs to be controlled; scripts at the bottom of the page will load after scripts earlier on the page, such as those needed for transforming text areas into WYSIWYG editors.

Passing Extra Variables to Templates

The variables listed for each of the previous `tpl.php` template files are all you need to support the normal functioning of your Drupal site. In case you would like to push other information into the template files, there is a mechanism for adding variables. The following function must be added to a file named `template.php` in your theme's directory:

```
function _phptemplate_variables($hook, $vars) {
  ...
  return $vars;
}
```

For Bluemarine, this would be in the file `themes/bluemarine/template.php`. The `$hook` variable is the name of the themable function being called and subsequently the root of the name of the template file to which the variables are headed. The `$vars` variable is an associative array containing the default variables as described in the preceding section. Thus, when the `theme('block')` function is called, `_phptemplate_variables` will also be called with the parameters `'block'` and an array of the variables associated with the `block.tpl.php` template: `$block`, `$id`, `$block_id`, `$zebra`, `$block_zebra`, and `$is_front`. At this point, you have the chance to add values to the array, or even change those that are already inside it. The `$vars` array that you return will determine which variables are visible to the `block.tpl.php` file. The same is true for each of the default `tpl.php` files, as well as any other template files that you may have added, such as node-type-specific files or overrides of themable functions.

Exercise 5-2 demonstrates how to pass extra variables to a template.

Exercise 5-2. Use Random Colors for Blocks

If you wanted to have each block on the page have a randomly chosen color, this would be a great opportunity to add the logic for choosing the color. Naturally, you could do this directly in the block.tpl.php file, but that would make the file harder to read for your graphic designer, who doesn't care how you determine the color, only that it is available in a nice, clean variable to be applied inside the template.

First, add the following _phptemplate_variables function to the template.php file in your theme. If the template.php file doesn't exist, create it (make sure to begin the file with <?php):

```
function _phptemplate_variables($hook, $vars) {
  switch ($hook) {
    case 'block':
      // generate a random color string like #26295d
      $color = '#';
      for ($i = 0; $i < 3; $i++) {
        $r = dechex(rand(0, 255));
        $color .= strlen($r) < 2 ? '0'.$r : $r;
      }

      // add the $color variable to the $vars array
      $vars['color'] = $color;
    break;
  }
  return $vars;
}
```

Next, update the block.tpl.php file in your theme with the following code, which uses the new $color variable to create a border around each block (changes are highlighted):

```
<div class="block block-<?php print $block->module; ?>"
  id="block-<?php print $block->module; ?>-<?php print $block->delta; ?>"
  style="border:5px solid <?php print $color ?>;">

  <h2 class="title"><?php print $block->subject; ?></h2>
  <div class="content"><?php print $block->content; ?></div>
</div>
```

Now when you access your site, every block should have a border with a randomly chosen color.

Manipulations at this point in the code are useful mainly for adding decoration or elements that are external to your site's logic. Most of the page execution code has been run by the time _phptemplate_variables gets called, which means it is quite limited in its possibilities. Furthermore, keep in mind that this is the theme for your site, which, by definition, should concern itself exclusively with visual elements and layout. Nevertheless, for tasks like using random colors for blocks, it is a useful place to make customizations.

Overriding Themable Functions

The preceding section demonstrated how to work with the default tpl.php files to modify your theme. Each of these files represents an override to a themable function from the Drupal core. While theme_page, theme_node, theme_comment, theme_box, and theme_block may be the most important themable functions, and thus have the greatest and most direct impact on the appearance of your site, they are by no means the only functions that are available for modification. Core Drupal includes dozens more themable functions, and most contributed modules add to the list as well. Learning how to find and override any themable function you wish is essential to having full mastery over your Drupal site.

How to Find Themable Functions

Finding themable functions, at the most basic level, is easy. You just open the code and search for function theme_. Everything that turns up is a themable function and can be overridden. This isn't much consolation, however, when you are looking at your site and you want to change a particular HTML snippet in a particular way. How do you know which themable function is responsible for a given widget or element in your Drupal site? Unfortunately, Drupal doesn't provide an easy built-in method for doing this. However, there is an easy way to fix this, and doing so gives you a good opportunity to peer further into the world of Drupal theming. Exercise 5-3 gives you a tool for identifying themable functions.

Exercise 5-3. Identify Themable Functions

The goal of this exercise is to modify the function responsible for calling themable functions in such a way that allows you to see in the HTML output which function was called. To do this, you will wrap the output from each call to a themable function in HTML comments like this:

```
<!-- BEGIN: theme_foo -->
result of the themable function
<!-- END: theme_foo -->
```

This way, you can look at the source code of a generated page and know exactly which themable function to override in order to change the output. This will be a handy tool while designing the theme for your site, but you won't want to use it on a production site.

To begin, locate the includes/theme.inc file and make a backup copy, which you will use later to restore your Drupal installation to its original state when you're finished with this exercise. In theme.inc, find the theme() function around line 160. This is the function that is responsible for determining exactly which themable function to call. It looks first for a function specific to your theme, then to the theme engine, and finally to the default theme_foo function, calling the first one found. Replace the theme() function with the following code:

```
function theme() {
  global $theme, $theme_engine;

  if ($theme === NULL) {
    // Initialize the enabled theme.
    $theme = init_theme();
  }
```

```
    $args = func_get_args();
    $function = array_shift($args);

    if (($theme != '') && function_exists($theme .'_'. $function)) {
      // call themable function
      $function = $theme .'_'. $function;
    }
    elseif (($theme != '') && isset($theme_engine) &&
      function_exists($theme_engine .'_'. $function)) {
      // call engine function
      $function = $theme_engine .'_'. $function;
    }
    elseif (function_exists('theme_'. $function)){
      // call Drupal function
      $function = 'theme_'. $function;
    }

    $output = call_user_func_array($function, $args);

    if (trim($output)) {
      return "<!-- BEGIN: $function -->\n$output\n<!-- END: $function -->\n";
    }
  }
```

The beauty of Drupal's theme mechanism lies in the code `call_user_func_array($function, $args)`, which executes the function `$function` (the dynamically chosen themable function) with the parameters found in the array `$args`. This code differs from the original mainly in that it stores the product of this call in a variable `$output`, and as long as `$output` is more than mere white space, wraps it in the HTML comments as discussed earlier.

The final result is that your site should look the same as before in the browser, but when you view the source code, every section of HTML will be nested in comments identifying the specific themable function that was responsible for that segment of the output. Here is an example:

```
<!-- BEGIN: phptemplate_block -->
  <div class="block block-user" id="block-user-1">
  <h2 class="title">admin</h2>
  <div class="content"><div class="menu">

  <!-- BEGIN: theme_menu_tree -->
    <ul>

    <!-- BEGIN: theme_menu_item -->
      <li class="collapsed">

      <!-- BEGIN: theme_menu_item_link -->
        <a href="?q=node/add" >create content</a>
      <!-- END: theme_menu_item_link -->
      </li>
    <!-- END: theme_menu_item -->
```

```
[...]

   </ul>

   <!-- END: theme_menu_tree -->
   </div></div>
   </div>

<!-- END: phptemplate_block -->
```

This is an excerpt of the HTML that renders the main navigation menu using the Bluemarine theme. Notice how easy it is to identify which themable function generates which HTML. You can see, for example, that the *create content* link was generated by a function named `theme_menu_item_link`. Searching the codebase for `function theme_menu_item_link` will guide you to the `includes/menu.inc` file, where you can view and dissect how the HTML was made.

You can find functions starting with the name of the theme engine, `phptemplate`, either in the theme itself (in the form of a function in `template.php` or as a `tpl.php` file) or in the theme engine (as a function in `phptemplate.engine` and corresponding `tpl.php` file). To find the code that handles the call to `phptemplate_block` in the previous example, you must first look for a `block.tpl.php` file in the theme's folder, `themes/bluemarine/block.tpl.php` in this case. In its absence, look for a `phptemplate_block` function in the theme's `template.php` file. If that also doesn't exist, then you can be certain that the theme engine itself is handling the call in the form of a `tpl.php` file, `themes/engines/phptemplate/block.tpl.php`.

Techniques for Overriding Themable Functions

Once you have found a themable function that you would like to override, you have two variations on how to go about doing it.

The first variation is to provide an alternative function in your theme that will be used instead of the functions provided by Drupal or by the theme engine. In general, this involves creating a function with the naming convention *namespace*`_foo()`, where `namespace` is the name of your theme engine and `foo` is the name of the function. Review Exercise 5-1 earlier in the chapter for an example of creating a `phptemplate_breadcrumb($breadcrumb)` function that overrides the `theme _breadcrumb($breadcrumb)` function.

The second way to override a themable function in your theme is actually an extension of the first way, but puts the code and logic for generating the output into a `tpl.php` template file instead. You still provide a function following the same naming convention, but instead of putting the logic for the output there, in the function, you use it to call the template file instead.

The second approach has several advantages over the first method. It is vastly easier to output large amounts of HTML from a template file rather than a PHP function, since you don't need to quote and escape everything. This is the largest advantage. Beyond that, switching and swapping `tpl.php` files between themes is easier and more portable than using copy and paste to move and rename themable functions into your theme, and template files are easier for people with weak PHP skills to work with.

For both approaches, you will need to create a file in your theme folder named `template.php` if it doesn't already exist. This is where Drupal will look for themable functions that are specific to the current theme. In the case of the Bluemarine theme, the path to this file will be themes/bluemarine/template.php. Here is the override to the breadcrumb function from Exercise 5-1:

```
<?php
function phptemplate_breadcrumb($breadcrumb) {
  $output = '<h1>Hello World!</h1>';
  $output .= implode(' / ', $breadcrumb);
  return $output;
}
?>
```

Compare that to the original theme_breadcrumb function from includes/theme.inc:

```
function theme_breadcrumb($breadcrumb) {
  return '<div class="breadcrumb">'. implode(' Â» ', $breadcrumb) .'</div>';
}
```

Notice that the new breadcrumb function takes the same parameter ($breadcrumb) and applies essentially the same logic as the original, but chooses to embellish the output in a different way. This is the responsibility of the theme developer who ventures to write new themable functions. You need to understand the original functionality, and, as far as desired, reproduce it in the override, including handling all of the input parameters.

The previous code demonstrates the first approach to overriding themable functions: writing new functions in template.php. A better implementation would be to create a breadcrumb.tpl.php file instead. The path to this new file would be themes/bluemarine/breadcrumb.tpl.php, and here is what it would look like:

```
<h1>Hello World!</h1>
<?php print implode(' / ', $breadcrumb); ?>
```

Notice a few things about this code. First, it is much shorter than the function version. Second, it isn't necessary to store all of the output in a variable. Third, pure HTML, such as the <h1>Hello World!</h1>, doesn't need to be quoted. This last point is especially practical when you consider more complex HTML that involves quotation marks or line breaks, both of which need to be escaped with backslashes and special characters in functions. Template files are also easier to edit in programs such as Dreamweaver, and therefore nicer for graphic designers who get the shivers when confronted with too much PHP code. You also end up with a collection of template files that can be used again for another theme, allowing you to build a theme library and reuse your code.

To let PHPTemplate know that it is to use the breadcrumb.tpl.php file, you need to add the following function to the file themes/bluemarine/template.php:

```
function phptemplate_breadcrumb($breadcrumb) {
  return _phptemplate_callback('breadcrumb',
    array('breadcrumb' => $breadcrumb));
}
```

The _phptemplate_callback function is PHPTemplate's mechanism for finding and including tpl.php files. Any time you want to use a template file, a call to this function is required. The first parameter to _phptemplate_callback is the name of the themable function you wish to override, minus the theme_ part. In this case, you wish to override the theme_breadcrumb function, so the first parameter becomes 'breadcrumb'. If you had set out to override the theme_status_messages function, the first parameter would be 'status_messages'. The second parameter is an associative array of the variables that you wish to pass to the function. This will usually correspond one-to-one with the parameters that the original themable function requires. The function theme_breadcrumb($breadcrumb) receives one variable $breadcrumb, and so the array becomes 'breadcrumb' => $breadcrumb.

Now when theme('breadcrumb', $breadcrumb) is called, the function phptemplate_breadcrumb will be invoked, which will in turn lead to the inclusion of the breadcrumb.tpl.php template file. Does that sound complex? Complexity is the price to pay for flexibility, in this case.

Adding Custom Regions for Blocks

Blocks can appear anywhere you want them to in your theme. By default, Drupal offers five regions to which blocks can be assigned: left sidebar, right sidebar, header, content, and footer. With just two quick alterations to your theme, you can add custom regions to this list, allowing you to place blocks anywhere on the page.

The first step for adding a custom block is to add a function to your theme's template.php file. This function is named *theme*_regions(), where *theme* is replaced with the actual name of your theme. For Blumarine, this would be bluemarine_regions(). The function must return an array of custom regions that will be added to the list of available regions when you configure blocks from the block administration page (admin/block).

The second step is to add a line of PHP to your page.tpl.php file where you want blocks in the custom region to appear:

```
<?php print $custom_region; ?>
```

This will print all of the code for the blocks that have been assigned to that particular region. You may add as many custom regions to your theme as you like. Exercise 5-4 demonstrates how to do this.

Exercise 5-4. Add a Custom Block Region to a Theme

This exercise shows you how to add a custom region to your Bluemarine theme. The region will be added directly above the content area, complementing the block region named *content* that appears below the content area.

First, if you don't already have a template.php file in your theme, create one. Make sure that it is a true PHP file and starts with <?php.

Next, add this function to the template.php file:

```
function bluemarine_regions() {
  return array(
    'content_top' => t('content top')
    );
}
```

Finally, update the `page.tpl.php` file with the line of code shown in bold:

```
<div id="main">
  <?php print $content_top; ?>
  <?php print $breadcrumb ?>
  <h1 class="title"><?php print $title ?></h1>
  <div class="tabs"><?php print $tabs ?></div>
  <?php print $help ?>
  <?php print $messages ?>

  <?php print $content; ?>  <!-- this is the other block region -->
</div>
```

Now when you navigate to *administer* ➤ *blocks* (`admin/block`), you'll be given an additional option for where to place blocks, a shown in Figure 5-6.

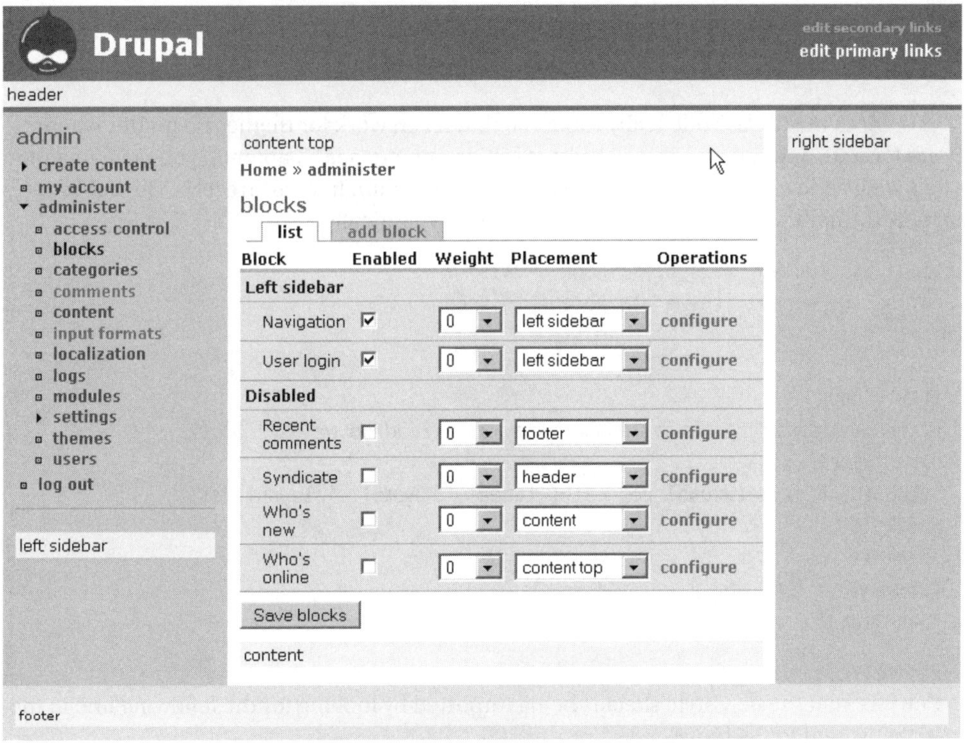

Figure 5-6. *Adding a block to the Bluemarine theme*

Using CSS for Themes

Drupal has been designed from the ground up with CSS in mind. If you are adept at using CSS to style your web pages, you will find the HTML generated by Drupal to be very easy to work with and the style sheets from existing themes helpful starting points for your own design work. Here, I will focus on some basic information that will help you find things a bit quicker while working with Drupal's style sheets.

A Custom CSS File

Drupal will automatically search the theme folder for a file called style.css. If it is found, it will be imported automatically; there is nothing you need to do to guarantee this behavior. However, you may want to import additional style sheets. Perhaps you would like to have one called style.css that governs typesetting, color, and graphical elements to be imported automatically, and another called layout.css that deals exclusively with positioning and spacing.

To add a custom .css file, in your theme's template.php file (if you don't have one, create one in your theme's main directory), call the following function:

```
theme_add_style($stylesheet, $media = 'all');
```

Replace the $stylesheet variable with the relative path to the file you wish to import. To import the file themes/bluemarine/layout.css, for example, you would use this line (the function's optional $media parameter will default to all):

```
theme_add_style('themes/bluemarine/layout.css');
```

In order to make this code really robust so that it can work for themes no matter where they are located, and even work in a multisite environment (see Chapter 6), you need to add the following code to the _phptemplate_variables() function in template.php. The bold segment gets the path to the current theme's directory dynamically:

```
function _phptemplate_variables($hook, $vars) {
  // bring the global $theme variable into scope
  global $theme;

  switch ($hook) {
    // theme('block') gets called on every page load so we use 'block'
    case 'block':
      theme_add_style(drupal_get_path('theme', $theme). '/layout.css');
    break;
  }

  return $vars;
}
```

Confirm that the new style sheet is being imported by looking for the following line in the HTML that is sent to the browser:

```
<style type="text/css" media="all">@import "themes/bluemarine/layout.css";</style>
```

Style-Only Themes

One of the fantastic features that Drupal offers is the ability to build themes based entirely on one CSS file. The standard themable functions and tpl.php files all serve to generate HTML according to the theme designer's exact wishes, yet HTML is far from the last word concerning how a page will actually look. In terms of web design, the CSS has a far greater impact overall than the mere HTML, which provides structure to the content, but not much else. That is why the ability to reuse the HTML and build multiple themes on top of it is especially helpful.

Top-level themes earn their status as a theme by virtue of the `page.tpl.php` file, which is the minimum requirement to qualify as a PHPTemplate theme. You create a CSS theme by adding a directory inside a top-level theme like Bluemarine or Pushbutton. Inside the subfolder, place a `style.css` file, and you've created a whole new theme! Visit `admin/themes` to verify its existence.

The new CSS theme will use the HTML generated by the top-level theme and apply the `style.css` file in the subfolder. The theme will take its name from the name of the subfolder. For example, the file `bluemarine/greenmarine/style.css` would cause an entire new theme called Greenmarine to register on the `admin/themes` page. It would be identical to Bluemarine in terms of HTML, but could look completely different, based on whatever rules are found in the `bluemarine/greenmarine/style.css` file.

This type of CSS theme also has the minimum requirement of having a `page.tpl.php` file at its disposal; it borrows the file from its parent directory. All of the other `tpl.php` files, as well as themable function overrides in `template.php`, will apply to the CSS theme. For an example of this in action, check out the CivicSpace theme available at `http://drupal.org/project/civicspace_theme`.

■ **Note** When adding a CSS theme, you need to visit `admin/themes` once before Drupal will recognize the new theme.

Drupal.css: The Drupal Style Sheet

Some of the style information that applies to a Drupal site is considered so basic that it is not left to the theme, but is instead stored in a `misc/drupal.css` file, which applies to every page loaded in every Drupal site. The file contains style rules that apply to elements that directly affect functionality, such as menu styles, tabs, auto-complete fields, and collapsible fieldsets. These are elements that need styles to be useful to the end user and generally don't need to be changed on every Drupal site.

Seeing Drupal.css Styling

To get a feel for the role that `drupal.css` plays on your site, you can try a small exercise. Rename the `themes` folder to `_themes` and click around your site for a while. Are you surprised that your site still works? Don't forget that all of the basic functions to generate HTML are in the core include and module files, and that the themes, which you've effectively hidden from Drupal by renaming the `themes` folder, are intended only to shape that output or modify it if needed. What you will notice in this new, themeless world, is that not all elements are without styling. Figure 5-7 shows some examples of items styled by `drupal.css`.

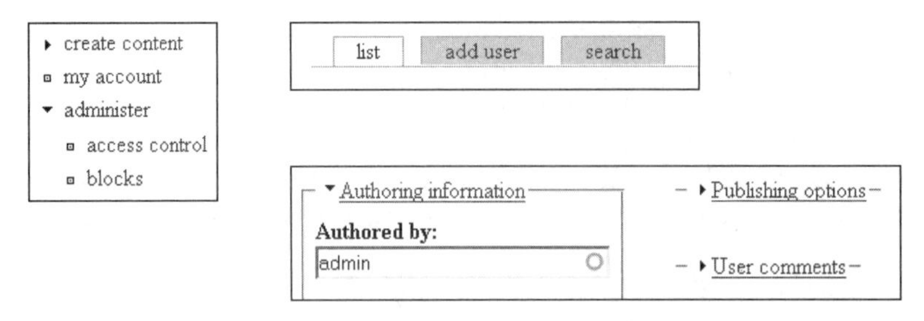

Figure 5-7. *Menu items, tabs, auto-complete fields, and collapsible fieldsets styled by drupal.css*

These styles come directly from `misc/drupal.css`. If you wish to change any of them, you shouldn't edit the `drupal.css` file directly, for several reasons:

- Upgrading to a newer Drupal version will be difficult. You will need to remember that you made the changes and merge your altered file with the newer file that comes with the upgrade.
- As I will discuss in the next chapter, several sites can be run from one codebase. If you change `drupal.css`, the changes will affect all of the sites you run on that particular codebase.
- It isn't necessary to change `drupal.css`. The nature of CSS means that writing the same or more specific rule in another style sheet, such as your theme's `style.css`, will override the rule in `drupal.css`.

If what you are interested in achieving is modifying or altering the rules defined in `drupal.css`, the best method is to copy the rules into `style.css` in your theme and change them there.

Removing drupal.css

Sometimes, you might want to get rid of `drupal.css` altogether for a site. Perhaps you want to view the site on a device for which none of the styles make sense, and instead of overriding them all, you simply want to avoid loading the style sheet to begin with.

Deleting `drupal.css` will cause 404 Not Found errors to be written to your logs every time a page loads, so don't do that. The solution relies on the very techniques that this chapter has been discussing all along, namely overriding themable functions. The function in question is named `theme_stylesheet_import`, is found in `includes/theme.inc`, and is responsible for printing the tags that import style sheets.

To block `drupal.css` from being loaded, you need to override the `theme_stylesheet_import` function in your theme's `template.php` file. For Bluemarine, this will be `themes/bluemarine/template.php`, and the function will be named `phptemplate_stylesheet_import`. Here is the modified function:

```
function phptemplate_stylesheet_import($stylesheet, $media = 'all') {
  if ($stylesheet != 'misc/drupal.css') {
    return theme_stylesheet_import($stylesheet, $media);
  }
}
```

Comparing this to the original function, you will see that the difference lies with the `if` clause, which checks to see if `misc/drupal.css` is being loaded. While this may seem like a lot of work to do just to avoid loading one style sheet, it is the recommended method to achieve the goal, as it guarantees your upgrade path and doesn't interfere with Drupal's ability to host multiple sites on one codebase.

Creating a Custom Favicon.ico

This is a tip for everyone who runs a Drupal site: make a custom `favicon.ico` file for your theme. A `favicon.ico` is a 16-by-16 image that is sent to the browser for use in the address bar, bookmarks, and tabs to help identify the site. Many people forget to change the `favicon.ico` and end up with Drupal's smiling water drop by default, as shown in Figure 5-8.

Figure 5-8. *Drupal's icon is used as the icon in the address bar, by default.*

All that you needed to replace this icon is a 16-by-16 `.ico` file named `favicon.ico` in your theme's directory. Drupal will look in your theme to see if you've made a `favicon.ico` file. If it doesn't find a custom icon, it will use the default `favicon.ico` file in the top directory.

Using Theme-Related Modules

Having ultimate control over the theming of your web site is important, but many times, it would be nice if you could use prebuilt tools to handle some common tasks. Fortunately, several contributed modules are aimed at giving you more power and flexibility over the looks of your site. Here are five such modules that can be downloaded from the contributed repository on `Drupal.org`:

Blog Theme: If you have multiple themes activated for your site, registered users will be able to choose which theme they wish to use. The Blog Theme module (`http://drupal.org/node/19248`) capitalizes on this to make blog postings on the site more personalized. When this module is installed and activated, blog postings will be displayed in the author's chosen theme.

Themedev: The Themedev module (`http://drupal.org/project/themedev`) comes packaged with a number of diagnostic style sheets that, when loaded, augment a page by highlighting various elements. The administrator can turn the style sheets on or off in a role-based fashion, so that you can create a special user role for the theme designer. The style sheets include tools to highlight page structure, list structure, and table structure. They can also highlight tags that are deprecated in XHTML 1.0 Strict, tags that are commonly misused, and constructions that could hinder usability. Figure 5-9 shows an example of using the Themedev module.

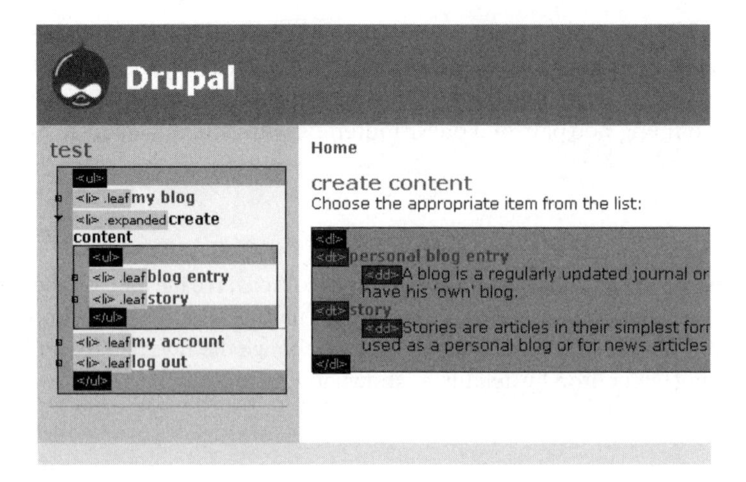

Figure 5-9. *The Themedev module in action*

Theme Editor: With the Theme Editor module (`http://drupal.org/project/theme_editor`), the themes that are found in the `themes` directory serve as a sort of template repository on which an arbitrary number of new themes can be created and developed, all from the web interface. When a new theme is created, the user is asked to choose an existing theme, which will then be copied into a working directory and renamed. All of the text files can be edited directly in the browser, and new files can be added to the directory via HTTP upload. This is a useful module in several circumstances. Perhaps you would like to allow users on your site to have control over their own theme without granting them FTP or shell access to the server. Or perhaps you've hired a developer to edit your theme and want to allow him to work on the theme directly with the browser.

■ **Caution** Don't forget that anyone who can edit theme files can run PHP code on your server. Letting the general public use the Theme Editor module is a severe security risk.

Sections: A common request seen on `Drupal.org` is to add a mechanism that allows for different themes in different sections or areas of a site. Perhaps the forums should look different from the book pages. Maybe the front page should have its own theme distinct from the rest of the site. Or perhaps the tables and controls in the administrative sections of the site don't work well in the theme that looks good for the content areas of the site. The Sections module (`http://drupal.org/project/sections`) allows you to define sections of your site that have distinct themes. The pages that are included in these sections are defined by using paths, just as block administration is done. Using a path of `admin*`, for example, will define a section that includes all of the administrative pages, allowing you to pick a theme that works well for the wide tables, while leaving untouched the main theme that makes your blog sparkle and shine.

Taxonomy_theme: Another strategy for assigning a theme other than the main theme to a page is through the taxonomy system. Using the Taxonomy_theme module (http://drupal.org/project/taxonomy_theme), the administrator has the chance to associate themes with taxonomy terms. When a node is viewed and has been categorized with one of these terms, the theme of the page is taken from the term. This system would be useful on a site where the design and presentation need to change depending on the content of the posts.

Summary

This chapter described how to install and create Drupal themes. It covered a lot of ground, and I will briefly summarize the main points here.

The theming system that governs the look and feel of your Drupal site is built on themable functions—functions in the core modules and includes that are responsible for generating HTML output. The HTML that is produced by these fundamental functions is adequate to run a site and ready to be styled using CSS. Themes are groups of files organized by folders in the themes directory that represent alterations and enhancements to the core themable functions and the HTML they generate.

Administrators can decide which of the themes available in the themes directory are activated. If more than one theme is activated, users will be able to choose which theme is to be used for them when they visit the site.

Various strategies have been developed for managing the interactions between themes and the underlying themable functions. As a result, various theme engines are available. PHPTemplate is the standard engine and is part of the standard Drupal download.

Most of the work done in designing the look of a Drupal web site will be achieved using CSS and binary image files. Every theme has a style.css file, which can be customized to make themes unique. Other style sheets can be added using the function theme_add_style.

Themable functions from the core include files and modules can be overridden by adding new functions that follow a naming convention that combines the name of the active theme with the name of the themable function. For PHPTemplate-driven themes, these new functions are placed in the theme's template.php file. Theme overrides can also be achieved in the form of tpl.php template files, a strategy that has many advantages for designers and site administrators.

The most common themable functions have been overridden by PHPTemplate automatically. These functions include theme_page, theme_box, theme_block, theme_comment, and theme_node. Any PHPTemplate-driven theme must provide, at a minimum, an override for theme_page. This is done by including a page.tpl.php file in the theme's directory. If other tpl.php files for these common functions are found in the same directory, they are used instead of the underlying themable function.

The node.tpl.php template, which overrides the function theme_node, can have node-type specific variants, which follow a naming convention. The file node-blog.tpl.php, for example, will provide an override that is specific to blog nodes. Any node type can be themed in this way.

You can create style sheet-only themes (styles) by making a subdirectory in a theme and adding a style.css file to it. The theme will rely on the tpl.php templates and theme overrides from the parent directory, but the style.css file in the subdirectory will be used.

Several modules can assist you in various theming tasks or augment the theming system in some way. With so many tools, you usually have several ways to achieve any particular goal concerning the appearance of your web site.

In the next chapter, I will describe some of Drupal's features regarding hosting and maintaining sites. This will include how to set up multisite hosting, schedule cron tasks, use different backup strategies, and get help and find resources on `Drupal.org`.

CHAPTER 6

Maintaining Your Site

By now, you are enjoying your Drupal site quite a bit. You can create many types of content, are attracting new users to your online community, have developed a gorgeous theme, and have installed a dozen contributed modules to add all sorts of great new features. Congratulations! Isn't Drupal fun? You're not quite finished, though. Some aspects of Drupal won't work right without enabling automated tasks to run, and I haven't discussed some of Drupal's most interesting configuration options yet. For example, Drupal is capable of running any number of web sites from one installation. This is exceptionally useful after you've made your first successful site and want to repeat your success. It also makes maintaining the code much easier, as there is only one set of scripts for all your sites.

Somewhere in the back of your mind, you might be aware of the importance of making backups of your data, but what have you actually done to guarantee that you can recover from a server disaster? If your backup and recovery plan leaves something to be desired, read on. This chapter guides you through a practical backup strategy that will save you much heartache and trouble if you ever need to restore your site.

Upgrading your Drupal installation and testing new features can be a tricky business. Here, I'll give you practical advice and instructions on how to go about both of these tasks in a way that minimizes the risk of inadvertently breaking your production site.

The final section in this chapter looks at how to find help on the Web and some of the resources available on `Drupal.org`. I then close this part of the book with some thoughts about the Drupal community and how the software that runs Drupal sites directly contributes to the unity and involvement of the people who use and develop Drupal.

Scheduling Automated Tasks

A number of Drupal features and maintenance tasks are designed to be done at regular intervals on an ongoing basis. These are tasks that need to be executed periodically and include updating the search index, updating aggregator feeds, closing polls, and discarding old logging information. As you can see, these are important and vital functions for most Drupal web sites.

Drupal is programmed in PHP, and PHP running on a web server like Apache offers no solution to the problem of scheduling tasks to be run at repeating intervals—that just isn't what Apache and PHP were designed to do. Therefore, you need to use other tools to trigger the tasks.

The cron program is the most common tool used for scheduling these tasks for Drupal. The cron program is used on UNIX-based machines to launch programs and scripts on a scheduled timer.

Introducing Cron.php

In the base directory of your Drupal installation you will find a file named `cron.php`. This is a normal `.php` file that you can call in your browser, instead of the normal entry point to your Drupal site (`index.php`), by using a URL like `http://www.yoursite.com/cron.php`. The `cron.php` file has the responsibility of triggering all of the scheduled maintenance tasks. It does not return a Drupal page, as calls to `index.php` do, but instead executes whatever tasks are scheduled and returns an empty page.

You must call `cron.php` in order to achieve tasks like updating the search index and discarding old log files (I'll describe how to call `cron.php` in the next section).

Failure to do these tasks will result in a slowdown in your site's performance over time, as the history and logging tables get larger and more expensive to search and sort. Call `cron.php` periodically, even if only once a week, for any Drupal site that you run.

Table 6-1 lists the core modules that rely on `cron.php` and what gets done when it gets called (see Chapter 3 for details on how to use Drupal core modules).

Table 6-1. *Core Modules That Rely on Cron.php*

Module	Tasks
Aggregator	The Aggregator module lets you set a schedule for updating and importing syndication feeds. When `cron.php` is run, the Aggregator module updates the appropriate feeds according to the schedule you set.
Drupal	When `cron.php` is run, the Drupal module updates the sites directory with any sites that are using your site as a directory server, and pings the site listed as the directory server for your site.
Node	The history table in the database is used to track which content has been viewed by each user. This allows Drupal to mark content as new on an individual user basis. When `cron.php` is run, old entries are removed from the history table, thus preventing it from growing to unmanageable sizes.
Ping	When `cron.php` is run, the Ping module notifies `pingomatic.com` of updates to your site.
Poll	When `cron.php` is run, the Poll module closes polls that have expired.
Search	When `cron.php` is run, the Search module updates the search index based on new content.
Statistics	When `cron.php` is run, the Statistics module maintains the access log and the node counter.
Watchdog	When `cron.php` is run, the Watchdog module deletes old watchdog entries.

Many contributed modules also make use of `cron.php` tasks. Make sure to consult a module's documentation to see whether `cron.php` tasks are required and if there are special considerations with regard to timing.

CRON.PHP AND SECURITY

Is cron.php a security risk? Couldn't someone call cron.php over and over again and thus overload the system? Fortunately, this isn't as worrisome as many first assume. Each cron task maintains its own schedule for updating various things such as search and aggregator tasks, so the tasks themselves are run only on that schedule, no matter how often cron.php is called. If someone were to call cron.php repeatedly, the first call would trigger all the scheduled tasks set to run, but then the second and subsequent calls to cron.php would return having done nothing. In the end, calling index.php is more expensive in terms of server load, and therefore the more likely target of a denial-of-service attack.

If you want to prevent cron.php from being accessed from the Web, and allow it to be accessed only from the server itself, you can add this directive to your Apache httpd.conf file:

```
<Location cron.php>
  Order deny,allow
  Deny from all
  Allow from 127.0.0.1
</Location>
```

■ **Note** When deciding how often to call cron.php and execute the scheduled tasks, pick the lowest frequency that is practical for your site. Make a list of the modules that rely on cron (consult the list in Table 6-1 and the documentation for contributed modules) so that you have a clear idea of what is happening when it is called. For tasks like updating the search index, a frequency of every hour for busy sites will most likely be adequate. For tasks like querying the mail server to see if the site has received incoming messages (see the Mailhandler module, available from http://drupal.org/project/mailhandler), a frequency of every 3 to 5 minutes is more realistic.

Calling Cron.php

One option for calling cron.php is to simply load it using your browser. This quickly gets tiring, and it is unlikely that you will be able to keep your search index up-to-date using this method. A better solution includes two types of external programs: a program that can load cron.php via HTTP, like a web browser, and a program that can schedule and trigger the task on a regular basis.

There are many ways to arrange to have cron.php called regularly enough to keep your Drupal site shipshape. Since all except the most obvious method is at least partially dependent on the operating system of the server and the other software programs it has installed, setting up a cron.php schedule is a common source of confusion. Here, I will discuss several different strategies to address all of the common scenarios.

Poor Man's Cron: The Poormanscron Module

For many people, the Poormanscron module (http://drupal.org/project/poormanscron) is the easiest choice for addressing the cron issue. The module is a snap to install. You just need to move it to the modules directory, activate it, and set some basic configurations, such as how often it should run. When people visit your site, the Poormanscron module triggers the cron tasks, exactly as calling cron.php would do.

The main drawback to this approach is that it makes the cron tasks dependent on your site having visitors. This isn't a suitable solution if your site requires modules to do tasks like retrieving mail messages from the mail server (the Mass Mailer module, http://drupal.org/project/massmailer, does this). When deciding whether to use the Poormanscron module, ask yourself if there are times of day when your site will be receiving little or no traffic, and whether there are cron tasks that need to be done during those times. If there are, then you should find a different solution. The Poormanscron module also adds a very small amount of overhead to every page request, though this is trivial and shouldn't play a role when you're deciding whether to use it.

GNU/Linux Solutions

The part that confuses most people about using cron for your Drupal installation is that the cron program is responsible only for the scheduling. You need a second program to actually call the cron.php file. wget, lynx, and curl are three candidates for this second program, and you are free to choose which one works best for you. You need to configure the program to call the URL of the cron.php file via HTTP. It is important to allow the web server to handle the request instead of calling cron.php from the PHP command line, because the web server provides key information, such as the host name, that will otherwise be missing.

The easiest tool for sending an HTTP request to cron.php is wget (http://www.gnu.org/software/wget/wget.html). To find out if you have wget available, issue the following command:

```
# whereis wget
```

If it is installed, you will see a line like this:

```
wget: /usr/bin/wget
```

You can test that you have permissions to use it by issuing a command like this:

```
# wget -S --spider drupal.org
```

-S tells wget to print the output to the console, and --spider tells wget not to retrieve the response, just the headers. The result should look like this:

```
# wget -S --spider drupal.org
--16:53:14--  http://drupal.org/
           => `index.html'
Resolving drupal.org... 217.67.229.126
Connecting to drupal.org|217.67.229.126|:80... connected.
HTTP request sent, awaiting response...
  HTTP/1.1 200 OK
[...]
```

If you have gotten this far, wget is the best tool for you. You will most likely be able to use cron and wget to access cron.php in your Drupal installation. Here is the command to use to have wget call cron.php in the appropriate way:

```
/usr/bin/wget -q -O /dev/null http://www.yoursite.com/cron.php
```

The /usr/bin/wget part needs to be modified to match what was returned by the whereis wget command. The -q flag tells wget to be quiet (not to output its activities and status). The -O flag tells it to send whatever headers and output come from the web site to the destination that follows. In this case, the destination is /dev/null, which means the output will be discarded. Finally comes the correct URL to your cron.php file. Test the command in your shell, and then confirm from your Watchdog logs (Drupal path admin) that cron.php has actually run. If all is well, you will see the message "Cron run completed."

If you haven't had any success with wget, you can explore using the cron-lynx.sh or cron-curl.sh scripts in your Drupal's scripts directory. These depend on the lynx and curl programs, respectively. Refer to Drupal.org (http://drupal.org/node/23714) for further instructions. Alternatively, you might want to explore using a free web-based service, such as Webcron (http://www.webcron.org/).

After selecting the tool to call cron.php, you need to set up your cron schedule and task. A typical cron schedule looks like this:

```
30 * * * *
```

The places correspond to minute, hour, day of the month, month, and day of the week, so this command would run at the thirtieth minute of every hour, every day, every month, every week. In other words, once an hour at 30 minutes past the hour. This is very much along the lines of what a typical Drupal site needs. But perhaps your site has more traffic, or uses a cron task to retrieve mail from the mail server to be published to the forums. In that case, you will want to run cron a little more often:

```
*/2 * * * *
```

This runs the task every two minutes. Note that the varying parts are separated by a space.

The cron task to run is specified after the scheduling part. If you decide to use wget as the program to call cron.php, this is the command:

```
30 * * * /usr/bin/wget -q -O /dev/null http://www.yoursite.com/cron.php
```

Now you are finally ready to put the command in the crontab file. Use crontab -e, which will open your crontab file and insert the full command on a new line at the end. That should do the trick! Refer to cron's documentation (http://www.unixgeeks.org/security/newbie/unix/cron-1.html) for more complete information.

Windows Solutions

Windows has a tool called the Windows Task Scheduler, which you can use to launch a web browser and access cron.php. For excellent instructions on configuring the Windows Task Scheduler, see the "Configuring Cron Jobs on Windows" article at Drupal.org (http://drupal.org/node/31506).

Although Windows does not ship with the cron program, you have the same options as UNIX users, thanks to Cygwin (which gives you the power of cron, wget, lynx, and curl on Windows) and web-based cron services. Here are some resources to consider:

- Cygwin, a Linux-like environment for Windows: http://www.cygwin.com/.
- Cron for Windows: http://www.kalab.com/freeware/cron/cron.htm
- Web-based cron: http://webcron.org/

Running Multiple Drupal Sites

Running multiple web sites can be very time-consuming for administrators. Installing the scripts for new sites, patching security updates, upgrading to new releases, and tracking what version of which module is installed all adds up to a lot of work. Drupal addresses this problem by allowing you to run an arbitrary, unlimited number of web sites on the same installation. That means you need to install Drupal only once, and upgrading, patching, and installing new modules is exponentially more efficient since the tasks for all of your sites need to be done only once.

Before you can use Drupal's multisite features, you need to explore how to make your various domains resolve to the same document root (where Drupal is installed). If you are administering your own server, you can do this with Apache and virtual hosts (see `http://httpd.apache.org/docs/1.3/vhosts/name-based.html`). Hosting companies use terms like *aliased domains* and *parked domains* to describe this configuration. If you have access to the server through a control panel like CPanel (`http://www.cpanel.net/`) or Plesk (`http://www.➥sw-soft.com/en/products/plesk/`), configurations of this nature are usually possible, but you should ask your hosting company for directions on how to make various domains resolve to the same source directory.

The first step to setting up a new web site to run off of an existing Drupal installation is to configure the web server to direct requests for the new URL to the existing Drupal document root.

Directing Requests for Multiple Sites

In order for you to be able to run many web sites off of one Drupal installation, your server needs to be told to direct requests from multiple domains to the same place. With such a configuration, the following domains would all get sent to the same document root directory and would thus all be handled by the same `index.php` file:

- `www.yoursite.com`
- `www.secondsite.com`
- `subdomain.yoursite.com`

Once this is the case, you can then configure Drupal to use the domain to determine which configuration file to load, and thus which web site to display.

The Apache web server refers to this type of configuration as *virtual hosting*, or *vhosts*. You can configure your Apache server to direct multiple domains to the same document root. The following snippet from an Apache `httpd.conf` file is representative of the goal at hand:

```
# Substitute your IP address
NameVirtualHost 111.22.33.444

<VirtualHost 111.22.33.444>
  DocumentRoot /absolute/path/to/drupal
  ServerName yoursite.com
</VirtualHost>
```

```
<VirtualHost 111.22.33.444>
# note that the DocumentRoot is exactly the same for both VirtualHosts
  DocumentRoot /absolute/path/to/drupal
  ServerName secondsite.com
</VirtualHost>
```

If your site is being hosted by a hosting company that doesn't let you edit the `httpd.conf` file, you need to explore what options the service offers for achieving the same thing. Some call these *aliased domains*; others call them *parked domains*. The basic principle is always the same, however: each of the various domains is sent to the same document root in order to be handled by your Drupal installation. Ask your hosting company for advice concerning virtual hosts, or refer to your web server's documentation for more information. The various options are vast and depend on the exact operating system and web server that is hosting your site.

Creating a sites Subdirectory

Your Drupal installation has a folder named `sites`. The `sites` folder is where Drupal looks to see what domains and subdomains it is supposed to handle. During installation, I instructed you to use the `sites/default/settings.php` file for your site configuration. This is fine, as long as you need to run only one site with your Drupal installation.

Now, since you are learning to run multiple sites, you need to create a subdirectory in the `sites` folder for every site that you wish to run with this installation. Each of these subdirectories will bear the name of the domain. Each subdirectory contains a separate `settings.php` file (the configuration file), as well as other resources such as custom modules or themes.

When Drupal receives a request from the server, it looks through subdirectories of `sites` and uses their names to match the incoming URL to the correct configuration file and other resources. Once Drupal has matched a domain with a subfolder in the `sites` directory, it will use the resources (modules, themes, and so on) in that directory before using any corresponding resources in the shared codebase. This allows you to have web sites that share the majority of the codebase but use different versions of a certain module or have different themes available.

At the very minimum, each of the subdirectories representing different sites must have a `settings.php` file. This is where Drupal gets the information needed to make the database connection, and also where the `$base_url` variable is defined. These two bits of information are the bare minimum configuration information that Drupal needs in order to get running. The directory structure shown in Figure 6-1 represents three different sites:

- `sites/default/settings.php`
- `sites/domain.com/settings.php`
- `sites/otherdomain.net/settings.php`
- `sites/thirdsite.org/settings.php`

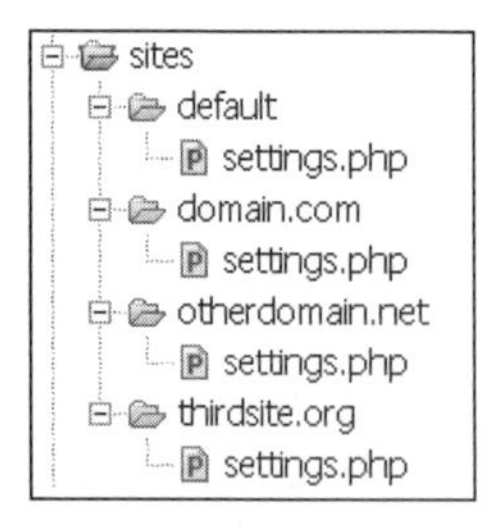

Figure 6-1. *Directory structure with sites subdirectories*

Each of the sites—`domain.com`, `otherdomain.net`, and `thirdsite.org`—would have its own database, and they would function as three completely and unrelated sites. If Drupal ever received a request from the web server that asked for a different domain—one that didn't match any of the three domain-specific configuration folders—the `settings.php` file in the `default` directory would be used.

The steps for adding a new site are as follows:

1. Configure the web server to direct requests for the new URL to the Drupal document root.
2. Create a subdirectory in `sites` for this new domain.
3. Copy the `sites/default/settings.php` file into the new subdirectory and modify it according to the configuration instructions in Chapter 1. This involves, at a minimum, setting the database connection configuration and the `$base_url` parameter.
4. Create a `files` directory in your new subdirectory: `sites/yoursite.net/files`. This will be used to keep uploaded files for `yoursite.net` separate from those for the other sites.
5. Update the File System Path setting on the site settings page (`admin/settings`) to reflect the `files` subdirectory change. The path will look like this: `sites/yoursite.net/files`.

Table 6-2 shows some examples of domains, the subdirectory of `sites` that you should create, and the `$base_url` variable for `settings.php`.

Table 6-2. *Examples of Subdirectories and Base URLs for Domains*

Domain	Subdirectory	$base_url
`www.domain.com`	`domain.com`	`http://www.domain.com`
`www.yoursite.net`	`yoursite.net`	`http://www.yoursite.net`
`blog.domain.com`	`blog.domain.com`	`http://blog.domain.com`

Every domain/site that you want to run off of a single Drupal installation needs its own database. Refer to Chapter 1 for the instructions on creating databases and importing the table definitions. The details for the database connection (user, password, and database name) need to be updated in the appropriate `settings.php` file that you created in a subdirectory of `sites`.

HOW DRUPAL FINDS SETTINGS.PHP

Exactly how does Drupal match incoming URLs with directories in `sites`? Drupal treats the domain of the incoming request as a hierarchical construct (which it is), and leaves open the possibility that you will configure your sites in the same way. The domain is therefore systematically broken down into less specific fragments until a matching configuration directory is located. The first configuration directory that is found is used. If no matching configuration directories are found, the default directory is used.

The URL `http://www.testsite.com/drupal` is a typical base URL for a site, hosted at `www.testsite.com` and installed in a subdirectory called `drupal`. The fragments that will be used for matching when looking for `settings.php` are `www`, `testsite`, and `com`.

Here is an example of a URL and the steps Drupal will take to find the proper configuration directory:

```
http://www.testsite.com/drupal
```

1. `www.testsite.com`
2. `testsite.com`
3. `com`
4. `default`

Drupal looks for directories in the `sites` folders with names from the list and uses the first match found. It is interesting to note that you could have a configuration directory named `sites/com` that would not only handle the URL in this example, but also handle any other `.com` URL that came to your site.

Once you have created and configured a `settings.php` file in the appropriate subdirectory of `sites`, including creating the database and importing its definition, you should be able to access the new site in the normal fashion by entering its domain in your browser.

■ **Note** When running many sites off of the same codebase using the multisite functionality, you should take care to make separate directories for each site to store uploaded files. A good location for these files is in the `sites` directory, in the appropriate site-specific subdirectory: `{`*`drupal installation`*`}/sites/yoursite.com/`**`files`**.

Using Site-Specific Modules and Themes

Each site configuration can have its own site-specific modules and themes that will be made available in addition to those installed in the standard `modules` and `themes` directories. To use site-specific modules or themes, simply create a `modules` or `themes` directory within the site configuration directory. For example, if `sub.example.com` has a custom theme and a custom module that should not be accessible to other sites, the setup would look like Figure 6-2.

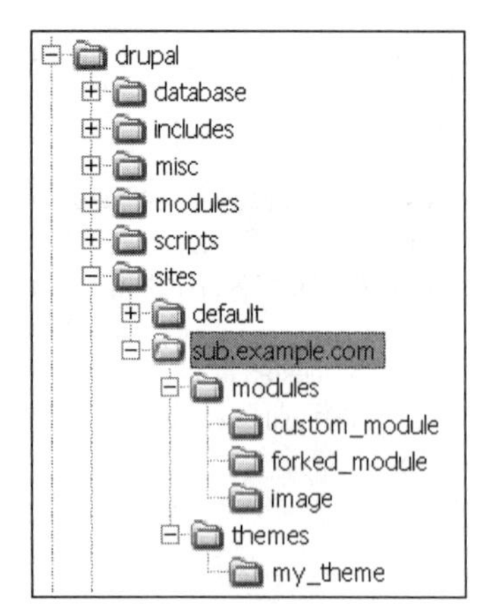

Figure 6-2. *Site-specific custom modules and themes*

■ **Note** If you install a custom module in a site-specific directory, you will need to visit `admin/modules` before Drupal will recognize it. Make sure to enable the module while you are there. Similarly, if you install a site-specific theme, you will need to visit `admin/themes` before Drupal will know it is there.

Sharing a Database Among Multiple Sites

Drupal makes great efforts to allow you to run multiple sites from the same installation. Because each installation requires its own database, the number of sites you can run on some hosting plans would be limited by the number of databases the web hosting service allows you to make. Some hosting plans allow for only one database. How can people in this situation take advantage of Drupal's multisite configuration features? Fortunately, there is a relatively simple solution. Through the use of table prefixes, you can load the tables for two or more Drupal sites into the same database and instruct each site which prefix to use, thus uniquely identifying the tables within a shared database.

In Figure 6-3, you can see how the tables are prefixed with either `db1_` or `db2_` and that the list of tables repeats. This is the setup that you can use if you need to use the same database for multiple Drupal installations.

Setting up the database with prefixed tables requires that you edit the `database.mysql` or `database.pgsql` file that is used during installation. This would be quite laborious if it had to be done by hand. Thankfully, you can use a script that automates the process.

Table
db1_access
db1_accesslog
db1_aggregator_category
db1_aggregator_category_feed
db1_aggregator_category_item
db1_aggregator_feed
db1_aggregator_item
db1_authmap
db1_blocks
db1_book
db1_boxes
db1_cache
db1_term_hierarchy
db1_term_node
db1_term_relation
db1_term_synonym
db1_url_alias
db1_users
db1_users_roles
db1_variable
db1_vocabulary
db1_vocabulary_node_types
db1_watchdog
db2_access
db2_accesslog
db2_aggregator_category
db2_aggregator_category_feed
db2_aggregator_category_item
db2_aggregator_feed
db2_aggregator_item
db2_authmap
db2_blocks
db2_book
db2_boxes
db2_cache

Figure 6-3. *One database with prefixed tables*

Setting Up the Database for Prefixed Tables

The easiest way to prepare your database definition file, whether it is the main definition file (`database.mysql` or `database.pgsql`) or the database definitions for a contributed module, is by running the `prefix.sh` script. The script accepts two parameters, and you must instruct it to direct its output to a new file. The first parameter is the prefix that you would like to prepend to all of the table names in CREATE TABLE and INSERT statements in the file, and the second parameter is the original file with the SQL statements inside. Here is an example invocation of the script for GNU/Linux systems:

```
./scripts/prefix.sh db1_ ./database/database.mysql > ./database/db1_database.mysql
```

■ **Tip** To run the prefix.sh script on Windows, use a program such as Cygwin (http://www.cygwin.com/).

When run from within the base Drupal installation directory, this will launch the script and apply the database prefix db1_ to all table names in the database.mysql file. The resulting file will be named db1_database.mysql and can be found in the database directory. Here is an excerpt from database.mysql:

```
CREATE TABLE aggregator_category_feed (
  fid int(10) NOT NULL default '0',
  cid int(10) NOT NULL default '0',
  PRIMARY KEY (fid,cid)
) TYPE=MyISAM;
```

And here is what the same portion of db1_database.mysql looks like:

```
CREATE TABLE db1_aggregator_category_feed (
  fid int(10) NOT NULL default '0',
  cid int(10) NOT NULL default '0',
  PRIMARY KEY (fid,cid)
) TYPE=MyISAM;
```

You can use the prefix.sh script to prepare the database updates for contributed modules as well. This command will add the prefix db2_ to the database definition for the Flexinode module (you must have the Flexinode module installed in modules/flexinode/, as described in Chapter 4):

```
./scripts/prefix.sh db2_ ./modules/flexinode/flexinode.pgsql >➥
./modules/flexinode/db2_flexinode.pgsql
```

After running the prefix.sh script, you can then import the generated SQL files into the database, and you will have the appropriate table prefixes.

Sharing Prefixed Tables

The key to telling Drupal about table prefixes is found in the settings.php file for your site. The $db_prefix variable is set to an empty string by default. You must edit the settings.php file and assign $db_prefix a value if you intend to use prefixed tables. For example, if you ran the prefix.sh script with the prefix db1_, you should update the $db_prefix variable like this:

```
$db_prefix = 'db1_';
```

As each site can have its own prefix, and you can import many prefixed versions of Drupal's tables into one database, this is the solution if you have only one database available from your hosting company.

The `$db_prefix` variable is more flexible, however, and can alternatively take an array of prefixes and table names. This makes a whole different set of configurations possible.

For example, the Location module (discussed in Chapter 4) comes with a `zipcodes` table that is quite large and is read-only. Drupal never writes data to this table; it uses the table only to look up locations. It would be redundant and wasteful to import this table for every Drupal site that you run, so an elegant solution is to have all of your Drupal installations share it. You can achieve this through use of the `$db_prefix` variable.

When using the array syntax for `$db_prefix`, the keys are the names of tables and the values are the prefixes:

```
$db_prefix = array(
  'table_name1'   => 'prefix1',
  'table_name2'   => 'prefix2',
  [...]
);
```

The key `default` defines the default prefix that will be used for every table whose prefix isn't explicitly defined in the array. These two definitions are equal:

```
$db_prefix = 'demo_';
$db_prefix = array('default' => 'demo_');
```

Now when you install the Location module, you can use the `prefix.sh` script to add a prefix to the `zipcodes` database table. This makes configurations like those shown in Listings 6-1 and 6-2 possible, where two different sites share a common table.

Listing 6-1. *Sharing the Zipcodes Table, Site 1*

```
$db_prefix = array(
  'default'   => 'site1_',
  'zipcodes'  => 'shared_'
);
```

Listing 6-2. *Sharing the Zipcodes Table, Site 2*

```
$db_prefix = array(
  'default'   => 'site2_',
  'zipcodes'  => 'shared_'
);
```

Using this configuration, you can have two sites in the same database, each with its own separate and independent tables, with the exception of the `zipcodes` table, which is shared. This is a very useful approach, and the next sections offer two more suggestions for interesting opportunities to share tables.

Sharing User Information

The idea of an online community can be greatly enhanced if the community spans multiple sites. One problem that plagues the Internet in this respect is the requirement that visitors must log in to every site they visit, often with different usernames and passwords. With database prefixing, you can sidestep part of this problem by allowing your visitors to use the same username and password for multiple sites. Listing 6-3 shows the `$db_prefix` definition that makes this possible.

Listing 6-3. *Sharing User-Related Tables*

```
$db_prefix = array(
  'default'      => 'site_',
  'users'        => 'shared_',
  'sessions'     => 'shared_',
  'role'         => 'shared_',
  'authmap'      => 'shared_',
  'sequences'    => 'shared_',
);
```

To share user information, follow these steps:

1. Use `prefix.sh` to create a new database definition file called `shared.mysql` with the `shared_` prefix. All you really need are the definitions for the six `shared_` tables from Listing 6-3. The rest of the table definitions can be deleted.
2. For every site that you want to share usernames and passwords, run `prefix.sh` again to create database definition files that each has a unique prefix that corresponds to an individual site.
3. Import all of the database definitions into the same database.
4. For each site, you will need a separate subdirectory in the `sites` folder, as described earlier in this chapter.
5. For each site, update `settings.php` with the code from Listing 6-3 for the `$db_prefix` variable. Update the value given for `'default'` to match the prefix of the particular site.

■ **Caution** Sharing tables between sites has profound effects in terms of how your sites behave, and some combinations of table sharing will lead to data inconsistency and broken sites. It is a technique that is recommended only for advanced users who are intimately familiar with the inner workings of Drupal.

Sharing Spam Tables

Another very effective set of tables to share are those involved with the Spam module. Because the Spam module becomes more effective the more spam it is fed, it benefits all sites involved to share spam information. Say a spammer hits Site1 with spam comments and the administrator marks them as spam. If Site2 shares the spam tables, it will be automatically protected from this spammer's attacks.

Listing 6-4 shows the `$db_prefix` variable configured to share spam tables.

Listing 6-4. *Sharing Spam Tables*

```
$db_prefix = array(
  'default'          => 'site_',
  'sequences'        => 'spam_',
  'spam_tokens'      => 'spam_',
  'spam_statistics'  => 'spam_',
  'spam_comments'    => 'spam_',
  'spam_custom'      => 'spam_',
  'spam_nodes'       => 'spam_'
);
```

Sharing Tables Across Databases

The previous solutions are useful for getting around restrictions on the number of databases that you can create, but they are less than ideal if no such restriction exists. In general, it is better to make separate databases for individual Drupal installations, as the portability and user management issues are greatly simplified.

■ **Note** The solution shown in this section is specific to MySQL databases and will not work on PostgreSQL.

If you have many Drupal sites running from separate databases, you may find cases where it is useful to share tables among databases. As noted in the previous section, a good example is the `zipcodes` table in the Location module (discussed in Chapter 4), which is read-only and quite large. Importing the `zipcodes` table into every one of your databases would be wasteful and redundant. This makes it a perfect candidate for being shared by all of your sites that use the Location module. The solution involves creating a new database dedicated to the zip code information. It's similar to the solution offered in the previous section, but preferred in situations where it is possible to create multiple databases.

The secret ingredient in this configuration lies in the `$db_prefix` variable. Instead of using the prefix as a means for identifying a prefixed table in the same database, it can be used to change databases altogether, as shown in Listing 6-5.

Listing 6-5. *Using Prefixes to Select Databases*

```
$db_prefix = array(
  'default'     => 'db_site1.',
  'zipcodes'    => 'db_zipcodes.'
);
```

Listing 6-5 assigns the default prefix to `db_site1.` (note the period after the database names). This trick works because MySQL will then look for `db_site1.some_table`, which, in effect, says, "Use `some_table` from the `db_site1` database." The value you use for the prefix corresponds to the name of the database to be used (plus the dot). This is also the database part of the `$db_url` variable in `settings.php`:

```
$db_url = 'mysql://username:password@localhost/database';
```

The caveat is that the `db_site1` and `db_zipcodes` databases will both be accessed with the same username and password pair; there is currently no method for configuring separate database connections for individual tables. Use your database administration tool or the following MySQL command to grant access to the `db_zipcodes` database for the username that you use to access the main database:

```
grant select on db_zipcodes.zipcodes to username@localhost;
```

Since the `db_zipcodes` table should be read-only, the `SELECT` privilege is sufficient. Whenever the `zipcodes` table is needed by this site, it will use the `db_zipcodes` database; in all other cases, `db_site1` will be used.

Making Backups

Whether you are running your own server or have hired a hosting company, you should carefully consider the safety of your data, and it is always prudent to expect the worst. Servers will malfunction, and hosting companies may go out of business and simply unplug their machines without warning (this actually happened to me). In these cases, your sites will simply be gone. You need to take responsibility for having all of your data and resources stored somewhere that you can get to, even if your hosting company falls off the face of the earth. This rules out depending entirely on the backup services that most hosting companies offer. Take matters into your own hands. The harder you work on a site, the more you will suffer if it gets destroyed.

A Drupal site is a complex organism. The more configuration, customization, and extending you do—whether in the form of themes, modules, or settings—the more complex and unique your site becomes. The goals of your backup strategy should be twofold:

- You should strive to never lose any data.
- You should be able to set up a clone of your site as quickly as possible, ideally by having a mirror image of the site waiting in the wings for the disaster to strike.

Achieving a backup plan that fully satisfies both of these goals is not trivial, and the instructions I provide here do not give a complete solution for either goal. However, this discussion will highlight the issues at hand and provide a solution that can work with small sites, where it might not make sense to implement more elaborate solutions.

Any Drupal site has two main components: the files on the file system and the database. Of the two, the database is by far the easiest component to back up. The file system is more complex for the following reasons:

- Its properties will vary based on operating system.
- It contains the files that are uploaded to your site. These can accumulate and represent a significant amount of data.

- For advanced installations, the file system may contain soft links or may keep files in far-flung corners of the directory structure. Depending on how you have configured your site, it may be impossible to simply make a copy of one directory and be finished.

Despite the complexity of the file system, you won't be able to restore your site from a disaster without a copy of it, so your strategy must include backing up both your database and your file system.

Making Database Backups

Making a database backup is not only the easier of the two backup tasks that need to be done, but it also has many helpful tools available to ease the burden. The most common solution involves exporting the contents of the database as a SQL dump, and then moving the dump to an off-server location (such as your local machine). Here, I'll review three database backup tools, which are available through the Database Administrator module, CivicSpace Labs, and phpMyAdmin or phpPgAdmin.

Database Administrator Module

The Database Administration module (dba), introduced in Chapter 4 and available from `http://drupal.org/project/dba`, can help you keep a backup copy of your data by using a `cron.php` task to generate a database dump, zip or tar it, and mail it to you. This is a super option as long as your database isn't too large and your e-mail service can handle large attachments. When your data starts taking up many megabytes of space in zipped format, you'll need another solution, but the dba module will fill the gap until that time. See Chapter 4 for details on configuring and using the dba module.

Database Dump CivicSpace Style

CivicSpace Labs offers a nice script for GNU/Linux users that makes dumping your MySQL database quite easy. You can download the file, named `drupalsqldump`, from the CivicSpace Labs web page (`http://civicspacelabs.org/home/files/drupalsqldump`), or you can use the `wget` tool to load it directly onto your server:

```
wget http://civicspacelabs.org/home/files/drupalsqldump -O drupalsqldump.sh
```

After running this command, you have a file named `drupalsqldump.sh` in the current directory. To execute the file, you need to run this command, which makes it executable:

```
chmod +x drupaldumpsql.sh
```

The script takes the path to your site's configuration file (`settings.php`) as an argument, and you need to direct the output to the appropriate backup file:

```
path/to/drupalsqldump.sh /path/to/sites/yourdomain/settings.php > backup.sql
```

You can then use FTP or SCP to transfer the `backup.sql` file to an off-site location.

For more information about using the `drupalsqldump` tool from CivicSpace Labs, see `http://civicspacelabs.org/home/upgrade/testsite/commandline`.

phpMyAdmin and phpPgAdmin

Anyone using phpMyAdmin (`http://www.phpmyadmin.net/home_page/`) or phpPgAdmin (`http://phppgadmin.sourceforge.net/`) to administer the database might be satisfied with the export functionality that these programs offer. If you decide to rely on these tools for your database backup, you must have iron discipline and make the backup on a regular schedule.

For details on making database backups with phpMyAdmin or phpPgAdmin, try these tutorials:

- For phpMyAdmin: `http://codex.wordpress.org/WordPress_Backups#Backing_Up_Your_WordPress_Site`
- For phpPgAdmin: `http://phppgadmin.sourceforge.net/?page=faq`

Making File System Backups

The database backup is only half of the backup equation. Without the files stored on the server, your site can never be completely restored after a disaster. The files in question fall into two general categories: those used by Drupal to run and present your site, and those uploaded to the site as content.

The files in the first category include the scripts that were delivered with the Drupal installation, contributed modules that you may have installed, customized themes, and the configuration file (`settings.php`). From the standpoint of a backup strategy, these files are relatively easy to deal with. Their volume doesn't increase even as site traffic grows, and you know every time they change since you make the changes yourself. If you simply take the time to manually copy these files to your local machine every time you install something new or make a change, you're already ahead of the game.

The files in the second category—the files uploaded as content to your site—can be more problematic. They can change regularly as your site visitors upload more and more content, and their volume can become quite large. (My personal blog, for example, amassed 1GB of images in slightly over a year of operation.) The strategy for making backups of these files must be different from the strategy for backing up script files, because of the frequency of change and because of the practical limitations of moving large masses of data across the network.

The Filesystem Backup module and the GNU/Linux `cp` command are two tools that you can use to make file system backups.

Filesystem Backup Module

The Filesystem Backup module (`http://www.drupal.org/project/fbu`) was written to deal with the problem of identifying newly added or modified files on the file system, as well as moving them off-site to a safe location. This module sends any new or modified files to the administrator as zipped attachments to an e-mail message. The attachments are all uniquely numbered, and when they are extracted in the order received, will re-create the entire Drupal installation on your local machine. This is a way of automating the backup process for people who may not have sufficient server access (in shared hosting environments) to implement an automated backup routine using shell scripts.

■ **Note** The Filesystem Backup module will not work on some shared hosting environments due to its dependency on third-party libraries from the PEAR project. Refer to the module's `README.txt` file for the latest information on which libraries these are, and how to install them. In the case that your host doesn't have the required PEAR libraries, you can investigate using shell commands to make the backups on the server and moving the backups using FTP or SCP.

GNU/Linux cp Command

The GNU/Linux `cp` command will copy your site's files (scripts and uploaded files) to a backup directory. Make sure the backup directory exists beforehand. Here's the syntax:

```
cp -R -u --copy-contents /path/to/site/* /path/to/site/.htaccess /path/to/backup
```

The first path, `/path/to/site/*` will copy all of the files in your site's directory except `.htaccess`. The second path, `/path/to/site.htaccess`, takes care of the `.htaccess` file. The third path is the directory (which must already exist) where the backup is to be stored. The `-R` flag sets the command to be recursive. The `-u` flag states that if a file already exists in the destination folder (from a previous backup, for example), it will be replaced only if the source is newer. This makes repeated applications of the `cp` command more efficient and better suited for an automated backup plan. Depending on whether you are using symbolic links, you need to decide whether to set the `--dereference` or `--no-dereference` flags. The `--dereference` flag will follow and copy symbolic links.

Moving Your Backup

Once you have created backup copies of your site's files and database on the server, it is imperative that you move the backup off your server and have it available to you locally. The most straightforward strategy is to zip or tar.gz the backup copies into an archive and use FTP or SCP to download them from the server.

Most hosting companies also offer some sort of backup facility, and it is usually worthwhile to talk with their representatives and get assistance setting up your backup plan. Any hosting plan worthy of running a complex CMS like Drupal will allow you to have FTP access. See Chapter 1 for some tips on using FTP to move files to and from your server.

■ **Tip** Advanced Linux users should consider using `rsync` (available for download from `http://samba.anu.edu.au/rsync/download.html`) to assist in making remote copies of their backups. See `http://www.mikerubel.org/computers/rsync_snapshots/` for more information.

Maintaining a Test Site

As your Drupal site grows and develops a community of users who contribute content, it will become increasingly important that the site be available and online, running problem-free, at all times. At the same time, you will be constantly thinking of new ways to use and expand your site to enhance its value. Many of these enhancements will come in the form of extra modules, but you may also want to tweak the themes or do custom programming. No matter what the details are, if you intend to add features to a production site, you need a test site.

A test site is a functional clone of your production site that serves as a test bed for the changes you plan on making on the production site. It gives you a chance to experiment without alienating your users when the experiment goes wrong. Although it seems like a lot of work to set up and maintain a test site, it is very much in your best interest to do so.

The basic steps to make a test site are as follows:

1. Make a backup of your existing files and database, as described in the previous section.
2. Copy the files to a `test-site` subfolder or to an alternate document root (using a virtual host) on your server or to a test server (this can be your local machine).
3. Create a test database and import the data from your live site.
4. Update configuration settings for the test site.

You can host a test site several places:

- The best scenario is on a dedicated test server that is a clone of the production environment.
- If you are using managed hosting and can create subdomains, use a subdomain and a separate document root.
- If you are using managed hosting and cannot create subdomains, you can use a subdirectory within your main document root.
- The easiest method is to use your local machine. In this case, it is best if your local machine is configured similarly to the production server.

Most of the issues you will be testing can be replicated without needing to consider issues like operating system and installed libraries, but some functionality, such as working with e-mail features (see the Moblog, Mass Mailer, and Mailhandler modules) and functionality that depends on third-party libraries (image manipulation, working with media files, and PEAR libraries) will make it important that your test environment be as close to the production environment as possible. In these cases, it is usually most practical to set up a test site on the production server (unless you have the resources to have a dedicated test server; in which case, it should be configured exactly the same as the production server).

I'll assume for the rest of the discussion that you will simply create a subdirectory on your production server, as this is the easiest, does not require any Apache or web server configuration, and guarantees that the test environment is the same as the production environment.

Creating the test_site Subdirectory

To store your test site's files, create a subdirectory on your server named `test_site`:

```
yourdomain.com/test_site/
```

It is also a good idea to hide the `test_site` directory from the public by making the directory password-protected, using web server authentication or the Drupal Securesite module (`http://drupal.org/project/securesite`).

■ **Tip** The Securesite module allows you to password-protect your entire site so that only authorized users can access it. Permissions are role-based. This is a good solution if you want to protect your test site and allow a group of beta testers to have access to it.

Creating a Copy of the Site Database

Refer to the previous section earlier for instructions on creating a backup copy of your Drupal database. The backup copy of your live site can be used as the basis for creating your test site.

Next, create a new empty database and import the backup database into it. Chapter 1 gives you full details for installing a Drupal database. The only difference is that instead of using the `database.mysql` or `database.pgsql` file for the definitions, you use the backup of your live site.

Copying the Files to the test_site directory

The next step is to copy all of the files from the production site into the `test_site` directory. For GNU/Linux users, the easiest way to do this is by using shell access to the server and running the following command:

```
cp -u --copy-contents /path/to/site/* /path/to/site/.htaccess /path/to/test_site
```

Updating the Test Site's Configuration Settings

The `settings.php` file determines which database to use and the `$base_url` for the site. It is in a subdirectory of the `sites` folder, and because you just copied it along with all of the files from the production site, it still has the details for the production site. You will need to find all of the settings that are specific to the production site and adjust them to work with the test site.

The first of these settings is the database connection information. Update this variable with the test user, test password, and test database name for the database you created for the test site.

```
$db_url = mysql://test_user:test_pass@localhost/test_site_db';
```

Because the test site is in a different folder than the main site, you will need to update the `$base_url` variable as well. Here is what it should look like for a test site that is in a subfolder of the main site:

```
$base_url = 'http://www.yourdomain.com/test_site';
```

These are typically the only two adjustments you will need to make to the test's sites configuration settings.

■ **Note** For detailed instructions for setting up Drupal test sites, see `http://drupal.org/creating-drupal-test-sites`.

Accessing the Test Site

Navigate to `http://www.yoursite.com/test_site`, and you should see a working copy of your live site. You are now set up to try new modules, adjust the theme, and test new code on a test site—without affecting your main site.

When you are happy with the changes you have made on the test site, you can deploy them to the production site with confidence, as you have already tested your work. But do note that "confidence" should be tempered with a dose of paranoia. Always be vigilant for changes that will be hard to reverse or that depend on the state of the database. You can be truly confident only if the backup of your production site is recent and you are adept at hunting down and isolating the unexpected problems that seem to be so common in software development.

Updating Drupal

Drupal is under constant development from a growing community of programmers around the world. Bugs get fixed and features are added. Historically, major point releases (4.5, 4.6, 4.7, and so on) have appeared every six months, usually with several minor point releases following (4.5.5 was released shortly before the time of this writing, approximately one year after 4.5.0 was released).

Eventually, you will probably want to update your site to take advantage of improvements available in a new release. How smoothly a site update goes depends a lot on your level of preparation. This section shows you how to upgrade a Drupal site, with some tips on making the process as easy as possible.

■ **Note** This section describes all of the general steps that you need to take to update your Drupal installation. For precise instructions, refer to the documentation found on `Drupal.org` pertaining to the actual release to which you are updating.

Tracking Your Changes

The first piece of advice concerning updating addresses how you manage your Drupal site prior to the update. Drupal is attractive due to its extensibility (contributed modules and themes) and for its ease of customization (hacking the code and writing your own themes or modules). It is a fantastic solution for creating unique and one-of-a-kind web sites. The problem with unique, one-of-a-kind web sites is that they defy the efforts of the core development team to provide a clean update path when new versions are released.

To secure your update path and to avoid the situation where you accidentally delete changes that you made while customizing your site, you need to take the initiative to track your changes. Your web site needs some sort of journal or diary to record all of its major events. This can be as simple as a `SITE-CHANGELOG.txt` file that you maintain, diligently noting every line of code you alter and every module you install, to a full version control system such as CVS (`http://www.nongnu.org/cvs/`), Subversion (`http://subversion.tigris.org/`), or Monotone (`http://venge.net/monotone/`).

■Tip A far better solution that a manually edited `SITE-CHANGELOG.txt` file is to keep your site under version control of some sort. See the Drupal handbook for tips on using CVS for this purpose (`http://drupal.org/node/5123`).

Suppose that you installed Drupal for the first time shortly after the 4.6 release. You created a stunning image gallery with your digital photos and worked hard to promote your site. Before long, you started getting large numbers of visitors, but noticed that performance of the site was degrading under the load. Upon inspecting your server log files, you come to the conclusion that people hotlinking to your images were creating an unacceptable strain on the server, and you search `Drupal.org` for possible solutions. You find the answer after reading an informative post (`http://drupal.org/node/20716`) by someone who had the same problem, and proceed to edit the `.htaccess` file with the changes suggested. All is fine, and you make no other changes to your site for six months. Then, attracted by the new features in Drupal 4.7, you decide to update. You follow this bit of advice straight from the `INSTALL.txt` file that comes with Drupal:

```
3. Remove all the old Drupal files. Then unpack the new Drupal
   files into the directory that you run Drupal from.
```

The update works, your site is running 4.7, you attract even more users, and your server is once again crushed by people hotlinking to your photographs. What happened? Somewhere in the six months that passed between Drupal versions, you forgot about the small change you made to `.htaccess`, and as part of the update process, replaced your custom file with the generic version delivered with Drupal. No big deal—just a couple hours lost. But now suppose that you had made dozens of similar tweaks and changes. If there were a record of all the changes you had made, at least you would be able to re-create the changes on the updated site. A version tracking system includes tools that let you merge these changes into the newer source code.

The need for tracking your changes should be clear. Drupal cannot provide this service for you, so you'll need to come up with a creative solution that suits your needs and working style.

■Tip Record the date when you download Drupal. This date will help you decide which steps in the update script need to be executed. While a new version of Drupal will attempt to detect this information automatically, you won't be able to double-check this step if you don't yourself know when you downloaded and installed the old version.

Testing the Update

The next piece of advice regarding updating Drupal is to use a test site and perform the update on it before trying it on your production site. Having a clone of your production site is a great way to test updates and lets you discover potential problems in advance, saving you and your site visitors the headaches of having a broken production site.

In addition to the test site, you should also create a full backup of your site prior to attempting any update. You need to know that whatever happens during the update, you can revert to the functioning prior state of the site quickly if problems arise. Refer to the earlier sections in this chapter that cover creating backups and setting up a test site.

Performing the Update

In order to explain why these elaborate precautions I just recommended are vital, let me describe what actually happens when you update your Drupal site to a new major point version (4.6 to 4.7, for example). A web application, such as Drupal, is a combination of code (the scripts that run the site), state (the data in the database), and resources (uploaded files on your file system). The web application is dependent on all three of these elements working together; changing one without changing the other two to match will simply break everything.

During an update, the first step is always to replace the code on your site. This is the only aspect of the three-part equation that the Drupal developers can control, as the state of your database and the resources on your file system are unique to your site. Once the code on your site has been replaced, your site is broken. The database and file system resources don't match what the code is expecting. In order to fix this, Drupal is provided with an `update.php` script in the base directory of the installation. It is responsible for triggering the update process, whereby the database and file system resources are systematically altered and updated until they match what the code is expecting. Depending on how intensely Drupal was developed since the last time you updated, these changes can be quite severe.

When everything works well, updating is as easy as unpacking the new files and running the update script. If something doesn't work, however, and the update process stalls in the middle, your database and file system resources are left in an undefined state, and you may or may not be successful in completing the update through debugging and making changes manually. In this case, you will be very happy if you have a backup from which you can restore your old site, and very unhappy if you skipped that step.

Here are the steps for updating.

Review Changes for the Update

Review the list of changes for the new release. Sometimes, new features are added that make features of your old site redundant. For example, the Upload module that was added to version 4.6 made the contributed module of a similar name redundant, and people using the contributed module needed to update their uploaded files to use the new core feature.

Inventory Your Contributed Modules

Take inventory of your contributed modules and check to see that they have also been updated. You can do this by monitoring the downloads page (`http://drupal.org/project/Modules`) for the new release to which you wish to update. If the module doesn't appear on the list, it hasn't been updated yet.

Since the contributed modules each represent an independent software project and are only loosely coupled to the core development cycle, it is critical that you consider the update path for each and every one that you have installed before deciding to update. If, for example, your site is fundamentally dependent on the foo module, and the foo module maintainer is no longer actively working on the module, you may not want to update, as losing the use of this one module would significantly detract from your site.

Thankfully, the most popular contributed modules are actively maintained and usually keep up with major Drupal releases. In the worst case, there are always instructions (`http://drupal.org/upgrading`) for updating modules, so you could try to do it yourself, or hire someone to do it for you (`http://drupal.org/drupal-services`).

■Note The Drupal development philosophy mandates that the top priority is making the current release as good as it can be and worrying about updating the contributed themes and modules later. Backward compatibility is *not* guaranteed.

Deactivate Contributed Modules

Navigate to `admin/modules` and deactivate contributed modules. Contributed modules can interact with your core Drupal site in complex ways, and should thus be disabled during the core update process. Each contributed module will need to be updated on its own, later. You can find instructions for how to do this in the documentation for the individual modules.

Log In to Your Site

Log in to your site as administrator (user number 1). It is important that you have a browser (with cookies enabled) window open that stores the cookie for an open session with this user. Without this, you will be denied the permission to run the update script.

If you need to run the update script without being able to log in as the administrator (which happens when people forget to log in before starting the update process, or otherwise skip this step), you can turn off the access check by editing the `update.php` script on your server. Find the following lines of code:

```
// Enforce access checking?
$access_check = TRUE;
```

Change `TRUE` to `FALSE`. Now you can run the script without logging in. If you turn off the access check in the update script, any user on the Internet can run it. Since this could have a potentially disastrous effect on your site, you must, at a minimum, edit the code to read `TRUE`, once again. A more secure precaution would be to remove the `update.php` file from your server altogether after you have finished updating your site.

■Caution If you disable the `$access_check` variable in `update.php` for the sake of an update, make sure to enable it again (set its value to `TRUE`) when you are finished.

Replace Old Script Files

The next step is to replace the old script files with the new distribution that you downloaded from `Drupal.org`. This can be accomplished most easily by moving the Drupal `tar.gz` file into the base of your installation and running the `untar` command. Here are the GNU/Linux commands to run from a shell to get the Drupal distribution and untar it (replace `x.x.x` with the version number to which you are updating):

```
wget http://drupal.org/files/projects/drupal-x.x.x.tar.gz
tar -zxvf drupal-x.x.x.tar.gz
```

If your `settings.php` file is in the `settings/default` folder, make sure to have a backup on hand, since the preceding command will overwrite it. If your `settings.php` file is in a folder named after the site you are running, such as `yoursite.com`, this will not be a problem, and you can run the `tar` command without concern. This is an important point, as the upgrade script depends on the `settings.php` file (`conf.php` in Drupal 4.5 or earlier) to establish the database connection. It would be inconvenient for you to delete or overwrite this file, so double-check that it is still in place before moving on to the next step.

Caution The instructions that are offered in the `UPDATE.txt` file say to "Remove all the old Drupal files. . . ." This does *not* mean that you should remove the `files` directory or its contents, or any custom themes or modules that you have developed. It means "Remove the files that came with your original Drupal download."

Run the Update Script

Access `update.php` in your browser. Click the link *run the database upgrade script.* The update script is a chronological set of changes to be made, starting from early Drupal versions all the way to the most current version. Each change has a date associated with it. Drupal will look to see what your update history has been (the last time you ran this update script, a value that is stored in the database) and will suggest a starting date for your update process.

If Drupal is unable to recognize the correct date, this is where your records will prove to be useful. When did you install Drupal? When was the last time you altered the database schema in any way? Pick a date that precedes or matches your installation or the last update.

When you've settled on a date, click *Update*, and the script will run. The update script is primarily focused on updating the database schema. Typical output for a successful update looks like the screen shown in Figure 6-4.

Drupal database update

- main page
- administration pages

2005-04-08: first update since Drupal 4.6.0 release

```
ALTER TABLE {vocabulary} ADD tags tinyint(3) unsigned default '0' NOT NULL
OK
```

2005-04-10

```
ALTER TABLE {sessions} ADD cache int(11) NOT NULL default '0' AFTER timestamp
OK
```

2005-04-11

```
ALTER TABLE {boxes} DROP INDEX title
OK
ALTER TABLE {boxes} ADD INDEX title (title)
OK
```

Figure 6-4. *The Drupal update screen*

Test Your Site

After running the update.php script, you should test your site (with the contributed modules still turned off) and confirm that things are alright. If you find any bugs or issues at this point, it is better to address them before getting to the business of updating the contributed modules, as everything is dependent on the core system.

Update Contributed Modules

Once the Drupal core is up and running, it is time to update the contributed modules. Make sure you download the version of the modules that corresponds to your new, updated Drupal installation. For each module, look for README.txt, UPDATE.txt, and INSTALL.txt files to address how to go about updating to the current version.

The difficulty here is that it is up to the module's author(s) and the community at large to provide the information and scripts necessary to do an update. Expect to find different levels of completeness and support among the contributed modules. For popular modules by well-respected module authors, this won't be a problem, and most of the time, updates will be relatively painless. Regardless, you should update your contributed modules one at a time, testing the functionality of each one before moving on to the next. In the ideal case, you will do this on your test site before attempting the updates on a production site.

Maintain Your Updated Site

Now that you have updated your site, don't forget to plan for the future: make a backup of your database and your file system, write to your log what changes you've made (or check the new version into your version control software), and use the backup to set up a test site!

Getting Drupal Support

Documentation isn't worth anything if you don't know where to find it, and sometimes all the documentation in the world isn't as useful as being able to ask someone for advice. Knowing where to look and whom to ask will greatly enhance your success and enjoyment as a Drupal site administrator.

Not surprisingly, the main resource for Drupal documentation and help is `Drupal.org`. Here is a quick tour of the most important resources to be found there.

Projects: Keeping up with the latest releases and browsing the various offerings for modules and themes is fun and informative. Projects include the Drupal project itself, contributed modules, contributed themes, and translations. Each of these subprojects can be browsed by the Drupal version you're interested in (4.6, 4.7, cvs, and so forth). You can see the entire range of offerings on the Projects page at `Drupal.org` (`http://drupal.org/project`).

Bugs, issues and feature requests: Did you find something wrong with Drupal or a contributed module? Do you have a great idea for how a component can be improved? Perhaps there is a feature you are missing? For these cases, please file an issue (`http://drupal.org/node/add/project_issue`). Make sure to specify the component and version to which it applies, as well as how you found the problem to begin with. This is also the proper way to submit patches to existing code.

Forums: The forums on Drupal.org (`http://drupal.org/forum`) are the main place to turn when you want to ask "how-to" questions, assess whether Drupal is right for you, or present your newly created Drupal-powered site. The forums are also a great place to look for opportunities to use your Drupal wisdom to answer questions for others who might be just starting out. The forums form the backbone of the Drupal user community.

Drupal handbooks: The Drupal handbooks (`http://drupal.org/handbooks`) are the official documentation for the project. They are written and contributed by normal users who have taken the time to learn about Drupal and write about their experiences for the benefit of others. Because the text is covered by a Creative Commons Attribution-ShareAlike2.0 license (`http://creativecommons.org/licenses/by-sa/2.0/`), you are free to make copies of the work and use it in a very flexible manner. Drupal aids you in this by offering several export features, including printer-friendly, DocBook XML, and OPML views. If you want to contribute to the documentation, all you need is a Drupal user account.

Mailing lists: Several Drupal-related mailing lists are available (`http://drupal.org/mailing-lists`), ranging from a monthly newsletter to focused discussions on support, documentation, infrastructure, and development. If you need help, join the support list. Volunteers from the community try to keep up with everyone who needs help getting Drupal going, and your expert voice is always welcome. If you want to discuss the way the Drupal.org web site is put together, or how to best document the Drupal software, join the infrastructure or documentation lists. If you want to participate in a discussion on how to program Drupal and see the latest discussions about where the Drupal codebase is going, the development list is for you. Each mailing list also has an archive that you can search to catch up on previous discussions or find answers to your questions.

DrupalDocs: If you are keen on learning how to program Drupal modules or customize Drupal code, you'll be interested in exploring DrupalDocs (`http://drupaldocs.org/`). That is where the Drupal API references are kept, showing you all of Drupal's functions and explaining how to use them. The documentation also includes excellent discussions and articles that describe the way the code is put together, explore the various subsystems such as the database abstraction layer and the menu system, and give plenty of code examples to help you write your own custom modules. (See `http://drupaldocs.org/api/head/group`.)

CVS repositories: All Drupal code is kept in revision control with CVS. If you have a CVS client, you can check out the code directly from CVS (`http://drupal.org/node/320`). Furthermore, the repositories are displayed online as web pages (`http://cvs.drupal.org/viewcvs/drupal/`), meaning you can browse through the many files that make up Drupal, see how they've evolved in time, and check when the latest changes were made. If you are a programmer and have written a Drupal module or theme that you want to share with the community, you can apply for commit access to the contributions repository (`http://drupal.org/cvs-account`). Make sure to describe in detail what you wish to contribute; expressing your intentions clearly, or perhaps pointing to a demonstration of the code you want to commit, will speed the process of getting your CVS account.

■ **Note** One of my personal favorite pages on the `Drupal.org` site is the history of CVS commits (`http://drupal.org/cvs`). To some of us, seeing what code is being worked on and how Drupal is evolving is daily reading.

IRC: Many of the most active members of the Drupal community can be found on one of the IRC channels dedicated to Drupal at Freenode.net (`http://freenode.net/`). Join either the `#drupal-support` (for help with using and administering Drupal) or the `#drupal` (for development) channels to meet with Drupal experts and enthusiasts for real-time chatting.

Planet Drupal: A great way to stay on top of what is happening in the Drupal world is to visit the Planet Drupal page (`http://drupal.org/planet`). Planet Drupal is a special collection of feeds aggregated from the personal blogs of many individuals who are active in the Drupal community.

The Drupal Community

Building a successful online community is a challenge. How do you know when you've succeeded? Statistics from your server logs won't tell you—plenty of sites on the Internet get thousands of visits a day but couldn't be considered communities. Likewise, you can't measure your community based on how many posts or comments are on a site. I've visited many sites and left comments, never to return and read another article or see if someone has replied to my comment. And there you have the first clues as to what makes a successful online community: can you participate in some way? Do you want to come back? Are you interested in seeing how others in the community react to what you've said or done? Are you interested in what the others in the community are doing?

The vibrant and growing Drupal community is one that spills over the confines of Drupal.org. There is no doubt that Drupal.org plays a central and crucial role in forming and defining the Drupal community, but there is so much more to it than that. Several other sites focus exclusively on Drupal's software (http://www.bryght.com, http://www.civicspace➥labs.org, and http://www.civicactions.com), and these must be included in any definition of the Drupal community. In fact, anyone who writes on the Web about Drupal becomes part of the community via aggregator sites like Technorati and Planet Drupal.

When people write about Drupal on the Web, and especially if they allow visitors to leave comments on their site, they are initiating a conversation. It is common for people, having found a blog post about Drupal, to leave comments on the blog engaging the blog owner, perhaps answering questions, providing guidance, sharing resources, and so on. This type of web-based dialogue highlights the attractive power of the community, as well as the effectiveness of tools such as feed aggregation.

What are the functional elements of the Drupal community? There is a central place (Drupal.org), a cause (great software), a community awareness (the aggregated writings about Drupal from around the Web), and motivated individuals who believe in the cause.

The Drupal community is not just virtual. The people who identify themselves most strongly with the Drupal community organize and attend real-life events. Whether at conferences, user groups, or ad hoc meetings, members of the Drupal community often take the opportunity to get together. When they do, they usually share their experiences online with the community using Drupal.org, thus bridging the gap between the virtual and the real-world aspects of the community. This would suggest that online communities benefit when the tools are available for organizing real-world events. This includes calendars for dates and times, private messages for working out details, and a way for everyone to be involved by adding to a web site and sharing their ideas. This can be seen in other online communities as well. For example, Craigslist (http://www.craigslist.org/) is very much about making real-world contacts happen.

Communities reward members who make positive contributions and discourage abusers. This seems to happen naturally due to human nature, but successful online communities give the humans tools to express their nature. The reward of having other community members appreciate your posts and respond to your comments seems to be great enough to motivate people to keep coming back and become more and more involved in the community.

A community preserves an identity. Drupal rewards its developers by tracking how many CVS commits they've made, or by letting people announce what roles they've played in developing or supporting Drupal. You can also monitor a particular member and closely follow what he or she has posted. A long-term sense of identity on a site is critical for the individuals to stay motivated to come back and participate.

Drupal, which has focused on community building since its inception, gives you the tools to shape your community the way you want it. While you can think about Drupal in terms of its usefulness as a content management system, or its practicality as a publishing platform, or its suitability as a web application framework, the most Drupal-like question to ask might be, “What kind of online community do I want to create?”

PART 2

phpBB

CHAPTER 7

Introducing phpBB

If you look at the web sites that attract immense traffic consistently, you'll find that their respective webmasters have implemented a message board of some kind to augment the content they serve. These days, it's surprising to run into a web site that *doesn't* host forums of some kind! Forums are an easy and popular way to implement a community on your site. Properly run, forums can reap considerable rewards in terms of first-time visitors and, most importantly, repeat traffic. Running a forum on your web site can be a very engaging experience, with the opportunity to collaborate with people all over the world right on your site; best of all, you can do it for free with an immensely popular Open Source forum script known as *phpBB*.

This chapter will discuss common terminology used in the world of message board administration, a few important habits to pick up to help drive your community to success, items to take into consideration when choosing the software your message board should run on, and an overview of why you should use phpBB as your forum solution.

The Basics of Running Your Own Forums

To make your message board venture succeed, you'll want to have a grasp of the important concepts of successful message board administration.

Some Forum Administration Lingo

Message boards, like anything else, come with their own brand of lingo. I'll take you through some of the more common terminology that you'll encounter in the world of forum administration. If you're experienced with message boards, feel free to skip this section (or skim it for fun). If not, these are some good terms for you to get acquainted with, as you'll undoubtedly be exposed to them.

Forum: An organizational area for posts on your message board with a common theme.

Archive: A special type of read-only forum that holds old posts generally deemed worthy of keeping around by a moderator.

Category: A group of forums that (ideally!) share a common theme, typically displayed on the front page of a message board.

Topic/Thread: A string of related posts that live in a forum.

Administrator: This person controls all aspects of the message boards, including the forum software and possibly even the underlying server hardware.

Moderator: A user the administrator entrusts with running the day-to-day operations of a specific forum. Moderators may be experts in the field their forum may cover, for example.

Super moderator: A user the administrator designates who can moderate all of the forums on the message board. Some administrators choose to make all their moderators super moderators, while others give this title to possibly one other person.

Signature/"Sig": Users can optionally affix a signature to each of their posts, which may contain a quote, an image known as a *tag*, or pretty much anything else they want.

Hack: Also known as a *modification* (or simply *mod*), hacks are not as bad as they may sound. Hacks generally add new features to the board. This old-hat terminology lives on despite the mainstream media's confusion of *hackers* with *crackers*, which are criminals. Don't get the two confused. A phpBB hacker generally implements lots of new features for the board software and releases them to the public.

Script kiddie: Script kiddies are crackers that exploit and deface web sites and message boards for fun and bragging rights. Sometimes, script kiddies can cause lots of damage. As a message board administrator, you should secure your board as if you are under constant threat from script kiddies and other, more sophisticated, threats, because you are.

Troll: A user generally intent on causing havoc on your board. Trolls like to start arguments or generally act disrespectful to everyone. They have existed on the Internet (and in real life, for that matter!) since the beginning of time. Get used to them! You'll see more than your share while you administer a message board.

Bot: Bots are a relatively new phenomenon in the fight for message board security; the typical bot registers new accounts on message boards automatically in order to boost their search engine rankings. Some bots are sophisticated enough to spam certain types of message boards. If you enable the proper validation in phpBB, you won't have to deal with these. (I'll cover defense against bots at length in Chapter 10.)

Organizing Your Forums Logically

Time is money, and you will need to put a lot of time into your message board to make it worth your while and be something special. Generally, you need to pay very close attention to how you decide to organize your forums. Keep your forums in line with the main content of the rest of your web site. People are on your site because they are interested in what your site has to say on a particular topic, and having a forum for their discourse will be a boon to your traffic (and repeat traffic). It's a good idea to make a map of your site's content (if you don't have one already) and model your forums and categories against that map.

Respecting Your Bread and Butter: Your User Base

It's very important that you visit your forum frequently to keep up with what is going on. Abandoning your board is the worst thing for it. People feel comfortable seeing their "fearless leader" stick around their board, so they don't feel left out in the cold. If your members report problems, make an honest attempt to resolve the issues. Make them feel at home in your community. It's a good idea to welcome them aboard, as this creates a personal rapport. Always act in a professional manner, and remember that you only get one chance to make a first impression. Your users ultimately define the difference between a successful message board and a miserable failure—if you keep that in mind, and act accordingly, you'll have done well for yourself.

Keeping Things Familiar

You would do very well to make sure your forums visually resemble the rest of your site. Ideally, you will be able to create a template that closely matches the design of the rest of your site, create forums whose topics closely reflect whatever services or products your site may deliver, and apply it to your community. Keeping continuity between the two areas of your site not only will help your users feel right at home, but could also have the added effect of further visits to your site's main content, which can only help. Continuity is a must for professionalism on your site. Leaving the default theme will not necessarily make your site stand out and be appealing.

Keeping Things Fresh

At the very least, it's critical that you keep your forum software current. If you don't, you open yourself up to security problems and a nightmare that no forum administrator wants to experience: a board hijacking. Additionally, introducing new features via modifications (also known as *mods* or *hacks*) every once in a while is a smart idea. You could also add new smilies from time to time to appease your users. People love new stuff, and it keeps them coming back every time.

Using a Quality Script

Finally, it's important that the forum script you choose is of high quality. Forum scripts that are buggy detract from the users' experience. Make sure your script is easily maintained and upgraded to help facilitate running a well-patched and secure board, and make sure your script has a large support network in case something goes wrong. Lucky for you, I've made this search easy, as I'm covering such a script in this part.

Enter phpBB

The first version of phpBB grew out of the need for a PHP-based message board script that visually resembled the gold standard of message boards in 2000, Infopop's Ultimate Bulletin Board. The board caught on with users as a simple, easily run script, and the rest is history. Since those humble beginnings, phpBB's popularity has grown tremendously, with a vast online community of developers, gurus, and code hackers. It's been translated into over 25 languages, and had over a thousand modifications and templates coded for it. People have coded entire content management systems around it, showing how popular phpBB is with the online community. Figure 7-1 illustrates a default installation of phpBB 2.0.

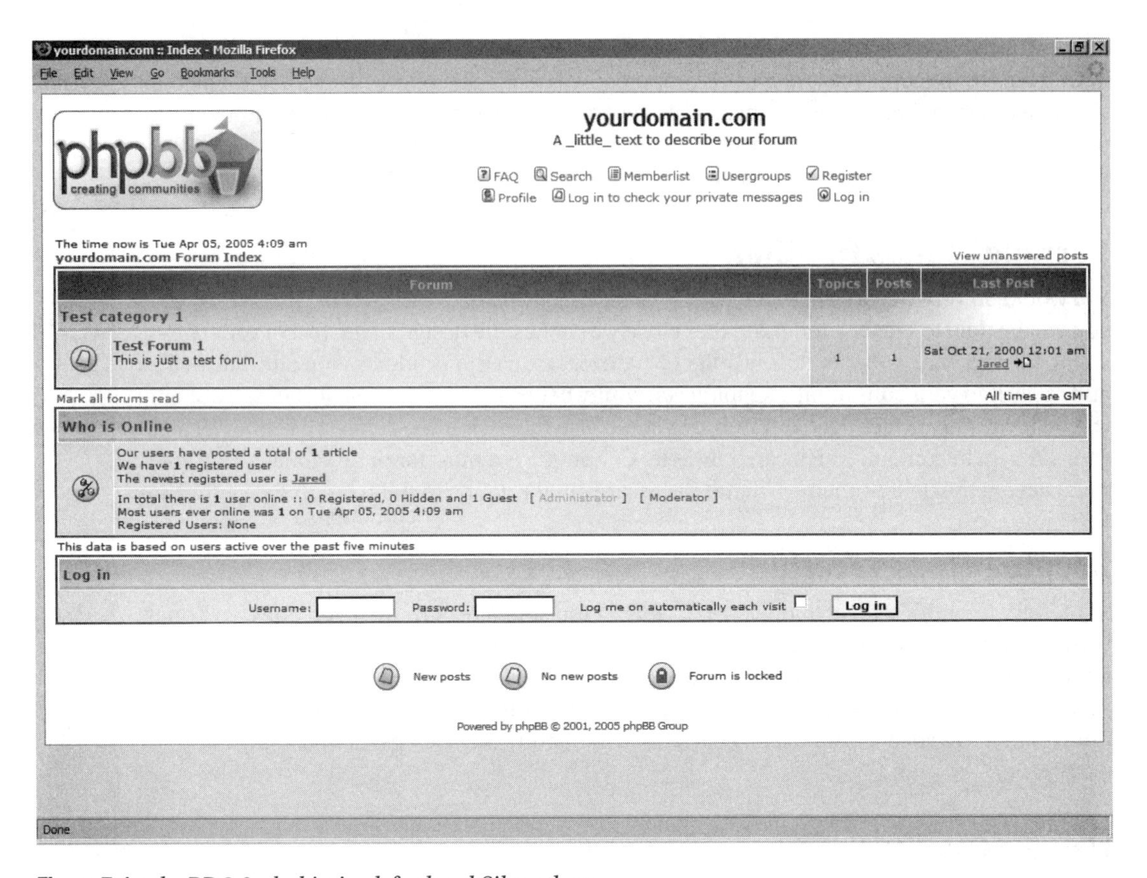

Figure 7-1. *phpBB 2.0, clad in its default subSilver theme*

The Million-Dollar Question: Why Use phpBB?

An almost overwhelming array of forum solutions are available on the Internet—the question is, why use phpBB?

> **phpBB is very easy to get started with**: Installation (which I will cover in the next chapter) is, in an overwhelming majority of cases, a three-click affair that takes less than five minutes to complete, after which you will have a fully functioning community ripe for the customizing.
>
> **phpBB runs on your own server**: Unlike hosted forum solutions, phpBB allows you to modify everything about it, including the core source code that drives the script if you see fit. Running the script on your own server puts your community on your terms and no one else's. You aren't limited by arbitrary size limits, required to display advertisements, or stuck playing the waiting game for a feature you may desperately want. You have every right to modify your phpBB to your heart's content.

phpBB has a far-reaching support network: The phpBB community is massive and vibrant, and offers great support and documentation on a wide range of phpBB topics absolutely free of charge. There are hundreds of supported modifications and templates available so you can make your board stand out. Plus, phpBB is actively maintained and developed, so you are never left with a stale board (provided, of course, you update it). If you have a question about your board, chances are you will find an answer quickly.

phpBB scales well to fit the needs of your site: phpBB 2.0.x has a track record of consistently good performance on high-traffic sites, and has modifications available to help it perform even better for incredibly busy boards. Plus, the upcoming phpBB 3.0 series will feature even further improvements in performance for busy boards, with additional options to optimize for speed.

phpBB runs on many different database systems: Most people run phpBB on top of a MySQL database, but this does not necessarily have to be the case at all. Thanks to phpBB's modularized database abstraction, you can just as easily run phpBB with PostgreSQL, Microsoft SQL Server 2000, or even Access via ODBC for the masochists among us.

phpBB is absolutely, positively, 100% free: There are an increasing number of forum scripts out there that require a steep licensing fee in order to run the software, plus a recurring yearly charge to continue access to updates—and I haven't even gotten into support contracts yet! Being Open Source and a GNU General Public Licensed product, you can breathe easy knowing that the copy of phpBB you download today, and any upgrades in the future, will be totally free for you to obtain, customize, and modify. You can be at ease knowing you can get questions about your forum answered from experts with no expensive support contract necessary.

phpBB's Feature Set

phpBB 2.0.x, the current release, has a very solid array of features for a stable and quick forum experience.

End-User Features

Browse forums and topics with ease: Smart post marking helps to distinguish exactly what's been read and what's left to take a look at. Users can mark a single forum as read or mark them all read in bulk. Jumping to the first unread post helps users pick up where they left off in a thread.

Posting messages made simple: Posting messages in phpBB is like using a rich-text editor, with formatting buttons and clickable smilies. Users can also place graphical polls in their topics with little effort. Using BBCode, users can insert formatting into their messages without having to know HTML code. This is a win-win for the user and the administrator, as the administrator does not have to worry about a user using HTML or JavaScript to damage the board. If desired, the administrator can enable HTML and limit the tags that can be used, if the user base can be trusted enough.

Highly customizable profiles: Users can express themselves with signatures, avatars, and personal profiles. Additionally, the administrator can configure rankings based on post count or group memberships for further community building.

Private messaging: Users have the ability to send private messages to each other, with an administrator-configured limit on inbox size. Users can use all the formatting of a regular post, including smilies, in their private messages. phpBB notifies users of new private messages with an optional pop-up window and a counter in the header section of each phpBB page. Additionally, administrators can disable a user's ability to send private messages.

Powerful forum search: The phpBB search tool can search for keywords and authors, and display search results either in a list with post text or in a topic list. phpBB highlights your search terms in your results to make locating your keywords much easier.

Who's online: Users and administrators alike can see who's browsing the forums at any given time. Additionally, administrators have the option of seeing the IP address of online users in the administration panel to help with security.

Administrative Features

phpBB is equipped, by default, with a great deal of functionality for customizing and operating your community. You can even add additional features via modifications, if you so desire. phpBB's administrative features permit you to

Decide who is allowed to do what: Using the permissions system, you can set your forums to be registration-only, and configure what types of users can do what. You can go as far as restricting guests from viewing certain forums, if you desire. Paired with the groups system, permissions are a pervasive feature in phpBB.

Manage groups of users: You can use phpBB's usergroups feature to apply common characteristics, such as permission levels, to a group of people, such as your moderators. You can assign groups as moderators of forums, which is particularly useful if you want to have a group that can moderate every forum.

Keep forums clean with automatic pruning: You can set certain forums to automatically clean themselves up with phpBB's automatic pruning (commonly referenced in phpBB as *autoprune*) feature, which identifies inactive threads and eradicates them, helping to keep your community operating smoothly and to eliminate deadwood.

Mass e-mail your members: If you have a major announcement about your boards, you can simply use the mass e-mail feature to contact your members. You can also limit contact to certain groups in contrast to all users in bulk.

Back up and restore your database without tangling with command-line utilities: phpBB's administration panel offers backup and restore functionality, which dumps the contents of your phpBB database to a file on your hard drive. This functionality is especially useful for people who may or may not have command-line access to their server, as not all hosts provide that functionality.

Add a theme to your board: You can use the basic color and CSS controls in the theme administration system to make basic changes to your board's appearance, or you can install entirely new templates for even further customization. Additionally, phpBB permits you to modify the source code to all its templates, allowing a nearly unlimited level of flexibility. If you wish, phpBB permits you to export your finished themes to a file for release purposes.

Set up the rank and file: You can set up a list of rank milestones for users to reach when they reach certain post counts. Additionally, you can assign special ranks to certain users if you desire.

Manage every facet of a user's profile: You can edit any user's profile in its entirety, activate their accounts, disable their ability to send private messages, and much more. You can set permissions on a specific user if you wish.

Ban offenders and make sure they don't return: phpBB offers banning of specific users, IP ranges, e-mail addresses, and e-mail domain names. You can disallow special names, such as "admin," if you wish.

phpBB's Security Features

Security on your message board should be paramount. phpBB provides many features to assist you in tightening your community's security to keep miscreants out. In Chapter 10, I will go into further detail on how to secure phpBB. For now, I'll give you a brief introduction to phpBB's security features, which include the following:

Visual confirmation: phpBB's later releases come bundled with a visual confirmation system, which aids as a deterrent against automated registration "bots" that use your member list as ad space for shady web sites that are interested in increasing their search engine placement. Humans should be the only people using your forums, and visual confirmation helps in ensuring that is the case.

Selectively enable HTML: If you wish to permit the usage of HTML in forum posts, you can at least disable certain tags (such as `<script>`) to prevent problems with rogue JavaScripts.

Enable account validation via user or admin action: You can require a valid e-mail address of your users, and also require that your users self-validate their accounts before they begin posting. This helps to cut down on troll accounts by tying the account to an e-mail address, which also locks that e-mail address out from being used for additional account registrations. You can also require administrative authorization of all new accounts, which can be necessary in severe instances.

phpBB's Customizability

The open source nature of phpBB helps it be one of the most customizable forum platforms around. We will spend Chapters 11 and 12 on customizing phpBB. Here's an overview of what helps make phpBB easily customized:

Flexible template system: phpBB's template system is remarkably flexible and allows for a great deal of creativity in layout. You can use the template system to make phpBB easily fit the look of your existing web site. Continuity is a plus toward an aura of a job well done.

Vast modification community: You can hack (modify) your boards however well you want. And with literally hundreds of hacks available for your phpBB, it's likely that any feature you want that phpBB may not provide is out there, ripe for the picking. With a solid support community, installing modifications is incredibly simple, and you have lots of people to help you out in case something goes wrong.

phpBB's Scalability

When choosing message board software, you want to have a solution you can implement and grow with for years to come. Scalability and reliability are important traits of any good forum software, and phpBB has both.

phpBB scales well: Your phpBB is only limited by the limitations of your hardware. It performs reliably under stress and can handle high post volume. For those who operate ultra-high-traffic boards, power users in the modification community have published lots of performance tweaks to get even more power out of your phpBB. phpBB is also designed and bundled with database drivers to run on high-end database systems such as Microsoft SQL Server and Oracle, and can be extended to more databases.

As you can see, phpBB has a remarkable set of features. My job is to take you through those and help put them to work for you in creating your community.

What We'll Accomplish

Here's a list of what I'd like to accomplish with you, the reader, as you navigate this part of *Building Online Communities with Drupal, phpBB, and WordPress*:

Installation and initial configuration: I'll walk you through the ins and outs of experiencing the painless phpBB installation. I'll introduce you to the main attractions in the phpBB Administration control panel so you can set up shop and begin to establish your community. Finally, you'll get a tour of the basics of managing forums, setting up basic permissions, and establishing moderators.

Harnessing the power of phpBB's end-user features: As a phpBB administrator, you should know the ins and outs of phpBB's end-user features for those inevitable questions. Never fear—I'll take you through a tour of those features and share some tips and tricks for making them work better for you.

Securing and maintaining your board: The key to being an effective phpBB system administrator is keeping your board secured and maintained properly. I'll show you how to keep your phpBB updated with minimal problems. You'll get the full tour of phpBB's user management features. Finally, I'll discuss in-depth the best practices for keeping your phpBB secure from hackers, and show you some techniques for minimizing the impact from those annoying auto-registration robot scripts out there.

The ins and outs of installing and creating hacks: I'll show you how to use the phpBB hack template to install modifications to your board. You'll get the benefit of my experience with hacking phpBB's code to make it work the way you want it with a tour of the built-in phpBB programming interfaces. I'll introduce you to several modifications I feel you can't live without. Plus, I'll show you how to document your own modifications so you can release them to the world so others can use your features.

Harnessing the power of the phpBB template system: Using phpBB's template system is an essential for your board to get the professional look you covet. You'll get the full walkthrough of phpBB's template variables and control structures so you can make your forums look the best they possibly can.

Looking Toward Olympus

In addition to my coverage of the phpBB 2.0 series, I'm also going to provide a preview of the next-generation phpBB software, to be known as phpBB 3.0.0 and currently codenamed Olympus. As of this writing, the only pre-release versions of phpBB 3.0.0 are development versions pulled straight from the phpBB source code repository, so bear in mind that a lot of things could change between now and then. Figure 7-2 is a screenshot of a preview version of phpBB 3.0.0, known in its development stages as phpBB 2.2.

phpBB 3 is a major overhaul of the phpBB software with a noticeable performance improvement, a revamped template system, and tons of new features designed to make using and administering the forums easier. Some of the more notable features include the following:

Revamped User Control Panel: Instead of having separate areas to edit your profile and check your private messages, phpBB 3 offers a unified User Control Panel, similar to what is found in commercial products such as vBulletin. The UCP currently offers modules for editing your profile, checking private messages (which has been vastly improved in this version), managing forum subscriptions, and a "buddy list" of people on the board that you are friendly with. Plus, the new UCP is fully modular, so more modules can, and likely will, be written for it to further extend the functionality of the board. You'll be able to specify your birthday and see it and others' birthdays in a special section in the forum index (if the administrator so chooses).

Attachments: Attachments finally will make it into phpBB as a core feature in this version. Attachments have been around as a modification to existing phpBB 2 series boards, but the phpBB 3 series integrates them and integrates them well, with even a User Control Panel module for managing your attachments.

Revamped private messaging: As alluded to previously, private messaging has been seriously revamped in this version. You can save drafts of private messages, add storage folders, and even set up rules for filtering incoming private messages much like you do with your e-mail. It is already among the most flexible of private messaging systems, even in this early stage.

"Friends and Foes": You can set up a list of who you like on the board for easy private message access, or set up a list of people you don't like so you can ignore their posts automatically. This feature should be a boon to keeping peace on a board like never before.

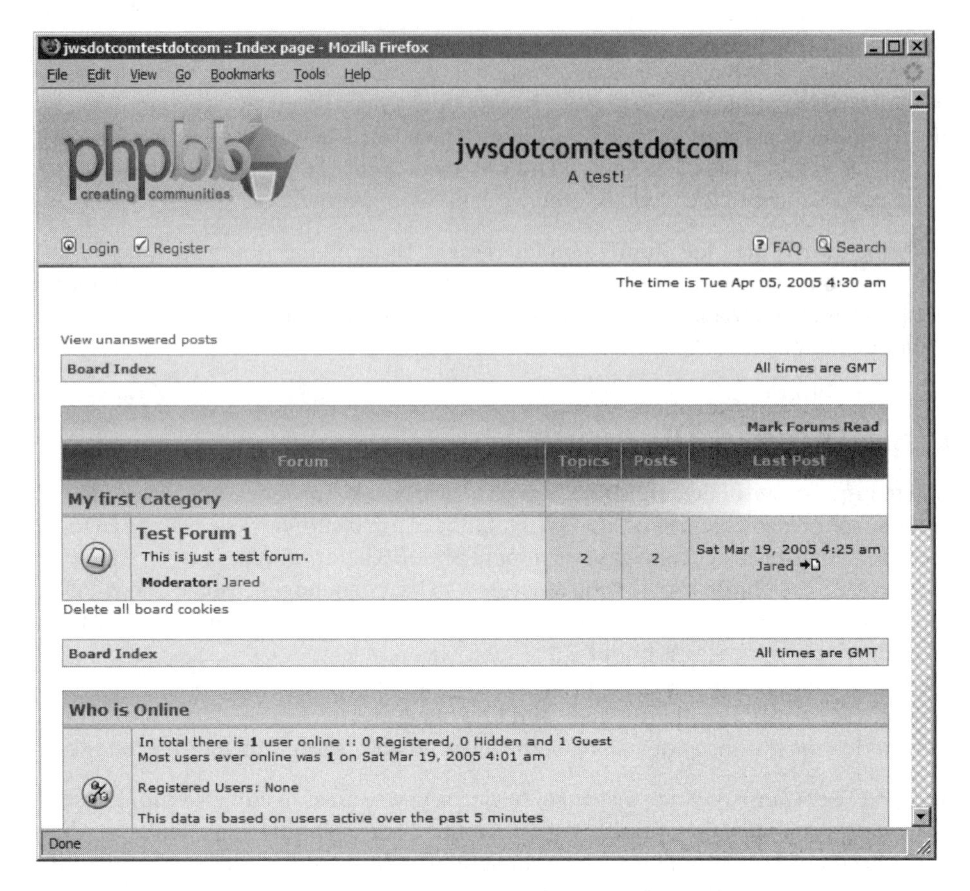

Figure 7-2. *phpBB 3.0.0, codename Olympus, in all its pre-release glory*

Revamped forum Administration panel: The Administration control panel in this version has been seriously revamped as well. All administrative actions are now logged, and those logs are fully configurable. You can set access control lists for specific forums, making for unprecedented configuration of permissions. There are plenty of new settings for optimizing the board for server load, which will be a major help to exceptionally high-traffic boards. You can even add new BBCode tags via the administration panel. Administrators will find they have unparalleled control over their board in this version.

Lots of posting enhancements: You can now define post icons to be shown next to a post, similar to features found in UBB and vBulletin. phpBB also visually delineates what threads you have posted in. You can report misguided posts to moderators for further action.

Security enhancements: As mentioned before, permissions have been totally revamped, and you can apply permissions to more facets of the board, including the member list and the search functions, which some automated robot scripts have been known to abuse. The administration panel uses extra checking to prevent unauthorized logins. Visual confirmation is very pervasive in this release, making you type in a special code to verify that you aren't an automated robot that's designed to sign up on all sorts of sites to help their Google results.

phpBB 3.0 will prove to be an exciting release. In addition to the preceding features, expect a brand new theme to be unveiled at release, which promises to be an exciting event.

At the time of this writing, the phpBB Group has not publicly committed to a release date, so estimates are our best hope. The current estimation is that we will see phpBB 3.0.0 in early 2006, but only time will tell. As a result, the features described in each phpBB 3.0 preview section at the end of each chapter will contain a standard disclaimer reminding you of the software's pre-release nature, because procedures and the interface can (and most likely will) change between the time of this writing and the time phpBB 3.0 is released to the public.

Summary

In this chapter, I've introduced you to the basic concepts and lingo involved in forum administration. I've showed you the important qualities in any good piece of forum software, and shown you how phpBB fits that mold. In the next chapter, I'll walk you through the process of installing your phpBB and making it operational. I'll take you through every nuance of the installation process, and give you a guided tour of the phpBB administration panel. You'll learn how to make basic configuration adjustments, create forums, and assign them moderators, all in an effort to get a basic community underway. Finally, I'll also preview the phpBB 3.0 installer and administration tools.

CHAPTER 8

Installing and Configuring phpBB

Now that you've been introduced to the basics of message board administration, it's time to bring your community online. I'll walk you through the entire phpBB setup process, from ensuring that your host has what it takes to run phpBB to having live forums that are ready for your visitors, with as little aspirin as possible. Additionally, I'll preview the new setup routine for phpBB 3.0. Let's get started!

Installing phpBB

Installing phpBB is as simple as running its install script. However, to ensure that the process goes smoothly, you need to do a little preparation. This includes making sure your system meets phpBB requirements, obtaining phpBB, and preparing your server.

Meeting phpBB Requirements

Before you install phpBB, make sure that your host has the necessary software in place to run the install script. Luckily for you, phpBB's requirements are very modest, and any host worth paying for will run phpBB like a champ. Whether you're shopping for a hosting service for your phpBB or configuring your own dedicated server to run phpBB, it's smart to check a few details to help ensure a smooth installation.

Operating System and Web Server: Anything *nix + Apache

The so-called LAMP platform—Linux, Apache, MySQL, and PHP—has a track record of being very reliable, fast, and cost-effective for your web applications. Many hosting services offer such a configuration in their packages. LAMP's track record is why you will find excellent free applications, such as phpBB, are designed with that environment in mind.

The Apache version you use does not matter that much. Some people think that Apache 1.3 outperforms Apache 2.0 when serving PHP pages, but your mileage may vary considerably. phpBB is compatible with both versions of Apache, so as a phpBB administrator, you should not concern yourself too much over which version of Apache to run (unless, of course, it's your box).

Linux hosting is extremely common and reliable. It's also relatively inexpensive and provides a great return on your investment in terms of uptime and performance. You may also come across plans that offer hosting on a BSD-based server. BSD operating systems generally offer improved performance, reliability, and security over a Linux server.

If you decide to use a Windows Server-based host, rest assured that phpBB does indeed run under Internet Information Services (IIS), but you will experience a small delay when you log in to your forum, and performance is not guaranteed. Plus, if you run into a problem with your board, it may be harder to troubleshoot under IIS, mainly due to the nature of the community, which typically uses Apache. If at all possible, install Apache on Windows and avoid IIS altogether (which I generally recommend due to IIS's history of being vulnerable to attack).

PHP Interpreter: Version 4.4

The current releases of phpBB, as of this writing, are fully supported on the 4.*x* series of the PHP engine. I recommend that you have at least PHP 4.3.10 installed, because earlier revisions of PHP prior to 4.3.10 are vulnerable to some nasty exploits (manifested in the form of the Santy worm in late 2004, which targeted phpBB installations and defaced them).

■ **Caution** The most recent versions of phpBB 2.0 no longer support PHP 3. If you still have PHP 3 installed on your server, note that it is not actively maintained. I strongly recommend that you migrate to the 4.3.*x* series.

While PHP 4.3.10 is a good minimum, shoot for PHP 4.4, which offers improved performance and contains all of the features of the PHP 4.3 series. If you lease space from a hosting service and find an earlier version of PHP installed on your server, I recommend contacting your host provider and lobbying heavily for an upgrade to PHP 4.4. If you run your own box, it's time to bite the bullet and brave a little downtime to upgrade PHP—the security of your box should be worth it. (Security is covered in Chapter 10.)

■ **Note** In late 2004, the PHP project released the first iteration of the PHP 5 series of interpreters. The latest versions of phpBB 2.0 currently operate under PHP 5 with no known ill effects; however, this configuration, as of this writing, is not officially supported by the phpBB Group. The upcoming phpBB 3.0 (code-named Olympus), tentatively slated for release in early 2006, will fully support PHP 5.

Database: MySQL

MySQL is by far the most widely used database in the phpBB universe. Like phpBB, it is released under the GNU General Public License (GPL). MySQL 4.1 includes a number of performance and feature improvements. It's still a new release, so some hosts may not have migrated to it yet. If your host doesn't have MySQL 4.1, don't fret; phpBB works at the very least with 3.23.58 (which is the version my production host uses).

Although MySQL does not come with some of the power-user features of PostgreSQL and Oracle, it still performs just fine for a great majority of users. Plus, MySQL is a part of just about any Linux hosting package that you'll find.

Obtaining phpBB

phpBB is primarily obtained via download from `http://www.phpbb.com`, but you can also acquire it through sites such as `http://www.phpbbhacks.com` if you so desire. phpBB is distributed in several flavors:

Full package: If this is your first time downloading phpBB, you want the full package. This package contains everything you will need to install phpBB on your server. For the installation described in this chapter, you need to download this package.

Changed files only: If you are upgrading your phpBB to a new version, this package helps you migrate to the new version with the minimal files necessary. You can use this package only to upgrade an older version of phpBB. It consists of compressed files that contain the changes from every old version to the latest version, which is useful if you've missed a round or two of updates. Upgrading is covered in Chapter 10.

Patch file only: If you have shell access to your server, you may elect to use this file to upgrade your version of phpBB using the UNIX `patch` utility, rather than uploading multiple files.

The phpBB Group offers three versions of each package, compressed with a different algorithm. Feel free to pick the file of your choice. If you are on Linux, you may want the `.bzip` packages. Windows users will likely wish to use the `.zip` files.

Further down the download page, you will see that many translations of phpBB are available for just about any language you may ever want. If you wish to display your board in another language, feel free to download its corresponding language pack. You can install as many language packs as you wish, and you can install language packs at any time after initial installation.

After you've downloaded phpBB and whichever language packs you want, decompress phpBB to a folder on your hard drive. If you obtained language packs, decompress those to the `/languages` directory where you decompressed phpBB.

Now that you have phpBB, it's time to get your server ready for installation.

■ **Caution** Some Linux distributions now ship with a phpBB2 package. Resist the temptation to use it! The package may not put phpBB where you want it to be installed, could complicate adding modifications to your board, and could cause your custom work on your installation to be lost automatically when upgrading the package.

Preparing Your Server

Now that you have the phpBB software downloaded to your hard drive, you can upload it to your server. But first, take a moment to set up your database.

Setting Up a Database for phpBB

Creating a database for phpBB is a fairly trivial matter. I recommend that you use a totally separate database for your phpBB installation, if at all possible. The database will be accessed frequently and will grow, and database performance can suffer if you have more tables than necessary in the database. In addition to performance benefits, using a separate database is a boon to security; if a miscreant should break into your board, the damage is far more likely to be limited to just the phpBB database, rather than affecting the whole site's database, which could lead to real trouble.

The method for creating a database varies from host to host. Most hosts using the cPanel control panel system have a MySQL option you can select, which permits creation of a database via a form. Ultimately, your best bet is to check with your host providers on their *modus operandi* for creating a database.

If creating an additional database isn't an option, phpBB plays very well with existing data in the database by attaching a prefix of your choice (the default is `phpbb_`) to each of phpBB's tables in order to provide a distinguishing characteristic. Also, this functionality lets you run additional instances of phpBB inside the same database.

Uploading phpBB to Your Server

Now it's time to put the phpBB script in your web space on your server. Start the FTP client of your choice and connect to your server. Before you start uploading the files, you need to check your client's upload settings. Most modern FTP clients can automatically determine whether they are uploading plain text or binary data, and negotiate the connection as appropriate, so you do not need to bother with uploading certain file types separately from others. Check your transfer type setting, usually found in the Options dialog of your program, to make sure it's set for Auto. Next, navigate to the directory where your public web files are placed (typically called `www`, `public_html`, or `htdocs`), and then simply upload the entire `phpBB2` folder to that location.

■ Tip If your client can't automatically select the transfer type, you are better off trying a new FTP client. I use and heartily recommend SmartFTP, which handles this with incredible ease. You can obtain it free for personal use from `http://www.smartftp.com`.

After uploading, you may wish to consider renaming the `phpBB2` folder to something a little more user-friendly, such as `forums`. It's not necessary, but it's a nice, professional touch—`forums` seems to be a more logical choice to house your board than `phpBB2`.

Making the Configuration File Writable

After you've completed the upload, make the following writable by the web server:

- `/config.php`: This file contains the configuration data for the database, and it is written only during installation.
- `/images/avatars/uploads/`: This directory does not exist by default in the phpBB installation. If you wish for users to be able to upload avatars directly to your server (explained in detail in Chapter 9), feel free to create this directory and make it writable.

You can use your FTP client to make files writable. For example, in SmartFTP, right-click the file you want to make writable, select Properties, and check the Writable box under Group. Depending on your server configuration, you may also need to check the Writable box under Public.

■ **Caution** Check with your hosting service to ensure that it is taking the proper precautions to protect files you make public, as this can be a security risk. Most host providers are on the ball with ensuring the security of your account, but it never hurts to ask.

Now that you've made the necessary files writable by the server, it's finally time for the easy part: running the phpBB install script.

Running the Install Script

The phpBB install script is located in the `/install` subdirectory where phpBB is installed. Get your database information from your host handy, open a web browser, and navigate to the following URL (making the appropriate substitutions for your domain name and path to phpBB):

`www.`*`yourserver`*`.com/`*`yourphpBBpath`*`/install/install.php`

When you arrive at `install.php`, you will be presented with the form shown in Figure 8-1.

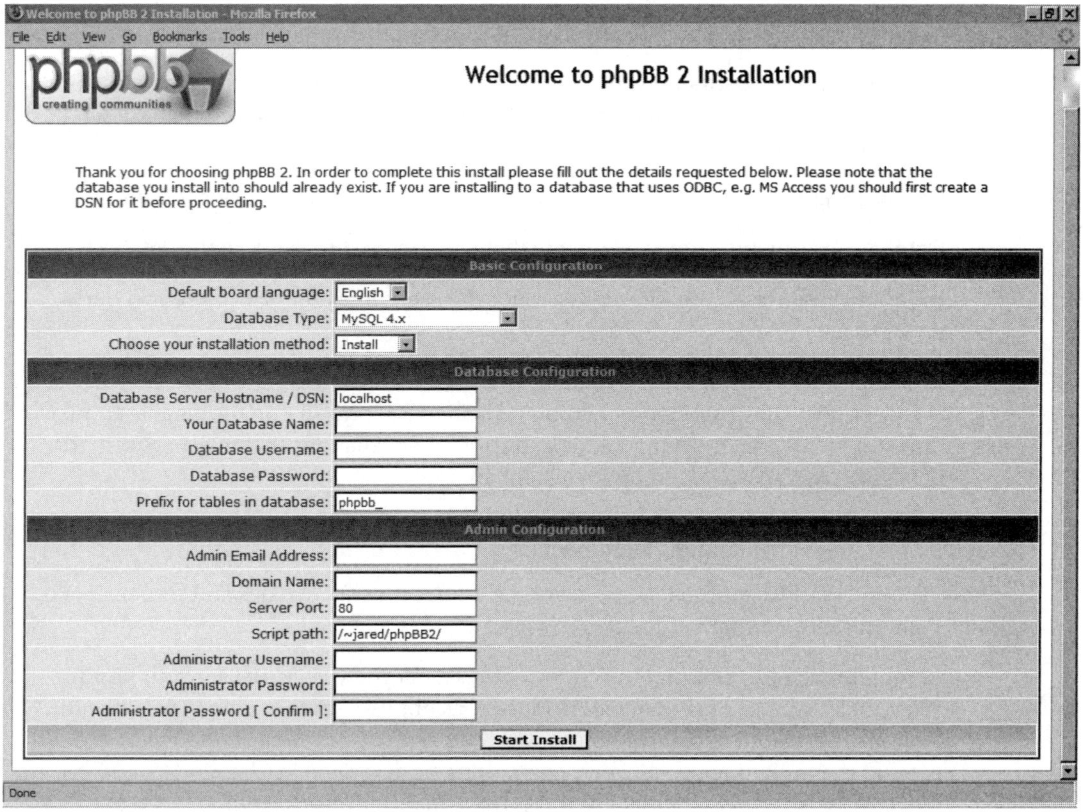

Figure 8-1. *The first page of the phpBB installation script*

Here's a guide to completing the phpBB installation form.

Completing the Basic Configuration Section

In most cases, this part of the form defaults to the settings that you'll be using. Typically, the only field you may change is the Database Type field.

Default board language: In most cases, you will leave this as English. However, if you uploaded additional languages, you can set one of those languages as the default if you wish.

Database Type: Here, you tell phpBB which kind of database driver to use. If you are using MySQL, you need to check if your server still uses MySQL 3.*x* or if it has been upgraded to MySQL 4.*x*, as phpBB has a specific driver for MySQL 4. You can ask your host provider, or you can use phpMyAdmin, a popular web-based MySQL administration tool, to check the version.

Choose your installation method: In most cases, you will leave this as Install. The Upgrade option is for those upgrading from phpBB 1.4.4. This chapter describes a new installation (the Install option).

Completing the Database Configuration Section

Here, you will need the database connection information that you collected from your host.

Database Server Hostname/DSN: phpBB assumes that you will use `localhost` as the database server. In most configurations, this is correct; however, if the database server is hosted elsewhere, insert the name of the database server.

Database Name: Enter the name of the database that you plan on using for phpBB.

Database Username: Enter a username that you can use for access to the database.

Database Password: Enter the password for the username that you entered on the previous line.

Prefix for tables in database: Generally, you will do well to leave the default set to `phpbb_`. However, if you are installing an additional instance of phpBB into the database, you must use a different prefix than used by any other installations that may persist in the database; otherwise, nasty things will happen.

Completing the Admin Configuration Section

Here, you will set up a few final items, including information for cookies and your own personal administrator account.

Admin Email Address: Enter the e-mail address that you wish to use for your phpBB account. Make sure you enter a valid address, as phpBB uses this address for several administrative purposes, including password resets, notifications of new registrations (if you set phpBB to screen all new registrations, as described in Chapter 10), and private messages sent to you. Additionally, this is the e-mail address that is appended to e-mail sent from the board.

Domain Name: This will already be filled in for you. This is for cookie purposes, and in most cases, you won't have a reason to change it.

Server Port: Again, phpBB's installer fills this in for you, and it's best to leave this value as is, as this port is determined automatically.

Script path: Another "gimme" courtesy of phpBB. Again, there's really no reason to change this path.

Administrator username: Enter the username you wish to identify yourself with on your board. You can use the Administration panel to change this later, if you wish.

Administrator password: Enter a strong password (using a mix of numbers, letters, and symbols) for your administrator account. In the next field, confirm that password.

Starting the Installation

Verify that all the fields in the installation form are filled in, take a deep breath, and click Start Install. With any luck, phpBB will be installed, and you'll see a screen like the one shown in Figure 8-2.

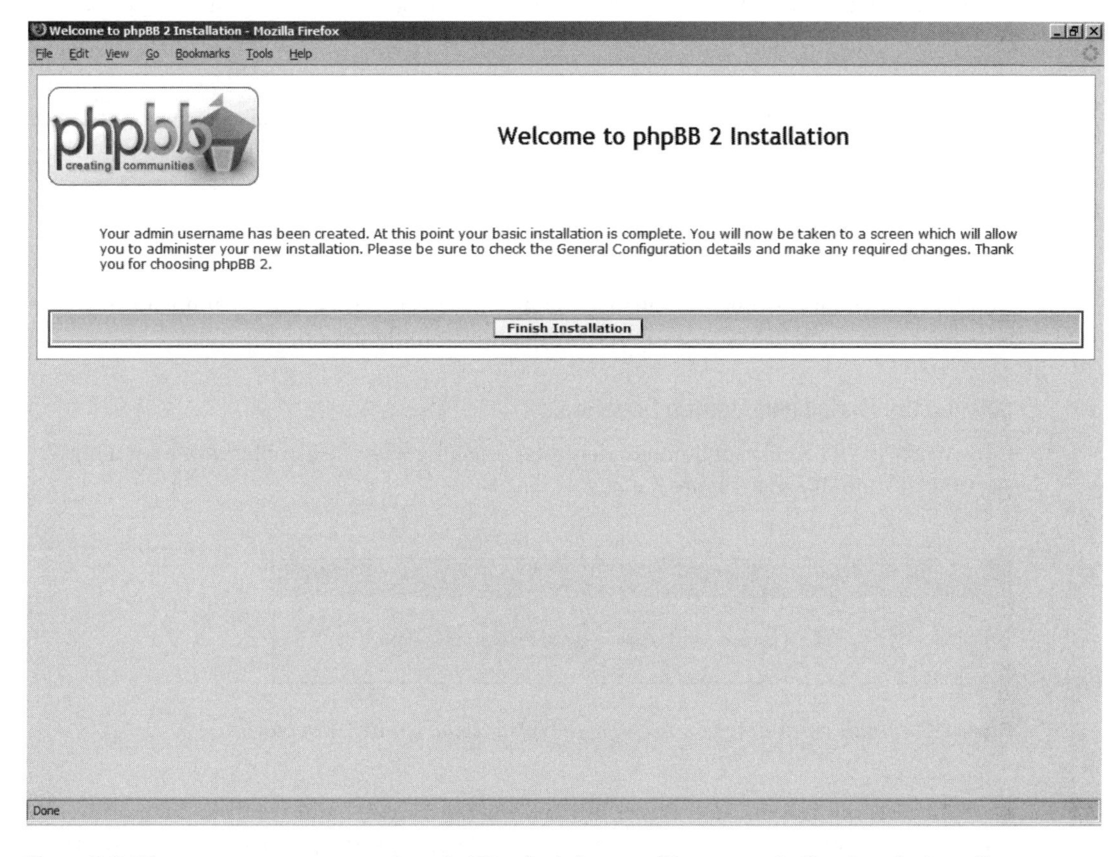

Figure 8-2. *The screen every prospective phpBB administrator likes to see, indicating the installation was a success*

If you see the screen with the Finish Installation button, congratulations! You're just a couple tasks away from having a fully functional phpBB setup. Go ahead and skip to the section named "Performing Post-Installation Chores" for what to do next.

Troubleshooting Installation

Perhaps when you clicked the Start Install button, you saw something very different from the display in Figure 8-2, such as Critical Error with a bunch of MySQL error messages. Here, I'll take you through a few common errors that you might encounter along the way.

Access denied for *user*@localhost (Using password: YES): MySQL ran into a problem letting you use the database with the database username and password you specified in installation. You should examine your database username and password settings to ensure that they're correct, and make sure the username and password you supply have rights to access that particular database.

Not a valid MySQL-Link Resource...: This is an obscure message that doesn't tell you exactly what the problem is. Check to make sure you have the correct database name entered into the form. If the database name is correct, make sure that you have the right server settings.

Unable to write config.php: If phpBB tells you to download `config.php` because it couldn't be written, go ahead and do so. This is the installer's fallback method when the `config.php` file is unwritable by the server.

Performing Post-Installation Chores

Now that you've successfully run the install script, you need to do a little cleaning up and securing of the board before you continue with phpBB configuration.

Deleting the /install and /contrib Directories

If you click Finish Installation immediately after finishing with the installer, you'll see a message like the one shown in Figure 8-3.

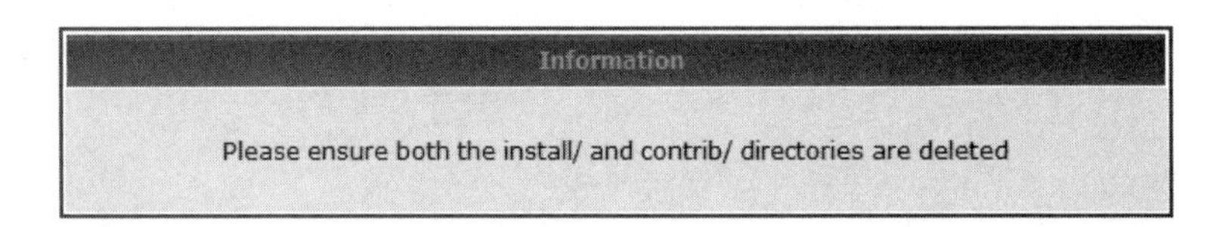

Information
Please ensure both the install/ and contrib/ directories are deleted

Figure 8-3. *phpBB reminding you to delete the /install and /contrib directories*

Why won't phpBB run after this point? Leaving the `/install` and `/contrib` directories provides a great way for a hacker to overwrite your database settings and cause havoc. At this point, anyone can rerun the installer and hijack your board. So, it's *vital* that you remove these directories. Simply log in with your FTP client or with your shell, navigate to where phpBB is located, and delete the `/install` and `/contrib` directories.

Making config.php Read-Only

Another extremely important step to take immediately after installation is to remove the write permissions from `config.php`. With your FTP client, remove the `write` attribute from `others` and `group`. This way, no one other than you can overwrite your `config.php` file, which makes your board more secure.

Logging in to phpBB

After you've finished those two tasks, click *yourdomain.com Forum Index*, and behold—you have a *working* phpBB! Figure 8-4 shows the forum index page.

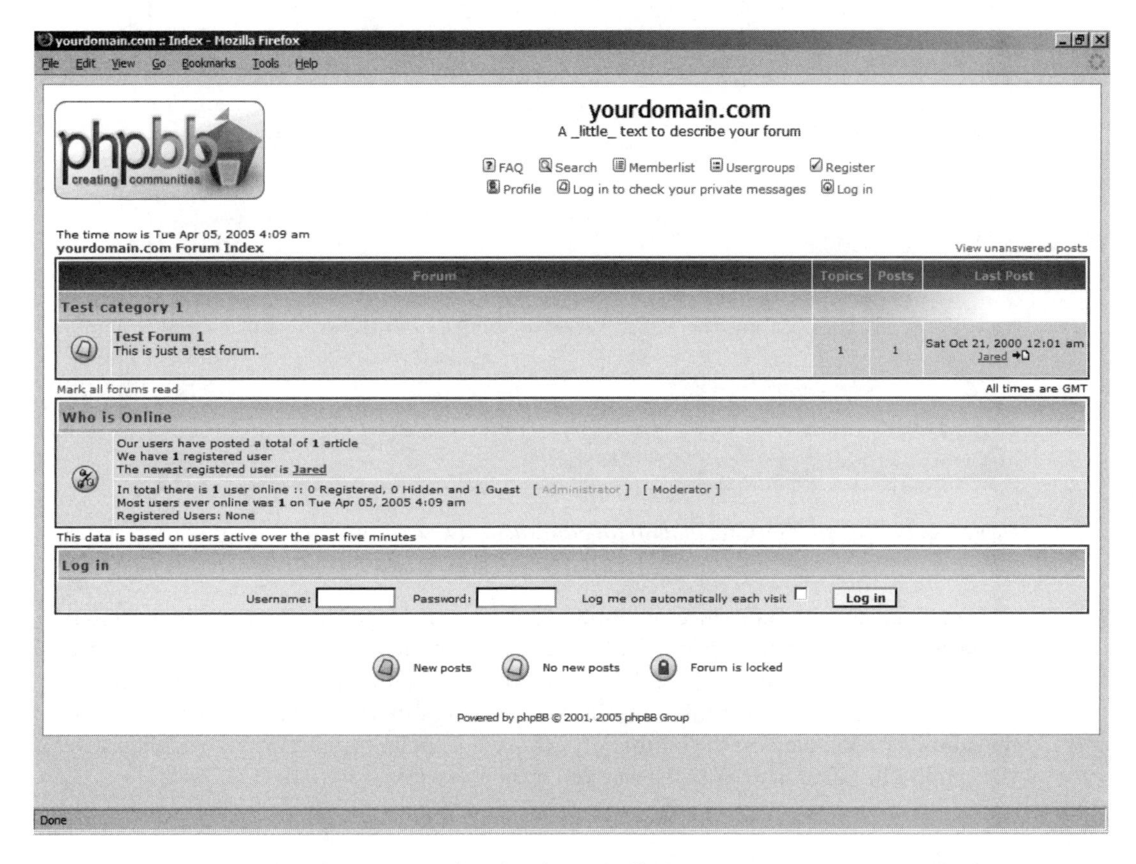

Figure 8-4. *A plain-vanilla phpBB, immediately after installation*

You can use the Log In form at the bottom of the forum index page to quickly log in to your account. Log in using the administrator username and password you created during the installation, and then click the Log in button. You can also set phpBB to remember your session and log you in on every visit. This utilizes cookies, so make sure you have them enabled. After you've logged in, your screen should resemble Figure 8-5.

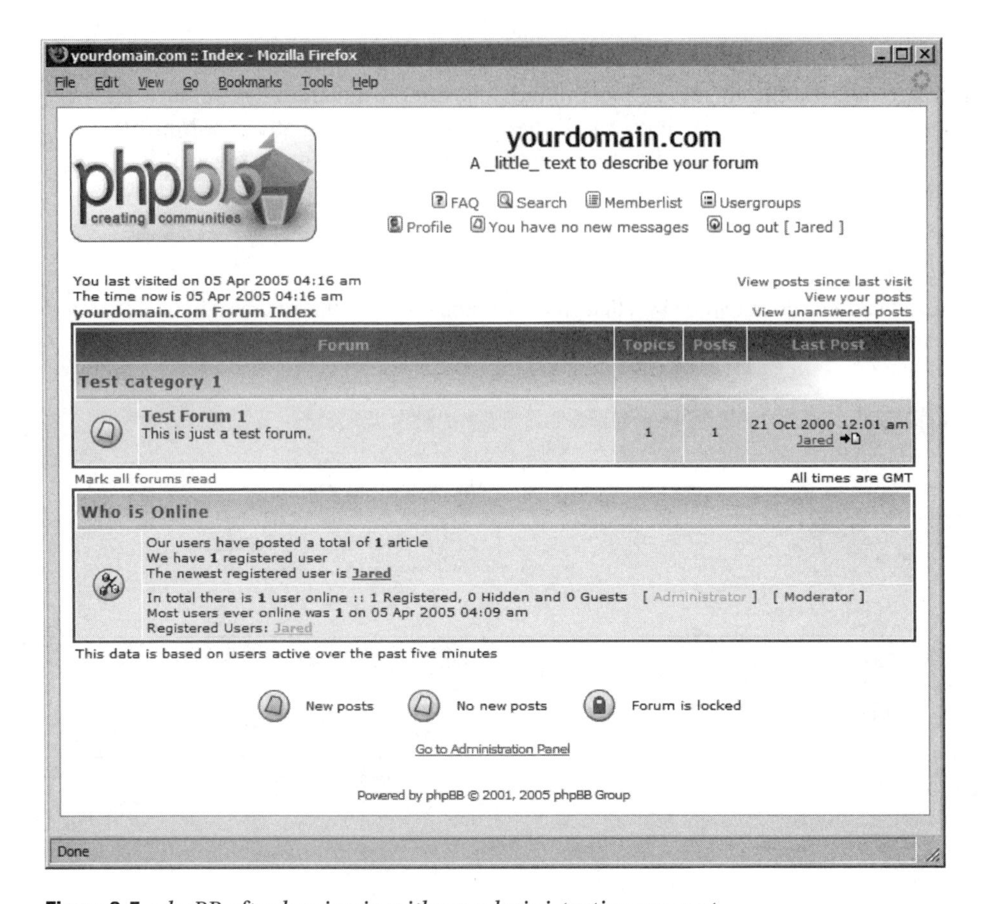

Figure 8-5. *phpBB after logging in with an administrative account*

You'll notice a few differences in phpBB while you are logged in. The navigational links in the header of each phpBB page now list the number of new private messages you have, display the option to log out, and hide the Register option. Additionally, your name will show up on the online users list. The most important change you should notice, though, is the link to the Administration panel at the bottom of each page. That link is your ticket to configuring your phpBB installation to work the way you want it to work.

Configuring phpBB

Now that you've installed phpBB, the time has come to make it yours by changing settings and styles of the board to personalize it, creating forums and categories to organize those forums, and setting up the rules for what you want people to be able to do. phpBB is unbelievably configurable. Here, I'll walk you through the steps common for just about every phpBB installation. In Chapters 9 and 10, I'll provide more details about configuring phpBB to suit your preferences and for improved security.

Using the phpBB Administration Panel

To access the phpBB Administration panel, log in to your forums with your user account (if you aren't already logged in) and click the *Go to Administration Panel* link at the bottom of the page. Your screen should resemble Figure 8-6.

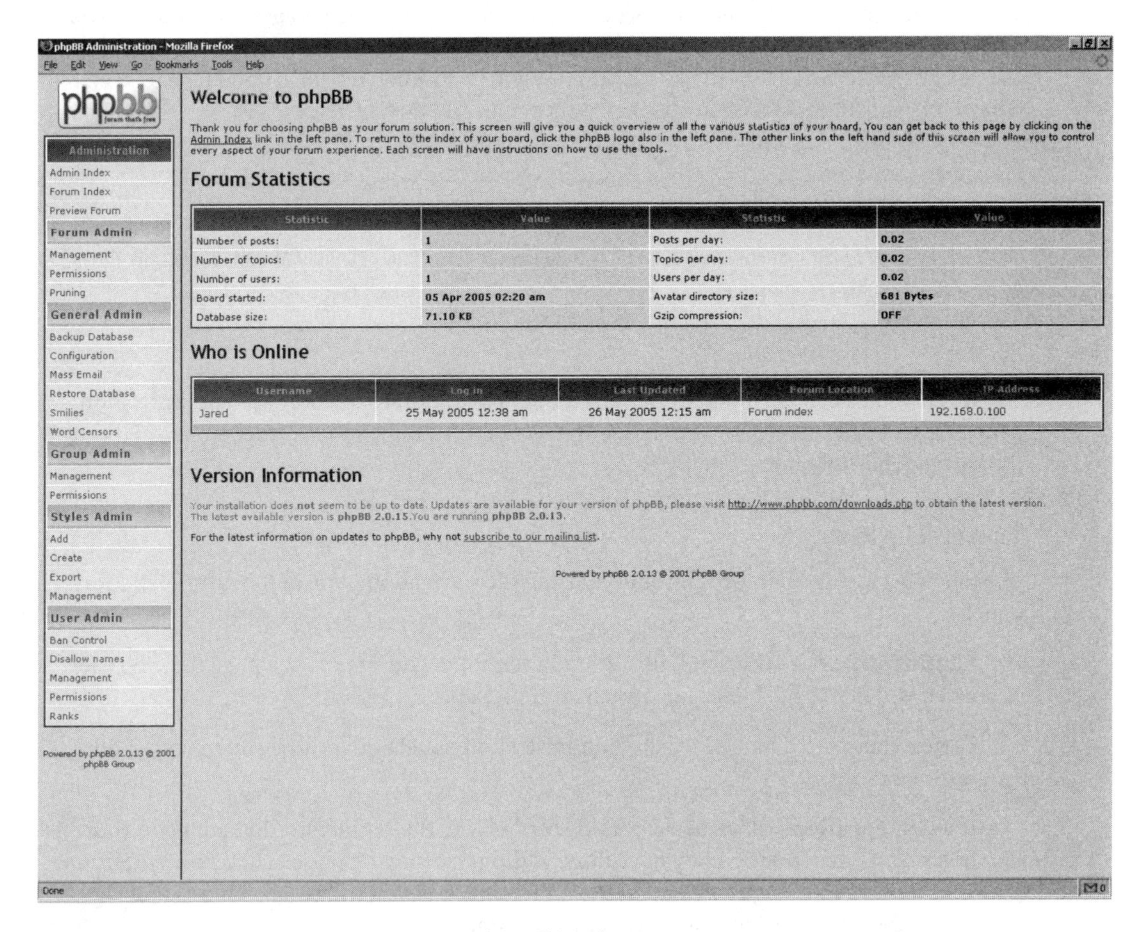

Figure 8-6. *The phpBB Administration panel in all its glory*

phpBB's Administration panel is laid out in a straightforward manner. The left pane contains all the navigational links for the various options for phpBB; this will remain on your screen as you work in the Administration panel.

The front page of the phpBB Administration panel offers a few useful statistics on forum activity and information about the state of your board. phpBB calculates the average signups per day, average posts per day, when your board was started, and a few additional tidbits of information that can help you determine if you need to tweak your marketing or upgrade your server hardware. You'll also notice an enhanced version of the Who's Online feature. In addition to the usual statistics about who's online and where they are, you also get a look at the IP addresses of the users as they browse the forum, with a link to a network tools site that lets you perform WHOIS queries, pings, and traceroutes on that particular IP. This link can be useful, for example, if the IP address is of someone who is causing problems on your board, and you need to get in touch with the user's Internet service provider.

Another nice feature, found in later revisions of the phpBB 2 series, is an upgrade notification, which shows you when your phpBB version is outdated (you can see this in Figure 8-6). The upgrade notification checks `phpBB.com` for updates every time you enter the Administration panel, so you can rest assured that it has all the latest information. This frees you from checking `phpBB.com` daily for major version revisions (although it's still a good idea to keep tabs on the site for interim security fixes, as they can and do happen).

■ **Caution** If your version of phpBB doesn't have the upgrade check functionality in the Administration panel, chances are your installation is incredibly outdated (and is most definitely at risk for security flaws!). An upgrade is highly recommended.

It's easy to be overwhelmed by the vast amount of options offered by the Administration panel. Here's a brief overview of the functionality of the Administration panel, accessed through the navigational links in the left pane.

Top-Level Options

The following are the first three options listed in the navigation pane of the Administration panel:

Admin Index: The very first link, Admin Index, takes you back to the page that you saw when you first logged in to the Administration panel.

Forum Index: This link closes the Administration panel and returns you to your main forum index page.

Preview Forum: If you've been working furiously in the Administration panel on your board and want to see what you've done without closing the panel, click *Preview Forum*. Your forum index page will load in the right pane, and you will still be able to quickly access the administrative options in the left pane.

Forum Administration Options

The following are the links listed under Forum Admin in the navigation pane:

Management: This link takes you to the Management panel, which allows you to create, reorder, and delete forums and categories. You'll use this tool a lot as you set up your forums.

Permissions: Use the Permissions panel to apply the necessary posting rights to each of your forums. You can use Simple Mode, which provides a list of preset permission scenarios that reflect the most common forum configurations, or Advanced Mode, which gives you fine-grained control over who can do exactly what.

Pruning: Pruning helps you keep your forums clean and running smoothly by removing old, dead posts. If you find your forum is outgrowing your server, and you can't change the server situation, pruning is a very useful feature.

General Administration Options

The following are the links listed under General Admin in the navigation pane:

Backup Database: phpBB comes bundled with a backup feature that permits you to save the contents of your forums to a text file that can be easily restored by your database server. This is an extremely useful feature, as it saves you a trip into your server's database management software (for example, phpMyAdmin).

Configuration: The Configuration panel is another workhorse as administration panels go, particularly during your initial setup phase. Here, you give your site a title, define user validation policy, set up avatars, and much, much more. You'll be using this panel to configure your phpBB installation in the next section of this chapter.

Mass Email: If you want to do mass e-mailing to your user base or just a particular group of people on your board, you can use the Email panel to do just that.

Restore Database: The natural counterpart to the Backup Database function, the Restore Database panel restores a backup you've made to your database. It overwrites anything phpBB-related in your database, so be absolutely sure you want to restore a backup before initiating a restore operation.

Smilies: You can use the Smilies panel to effortlessly add, remove, and modify the code for those infamous smilies that have become a staple of forums everywhere.

Word Censors: The Word Censors panel allows you to specify words that you find inappropriate for your forum audience and replace them with something you'll find a little less objectionable.

Group Administration Options

The following are the links listed under Group Admin in the navigation pane:

Management: Use the Management panel to create user groups, which permit you to group members together for a variety of reasons, the most popular being to keep a set of permissions consistent between a group (for example, super moderators).

Permissions: Use this tool to assign a group the rights to perform actions on certain forums, such as moderating them.

Styles Administration Options

The following are the links listed under Styles Admin in the navigation pane:

Add: You can add newly uploaded styles to your database using this function. It automatically looks in your `templates` directory on the server, determines which styles are available to be installed, and adds them to a list that lets you add them to the database.

Create: If you want to add a new color scheme for a template that you've already installed, you can use this panel to create a new style. It displays a form with many attributes to fill in, including many different color and font classifications.

Export: If you've created a color scheme in the Create panel that you would like to release, or just want to have a backup of, you can save it in phpBB's text-based styles format by using the Export utility. Styles exported in this format can be added with the aforementioned Add panel.

Management: The Management panel enables you to add, edit, and uninstall styles and templates from your board's database.

You'll learn how to tackle the phpBB styling system, including using these administration panels, in Chapter 12.

User Administration Options

The following are the links listed under User Admin in the navigation pane:

Ban Control: If you run into troublesome users, such as people who keep coming back to harass your board, hop into Ban Control and put a stop to them. phpBB lets you ban users by e-mail address, e-mail domains, IP ranges, and usernames. You'll learn about the ban controls in more detail in Chapter 10, where I'll discuss security strategies for phpBB.

Disallow Names: Most people would rather not have a user register their name as "Forum Administrator." The Disallow Names feature permits you to block names that you would rather not have John Doe User register. You can even use wildcards (*) to disallow usernames with a string you specify (such as `*admin*`).

Management: The User Management panel allows you to edit all facets of users' accounts, including their public profiles. You can activate and deactivate accounts, enable or disable users' rights to send private messages, reset passwords, set rankings, delete users, and so on.

Permissions: The Permissions panel lets you give a user administrator and moderator privileges. Additionally, switching over to Advanced Mode gives you fine-grained control over who can do what in every forum, including whether to allow each user to read, post, and/or moderate in each forum.

Ranks: The Ranks panel permits you to set up a ranking system for your forums based on post count, as well as create special ranks you manually set for a user in the User Management panel.

Configuring Basic Settings

Before you set up your community's forums and categories, head into the Configuration panel under General Admin and set up a few essentials. When you click the *Configuration* link, you'll see the General Configuration panel, as shown in Figure 8-7.

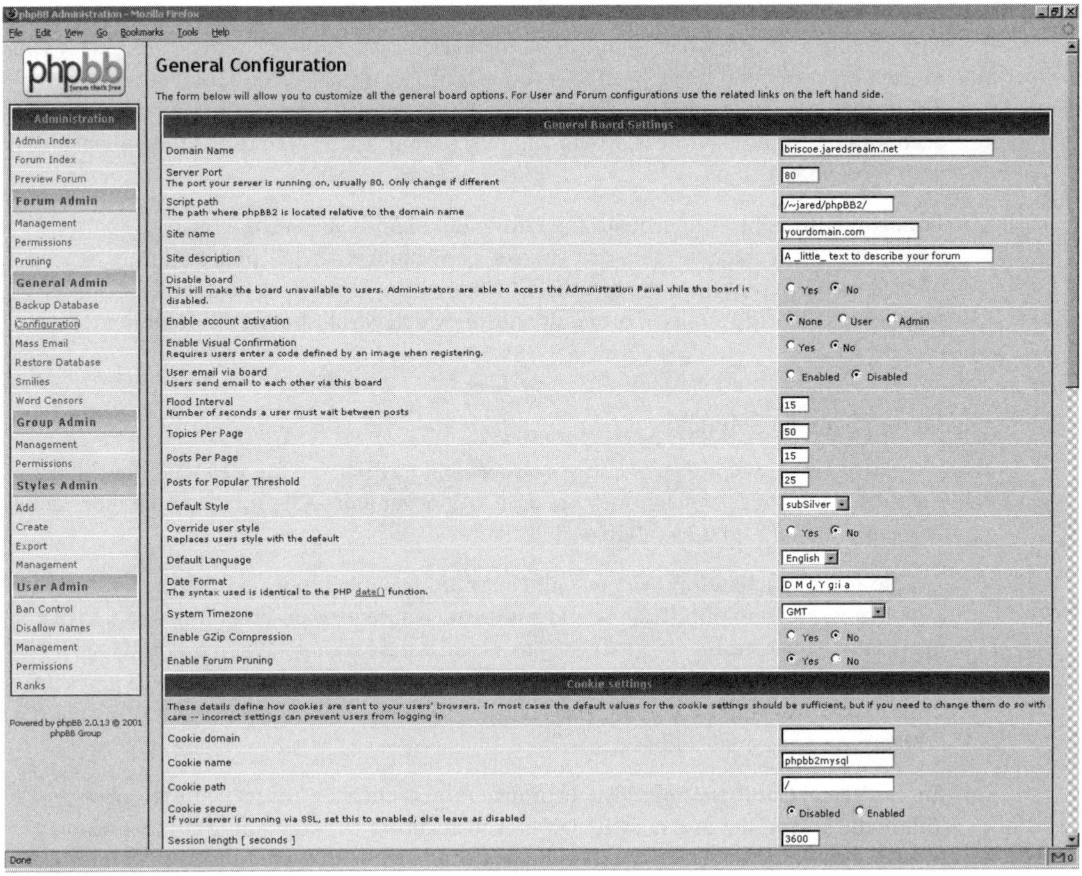

Figure 8-7. *The General Configuration panel, filled in with installation defaults*

Note the default values are filled in. You should be in good shape leaving a vast majority of these options alone; however, you'll definitely want to change a few things. I've grouped these changes as cosmetic and security, plus one "performance boost" adjustment.

Making Cosmetic Changes

Unless you are the owner of `yourdomain.com`, you'll want to make some of the following cosmetic changes to your phpBB configuration:

Site name: Fill in the title of your web site here. The site name is the big bold text on the top-right portion of the header in the subSilver template (phpBB's default template).

Site description: Fill in a slogan for your site, or describe it briefly. In the subSilver template, this information displays directly underneath the site name.

System Timezone: Change this to reflect the time zone you wish to use as the default for all accounts and for guests. Typically, the default time zone is set to the administrator's time zone.

Admin Email Address: At the very bottom of the page, under the heading Email Settings, you are able to specify an e-mail address to be used as an "official" e-mail address for your forums. I recommend that you change this value to an e-mail account that acts as a catch-all for your domain, as phpBB's setup routine fills the information in with your administrator account's registration address, which you may or may not wish to use as the official e-mail address of your forums.

Email Signature: Just underneath the Admin Email Address setting, you're given the opportunity to replace the generic "Thanks, The Management" e-mail signature, affixed to each message sent from the forums, with something a bit more personalized. Little touches like this add a hint of professionalism, which we all should shoot for in our communities.

Configuring Security Settings

Over the years, I've found a set of security settings that have served me well, and now I'll pass those along to you. These explanations are brief, but never fear—I'll provide much more detail on the security benefits of these changes in Chapter 10.

Enable account activation: With account activation enabled, new registrants receive an e-mail message from phpBB at the address the registrant provides, requiring them to confirm that the new phpBB account is tied to a valid e-mail address. When users change their e-mail address, phpBB sends another e-mail message to the new address and requires the users to reactivate their accounts. This feature also prevents users from registering multiple accounts on one e-mail address.

Enable Visual Confirmation: Visual confirmation is another "must." Scripts, called *bots*, automatically register and post at web sites to advertise sites for a boost in their Google ratings. Enabling visual confirmation helps to deter these bots from using your board as a traffic driver. This requires users who register to enter a code from a randomly generated image to verify that they are indeed human. You'll save a lot of time cleaning out dead accounts thanks to this feature.

User email via board: Enable this feature as well. Instead of using easily harvested mailto links to users' e-mail addresses, this feature permits registered users to send e-mail to other registered users via the board, without ever seeing an e-mail address. It's one less way for your users' e-mail addresses to become spam magnets.

COPPA: If you are in the U.S. and plan on running a board that could interest users under the age of 13, you should make sure you have the Children's Online Privacy Protection Act (COPPA) information filled in so you can ensure that you comply with all pertinent U.S. regulations concerning minors registering on your site. These settings appear near the very bottom of the page, just above the Email Settings section.

Getting a Nifty Performance Boost

Finally, here's a setting I highly recommend you use on any board you create whenever possible. You save a lot of bandwidth and get much better performance from the board with the following option:

Enable GZip Compression: Turn this on. The bandwidth savings are quite nice, and the performance penalty is unnoticeable on all but the busiest boards. This function uses the server to compress the page and send it to the user. Older browsers have been known to fumble a bit with gzip-compressed pages, but most of them are no longer in use across the Internet, so enabling this feature should be safe.

Now that you have some of the basic settings configured to your community's tastes, let's start creating some forums!

Creating Your Forums

You're ready to get started with your forums and categories. You'll be creating those in a short while, but right now is a good time to think about how you want your community organized.

Considering the Organization of Your Forums

phpBB offers the ability to place your forums in different categories, providing possibilities for logical organization of your forums. Here are some guidelines to follow when creating your forums.

Think Big, But Start Small

Having too many specific forums for each little topic is not a good idea. It's generally best to create forums that have a broad reach in a particular topic at first. As the community evolves and, ideally, the number of conversations increase, you can then reevaluate your individual forums and break them down as you see fit. The less specific the forums, the better. That way, your users will be more likely to post in the right forum at first, and they won't experience the shock of having their post moved by a moderator.

Avoid Category Overload

Stick to broad topics. Try to avoid having categories with one or two forums in them. If your categories are that specific, chances are there is a broader category topic that you can bring more forums under.

Have Announcements, Feedback, and Private Staff Forums

An announcements forum is a good idea when you have new features or policies to announce. I recommend permitting users to reply to topics in this announcements forum so you can get immediate feedback on a new feature. It helps users feel that they're involved.

Additionally, you should create a separate forum for feedback and general questions to the staff. While users could use private messages to ask these questions, inviting them to ask in the open permits multiple staff members to comment. Sometimes, veterans of your board can answer a user's question before a staff member gets to it. And what administrator realistically wants to come home to a stuffed private message box from a user asking why her avatar doesn't work?

Finally, a private staff forum is another one of those "must-haves." phpBB provides all the permissions to make this happen, and it's a very smart thing to do. You and your staff need a sounding board for issues in your community—one that the members don't see. It's part of good teamwork, and it's crucial as your forums grow.

Now that you have some guidelines, let's create some working forums!

Adding Forums

Log in to the Administration panel, click *Management* under Forum Admin in the navigation pane, and take a look at the screen. Chances are it resembles Figure 8-8.

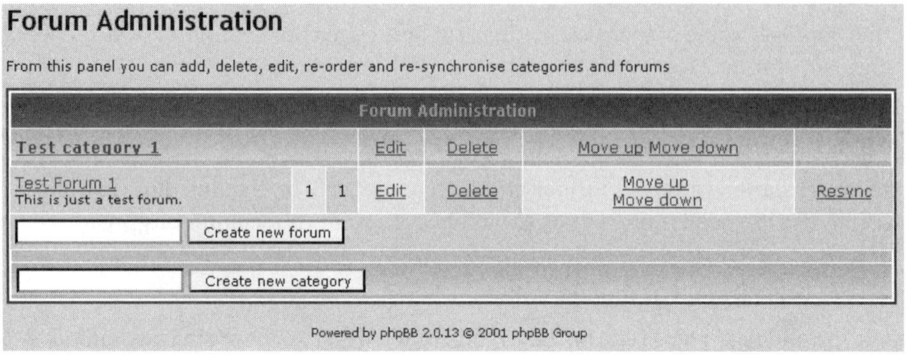

Figure 8-8. *The Forum Administration panel*

When you installed phpBB, it created a sample category and forum for you. You can feel free to delete those if you wish. They were intended only as a brief demonstration that, in fact, your board works.

Since you know your board works, it's time to get started creating categories. At the very bottom of the form, you'll see a text box with a button next to it labeled Create new category. Fill the text box with the title of the category you wish to create. I'll call mine Forum Announcements, but feel free to call yours whatever you like. Click the Create new category button, and you will get a confirmation message, saying that the "forum and category information was updated successfully." Click the first link to return to the Forum Administration panel, and your categories list should now look something like Figure 8-9.

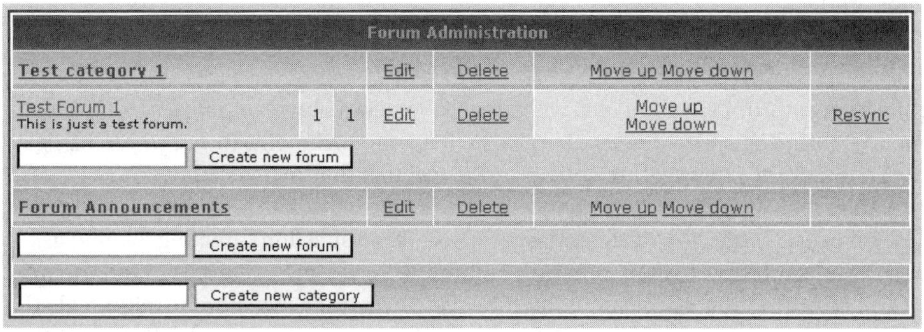

Figure 8-9. *The Forum Administration panel, featuring the newly created category*

If you don't like the position of your category, feel free to use the links to move it up and down. You can use the *Edit* link to change the title, or if you decide that you don't want that category, you can delete it.

At the end of each category, you see a text box with a Create new forum button next to it. As you've guessed, that's how you create a new forum within that category. Fill in the title of the forum you wish to create, and then click the Create new forum button. You'll see a form requesting additional information about the forum you wish to create, as shown in Figure 8-10.

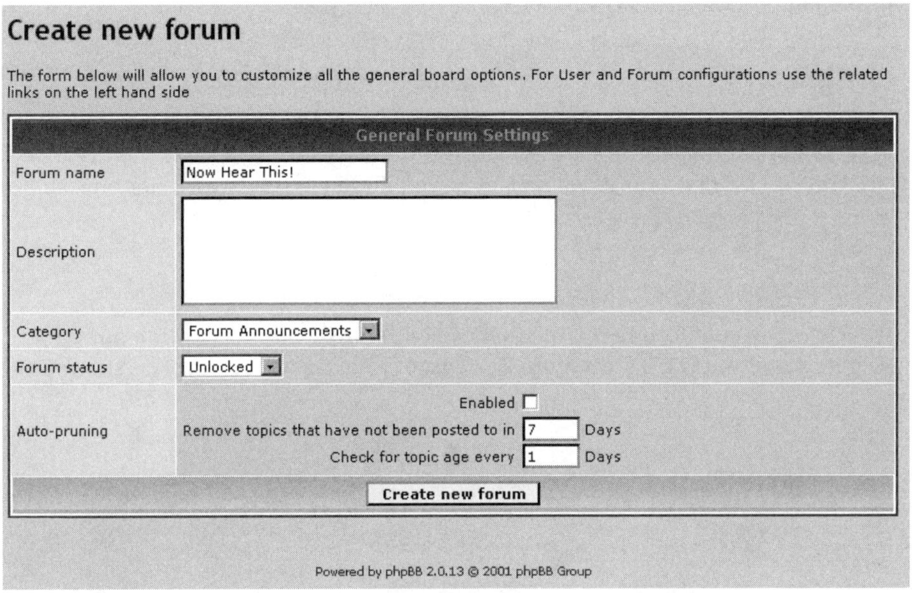

Create new forum

The form below will allow you to customize all the general board options. For User and Forum configurations use the related links on the left hand side

General Forum Settings

Forum name: Now Hear This!

Description

Category: Forum Announcements

Forum status: Unlocked

Auto-pruning: Enabled
Remove topics that have not been posted to in 7 Days
Check for topic age every 1 Days

Create new forum

Powered by phpBB 2.0.13 © 2001 phpBB Group

Figure 8-10. *The form for additional information about your new forum*

This form contains the following fields:

Forum name: This field is filled in for you. You gave the forum a name on the previous page, and that information is carried over to this page. If you decide that you don't like the name of your forum, you can change it at this point.

Description: You'll need to add a brief description of what the forum entails for your users.

Category: If you have second thoughts about which category you wish to put this forum in, you can change that in the Category drop-down menu.

Forum status: In most cases, you will wish to leave the forum unlocked, unless you are creating a forum for archival purposes that you don't want anyone posting in.

Auto-pruning: Leave auto-pruning, a feature that automatically removes dead topics on a schedule you specify, off for now, as this feature is far from ideal for fledgling boards.

Naturally, you can always return to this form and change any of these settings.

Click the Create new forum button, and you'll see the familiar success screen. Return to the Forum Administration panel, and your new forum should appear in its proper category, as shown in Figure 8-11.

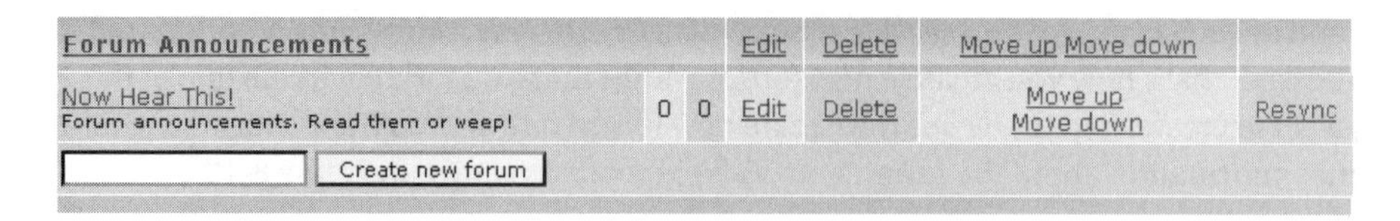

Figure 8-11. *Your new forum in all its glory*

The rest is pretty straightforward. Repeat these steps to add your forums until you are satisfied with your changes. Feel free to edit and delete at will. I recommend using the *Preview Forum* link in the navigation pane to see the changes from the user's perspective, as discussed shortly. Once you are satisfied with all your changes, you'll want to set permissions on your forums.

Setting Permissions on Forums

Now you need to set up your forums' permissions. Click *Permissions* under Forum Admin in the navigation pane, and you'll see a drop-down list of your available forums, as shown in Figure 8-12.

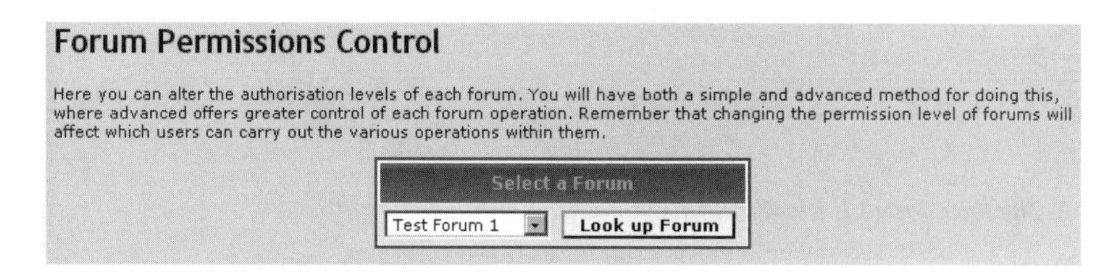

Figure 8-12. *The initial Forum Permissions panel*

You'll want to set the permissions on each forum, unless you wish to permit guest posting on your board (which I strongly discourage for security reasons). Select the first forum in the list, and then click the Look up Forum button, which will take you to the permissions screen in Simple Mode, as shown in Figure 8-13.

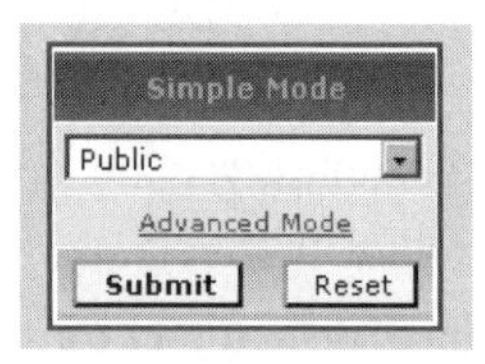

Figure 8-13. *The Forum Permissions panel in Simple Mode*

I recommend sticking with Simple Mode for now. You will delve further into the finer-grained permissions possible with phpBB in Chapter 10.

My recommendation for the vast majority of your forums is to set them to the Registered mode. This permits the public at large to read your forums but not post new topics or respond to them. Among other benefits, this deters people from stopping in to post spam and other undesired messages. If you don't wish for the public to see some of your forums, you can use the Registered [Hidden] option. Use that option conservatively, as it generally is better to permit guests to read your forum so they can have an idea what that forum covers before they register.

If you create a staff-only forum, as I suggested earlier, I recommend you set it to Moderators [Hidden], as that will hide the forum from the general public but permit your moderators and administrators to see it. In this case, regular users don't need to see the staff room, since they can't get into it.

Previewing Your Forums

Use the *Preview Forum* link in the navigation pane to take a look at your forum structure. Figure 8-14 shows an example of a forum preview.

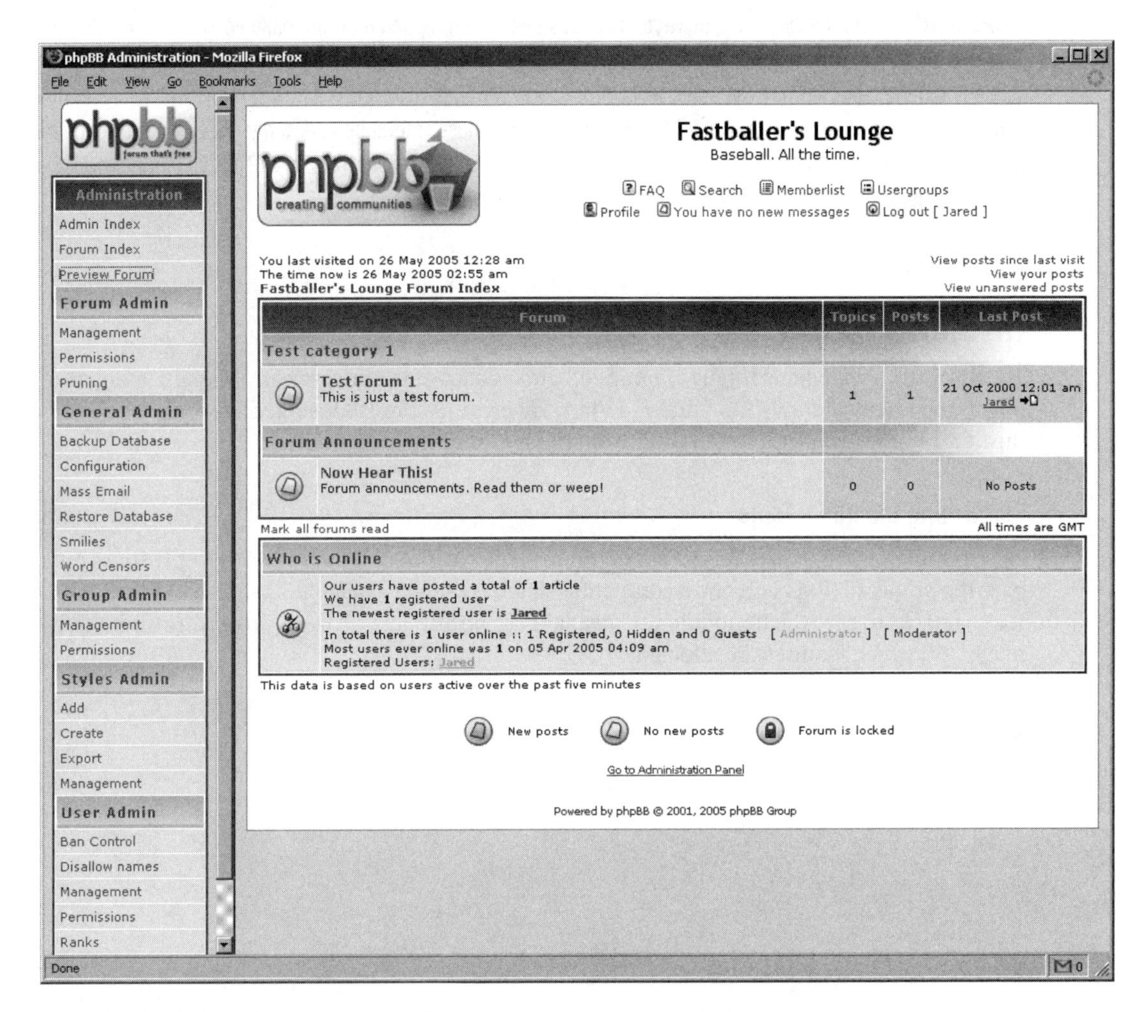

Figure 8-14. *The humble beginnings of my community, Fastballer's Lounge*

You can use the links in the Forum Administration panel to rearrange your forums and categories accordingly. The *Move up* and *Move down* links change their order. To move a forum out of one category into another, click the *Edit* link, and then choose a different category on the forum's setup form. Once you are satisfied with how things look, try logging out. Make sure all your permissions work as you wish, and then log back in.

Touring the phpBB 3.0 Installer and Administration Panel

For the curious reader, I'll conclude this chapter with a sneak preview of the next generation of phpBB, version 3.0, code-named Olympus. I will describe installing and configuring a phpBB 3.0 board, and the changes and improvements version 3.0 delivers.

■ **Caution** The screenshots and instructions in this section are based on prerelease versions of phpBB 3.0. They are all subject to change at any time, as phpBB 3.0's features are still in flux. Things could be added or deleted, and the installer could be massively overhauled overnight. Also, some items in the prerelease version of phpBB 3.0 may display "phpBB 2.2" or even "phpBB 2." Those references primarily exist as a reference to the development version of 3.0, which the phpBB development team dubs *version 2.2* or even just *phpBB 2*. These inconsistent references will eventually be fixed to read *phpBB 3.0*.

Installing phpBB 3.0

The phpBB 3.0 installer is totally revamped. It takes a lot of the guesswork out of installing the board and is considerably more helpful than any previous phpBB installer. Let's take a tour of the new phpBB installer. I'll walk you through my installation experience.

Performing the Initial Tests

New to the phpBB 3.0 installer is a set of initial tests that run on your server to verify that you have the proper PHP version and a compatible database server available, as shown in Figure 8-15. It also checks to see which modules are available to phpBB for use in its various features, and it tells you which features are affected.

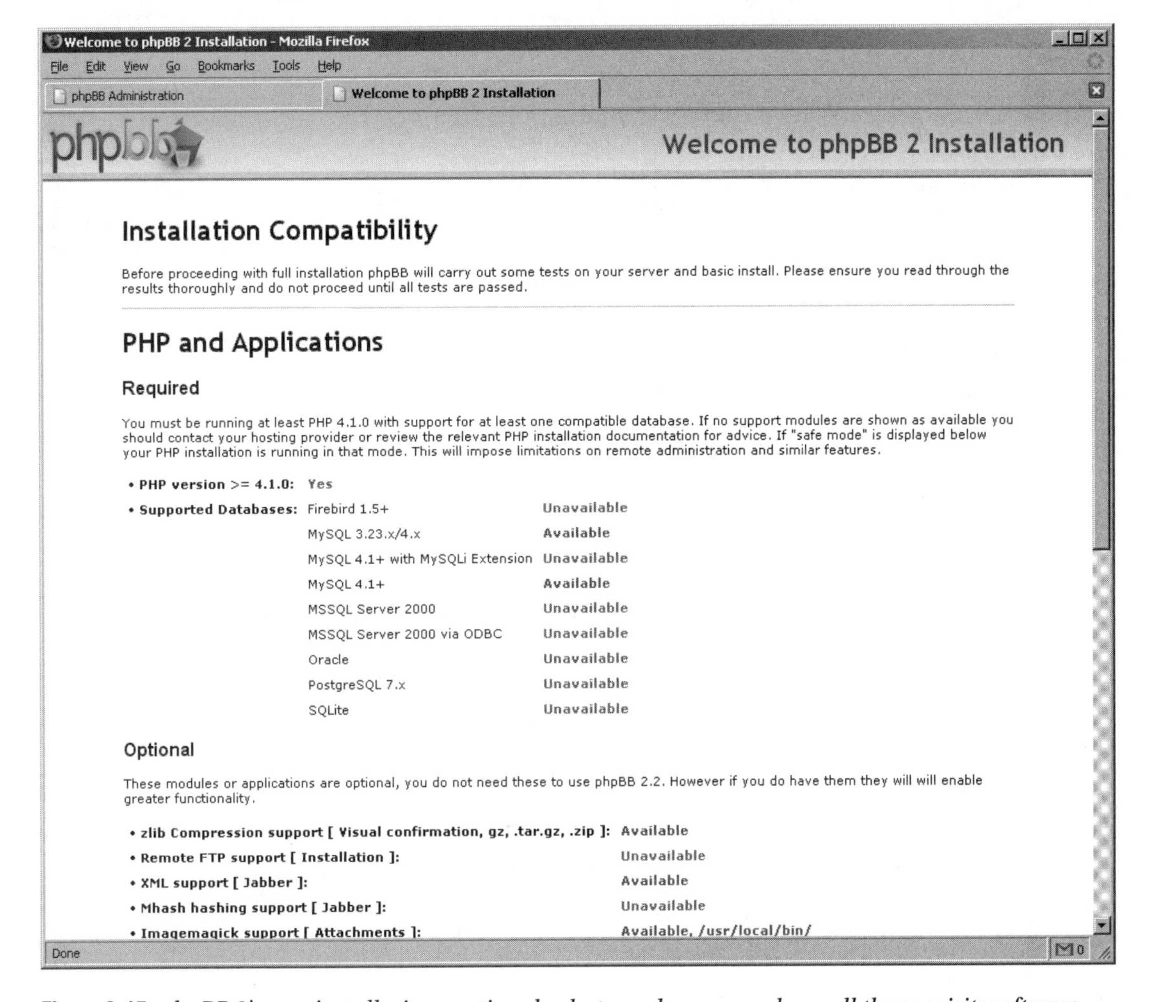

Figure 8-15. *phpBB 3's new installation routine checks to make sure you have all the requisite software.*

The installer also tests to make sure that the proper files and directories are writable by the web server. For phpBB 3.0, you'll want to ensure that the cache, files, and store directories are writable, as is `config.php`, as you have done for phpBB 2.0. The installer will test for this, as shown in Figure 8-16, and complain accordingly if it can't write to the files.

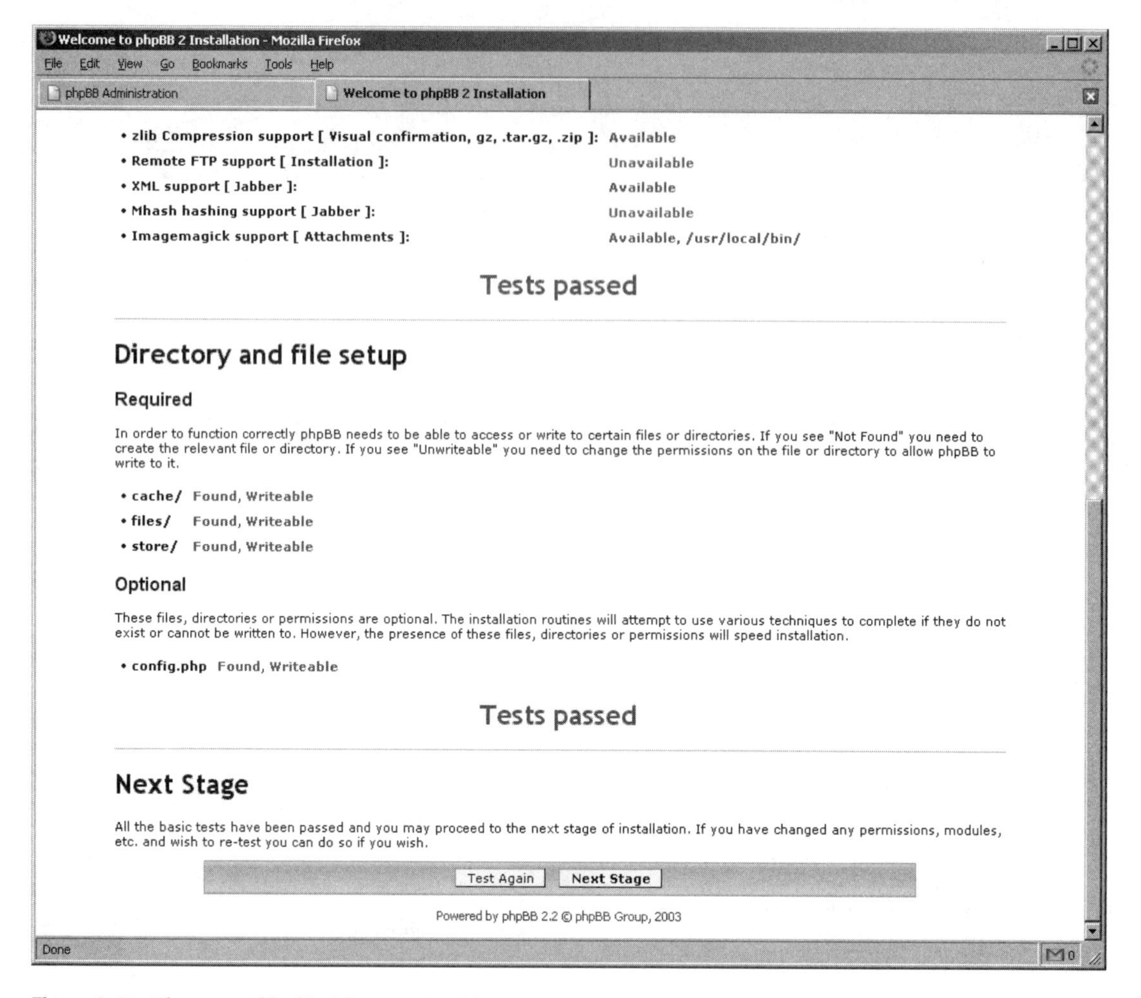

Figure 8-16. *The second half of the preinstallation test suite. I changed the permissions on those directories only because the tests failed the first time.*

Since I've passed all the tests, I have the option to continue to the next stage. So let's do that!

Configuring the Basics

Entering server information and administrator account details for phpBB 3.0 is similar to filling in the form in phpBB 2.0. However, there's one nice change in this form, shown in Figure 8-17, which is the Test Connection button at the bottom of the Database Configuration section. You can make sure your database details work properly before you try to perform the installation. The phpBB team has pulled out all the stops in this release to help ensure a fully successful installation, and this is just another example of that. As before, you can leave the prefilled fields intact.

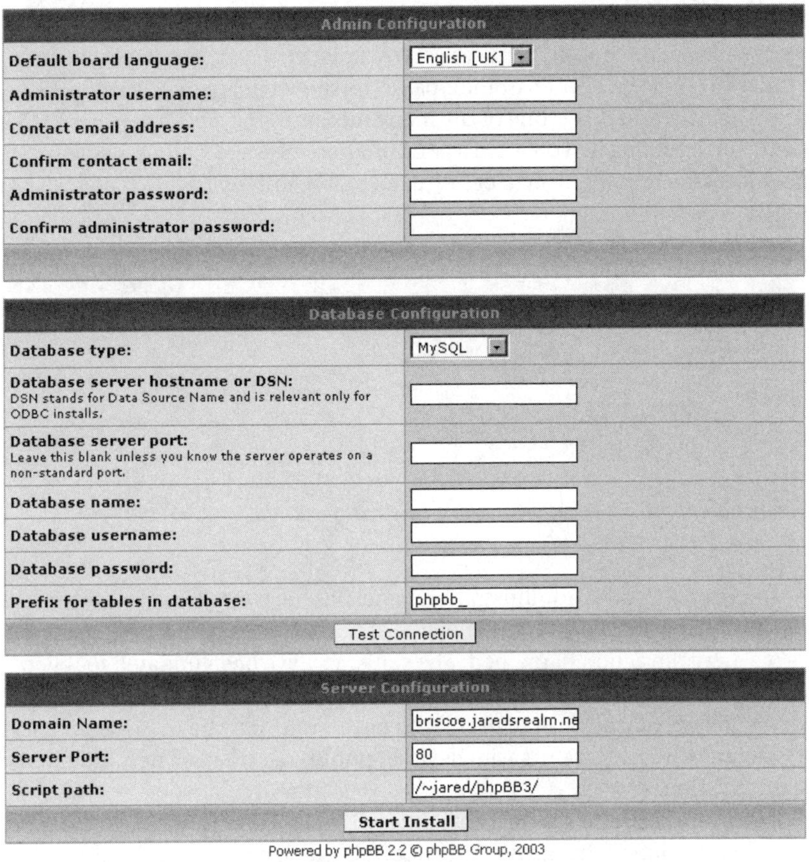

Admin Configuration

Default board language: English [UK]
Administrator username:
Contact email address:
Confirm contact email:
Administrator password:
Confirm administrator password:

Database Configuration

Database type: MySQL
Database server hostname or DSN:
DSN stands for Data Source Name and is relevant only for ODBC installs.
Database server port:
Leave this blank unless you know the server operates on a non-standard port.
Database name:
Database username:
Database password:
Prefix for tables in database: phpbb_
Test Connection

Server Configuration

Domain Name: briscoe.jaredsrealm.ne
Server Port: 80
Script path: /~jared/phpBB3/
Start Install

Powered by phpBB 2.2 © phpBB Group, 2003

Figure 8-17. *Basic configuration for phpBB 3.0 (notice the new Test Connection button underneath the database information)*

Hold your breath—I'm going to start the install! As you can see in Figure 8-18, it worked, largely because I had the chance to do all the tests beforehand. The installer is vastly improved.

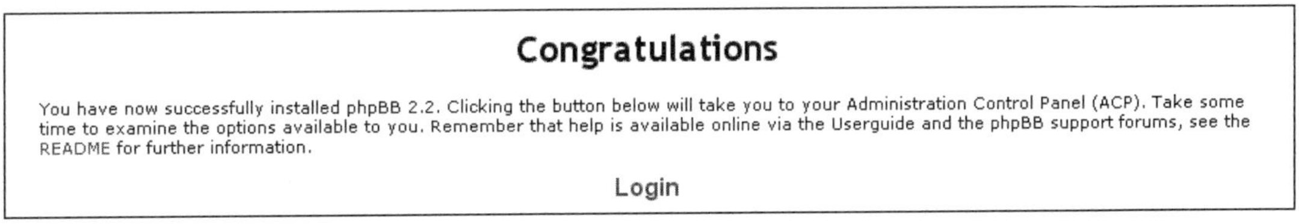

Congratulations

You have now successfully installed phpBB 2.2. Clicking the button below will take you to your Administration Control Panel (ACP). Take some time to examine the options available to you. Remember that help is available online via the Userguide and the phpBB support forums, see the README for further information.

Login

Figure 8-18. *It just works. You can't ask for much else.*

Now let's kick the tires on this new installation and see what it can do.

Configuring phpBB 3.0

As with post-2.0.15 versions of the phpBB 2.0.*x* series, you must now reauthenticate yourself with the board in order to enter the Administration panel, as shown in Figure 8-19. phpBB 3.0 is all about increased security, and this is one of the many measures the developers have taken to keep intruders out. Once you log in, you'll see a confirmation message stating that your authentication was successful and that you're being taken to the Administration panel.

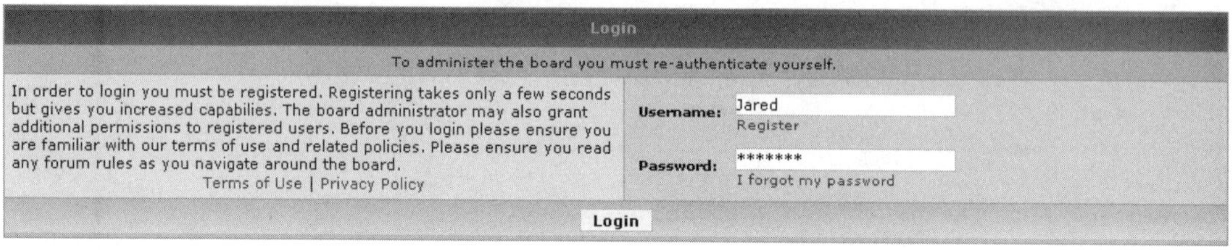

Figure 8-19. *Reauthentication is now required to enter the Administration panel.*

As you can see in Figure 8-20, the Administration panel has been totally revamped. Administrative actions are now logged with the user, the action the user performed, the time, and the IP address of where the action happened. The statistics have been updated to reflect new features such as attachments, and you can refresh these statistics using a drop-down menu. Finally, you are presented with a list of users who have yet to activate their accounts. This is particularly useful for administrators who have set phpBB to screen all new members and require manual activation.

The left pane of the Administration panel is bustling with all sorts of new categories and features. With this reorganization of the navigation pane, it is much easier to find the function you are looking for, as the headings and links generally make more sense.

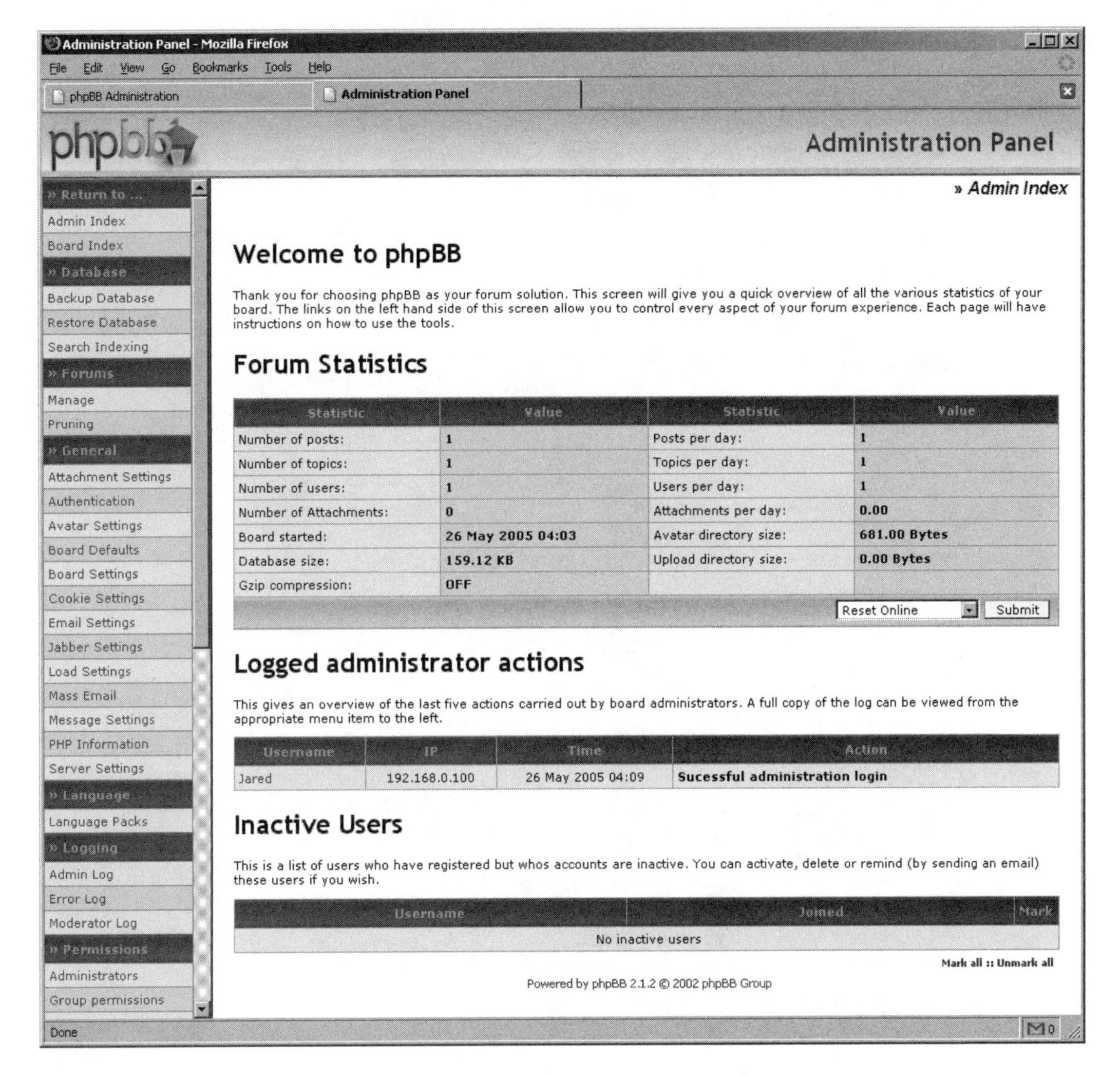

Figure 8-20. *A glance at the revamped phpBB 3.0 Administration panel*

Finding General Configuration Settings

The items under General Admin in phpBB 2.0's Administration panel are now available in two locations in phpBB 3.0: Board Defaults and Board Settings. The Board Defaults group deals with the settings the users will pick up when they first sign up, as shown in Figure 8-21. This is where you configure the time zone, default theme, and other useful options for users.

Board Defaults

These settings allow you to define a number of default or global settings used by the board. For example, to disable the use of HTML across the entire board alter the relevant setting below. This data is also used for new user registrations and (where releva guest users. Please note that registered users can override some of these options with their own settings.

Board Defaults	
Default Style:	subSilver
Override user style: Replaces users style with the default.	Yes (•) No
Default Language:	English [UK]
Date Format: The date format is the same as the PHP date function.	D M d, Y g:i a
System Timezone:	[GMT] Dublin, Edinburgh, Iceland, Lisbon, London, Casablanca
Enable Daylight Savings Time:	Yes (•) No
Private Messaging: Enable or disable private messaging for all users.	(•) Yes No
Allow Topic Watching:	(•) Yes No
Allow Forum Watching:	(•) Yes No
Allow Username changes:	Yes (•) No
Allow Attachments:	(•) Yes No
Allow HTML:	Yes (•) No
Allowed HTML tags: Separate tags with commas.	b,i,u,pre
Allow BBCode:	(•) Yes No
Allow Smilies:	(•) Yes No
Allow Signatures:	(•) Yes No
Maximum signature length: Maximum number of characters in user signatures.	255
Allow Disable of Censors: User can disable word censoring.	Yes (•) No
Allow bookmarking topics: User is able to store personal bookmarks	(•) Yes No
Submit Reset	

Figure 8-21. *phpBB 3.0 Board Defaults options*

As shown in Figure 8-22, the Board Settings group contains the settings for the community's title and description, COPPA information, account activation policies, visual confirmation, and much more.

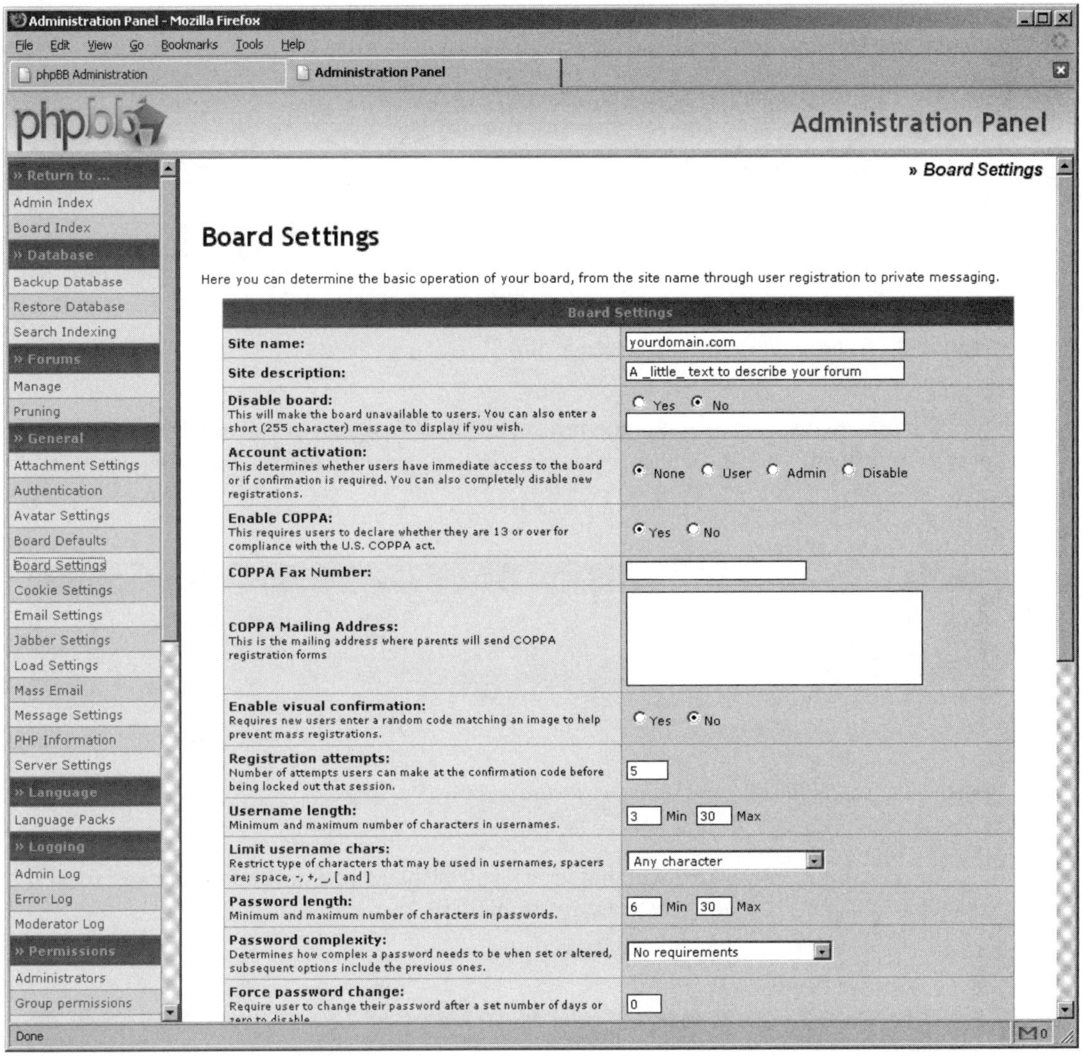

Figure 8-22. *phpBB 3.0 Board Settings options*

Creating Forums, Sub-Forums, Sub-Sub-Forums. . .

When configuring forums for phpBB 3.0 for the first time, you may be thrown off by the fact that there are no categories! phpBB 3.0 introduces sub-forums, which take the place of categories and also allow you to nest forums within forums.

Sub-forums are a strange concept to get used to at first, but when you get the hang of them, sub-forums quickly turn into an organizational boon for your site. Say you have an archive for one particular forum. Instead of having the archive on the forum index page, you can now have the archive live inside the main forum, so it doesn't take up room on the front page. That's one of many possible uses for a sub-forum.

So how do you create forums in phpBB 3.0? First, click the *Manage* link under Forums in the navigation pane, and you'll see the screen shown in Figure 8-23.

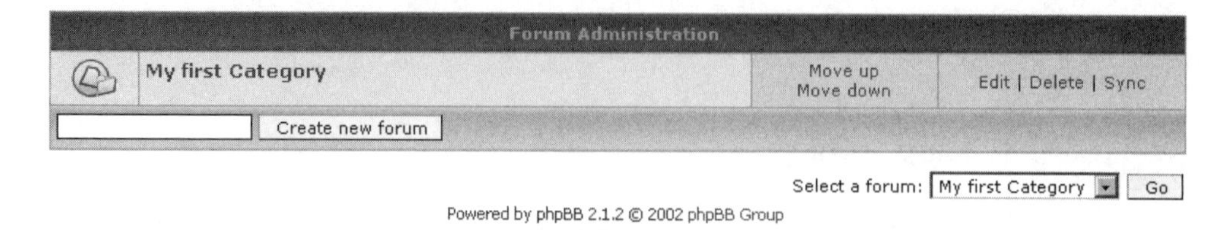

Figure 8-23. *Is that a category, or is that a forum?*

You can create a forum at that top level to act like a category, or you can click the category's name. If you click the category's name, you'll see a screen like the one in Figure 8-24.

Board Index -> My first Category
Forum Administration
Test Forum 1
This is just a test forum.
Topics: 1 / Posts: 1
Move up
Move down
Edit | Delete | Sync
Create new forum
Select a forum: My first Category
Go

Figure 8-24. *Inside the My First Category forum*

You can then create a forum at that level if you wish. Or, you can go into that test forum, as shown in Figure 8-25, and create a sub-forum there.

Board Index -> My first Category -> Test Forum 1
Forum Administration
Test Forum Archive
Create new forum
Select a forum: Test Forum 1
Go

Figure 8-25. *Inside the Test Forum 1 forum*

Wherever you decide to create a forum, you'll notice an explosion of options, compared with those available in phpBB 2.0. Figure 8-26 shows the phpBB 3.0 form for creating a new forum.

» *Create new forum*

In phpBB 2.2 there are no categories, everything is forum based. Each forum can have an unlimited number of sub-forums and you can determine whether each may be posted to or not (i.e. whether it acts like an old category). Here you can add, edit, delete, lock, unlock individual forums as well as set certain additional controls. If your posts and topics have got out of sync you can also resynchronise a forum.

Create new forum

The form below will allow you to customise this forum. Please note that moderation and post count controls are set via forum permissions for each user or usergroup.

Board Index -> My first Category -> Test Forum 1

Forum Settings	
Forum Type:	Forum
Forum Status:	Unlocked
Parent Forum:	Test Forum 1
Forum Name:	Test Forum Archive
Description: Any markup entered here will displayed as is.	
Please click to view the forum rules: You are able to enter the URL of the page/post containing your forum rules here. This setting will override the Forum Rules text you specified.	
Forum Rules: Forum Rules are displayed at any page within the given forum.	Parse BBCode / Parse Smilies / Parse Links
Forum Image: Location, relative to the phpBB root directory, of an image to associate with this forum.	
Forum Style:	Default Style
Enable search indexing: If set to yes posts made to this forum will be indexed for searching.	Yes / No
Enable Topic Icons:	Yes / No
Enable Auto-Pruning: Prunes the forum of topics, set the frequency/age parameters below.	Yes / No
Auto-prune Frequency: Time in days between pruning events.	0 Days
Auto-prune Post Age: Number of days since last post after which topic is removed.	0 Days
Auto-prune Post Viewed Age: Number of days since topic was viewed after which topic is removed.	0 Days
Prune Old Polls: Removes topics with polls not voted in for post age days.	Yes / No
Prune Announcements:	Yes / No
Prune Stickies:	Yes / No
Topics Per Page: If non-zero this value will override the default topics per page setting.	0
Forum Password: Defines a password for this forum, use the permission system in preference.	
Confirm Forum Password: Only needs to be set if a forum password is entered.	
Submit / Reset	

Powered by phpBB 2.1.2 © 2002 phpBB Group

Figure 8-26. *Creating a new forum in phpBB 3.0 (notice all the brand-new options!)*

Feel free to add forum rules. At this time, phpBB does not provide a template for those rules. You add the forum rules by entering them directly into this box. If you have a custom image for the forum, you can use the new Forum Image option to include that as well. You have much more control over the pruning options, too. If you want a quick-and-dirty private forum, you can use the Forum Password field to assign a password to it. phpBB recommends that you use permissions rather than this password feature, but it's there if you need it.

Setting Forum Permissions

After filling in the settings and continuing, phpBB will tell you it created the forum, and it gives you a link to start filling in permissions—another nice touch (before, you had to remember to set permissions). Permissions in phpBB 3.0 are vastly expanded over version 2.0, with the introduction of access control lists (ACLs). The new ACLs work with both individual users and user groups, as shown in Figure 8-27. You can add groups or users to the list and apply permissions to each object.

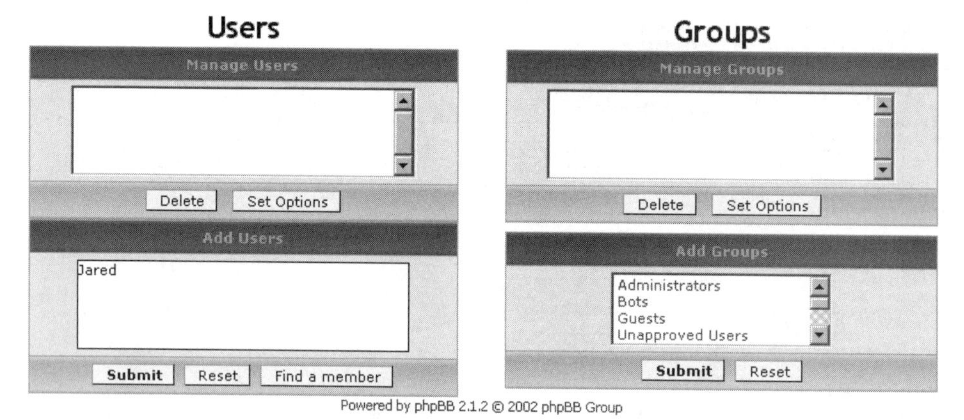

Figure 8-27. *The first permissions screen, where you select the user or group you wish to set access rights for*

When you click Submit, don't panic. There's an enormous list of permissions here, allowing you to restrict (or permit) more than you ever thought possible, as shown in Figure 8-28. Luckily for us, phpBB 3.0 explains each permission in a far easier to understand fashion than in previous versions. You can use the Presets menu to turn them all on or off. Don't be surprised if the final release of phpBB 3.0 comes with even more presets. The form at the very bottom permits you to set your own presets—yet another one of those nice touches.

» *Permissions*

Permissions are based on a simple YES / NO system. Setting an option to NO for a user or usergroup overrides any other value assigned to it. If you do not wish to assign a value for an option for this user or group select UNSET. If values are assigned for this option elsewhere they will be used in preference, else NO is assumed.

Permissions

Selected User: **Jared**

Here you can alter which users and groups can access which forums. To assign moderators or define administrators please use the appropriate page (see left hand side menu).

Presets: Select ->

Option	Yes	Unset	No
Can see forum	○	◉	○
Can read forum	○	◉	○
Can post in forum	○	◉	○
Can reply to posts	○	◉	○
Can quote posts	○	◉	○
Can edit own posts	○	◉	○
Can lock own topics	○	◉	○
Can delete own posts	○	◉	○
Can bump topics	○	◉	○
Can create polls	○	◉	○
Can vote in polls	○	◉	○
Can change existing vote	○	◉	○
Can post announcements	○	◉	○
Can post stickies	○	◉	○
Can attach files	○	◉	○
Can download files	○	◉	○
Icons	○	◉	○
Can post HTML	○	◉	○
Can post BBCode	○	◉	○
Can post smilies	○	◉	○
Can post images	○	◉	○
Can post Flash	○	◉	○
Can use signatures	○	◉	○
Can search the forum	○	◉	○
Can email topics	○	◉	○
Can rate posts	○	◉	○
Can print topics	○	◉	○
Can ignore flood limit	○	◉	○
Increment post counter	○	◉	○
Posts are moderated	○	◉	○
Can report posts	○	◉	○
Can subscribe forum	○	◉	○

Update Cancel

Presets

To update or delete an existing preset select it from the list.

Select preset: Select ->

Preset name:

Save Delete

Powered by phpBB 2.1.2 © 2002 phpBB Group

Figure 8-28. *phpBB 3.0 has many policies for the user. Thank goodness for presets!*

Clicking the Update button does what you expect: it updates the permissions for the user. It's a very cool system, and an unbelievably powerful one.

So what exactly happened? When you visit the test forum, sure enough, there's another forum inside it, as shown in Figure 8-29. It's a great method of organization.

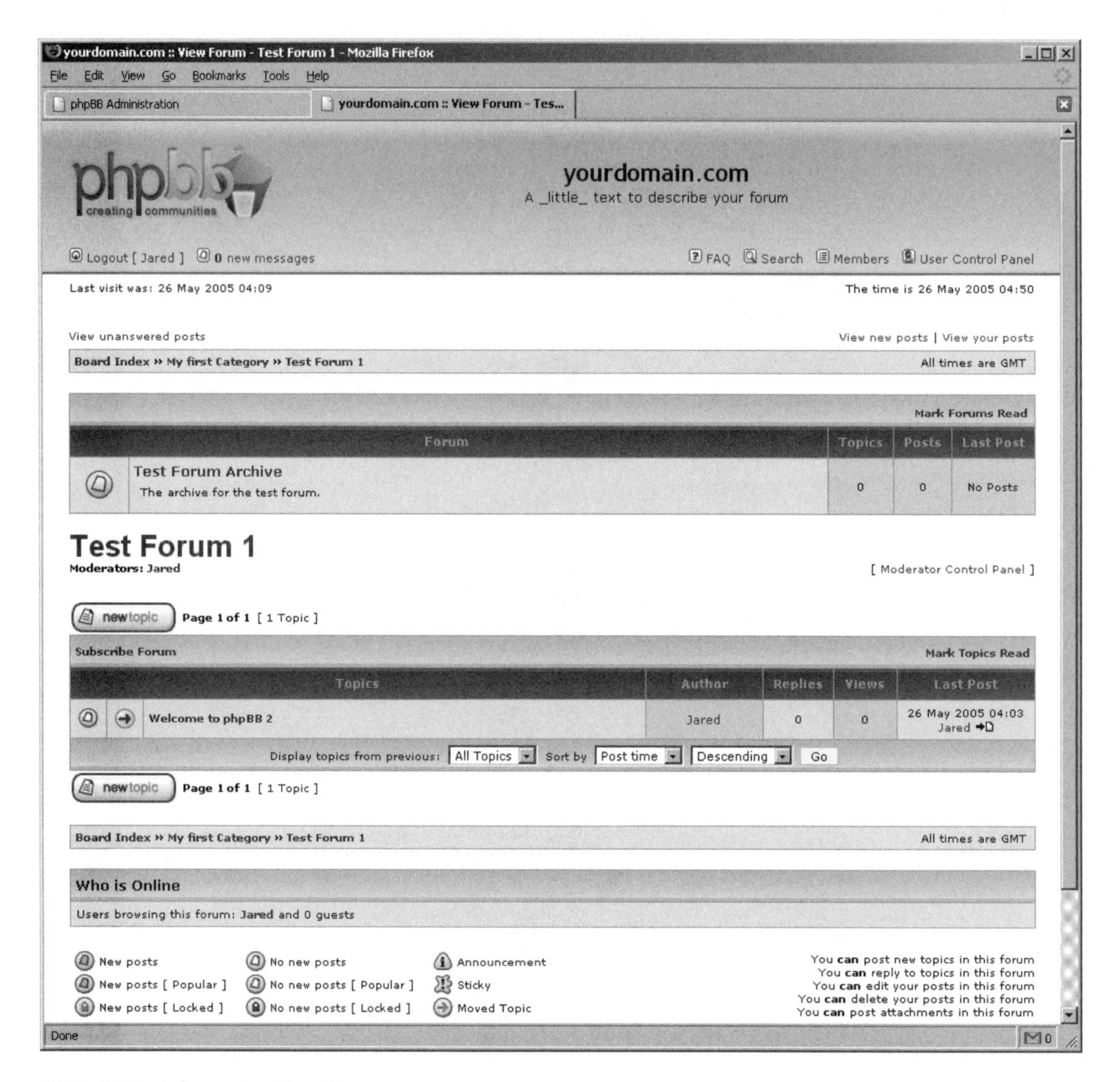

Figure 8-29. *A forum inside a forum*

As of this prerelease version of phpBB 3.0, it appears you can have as many levels as you want, which might be counterproductive. Ideally, two levels is quite enough. Anything more than that might make things too complex.

■ **Tip** If you absolutely must have sub-forums in your phpBB 2.0 installation, rejoice! There is a modification available for the phpBB 2.0 series that installs a sub-forum feature on your board. It has been well tested and works remarkably well. Obtain it from a site such as `http://www.phpbbhacks.com`, and then flip ahead to Chapter 11 to find out how to install it.

Summary

You've now worked through installing and configuring phpBB. You've set up your forums and configured what your users can and cannot do in those forums. In other words, you now have a working board ready for posting! The next step is to familiarize yourself with the many end-user features that phpBB has to offer to your members, which is the topic of the next chapter. Additionally, I'll take you through more administrative functions you may use on a regular basis, which will further assist you in building a dynamite community for your web site.

CHAPTER 9

Touring phpBB's Features

One of the keys to success of managing your phpBB community is having a grasp of the phpBB software's feature set. While phpBB's end-user features are generally straightforward, they are also quite powerful. Knowing the ins and outs of these features will help you explain and fix problems you (or your users) may run into in the day-to-day operations of your forum.

In this chapter, I'll walk you through mastering the end-user features that will help you guide users having difficulty adjusting to your forums, and discuss the administrative options related to these features. I'll also preview the phpBB 3.0 feature set.

Reading and Posting to Forums

Making posts and reading them are absolutely the most basic functions to a message board. phpBB offers enhancements to these seemingly simple functions to make you and your users' lives much easier. Knowing how a particular function works can be a huge help when someone has a question as to why it's behaving that way.

Using the Forum Index

The Forum Index page is the front page to your forums and contains some very useful time-saving features. It has links to quick searches (some of which are available only to registered users, as explained in the "Searching Forums" section later in this chapter), a convenient login form, and a look at who is browsing the forums with the Who's Online feature.

The forums tell you when the last post was made and who made it, and if there is anything new since your last visit (if you are logged in). The Forum Index page also showcases the newest member to the board, which is a very useful feature in building your community, as it gives users the opportunity to welcome the new users. Finally, the Forum Index page gives some brief statistics on how many users have ever been online at the same time, which can be a fun fact to have.

Marking Forums As Read

When registered users read forums, phpBB automatically keeps track of the posts they've read in cookies stored on the users' machines. Users have the ability to mark a forum or all forums as read via links on the forum or index pages, respectively.

While rare, problems with the marking feature can arise. If users are having problems with this feature, they likely are not accepting cookies from your site. If this problem becomes widespread, you may wish to check the session length under the Cookie Settings options accessed through the *Configuration* link under General Admin in the Administration panel. If you have this set to a smaller value, the session will time out sooner, and posts may be reset as read automatically.

Watching Topics

Watching topics permits users to receive e-mail notifications on replies to those topics. Users must be registered and logged in to use this feature.

Users can elect to watch topics they choose by clicking a *Watch this topic for replies* link near the bottom of every topic view page. A user can also enable the topic watch feature for a particular topic by checking the "Notify me when replies are posted" check box when replying to a thread (see Figure 9-1, shown later in this chapter). To stop watching a topic, the user can revisit the topic and click the *Stop watching this topic* link.

Formatting Posts Using BBCode

phpBB provides a potent and safe HTML substitute, known as BBCode, so users can format their text (bold, italic, underline, and so on) without exposing your board to the possibility of malicious HTML. BBCode is usable in forum posts, private messages, and signatures (small lines of text registered users can optionally attach to every post). The BBCode system is incredibly powerful and easily customized via phpBB's template engine, which I will discuss in Chapter 12.

Table 9-1 outlines the available BBCode in default installations of phpBB 2.0. As Table 9-1 illustrates, BBCode tags are used much like HTML. Note the usage of square brackets versus HTML's angle brackets.

Table 9-1. *BBCode Available in phpBB 2.0*

BBCode Tag*	Formatting Result
`[b]Bold text.[/b]`	Creates bold text
`[i]Italic text.[/i]`	Creates italic text
`[u]Underlined text.[/u]`	Creates underlined text
`[quote]Quoted text[/quote]`	Puts text in a smaller font, indented, and set off by a box
`[code]Program code[/code]`	Sets off text similarly to quoted text, and displays it in monospace
`[list][*]Item in the list[/list]`	`[list]` starts the list; `[*]` is an item in the list
`[list=a][*]Alphabetized list[/list]`	Same as a regular BBCode list, but makes an alphabetically ordered list
`[list=1][*]Numbered list[/list]`	Same as a regular BBCode list, but makes a numerically ordered list
`[img]http://path/to/image[/img]`	Embeds an image in a forum post
`[url]http://path/to/link[/url]`	Embeds a link in a post
`[url=http://link]Link text[/url]`	Links the text between the `[url]` tags to `http://link`
`[color=colorname]Text[/color]`	Changes the text between the `[color]` tags to whichever color name (red, blue, and so, on) or hexadecimal code (as in HTML) you specify
`[size=pointsize]Text[/size]`	Changes the point size of the text to the number you specify

**Some installations of phpBB across the Internet may contain modifications that add additional BBCode or modify the behavior of existing BBCode. This table lists the base set of BBCode tags.*

Users can access BBCode two ways: manually type in the code or use phpBB's formatting toolbar, available in the post form, which looks like Figure 9-1 (clad in the default subSilver style).

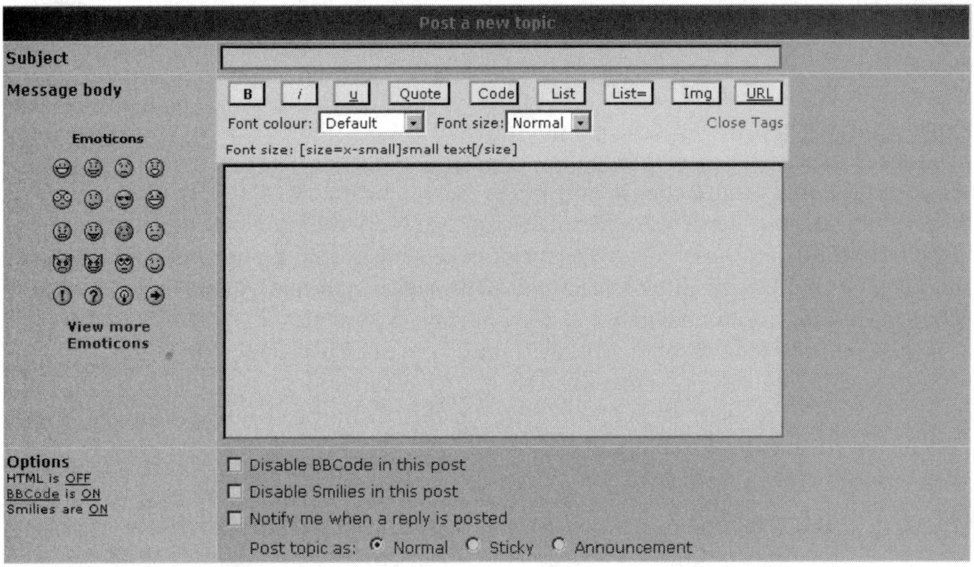

Figure 9-1. *The BBCode formatting toolbar on the post form*

The phpBB formatting toolbar offers full control over BBCode directly from the form. To get an explanation for each formatting option in the toolbar, simply hover the mouse over its button, and a description will appear in a line above the text box.

Users have the option of disabling BBCode in each of their posts by setting the corresponding option in their profile (as discussed in the "Setting User Preferences" section later in this chapter), or they can turn BBCode off in an individual post by checking the "Disable BBCode in this post" check box located at the bottom of the post form. To see the results of their formatting before making a live post, users can select the Preview button in the post form (before choosing the Submit button). When they are satisfied with their formatting, they can submit their post.

Working with Emoticons (Smilies)

phpBB offers optional graphical emoticons to replace the common Internet punctuation faces such as :-) that have permeated e-mail for years. phpBB contains more than 20 emoticons by default, with the option to add plenty of others.

To add an emoticon to a post, you can simply type the emoticon code that corresponds to the image you wish to use. Alternatively, you can use the clickable emoticons that sit on the side of the post form. phpBB shows only a few of the emoticons on the post form by default. If you wish to work with more emoticons, you can click *View more Emoticons*, and a window will pop open with the full suite of additional emoticons. You can click an emoticon in the pop-up window, and the appropriate code will be added. If users report problems with this window, their pop-up blocker probably stops that window from appearing.

As the administrator, you can use the Smilies (phpBB uses the terms *emoticons* and *smilies* interchangeably) option in the Administration panel to add or remove smiley codes at your leisure. To add a code for an emoticon, click the *Add a new Smiley* button at the bottom of the form. You will be prompted for the code, the smiley image file (which must reside in `images/smilies`), and a description of what the emotion expresses. Click Submit, and the code will be added.

Alternatively, you can add more emoticons en masse by installing Smile Packs, which come complete with the necessary codes, descriptions, and images. All you need to do is unzip the Smile Pack file you wish to import into the `images/smiles` directory under your phpBB root. Then go to the Smilies panel, click *Import Smiley Pack* at the bottom of the form, and select the pack from the drop-down menu. You can choose to overwrite your existing set of emoticons, and choose to resolve conflicts by replacing or keeping existing emoticons. After you click Import Smileys, phpBB will automatically add all the codes in the pack to the board, and they will be available for use immediately.

If you would like to release your installed emoticons as an installable Smile Pack, you can use the *Export Smile Pack* option to make it so. phpBB generates a `smiles.pak` file, which you rename to whatever you like, keeping the `.pak` extension. Then you create a zip file with your emoticon images and the `.pak` file, and release it at will.

Making Topics Sticky and Posting Announcements

Users with the proper permissions in a forum have the option when creating a new topic to make it normal, sticky, or an announcement, as shown at the bottom of Figure 9-2. Sticky and announcement topics are denoted with special icons, and are "stuck" (hence the term *sticky*) at the top of each forum. Announcements in multipage forums appear at the top of each page in the forum. Sticky topics appear only at the top of the first page.

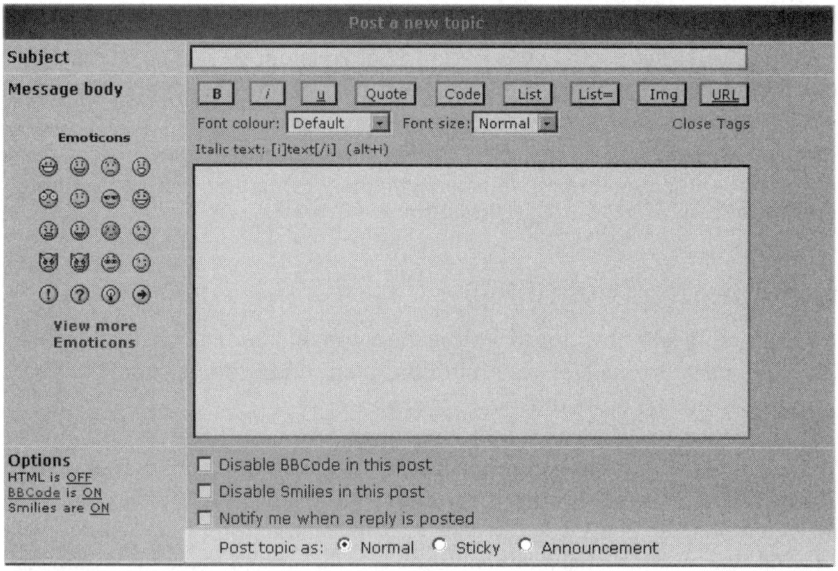

Figure 9-2. *The options for setting a sticky or announcement post are highlighted.*

The rights to stick topics or make them announcements are set through the permissions system, introduced in the previous chapter. The default permissions for sticking posts and creating announcements permit administrators to do this anywhere and moderators to do this in their assigned forums. phpBB's default settings are generally reasonable for most communities, but if you wish to alter these settings, see Chapter 10 for details.

To remove sticky or announcement priority from a topic, simply edit the first post in the thread and change the options accordingly. You can also use this functionality to bump sticky topics up to announcement status and vice versa.

Attaching Polls to Topics

When posting a new topic, phpBB gives you the option to add a poll to the topic. The form that adds the poll resides at the bottom of the post form, as illustrated in Figure 9-3.

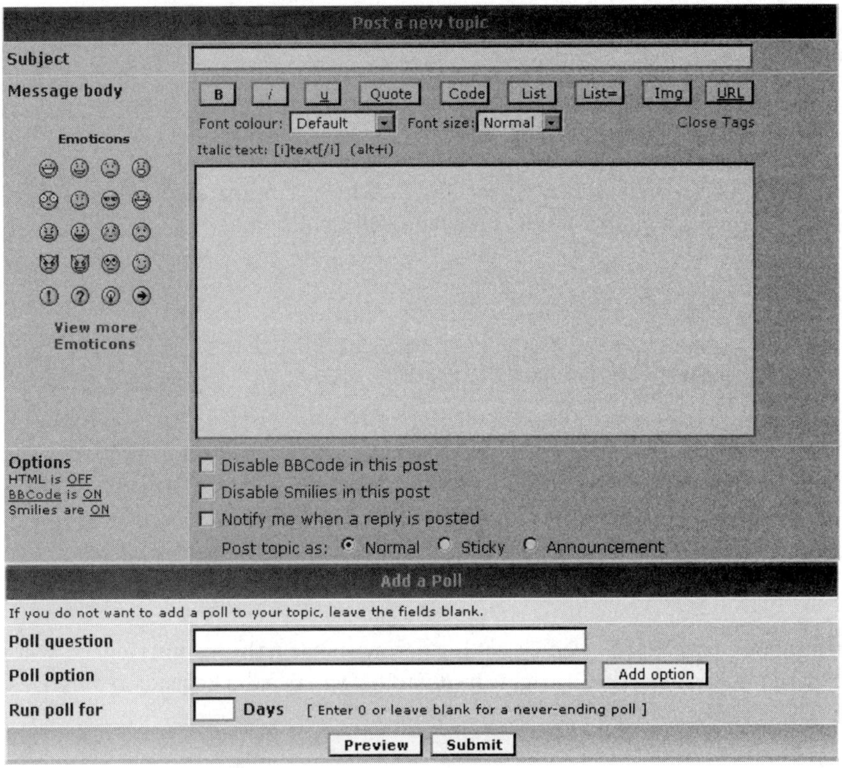

Figure 9-3. *The options for adding a poll for new topics*

Adding a poll is straightforward. You enter the poll question, and then enter an option. Add options to the poll by clicking the Add option button next to the text field of your new poll option. You can optionally set your poll to close after a period of time you specify (in days). When you are finished setting up your poll, click Submit, and it will post your topic with the poll, as shown in Figure 9-4.

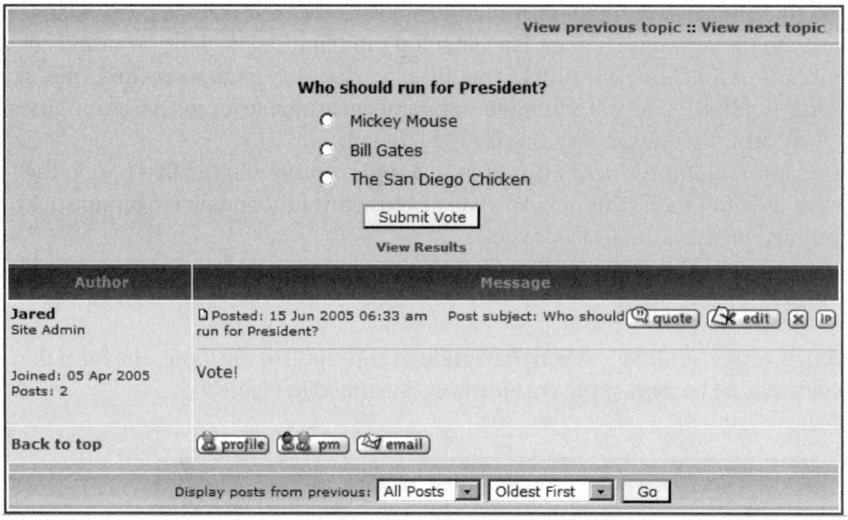

Figure 9-4. *A poll that you have not voted in yet*

After voting (or if you abstain by clicking *View Results*, which is ultimately a null vote), you can see how your poll is going. Figure 9-5 shows how the poll results look.

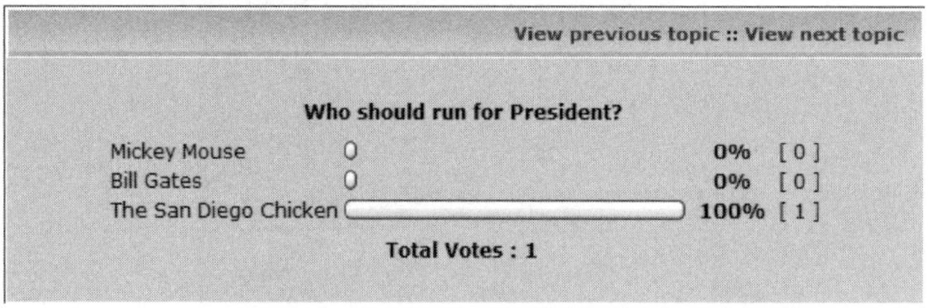

Figure 9-5. *The poll results*

Polling can be allowed and disallowed via setting permissions on the forum. Generally, users with posting rights also have polling rights by default, if you use the Registered preset.

Editing Posts

phpBB provides the ability to edit individual posts after they have been posted to the forum. Unless permissions dictate otherwise, users are generally permitted to edit their own posts.

phpBB provides a message at the bottom of the post stating it has been altered when an edit is made after the post's first five minutes of life. Posts edited by moderators and administrators do not display the "post edited" notification. This puts a bit of burden on the moderators and administrators of the forum not to abuse their power and edit posts, knowing that the post is edited blindly and without being logged.

Creating User Profiles

phpBB's user profiles allow for a great deal of personalization for your members. I'll walk you through the user profile options phpBB makes available to registered users.

Entering Registration Information

The information contained in the Registration Information section is the basic registration data required to establish an account on a phpBB forum. Figure 9-6 illustrates this section of the Edit Profile form.

Registration Information	
Items marked with a * are required unless stated otherwise.	
Username: *	**Jared**
E-mail address: *	jared@jwswebenterprises.com
Current password: * You must confirm your current password if you wish to change it or alter your e-mail address	
New password: * You only need to supply a password if you want to change it	
Confirm password: * You only need to confirm your password if you changed it above	

Figure 9-6. *The Registration Information section contains the basic information for a user account.*

If you permit users to change their username, then the Username field will be editable. If users decide to change their e-mail address and e-mail verification is enabled, they will need to reactivate their account. I will discuss e-mail verification in detail in Chapter 10, as that is an important step in securing your board.

Adding Profile Information

The fields in the Profile Information section of the Edit Profile form, shown in Figure 9-7, contain the information that is publicly viewable when viewing a user's profile or perusing the member list. Users can fill out as much or as little of the information as they please—it is all optional.

Users can also add a custom signature to append to each of their posts. Your policies on allowing HTML, BBCode, and smilies pertain to signatures as well. The default limit is set to 255 characters. This is a comfortable limit, which you are free to adjust using the General Board Settings options accessed through the *Configuration* link under General Admin in the Administration panel. It is generally good practice to keep the signature size around the default limit, or perhaps even under it. This helps prevent posts that have more signature than substance, if that is important to you.

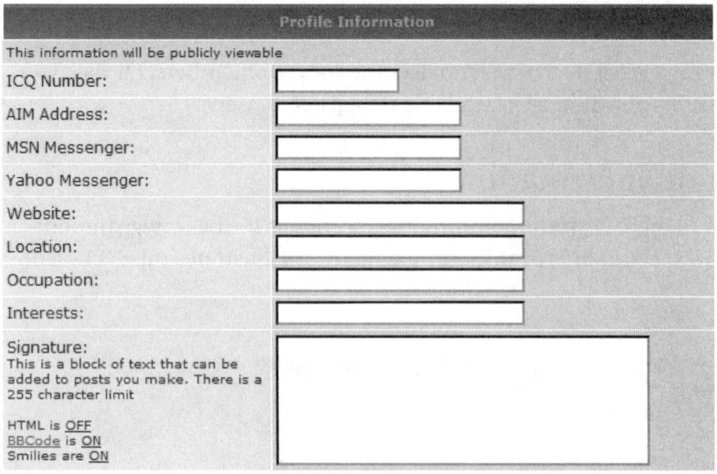

Profile Information
This information will be publicly viewable
ICQ Number:
AIM Address:
MSN Messenger:
Yahoo Messenger:
Website:
Location:
Occupation:
Interests:
Signature:
This is a block of text that can be added to posts you make. There is a 255 character limit
HTML is OFF
BBCode is ON
Smilies are ON

Figure 9-7. *The Profile Information section contains optional, publicly available information about a user.*

Setting User Preferences

The Preferences section of the Edit Profile form, shown in Figure 9-8, allows users some control over how phpBB behaves. I'll provide a brief description of each of the preferences and suggest the best practices with them.

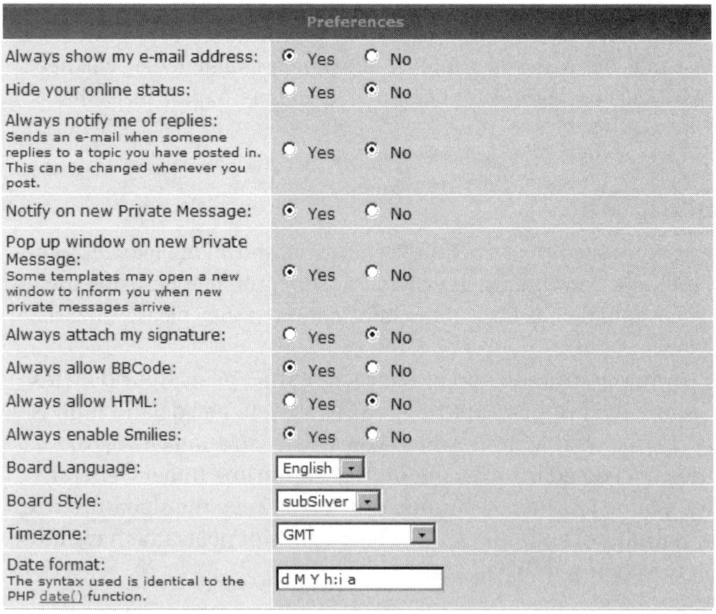

Preferences
Always show my e-mail address: Yes No
Hide your online status: Yes No
Always notify me of replies: Sends an e-mail when someone replies to a topic you have posted in. This can be changed whenever you post. Yes No
Notify on new Private Message: Yes No
Pop up window on new Private Message: Some templates may open a new window to inform you when new private messages arrive. Yes No
Always attach my signature: Yes No
Always allow BBCode: Yes No
Always allow HTML: Yes No
Always enable Smilies: Yes No
Board Language: English
Board Style: subSilver
Timezone: GMT
Date format: The syntax used is identical to the PHP date() function. d M Y h:i a

Figure 9-8. *The Preferences section is where users can choose some preferences for how phpBB should behave.*

Always show my e-mail address: The default is Yes, to show your e-mail address. I heartily recommend changing your answer to No for this question. It potentially opens up your e-mail address to unwanted messages, most notably spam messages. There's enough spam on the Internet, so why potentially expose yourself to more?

Hide your online status: Users can set their visibility to the Who's Online list with this preference. The default is No. Even if it's set to Yes, board administrators can still see the user logged in. The user is denoted with italics as being hidden.

Always notify me of replies: Users have the ability to be notified by e-mail of replies on every topic they post in, effectively enabling the topic watch feature for each of these threads. This can cause increased e-mail traffic, especially if you have a busy board, and could delay registration e-mail and other important correspondence from your board if a great deal of users take advantage of this feature. phpBB sets this to No by default.

Notify on new Private Message: When a user receives a new private message, the default behavior is for phpBB to send an e-mail to the user stating that he has a new message in his Inbox. Users can select No to turn off this feature if they wish.

Pop up window on new Private Message: Templates (including the default subSilver) offer the option to pop up a window when you receive a new private message. You will need to check with your template author (if applicable) if that feature is offered with your template. This feature defaults to Yes, although users with pop-up blockers may never see these notifications.

Always attach my signature: If the user has a blank signature, phpBB will automatically default this option to No. If the user fills in the signature box, phpBB will see this and set the option to Yes, as most users generally wish to attach their signature to each post. If this isn't the case, the user can switch the preference off and attach her signature selectively.

Always allow BBCode: phpBB defaults to leaving BBCode on all the time, and I generally recommend leaving this option set to Yes. Users can shut off BBCode if they find they don't want it in their posts, particularly if the forum administrator permits HTML. If you disable BBCode for your board in the Administration panel, this setting has no effect.

Always allow HTML: This defaults to No, so HTML isn't allowed. If you have HTML disabled in the Administration panel (highly recommended), this setting has no effect. BBCode is highly encouraged over HTML, as errors in BBCode are far less likely to break the layout of your board.

Always enable Smilies: If users do not like the graphical smilies provided by phpBB, they can turn off that feature for all their posts by changing this option to No. This may be useful for your members who do not have a broadband connection.

Board Language: If you have multiple language packs installed, users can set their preferred language to read phpBB here. This defaults to whichever language you set as the default in the Administration panel.

Board Style: If you have multiple styles installed on your board and you do not force one style over the others, users can choose which style they wish to use on the board. This is strictly a per-user setting and does not affect the board globally.

Timezone: Users have the ability to customize times to their own time zone. Note that if you change the global time zone of the board in the Administration panel, that change will not take effect for existing users; it affects only new registrations. Additionally, note that phpBB 2.0 does not support automatically compensating for Daylight Saving Time (DST), so users will need to adjust their time zone settings accordingly. (phpBB 3.0 will support automatic DST changes.)

Date format: phpBB offers fine-grained customization of the date format using the exact formatting offered by the PHP `date()` function. The default setting can be changed by the administrator; like the other options, these defaults kick in only on new registrations. A guide to the syntax for the date format is provided in a link to the corresponding `php.net` page for the `date()` function.

Choosing Avatar Options

phpBB offers many options for displaying avatars, as Figure 9-9 illustrates. You can permit users to upload avatars to the server from their hard drives or another web site, or link to avatar images on remote sites. Alternatively, you can provide a gallery of avatars for your users to peruse and select from. You can pick and choose which options you wish to enable by using the Configuration panel in the Administration panel, under the heading Avatar Settings.

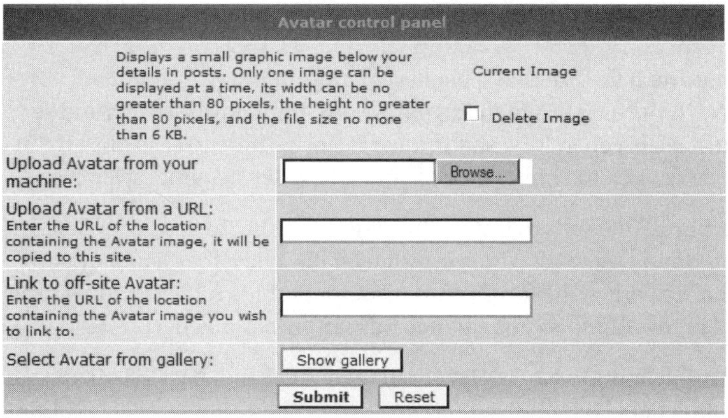

Figure 9-9. *phpBB Avatar options*

Permitting users to upload their avatar images to your server is by far the most convenient method for your users. In order for this option to work, you must make sure the upload directory you've specified (typically `images/avatars`) is writable by the web server; otherwise, your users will have problems uploading files. This option is less than desirable if your server is strapped for disk space. You can specify a hard limit on the size of files uploaded to your server under the Avatar Settings section in the Configuration page of the Administration panel.

Enabling remote avatars permits users to link to images hosted on other servers as their avatar image. This approach helps take the load off your server, but there is an increasing resistance against cross-linking images from other servers. More and more hosts use server-based measures to prevent hotlinking from their servers. To add insult to injury, phpBB does not always take into consideration the pixel-size limitations specified in the Administration panel, so users may select avatars that do not necessarily agree with your layout. You can edit avatars via the *Management* link under User Admin in the Administration panel.

You can also gather a gallery of your own hand-selected avatars and make them available for your users. This is especially useful if your site has a particular theme and you wish to have your avatars fit that theme. You add images to the gallery by putting them in the directory specified in the Avatar Settings in the Administration panel (the default is `images/avatars/gallery`). Creating directories underneath the main gallery root creates categories in which you file your images. Figure 9-10 illustrates a Random gallery with a couple of images. To select an image from the gallery, the user clicks the radio button underneath the image, and then clicks Select avatar. phpBB assigns this as the user's avatar.

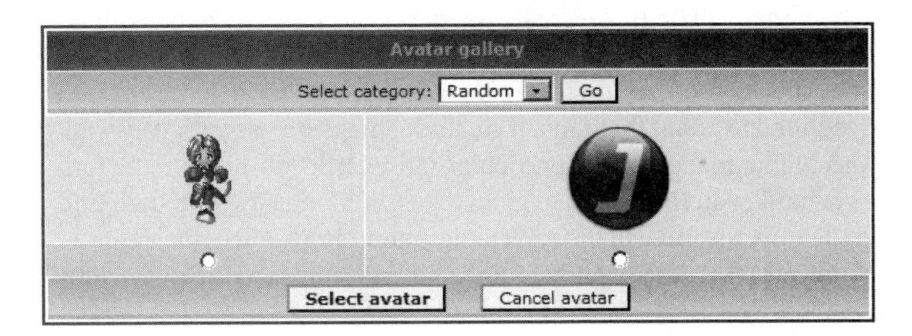

Figure 9-10. *An avatar gallery*

phpBB gives users a bit of a runaround when they wish to change their avatar. You must delete any existing avatar before you change it to a new one. To delete your avatar, check the Delete Image check box in the Avatar control panel section of the Edit Profile form (see Figure 9-9, shown earlier) and click Submit, as if you were editing your profile. Then, you must reenter the Edit Profile form and select your new avatar. Just make sure your users are aware of this procedure, and all will be well.

Administering User Profiles

As a forum administrator, you have the ability to edit every facet of every user profile, including the username and password. Additionally, you have the ability to activate and deactivate accounts at will, disable a user's ability to display an avatar and send private messages, and much more. You can set a rank for the user as well, and delete accounts from there.

Creating a Ranking System

As mentioned in the previous section, you can assign special ranks to users. Alternatively, you can create a ranking system that automatically updates a user's rank when he reaches a certain post count. You accomplish this by using the Rank Administration utility in the Administration panel, illustrated in Figure 9-11.

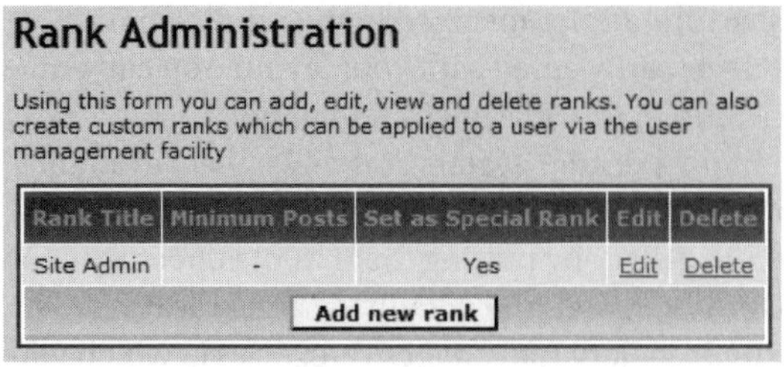

Rank Administration

Using this form you can add, edit, view and delete ranks. You can also create custom ranks which can be applied to a user via the user management facility

Rank Title	Minimum Posts	Set as Special Rank	Edit	Delete
Site Admin	-	Yes	Edit	Delete

Add new rank

Figure 9-11. *The Rank Administration panel*

To add new ranks to the list, click the Add new rank button toward the bottom of the page. That button takes you to a form that will help you create the new rank. Give the rank a title. If you plan on using this rank as something you will assign to specific users, rather than basing it on post count, set the Set as special rank option to Yes. If you set this to No instead, enter the minimum number of posts required to attain that rank. If you have images to use with your ranks (such as stars), fill in the path to the image for that particular rank. Click Submit, and the rank will take effect. If it is a special rank, you then need to go to the User Management panel, find the user you wish to assign the rank to, and use the rank assignment drop-down box at the bottom of the form. Users with special ranks assigned to them are not subject to the post count-based ranking system.

Private Messaging with phpBB

Private messages offer a spam-safe, simple solution to registered users of your board who want to exchange personal messages. For users who don't wish to reveal other contact information to the rest of the board, private messages come in very handy. They can be used as a point of contact by you, the administrator, for example, when you find a user is exceeding the bounds of how you feel he should conduct himself. It is exceedingly important to stress the usage of private messages on your board, and as such, understanding the inner workings of phpBB's private messaging system can be incredibly beneficial.

On the other hand, if you are an administrator who would rather not use private messages, phpBB permits you to disable them. In the Administration panel, select *Configuration* under General Admin, and scroll down to the Private Messaging section. From there, you can set private messaging to the Disabled option and save your changes.

■ **Tip** The option to disable private messages can be advantageous if your board is under siege from people who are using them to spam your members. Additionally, if you need to perform any maintenance on your private message database tables, disabling these messages is a good idea before doing so, as this will ensure the private message tables remain untouched throughout your maintenance period.

Reading and Managing Private Messages

When you enter the private messaging system in phpBB, you will be greeted by the Inbox, shown in Figure 9-12. All of phpBB's private message boxes look similar to the Inbox. As with a forum, you click the subject of a message to read it. The message is then marked as read when you return to the folder.

Figure 9-12. *The Inbox is the starting point of phpBB private messaging.*

If you use private messages on a regular basis, it's important to manage them. Keep a close eye on your folder usage, indicated in the top-right corner of the screen. If you fill up your Inbox, you will continue to receive new messages at the expense of older messages, which are irrevocably purged to make way for the newer messages. Size limits also apply to the Savebox and the Sentbox folders. By default, phpBB permits you to store 50 private messages in the Inbox, and 25 messages each in the Savebox and Sentbox. However, you can increase or decrease these folder size limits as demand requires, using the Private Messaging options accessed through the *Configuration* link under General Admin in the Administration panel.

Managing your private messages is a simple task. Under the Mark column on the far right of your folder view, you can select messages to save or delete. Alternatively, if you wish to mass-move or mass-delete your messages, click the *Mark all* link in the bottom-right portion of the form. *Mark all* and *Unmark all* will select and deselect, respectively, all the messages displayed in your folder. You can then click the Save Marked or Delete Marked button. Saving your messages transports them to the Savebox, where they are held for retrieval later. To erase the entire contents of your folder, simply click the Delete All button, and your folder will be cleared out.

■ **Tip** If you or one of your members report a user sending abusive private messages, you can use the User Management tool in the Administration panel to disable the abusive user's ability to send private messages.

Sending Private Messages

Sending a private message is just like making a post on the forum, with a few important differences. As you can see in Figure 9-13, a Username field is added to the standard post form. You can enter the username of the user you wish to send the message to, or click the Find a username button, which opens a window in which you can perform wildcard searches to get the name exactly right. After entering the name, you can enter your message. All the standard formatting and smiley controls apply. Formatting rules are consistent with the rules for posting on the forum at large. You can preview your private message. When you're ready, click Submit to send the message.

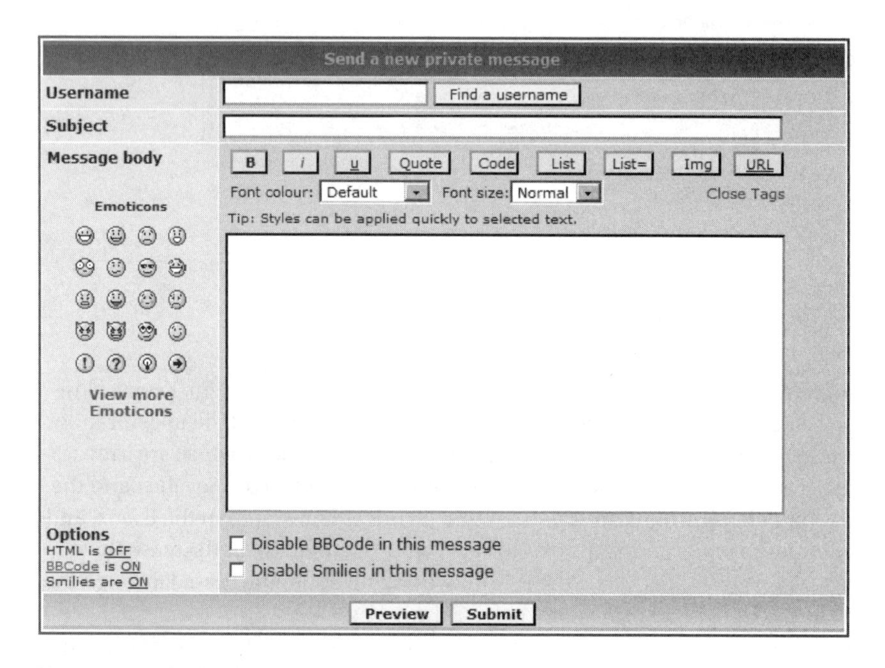

Figure 9-13. *The form to send a private message*

When you send a private message, the sent message is listed under your Outbox until the intended recipient reads the message. If you feel you sent your message in error, you can enter the Outbox and delete the message you sent, effectively canceling the message. If you do not see the message in the Outbox, it likely has already been read, and thus moved to the Sentbox, which is analogous to the Sent Items folder in e-mail clients such as Microsoft Outlook. At this point, you cannot cancel sending the private message.

Searching Forums

phpBB's search feature is incredibly powerful, with keyword and author search, two methods of viewing your results, and good filtering of results. The search feature builds an index of keywords from the posts made in the forums and uses that index to perform the search. phpBB does an admirable job of keeping this index up-to-date without any administrator intervention. Here, you will learn how to use phpBB's search feature to your advantage.

Performing a Search

The Search Query form, shown in Figure 9-14, paints what could be a slightly intimidating picture to your users, but it's actually quite simple to use. You can search on keywords, author, or posts by an author with your chosen keywords. As long as there is some criteria in one of the text boxes at the top, the search will execute.

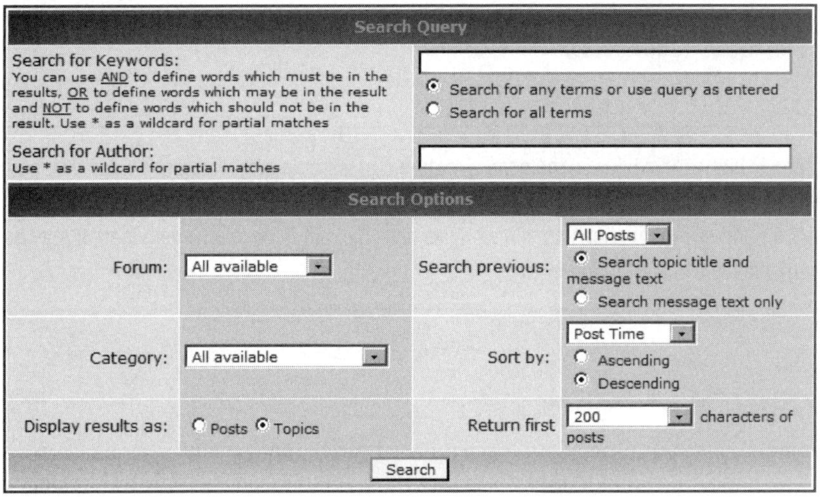

Search Query
Search for Keywords:
You can use AND to define words which must be in the results, OR to define words which may be in the result and NOT to define words which should not be in the result. Use * as a wildcard for partial matches
Search for any terms or use query as entered
Search for all terms
Search for Author:
Use * as a wildcard for partial matches
Search Options
Forum: All available
Search previous: All Posts
Search topic title and message text
Search message text only
Category: All available
Sort by: Post Time
Ascending
Descending
Display results as: Posts Topics
Return first 200 characters of posts
Search

Figure 9-14. *The phpBB search feature, ready for your query*

If you wish to further narrow your search, you can specify additional search options. You can constrain your search to one forum or a category containing multiple forums (as delineated in the Forum Index page). You can tell phpBB to search the topic title and message text or only the message text. Additionally, you can specify searching all topics or constraining the time period in which you search, from one day to the last year.

phpBB also provides several options for displaying your results. Returning results as posts, as illustrated in Figure 9-15, displays a preview of posts returned by the search engine, with your search terms highlighted. Returning results as topics, as shown in Figure 9-16, displays the results in topic form. In every case, when you click a result, phpBB takes you to the topic, and the keywords you searched on are highlighted in the page, making it fast and easy to find the post you're seeking.

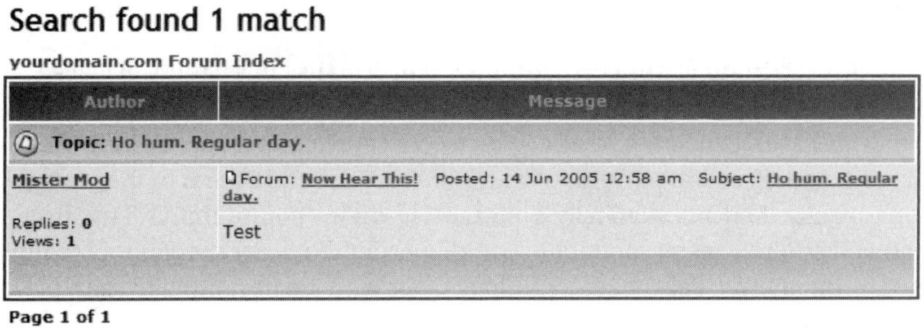

Search found 1 match
yourdomain.com Forum Index
Author | Message
Topic: Ho hum. Regular day.
Mister Mod
Forum: Now Hear This! Posted: 14 Jun 2005 12:58 am Subject: Ho hum. Regular day.
Replies: 0
Views: 1
Test
Page 1 of 1

Figure 9-15. *Returning search results as posts*

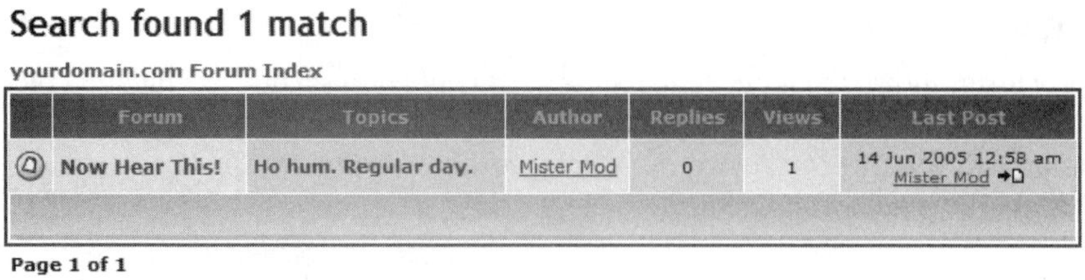

Search found 1 match

yourdomain.com Forum Index

	Forum	Topics	Author	Replies	Views	Last Post
	Now Hear This!	Ho hum. Regular day.	Mister Mod	0	1	14 Jun 2005 12:58 am Mister Mod

Page 1 of 1

Figure 9-16. *Returning search results as topics*

Caution On extremely high-traffic boards, the search feature can become quite database-intensive, and performance could suffer as a result. Such problems are largely related to limitations on your database server. phpBB is built to work around such limitations as efficiently as possible, but in case of severe load, it may be necessary to temporarily disable search functionality.

Conducting Special Searches

phpBB's search engine is also equipped with three types of predefined special searches. Any users—guests or registered—are able to find posts that have yet to receive a reply by clicking the *View unanswered posts* link in the top-right portion of the page, just above the forum and category listing. Registered users can perform two additional searches:

- A search for all new posts since the user's last visit (very useful for catching up with recent activity, especially after a long layoff from the forum)
- Affectionately nicknamed "ego search," a search in which the user can find all his own posts on the forum

---

Tip If your board has a lot of traffic, you can eliminate these special search links in the template, so that users won't click them and add even more load. Chapter 12 provides details on editing templates.

Grouping Users

phpBB offers a versatile user group feature that administrators can use in a variety of ways. User groups are most commonly used to lump together users who have the same permissions, which can be a great timesaver. Instead of hunting down users and assigning them individual permissions to do certain things on the forum, you are able to simply add them to the group, and the permissions are attached automatically. For example, on my communities, I use user groups to put together a group of super moderators, and I permit the super moderators group to moderate all forums on my site. I also have a group of users who are permitted to see a private forum.

In Chapter 10, I will discuss using user groups as a tool to secure your board. For now, I'll discuss the mechanics of setting up and modifying user groups.

Setting Up User Groups

Only an administrator can create a user group. To create a new user group, log in to the Administration panel. In the navigation pane, click *Management* under Group Admin. You will see a panel that resembles Figure 9-17.

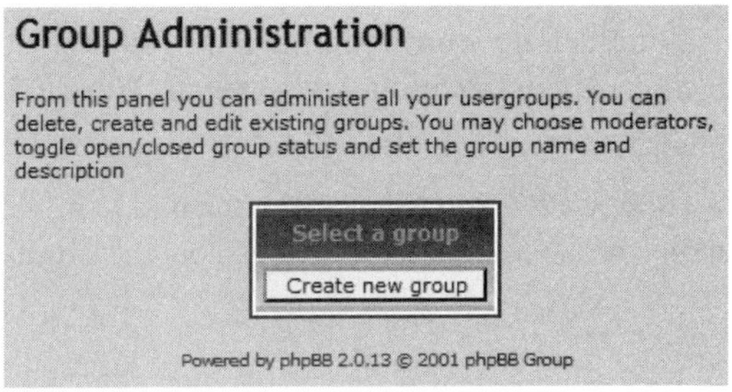

Figure 9-17. *A noticeably barren Group Administration panel*

To create a group, click the Create new group button. You'll see the form shown in Figure 9-18, where you are prompted for a few details about your new group.

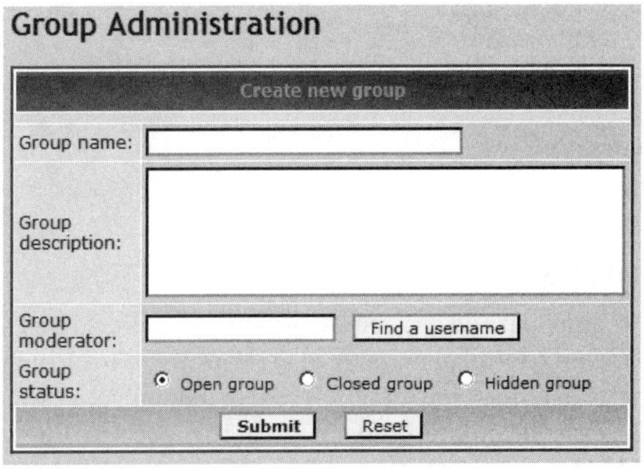

Figure 9-18. *The form for creating a new group*

This form is straightforward, for the most part. Give the new group a name and describe it. The group moderator is someone who you wish to manage the day-to-day operations of the group. If you are creating a group of people who will have permissions to moderate the board, you will probably want to make yourself or another highly trusted member the group moderator, as this person is empowered to add and remove group members. If you are creating a largely social group who will have limited power on the board, you can give the group moderator title to the leader of that pack, who will then have the option of adding and removing members. As a measure of checks and balances, all administrators, regardless of their group moderator status for a particular group, are able to perform group moderator functions.

The final set of options set the status of the group:

- An open group is a group that members can request to join. All potential memberships are subject to the approval of the group moderator.
- A closed group does not permit members to freely request to join. The group moderator must manually add members to a closed group.
- A hidden group is like a closed group. In addition, it does not show up in the publicly available list of user groups in the Group control panel, so nonmembers won't know it exists.

After you set up the group up as you desire, click Submit. You will get a confirmation message, and all will be well. Now, let's venture out of the Administration panel and explore the Group control panel.

Viewing Groups

Figure 9-19 illustrates what you will see after you create a group if you did not make yourself the group moderator. If you did make yourself the group moderator, you will see a list of groups of which you are a member. If there are also groups that you aren't a member of, you will see those groups listed as well.

Figure 9-19. *The Group control panel's initial page*

Modifying and Removing Groups

The group moderator (and forum administrator) can add and remove group members, as well as open, close, and hide a group from the Group control panel, shown in Figure 9-20. To change the status of the group, select your preference of group type (open, closed, or hidden) and click Update. To add members, you can type the exact username of the member in the box on the bottom-left side of the screen and click Add Member. Alternatively, you can click the Find a username button, and phpBB will display the username search box, where you can search for the user you wish to add. After you find the user in that list, click Add Member.

Administrators have further power over groups through the Administration panel. There, you can change the name, description, and moderator of the group, as well as the group's status. You can also remove a group from the board. To remove a group, log in to the Administration panel, and go to the Group Management panel. Select the group you wish to delete from the drop-down list, and click the Look up group button. At the bottom of the form, you'll see a check box to delete the group. Check that box, and then click Submit. The group will be deleted.

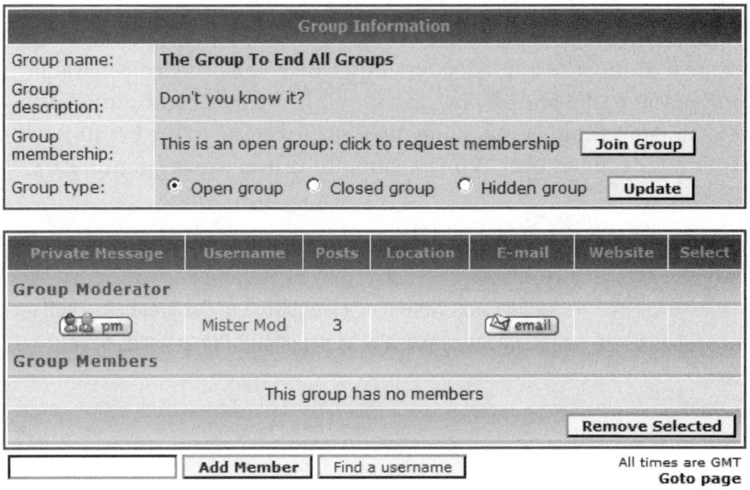

Figure 9-20. *The Group Information section, from a moderator's point of view*

Visiting Other Points of Interest

The following are some other features of interest to end users:

> **FAQs**: phpBB offers an extensive list of frequently asked questions (FAQs) about the software built in with each installation. The link is available in the header of each page on the board, and provides a quick online reference guide to some of phpBB's features. As a phpBB administrator, you should be familiar with the contents of the FAQs and be ready to direct your users there, as it is a valuable resource.

> **Member lists**: The Memberlist page does exactly as the name suggests: it lists all the registered users of your community. You are able to sort this list by several criteria, including joined date, post count, and username. phpBB also provides a presorted Top Ten Posters by post count. This can be useful if you are interested in promoting the top contributors in your community.

■ **Tip** Some unscrupulous folks see that their site is linked in the phpBB member list, and register accounts on many boards across the Internet to help boost their Google page rank. The Restrict Guest Access modification (`http://www.phpbbhacks.com/download/1415`) limits viewing of the member list to registered users, thus removing this incentive. See Chapter 11 for details on installing modifications.

> **Who's Online**: The Who's Online feature keeps track of user activity on the board, accurate to about five minutes. Visiting the Who's Online page shows you a list of users, the time of their last activity, and their location. This can be a fun feature for those who are curious. Remember that those who hold their privacy dear can elect to hide themselves from the Who's Online feature by making a change to their profile.

Touring phpBB 3.0 Feature Upgrades

phpBB 3.0 brings with it a great number of upgraded features, which will bring considerable advances in ease of use and power to the phpBB platform for both end users and administrators. End users now have a one-stop shop for managing their user account in the brand-new User Control Panel. The user interface has been refined, smoothing over a lot of phpBB 2.0's quirks.

■ **Caution** The usual disclaimer applies: This section was written when phpBB 3.0 was prerelease software, so items covered in this section could easily change drastically as the phpBB Group heads toward final release of the new version.

Introducing the Board Index

The Board Index, formerly known as the Forum Index in phpBB 2.0, has undergone several enhancements. The Who's Online summary at the bottom of the Board Index page has the ability to display search engine bots traversing your site.

phpBB now permits users to optionally enter their birthday into their user profile. phpBB keeps track of these birthdays and announces them just underneath the Who's Online section on the Board Index.

As I mentioned in Chapter 8, phpBB 3.0 now has support for sub-forums. You will know when a forum has a sub-forum underneath it by a special icon (currently, at the time of this writing, a standard phpBB forum icon with a folder overlay).

If you or your users experience problems with phpBB's tracking cookies, there is now a link on the Board Index to clear all board cookies. This can help dramatically when troubleshooting cookie problems (a feature noticeably missing from phpBB 2.0).

The links to the special searches (unanswered posts, your posts, and new posts) are now global links, along with a new breadcrumb navigational system that does a better job than phpBB 2.0 did in terms of helping you find your way back from deep points to the Board Index.

Posting and Reading in phpBB 3.0

phpBB 3.0 offers many new enhancements to making posts and reading topics. Here's an overview:

Topic icons: You can now select a topic icon to sit next to the topic title in the forum view, which acts as sort of an emoticon for your posts. You, as the administrator, have full control over how many topic icons are available, if you decide to allow the feature. The topic icon functionality works a great deal like the emoticon functionality, right down to being able to create a topic icon pack.

Drafts: This is one of the neater features of phpBB 3.0, which permits you to save working copies of your forum posts before making them public, much like making revisions to an article. You can view your drafts via the User Control Panel (described in the next section). This can be incredibly useful if you're writing a post but need to step away from the computer, because you can ensure that your message won't be lost. Simply click Save at the bottom of the post form, and your post will be saved to your Drafts folder, where you can retrieve it and continue working on it later.

Font color picker: When you're creating or editing a post, you can now choose colors from a color picker. This is more flexible than using a drop-down list of predefined colors (or remembering hexadecimal codes!).

Flash BBCode: BBCode now offers an option to embed Macromedia Flash animations into posts, which could be good or bad depending on your position on Flash. (If you dislike Flash, the Flash BBCode is easily disabled via permissions.)

Poll creation: The phpBB Group has streamlined the process for creating polls. No longer do you need to keep clicking Add option to add responses to your poll. Now you can just press Enter inside the text box, and phpBB will know to add the option. The polling engine also permits users to change their responses if you want to allow that. Additionally, you can create polls that permit more than one response.

Global announcements: phpBB 3.0 introduces global announcements to the base product, which permit administrators and other authorized personnel to make announcements to every forum. Previously, administrators were permitted to post announcements in only one forum at a time. Many people opted to hack this functionality into phpBB 2.0 using a modification written shortly after phpBB 2.0's release, demonstrating the popularity of the feature.

File attachments: Another old modification (which ships with phpBB 2.0 releases as a contributed package) is now a part of the base product as well. File attachments make their debut as an integrated feature in phpBB 3.0. This permits authorized users to attach certain administrator-defined file types to posts they make. This functionality can be very useful when you're posting an image in a thread and the image is either hosted somewhere else or does not have any hosting. As with a great majority of the features in phpBB 3.0, this feature can be heavily regulated via the Administration panel.

■ **Note** File attachments can be a risky proposition; in fact, early versions of the modification introduced security holes into the board. The phpBB Group has taken great care to ensure that their implementation of file attachments in phpBB 3.0 is a safe and secure method, and administrators should have no problems rolling the feature out to authorized users.

Reporting of offensive posts: If you come across a post you find offensive, you can use the new report functionality to contact the moderators of the forum in which the offensive post resides. They will get a notification via e-mail (or via private message if you prefer; this can be set in the Preferences area of the User Control Panel), stating the location of the topic and what is wrong with it. This allows moderators to act faster in cleaning up any problems that might arise.

Introducing the User Control Panel

The new User Control Panel represents the nerve center for user functions in phpBB 3.0, and it is amazingly informative. The new Overview page, shown in Figure 9-21, gives you the low-down on forum announcements from administration, lets you see what topics you are watching (a great improvement from phpBB 2.0, in which you hadn't a clue as to what topics you were watching), lets you revisit drafts of posts you are working on, and much more. Additionally, all the profile-editing tools from phpBB 2.0 are available here.

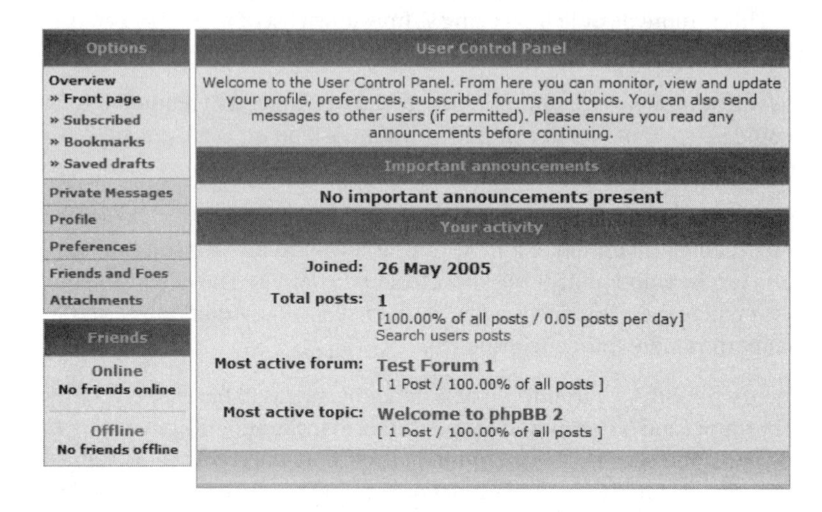

Figure 9-21. *The new phpBB 3.0 User Control Panel*

The User Control Panel includes a new Friends and Foes feature, something like a buddy and block list for those familiar with instant messaging programs. Private messaging is also an integral part of the new User Control Panel. Best of all, this panel is fully extensible, making writing modifications for it a cinch. (I'll discuss modifications in Chapter 11.)

User Profile Enhancements

phpBB 3.0 breaks the formerly consolidated user profile into four separate pages to cut down on clutter and form overload:

- Profile, which contains your publicly viewable information such as web site address, instant messaging contact information, and your birthday (a new addition)
- Registration Details, which has settings that deal with your username, password, and registered e-mail address
- Signature, where you can customize your signature for each one of your posts (now featuring the formatting toolbar and color picker found in the posting interface)
- Your Avatar, which provides nearly identical avatar-picking functionality to that in phpBB 2.0

A New Home for Preferences

Your user preferences are now in their own special Preferences section in the User Control Panel. Preferences are broken down into three separate categories:

- Personal Settings, which contains personal preferences and privacy settings, as well as date formatting (including the much-needed DST support) and language choice.
- Viewing Posts, which lets you enable and disable various elements of posts made on the board, such as Flash animations, signatures, and even word censoring. You can select a default topic and post ordering as well.
- Posting Messages, which includes the default options for creating posts (such as leaving BBCode on by default, automatically attaching your signature, and enabling notifications automatically).

These options have not changed since phpBB 2.0 thus far, but as I've said before, that may not be the case by the time phpBB 3.0 is released.

Friends and Foes

The Friends and Foes feature is a buddy list and ignore list, respectively. Your friends list shows up in your User Control Panel. When your friends are online, they are listed in the Online column, with a quick link to private messaging so you can see how they're doing.

Adding a user to your Foes list effectively blocks their communication and even the posts they make in the forum. It is a full-fledged ignore list, so you don't have to listen to a troll's bickering.

Attachments

The User Control Panel also keeps a running list of the attachments you post in threads. This functionality is useful when you wish to look for a file that you have attached. The User Control Panel keeps all this information referenced in one place, so you know how many attachments you've posted.

Private Messaging in phpBB 3.0

By far, the most renovation was saved for the private messaging system, as shown in Figure 9-22. With the features it now packs, phpBB 3.0's private messaging system rivals some e-mail clients in terms of power.

Figure 9-22. *The new Private Messages Inbox*

Multiple Folders and Rules

Put simply, phpBB 3.0 will allow you to manage your private messages in the much the same way that you manage your e-mail. The single Savebox is a thing of the past, replaced with the option to create multiple folders to save and organize your private messages, as shown in Figure 9-23.

The new rules feature really makes the private message system shine. With rules, you are able to redirect incoming private messages to a folder of your choice or the trash, mark the message for further action, or mark it as read. Additional message-filtering functionality cannot be ruled out for the final release. Right now, busy phpBB administrators inundated in a deluge of private messages are rejoicing at the thought of automatic organization!

Creating a rule is typically a four-step process, analogous to Microsoft Outlook's Rules and Alerts Wizard, though on a smaller scale:

1. Select an attribute to check, as shown in Figure 9-24.
2. Narrow down the search pattern, as shown in Figure 9-25.
3. Enter the pattern to match, as shown in Figure 9-26.
4. Select an action, as shown in Figure 9-27.

And that's it. You'll see the new rule you defined, as shown in Figure 9-28.

Add new Rule
If: Subject Next
Defined Rules
No rules defined
Rename folder
Rename folder: Junk (0 from 50 messages stored)
New folder name:
Rename
Add folder
Add folder:
Add
Remove folder
Remove folder: Junk (0 from 50 messages stored) And
Move messages from removed folder to Inbox (0 from 50 messages stored)
Delete all messages within removed folder
Remove
Folder Options
If Folder Full: Delete Oldest Messages
Move to Folder: Inbox (0 from 50 messages stored)
Do not accept new messages (New messages will be held back until enough space is available)
Default Action: This Action will be triggered if none of the above is applicable
Do not accept new messages (New messages will be held back until enough space is available)
Change

Figure 9-23. *Adding a new folder to Private Messaging*

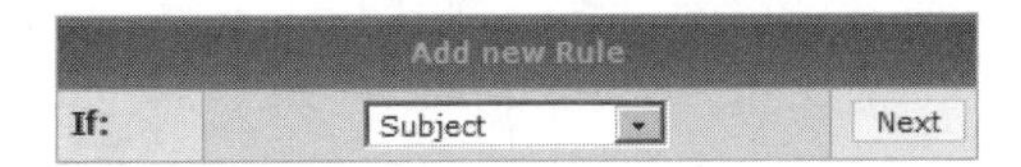

Figure 9-24. *Selecting an attribute to check*

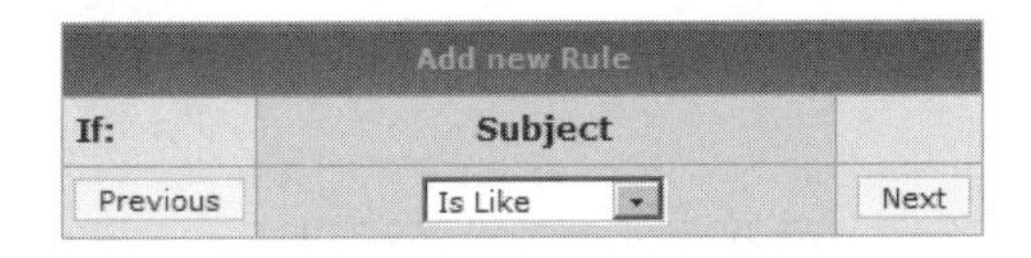

Figure 9-25. *Narrowing down the search pattern*

Add new Rule
If: Subject
Is Like
Previous Free Muffins! Next

Figure 9-26. *Entering a pattern to match*

Add new Rule		
If:	Subject	
	Is Like	
	Free Muffins!	
Previous	Mark Message	Add Rule

Figure 9-27. *Selecting an action*

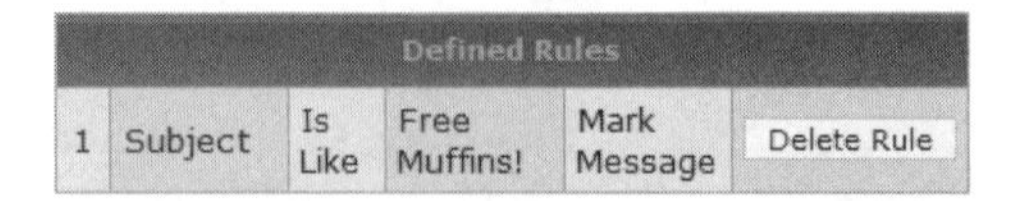

Figure 9-28. *Adding a rule for private messages*

Posting Interface

The upgrades to the posting interface in phpBB 3.0 really shine when writing private messages, as the same features are carried over. As mentioned before, phpBB 3.0 sports new drafts functionality, and that applies to the private message system as well. Note the link on the sidebar in Figure 9-29, PM Drafts, as well as the Save button at the bottom of the form. Just as with forum posts, you can save private messages to return to later.

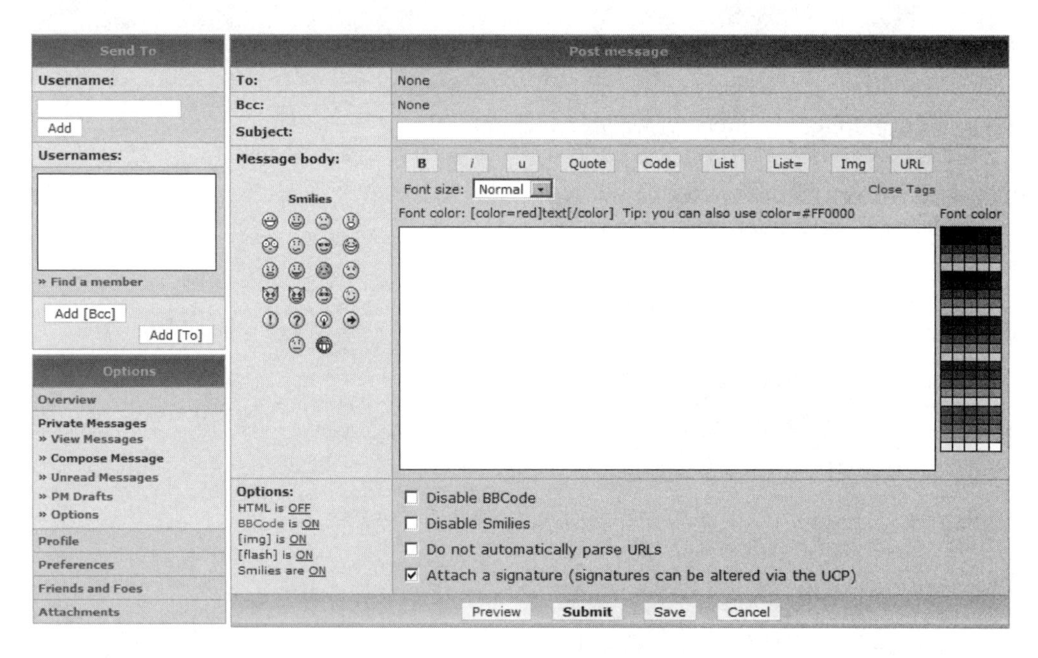

Figure 9-29. *The upgraded private message composition window*

In addition to the rest of the new features, the composition form's sidebar also features a quick search option for unread messages and reading your drafts. The *Options* link takes you to the form for creating new rules, adding new folders, and defining the behavior you wish phpBB to exhibit when your Inbox becomes full.

Previous versions of phpBB destroyed older messages to make room for the new ones. phpBB 3.0 gives you several options to handle full Inboxes:

- Redirect new messages to another folder with more space.
- Hold new messages until some space is cleared.
- Stick with the old way and start deleting old messages to make room for the new ones.

The phpBB default setting in the Administration panel is to hold new messages, and I do not recommend changing that option, as data loss is a very nasty thing.

Private messaging now supports multiple recipients, including sending blind carbon copies of private messages to people.

The most important aspect of all these enhancements is that each new option is incredibly administrator-configurable. The administrator can disallow mass private messaging, limit the editing time on private messages, and much more.

Searching with phpBB 3.0

phpBB 3.0's search features have been modestly upgraded to be more robust under load and to handle sub-forum searching. phpBB 3.0 also caches searches you have carried out and displays them on the search form for you, so you can revisit a previous search with one click—yet another example of the timesaving tweaks and polish being implemented in the next revision of phpBB.

Another nice addition to phpBB 3.0's search facilities is a new section in the Administration panel that permits you to allocate a minimum and maximum size of the index, specify words you do not wish to be indexed, and re-create the search index. phpBB 2.0 did not permit you to do much work on this index, as it handled most of the operations itself. Now, if you wish to alter the search index for some reason (if it is getting too large for your liking, for example), you have the tools to work on it.

■ **Caution** Modifying the search index could adversely affect search performance. Additionally, rebuilding the index is a time and resource-consuming task that should not be undertaken during peak hours of activity, nor performed often.

Summary

In this chapter, I've discussed many of phpBB's available features to end users and administrators, with the goal of helping you implement and troubleshoot them effectively in your community. The chapter covered the basics of posting topics, replies, and polls. It then discussed user profiles and avatars, and how to troubleshoot those. Next, you had an in-depth tour of the private messaging system, which often is a major part of your forum experience. Finally, you were introduced to the upgrades to these features in the upcoming phpBB 3.0 release.

The number one thing forum administrators should be concerned with is the security of their message board. In the next chapter, I'll detail strategies and tips on securing your phpBB installation. I'll also introduce you to important maintenance tasks that will ensure that your phpBB community runs as smoothly and efficiently as possible over the long haul, so you can reduce your risk of serious problems. You will also be introduced to the vast expansion of power phpBB 3.0 will provide you to optimize and secure your board for the rough reality of the Internet.

CHAPTER 10

Securing and Maintaining phpBB

Among the most important tasks you will perform with phpBB are the jobs you will handle behind the scenes: maintaining the less-than-glamorous but absolutely necessary routine maintenance schedule and vigilantly keeping the board's defenses against hackers and malicious users up-to-date. This chapter is dedicated to guiding you through these important tasks for keeping your community operating smoothly and safely, so your members can participate with confidence.

Generally, a secure phpBB is up-to-date with the latest patches, has tightly assigned permissions, and has a limited number of people with administrative power. phpBB provides many facilities to help ensure the security of your installation. It ultimately is up to you, as the phpBB administrator, to implement a security policy that you believe is best for your forums. My job in this chapter is to empower you with the tools to do just that and give you a few pointers along the way. I'll also introduce you to phpBB's tools for maintaining your board and tuning its performance.

Implementing Security Strategies

Having smart security strategies in place at the beginning can go a long way toward reducing headaches later. Here, I will suggest a few practices that can help you keep your board's power structure in order, keep tabs on who does what, and keep dictionary-attacking "script kiddies" at bay. Feel free to adjust these strategies for your own tastes as you see fit.

Best Practices for Delegating Power

As your board grows, you will undoubtedly wish to bring members of your community onto your forum staff in varying roles. As you delegate power to members to moderate and, perhaps, administer your forum, keep in mind the following guidelines:

Appoint only members you trust to be responsible: It seems like a no-brainer, but if you have any doubts that someone will behave responsibly in a position of power on your forum, he isn't the person to appoint to a staff position. Moderators will have total control over the content in their forums. Additionally, they will be able to view members' IP addresses, so it is particularly important to appoint someone you know you can trust with sensitive information.

Appoint members that visit regularly: Your moderators should be around your community on a regular basis so that their assigned forums are properly maintained. I'll leave it to you to define "regular basis."

Limit moderators to one or two forums at first: It's tempting to create "supermoderator" positions—moderators who control every forum—and give every moderator free reign. However, especially in the formative stages of your community when you may or may not know your staff members well, you will want to keep moderators limited to one or two forums. They will not be able to use their powers outside those forums, and that's an important step in securing your forums.

Keep supermoderators to a minimum: If you wish to create supermoderator positions, with power over all forums, appoint just enough (one or two is usually plenty, but that can vary depending on traffic) to provide backup to existing moderators. Ideally, you should appoint supermoderators only when your board's traffic increases to the point where you need a couple people to back up the moderators.

Use extreme caution when appointing additional administrators: As your board grows and the administrative tasks increase, you won't have a choice but to add another administrator or two. Appoint someone who you can trust and have worked with (preferably a moderator). Administrators should have enough technical savvy to operate the board's controls, know how to fix problems, and know how to avoid problems. Administrators should also know how to put on a good public face, as they will likely be contacted often by new members who may be unfamiliar with the phpBB software. (I consider prior experience with the board software a major plus in an administrator.)

How to Audit Moderators and Administrators

Keeping an eye on who is permitted to do what is incredibly important. Sadly, phpBB 2.0 does not contain an easy way to audit the number of people with administrator or moderator rights. I typically resort to periodically running two simple SQL queries using the phpMyAdmin front end to MySQL. Here, I'll explain how to run those queries.

■ **Note** Contact your hosting provider to determine the location of phpMyAdmin on the server, as this location varies from host to host.

When you have phpMyAdmin open, select the database you created for phpBB (when you installed phpBB, as described in Chapter 8) by clicking the name of the database in the left pane. This will load a listing of this database's tables in the main area of the window. Newer versions of phpMyAdmin (which most hosts run) have a SQL tab just above the area where the tables of the database are listed. Click that tab, and you'll be presented with a SQL query box, which should resemble Figure 10-1.

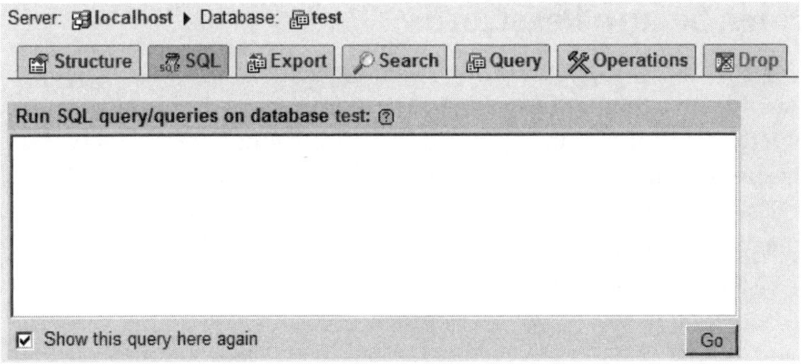

Figure 10-1. *The SQL query box in phpMyAdmin 2.6.1*

You'll input a raw SQL query here. In the query box, type the following line to check who has administrator rights, substituting <*yourprefix*> with the database prefix you selected while setting up your phpBB (typically `phpbb`):

```
SELECT user_id, username FROM <yourprefix>_users WHERE user_level = 1
```

To check to see which users have moderator permissions, run this query:

```
SELECT user_id, username FROM <yourprefix>_users WHERE user_level = 2
```

The queries return the user ID number assigned by phpBB at registration and the username of the empowered users, in a table structured like the one shown in Figure 10-2.

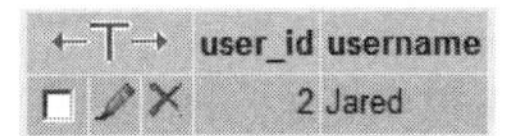

user_id	username
2	Jared

Figure 10-2. *The results of running the administrator query*

■ **Tip** If you find SQL queries cumbersome and inconvenient, as most people do, a far more graceful alternative to running these queries exists as a modification to the board. Visit `http://www.phpbbhacks.com/download/2977` to download the feature, and flip ahead to Chapter 11 for pointers on installing it.

Auditing on a regular basis is a good method for detecting people who may have surreptitiously gained administrative or moderator access without your knowledge. If you find people who are administrators that you don't want as administrators, you can edit their permissions (see the "Setting Per-User Permissions" section later in this chapter) and remove their rights. Then be sure to read the "Installing Updates" section, coming up soon, as you may have a security flaw.

Guidelines for Strong, Secure Passwords

A strong password policy, particularly for people with power, is crucial to security. Having staff members rotate passwords on a regular basis is good common sense. Using strong passwords—with a mix of letters, numbers, and symbols—helps prevent hackers' dictionary attacks. Thankfully, if they should break in, hackers cannot glean passwords from the database, as phpBB encodes passwords in the database using the MD5 one-way algorithm. This prevents intruders from deciphering the passwords in the database should they get that far. This also means that if you forget your password, you will need a new one.

■ **Note** The MD5 one-way algorithm has its advantages and its disadvantages. Passwords must be stored in the phpBB database, but in their encrypted form. When someone logs in to the forum, the password she supplies at login time is encrypted, and that is compared with the encrypted password stored in the database. No decryption takes place, because the MD5 algorithm is a one-way encryption. This has the advantage of passwords being unlikely to be decrypted (never say never!) should any malicious intruder break into your database. However, this means that any passwords cannot be e-mailed to the forgetful board user, which is a small price to pay for the level of security MD5 affords.

Installing Updates

All the permissions in the world won't help you if your board has a flaw in its security, which could let Joe Hacker simply slip past those permissions! Fortunately, the phpBB Group regularly publishes updated versions of phpBB that contain security and other bug fixes. Keeping up with these updates, as tedious as it may be (especially if Chapter 11 inspires you to install a ton of modifications), is quite important, as updates have been known to be released in rapid succession. While installing updates can sometimes be a pain and an inconvenience, it is even more inconvenient and painful to catch up with a few updates in succession.

Keeping Abreast of Updates

The phpBB Group uses several methods of notifying administrators when phpBB upgrades are released. phpBB versions 2.0.13 and later sport an update check, direct from `phpBB.com`, on the front page of the Administration panel, as shown in Figure 10-3.

Version Information

Your installation does **not** seem to be up to date. Updates are available for your version of phpBB, please visit http://www.phpbb.com/downloads.php to obtain the latest version.
The latest available version is **phpBB 2.0.16**.You are running **phpBB 2.0.13**.

Figure 10-3. *phpBB's upgrade notification message (note that this installation of phpBB 2.0.13 is outdated and should be upgraded)*

If you are running the latest release of phpBB, you'll see a message in green stating that your software is up-to-date and that no further upgrades are available. If not, you'll see the message in Figure 10-3, colored in red, notifying you that a newer version is available.

■ **Tip** If the Administration panel lacks the update check, as shown in Figure 10-3, you'll want to point your browser at `phpBB.com` to download the latest available version posthaste. Versions of phpBB earlier than 2.0.13 can be dangerously vulnerable to attack.

If you prefer, you can have update notifications delivered directly to your Inbox. Simply visit `http://www.phpbb.com/support/`, and enter your e-mail address in the field for the mailing list. You will then be notified via e-mail of security fixes and new versions when they become available.

Obtaining Updates

You obtain upgrades to phpBB in a similar fashion to how you initially obtained the full phpBB package: through the `phpBB.com` Downloads page. Instead of downloading the full package, this time you'll want to download the changed files only package, which as you might expect, contains only the changed files leading up to the current version.

■ **Caution** The changed files only package can be quite large in size, upwards of 4MB. This is because the package contains updates specific to each older version of phpBB 2, starting all the way with phpBB 2.0.0. If you connect to the Internet using a dial-up modem, you may find it easier to simply download the full package and remodify your board, or use the patch file only package.

On the other hand, if you have a lot of modifications installed and have access to a UNIX command line, you may wish to spring for the patch file only package, which contains files specifically designed for use with the UNIX `patch` utility. This utility can save you a great deal of time when dealing with a heavily modified board.

Upgrading with the Changed Files Only Package

The changed files only package is generally the most straightforward and reliable method of upgrading your board. To download it, choose the file you wish to download (on Windows, the safest bet is the `.zip` file; on UNIX or Linux, either the gzip or bz2 compressed files will do) by clicking its icon. Download the file to a safe place, and then open it. Figure 10-4 illustrates what the changed files only package contains at the point of the latest release at the time of this writing.

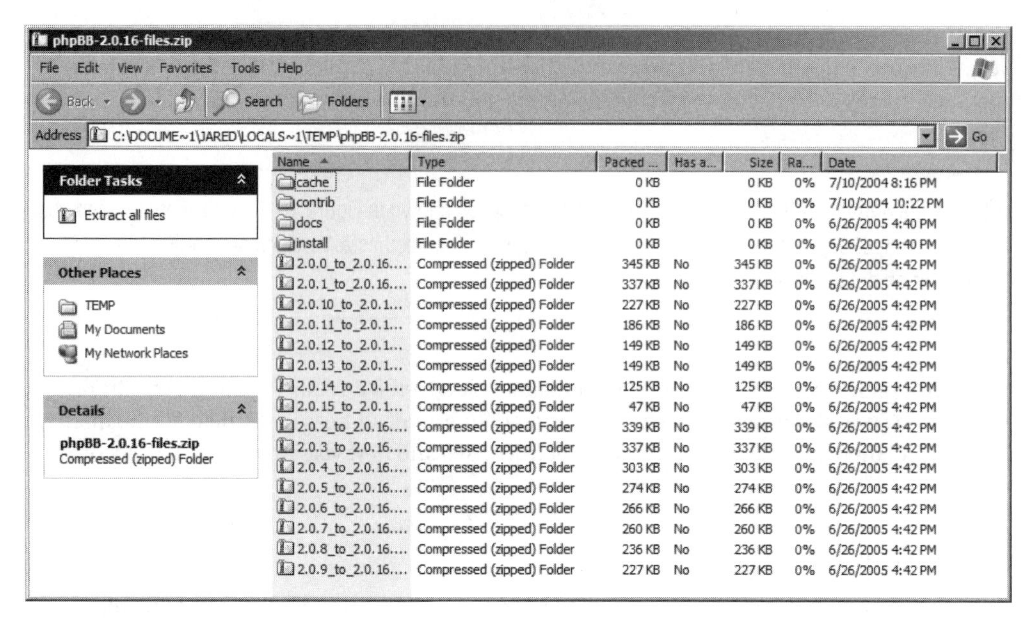

Figure 10-4. *The contents of the changed files only package*

The changed files only package contains the following:

- `cache`: A directory that exists as part of an optional file-based template-caching system. (I will discuss the template-caching systems available in the "Using Template Caching" section, later in the chapter.)
- `contrib`: A directory that contains the template-caching implementations and a database diagnostic tool.
- `docs`: A directory that contains late-breaking documentation and release notes for the updated version of phpBB you are about to install.
- `install`: A directory that contains the necessary upgrade scripts to complete the process of updating your board to the new version.
- `2.0.`*`x`*`_to_2.0.`*`y`*`.zip/.tar.gz`: A series of compressed files containing all the changed files from version 2.0.*x* (where *x* is the older revision of phpBB) to the newer version (represented as 2.0.*y*), which is phpBB 2.0.17 at the time of this writing.

Expanding the Updated Files

Now that you've downloaded and examined the upgrade package's contents, it's time to expand the appropriate files and upload them to your server.

Caution Now is an excellent time to back up the files from your existing installation to a safe place (especially if modifications are installed), just in case something doesn't work out as planned. You may even wish to perform a database backup using the backup tool in the Administration panel for added safety, as discussed in the "Backing Up and Restoring Your Database" section later in this chapter (though phpBB point releases rarely, if ever, see any wholesale database changes). Backing up is a good habit to get into, and you're better off safe than very, very sorry later.

I recommend creating a separate folder for the files you are about to expand. This helps you remember which files and folders have been updated and which ones haven't, saving you from possible confusion and uploading more than necessary.

You won't expand everything in the package—far from it. You will need to expand the `install` directory and its subdirectories, which contain the database upgrade script, and the appropriate `2.0.x_to_2.0.y.zip` archive, where `2.0.x` is the version of phpBB you are running. For example, if you are upgrading a phpBB 2.0.13 to version 2.0.16, you'll choose the `2.0.13_to_2.0.16.zip` file. This file contains all the changes between versions 2.0.13 and 2.0.16. The upgrade to the latest version of phpBB is cumulative; therefore, it is unnecessary to install 2.0.14 and 2.0.15 to upgrade to 2.0.16 from 2.0.13, for example.

Considering Your Modifications

If you haven't installed any modifications (discussed in detail in Chapter 11), you can safely skip this section. If you have, you must take into consideration the modifications you have installed. It is always a wise idea to check with the author's homepage or distribution site where you obtained your hacks to see if new versions are available for the upgraded version of phpBB.

Although the members try to minimize disruption, sometimes the phpBB Group is forced to make a change between revisions that can have an adverse effect on an existing hack. Other times, an outdated version of a modification could introduce a security hole that the new release was supposed to fix, which would certainly be counterproductive! Fortunately, volunteers at various hack distribution points, such as `phpBBHacks.com` and `phpBB.com`, verify that the most popular modifications work with the new release within a day.

Since the files in the changed files only package are clean, unmodified files, installing them directly over your modified board may produce adverse results of varying severity, depending on how many hacks you've installed and the complexity of your hacks. You will need to reinstall any modifications you've made to any of the changed files. If upgrades are available, reinstall the updated modification using the new files you've just expanded.

Uploading the Upgrade

Now that you've verified your modifications (if necessary), you're ready to upload the files to the server. Fire up the FTP program of your choice (I use SmartFTP, `http://www.smartftp.com`), connect to your host's FTP server, navigate to where your phpBB version is currently installed, and upload the files you extracted from the package to your server, overwriting anything with the same name (overwriting is not a risk as long as you've backed up your files). This could take a few minutes, depending on your connection speed.

Running the Upgrade Script

After the upload has completed, you need to take one more step. Go to the following URL (substituting *yourdomain.com* and *your_phpBB_path* accordingly):

```
http://<yourdomain.com>/<your_phpBB_path>/install/update_to_latest.php
```

This script performs any changes necessary to the database and updates a database field with the latest version. This allows the reporting tool in the Administration panel to report accurate version information. After the script has run, which usually takes no longer than a few seconds, reenter your FTP program and delete the `install` and `contrib` folders, as you no longer need them.

Congratulations, your upgrade is complete! Now is a good time to test your board and make sure that everything is working as anticipated, especially if modifications are involved.

If you run into problems, make sure you didn't miss uploading any files or incorrectly edit one of them when reinstalling modifications. If you've verified your installation instructions for a modification and it still isn't working, you may wish to remove it temporarily and get in touch with the author of the fix and see if there are any incompatibilities.

Upgrading with the Patch File Only Package

Installing upgrades to heavily modified phpBB installations can be a royal pain in the neck. You must manually go through each file and remodify it, making sure that nothing new is broken in the process. It gets to be a very tedious process after a while, and the possibility of human error is great. If you have one of these boards and need to perform upgrades to it, lack patience, and have access to a UNIX command line, you can use the patch file only package provided by the phpBB Group to quickly upgrade your board, thanks to the `patch` utility.

The first step is, as always, to back up a current copy of the board software to a safe place, in the event the `patch` utility does not work as planned. The phpBB Group recommends that you have a copy of the changed files only package handy, in the event the `patch` upgrade fails in spots (a rare occurrence).

Next, create a separate folder to hold your files, and extract the contents of the `/install` directory there. You'll also extract the `.patch` file that corresponds with your current version of phpBB. Extract the `.patch` file to the folder you specify, and then run the following command at the command line:

```
patch -cl -d <path/to/your/phpbb> -p1 < 2.0.x_to_2.0.y.patch
```

where *x* represents the current revision of phpBB you are running, and *y* is the latest release of phpBB you are patching.

With any luck, you'll get through the patching process without problems. If a file fails to patch, extract its corresponding file from the changed files only package and copy over it. In this scenario, unfortunately, you will need to reapply modifications to the file manually.

After running `patch`, visit this URL:

```
http://<yourdomain.com>/<your_phpBB_path>/install/update_to_latest.php
```

This will verify the database for the new version of the software. Test your board thoroughly, especially in places where modifications were made. With any luck, you will be up and running without any problems.

Mastering phpBB Permissions

Now that your board is at the latest software revision, it's time to go through and perform an audit of your forum and member permissions. Here, I'll discuss how to harness the power of the phpBB permissions system and use it to your advantage.

Using Advanced Forum Permissions

Back in Chapter 8, you learned how to create new forums and set basic permissions on them using the Simple Mode of the permissions screen. While the permission presets cover the most common usages, chances are you will want to delve into the more advanced options phpBB offers.

The first step is to become acquainted with the permissions system's Advanced Mode, illustrated in Figure 10-5.

■ **Note** Regardless of permission settings, administrators automatically have access to all forum features, and they cannot be denied access to those features.

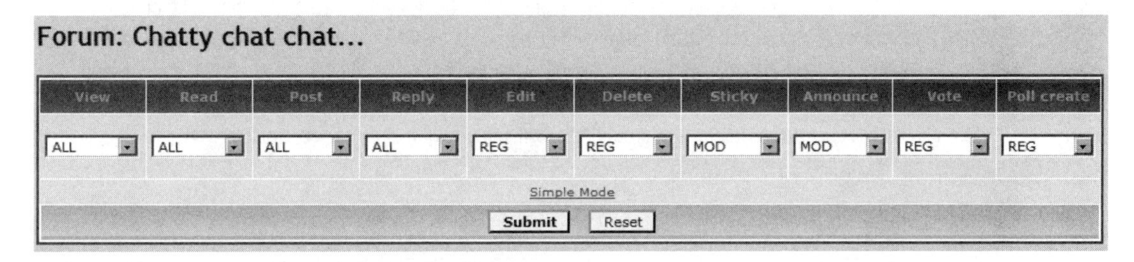

Figure 10-5. *Advanced forum permissions*

To set permissions for a specific action, use the drop-down options available underneath each category (View, Read, Post, and so on). The five possible options you can set are described in Table 10-1.

Table 10-1. *phpBB Permission Options*

Option	Description
ALL	All users, logged in or not, will be able to use the specified feature.
REG	Only registered users who are logged in will be able to use the specified feature.
PRIVATE	Users or user groups with specific permissions in this forum have access to features marked as private.
MOD	Moderators and administrators will have access to the feature.
ADMIN	Forum administrators will have access to the feature.

After setting the permissions you want, click Submit, and your changes will be successfully applied. You can test your permissions by logging out and logging back in as a normal user.

■ Tip When setting permissions on your forums, it's a great idea to have a generic user account and a moderator account for testing your permissions. Since having administrative rights trumps all permissions, you need to have a way to get some idea of what to expect when other users and moderators interact with your forum.

ADVANCED PERMISSIONS IN ACTION: AN ANNOUNCEMENT FORUM

Many communities offer a forum dedicated to moderators and administrators posting announcements concerning the board. Some communities lock out all posting by nonstaff members. phpBB's permissions system gives you a unique opportunity to create an announcement forum that restricts creation of new topics to administrators and moderators, but permits registered users to give feedback on those posts. Putting feedback posts on specific announcements in their own topics helps keep the rest of your forums on topic.

First things first: you need to create your forum in the Forum Administration panel. (For a refresher on creating forums, see Chapter 8.) Keep the forum unlocked and do not enable auto-pruning. Next, go to the Forum Permissions panel and select the forum you just created. You'll need to use Advanced Mode, as the permissions are very fine-tuned. As shown in the following example, I'm going to let all users see and read the forum; registered users post replies, edit their own posts, and vote in polls; moderators and administrators make new topics, delete posts, and create new polls; and administrators give priority (sticky/announcement flags) to topics.

Forum: Now Hear This!

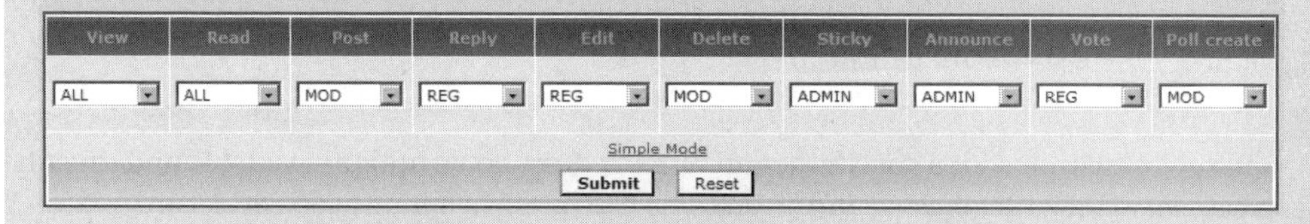

Feel free to adjust these permissions as desired. For example, if you want only administrators to be able to make forum-wide announcements, set the Post permission to ADMIN.

Click Submit, and then log in as a regular user. You'll notice that you don't have permission to create a new topic in the forum. Now, log in with your administrator account, and try again. This time, it works! Your regular users should still be able to reply to topics in that forum, which you can test by creating a topic and logging back in with your regular account and trying a reply.

You now have a unique forum for your users to sound off about your announcements in the proper threads, which encourages discourse between the staff and the users, and ultimately fosters a healthy community.

Setting Per-User Permissions

phpBB gives administrators the option to assign permissions to forums with Private permissions on a per-user basis, through the User Permissions Control panel. Here, you can also designate users as forum moderators.

Like the Forum Permissions panel, the User Permissions Control panel comes in Simple Mode and Advanced Mode. Figure 10-6 illustrates the permissions of a generic user, Joe Blo, in Simple Mode, and Figure 10-7 displays the same user's permissions in Advanced Mode.

User Permissions Control

Username: Joe Blo

User Level : User

Usergroup memberships : None

Permissions

Here you can alter the permissions and moderator status assigned to each individual user. Do not forget when changing user permissions that group permissions may still allow the user entry to forums, etc. You will be warned if this is the case.

Forum	Simple Permissions	Moderator status
Chatty chat chat...		Not Moderator
Now Hear This!		Not Moderator
G-14 Classified	Disallowed Access	Not Moderator

Advanced Mode

Submit Reset

Powered by phpBB 2.0.13 © 2001 phpBB Group

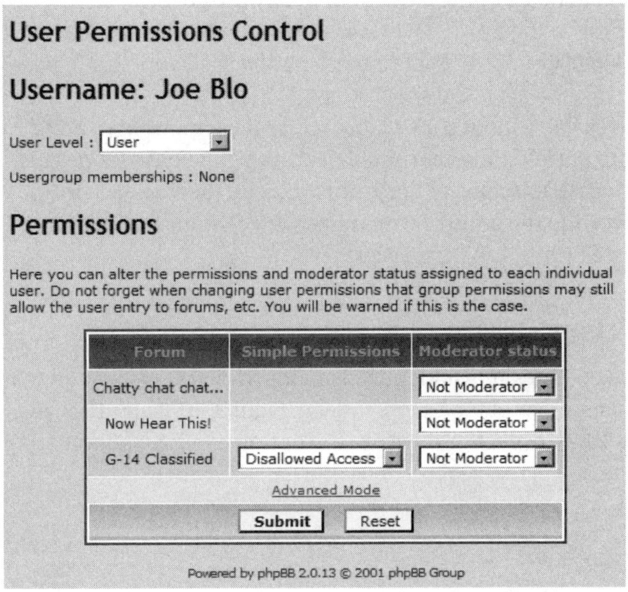

Figure 10-6. *Joe Blo's permissions, in Simple Mode*

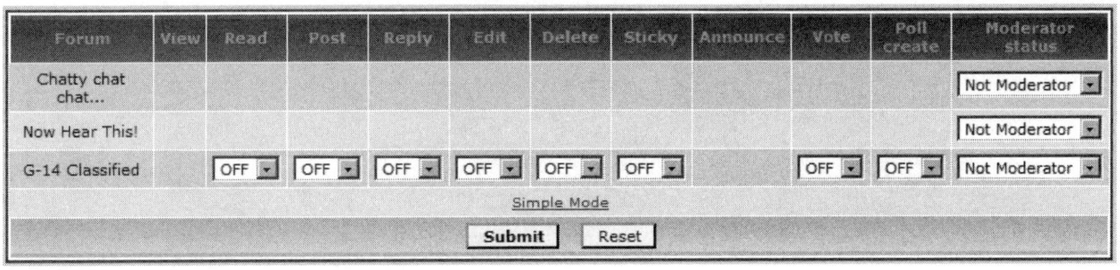

Forum	View	Read	Post	Reply	Edit	Delete	Sticky	Announce	Vote	Poll create	Moderator status
Chatty chat chat...											Not Moderator
Now Hear This!											Not Moderator
G-14 Classified		OFF	OFF	OFF	OFF	OFF	OFF		OFF	OFF	Not Moderator

Simple Mode

Submit Reset

Figure 10-7. *Joe Blo's permissions, in Advanced Mode*

Note three things about the user permissions screen in this example:

- Joe Blo is currently a regular user, changeable to Administrator via the drop-down box in the top-left corner.
- Joe is not a moderator of any forum.

- The G-14 Classified forum has more options than the other two forums. In the Simple Mode, it has another drop-down box available. In the Advanced Mode, each permission can be set separately.

In this example, I've set the permissions in the G-14 Classified forum to PRIVATE (except for the View and Announce functions) to enable per-user permissions in the forum. In Simple Mode, I can simply allow or disallow access across the board. In Advanced Mode, I can get a little more nitpicky: I can set whether Joe is able to read posts, make posts, edit posts, and the like. If I had set up the G-14 Classified forum as a hidden forum, I could also control whether Joe would be able to see it. If I wanted to make him a moderator of any forum, I can simply click the drop-down box corresponding to the forum I wish for him to moderate, change it to Is Moderator, and click Submit. Clicking Submit saves all changes for the user, and the changes take effect immediately.

Setting per-user permissions gives you a lot of control, but it can get somewhat tedious. In most cases, you will use user group permissions, explained next, as a good base for permissions for multiple users. After granting permissions to the group, you can then go back to an individual user's permissions and override the group permissions with custom settings, as per-user permissions take precedence over group permissions.

Using Permissions with User Groups

In terms of permissions, user groups operate almost identically to individual users, except that the permissions are applied to every member of the group. Indeed, Figures 10-8 and 10-9 are almost identical to Figures 10-6 and 10-7, respectively, except the option to assign administrator standing is not present for groups.

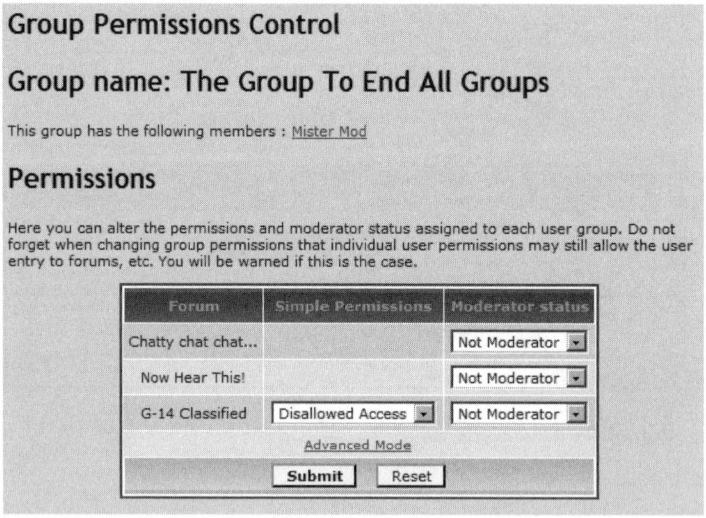

Group Permissions Control

Group name: The Group To End All Groups

This group has the following members : Mister Mod

Permissions

Here you can alter the permissions and moderator status assigned to each user group. Do not forget when changing group permissions that individual user permissions may still allow the user entry to forums, etc. You will be warned if this is the case.

Forum	Simple Permissions	Moderator status
Chatty chat chat...		Not Moderator
Now Hear This!		Not Moderator
G-14 Classified	Disallowed Access	Not Moderator

Advanced Mode

Submit Reset

Figure 10-8. *Group permissions, in Simple Mode*

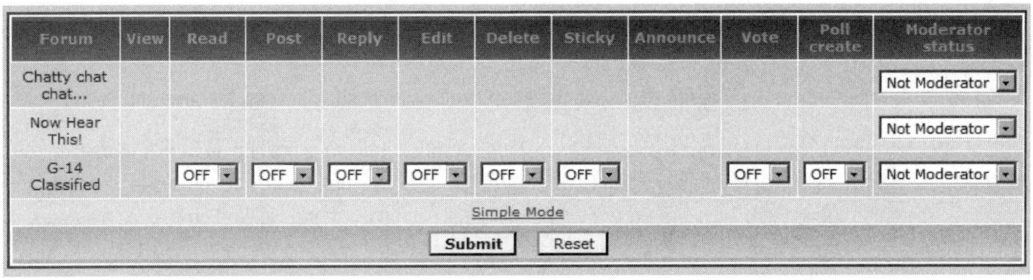

Forum	View	Read	Post	Reply	Edit	Delete	Sticky	Announce	Vote	Poll create	Moderator status
Chatty chat chat...											Not Moderator
Now Hear This!											Not Moderator
G-14 Classified		OFF	OFF	OFF	OFF	OFF	OFF		OFF	OFF	Not Moderator

Simple Mode

Submit Reset

Figure 10-9. *Group permissions, in Advanced Mode*

Group members are listed at the top of the permissions screens, so you know to which members you are assigning those permissions. As with user permissions, you can assign specific permissions in private forums and give a whole group moderator access to a forum.

Sites such as `phpBBHacks.com` and the official phpBB web site leverage this functionality to give specific teams of staff permission to moderate their assigned forums, without needing to labor through giving moderator rights to individual users. This has the added benefit of cutting down on clutter on the Forum Index page, too, as you can maintain order in your list of moderators underneath each forum. Otherwise, you end up with a considerably large string of users that just takes up space and makes your forum look a little more visually busy, which generally you wish to avoid.

A particularly useful application of user groups is for creating supermoderators. As I mentioned earlier in this chapter, a supermoderator is generally a moderator who has permission to moderate all forums in the community. phpBB 2.0 does not come with integrated supermoderator functionality, however. The workaround is to create a user group, named something like Super Moderator, assign your trusted users to this group, and then make the group moderator of the forums you wish these users to moderate. The upside to this approach is that you can restrict supermoderators' power in certain forums (leaving those for administrators to control), while other supermoderator implementations do not permit these kinds of restrictions.

■ **Note** As of this writing, phpBB 3.0 returns the traditional Super Moderator user level, so you will not need to create a special group to implement this role. The option to do so still exists, though.

Managing Registrations

In addition to the flexibility of the permissions system, phpBB provides other options for managing and securing the registration system, to further prevent miscreants from raising havoc in your community.

WHY REQUIRE REGISTRATION ON YOUR COMMUNITY?

More and more forums on the Internet require registration to be given posting access, for several reasons:

- **Registration helps weed out troublemakers**. Forums with anonymous posting are much more likely to take heat from miscreants who wish to disrupt the community's operation than forums that require registration. While there is no silver bullet for stopping trolls and spammers, registration creates a greater sense of accountability and gives the administrator more tools for stopping problem users from continuing their activities.
- **Registration keeps humans in and bots out**. Combined with tools such as visual confirmation, registration ensures that the only ones posting on your site are human beings, not advertising bots. More and more administrators are installing modifications to require registration for functions such as the member list and search, which are frequently used by bots. (phpBB 3.0's permissions system will include provisions for doing this without modifying the source code.)
- **Registration builds community**. Finally, users will typically not go through the trouble of registering if they don't intend on returning at least once. Registering users allows them to create a profile and get to know their fellow members, which promotes camaraderie and helps populate your community. Plus, moderator candidates must be registered users anyway, so it makes sense to register all posters.

Validating New User Accounts

The General Configuration section of the Administration panel contains an option to enable new account activation. You can disable the feature, which I discourage you from doing, as it opens you up to a myriad of unwanted registrations. Rather, my recommendation is to enable either user validation, which requires users to provide a valid e-mail address to activate their account, or enable administrator validation, which notifies the forum administrators that a new account is created and needs to be approved.

Enabling e-mail validation limits an e-mail address to just one associated account, which is good for sanity purposes. It is a must in this day and age of automated registration bots, which create mass accounts on various web services that are ultimately designed to abuse search engines' indexes. Additionally, it keeps the onus on users to keep their account information up-to-date, as a valid e-mail address is required to recover passwords.

Enabling Visual Confirmation

Another weapon in the war against illegitimate registrations is the visual confirmation process, which generates a random code embedded in a somewhat distorted image, as shown in the example in Figure 10-10. This ensures that programs creating accounts cannot successfully complete registration, but humans can. The validation code must be entered correctly in order for registration to continue. This feature was backported from phpBB 3.0 to recent versions of phpBB 2.0.

Figure 10-10. *The visual confirmation image*

The option to enable visual confirmation lives directly underneath the option for account activation, in the General Configuration section of the Administration panel.

■ **Note** If you do not have Enable Visual Confirmation as an option, you need to upgrade your phpBB installation. See the "Installing Updates" section earlier in this chapter for information about how to do just that.

Be aware that using the visual confirmation system may impede users that require the assistance of a screen reader, as the screen reader will be unable to interpret the contents of the image. phpBB recognizes this can be a problem and provides a link to the administrator e-mail address you provided when you set up phpBB (which you can change through the Administration panel, under Configuration). This gives users who may have difficulty with your image the opportunity to contact you to assist with registration. If you are contacted by a user who is having problems with visual confirmation, simply register the account for her under her e-mail address. phpBB will e-mail the user directly with the requisite registration information. Despite the potential for this problem, I still heartily endorse using visual confirmation in your registration form.

Disallowing Usernames

Another useful tool in regulating registration is to disallow certain usernames from being registered. I recommend disallowing names such as *admin*, *moderator*, and the like.

To restrict usernames, enter the Administration panel and click *Disallow names* under the User Admin heading in the navigation pane. You are then taken to a simple form, where you can add or remove names that you have disallowed. You can disallow groups of names using the wildcard character (*).

Managing Your Ban Lists

In the course of using phpBB, you will inevitably ban someone from using your site. The Ban panel, illustrated in Figure 10-11, helps you manage your lists of the banished.

You have several methods at your disposal for banning users:

Banning by username: This is straightforward. You simply ban the user's account by selecting his name. This is effective at shutting down an account, but the user can easily come back by registering under a different name.

Banning by e-mail address/domain: You can ban specific e-mail addresses (such as `troublesome@`*`domain`*`.com`) or use wildcards to block whole domains (such as `*@`*`domain`*`.com`). This can help screen out people who use free e-mail services to open accounts, particularly if you have validation enabled.

Banning by IP address/range: This is the most effective method of banning a user, but also the most dangerous, especially if you ban by range. To ban an IP address from your forum, simply enter the IP address (which you can glean from a user's post, explained in "Using the IP Manager" section later in this chapter) and click Submit at the bottom.

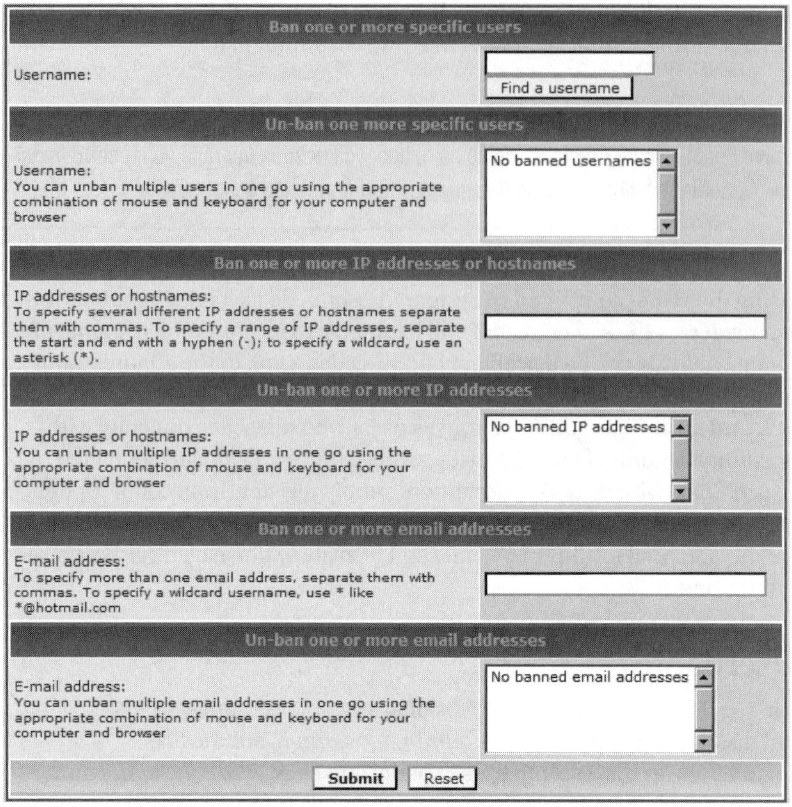

Ban one or more specific users

Username:

Find a username

Un-ban one more specific users

Username:
You can unban multiple users in one go using the appropriate combination of mouse and keyboard for your computer and browser

No banned usernames

Ban one or more IP addresses or hostnames

IP addresses or hostnames:
To specify several different IP addresses or hostnames separate them with commas. To specify a range of IP addresses, separate the start and end with a hyphen (-); to specify a wildcard, use an asterisk (*).

Un-ban one or more IP addresses

IP addresses or hostnames:
You can unban multiple IP addresses in one go using the appropriate combination of mouse and keyboard for your computer and browser

No banned IP addresses

Ban one or more email addresses

E-mail address:
To specify more than one email address, separate them with commas. To specify a wildcard username, use * like *@hotmail.com

Un-ban one or more email addresses

E-mail address:
You can unban multiple email addresses in one go using the appropriate combination of mouse and keyboard for your computer and browser

No banned email addresses

Submit Reset

Figure 10-11. *The Ban panel*

Use extreme caution when banning IP addresses (and especially ranges of IP addresses). Users on dial-up connections typically have their IP address change every session, so banning an IP address may be useful briefly but then ban an innocent person later. Banning ranges of IP addresses could potentially block an entire Internet service provider, so do that only if you really must. You can use sites such as `samspade.org` or `network-tools.com` (which phpBB's Administration panel references) to run WHOIS queries on IP addresses, so you can find out the range that they cover. Then you'll be able to avoid inadvertently banning whole cities or providers. It's a good idea to keep the list of banned IP addresses relatively short and trim. In most cases, once a troublemaker has been banned for a while, she will move on to another forum to cause problems. You don't want to inadvertently lose visitors due to overzealous banning.

Moderating Your Forums

Effective moderation is the key to every successful community. Moderation must be firm but fair, and it should always be professional. Here, I will show you the tools you can use to moderate posts on your site. I will leave it to you, the community administrator, to develop a policy on moderation that you feel is fair to your members.

Moderating Individual Posts

On the bottom of each View Topic page, administrators and moderators will (under the default subSilver template) see icons such as those shown in Figure 10-12.

Lock Unlock Move Delete Split Topic

Figure 10-12. *The icons found at the bottom of each View Topic page, visible to moderators of the forum and administrators only*

Here is a rundown of those moderation options and a little guidance on when to use them:

Locking a topic: This is an option generally employed when the topic in question is straying too far off track or is becoming heated, or topics that the moderator wishes to prevent replies to for some other reason. Once you lock a topic, it can no longer be replied to, nor can users edit their posts within the topic. Moderators have the option of unlocking the topic later, if they wish.

Moving a topic: This generally happens when a topic's subject matter isn't consistent with the purpose of the forum in which it was posted. When a moderator moves a topic, phpBB gives the option to leave a link in the original forum to the topic's new location with a "Moved" notation next to it. If you don't use this option, people might think their topics just randomly disappeared or were deleted, when those topics were just moved to another forum.

Deleting a topic: This removes a topic permanently and subtracts the number of posts deleted from the post counts of the forum and of the users who posted the topics. More and more communities are beginning to forego deleting offensive topics outright in favor of moving them to a hidden forum. This allows staff members to examine an offensive post and possibly use it as evidence in banning or, in extreme circumstances, reporting incidents to Internet service providers or law enforcement.

Splitting a topic: This is a good way to salvage a thread that has gone astray or remove posts that may be offensive to a hidden location for further discussion by staff. Splitting a topic takes posts out of one topic and generates a new topic from those posts. You can split off the end of a topic, or even take posts right out of the middle. The first post in the original topic can never be split out. Figure 10-13 illustrates the split topic function in action.

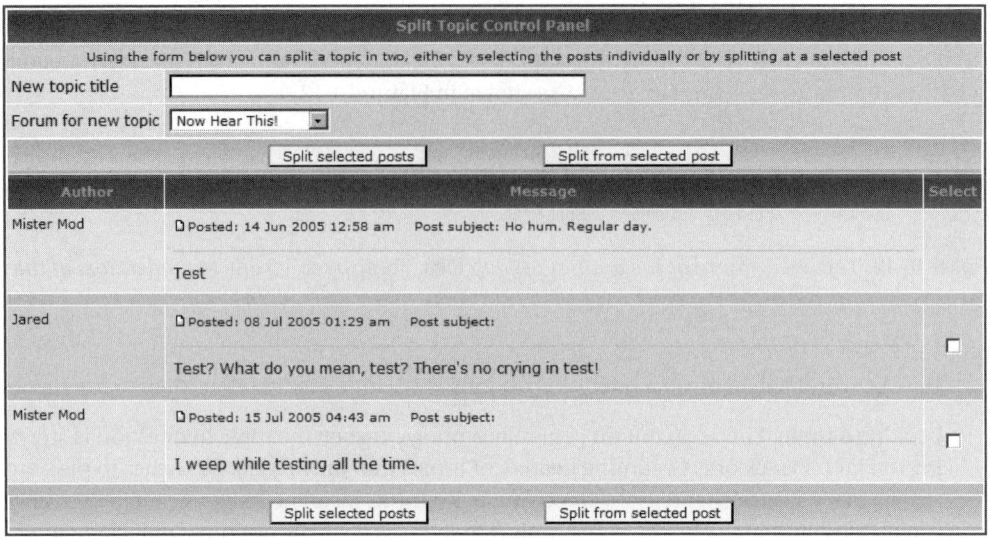

Figure 10-13. *Splitting a topic*

Performing Mass Moderation

If, for some reason, you need to perform moderation actions on many topics *en masse*, you don't need to worry about acting on each topic separately. phpBB provides facilities for mass moderation in the Moderator Control Panel, affectionately referred to by the phpBB community as the Mod CP.

You access the Mod CP for your forum by clicking the *Moderate this forum* link in the permissions block, typically located on the lower-right side of each View Forum and View Topic page. The Mod CP shows a list of topics, much as a regular forum view does, with options to perform mass actions on them, as shown in Figure 10-14.

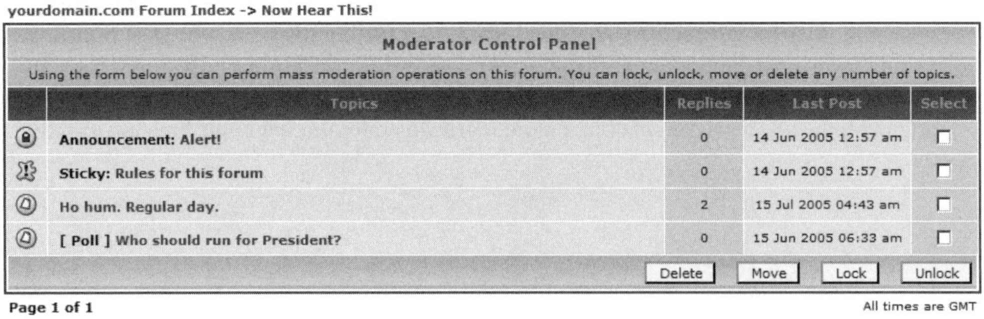

Figure 10-14. *The Moderator Control Panel, ready for mass-moderating fun!*

To delete, move, lock, or unlock multiple topics at once, check the check box on the far right corresponding to the topics on which you wish to perform the action, and then click the appropriate button for the action. Clicking a topic's title takes you to the Split Topic Control Panel (see Figure 10-13), the same location you arrive at when you click the Split Topic icon at the bottom of a View Topic page.

The Mod CP's mass moderation functions operate almost identically to performing the operations one by one. Be sure to heed the confirmations accordingly, as mass actions (particularly mass deletions) can take some time to recover from if you make a mistake.

Using the IP Manager

For security purposes, phpBB records an IP address with each post made, corresponding to the user who made the post. To access the IP address associated with a particular post, click the tiny IP icon in the extreme top-right corner of the post. This brings you to a screen similar to Figure 10-15.

Tip Stunningly, phpBB lacks the ability to track the IP address of users when they register, which can be important if users are registering accounts for malicious purposes, but not necessarily posting. This is a glaring omission, which luckily can be rectified by installing a modification known as Log Registration IP. I consider it vital, and I highly recommend this feature, even if you do not install any additional ones. You can obtain the Log Registration IP modification from `http://www.phpbbhacks.com/download/2975`.

IP Information	
IP address for this post	
192.168.0.106 [1 Post]	[Look up IP address]
Users posting from this IP address	
Jared [1 Post]	search
Mister Mod [1 Post]	search
Other IP addresses this user has posted from	
192.168.0.100 [3 Posts]	[Look up IP address]

Figure 10-15. *The IP manager displaying the IP address associated with a particular post, with a cross-reference to other users who have posted from the same IP address*

phpBB's IP manager helps you, with reasonable accuracy, see if a user is masquerading with multiple identities on your site, which is useful in terms of bans. Clicking the *Look up IP address* link next to the IP address associated with the post permits you to see the host name of the user (in most cases), which typically identifies the Internet service provider he is using to access your site. From there, you can take that information to a site such as `samspade.org` or `network-tools.com`, run a WHOIS query, and determine an abuse address, for example. You can search on the posting history of users who have posted from that IP address. Finally, phpBB gives the other IP addresses the user has posted from, for further cross-referencing work.

Caution Treat users' IP address information with the utmost care. Releasing that information could put users in danger of having their computer attacked if they have not taken the proper precautions. Additionally, IP addresses, if configured by the Internet service provider, can give information that some users may believe violates their privacy, right down to the town where they are located. Respect your users' privacy and be responsible with IP address information.

Maintaining and Performance Tuning phpBB

Now that you have improved the security of your board, it's time to talk about those mundane maintenance tasks that administrators love to hate, but are vital to the smooth operation of your community. These include pruning dead posts, managing your database, and caching templates.

Pruning Dead Posts

As your community gets larger and more active, it will inevitably slow down. This is a fact of any forum system you will come across. phpBB, like most other forum software, permits you to reduce the size of your community via a process known as *pruning*, where posts with no activity after a certain cutoff date are removed from the system.

Caution Pruning a fledgling community is generally discouraged. This is because pruning may result in the community looking rather dead, and that is not the image you want to cast as you try to attract people to your site.

Archiving Posts

If you plan to prune your forums on any sort of regular basis, I suggest setting up locked forums for the posts that you wish to keep, and then move those posts into them. This is a process known as *archiving*. Setting up an archive forum is just like setting up a regular forum, except that you check the box to lock the forum. This prevents users (but not administrators or moderators) from posting or editing anything inside the forum, so that the data inside is preserved. After creating your archive forums, I recommend using the Moderator Control Panel to perform mass movement of topics to these forums to save some time. This way, the posts that you prize can stay well away from your digital pruning shears (ha, ha!) while the deadwood gets cut out.

Pruning Forums Manually

To prune a forum, enter the Administration panel and click the *Pruning* link underneath Forum Admin in the navigation pane. You'll be presented with a screen resembling Figure 10-16.

Select the forum you wish to prune (or leave it set to All Forums to prune *en masse*), and then click the Look up Forum button. This takes you to the screen shown in Figure 10-17.

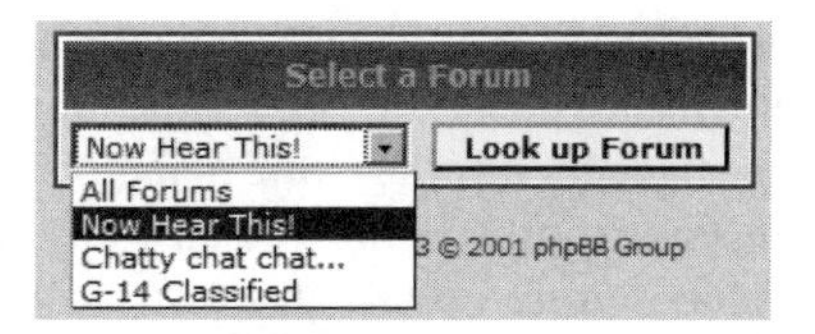

Figure 10-16. *Selecting a forum to prune*

Enter the maximum number of days for inactive topics in your forum to live, and then click the Do Prune button. The process may take a few seconds, as this is a database-intensive step.

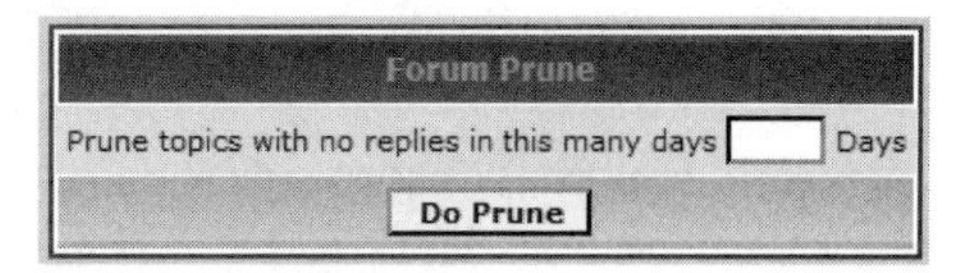

Figure 10-17. *The second part of pruning a forum, where you determine the cutoff*

When you reenter your forum, you should see that all of the inactive topics past the maximum age you specified are now gone. Repeat the process for each forum you wish to trim down. With any luck, you'll be running a little leaner and maybe even a smidgen faster.

■ **Note** Pruning—both manual and automatic—will not remove announcement or sticky posts, as those are considered having elevated importance and are designed to last a long time. To remove these posts, you'll need to manually delete them, or edit the first post in the topic and change the status of the posts you want to remove to Normal before you run the prune operation.

Pruning Forums Automatically

You can also set individual forums to automatically prune posts without user intervention. This option can be set while you are creating a forum or after the fact. Figure 10-18 shows an example of editing an existing forum.

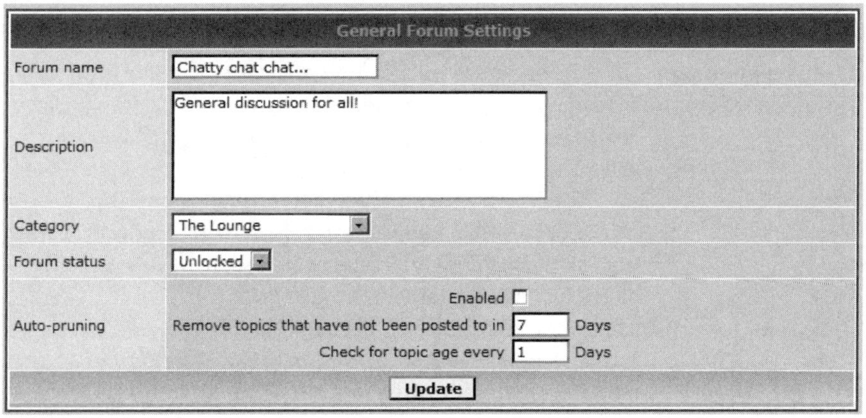

Figure 10-18. *Editing a forum, paying close attention to the automatic pruning options*

The bottom of the form contains the options for automatic pruning. To enable it, check the Enabled check box. You can set the maximum age (the default is seven days) and an interval for checking for topic age (the default is every day). Depending on how active you are about archiving topics and how much load your board takes, you may wish to adjust these settings. More frequent pruning will cause less of an immediate impact on your performance than pruning once over a long period of time. To save your changes, click Update.

When an administrator visits a forum, the auto-pruning feature will see if it needs to be run. If so, it will check the posts and delete them automatically.

Caution Auto-pruning occurs without warning. If you decide to enable this option in your forums, make sure you and your moderators regularly archive posts that you wish to keep, as you won't have any warning when phpBB is about to delete posts. If you are concerned about losing data in a forum, I recommend that you leave this option off and prune manually.

Managing Your Database

One of the most important tasks in administering phpBB is to keep your database healthy. The database is your bread and butter. Most databases do a fairly good job of taking care of themselves, but just like everything else, they require periodic maintenance. Keeping an eye on the database is quite important because when your database malfunctions, phpBB malfunctions, and your users won't like it one bit!

Note This section of this chapter relies on phpMyAdmin for performing some of these tasks. Now is a good time to check with your host provider about the location of your phpMyAdmin (or equivalent) database administration tool, how to log in, and the extent of the functionality available to you. I reference phpMyAdmin 2.6.1 here.

Optimizing and Repairing Database Tables

Over time, heavily accessed tables in your database will accumulate some sort of overhead. Predictably, this overhead can slow down your database operations a bit, causing it to perform less than optimally. Figure 10-19 illustrates phpMyAdmin showing a table with overhead.

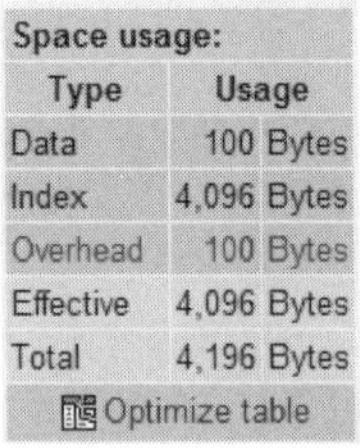

Space usage:

Type	Usage
Data	100 Bytes
Index	4,096 Bytes
Overhead	100 Bytes
Effective	4,096 Bytes
Total	4,196 Bytes

Optimize table

Figure 10-19. *phpMyAdmin looking at a table with some overhead*

Note the overhead of 100 bytes in this table. This is a minor occurrence, but it's worth optimizing anyway. Clicking *Optimize table* will fix the overhead. It's a good idea to check for this regularly in the `<prefix>_posts` table (where *prefix* represents the database prefix you selected during initial setup, usually phpbb), as that table is written to and read from incredibly frequently. You can easily optimize all tables that need work by viewing the full database (clicking the name of the database, in bolded black text, in the left pane takes you there), scrolling to the bottom of the page in the right pane, and clicking *Check overheaded.* This puts check boxes next to tables in which phpMyAdmin detects overhead. You can then click the drop-down menu and select *Optimize table.* Clicking Go at the bottom of the form runs the optimizations. You will, barring disaster, get an OK message from MySQL, indicating that the optimizations have been completed.

In rare instances, phpBB's tables may become damaged. This can happen due to a software error on the MySQL server side, a power glitch, or a random hardware issue. Signs of damage to your database tables include excessive slowness when browsing or odd SQL error messages when trying to use the forums. If you suspect damage has occurred, click Check all at the bottom of the main database page, and then select *Repair table* from the drop-down menu. Click Go, and you will get a confirmation message stating your tables were repaired. With any luck, your forum will perform better. If this turns out not to be the case, you may want to undo some of your recent modifications to see if they are causing problems. If even that doesn't work, there's a possibility you may have corrupted data in your database. Restoring a backup may be in order. Conveniently, that's the next task I'll cover.

Backing Up and Restoring Your Database

phpBB's Administration panel has useful facilities for creating a compressed backup of the contents of your phpBB database that you can download to your hard drive for safekeeping. This function is analogous to making a text dump of your database in phpMyAdmin or using the `mysql` command-line utility directly. You'll find the backup and restore utilities listed under the General Admin heading.

■ **Caution** I recommend disabling your board, through the Configuration panel, before backing up and restoring your database, as it will help to ensure the integrity of your backups and prevent data loss.

Click the *Backup Database* link to see the backup options, shown in Figure 10-20. These are quick and to the point. The first time you make a backup, you will want to do a full backup (of both the structure and data), as that file will contain the instructions to re-create the phpBB tables as well as re-create the data. If you have a broadband connection, there is no harm in backing up the structure and data every time. The other options—to create backups with the table structure only and the data only—can be useful for people on slower connections.

In addition to the phpBB tables, the backup utility also lets you list additional tables that you wish to back up. To do this, verify the names of those additional tables in the database, and then type them in the Additional tables text box, separated by commas.

Finally, you can choose whether to use gzip compression. I recommend, where available, using gzip compression on your backups. If you store a lot of backups of your forum, you'll be happy you

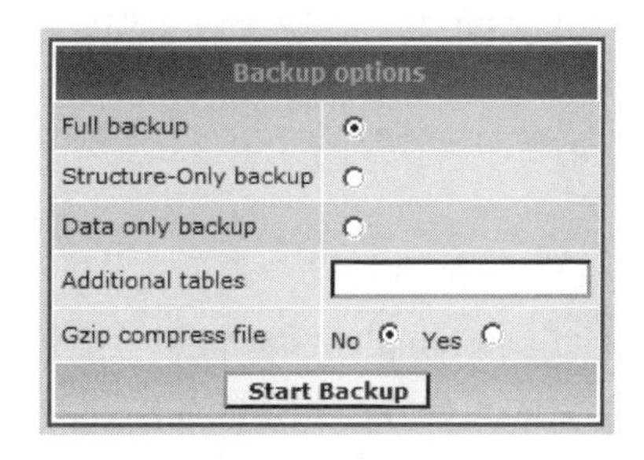

Figure 10-20. *The phpBB backup function*

selected the compression, especially if you have a slower connection. The trade-off is that the backup will take a little longer to get started.

Click Start Backup, and be patient, as it can take a few minutes to get the backup fully downloaded to your computer.

Once you've made a backup, restoring it is quite straightforward, as Figure 10-21 illustrates. This screen appears when you click the *Restore Database* link under General Admin in the Administration panel. From here, simply locate the compressed or uncompressed backup file on your computer, and then click Start Restore. phpBB uploads and, if necessary, decompresses the backup and restores it to the database. Be patient, as this process can take a few minutes.

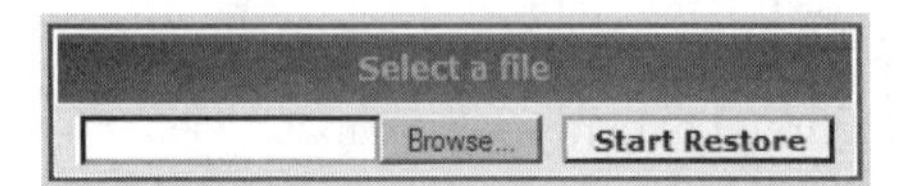

Figure 10-21. *Restoring a backup*

■ **Caution** If your database is quite large, the restore script may run afoul of your host's PHP script timeout. If you click Start Restore and nothing happens after five minutes, it's quite possible the script has terminated due to the timeout period, which is designed to stop runaway scripts. You can try breaking up the file (if it is compressed, use WinZip or WinRAR on Windows to decompress it first) and uploading separate text files. Contact your host provider if you have questions about its PHP timeout policies.

Using Template Caching

When the styling system made its debut in phpBB 2.0, there was a great deal of concern over increased server load due to the templates. Time has shown that phpBB's template engine is a solid performer under load, but the phpBB Group provides two options for caching templates: one for using individual files and the other to save template information to the database. These solutions will help decrease the strain on your server under periods of extreme duress.

■ **Caution** The phpBB Group has tested the caching systems, but as always, your mileage may vary. Back up the `template.php` file located in the `/includes` subdirectory under your phpBB path before proceeding, in case something goes wrong. Additionally, you can choose only one system or the other, not both.

Flat-File Template Caching

If you are going to use template caching, I recommend using the flat-file method, as it does not require further use of the database. Boards under duress already stress the database, so it's good to try to offload from the database when you can.

Extract template_file_cache.php from the /contrib folder from your phpBB installation package and place it in the /includes subdirectory. Remove the existing template.php file after ensuring it is backed up in a safe place, and rename template_file_cache.php to template.php. Next, you will need to upload the /cache subdirectory and its contents from your phpBB installation package to the server, and make it world-writable (777). As I discussed in Chapter 8, SmartFTP (http://www.smartftp.com) makes this task easy. Upload the newly christened template.php to your server (in the /includes subdirectory), and you will be finished. Visit a few pages on your board and take a look at the /cache subdirectory, and you should see some files inside, indicating caching is happening.

Database Template Caching

If you decide to go the database route, extract template_db_cache.php. Copy it over your existing template.php file (after making a backup of that file). In this case, you will not create a cache subdirectory, but rather a new table in your database. Log in to phpMyAdmin, select your phpBB database, and navigate to the SQL tab at the top. You'll be running another raw SQL query, shown in Listing 10-1, in this box. The *<your_prefix>* represents whatever database prefix you are using on your server, which defaults to phpbb.

Listing 10-1. *The SQL Query to Run in phpMyAdmin to Create the New Caching Table*

```
CREATE TABLE <your_prefix>_template_cache (
  template_name char(255) NOT NULL default '',
  template_handle char(50) NOT NULL default '',
  template_cached int(11) NOT NULL default '0',
  template_echo tinyint(1) NOT NULL default '1',
  template_compile text NOT NULL,
  PRIMARY KEY  (template_name)
)
```

Tip You can find this same query in the README.html file located in the /contrib folder of your phpBB installation or upgrade package. It will be easier and less error-prone for you to copy and paste the query than for you to type it straight in.

After creating the table, upload the enhanced template.php file to your includes subdirectory (as for the flat-file system). Visit a few pages of your phpBB, and open the template_cache table in your phpBB installation to ensure that there is activity in the table, indicating that the caching is working properly.

Uninstalling Template Caching

If, for some reason, you wish to uninstall the template cache system, simply copy the original template.php, either from your backup or the installation package, over the one that currently exists. This restores the old template functionality. Only then can you remove the /cache subdirectory or the template cache table, as removing those prior to restoring the original noncaching file can cause errors.

Introducing phpBB 3.0 Security and Maintenance Enhancements

phpBB 3.0 features a vastly improved set of options for hardening your board as well as performing maintenance. Additionally, the new version offers incredible performance improvements plus more tuning options.

■ **Caution** The standard disclaimer applies: as of this writing, phpBB 3.0 is still in prerelease form, with the permissions system under heavy construction. Screen shots and information here can and likely will change between now and final release.

Managing Permissions in phpBB 3.0

Back in Chapter 8, I introduced you to the new phpBB 3.0 permissions system with regard to working with forums. Additionally, you will be able to restrict all facets of a user's interaction with the board, including limiting access in the Administration panel, restricting private messages, and much more. Per-user and group permissions have been expanded considerably and are far more flexible than ever before.

Here are a few of the permissions enhancements:

The Founder: A new security feature in phpBB 3.0 designates the user who set up the forum as the community Founder. The Founder cannot, under any circumstances, lose administrative privileges. The Founder has the right, by default, to all objects, and other administrators cannot edit these preferences. This prevents malicious users from demoting every administrator and holding a board hostage, so to speak.

Administrative permissions for user groups: A glaring omission from phpBB 2.0 is the ability to assign a user group administrator rights. This is no longer the case in phpBB 3.0. As before, you can use user groups to assign moderator permissions, and also assign supermoderators in the same fashion. User groups have become much more useful in this release as a result of these changes, and they are my preferred method for designating permissions in phpBB 3.0.

Piecemeal administrative/moderator power: phpBB's permissions system breaks the mold of "one-size-fits-all" permissions for moderators and administrators and now permits you to assign or revoke individual rights to users or groups. For example, you can set someone to be able to access the Administration panel to ban users and edit user accounts, but not view the system logs.

Using Strengthened Security Features in phpBB 3.0

phpBB 3.0 offers a dazzling array of enhancements to other facets of security beyond the permissions system. There are now logging features that record activity by your staff, temporary banning, post reporting, and much, much more.

The following is a sampling of the new security features:

Auditing features: phpBB 3.0 now takes stock of all actions performed by administrators and moderators and places them in a system log. As shown in the example in Figure 10-22, you are now able to see exactly when administrators log in to the Administration panel and what actions they perform. This is an obvious boon to security and helps to provide accountability for when something goes wrong in the Administration panel. Similar logging exists for moderator actions, as well. In addition to these logs, phpBB also takes stock of all board errors that are encountered to aid in troubleshooting.

Display entries from previous: All entries | Sort by: Date | Descending | Go

Username	IP	Time	Action	Mark
Jared	192.168.0.106	15 Jul 2005 05:00	**Sucessful administration login**	☐
Jared	192.168.0.106	07 Jul 2005 02:10	**Sucessful administration login**	☐
Jared	192.168.0.100	15 Jun 2005 08:04	**Sucessful administration login**	☐
Jared	192.168.0.100	15 Jun 2005 08:03	**Sucessful administration login**	☐
Jared	192.168.0.100	15 Jun 2005 06:57	**Sucessful administration login**	☐
Jared	192.168.0.100	15 Jun 2005 05:02	**Sucessful administration login**	☐
Jared	192.168.0.100	26 May 2005 04:50	**Added or edited Forum access** from Test Forum Archive » Administrators	☐
Jared	192.168.0.100	26 May 2005 04:49	**Edited forum details** » Test Forum Archive	☐
Jared	192.168.0.100	26 May 2005 04:48	**Added or edited Forum access** from Jared » %s	☐
Jared	192.168.0.100	26 May 2005 04:39	**Created new forum** » Test Forum Archive	☐
Jared	192.168.0.100	26 May 2005 04:09	**Sucessful administration login**	☐

Delete Marked | Delete All

Figure 10-22. *An administration log from phpBB 3.0*

Authentication plug-ins: Authentication plug-ins are another new option to phpBB 3.0. Previously, the only method provided was to use phpBB's own database. That has all changed in the 3.0 world, with the addition of Apache `.htpasswd` authentication, as well as authentication against an LDAP server that you specify. A phpBB installation that authenticates against a Windows Server 2003 Active Directory would be nothing short of sweet, particularly in an enterprise setting, and that is theoretically possible with this version.

Validation options: The phpBB 3 Server Settings panel permits a few new validation options to be set for sessions. The option exists for setting a minimum threshold for how much an IP address can change in a session without the session being invalidated. This is incredibly useful for combating problems with America Online users, who sit behind rotating proxy servers, which sometimes change their IP addresses on each click. This has caused problems in the past, and you are now free to customize the feature (or even disable it). You can now restrict sessions to one browser; if the user opens a new session on another browser, she is logged out of the original browser.

Performance Tuning in phpBB 3.0

phpBB 3.0 enables easier tuning of the board to favor performance. You are now able to set the board to disable certain features under specific load conditions, or always disable some features. You can even tell phpBB not to operate until high-load situations subside. This is accomplished in the Server Settings control panel, shown in Figure 10-23.

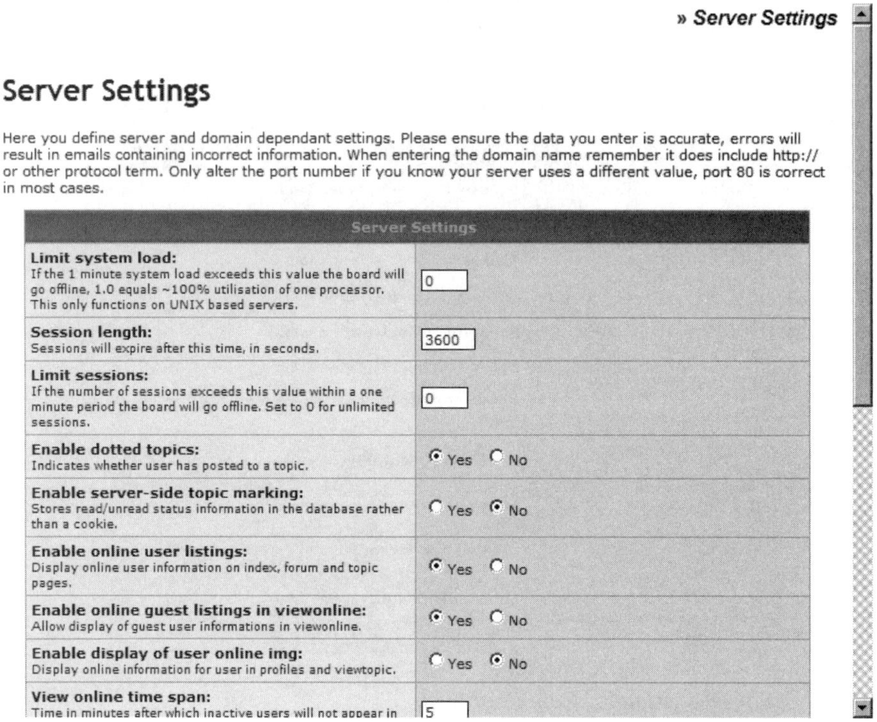

» Server Settings

Server Settings

Here you define server and domain dependant settings. Please ensure the data you enter is accurate, errors will result in emails containing incorrect information. When entering the domain name remember it does include http:// or other protocol term. Only alter the port number if you know your server uses a different value, port 80 is correct in most cases.

Server Settings	
Limit system load: If the 1 minute system load exceeds this value the board will go offline, 1.0 equals ~100% utilisation of one processor. This only functions on UNIX based servers.	0
Session length: Sessions will expire after this time, in seconds.	3600
Limit sessions: If the number of sessions exceeds this value within a one minute period the board will go offline. Set to 0 for unlimited sessions.	0
Enable dotted topics: Indicates whether user has posted to a topic.	(•) Yes ( ) No
Enable server-side topic marking: Stores read/unread status information in the database rather than a cookie.	( ) Yes (•) No
Enable online user listings: Display online user information on index, forum and topic pages.	(•) Yes ( ) No
Enable online guest listings in viewonline: Allow display of guest user informations in viewonline.	(•) Yes ( ) No
Enable display of user online img: Display online information for user in profiles and viewtopic.	( ) Yes (•) No
View online time span: Time in minutes after which inactive users will not appear in	5

Figure 10-23. *The Server Settings control panel*

The options are relatively self-explanatory. You have a lot of flexibility in shutting down phpBB features that you may find to be performance-sapping. Additionally, phpBB 3.0 gives you unparalleled control over the search indexing feature, which is a major change from phpBB 2.0, as it did not permit you to manage the feature at all. You now can tweak some of the indexing settings to further improve performance, or even disable searching entirely if it becomes a major performance problem.

Pruning in phpBB 3.0

As you might expect, the pruning feature is much improved over phpBB 2.0 as well. There's now the option to prune users as well as forums, and forum pruning has been expanded nicely.

Pruning Forums

The updated forum pruning utility is illustrated in Figure 10-24. Note some of the new features it offers.

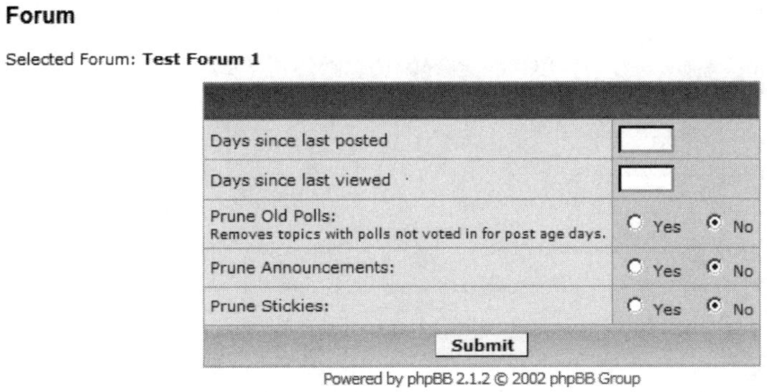

Figure 10-24. *phpBB 3.0's pruning utility, operating on Test Forum 1*

In Figure 10-24, I've selected Test Forum 1 as the forum I want to prune. You'll notice that phpBB 3.0 now permits you to prune old announcements and sticky topics, in addition to the regular topics. Previously, phpBB did not permit you to prune such topics. You can also prune topics by last view time, so that topics that no one reads can also go by the wayside. These options are also available when setting up automatic pruning in the forum's options.

Pruning Users

phpBB 3.0 introduces the option to prune inactive users. See Figure 10-25 for an illustration of this new utility.

You have a number of criteria to choose from, all of which can be combined. You can target specific usernames and e-mail addresses for pruning, or do mass-pruning of users based on last activity, join date, or post count. You have the option to simply deactivate accounts that the pruning utility finds, so that no data is lost. And, if you need to shrink the database, you can remove the accounts entirely.

■ **Caution** Deleting accounts is permanent. Have a backup handy if you use the prune feature to remove users!

» *Prune users*

Prune users

Here you can delete (or deactivate) users from you board. This can be done in a variety of ways; by post count, last activity, etc. Each of these criteria can be combined, i.e. you can prune users last active before 2002-01-01 with fewer than 10 posts. Alternatively you can enter a list of users directly into the text box, any criteria entered will be ignored. Take care with this facility! Once a user is deleted there is no way back.

Prune users	
Username:	
Email:	
Joined:	
Last active:	
Posts:	
Prune users: Enter specific usernames here, they will be used in preference to the criteria above.	
Delete pruned user posts: Removes posts made by deleted users, has no effect if users are deactivated.	○ Yes ● No
Deactivate or delete: Choose whether to deactivate users or delete them entirely, note there is no undo!	○ Delete ● Deactivate
Submit Find a member	

Powered by phpBB 2.1.2 © 2002 phpBB Group

Figure 10-25. *User pruning, a new feature in phpBB 3.0*

Backing Up and Restoring Databases in phpBB 3.0

Finally, the backup and restore functions have undergone improvements. You now can compress data in bzip format, which is another popular and tight compression algorithm on UNIX machines.

A great new feature for those with limited bandwidth has been introduced as well. You no longer need to download backups to your hard drive, as phpBB 3.0 offers the usage of a `/store` directory, where you can direct your backups to be saved. Dial-up users, rejoice! You also have the option to include or exclude (leading to a significant size savings) the search index.

■ **Note** To use the `/store` directory to hold your database backups, you will need to make it writable. You can do this using your FTP program or by issuing the `chmod ugo+w` command at a UNIX command line.

Restoration is still as simple as in earlier versions, with the additional option to load backups directly from the server.

Summary

The focus in this chapter was to make your board ready for the public. By using the permissions system and setting other critical options, you can harden your board's security to minimize disturbances. You've learned how to tune the forum's performance via pruning, archiving, and optimizing the database. And, you've seen an additional option in reducing load by introducing template caching.

In Chapter 11, I'll discuss the ins and outs of modifying the phpBB software. I'll introduce you to common modifications that I like to use whenever I set up a phpBB. I'll show you the best places to obtain modifications and get support for them. Additionally, for the curious and code-savvy, there will be an introduction to the phpBB codebase and database abstraction system, so that you can fashion your own modifications. Finally, I'll discuss how to document those modifications so you can contribute them to the phpBB community.

CHAPTER 11

Modifying phpBB

One of the key advantages of using a package such as phpBB to power your forum solution is that you can add modifications to the software. Your modifications can range from small changes to the software's behavior to adding entirely new features that you can offer your members. The hacking scene—not the scene commonly associated with malicious users breaking into computer systems, but rather the community of forum administrators who author and release such modifications commonly known as *hacks*—has thrived for each major piece of forum software for years. Some hacks add features so popular that they are officially added to subsequent releases of the software.

This chapter covers two aspects of modifying phpBB. The first section will discuss the mechanics of installing modifications to your phpBB software, and the second section will detail how to create hacks for your board and prepare them for release to the community, if you so desire.

Installing Modifications

A vast number of modifications are available for the phpBB software. The advantages to using existing modifications are numerous. You do not need to be an expert in PHP coding to install these modifications, and they have likely been put through a series of tests to make sure they work as advertised. Plus, you will have a whole community to consult if something goes wrong, which may not be possible if you write your own modifications.

Getting Ready to Install a Hack

Before you jump into modifying your board, you should perform a few tasks to make the modification process as smooth and uneventful as possible. You will be delving into phpBB's underlying source code now, so it does not hurt to be prepared!

Making Backups

When you install modifications, you change the behavior of your phpBB setup in some fashion by editing the source code. The gravity of this task means that you should make a backup of your existing phpBB script files and store it in a safe location. If something goes wrong, you can revert to the old copy immediately.

It also is a good idea to make a backup of your database's structure and data, as described in Chapter 10, as some modifications alter the database's tables. Nothing angers a member base, and of course, an administrator, more than massive data loss. The age-old adage applies: better safe than sorry!

Avoiding Excessive Downtime

When you modify your board, a little downtime is inevitable. Something may not work quite right, or you might have missed a line and caused something to go wrong. It happens to the best of us. While eliminating outages completely is probably impossible, you can do a few things to make your downtime short-lived and as little of an inconvenience as possible.

Use a test installation, separate from your production forums. Having a test board is a great idea, especially if you are just getting started with modifying phpBB. You can freely test features you wish to add and thoroughly test your modifications, without disturbing the day-to-day operations of your production site. Plus, you can simply upload the modified test copy of the board to your production site once you know it is stable, which will put in all the necessary modifications. (If your modifications require that you perform some updates to your database, you will still need to do that in addition to uploading the test copy.) Since phpBB 2.0 permits you to install multiple copies in the same database, there is no reason not to have a test board, especially if you plan to do a lot of modification work.

Schedule modification work for off-peak hours. If you have some time when your board is not heavily accessed, use that time to make changes to your board, if at all possible. That way, potential problems that can arise will have less of an impact on your operation.

Let your members know what's happening. Finally, let your members know that you will be adding new features to the board during your scheduled time window, and make them aware of the possibility of outages or other issues during that time. This is especially critical if you must perform your modifications during times of higher activity. It's a nice, common courtesy, and can help in advertising some of the new features you may add.

Acquiring Your Hacks

After your preparatory routine, it's time to start looking around the Internet for the modifications you wish to add. Most, if not all, phpBB administrators look at a few select "hack databases" from which they download modifications and get support for them. These sites offer modifications and templates listed by category. You can often find many new features to add to your installation at one of these sites. Also, any hack database worth your time also has a support forum, where many of the authors and other experienced phpBB administrators can assist you with problems you may encounter along the way.

■ **Tip** If you are browsing around the Web and see a phpBB board with a few nice modifications, but don't know what they might be called, feel free to ask the administrator. Most phpBB administrators will be happy to help you and point you in the right direction toward acquiring those modifications. It's a *community* for a reason!

Using the Two Top Hack Databases

The phpBB Group operates its own hack database, located at `http://www.phpbb.com/mods/`. If you already use `phpBB.com` for supporting your board software, it can be quite convenient to have your modification support in the same place. You can also find development guides and coding standards here as well, if you are adventurous enough to create your own hacks. The official phpBB hack database has a fair selection of hacks for you to choose from, divided into several categories. You can also download development tools from their database. Note that support on this site is limited to the hacks available in the official phpBB MOD Database.

If you are looking for a wider selection of hacks to download, visit `phpBBHacks.com`, located at `http://www.phpbbhacks.com/`. (Full disclosure: I do consulting with `phpBBHacks.com` and was once a support team member there.) This site offers a full array of modifications for all versions of phpBB, including the deprecated 1.*x* series. The support forums are top-notch as well, with a team of hack developers waiting to assist. The signal-to-noise ratio at `phpBBHacks.com`'s support forums is generally lower, mainly because it is not the official phpBB site, and thus concentrates most of its energy on modifying phpBB. `phpBBHacks.com` also offers a Site of the Month, which is usually a great example of a modified, professional-looking phpBB in action. I found it to be a wonderful resource when I was getting started with phpBB.

Getting Recommended Hacks

Some hacks out there really should be regular features of phpBB. Until that happens, you'll probably want to install those hacks on the phpBB boards you run. Other hacks provide cool features that you might find interesting. Table 11-1 lists some hacks that I recommend.

■ **Caution** A vast majority of hacks that use the database are written primarily for the MySQL database, as that is the most common database system used with phpBB. As a result, if you are using another system such as PostgreSQL or Microsoft SQL Server, you may run into differences in SQL syntax from MySQL and will need to port (or find a knowledgeable user to port) the necessary commands to the other database system.

Table 11-1. *Some Recommended Hacks*

Name	Description	URL*
Log Registration IP	Records the IP address of users when they first register. It provides elaborate cross-referencing tools inside the Administration panel, as well.	`http://www.phpbbhacks.com/download/2975`
Last Post Topic on Index	Displays the topic title of the thread where the last post was made on the forum index page, in addition to the date and the user. It uses permissions to ensure that privacy of forums is not breached, and also uses the word-censoring feature, if enabled, to curb offensive language.	`http://www.phpbbhacks.com/download/566`

Continued

Table 11-1. *Continued*

Name	Description	URL*
Global Announcement Hack	Permits authorized users to make an announcement that is seen in all forums, a feature conspicuously absent from phpBB 2.0.	`http://www.phpbbhacks.com/download/345`
Karma Hack	Permits authorized users to give users a karma rating and make comments justifying the rating. It can be useful in large communities where an assessment of problem users is needed. It can also be used to foster a reward system on your community.	`http://www.phpbbhacks.com/download/5317`
Email Topic to Friend	Enables users to e-mail links to topics, with a personal message enclosed. Again, this is another startling omission from the phpBB 2.0 feature set.	`http://www.phpbbhacks.com/download/936`
Birthday Hack	Permits users to optionally enter their birthday, and displays their age on their posts. Additionally, when the users' birthday arrives, they get greetings directly from your phpBB!	`http://www.phpbbhacks.com/download/187`
Restrict Guest Access	Denies guest access to profiles, user groups, the member list, the search function, and similar information. This can be incredibly useful when fending off illegitimate "bot" registrations and when your board is under high load.	`http://www.phpbbhacks.com/download/1415`

**These hacks were available from the listed URLs at the time of this writing, but their URLs may change in the future.*

Installing a Hack

Now let's try installing a hack. You'll install a popular modification, Quick Reply with Quote, which was written and released by phpBB community member Smartor. You can retrieve this hack from `phpBBHacks.com`, at `http://www.phpbbhacks.com/download/540`. This modification will place a Quick Reply box on each View Topic page, permitting users with permission to post in a forum the opportunity to write a response without clicking Post Reply. This particular flavor of Quick Reply (several exist) permits you to quote the previous message in the thread.

This hack is one of the easier ones to install. In addition to modifying core phpBB files, it also adds a couple lines to the English language file and a couple lines to a template. Thus, this hack serves as a fairly well-rounded demonstration of modifying your board, not only through code, but through styling as well. (Chapter 12 covers styling in more depth.)

Opening the Hack

You'll notice the hack came in a `.zip` file. A lot of hack sites distribute hacks as compressed files, normally in `.zip` format, to save bandwidth and for convenience. While the Quick Reply with Quote hack is only one file, some hacks contain multiple files (such as additional `.php` files).

You'll want to open the text file that came with the hack (in this case, it will be `Quick Reply with Quote Mod.txt`). This contains the steps for installing the hack. Figure 11-1 shows a Notepad window with this hack open.

```
Quick Reply with Quote Mod.txt - Notepad
File Edit Format View Help
## MOD Author: Smartor < smartor_xp@hotmail.com > (Hoang Ngoc Tu) http://smartor.is-root.com
## MOD Description: This will add a quick-reply form below every topics
##                  It will only display when user has the Reply access
##                  User have a option to quote the last message
## MOD Version: 1.1.3
##
## Installation Level: easy
## Installation Time: 5 Minutes
## Files To Edit: 3
##      viewtopic.php
##      language/lang_XX/lang_main.php
##      templates/template_XX/viewtopic_body.tpl
## Included Files: N/A
##############################################################
## Author Notes:
##
##############################################################
## This MOD is released under the GPL License.
## Intellectual Property is retained by the MOD Author(s) listed above
##############################################################
## Before Adding This MOD To Your Forum, You Should Back Up All Files Related To This MOD
##############################################################

#
#-----[ OPEN ]------------------------------------------
#
viewtopic.php

#
#-----[ FIND ]------------------------------------------
#
$template->pparse('body');

include($phpbb_root_path . 'includes/page_tail.'.$phpEx);

#
#-----[ BEFORE, ADD ]------------------------------------
#
//
// Quick Reply Mod
//
if ( ((!$is_auth['auth_reply']) or ($forum_topic_data['forum_status'] == FORUM_LOCKED) or
($forum_topic_data['topic_status'] == TOPIC_LOCKED)) and ($userdata['user_level'] != ADMIN)
)
{
        $quick_reply_form = "";
}
else
{
        if ( $can_watch_topic && $is_watching_topic )
        {
                $notify = 1;
        }
```

Figure 11-1. *The Quick Reply with Quote modification, opened in Notepad*

Note the format of this hack. Most hacks authored in the past few years will be presented in this same format, so each hack you install will look similar. The header is quite straightforward, giving the title of the hack, the author's name (usually with contact information as well), a description of what the hack does, the difficulty level along with the installation time, a list of files that need to be opened, and a list of files included. Make sure you heed the warning to back up your files!

The next section of the file contains the main instructions: which files to open, what to search for, and what to do with the piece of modified code (whether to add it somewhere, replace a line, and so on).

■ **Caution** When editing your phpBB files, make sure you use a plain text editor, and not something like Microsoft Word, which could damage your files. While Notepad is adequate for the job, for Windows users, something like EditPlus (shareware available from `http://www.editplus.com`, $30 registration) is better. EditPlus (and editors like it) is very handy for its color-coding abilities, which can help prevent a lot of common coding mistakes that simple editors such as Notepad can't point out to you.

Making the Changes

With the hack open on your desktop (in Notepad, EditPlus, or a similar text editor), start by navigating to the proper file—in this case, `viewtopic.php`—and following the instructions on where to insert code. The instructions are fairly straightforward. Look toward the end of the file to insert a large block of code. (For the sake of brevity, and acknowledging the changing nature of modifications, the code is not reprinted here.) After making the prescribed changes, save and close `viewtopic.php`.

Next, open `lang_main.php`, which will reside under `language/lang_english` for our purposes. These language lines will contain two strings used by this hack. In this instance, you're looking for a comment marked "That's All Folks" at the very end of the file. Above that, you'll insert the language lines specified in the next section of the hack. In the version of the hack available at the time of this writing, two lines are specified.

■ **Note** Feel free to substitute for other languages in which you have translations of phpBB. However, note that the text supplied with this particular hack is in English, so you will need to translate to your other desired language (or obtain a translation of the hack, if one is available).

Finally, open the `viewtopic_body.tpl` template file, which will place the form on the bottom of the View Topic page. Chapter 12 will delve into the details of working with template files, but for now, you'll be editing just this one file. If you have multiple active templates, you will need to edit the `viewtopic_body.tpl` file for each additional template as well, in order for the feature to be properly enabled across all templates. Look for the line `{S_TOPIC_ADMIN}`, and insert the final line specified in the hack below it. Don't worry about the meaning of these lines right now; Chapter 12 will educate you on the available template variables.

The final instruction is to save and close all files. Yes, that's right—you're finished! Upload your changes to the server, open your board, and go view a topic (while logged in, of course). With any luck, you'll have a new addition to your View Topic page, as illustrated in Figure 11-2.

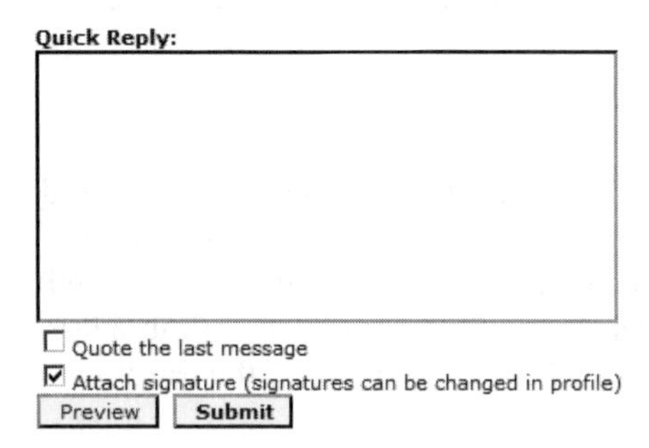

Figure 11-2. *The expected results of installing the Quick Reply hack: a Quick Reply box*

If you see something reasonably close to Figure 11-2, you've successfully installed the Quick Reply hack, and congratulations are in order. Feel free to give the box a try. Chances are, you'll like it.

Be sure to back up your newly hacked files, in case you decide to go for more modifications and they don't work out. This way, you can restore from a recent point if something goes wrong, so you won't lose *all* your work. This is excellent practice for each modification you install. Once you know that everything is working properly, you can feel free to clean up some of these developmental backup copies. Go ahead and check out my recommendations on additional modifications (listed earlier in Table 11-1) for more phpBB hacking fun!

If you see something other than Figure 11-2, don't panic. I've got some troubleshooting ideas for you.

Troubleshooting Hack Installation

So you went through all those steps, but instead of the modification, you got a cryptic PHP error message, or perhaps there's no sign of any changes. In that case, review the following troubleshooting steps:

Did you upload it? In the heat of the moment, it's easy to forget to upload. Make sure you uploaded the modification, and it's in the right place.

Did you insert template code? Most phpBB 2.0 hacks require work to be done on your template. If you are not using the subSilver template on your site, make sure you edit the templates that your site uses. If you don't, you likely won't see any result from any of your hacks.

Is all the code in the right place? Make sure all your code is properly placed within your files. Placement can be critical. Sometimes, the instructions are not as clear as they should be about where to put the code (it does happen).

Is all the code right? Rarely, bad code makes its way into a hack. While people test hacks before they go into the databases, sometimes something slips. Check with the hack author or the distributor before continuing.

Is there a version incompatibility? Sometimes, phpBB updates break existing hacks. If you have reason to believe this is a problem, contact the distributor of your hack or the hack author.

If you continue to encounter problems, you will probably want to restore your file from a backup (particularly if there is a parse error or other unsightly problem that PHP reports) and wait to see if a fix is released. Also, feel free to use the support forums located at the various hack sites. They are there to help!

PREHACKED BOARDS AND WHY YOU SHOULD AVOID THEM

Some groups independent of phpBB take the phpBB codebase, add a lot of modifications to it, and re-release it in a package commonly known as a "prehacked" board. These can be the pinnacle of convenience, adding in just about any feature you could ever want bolted onto your phpBB software in one easy-to-install package, with no code to sweat over. However, these prehacked boards have some serious disadvantages that outweigh their advantages.

For starters, prehacked boards typically come with a plethora of additional features that you may never need. With additional features comes additional bloat. Considering that the modifications applied probably have not had much mainstream performance testing, loading the package on your server when traffic is high could be quite a challenge. (Of course, this varies depending on who packaged the distribution.)

Another problem is that prehacked boards may or may not be totally secure. Some boards may use older phpBB codebases, which may be vulnerable to attack. If a critical update is made available by the phpBB team, there's no telling when that same update will be available for your prehacked package, as applying the official phpBB update may break your board.

Finally, distributions can come and go. If your prehacked phpBB maintainers decide to abandon their project, you could be stuck out in the cold with limited support and no updates, which is not safe when vulnerabilities strike.

You are better off sticking with an official phpBB release that *will* be updated and supported. With an official release, you have total control over the modifications—the freedom to add and remove features at will. With the prehacked packages, you are not necessarily afforded such flexibility.

Creating Modifications

Sometimes, the hacks out there just don't cut it—you can't find one that does exactly what you want. Some people (like myself) are incessant tweakers, who feel the need to change more of the board than typically is modified. In these cases, the alternative is to create your own modifications. This is a task for the self-motivated with enough time to thoroughly test the effects of the modification.

This section covers the basics of working with phpBB's various subsystems—the guts of phpBB, if you will—programmatically to create your own modifications, as well as how to package and submit them to the community. This section requires a fair amount of competency with PHP, object-oriented programming, and MySQL syntax. If you have any qualms about these topics, you should review a tutorial or consider purchasing a book such as *Beginning PHP and MySQL* by W. Jason Gilmore (Apress, 2004) before you start coding a hack.

■ **Note** Before you start coding your hack, do a thorough search of the hacks sites listed in Table 11-1, and make sure that your desired hack doesn't already exist. If it does, it may be better for you to install that existing hack, rather than trying to reinvent the wheel. Additionally, if you will be submitting your work to the community, this cuts down on the number of duplicate hacks and other potential issues that may arise between the original author of the hack and yourself. You can save yourself a lot of work and trouble by making sure you aren't duplicating someone else's work.

Getting Ready to Code

When coding for phpBB 2.0, the key is understanding the codebase and the conventions involved. The phpBB team developers envisioned phpBB 2.0 as an easily modified version of phpBB, with plenty of accessible methods to aid you in accomplishing your tasks. Grasping those is a good first step to being a successful phpBB 2.0 hacker.

When writing your hacks, a test installation is a must. For writing hacks, I recommend using a separate database from your production database entirely. This way, if you are making sweeping database modifications, there is zero risk of your production database being wiped out in a freak accident.

■ **Caution** *Never, ever, under any circumstances, do active hack development on a live installation!* Doing so can result in broken boards, frustrated administrators, and unhappy end users. Save yourself the grief and aspirin, and develop on only your test installation. Don't forget to have a backup handy, too.

Using the phpBB Coding Conventions

As I mentioned earlier, one of the keys to a successful phpBB installation is to adhere to the phpBB coding conventions. You can find the most recent updates to these on `http://www.phpbb.com/mods/`.

phpBB's built-in methods are, in a nutshell, designed to keep you from reinventing the wheel. They are also designed to provide a seamless experience for end users, which is important in terms of continuity and goes a long way toward professionalism. Writing hacks that don't use the built-in phpBB methods can cause strange problems, may not be easily ported between boards (an important consideration if you intend to release your work to the public), and may ultimately limit the usefulness of your modification.

The following sections discuss the methods phpBB uses for accessing data, using templates, working with sessions, getting user information, and giving feedback to your users.

Accessing the phpBB Database Abstraction Layer

The database abstraction layer provided by phpBB helps to simplify support for major database systems. PHP has groups of functions, such as `mysql_query()`, that correspond to whichever database type it is accessing. This can prove painful when writing blocks of SQL to support different databases; you will not only need to define different SQL (which you typically must do in any case), but you will also must implement the query method for each different database system. Undoubtedly, this can prove tedious, tiring, and error-prone.

In the phpBB world, you are provided with a `$db` object, which represents the database driver for your configured database type. This object is initialized every time you run phpBB and is globally available to you. The `$db` object eliminates the need to fumble through the different functions for different database systems; in other words, rather than using database-specific calls such as `mysql_query()` or `postgres_query()`, you only need to call `$db->sql_query()`. If necessary, you can check the loaded database driver using a `switch(SQL_LAYER)` construct, as demonstrated in Listing 11-1. This example depicts checking the `SQL_LAYER` and defining different SQL for each database system, if necessary. (For clarity, the SQL is omitted to better highlight the structure.)

Listing 11-1. *Defining SQL for Different Database Systems*

```
switch(SQL_LAYER)
{
   case 'postgresql':
                 $sql...
                 .
                 .
                 .
                 break;
   case 'oracle':
                 $sql...
                 .
                 .
                 .
                 break;
   case 'mysql':
   case 'mysql4':
   default:
                 $sql...
                 .
                 .
                 .
                 break;
}
```

This ability to check the SQL_LAYER is quite useful if you need to define SQL statements that vary from database to database. Table 11-2 lists the various possible SQL_LAYER values supported by phpBB 2.0.

Table 11-2. *Supported SQL_LAYER Values in phpBB 2.0*

SQL_LAYER Value	Corresponding Database
mysql	MySQL 3.*x*
mysql4	MySQL 4.*x*
postgres	PostgreSQL
mssql	Microsoft SQL Server, no ODBC
oracle	Oracle
msaccess	Microsoft Access database
mssql-odbc	Microsoft SQL Server using an ODBC connection

In most cases, modified SQL is not necessary. Most people do not have access to testing their SQL code against all the databases phpBB supports; this is why a lot of hacks only claim to work on MySQL, as they are largely untested on other systems. The hacks presented here are tested only on MySQL, which is the database you have been using for the examples in this book.

The abstraction layer provides all the functionality you need to get data to and from your database. Many methods are available to you to manipulate your data. Table 11-3 lists the functions you'll most commonly use when writing modifications, with their PHP equivalents.

Table 11-3. *Common Database Abstraction Layer Methods*

phpBB Method	PHP Equivalent	Description
`sql_query($sql)`	`mysql_query()`	Runs a query on your database using SQL statements defined in `$sql`. Returns the result of the query if it is successful, and `false` if a failure occurred.
`sql_fetchrow($query_id)`	`mysql_fetch_array()`	Returns a row of data as requested in the result of `sql_query()`, or `false` if a failure occurred. Use this function when you expect only one row of results. The data returned by `sql_fetchrow()` is an array indexed by field name. For example, to access the field `user_name` in the returned variable `foo`, use the notation `$foo['user_name']`.
`sql_fetchrowset($query_id)`	Multiple calls to `mysql_fetch_array()`	Works just like `sql_fetchrow()`, except it returns a multidimensional array containing multiple rows of data. Access the data returned by `sql_fetchrowset()` by using the notation `$foo[$i]['field_name']`, where `$i` is the number (starting with zero) of the result you wish to access. For example, to access the third result of a query on usernames, use the notation `$foo[2]['user_name']`.
`sql_freeresult($query_id)`	`mysql_free_result()`	Clears out the result of a query and enables you to start fresh. This is a good cleanup method to use, particularly after a large query, to help free memory and keep things running smoothly. Simply pass a result from `sql_query()` into the function to make it work. Returns `true` if successful, and `false` if a failure occurred.

The mechanics of these functions are not much different from those of the built-in PHP equivalents. For example, Listing 11-2 shows how to get a post title in PHP format, and Listing 11-3 shows how to use the phpBB abstraction layer to retrieve the same information.

Listing 11-2. *Retrieving a Post's Information Using Standard PHP*

```
<?php
$sql = "SELECT * FROM phpbb_posts WHERE post_id = 1234";
if($result != mysql_query($sql))     // check failure
{
   echo "Problem querying the database";
}
else
{
   $postdata = mysql_fetch_array($result);
   echo "The post's title is " . $postdata['subject'] . ".";
}
?>
```

Listing 11-3. *Retrieving a Post's Information Using the phpBB Abstraction Layer*

```
<?php
$sql = "SELECT * FROM phpbb_posts WHERE post_id = 1234";
if($result != $db->sql_query($sql))
{
   message_die("Problem querying the database.");
}
else
{
   $postdata = $db->sql_fetchrow($result);
   echo "The post's title is " . $postdata['subject'] . ".";
}
?>
```

Notice that these two versions are essentially the same. In most cases, the main differences are the names of the functions. The convenience here is that you will be able to perform the query with whatever database driver is available, not just MySQL.

You may also have noticed the use of the `message_die()` function in Listing 11-3 versus `echo` in Listing 11-2. `message_die()` is the standard, template-safe method of displaying error messages in phpBB, which is discussed next.

Using phpBB's Template System

When writing hacks for phpBB, interfacing with the template engine is about as inevitable as death and taxes. While this chapter will not specifically detail the creation of templates (a Chapter 12 topic), your modifications will need to perform some operations to properly integrate with the templating engine. Therefore, you should have some idea of how the template engine works.

When a phpBB page is started, all output is directed to an *output buffer*, which holds all output until the end of the page. At that point, the template engine dumps the buffer, and thus the page, into your web browser. In between, the programmer performs the various operations the page is to undertake, and writes all intended output to typical PHP variables. In most cases, when the main page's processing is finished, the page title variable is set, the page header file is included, and the page header processing is started. The page header then loads its specific template file, assigns its PHP output variables to special *template variables*, and parses the overall header to HTML. After returning control to the main page, the main page calls its template file, assigns its own PHP output variables to template variables, and tells the template engine to parse its template file into HTML. Finally, the page footer is included, and it is parsed into HTML. Shortly thereafter, the output buffer is dumped onto the screen, and you have a fully built phpBB forum page.

The template engine uses a few public methods to permit programmers to work with templates. Table 11-4 list the most common ones.

Table 11-4. *Common Template Engine Methods*

phpBB Method	Description
`assign_vars([array])`	Assigns an array of template variables for use in your page. These variables are, in turn, inserted in your templates and display content onscreen.
`assign_block_vars([array])`	Similar to `assign_vars()`, except this function is used in loops (such as in the Forum Index, View Topic, and View Forum pages, to name a few).
`set_filenames([array])`	Takes an array of filenames and associated identifiers that represent the files that make up the template.
`pparse($identifier)`	Parses the template file associated with the identifier that is passed in to HTML. This helps to produce the final output.

In developing your modifications, you will most likely be working with the `assign_vars()` and `assign_block_vars()` methods the most, as these create the necessary template variables for output. Listing 11-4 demonstrates how to assign template variables.

Listing 11-4. *Assigning Template Variables*

```
<?php
$one = "1";
$two = "2";
$three = "3";
.
.
.
$template->assign_vars(array('UNO' => $one,
                             'DOS' => $two,
                             'TRES' => $three)
                                        );
?>
```

As you can see, Listing 11-4 defines three PHP variables and assigns them the template variable names `UNO`, `DOS`, and `TRES`, using PHP's in-line array definition. Now, you can write a template calling these variables, as shown in the snippet of template code in Listing 11-5.

Listing 11-5. *Using Template Variables*

```
<p>I am counting!<br />
{UNO}<br />
{DOS}<br />
{TRES}<br />
```

Using the template code in Listing 11-5, the values 1, 2, and 3 will display accordingly. If you were to run Listing 11-5 through the template engine, it would look a little something like this:

```
I can count!
1
2
3
```

Working with phpBB Sessions

phpBB provides several facilities for working with sessions. A lot of these facilities are automatically called during the script execution and rarely need manipulation. However, you may need to work with these functions if your modifications use custom pages.

While browsing the phpBB code, you may have noticed the existence of an `append_sid()` function surrounding every hyperlink URI, like this:

```
$foo_uri = "<a href=\"" . append_sid($phpbb_root_path . "index.php") . "\">";
```

If you ever code a hyperlink in the phpBB source code, this is a necessary evil. The `append_sid()` function, when used around a URI, adds a session ID to the end of that URI to facilitate a continuous session for users who elect not to accept cookies in their browser. Typically, this session ID—an MD5 hash of a hashed version of the user's IP address—is passed via cookies from page to page, not requiring the passing of a session ID between URIs.

It is good practice to make sure `append_sid()` is used consistently whenever you create a new hyperlink, as forgetting to use this function can cause continuity issues with users who are logged in without cookies. If they click a link on your site that does not have the session ID built in, this can cause phpBB to generate a new session, which may result in problems with topic marking and other related functions.

Note The phpBB developers heard the call of its community, and they have dropped the `append_sid()` requirement in phpBB 3.0.

Getting User Information

phpBB offers some functions for getting user information. Two particularly useful ones are `get_userdata()` and `auth()`.

If you do a lot of work with users, you will find the `get_userdata()` function immensely helpful. You can pass either the username or user ID number of the user whose data you wish to retrieve to the function. phpBB will figure it out and return a value. If you wish, you can also pass a second, optional parameter called `force_str`. If you pass `true` in as the second parameter, it will force a username check. If the user ID or username was found, the function will return the user's data. If the user does not exist, the function returns `false`.

You are also able to retrieve permissions for a user or group by using the `auth()` function, which is the programming interface to the permissions system. This can help you write hacks that are dependent on the rights of a user. `auth()` takes four parameters:

- The level of authorization to check
- The forum ID to check authorization on
- A handle to the user's data (obtained via get_userdata())
- The forum object on which to check access control lists (if necessary)

If the permission is granted, auth() returns true; if not, it returns false. Table 11-5 lists the possible auth() values that you can check.

Table 11-5. *Available auth() Values*

Value	Explanation
AUTH_VIEW	Checks if the user is able to view the object (topic, forum, and so on)
AUTH_READ	Checks if the user is able to view and read the object in question
AUTH_POST	Checks if the user is able to make new topics in the forum in question
AUTH_REPLY	Checks if the user is able to reply to posts in the forum in question
AUTH_EDIT	Checks if the user is able to edit posts in the forum in question
AUTH_DELETE	Checks if the user can delete posts in the forum in question
AUTH_ANNOUNCE	Checks if the user is permitted to post announcements in the forum in question
AUTH_STICKY	Checks if the user is permitted to post sticky topics in the forum in question
AUTH_POLLCREATE	Checks if the user is permitted to create polls in the forum in question
AUTH_VOTE	Checks if the user is able to vote in polls in the forum in question
AUTH_ALL	Returns all auth() values in an array, permitting you to pick and choose between multiple authorization levels if needed

For example, Listing 11-6, which comes from viewtopic.php, gives an example of phpBB checking permissions on a topic.

Listing 11-6. *Using auth() to Check Topic Permissions, from viewtopic.php*

```
//
// Start auth check
//
$is_auth = array();
$is_auth = auth(AUTH_ALL, $forum_id, $userdata, $forum_topic_data);

if( !$is_auth['auth_view'] || !$is_auth['auth_read'] )
{
                if ( !$userdata['session_logged_in'] )
                {
                             $redirect = ( isset($post_id) ) ? POST_POST_URL . "=:➥
$post_id" POST_TOPIC_URL . "=$topic_id";
                             $redirect .= ( isset($start) ) ? "&start=$start" : '';
                             redirect(append_sid("login.$phpEx?redirect=➥
viewtopic.$phpEx&$redirect", true));
                }
```

```
                $message = ( !$is_auth['auth_view'] ) ? ➥
$lang['Topic_post_not_exist'] : sprintf($lang['Sorry_auth_read'], ➥
$is_auth['auth_read_type']);

                message_die(GENERAL_MESSAGE, $message);
}
//
// End auth check
//
```

In Listing 11-6, the first two lines do predefined queries to the database to see what kind of authorization level is available for the objects requested. In this case, the queries are sending the ID number of the forum you are in (as it corresponds to the database), the `$userdata` variable containing all pertinent information about the current user (logged in or anonymous), and additional information about the data in the topic (such as the topic's database ID number, so it can determine if the topic is locked, for example).

Next, the script checks to see if the current user's permissions permit the user to read or view topics in the forum. If one of these checks fails, phpBB then looks to see if a session is logged in on the computer. If this is the case, phpBB spits out an Access Denied error message and ends the script. If not, phpBB will redirect the user to the login screen, where the user has the opportunity to enter the username and password of a user with proper permissions to the forum.

Giving Feedback to Your Users When Something Goes Wrong

phpBB permits you to give feedback to your users via the `message_die()` function. It enables you to display a message to the user and then abort processing. It is useful for reporting failure conditions or other problems to the user, such as failed password validation or the user being banned. The function takes six parameters:

- Any of four constants:
  - `GENERAL_MESSAGE`, used to display a message that may convey a noncritical error or failure
  - `GENERAL_ERROR`, used for errors that occur in your pages
  - `CRITICAL_MESSAGE`, typically used when the system has basic configuration loaded but is unable to reach a session (this is used for banned users, for example)
  - `CRITICAL_ERROR`, when phpBB is encountering serious problems (database connectivity failures, for example)
- Message text, which should explain the situation that caused the error message
- A message title, which summarizes the situation (such as Critical Error, Banned User, or Warning)
- Optionally, the line an error occurred on, if necessary, for debugging purposes
- Optionally, the file the error occurred in, if necessary, for debugging purposes
- Optionally, the SQL statement that may have triggered the error, if necessary, for debugging purposes

Listing 11-7 shows an example of using `message_die()`, excerpted from `viewtopic.php`.

Listing 11-7. *Using message_die, from viewtopic.php*

```
<?php
.
.
.
if ( !($result = $db->sql_query($sql)) )
{
            message_die(GENERAL_ERROR, "Could not obtain topic information", '',➥
__LINE__, __FILE__, $sql);
}
.
.
.
?>
```

In Listing 11-7, `viewtopic.php` is trying to perform the first part of the query to the database. If this step fails, phpBB produces a General Error message, which notifies the user that topic information could not be identified, and gives the line of the file in which it failed, as well as the offending SQL statement. This permits the user to give debugging information to the developer. I recommend copious output of details in your error messages, as this can be of immense help to you as you work through creating your modifications, particularly if they are relatively large.

Releasing Your Modifications to the Community

An open-source community is only as successful as the quality of contributions it receives. While it is ultimately your call, I strongly encourage you to release any original modifications you make to the phpBB community at large. With your modifications released to the community, you help to cultivate the evolution of phpBB even further. Your work can receive criticism and enhancement. Plus, you never know when one of your features may be adopted in a future release! Here, I will give some pointers on how to release your modification to the community at large.

Using the Hack Template

The phpBB Group offers a hack template, which encourages consistency in each hack's installation instructions. You more than likely have noticed this template in the hacks you have browsed and installed. The consistency goes a long way toward opening the hack community to more and more people.

Listing 11-8 shows an example of a hack documented with the template. This hack will lead you through making two small modifications to the `lang_main.php` file for the English language pack.

Listing 11-8. *Using the phpBB Hack Template*

```
################################################################
## MOD Title:  Change Some Language Strings
## MOD Author: Jared Smith (foo@jaredwsmith.com)
## MOD Description:  Edits some language strings in lang_main.
## MOD Version: 1.0
##
## Installation Level: Easy
## Installation Time: 3 Minutes
## Files To Edit: 1
##         language/lang_english/lang_main.php
## Included Files: N/A
################################################################
## Author Notes:  This hack is basically useless, but proves
##                          a point fairly easily.
##
################################################################
## This MOD is released under the GPL License.
## Intellectual Property is retained by the MOD Author(s) listed above
################################################################
## Before Adding This MOD To Your Forum, You Should Back Up All
## Files Related To This MOD
################################################################

#
#-----[ OPEN ]------------------------------------------
#
language/lang_english/lang_main.php
#
#-----[ FIND ]------------------------------------------
#
$lang['Register'] = 'Register';

#
#-----[ REPLACE WITH ]----------------------------------
#
$lang['Register'] = 'Sign Up';

#
#-----[ FIND ]------------------------------------------
#
$lang['Too_many_registers'] = 'You have made too many registration attempts.➥
Please try again later.';

#
#-----[ AFTER, ADD ]------------------------------------------
#
$lang['Registration_required'] = 'Registration is required to use this board.';
```

```
#
#-----[ SAVE/CLOSE ALL FILES ]------------------------------------------
#
# EoM
```

While this example is a bit simplistic, it is fairly straightforward to follow, and it gives you a general idea of how the standard template operates. You fill in the appropriate header information (including your name and contact information, which is important). You then get started with the modification proper.

Use the OPEN directive to instruct the user to open the file. Always make sure you provide a good reference point for the user to find when giving instructions. Do not use line numbers, as they are subject to serious change between versions of phpBB or due to other modifications. If the same line appears in the same place throughout the file, give a few surrounding lines for the user to find in addition to that line, but don't give the user too much to look for. Finding the right balance between brevity and context is important.

At the end of the modification, make sure you instruct the user to save and close all files, as a good reminder. Be sure to have a look around the Web to see how others template their phpBB hacks, as they can also provide a good guide to how to do it.

Now that you've templated your hack instructions, it's time to start getting people to test your hack to make sure it's fit for release.

Beta Testing Hacks

When creating a hack designed for public consumption, letting the public test your hack and give feedback is a solid step toward releasing a robust modification. Many of the hacks-oriented sites on the Internet provide a forum for you to release your hacks for testing purposes and permit you to receive feedback. phpBB.com and phpBBHacks.com both provide forums for testing hacks in development.

Use these forums to your advantage, as they are there to help. You will get valuable insight on your work from seasoned phpBB hackers, who have "been there and done that." Plus, you can offer advice to others as you learn. Again, you have this tight community available to assist you, so take advantage!

Submitting Your Finished Work

When you have retraced the steps for your hack in the template, packaged them into a file, tested it, revised it, and tested it again, feel free to submit it to the various hack sites. The official phpBB site is a little more stringent with their submission requirements; use its modification validator tool at http://www.phpbb.com/mods/ to make sure your hack is up to snuff. Since you will have beta tested it extensively (I hope!), the hack should have no problem being accepted and used around the Internet.

After submitting your work and getting it accepted, make sure you make yourself available for support. This helps your public image, and also helps you further perfect your work. The better you support and keep your hack maintained, the more likely it will be adopted.

If you like phpBB hacking, feel free to create more modifications! Most hack authors have several different modifications to choose from, and they gain quite a bit of notoriety doing so (and who knows where that could lead?).

Looking Ahead to phpBB 3.0 Modifications

For the truly adventurous, this section examines some of the underlying changes in phpBB 3.0 that will affect the way modifications are written in the future.

phpBB version 3.0 will contain a number of programming changes that will make it even easier for people to modify the board. While the mechanics of installing modifications are not expected to change, creating modifications will be a bit different.

■ **Caution** This section's contents are based on a prerelease version of phpBB 3.0. The objects I briefly describe here have not been finalized yet and should be considered subject to change as of this writing.

As phpBB evolves, the aim is to make the code simpler to understand, not harder. You will find that phpBB 3.0's source code is even more thoroughly documented than phpBB 2.0. Additionally, the framework is being put in place to support PHPDoc-style documentation, which generates HTML pages that explain how methods work, why they exist, and how to access them. This will permit easily updated and accessible developer documentation, making hacking phpBB easier than ever.

Another change is that phpBB 3.0 places users and permissions into their own objects. Previously, phpBB 2.0 provided the `get_userdata()` function as a way to retrieve user information from the database. In phpBB 3.0, you will use a `user` object, similar to how you manipulate the database and template engine in the phpBB 2.0 world. This will make working with user data a lot more sensible and more encapsulated. Plus, `user` objects help as the programming front end to the advanced authentication plug-ins that phpBB 3.0 will provide.

Similarly, phpBB 3.0 will provide authentication and permissions information in an `auth` object. You will be able to retrieve all permissions information using an `auth` object, as well as access control lists for users and other items in the phpBB system. The `auth` object also provides phpBB's login services.

Finally, phpBB 3.0 will also work with sessions as objects, which will constitute a far more structured version of the phpBB 2.0 sessions system. You will have more flexibility with this system, compared to version 2.0. Sessions were a sticking point for a lot of budding programmers in phpBB 2.0, and having a `session` object (as it will be called in code) consolidates the functionality and makes it much easier to access and understand. On a related note, changes in the session system will permit you to forego the infamous `append_sid()` function, which plagues phpBB 2.0 hackers everywhere.

Summary

We're almost to the finish line for this part of the book. You've installed, configured, secured, and modified your phpBB installation. A truly great phpBB typically does not come clad in subSilver, however. Chapter 12 will take you through adding a touch of style to your community, helping to set it apart from the rest.

CHAPTER 12

Styling phpBB

Let's face it, making your board stand out from the crowd is the best way to attract people to your community. The first thing people will notice about your board is not the amount of hacks you have installed or the organization of your forums—it's how the board looks on their screen. You get only one chance to make a first impression, so why not do it with some style?

When you start to make decisions about the styling of your phpBB installation, you want to weigh your options and circumstances carefully. Is this a professional project? In that case, you'll probably want to bypass acquiring your themes from the Internet and just dive into the code for a slick, integrated look with your site. On the other hand, perhaps your phpBB board will stand alone from any other site, and just be a hobbyist project. In that case, you might want to download a theme that catches your eye, customize it a bit, and install it. It all boils down to just how much work you really want to do.

This, the final chapter in this part about phpBB, will take you through the process of styling your board. You'll learn how to obtain and install predefined styles for your phpBB installation, as well as how to create your own templates and styles if you so desire.

Acquiring Themes

Many sites in the phpBB community offer prefabricated themes free for downloading. These themes range from simplistic to elaborate, and everything in between.

If you don't have the time to do customizations or are unfamiliar with HTML and CSS coding, consider downloading and installing a theme package. While I heartily recommend going for the gusto and giving your phpBB board a full styling treatment, complete with integration with the rest of your web site, operating with a downloaded theme is still better than running with the stock subSilver look.

Finding themes for phpBB is just as easy as finding modifications for it. In fact, a lot of the same sites that offer modifications also offer themes for free download. Some of these sites may be quite familiar to you, especially after Chapter 11. Here are three sources that I recommend:

phpBB.com Styles: At this site (`http://www.phpbb.com/styles/`), you can find and get demos of more than 100 categorized styles, and it also has support forums. Additionally, you can find documentation for creating your own styles and a full listing of the default template variables phpBB offers (discussed in the next section).

phpBBHacks.com Templates: This site (`http://www.phpbbhacks.com/templates.php`) also offers a copious number of templates available for download, with support included. You can also use `phpBBHacks.com` to acquire graphics for your forums, such as rank images.

phpBBStyles.com: The greatest asset of this site (`http://www.phpbbstyles.com`) is the way it presents its demonstrations of styles. It uses a top frame with a drop-down list, which automatically switches the bottom frame to a preview of the style you've selected. You can then jump from that page to download the selected theme. `phpBBStyles.com` also offers some modifications, as well as a lively community largely devoted to customizing phpBB.

Just because you download a theme from the Internet doesn't mean you can't modify it. In fact, you're encouraged to personalize it in many cases! The next section explains how to do just that. If you don't feel that adventurous, that's okay, too. Feel free to skip ahead to the "Installing and Using Your Themes" section to learn how to install your theme into your phpBB database and then apply it to your site.

Creating and Modifying Themes

If you don't like the templates and styles available on the Internet, or you wish to integrate phpBB with the look of your web site, you'll need to create your own theme or modify an existing one. By creating your own themes, you are totally in the driver's seat as to how you want your board to look.

I'll tell you up front that working on a template for phpBB is serious business. Depending on how much you wish to customize your template, you may find that it requires as little as a couple days or as long as a month (or more!) to get the theme the way you want it. Like most projects, some parts of templating can be quite tedious, but your hard work will most certainly be worth it in the end.

■ **Caution** You'll want to make sure your HTML and Cascading Style Sheet (CSS) skills are up to snuff before you begin working with phpBB templates. phpBB 2.0 templates, by default, make liberal use of style sheets and somewhat advanced HTML to generate pages.

Putting in the extra effort to integrate phpBB with your web site will score major points with your visitors. A seamless integration of phpBB with the rest of your site gives your board an extremely professional appearance and establishes continuity, so people will remain familiar with your board's navigation as it relates to the rest of your web site. The results will show that you put a lot of time and energy into what you do, and that you take pride in it. Additionally, do you want to be just another one of the many phpBB boards out there running the default subSilver theme? Making your community stand out captures your visitors' interest, and they'll be more likely to come back for more.

In this section, I'm going to run with the assumption that you are shooting for an integrated look for your site. It's the course of action I recommend, as continuity goes a long way toward keeping visitors comfortable with your site's layout.

This section is also based on modifying subSilver. When you're working on your themes, I strongly suggest using the default subSilver style as your base. subSilver is well tested, actively developed, and well supported in the community. It contains implementations of all the pertinent template variables, and has plenty of documentation. You can do as little or as much to it as you want. Because subSilver is the default phpBB theme, having some continuity between it and your custom skin will help users adjust to your community more quickly, especially if they are familiar with other phpBB-based boards. Finally, modifying the default theme helps you avoid a sticky mess involving other template authors who may or may not wish for you to use their work as a base.

Caution If you are tempted to use FrontPage or another WYSIWYG HTML editor, resist at all costs! You run the risk of introducing a great deal of incompatible code. Additionally, these editors may try to reformat (and ultimately destroy) the `.tpl` files, which are not full HTML files, but rather snippets of HTML that phpBB's engine pieces together to build full pages. Avoiding WYSIWYG editors for special projects such as a phpBB template is always a smart move, as they just don't know how to handle these files. Stick with a text editor like EditPlus (`http://www.editplus.com`), and you won't go astray.

Working with phpBB's Template System

Before you begin creating or modifying a theme, you need to understand how phpBB uses templates. phpBB's styling system involves two components:

- The *template engine* does the work of putting together output from the phpBB script and individual template files (typically a header, body, and footer) to create the HTML pages you see while browsing your board.
- The *style system* operates from the database and, if your template is designed for it, permits you to use different color schemes and style sheets with the same template on the fly, without necessarily editing the template directly.

Note When I refer to *templates*, I'm talking about the physical files that make up a template set. When I refer to *styles*, I'm talking about the color schemes retrieved from the phpBB database that can be applied to individual templates. The combination of templates and styles are generally known in phpBB lore as a *theme*.

As you delve into the phpBB template code, you'll find the flexibility of the template system to work to your advantage, and you'll also find that it isn't much harder to work on a template than it is to create a static HTML page.

Theme Files

A full theme consists of its template files, style sheets (if needed), graphics, and theme configuration file. Table 12-1 lists the template files that come packaged with the subSilver template (`.tpl` and `.css` files), which is the basis for the customizations I'll describe in this chapter.

Note You will not be doing any work with the files in the `templates/theme/admin` directory in this chapter. You will not commonly want to modify those, although it is theoretically possible, because making changes to your administrative templates puts you at risk of rendering your Administration panel inaccessible.

Table 12-1. *subSilver Theme Content Files*

File	Description
agreement.tpl	Template file containing the HTML layout of the user agreement, shown when a user registers for the forum
bbcode.tpl	Template file containing the HTML that is substituted for BBCode in posts
confirm_body.tpl	A "yes or no" form shown when phpBB needs user input on an action before it can continue (such as when deleting a post)
error_body.tpl	Template file containing the HTML for noncritical error messages displayed by phpBB
faq_body.tpl	Template file containing the HTML for the FAQ list
groupcp_info_body.tpl	Template file containing the HTML that displays information about a user group
groupcp_pending_info.tpl	Template file containing the HTML that displays a list of pending group memberships
groupcp_user_body.tpl	Template file containing the HTML showing a user's group membership details
index_body.tpl	Template file that provides the HTML for the Forum Index page
jumpbox.tpl	A template "snippet" that contains the HTML for the forum jumpbox located in the bottom-right corner of most pages in phpBB
login_body.tpl	Template file for the login form
memberlist_body.tpl	Template file for the Memberlist page
modcp_body.tpl	Template file for the first page of the Moderator Control Panel, where topics are listed
modcp_move.tpl	Template file for the form that permits a moderator to move topics to another forum
modcp_split.tpl	Template file for the form that permits a moderator to split a topic into two separate topics
modcp_viewip.tpl	Template file that provides the view for the IP management utility
overall_footer.tpl	Template file for the main footer used on most pages in phpBB, which provides the copyright date and a link to the Administration panel (if applicable), and closes the page
overall_header.tpl	Template file for the main header used on most pages in phpBB, which provides the opening of the HTML page, style sheet information, meta tags, the Mozilla navigation bar, the site title and slogan, and other navigational aids
posting_body.tpl	Template file used to create the posting and private message sending form
posting_poll_body.tpl	Template file that provides the interface for creating a poll
posting_preview.tpl	Template file that provides the interface for previewing posts
posting_smilies.tpl	Template file that provides the expanded view of all available emoticons
posting_topic_review.tpl	Template file that generates the topic review frame on the posting page
privmsgs_body.tpl	Template file that generates the folder view for private messages

File	Description
privmsgs_popup.tpl	Template file that provides the content of the pop-up window that appears when a new private message is received
privmsgs_preview.tpl	Template file that provides preview functionality for sending private messages
privmsgs_read_body.tpl	Template file for reading a private message
profile_add_body.tpl	Template file for the form to edit user profiles
profile_avatar_gallery.tpl	Template file used in generating the avatar gallery
profile_send_email.tpl	Template file that provides the interface to sending e-mail to users (when "board e-mail" is enabled)
profile_send_pass.tpl	Template file for the page that sends new passwords
profile_view_body.tpl	Template file for the page where people view user profiles
search_body.tpl	Template file that contains the main search form
search_results_posts.tpl	Template file that is used for results displayed as posts
search_results_topics.tpl	Template file that is used for results displayed as topics
search_username.tpl	Template file used for searches for posts made under a given username
simple_footer.tpl	Footer file used in small pop-up windows and topic review
simple_header.tpl	Header file used in small pop-up windows and topic review
viewforum_body.tpl	Template file used for laying out the contents of a forum
viewonline_body.tpl	Template file used for displaying the Who's Online page
viewtopic_body.tpl	Template file used in laying out a topic page
viewtopic_poll_ballot.tpl	Template file containing a block of HTML for displaying a poll ballot
viewtopic_poll_result.tpl	Template file containing a block of HTML for displaying poll results
formIE.css	CSS file containing rules for modern browsers (Internet Explorer 4 and later; Mozilla browsers, and so on) that are ignored by other, older browsers (Netscape 4.*x*, Internet Explorer 3.0, and so on) to help maximize compatibility
subSilver.css	The master external style sheet for the subSilver theme

Table 12-2 lists the two configuration files that come packaged with subSilver and are found in generally any theme you may to create or install.

Table 12-2. *subSilver Configuration Files*

File	Description
subSilver.cfg	A PHP file that largely provides paths to images. When you create your own theme, you will rename this file to the name of your theme.
theme_info.cfg	A configuration file standard to all themes and generated from the database, and used when installing themes. It contains template and style information, a CSS filename, colors for certain objects, and fonts for certain areas.

Table 12-3 lists the language-neutral images supplied with subSilver, located in the `templates/subSilver/images` subdirectory.

Table 12-3. *subSilver Language-Neutral Images (in templates/subSilver/images)*

File	Description
`cellpic1.gif`	Background image most commonly used in subSilver category headers
`cellpic2.jpg`	Background image gradient used on the right side of table headings on the Forum Index page
`cellpic3.gif`	Background image used for subSilver table titles and headers
`cellpic.gif`	Does not appear to be used
`created_by.jpg`	Credit image for the subSilver theme (optionally, you can create one for your theme)
`folder.gif`	Image that represents topics with no new posts since the user's last visit that have not reached the hot topic threshold (by default 25 posts in a thread); used primarily in `viewforum.php` pages
`folder_announce.gif`	Image that represents topics marked as announcements that do not have any new posts since the user's last visit (there is no hot topic threshold for announcements or sticky topics)
`folder_announce_new.gif`	Image that represents topics marked as announcements that have new posts since the user's last visit
`folder_big.gif`	Image used on the Forum Index page to represent a forum with no new posts since the user's last visit
`folder_hot.gif`	Image that represents topics with no new posts since the user's last visit that have met the hot topic threshold
`folder_lock.gif`	Image that represents topics with no new posts since the user's last visit that have been locked by a moderator or administrator
`folder_lock_new.gif`	Image that represents topics containing new posts since the user's last visit that have been locked by a moderator or an administrator
`folder_locked_big.gif`	Image used on the Forum Index page to represent a forum that has been set to not permit any posting
`folder_new.gif`	Image that represents topics containing new posts since the user's last visit that have not reached the hot topic threshold
`folder_new_big.gif`	Image used on Forum Index page to represent a forum containing new posts and/or topics since the user's last visit
`folder_new_hot.gif`	Image that represents topics containing new posts since the user's last visit that have reached the hot topic threshold
`folder_sticky.gif`	Image that represents topics marked as sticky that contain no new posts since the user's last visit. (there is no hot topic threshold for sticky topics)
`folder_sticky_new.gif`	Image that represents topics marked as sticky that contain new posts since the user's last visit
`icon_delete.gif`	Image that appears on individual posts in `viewtopic.php` where the logged-in user has permission to delete a post (for example, a moderator could click this icon to delete an individual post)
`icon_latest_reply.gif`	Image that appears on the Forum Index and `viewforum.php` pages, in conjunction with a link to the latest reply in a thread
`icon_mini_faq.gif`	Image that appears on each forum page, next to the FAQ link in the default subSilver header

File	Description
icon_mini_groups.gif	Image that appears on each forum page, next to the usergroups link in the default subSilver header
icon_mini_login.gif	Image that appears on each forum page, next to the login/logout link in the default subSilver header
icon_mini_members.gif	Image that appears on each forum page, next to the memberlist link in the default subSilver header
icon_mini_message.gif	Image that appears on each forum page, next to the private message link in the default subSilver header
icon_mini_profile.gif	Image that appears on each forum page, next to the profile link in the default subSilver header
icon_mini_register.gif	Image that appears on each forum page, next to the register link in the default subSilver header (users who are logged in will not see this image or link)
icon_mini_search.gif	Image that appears on each forum page, next to the search link in the default subSilver header
icon_minipost.gif	Image that appears in individual posts next to the "Posted" time in a viewtopic.php page to indicate that this post is not new since the user's last visit
icon_minipost_new.gif	Image that appears in individual posts next to the "Posted" time in a viewtopic.php page to indicate that this post is new since the user's last visit
icon_newest_reply.gif	Image that appears next to titles of topics containing new posts since the user's last visit in a viewforum.php page; associated with a hyperlink that takes you to the first new post in a thread
index.htm	Page that displays the credit image, created_by.jpg, used to block outside readers from seeing the contents of your template directory
logo_phpBB.gif	phpBB logo image that appears on each phpBB page
logo_phpBB_med.gif	phpBB logo image that appears in the left pane of the Administration panel
msg_inbox.gif	Icon representing the Private Message Inbox in privmsgs.php
msg_outbox.gif	Icon representing the Private Message Outbox in privmsgs.php
msg_savebox.gif	Icon representing the Private Message Savebox in privmsgs.php
msg_sentbox.gif	Icon representing the Private Message Sentbox in privmsgs.php
spacer.gif	One-by-one transparent image used for spacing items
topic_delete.gif	Icon associated with link to delete a topic; displays for authorized users in viewtopic.php
topic_lock.gif	Icon associated with link to lock a topic; displays for authorized users in viewtopic.php
topic_move.gif	Icon associated with link to move a topic to a new forum; displays for authorized users in viewtopic.php
topic_split.gif	Icon associated with link to split a topic into two topics; displays for authorized users in viewtopic.php
topic_unlock.gif	Icon associated with link to unlock a topic; displays for authorized users in viewtopic.php
vote_lcap.gif	Image used to round out the left side of a poll percentage bar
vote_rcap.gif	Image used to round out the right side of a poll percentage bar
voting_bar.gif	Image used to fill in the middle of a poll percentage bar
whosonline.gif	Icon for the Who's Online feature, displayed on the Forum Index page

Finally, Table 12-4 lists the images that are language-specific. If you have installed additional language packs, you will want to ensure these images are translated as well. This table shows the files in the `lang_english` directory. Put images you port to other translations in a `lang_language` directory, where *language* is the language to which you are translating.

Table 12-4. *subSilver Language-Sensitive Image Files (in templates/subSilver/images/lang_english)*

File	Description
icon_aim.gif	Icon displayed in individual posts that represents a link that starts an AOL Instant Messenger conversation with the user who made the post, if the user volunteers that information in her profile
icon_edit.gif	Icon displayed in individual posts that is linked to the post editing functionality, if the logged-in user is authorized to edit the post
icon_email.gif	Icon displayed in individual posts that, depending on e-mail settings you choose in the Administration panel, is linked to a mailto: address for the user's registration e-mail, or links to a page from which you can send an e-mail
icon_icq_add.gif	Icon displayed in individual posts that permits you to add a user to their ICQ buddy list, if he volunteers his ICQ number
icon_ip.gif	Icon that links to the IP manager, permitting authorized users to get the IP address of the user making a post, if the user has permissions to view IP addresses of posts
icon_msnm.gif	Icon that links to the user's profile that contains MSN Messenger contact information, if this information is given
icon_pm.gif	Icon that permits users to send a private message to the user who made the post
icon_profile.gif	Icon that links to the profile of the user making a post
icon_quote.gif	Icon that links to the quote reply page for posts in open threads
icon_search.gif	Icon used on public user profile pages that links to a search query on the user's posts
icon_www.gif	If the user specifies a web site, icon that appears on her posts and profile
icon_yim.gif	If the user specifies a Yahoo! Messenger account name, the icon that appears on his posts and profile; clicking its associated link starts a Yahoo! Messenger chat session
msg_newpost.gif	Image associated with a link to send a new private message
post.gif	Image appearing on `viewforum.php` and `viewtopic.php` pages that starts a new post, if the forum or topic is not closed
reply.gif	Image appearing on `viewtopic.php` pages that links users to the reply page, if they are permitted to post and the topic is not closed
reply-locked.gif	Image appearing on `viewtopic.php` or `viewforum.php` pages that notifies the user that the topic is closed to further responses

Template Variables

The template engine's syntax is not incredibly complex. Studying the layout of the subSilver template will help you get used to the syntax quickly.

By far, the most common element you will deal with while writing your template is the insertion of *template variables* generated by the phpBB script for output in your page. More than 100 separate template variables are available. Here, I'll cover the most commonly used template variables. For a comprehensive list of every template variable supplied with phpBB (excluding template variables that may be created by code modifications) with brief descriptions, see `http://www.phpbb.com/styles/listvars.php`. This list is kept up-to-date when changes warrant, so you can be confident that it's reliable information.

Template variables generally come in the form `{VAR}`, where `VAR` is the name of the template variable as defined in the phpBB script file. If you are using a template variable defined inside a block (commonly seen on pages such as `viewforum.php` and `viewtopic.php`), the template variable will be formatted slightly differently: you'll see a line like `{myblock.VAR}`, where *myblock* is the name of the block in which the variable `VAR` is defined. (You'll learn more about blocks in the next section.)

Template variables are always denoted by the two curly braces surrounding the identifier. Therefore, you should use care when using curly braces in your layout. In fact, I recommend avoiding the usage of curly braces outside of template variables. If they are unavoidable, make sure you have one space separating the first curly brace from the word inside, and one space after the word in between. This way, phpBB will not attempt to execute the variable. If you use a template variable that isn't defined, phpBB will simply replace that variable with a blank space character.

When using template variables, you can stick them anywhere in the template file—in the `<head>` section of your HTML document, within a hyperlink, or anywhere else you wish a piece of text from phpBB to be output to the screen. For example, subSilver contains the following code snippet, which generates a title for the resulting HTML document from two template variables:

```
<title>{SITENAME} :: {PAGE_TITLE}</title>
```

The two template variables in this example are `{SITENAME}`, which will display the name of your site as you configured in the Administration panel when you first set up your board, and `{PAGE_TITLE}`, which is, predictably, the title of the page as set in the page's PHP code. This line displays in the title bar of the user's browser. So, for a site named MyForums on the Memberlist page, you'll see the following output in your HTML source after the previous code is parsed:

```
<title>MyForums :: Memberlist</title>
```

Notice the clean replacement of text.

Template variables are often small snippets of text, but they can also contain sizable chunks of HTML in some rare instances. I reiterate that you can use a template variable anywhere in a template file, as long as it will be defined for that file. Refer to Chapter 11 for details on creating template variables for use within your pages.

Be warned: not every template variable exists in all pages of phpBB. There are two types of template variables:

- *Global variables* are defined in `page_header.php` and `page_tail.php`, and are available to every page in your script.
- *Per-page variables* are defined in each individual phpBB page such as `index.php` or `viewforum.php`.

Template variables defined in files other than `page_header.php` and `page_tail.php` are not global to the entire script, and therefore take effect only for individual pages. Often, though, you'll find phpBB will generate template variables that have the same name on multiple pages. Don't confuse those with the global variables. When in doubt, consult phpBB.com's listing of template variables (http://www.phpbb.com/styles/listvars.php). In that listing, you can find which variable you want, and it will let you know the location appropriately.

Some, but not all, template variables have prefixes corresponding to the type of information they represent. Table 12-5 explains the prefixes you'll encounter.

Table 12-5. *Common Template Variable Prefixes*

Prefix	Description
U_	Variables beginning with U_ are URLs, which are typically used inside hyperlinks in HTML.
T_	Variables beginning with T_ are theme attributes, which correspond to the available customization options in the Styles Administration panel.
S_	Variables beginning with S_ are system variables. You'll rarely encounter these.
L_	Variables beginning with L_ represent strings that are taken from the active language file.

If you end up creating your own template variables, you'll want to make sure that the prefixes you use for your links and language strings are consistent with the prefixes shown in Table 12-5. This helps you know what a template variable represents without having to dig inside the phpBB code to find its definition.

Blocks

phpBB's template engine also supports blocks of code. Blocks are defined as HTML comments and are delineated with a BEGIN to start the block and an END to finish the block. One purpose of blocks is to define repeating data, such as the tables on many pages—index.php, viewforum.php, and viewtopic.php, to name a few. Here is an example of a repeating block:

```
<!-- BEGIN myblock -->
<br />{myblock.COUNTER}
<!-- END myblock -->
```

A repeating block is generally identified by the presence of block-specific template variables (the template variables prepended with *blockname.* before each variable name). These variables are local in scope to the block only, and they cannot be used outside the boundaries of the block.

The other reason to use blocks is to display when a certain condition is met, such as whether or not the user is logged in. Here is an example of a conditional block:

```
<!-- BEGIN switch_user_logged_in -->
<p>Welcome back to our community!</p>
<!-- END switch_user_logged_in -->
```

You'll find that the names of conditional blocks generally start with the prefix switch_ and the condition for executing the command. phpBB's template engine does not necessarily make decisions. Instead, it relies on flags set by the phpBB script to determine whether a block of code should run.

Defining blocks provokes a little nitpicking from the template engine. Block definitions must occur on their own line, and the code inside the HTML comment identifiers must be set off from each identifier by a space. Here is a great example of what *not* to do when defining blocks:

```
.
.
     </td>
   </tr>
</table><!-- BEGIN switch_user_logged_in-->
        You're logged in!
        <!--END switch_user_logged_in -->
```

Notice the problems with this example. Line 1 has the block delineation on the same line as other code; phpBB does not like this. Line 3 shows the END keyword is directly next to the opening HTML comment identifier, where it should be set off with one space. These kinds of errors are easy to make, but you need to be careful to avoid them, because they can cause problems, even to the point of malfunction.

Limitations on Using Templates

phpBB 2.0 templates have some limitations that you should be aware of before you start modifying or creating templates. Some of these limitations are due to the nature of its syntax; others are due to performance and reliability concerns.

Because the phpBB templating system uses HTML comments to denote blocks of HTML code, it is generally a good idea to place a C++-style comment (//) before the text of your HTML comment, after the opening marking (<!--). While using this comment style is optional, doing this rules out any chance of an errant comment causing problems. If you forget to do this, there's no real reason for concern, as long as you don't start the comment with BEGIN or END.

Additionally, phpBB 2.0 does not support inserting PHP code directly into a template. (phpBB 3.0 will support including PHP code on a limited basis.) To use PHP code in your phpBB pages, such as code that may rotate banners, you'll need to embed that code in one of the PHP script files (most likely page_header.php) and create a template variable to reflect the output of that portion of the script. After creating your custom variable, as described in Chapter 11, you can embed it in your template.

Creating Your Theme

Now that you've been introduced to the basics of using phpBB's template engine, it's time to dive into subSilver and start changing a few things around. First, you'll make a copy of the template, and then you'll start making your modifications.

Installing a Copy of subSilver

Start by installing a second copy of subSilver, under a different name. This permits you to watch your changes in real time as they unfold, while keeping the original subSilver template intact in case something goes wrong.

Make sure you rename the folder to something else (I'll call mine aSilver). Also be sure that you rename the subSilver.cfg file inside the directory to *foldername*.cfg, where *foldername* is the name you gave the subSilver copy's directory. For example, I'll have an aSilver directory, with an aSilver.cfg file. Do *not* rename subSilver.css to anything else! Go ahead and make aSilver the default style so you can see your changes as they happen. (See the "Installing and Using Themes" section for more details on installing themes to your phpBB board and setting the default style.)

Now it's time to consider some strategies for managing style customizations.

Considering Styling Customization Approaches

You can take a couple different approaches to handling styling customizations in phpBB. You can provide a static style sheet in a separate .css file. This approach is generally good if you are going for site integration. It does not permit you to make changes to colors and fonts using the Styles Administration panel, however.

If you are looking to possibly release your template, you'll want to keep the subSilver method of adding styles to the board intact. subSilver places the contents of its style sheet in the overall_header.tpl file, complete with references to appropriate template variables for the theme, which permit you to use the Administration panel to change some colors and fonts.

Go ahead and crack open overall_header.tpl in your copy of subSilver. The first thing you will likely notice is the large amount of CSS representing all the styles that control subSilver's layout. This CSS is controlled via the Administration panel. If you remove this CSS, you will lose that control. For site integration projects, removing the embedded CSS is perfectly fine, unless you wish to support multiple color themes. Otherwise, you'll want to customize the embedded CSS accordingly. Having a static style sheet generally reduces bandwidth usage. While smaller sites may not have problems with high-bandwidth usage, busier sites will likely prefer the static style sheet, which can be cached in the browser, so it is not downloaded with each page visit.

If you are doing a site integration project, you should take another step and create your own style sheet and use the <link> HTML tag to link it to your page in overall_header.tpl. This way, you can style everything from scratch. If you wish, you can stick with the built-in subSilver identifiers, or you can take a harder, but more powerful, route and rip out subSilver's CSS definitions and replace them with your own. This is the route I almost always take. While it is a lot more work to replace the subSilver CSS definitions with your own, the control you get is unparalleled.

Again, regardless of which path you take, *do not delete the subSilver.css file!* phpBB permits you to theme the Administration panel along with the rest of the site. This is fine, but removing the CSS file without altering any of the definitions can have incredibly strange consequences. If you decide to use a separate style sheet, make sure you don't disturb any of the theme settings in the Administration panel, as subSilver is perfectly fine for your behind-the-scenes work. Removing these values will cause the Administration panel to go haywire and become completely illegible (think black screens and one-pixel fonts, seriously!). If you are sticking with the subSilver definitions and theme-controlled colors, feel free to change those. You will notice that the Administration panel undergoes some changes as you do this; this is perfectly normal, as you're altering the settings for your theme in its entirety.

Caution Under no circumstances should you delete the subSilver.css file!

After you decide a strategy to use to attack the CSS, the next step is to dive into the HTML of the header and footer template files to do the bulk of the integration portion of the project.

Using Headers and Footers to Integrate with Your Site

Site integration projects generally require you to work the most on the header and footer files. You need both because `overall_header.tpl` opens most of your pages, and `overall_footer.tpl` closes them. When customizing your board, think of `overall_header.tpl` extending to where the body of the board begins.

For example, I like to employ a sidebar in my designs. If you have a sidebar on the left side of your site, this is the file where you would want that sidebar to show up. However, if the sidebar is on the right side of your site, you will want to edit `overall_footer.tpl` and insert it there instead, as that picks up where the body of the page left off.

The key to templating is that you are just editing one fragmented HTML page. Understanding the templating of the header and footer is critical, especially if you use tables for layout. If you forget to finish your tables in the footer, you may run into serious problems with your page breaking.

When editing the header, it's important to preserve the links to the specific pages of your forums (editing profiles, registration, and so on). Going through and doing wholesale deletions can be costly; for example, you may realize that you can no longer check your private messages easily.

Make sure you use the subSilver template as a guide, and check constantly to make sure you've kept the links. It's a smart idea not to replace the titles of the links with images or textual characters that are not localized to the language, unless you are planning on serving an English-only site. By replacing the `{L_. . .}` variables, you're removing the references to the localizations.

Optional items include the site title and slogan. I usually end up using an image to replace these. A smart idea would be to use the site title and slogan as the alternate text for any title image you may create.

Use the footer to round out the design, whether tabular or via style sheets. Feel free to add your site's standard footer, not disturbing the link to phpBB too much. After rounding out your design in the footer, take a look at your site.

You may be wondering about the `simple_header.tpl` and `simple_footer.tpl` files (briefly explained in Table 12-1). These are the simple header and footer used in the pop-up windows. If you've decided on full CSS replacement, you'll want to remove the subSilver CSS embedded in `simple_header.tpl` and replace it with what you are using. You might edit `simple_footer.tpl` only if you wish to modify the style of the copyright, as that is all that is displayed on that screen.

■ **Caution** *Do not delete the link to phpBB in the footer!* By doing that, not only are you denying credit where credit is due (I doubt you wrote the source code behind phpBB), but you are also putting yourself in jeopardy of not being able to receive support for your forums if you run into a problem. You're getting phpBB for free, and the least you can do is acknowledge the work the phpBB Group has put into it.

You now likely have a subSilver board wrapped in your site's colors and layout. That's good progress, and you've completed about half of the job. Now is a good time to visit your pages and make sure there are no major problems in terms of layout or other areas. I recommend using multiple browsers to do this, as some browsers will catch errors that others may ignore. If you find some problems with the layout, double-check that all the code you've inserted is correct and works well with the existing pages. You may find that you have additional tweaking to do in your header and footer templates. Generally, it's always better to get these major layout errors out of the way sooner rather than later.

After you've verified that your layout and the existing phpBB pages are in harmony, it's time to take on the other half of the job: tweaking the tables, images, and other miscellaneous items scattered throughout to fit your web site's design and color scheme.

Customizing Pages

You should concentrate on modifying the pages that are the most frequently visited, and thus templated: `index_body.tpl`, `viewforum_body.tpl`, `viewtopic_body.tpl`, and `posting_body.tpl`. How you make those pages look can largely dictate how the rest of the forum looks. Those four templates are the ones I recommend that you spend the most time on initially. (If the error box is the first thing your users see rather than the Forum Index page, chances are you have bigger problems to resolve at the moment.)

Try to stick to the subSilver coding where you can, but do feel free to edit the tables accordingly. When you find a style of tables that you like, you can then begin implementing that on other pages throughout the site.

Changing Graphics

After you have your code straightened out, you can change into graphic designer mode. You'll want to alter, in some way, the graphics listed earlier in Tables 12-3 and 12-4, to help your site's integration. If your site uses a dark-blue background in some of the tables and also the subSilver-colored graphics, you'll notice a serious clash. If you're integrating phpBB into your main web site, redoing the graphics is a must for the professional appearance you want.

You can search some of the phpBB styles sites for graphics that match your new custom template, or you can modify the existing graphics. If you are feeling really ambitious, you can try your hand at creating your own graphics. This can be a fun and rewarding way to put your stamp on your forums. Plus, there's no feeling quite like when you can honestly say, "Yes, I did all the graphics."

■ **Caution** If you decide to edit some of the language-sensitive graphics (listed in Table 12-4), make sure you can provide translations for each of the language packs you have installed. Failing to do so will likely result in inconsistency and a language pack that's effectively broken. Plus, you run the risk of alienating visitors who use those language packs.

When you change the graphics of your template, it is often easier to stick with the subSilver naming convention versus going with your own. This prevents you from having to do heavy editing on your template configuration file (the `*template*.cfg` file, where *`template`* corresponds to the name of the folder your template resides in) to reflect these changes.

For the Really Ambitious: Styling BBCode

One of the unique features of phpBB 2.0 is that the BBCode functionality is now fully customizable via the template mechanism. Previous BBCode implementations hard-coded the formatting into the software, so this is a welcome addition.

You can edit the blocks of BBCode by opening `bbcode.tpl` in your theme's directory. This step is entirely optional, but if done right, it can be a major enhancement to your board.

One of my favorite modifications for the BBCode template is to edit the `[URL]` BBCode to display the location of the hyperlink in an HTML `title` attribute inside the hyperlink. This way, when a user rolls over the link, the true destination of the link shows up in a tool tip. This can help foil pranksters and help cut down on people clicking links and then regretting that click. Here's how to do this:

1. Open `bbcode.tpl` and navigate to around line 58, which will begin with `<!--BEGIN url -->`.
2. Near the end of the hyperlink code, by `class="postlink"`, insert the following small piece of code before the right-angle bracket:

   ```
   title="{URL}"
   ```

3. Save `bbcode.tpl` and upload it to your server in the `templates/`*`yourtemplate`* directory.
4. Visit your board and look for a hyperlink embedded in one of the posts. With any luck, hovering over the hyperlink will display the target URL of the link in a tool tip. (All browsers since Internet Explorer 4.0, Netscape 6.0, and Mozilla will display these tool tips.)

Testing Your Templates

Now that you have customized your template, you will want to test it thoroughly to ensure there are no major problems. I recommend testing your template at different screen resolutions and in different browsers to ensure accessibility and platform parity between browsers. If at lower resolutions you have horizontal scroll bars on your page, for example, you will want to revisit some of your code to see if these can be prevented.

Remember that you want your community to be as clean-looking as possible in as many browsers as possible, to make it inviting to your users. With the recent rise in usage of alternative browsers, you can't afford to target your site to one particular platform, because that could make your community uninviting to those who choose not to use that platform.

Tip A Mozilla Firefox extension provides a very handy toolbar for debugging and testing your web sites, including your phpBB templates. Visit `https://addons.mozilla.org/extensions/moreinfo.php?id=60` to download and install the Web Developer Toolbar for Mozilla Firefox. It works with all current versions of Firefox and can be quite a lifesaver!

Getting Help with Templates

As you've seen, the phpBB template engine gives you a great deal of flexibility in styling just about every aspect of your community. For people just getting started with theming phpBB, having all these options can be overwhelming. You might run into problems or have questions on how to further expand the use of the template engine on your site. As always, the phpBB community is ready and willing to help you out when you run into problems.

Try the resources at sites such as `phpBBStyles.com`, which specializes in creating templates for phpBB. Often, sites like these contain extensive tutorials, tips, and tricks for templating your board. Naturally, they also have forums for discussion and help on creating themes. Sites like these often have showcases for getting feedback on templates, which is especially useful if you are considering releasing the template to the public. `phpBB.com` and `phpBBHacks.com` also provide extensive support for template authors, with similar information available on both sites. The support is out there—don't be hesitant to use it!

Installing and Using Themes

Whether you downloaded your theme from the Internet or created it from scratch, the next step is to get it installed to the phpBB database so the script actually knows how to use it. As with a lot of features in phpBB, the process is straightforward, making for a smooth transition.

Adding Templates and Styles to phpBB

Adding new themes to your board is as simple as extracting the theme to your hard drive, uploading the resulting folder, and selecting it from a list in the Administration panel. Here's how to do exactly that.

Preparing to Install the Theme

In most cases, you'll receive your templates in the form of a compressed file of some kind (usually a `.zip` file). You'll want to extract the contents of the compressed file to its own temporary folder, so you can upload it to the server. Make sure you enable the option to keep the paths of the folders intact (which your archive extraction program will usually have enabled by default). This will help you immensely when uploading to the server.

After you've extracted the files, you should see a folder with the name of the theme. Open that folder to see what's inside. Ideally, you will see a bunch of files with a `tpl` extension. Try to find a file that bears the name of the folder with a `cfg` extension. For example, if the folder's name is `SnazzyTheme`, you will want to locate `SnazzyTheme.cfg`, with the case and spelling (except for the file extension) identical to the folder name.

Next, open `theme_info.cfg` in any text editor and make sure you set the template name variable (the first one) to the name of the folder. This step ensures that phpBB will pick up the theme in its installer utility.

Prepackaged themes generally have these bases covered, but it never hurts to double-check, as it can save you some troubleshooting time later. If you find problems with a theme, make sure you notify the theme's author so he can fix the theme and redistribute it.

Uploading and Installing the Theme

After checking those few items, go ahead and upload the folder containing the corresponding template files to *<yourphpbbroot>*`/templates`. After uploading, log in to your Administration panel. In the navigation pane, click the *Add* link underneath Styles Admin. With any luck, you'll see one or more styles (depending on how many styles the template author bundled with the template file) available to be installed. In Figure 12-1, I'm given the option to install Athena and Athena Orange, two themes based on the Athena template, available from `phpBBStyles.com`.

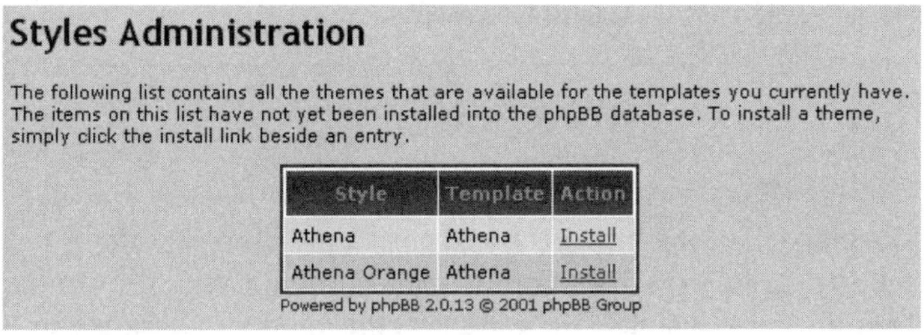

Figure 12-1. *The theme installation page*

■ **Note** If the style does not show up as an available theme, make sure the folder name and the `.cfg` file match each other properly. Case and spacing matter. Additionally, recheck the `theme_info.cfg` file and ensure the theme name is set to the name of the folder as well, and the path is pointing to the proper folder name.

To install a theme, click the *Install* link next to your desired theme's listing in the table. Installing a theme adds the information in its configuration file to the database, making it available to you and your users.

Using Your Themes

Congratulations! You've successfully installed a theme or two. Now that you've done that, you can make them available to your users, and perhaps even set one of these new themes as the default for your site.

Setting Your Preferred Theme

You can switch to the theme you wish to use on the board by editing your profile, scrolling down to the Preferences heading, and selecting the option in the Board Style drop-down list that corresponds with the name of the theme you wish to use. Figure 12-2 shows an example with two themes available.

Figure 12-2. *Setting the board style in the Preferences section of your profile*

By setting this theme for your profile, you are *not* changing settings for the rest of the board. This is purely a per-user setting. As a result, this feature works only for registered users. All guest users will see the default theme that you set up, as described in the next section.

Note If you see PHP error messages concerning `template.php` after switching to a new theme, the theme likely contains errors. Contact the author of the theme. If you wrote the theme, go through your header and footer template files to ensure there are no problems with syntax. If the error occurs on one specific page, edit the template file that page calls to make sure there are no mistakes causing the template engine to fail.

Setting a Default Theme

You can make a theme you've installed the default theme for all guests and users who don't otherwise have a preference set. To do this, go to the Administration panel and click the *Configuration* link under General Admin. Find Default Style, and select the option from the menu that corresponds to your desired theme. The screen should resemble Figure 12-3.

Figure 12-3. *Setting the default theme, board-wide*

Note that setting this option does not force the theme on all your users. They are still free to change to whichever themes you offer. Forcing the use of your theme is described next.

Note If users report they can't switch their theme, check to make sure you haven't locked down theme switching (see Figure 12-4). If that isn't the case, make sure your other themes are installed properly. Also remember that users must be logged in to switch themes.

Forcing Your Default Theme

If you wish to force your users to use your chosen theme, regardless of their theme preferences, you can set the Override user style option to Yes, as shown in Figure 12-4. This disables user theme switching on the board.

Default Style
Athena
Override user style
Replaces users style with the default
Yes No

Figure 12-4. *Setting the default theme to override user preferences, effectively shutting down user theme switching*

You may want to force a default theme if you wish to maintain only one template for your site. Also, you may wish to enable this option if your phpBB is well integrated into your site, or you have hacks that you've installed for your default template and not in any others. This way, you can ensure an optimum viewing experience for your community.

Touring phpBB 3.0 Templating Improvements

phpBB 3.0 introduces a few improvements to templating. A smarter and more flexible templating engine provides even more customization possibilities, with far fewer dives into the PHP scripting code required—a winning situation in terms of reliability and efficiency in development. The downside to these improvements is that existing phpBB 2.0 styles are considered totally incompatible with phpBB 3.0, and they will need to be reworked to accommodate the new version's changes.

■ **Caution** The information in this section at the time of this writing is based on prerelease software and is subject to change at any time.

For template designers, a lot has changed, and for the better. Here's a list of the new things you'll be able to accomplish with phpBB 3.0:

Use conditional structures: Potentially the biggest reason to switch to phpBB 3.0, from a designer's perspective, is the ability to use conditional structures, commonly known as *if statements*, directly in the templating engine. This will give designers unprecedented flexibility in customizing their templates without needing to touch a single line of raw PHP. This also benefits people working inside the core phpBB code, as virtually all of the formatting has been offloaded onto the templating engine. Previously, there was some work being done by the PHP script, but this is no longer the case. This is the landmark feature of the phpBB 3.0 template system, without a doubt.

Embed PHP: The phpBB Group has added the option to embed PHP code inside a template, which is welcome news to people who run ad-rotation code and other scripts inside their phpBB installation. Previously, these users had to edit the codebase and add a template variable to output the results of their scripts, and then edit their templates and add the template variable. While the phpBB Group still recommends that you use the template variables, as they will be fastest, the `INCLUDEPHP` directive will permit you to bring in PHP files from the outside. Or, you can declare a `PHP` block and execute a few lines directly inside the block. Either way, the flexibility is very nice.

Add common elements easily: Thanks to the new `INCLUDE` directive, templates are now able to include other template files directly. Previously, a great number of code hacks were required.

Some operational changes also impact designers. One is that phpBB 3.0 templates now use a standard `.html` extension instead of the `.tpl` extension. This helps people avoid having to set up their editors to do syntax highlighting on the `.tpl` files. The new extension also helps to set off phpBB 3.0 template files from phpBB 2.0 template files, which is a nice way to avoid any confusion.

Additionally, the Administration panel in version 3.0 is no longer skinnable, ending the days of all-black Administration panels due to mistakes creating themes. This is a very smart move on the phpBB developers' part!

Summary

In these six chapters, you've come quite a long way. You have installed and configured a stock phpBB installation, learned the ins and outs of phpBB's end-user features for your benefit as a user and as an administrator, learned best practices for keeping your phpBB stable and secure, modified your phpBB and installed additional features, and tied it all together with a style that puts a nice finishing touch on your hard work.

Now it's time to relax a bit and enjoy running your community. Get the word out on the various phpBB showcase forums around the Internet. Register your site in Google and the Open Directory (`http://dmoz.org`) so it can be found via search engines, and don't forget to watch for phpBB updates.

The next part of this book is about WordPress, a versatile blogging application that runs on the same platform as phpBB does.

PART 3

WordPress

CHAPTER 13

Introducing WordPress

This chapter provides an introduction to blogging and weblog software in general, and to the specific software you'll be using in this part of the book: WordPress. I'll begin with a little of the history behind blogging and blogging software. Next, I'll describe the types of blogging software available. Then I will present some of the common terminology used in connection with blogging and blogging software. Finally, I'll give you an overview of WordPress's main features.

A Brief History of Blogging

In the beginning was the Web. I know you know what the Web is, but you may not know that the first web site, created by Tim Berners-Lee, the inventor of the Web, is now recognized by some as the very first weblog.

Note Tim Berners-Lee's original server and content was located at `http://info.cern.ch/`, but is no longer available. The content has been archived at the World Wide Web Consortium site (`http://www.w3.org/History.html`). The page that could be described as the first weblog is at `http://www.w3.org/History/19921103-hypertext/hypertext/WWW/News/9201.html`.

Tim originally developed the Web as a more convenient way for people to publish their academic papers. More important, the Web provided a way to hyperlink between papers on *different* machines. People soon created gateways from the Web to the data already published using older technology like FTP, Gopher, and Wide Area Information Servers (WAIS). As more and more of this information came online, it became impossible to keep track of what there was and where it was.

Weblogs: Guides to the Web

On that original web server, Tim maintained a "What's New?" newsletter that included news about developments in the technology of the Web. He also wrote about, and linked to, new sites as they came online. Naturally, Tim's page included a brief description of these new places on the Web, and often Tim added his opinion of them. This style of web page—periodic, subject-specific, linking to interesting sites with commentary—is the very essence of the first weblogs.

After Tim's page, came the National Center for Supercomputing Applications (NCSA) "What's New" page (now archived at `http://archive.ncsa.uiuc.edu/SDG/Software/Mosaic/Docs/whats-new.html`), which ran from 1993 to 1996. Significantly, this page dated its entries, with the newest entries at the top of the page. Each month, NCSA started a new page and created a link to the previous pages, forming the archives.

As the Web grew, personal pages began to appear. They were created by people studying and working in universities, as these were often the only people who had access to the Web. Their sites usually contained links to papers and research materials pertinent to a their academic projects. Soon, as a natural progression, because people want to talk about themselves and share their interests, many of these pages became personalized. They contained items such as a bit of personal history or someone's opinion of the latest Star Trek movie and links to other Trek fans' pages. They also sometimes included links to the older pages, the archives.

With the growth and commercialization of the Web, personal pages soon became available to the general public. Companies began providing a little Web space to individuals, and pretty soon every Tom, Dick, and Harriet had their own homepage. These were filled with content such as pictures of their pets, detailed essays about themselves and their hobbies, or pages in praise of their favorite pop group. And always, there were links—links to other people who shared their passion, links to new and interesting pages on the Web, links to other people's pages of links, and so on.

People were publishing themselves. People were finding their voices and inviting the world to hear. These pages became the precursor to the other side of blogging: journals or personal diaries.

The Beginnings of Publishing Software

In those pioneering days, it wasn't easy to make your own web page. One of the earliest barriers to publishing web pages was the technology. You needed to learn the language of the Web, HTML, and the mechanics of publishing your pages, FTP. You could create web pages by hand, but soon there were many tools to help you with this endeavor.

As HTML and the Web matured, the techniques available to use on web pages grew at an incredible pace. Pages became more and more sophisticated. There were new ways to present your pages: JavaScript menus, frames, dynamic HTML, and more. The publishing tools evolved to keep up with these techniques. Each new page you created could take advantage of the newest tools and techniques. But what about your old pages?

Maintenance became a big problem. Should you go back and manually re-create your old pages in the newest style to match your site? Or should you leave them alone, even though they often looked out of place and disjointed? Many sites were abandoned after their initial creation because of this dilemma; the cost of maintenance was too high.

Commercial sites had already realized this problem and were solving it with big, complicated, and expensive content management systems (CMS). These systems were often created in-house or were prohibitively expensive for Joe Public. They were certainly not suitable for someone who only wanted to publish pictures of the new kittens or had decided that every page now needed to have that great animated butterfly GIF she just found.

True Weblogs

Weblogs as we now know them emerged in the late 1990s (the term was coined by Jorn Barger in 1997) in what is now the established weblog format: dated entries with the newest first, at the top of the page. The entries were links to interesting web pages, the latest news stories with commentary and opinions, or essays and personal stories. And they always had links to other people's weblogs. Early pioneers were Jesse James Garrett, Cameron Barrett, Peter Merholz, and Brigitte Eaton, among many others. But these sites were still essentially maintained by hand with page-creation applications or homegrown software.

In 1999, services like Pitas.com (`http://www.pitas.com/`), Blogger (`http://blogger.com/`), and Groksoup (no longer online) were launched, suddenly making it incredibly easy (and free) to create, publish, and maintain your own blog. Desktop software like Radio UserLand (`http://radio.userland.com/`) allowed you to publish your blog easily from the desktop. You could install server-based software like Greymatter (`http://www.noahgrey.com/greysoft/`) and Movable Type (`http://sixapart.com/`) on your own server or shared hosting service to publish your blog.

The final ingredient to the explosion of blogs and blogging is comments. Some blogging software allows you to have comments. Other blogging tools can make use of third-party services like HaloScan (`http://www.haloscan.com/`) or YACCS (`http://rateyourmusic.com/yaccs/`) for commenting. So much more than guest books, which were common and allowed you to get feedback on your site, comments allow you to get feedback on your individual stories. Was the review any good? What do other people think of the news item you just blogged about?

With blog publishing software and user comments, the Web became truly interactive. A simple post on your opinion of the latest blockbuster movie can trigger a conversation that continues for days. This involves not just each reader interacting with you, but also your readers interacting with each other. You can easily build up quite a community of like-minded people, or even unlike-minded people if you enjoy a good debate.

Weblogs as journals can also be used as a stream-of-consciousness publishing tool, where a blogger writes and comments on anything and everything. A lot of bloggers publish opinionated commentary on a wide range of topics. Other people blog as a means of keeping family and friends updated about their lives.

Today, it is easy to have your voice heard all the way across the world, to publish your thoughts and opinions, and to have anyone and everyone join your conversation. You simply pick any of several online services or choose one of many software packages, and you can be talking to the world in hours, if not minutes.

Weblog Software

Today's weblog publishing software can be broadly categorized in two ways: the type of software and the method of publishing. Here, I'll describe these categories, as well as the disadvantages and advantages of each publishing method.

Types of Blogging Software

Three main types of blogging software are available:

Desktop-based: These applications allow you to develop your content on your desktop, possibly offline, and publish to either a hosted service or your own server. Examples include Radio UserLand (`http://radio.userland.com/`), ecto (`http://ecto.kung-foo.tv/`), and iBlog (`http://www.lifli.com/Products/iBlog/main.htm`).

Hosted services: These services are web-based applications that allow you to edit content online, and then publish at the click of a button. Some, like Blogger (http://blogger.com/), allow you to publish to a companion web site or to FTP your files to your own server. Other examples are TypePad (http://www.sixapart.com/typepad/) and LiveJournal (http://www.livejournal.com/).

Self-hosted software: These are web-based applications installed on your own or a shared server, with which you edit online. Examples include WordPress, Movable Type, and Textpattern (http://textpattern.com/).

Publishing Methods

Weblog software uses either a static or dynamic publishing method. Each method has advantages and disadvantages.

Static Publishing

Software that uses the static publishing method stores your content in some kind of database, but then generates static HTML pages in a publishing step. Your main blog page, individual story pages, archive pages, and category pages are generated as flat HTML files and stored on the server, or even on a different server. These files are then served by the web server with no further requirement from the blog software. Blogger, Movable Type, and Radio UserLand, among others, are of this type.

The major advantage of publishing your blog to static HTML files is speed. All web servers serve static pages the fastest. If you have an extremely busy site, with an underpowered or an overloaded server, the difference will be quite apparent. With adequately powered servers, the speed increase is less significant. Another advantage of static publishing is that you don't need the content database on your web server. In practice, it may be located on the same machine, but that is not required.

On the downside, with pages published statically, adding a new story requires several of your pages to be regenerated; sometimes, it may require regenerating all of them. If you want to change the template used on your site—to add a new header or even just to correct a spelling mistake—every single page will need to be regenerated. This can be extremely slow. For a large site, even on a powerful server, this process can slow the server almost to a halt.

This also means that, if you want visitors to be able to comment on your stories, they will need to wait for the page to be regenerated with their new comments. This regeneration is not usually done immediately, as it may overload the server on a busy site. It could even be abused as a form of denial-of-service attack. Alternatively, you could use another service, often located on a different server (several companies provide this service), to handle your site's comments.

Lastly, generating hundreds or even thousands of flat files takes up a lot of space. The fixed parts of your pages—the header, sidebar, footer, and so on—are duplicated in every HMTL file. On a large site with thousands of files, this can consume a considerable amount of space.

Dynamic Publishing

Software that uses the dynamic publishing method has the content database serve the pages dynamically, generating them as they are requested by a browser. WordPress, Textpattern, and LiveJournal are examples of this type of software.

With dynamically driven sites, the content—your blog postings—are also stored in a database, but are used dynamically with each request to generate the HTML pages on the fly. Templates for your site are merged with the content to produce the pages sent to the visitor's browser. These generated pages are not stored on the server.

With this kind of system, any changes you make to your content or your template are immediately visible. When a visitor comments on a post you have made, the comments will appear immediately.

If the software provides a search function, it does so on the blog data itself and presents the page dynamically. If a new page is added, it is immediately available to be returned in the search results.

Archives are delivered on demand, with no need to have separate versions for weekly, monthly, by category, and so on. The whole setup takes up less space than pages published statically. You have a template file (or a series of them), but only one version. The content is dynamically inserted into the templates.

On the downside, this method is slower to deliver a given page. In practice, you will see it as slower only compared to static pages on the biggest of sites, or on particularly underpowered or overloaded servers. Also, blogs of this type require the database to be available to the running code. If that database becomes unavailable, there is no content to deliver, and the site stops working.

In conclusion, your choice of blogging software depends on what you want to do with it. A site that isn't modified too often and perhaps doesn't have too many comments, but does have a lot of visitors, would be best served by a blogging system that supports static publishing. A blog with dynamic content and a lively community contributing comments would be best served by a dynamic technology like WordPress. The many advantages to using WordPress for a community blog will become apparent as you progress through this part of the book.

Blogging-Related Terminology

In this section, I will briefly explain some of the terms associated with blogs and blogging. Some of them are specific to blogging; others are more generic.

Blog Comments: Comments are a feature available with some blogging software. They allow visitors to your blog to comment on your stories. Comments are usually visible after a user clicks a link, often one indicating how many comments there are or inviting the reader to leave a comment. Once the link is clicked, the comments are presented, usually in chronological order with the earliest comment at the top. This is the reverse of the order in which blog stories themselves are presented.

■ **Note** Comments can be abused by visitors who have messages to spout or grudges. Also, some people will attempt to spam your blog, usually with the intention of getting more exposure to links to their sites. I'll cover comment spam in detail in Chapters 14 and 15.

Blogrolls: Blogrolls are a convenient way to manage lists of links to other blogs and sites. These lists can often be displayed on your blog in a sidebar on the page. The links are usually to the blogs that you read regularly. Links to other blogs are often reciprocal: "You link to me, and I'll link to you." Getting your blog onto many people's blogrolls is good promotion for your blog.

Blogrolls can be served from external sites. Some blogroll services will integrate with most blogging software, whether or not it supports its own blogrolls. More sophisticated services and some blogging software allow you to maintain multiple list of links. Thus, you could have separate categories of links, for example.

Ping Notification: With ping notification, your blogging software reports to a central service each time you create a new post. The central service then displays a list of recently updated blogs. This allows people to check in with the central service and find blogs that have been recently updated.

Most blogging software supports pinging one or more central services. Many services are available, some offering quite sophisticated features. Some services maintain blogrolls, automatically marked to indicate which ones have been updated. The most famous recently updated ping notification list is probably the one at Weblogs.com (`http://weblogs.com/`). This originally listed only Radio UserLand blogs (it is owned by the same company), but now lists any blogs. One service, Ping-O-Matic (`http://pingomatic.com/`), when pinged by your blog software will ping dozens more services for you. Thus, you don't need to wait for your software to support all the services out there.

Blog Crawlers: Blog crawler services function in a similar fashion to ping notification services, but visit blogs that don't have the ability to ping the central service. They watch for changes to these blogs and update the recently updated listing as appropriate. These services cater to systems that don't ping and to homegrown or hand-edited blogs.

Metadata Services: Several new services receive pings from recently updated blogs and also actively crawl through those and other blogs, and then collate the data they've gathered in interesting ways. For example, they might list the most popular subjects about which people are currently blogging, the most talked about book, or the most popular blogs (based on which blogs everyone links to).

TrackBack: TrackBack was designed to provide a method of notification between web sites. If, for example, Anne has written a post on her blog that is a response to or comments on a post in Bob's blog, she may want to send a TrackBack to notify Bob. This is a form of remote comments. It is a way for Anne to say to Bob, "This is something you may be interested in." To do that, her blogging software sends a TrackBack ping (a small message sent from one web server to another) to Bob's software.

Pingback: Pingbacks are similar to TrackBacks, but were designed to solve some of the problems that people saw with TrackBacks. The most notable difference between the two is that Pingbacks do not send any content. Pingbacks are generally displayed with a blog's postings comments.

Both TrackBacks and Pingbacks allow a form of cross-blog communication, so the various readers of blogs that track and ping back each other can participate in a multisite conversation.

Syndication Feeds: Most blogging software supports a way of reading your blog contents other than with a browser. It uses the concept of *feeds*, which are XML-based presentations of your blog contents. They are consumed by *feed readers* or *aggregators*—special software that will regularly retrieve your blog's feed and compare it to the feed read last time. In this way, the software notices changes to your blog and highlights them to you.

Feed readers allow you to aggregate the feeds from all the blogs and news sites you regularly read and be informed in a central place of the ones that have changed. A simple click takes you to the site in question with its new content. Another advantage is that it takes a lot less bandwidth for a feed reader to download your XML feed than to grab your web page.

Some blogging software or their plug-ins allow you to incorporate the feeds into your own blog. This way, you could have the latest headlines in your own page automatically, instead of just a link to the latest industry news site.

Common formats for XML feeds are Really Simple Syndication (RSS), Atom, and Resource Description Framework (RDF). Most feed readers can understand them all. Feed readers are available for many platforms. Some are desktop applications like FeedDemon for Windows (`http://www.bradsoft.com/feeddemon/`), NetNewsWire for Mac OS X (`http://ranchero.com/netnewswire/`), and RSSOwl for UNIX and other platforms (`http://www.rssowl.org/`). Some are add-ons and plug-ins that add feed reader functions to other packages; for example, RSS Popper for Microsoft Outlook (`http://rsspopper.blogspot.com/2004/10/home.html`), Safari RSS for Safari on the Mac (`http://www.apple.com/macosx/features/safari/`), and Wizz RSS for Firefox on all platforms (`http://www.wizzcomputers.com/WizzRss.php`). There are also online feed aggregators, like Bloglines (`http://www.bloglines.com/`) and Syndic8 (`http://www.syndic8.com/`).

Podcasting: Podcasting is where you distribute audio or multimedia content (usually MP3 files) via your RSS feed. You can find tools that will let your readers subscribe to the RSS feed and automatically download the audio files to their MP3 players.

Permalinks: A permalink (contraction of the phrase *permanent link*) is a type of URL designed to refer to a specific information item (often a news story or weblog item) and to remain unchanged permanently, or at least for a lengthy period of time.

Permanence in links is desirable when content items are likely to be linked to from, or cited by, a source outside the originating organization. Permalinks are also desirable within organizations when the complexity of web sites grows to more than a modest number of pages. In particular, the growth of extensive commercial web sites built on database-backed CMS necessitated deliberate policies with regard to URL design and link permanence.

Moblogging: Moblogging is blogging photographs taken with a mobile phone camera. Often, these can be posted directly from the phone.

Why WordPress?

And so we come to WordPress, the blogging software this part of the book will be discussing. Why WordPress? WordPress is a state-of-the-art, semantic, personal publishing platform with a focus on aesthetics, web standards, and usability. That's quite a mouthful, but what does it all mean?

WordPress is *semantic* because it generates XHTML markup with *meaning*. It produces web pages that work without any style applied, work correctly with screen readers used by blind people, and validate by conforming to published web standards. This makes for lightweight pages that download faster onto a user's browser and that often appear on the screen quickly.

WordPress is designed from the start to look good. It comes with two themes, both of which are elegant and simple. It is always important that your readers have a pleasant experience when visiting your blog. Equally important, the WordPress administration interface is good looking, too. That's where you, as blog owner, will spend most of your time, and you will appreciate having a pleasant work environment.

If you have a little knowledge and a suitable hosting account, WordPress setup is quite literally a five-minute install. You will be up and running, and making your first post in a matter of minutes.

WordPress Features

WordPress includes the usual support for blogging, with comments, TrackBacks, and Pingbacks. Here is a summary of its main features:

- It supports multiple authors and registered visitors with the privilege to comment. You can configure different administration rights for each author.
- It supports a draft mode for your posts, so you can work on them until you are ready to publish.
- It supports protected posts, where a reader must supply a password to read the post.
- It supports private posts, visible only to you.
- It supports automatic Pingbacks, where all the links in an article can be pinged when the article is published.
- As well as categories for your posts, it also supports nested categories and multiple categories per post.
- It supports XML feeds in all the current formats. WordPress supports RSS, RDF, and Atom feeds. It also supports feeds by subject and by author, as well as feeds on comments.
- It has an integrated link manager, which supports categories, images, descriptions, notes, and XFN (XHTML Friends Network, `http://gmpg.org/xfn/`), as well as a built-in blogroll manager.
- It supports RSS enclosures for podcasting. WordPress supports podcasting in a simple, intuitive way.
- It generates standards-compliant XHTML and CSS, and uses nice-looking, search engine-friendly permalinks.
- WordPress supports typographic filters for proper formatting and styling of text. You don't need to learn HTML to enrich your postings.

HISTORY OF WORDPRESS

WordPress grew as the official successor to Michel Valdrighi's b2/cafelog blogging software. Michel started the b2 project around July 2001. The project's development progressed rapidly, and it built an extensive following. Cafelog.com, the home of b2, supported incredibly busy forums and built a great community. Many people helped report and fix bugs in b2. A few produced add-ons, hacks, and customizations to the core software.

In late 2002, Michel found he could not continue to develop b2 because of personal commitments. For a few months, b2 floundered after release 0.6. Some user frustration followed, and pretty much simultaneously, two forks of the project were proposed. b2evolution was started by François Planque, and WordPress was started by Matt Mullenweg and Mike Little (one of your humble authors). On May 23, 2003, Michel Valdrighi announced, "Matt Mullenweg and Mike Little are leading the new WordPress branch of b2. That is going to become the new official branch once they get a release out."

b2++, started by Donncha o'Caoimh, was another variant that began later. This project eventually became WordPress MU, or WordPress Multi User.

Michel later returned to online life and is now a contributor to WordPress.

- WordPress has a drop-in-and-go theme system. Upload one of the hundreds of beautiful themes people have developed and published, and start using it at the click of a mouse button. You can switch from one theme to another with a couple more mouse clicks.
- The administration interface is intuitive and simple to use. However, if you do get lost, there are help links on every page.
- WordPress has an extensible plug-in system, allowing developers to add to or change the software's functionality. Hundreds of plug-ins have already been developed, and many more are being created all the time. There are plug-ins for threaded comments, for adding a gallery to your post, to generate Amazon links, and much more.

WordPress Releases

The first non-beta release of WordPress was 0.7 in May 2003. This version was essentially an update to b2 version 0.6, but it already included semantically correct, validating default templates; a built-in link manager; a new administration interface; and other features.

Release 0.71 followed in June and added a 300% speed increase (honest!), draft and private posts, comment status, Outline Processor Markup Language (OPML) import of blogrolls, and many more improvements.

The WordPress developer team grew, and more releases followed over the next few months. January 2004 saw the leap to version 1.0, which heralded a massive increase in functionality: search engine-friendly permalinks, multiple categories, the much-touted quick installation, comment moderation, yet more improvements to the administration interface, and so on. By this time, the number of users was quite considerable. The forums were well established and quite busy.

May 2004 saw the next major release of WordPress. Version 1.2 was released with subcategories, automatic thumbnail creation for image uploads, the new plug-in architecture, localization, post preview, more importers, and the usual slew of bug fixes, speed ups, and tweaks. The administration interface was yet again improved.

Finally, version 1.5, the current version, was released in February 2005. This version introduced the powerful and flexible templates and theme system, with the default now the beautiful Kubrik theme by Michael Heilemann. This release also saw the introduction of even stronger anti-spam measures. Perhaps one of the most significant parts of this release is that you can now use WordPress to manage static pages on your site. The administration system got yet another overhaul after user feedback, this time introducing the Dashboard, a page displaying news feeds from WordPress's development blog and a summary of your recent posts, comments, and more.

Summary

This chapter provided an overview of blogging and blogging software, and then introduced WordPress, the software covered in this part of the book.

The next chapter will take you through a step-by-step installation of WordPress. I'll cover basic requirements and configuration, and explain some of the more advanced options. I'll introduce the project blog you'll build in this part of the book. Oh yes, I'll also walk you through making your first blog post!

CHAPTER 14

Installing and Configuring WordPress

In this chapter, I'll step you through a complete installation of WordPress. I'll list the minimum requirements and a couple of useful extras. After you have WordPress installed, I'll take you on a tour of WordPress options for configuring your blog. Finally, you'll make your first post to your blog.

Installing WordPress

Installing WordPress on your server is as simple as running its install script. However, first you'll need to make sure that your system meets WordPress requirements, obtain WordPress and some helper programs, and prepare your server.

Meeting the Requirements

Your system needs to meet some basic requirements to install and run a WordPress blog. The first is hosting. You'll need an account on a server somewhere. This may be shared hosting or your own server, if you have one. WordPress does work on Windows, especially with the same web server and database setup. But because it's the most common and, frankly, the simplest to set up, I'm going to concentrate on GNU/Linux-based hosting.

Your hosting server needs to have support for PHP version 4.1 or later and MySQL database server version 3.23.23 or later. I recommend Apache as a web server (version 1.3.23 or later), but any web server capable of supporting PHP should work. If you have support for `mod_rewrite` in Apache, you'll be able to use some especially useful features of WordPress. (See `http://httpd.apache.org/docs/1.3/mod/mod_rewrite.html` for more information about `mod_rewrite`.) You'll also need to be able to upload files via FTP and change permissions on your files and folders.

I don't have a recommendation for disk space or bandwidth. A 1,000-post blog with 2,000 comments and no pictures will fit comfortably in 10MB with room to spare. Bandwidth is too variable to call. Blog popularity ranges from 1 visit a week to 10,000 per day and higher.

A huge number of companies offer hosting. Shop around and get the best deal to suit your needs. Always go for more than you think you'll need, but stay within your budget. You never know—your blog may become very popular. The last thing you want is to be cut off for exceeding your bandwidth, just as you are building your community.

Obtaining WordPress

Next, you need to get a copy of WordPress. That's pretty easy. Mouse along to `http://wordpress.org/download` and download the latest `.zip` file. The latest release is also available as a gzipped tarball. If your desktop is a UNIX or Linux machine, this may be more appropriate for you. The files inside are all the same.

Obtaining Helper Programs

You will need an FTP program, a program to expand zipped files, and a text editor of some kind.

FTP is the term for the transfer of files from a client, in this case your PC, to a server—your hosting server. Actually the acronym stands for File Transfer Protocol, but it is commonly used as a verb, too. FTP software is readily available. In fact, it is likely that your current operating system already includes an FTP program. Unfortunately, it is probably a command-line-driven one. While command-line FTP is straightforward to use, it is much easier to work with a graphical application if you can. If your desktop is Windows, I recommend Filezilla (`http://filezilla.sourceforge.net/`) or SmartFTP (`http://www.smartftp.com`) for FTP. Plenty of other FTP programs are available..

You'll need a program to unarchive the WordPress installation files you download, because they are compressed in an archive. If you download the `.zip` file, you will need a program capable of expanding, or unzipping, the archive. WinZip (`http://www.winzip.com/`) is probably the most popular on Windows, but has a shareware license requiring you to purchase it after a trial period. I recommend 7zip (`http://www.7-zip.org/`), which is completely free.

For a text editor, I recommend nothing more elaborate than Notepad for now. Later, you might want to evaluate some of the specialized PHP and CSS editors.

Preparing Your Server

You'll need to take a few steps before you install WordPress on your server. These include gathering some information, creating a database, transferring the files, and setting file permissions. So, let's get started.

Gathering Information

Before doing anything else, you will need to gather some information and make a fairly simple decision.

From your hosting service you will need the following information:

- Your login and password for FTP (you should have been given those when you signed up for your hosting)
- The name of your database, if one has already been created for you, and your database login details

The decision you need to make is simply where to put your blog. By that, I mean that you must decide if your blog will be the only thing on your web site or whether you will want to also have other pages, such as Drupal or phpBB sections. It comes down to the URL of your blog. Will it be `http://example.com/` or will it be `http://example.com/blog`? I almost always recommend the latter (of course, you may wish to call it `journal`, `diary`, `news`, or something other than `blog`), because it leaves your options open for future changes.

Creating a Database

Now you need a database. Some hosting services allow you to have only one database. Often, this is already created for you when you sign in to your administration page. Others allow you to create your own database. If you have the choice of multiple databases with your own name, I suggest you create one called `WordPress`, if you can, but it doesn't matter *what* its name is, as long as you *know* that name. If you are creating a brand-new database, don't forget to give your *database user* account permission to access it.

These steps are usually carried out through some kind of control panel—software running on your server to allow you to administer your hosting space—provided by your hosting service. Hosting services provide many different control panels or administration pages. Although you rarely have a choice of which one you get, they should all be capable of allowing you to administer your database in various ways. Two of the most common control applications are Plesk (`http://www.sw-soft.com/en/products/plesk/`) and cPanel (`http://www.cpanel.net/`). Figures 14-1, 14-2, and Figure 14-3 illustrate adding a new database and user with the Plesk control panel.

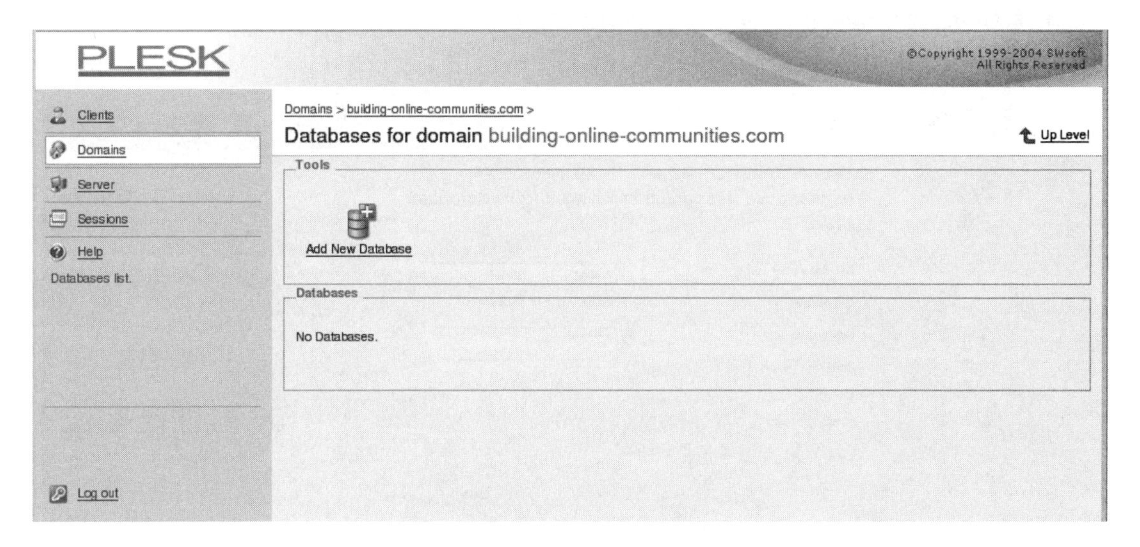

Figure 14-1. *Adding a new database icon in the Plesk control panel*

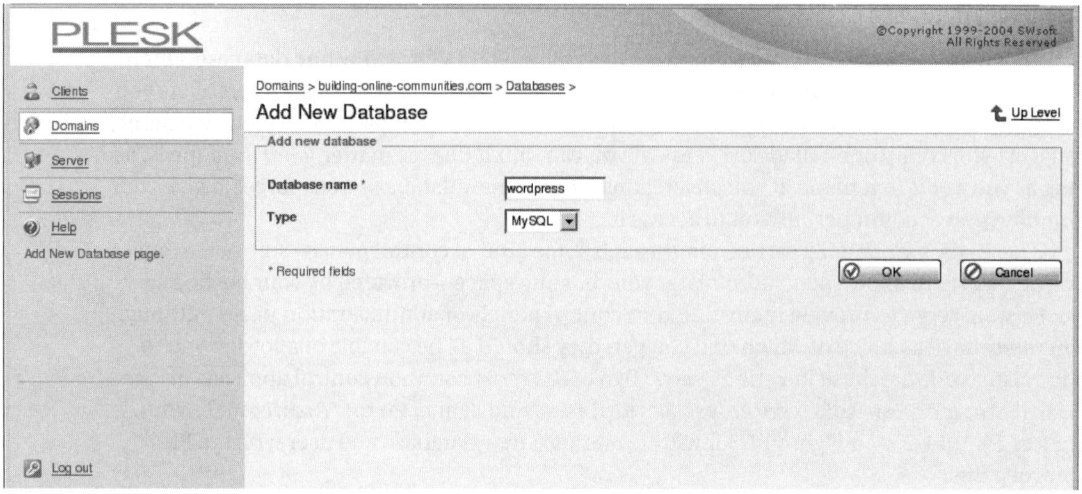

Figure 14-2. *Filling in the database name and selecting the type*

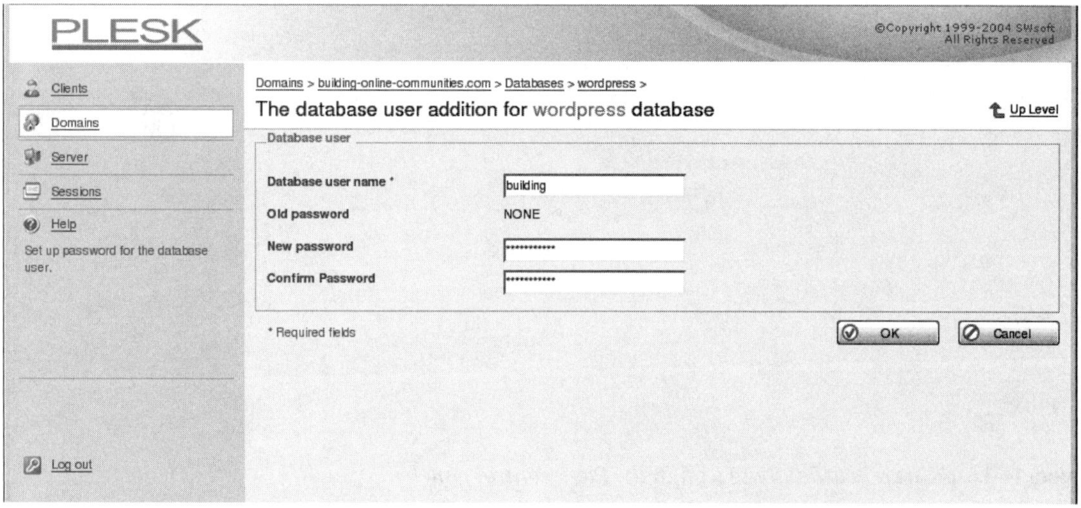

Figure 14-3. *Adding a user to the database*

If you have the option, create a database user specifically for the use of WordPress. That is, if you can, create a user and assign that user privileges to access the WordPress database you just created.

In the end, it doesn't actually matter whether you use an existing database or set up a new one. WordPress will quite happily share a database with any other application, including another installation of WordPress.

Extracting the Files

Before you transfer the WordPress files to your server, you'll need to expand the archive. The file you downloaded from the WordPress site is an archive, or a compressed collection of files. Then you will need to use FTP to transfer the WordPress files you downloaded earlier to your server. These tasks require the FTP program and expansion software I mentioned earlier as requirements.

Extract the WordPress files from the archive into a convenient folder, such as `C:\wpwork` or `C:\My Documents\wpwork`. You'll need this folder to work through the examples in this book. You should have approximately 160 files in various folders within `C:\wpwork`. You'll need to copy one of them and edit it before you upload the files.

Editing the Configuration File

Find the `wp-config-sample.php` file and make a copy of it called `wp-config.php`, saving it in the same directory. Load that copy into an editor program—a text editor, not a word processor. As I noted earlier, Notepad will work fine for now, if you don't have a specialized text editor. In this file, you need to change the dummy database connection settings to the real values. Find the part of the file that looks like Listing 14-1.

Listing 14-1. *MySQL Settings in wp-config.php*

```
// ** MySQL settings ** //
define('DB_NAME', 'wordpress');     // The name of the database
define('DB_USER', 'username');     // Your MySQL username
define('DB_PASSWORD', 'password'); // ...and password
define('DB_HOST', 'localhost');     // 99% chance you won't need➥
to change this value
```

Fill in the details for the database name, database user, and password from the information you gathered earlier. As the comment says, it is very unlikely you will need to change the host setting. I have found only one hosting service that required the host setting to be changed. If you do need to change that setting, your hosting provider will have supplied that information along with your other details. You should end up with something like the settings shown in Listing 14-2.

Listing 14-2. *MySQL Settings Populated in wp-config.php*

```
// ** MySQL settings ** //
define('DB_NAME', 'wp_example');     // The name of the database
define('DB_USER', 'wp_db_user');     // Your MySQL username
define('DB_PASSWORD', 'secret'); // ...and password
define('DB_HOST', 'localhost');     // 99% chance you won't need➥
to change this value
```

If your installation of WordPress is going to share a database with another WordPress installation—that is, if you plan to keep the data tables for multiple WordPress installations in the same database—you'll also need to change the prefix setting just below the database connection setting, which looks like this:

```
$table_prefix  = 'wp_';   // example: 'wp_' or 'b2' or 'mylogin_'
```

to this:

```
$table_prefix  = 'example_';   // example: 'wp_' or 'b2' or 'mylogin_'
```

Now save the changes made in wp-config.php file.

Note You need to change the prefix setting in wp-config.php only if your WordPress installation is going to be sharing a database with another installation. If some other software is using the database, you don't need to change this setting, as WordPress and the other program should not have conflicting table names.

Next, create a brand-new file called dothtaccess.txt in the same folder as wp-config.php. It should be an empty file, but if you're using Notepad, it won't let you create an empty file! Simply press Enter a couple of times to get around this restriction. You can create the file in Windows Explorer if you wish. Simply right-click, choose New ➤ Text Document, and name it dothtaccess.txt.

Transferring the Files

You are now ready to transfer the files onto your server. Using your FTP software, upload all the WordPress files to you web server, storing them in the folder you decided on earlier, as shown in Figure 14-4. This folder will be the one your hosting company told you is the place to put your web pages or a subfolder. You may need to create the folder first, if it does not already exist.

Next, on the server, rename the dothtaccess.txt file you uploaded to .htaccess—a leading period (or full stop), followed by the name htaccess with no extension. This is a special file that will be used later to give some special instructions to the Apache web server software.

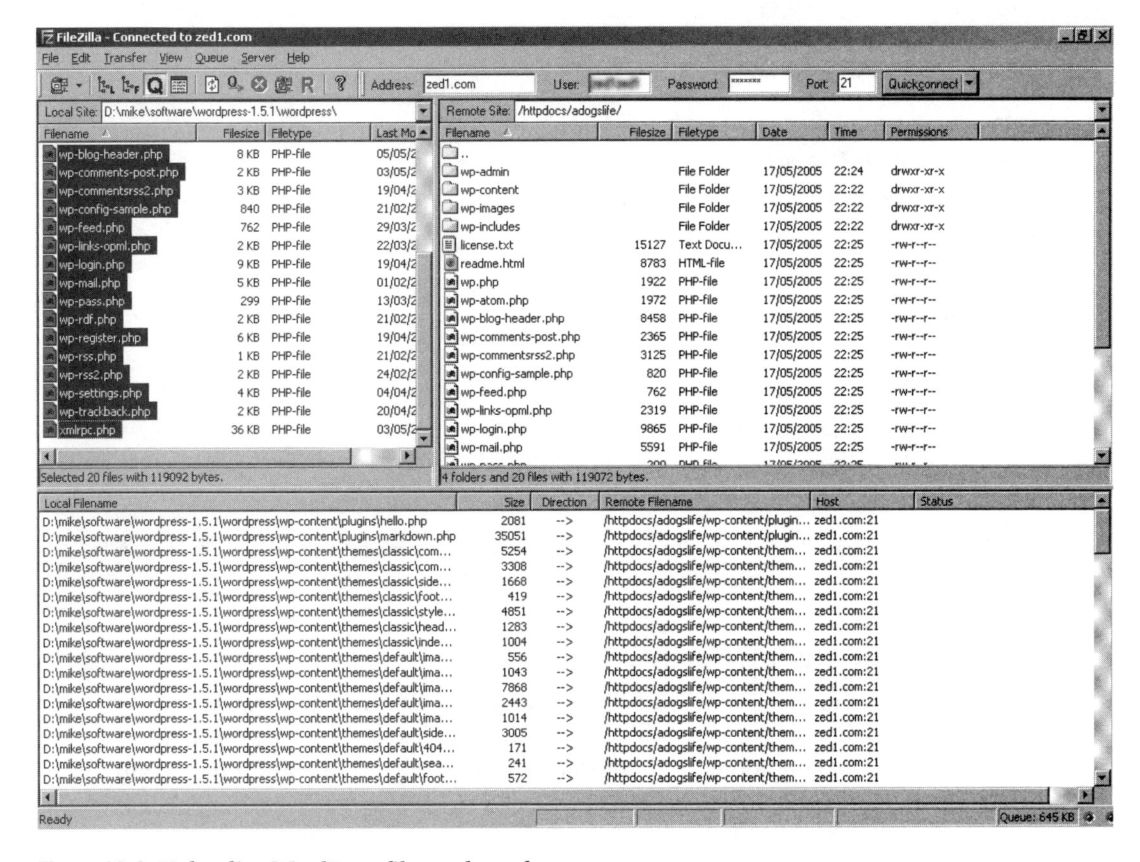

Figure 14-4. *Uploading WordPress files to the web server*

Setting File Permissions

Before you put away the FTP program, you need to check your permissions on certain files and directories. By default, files you upload to your server and directories you create on it are owned by you, or rather your account on the server. This is correct and as you might expect. However, the web server, Apache, usually runs as a different user, often `apache`, `httpd`, or `nobody`. This means that software running under Apache—in this case, WordPress—doesn't normally have permissions to modify or delete files, nor to create new ones. To fix this, you need to change the permissions of some of the WordPress files. You will most likely need to give full access to those files. You will also need to give write access to a couple of folders, so that WordPress can create new files.

Depending on your FTP software, you will either need to set the file permissions to a numeric value such as 666 or 777, or check the R (read), W (write), or X (eXecute) permissions for U (user or owner), G (group), and O (other). The numeric value 666 represents read and write permissions for user, group, and other. The 777 value represents read, write, and execute permissions for user, group, and other.

Table 14-1 shows which files and folders need their permissions set and what type of permissions should be applied. Note that a folder name with an asterisk following it signifies that all the files in that folder need their permissions adjusted.

Table 14-1. *File and Folder Permissions*

File/Folder	Mode
.htaccess	666
wp-content/themes/classic/*	666
wp-content/themes/default/*	666
wp-content/themes/default/images*	666
wp-content	777
wp-content/plugins	777
wp-content/themes	777
wp-content/themes/default	777
wp-content/themes/default/images	777
wp-content/themes/classic	777

These changes will allow you to edit the themes that come with WordPress and to install new themes and plug-ins later. Next, you'll finish installing WordPress.

Running the Install Script

You are now ready to install WordPress on your server. You have created a database, given permissions to your database user, uploaded the WordPress files, created a couple of new files, and set permissions appropriately. Although reading through these instructions, it seems like a lot of work, if you are already familiar with these tasks, this whole process really does take only five minutes! Have heart, you are nearly there.

Go to your web browser and type the following address into the address bar (assuming you installed in the `blog` directory):

```
http://yourdomain/blog/wp-admin/install.php
```

This will load the WordPress install script, as shown in Figure 14-5. Click First Step, and you will be prompted for the title of your weblog and an e-mail address.

As shown in Figure 14-6, type in a suitable name—Wendy's Weblog, Tuxedo News, or whatever you want to call it. Don't worry—you can change the title later. Make sure the e-mail address you enter is valid. Your administrator (admin) password will be sent to it. Click the Continue to Second Step button to move to the next step.

Next, you will see a progress screen as the install script creates your database tables for you. In practice, it is so fast that all you will see is the "Finished!" message. You will see instructions for logging in to your new blog. Make a careful note of the password. For security reasons, it is a randomly generated one.

■ **Tip** When I'm setting up a new WordPress blog, I select the password with my mouse and copy it to the clipboard (by pressing Ctrl+C). Then I can simply paste it into the login form.

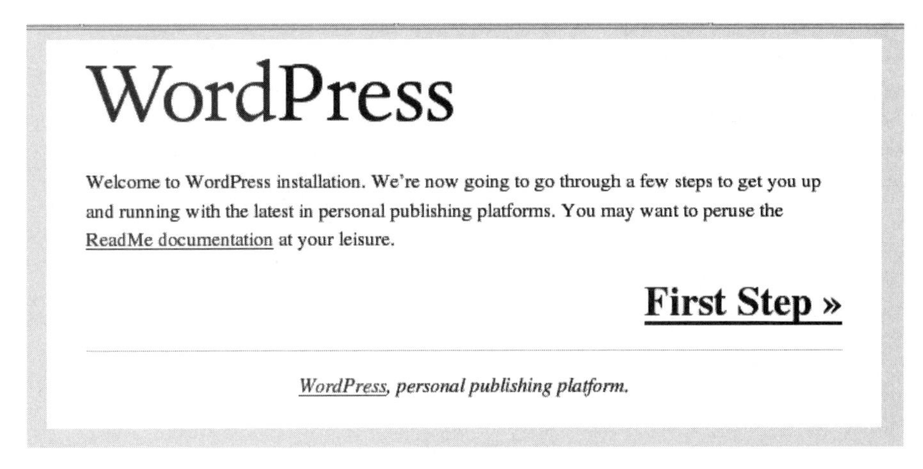

Figure 14-5. *The first screen of the WordPress install script*

Figure 14-6. *Install step 1*

Logging In

Now, click the link to `wp-login.php`. You will see the standard WordPress login screen. Enter the username of admin and the password from the previous page, as shown in Figure 14-7. Then click the Login button.

WordPress

Username:

admin

Password:

******

Login »

« Back to blog   Lost your password?

Figure 14-7. *The WordPress login screen*

Introducing the Dashboard

You should now see the WordPress Dashboard, as shown in Figure 14-8. This is the page that greets you every time you log in to your blog.

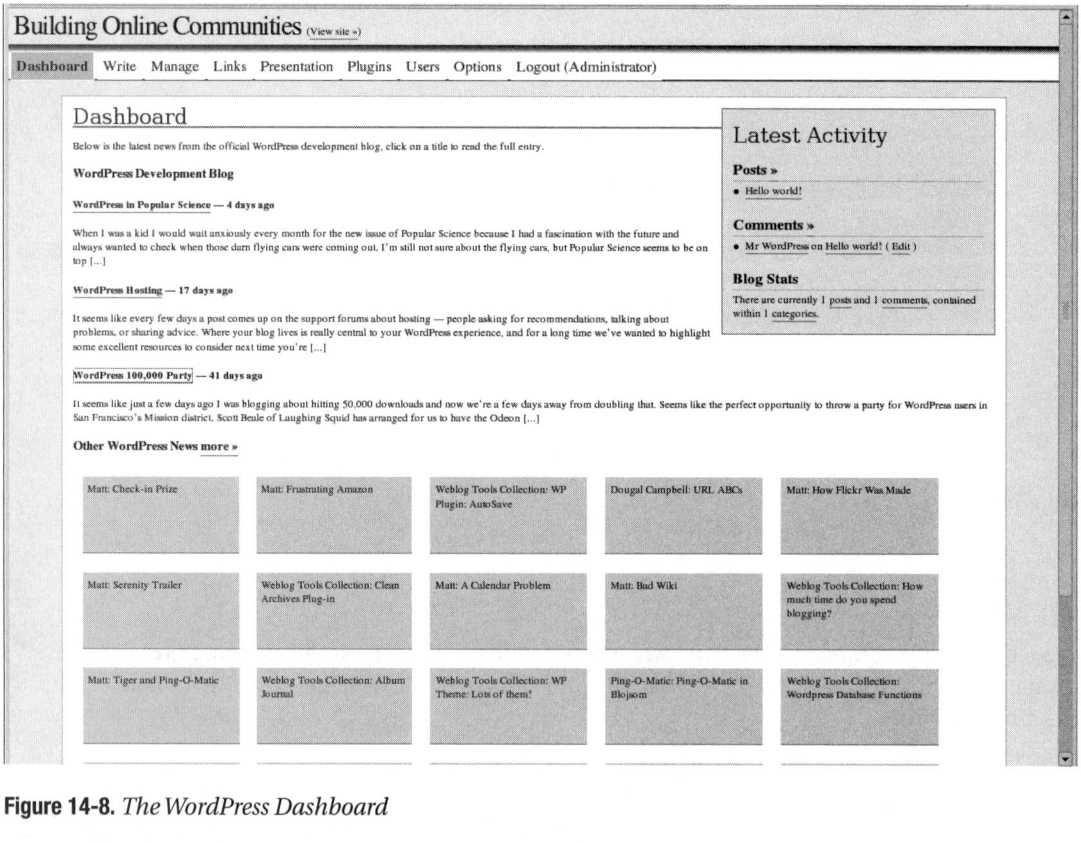

Building Online Communities (View site »)

Dashboard Write Manage Links Presentation Plugins Users Options Logout (Administrator)

Dashboard

Below is the latest news from the official WordPress development blog, click on a title to read the full entry.

WordPress Development Blog

WordPress in Popular Science — 4 days ago

When I was a kid I would wait anxiously every month for the new issue of Popular Science because I had a fascination with the future and always wanted to check when those darn flying cars were coming out. I'm still not sure about the flying cars, but Popular Science seems to be on top [...]

WordPress Hosting — 17 days ago

It seems like every few days a post comes up on the support forums about hosting — people asking for recommendations, talking about problems, or sharing advice. Where your blog lives is really central to your WordPress experience, and for a long time we've wanted to highlight some excellent resources to consider next time you're [...]

WordPress 100,000 Party — 41 days ago

It seems like just a few days ago I was blogging about hitting 50,000 downloads and now we're a few days away from doubling that. Seems like the perfect opportunity to throw a party for WordPress users in San Francisco's Mission district. Scott Beale of Laughing Squid has arranged for us to have the Odeon [...]

Other WordPress News more »

Matt: Check-in Prize

Matt: Frustrating Amazon

Weblog Tools Collection: WP Plugin: AutoSave

Dougal Campbell: URL ABCs

Matt: How Flickr Was Made

Matt: Serenity Trailer

Weblog Tools Collection: Clean Archives Plug-in

Matt: A Calendar Problem

Matt: Bad Wiki

Weblog Tools Collection: How much time do you spend blogging?

Matt: Tiger and Ping-O-Matic

Weblog Tools Collection: Album Journal

Weblog Tools Collection: WP Theme: Lots of them!

Ping-O-Matic: Ping-O-Matic in Blojsom

Weblog Tools Collection: Wordpress Database Functions

Latest Activity

Posts »

- Hello world!

Comments »

- Mr WordPress on Hello world! (Edit)

Blog Stats

There are currently 1 posts and 1 comments, contained within 1 categories.

Figure 14-8. *The WordPress Dashboard*

The Dashboard has several main areas. At the top of the page is the name of your blog and a link to view the web site. Resist clicking that just yet; let me take you through the rest of the page first. Below your blog title is the main menu bar. This contains links to all the main areas of the blog administration interface.

Below that is the main part of the Dashboard page. On the left, taking up a sizable portion of the page, are the three most recent posts from the WordPress development blog. Here, you will see news of any new versions of WordPress, news of security fixes, and so on. Below that are links to other stories from around the WordPress world.

On the right side of the page is a Latest Activity panel. This panel lists the last few posts and the last few comments from your blog. Right now, you will have only one of each, which the install script created for you. Below that you will see some blog statistics: number of posts, comments, and categories.

Changing the Admin Password

The first thing to do with your newly installed blog is to change the admin password to something you will remember. Click the Users tab across the top of the page. You'll see a form with space to enter a lot of personal details about yourself, as shown in Figure 14-9. Near the bottom are the fields to enter a new password. You need to enter the password twice. This is to check that you didn't mistype it.

You can go ahead and enter your other details while you are on the page. By default, none of these details other than your nickname and web address are ever visible on your blog. When you have finished entering all your details click Update Profile to save your changes.

Now you're ready to configure WordPress.

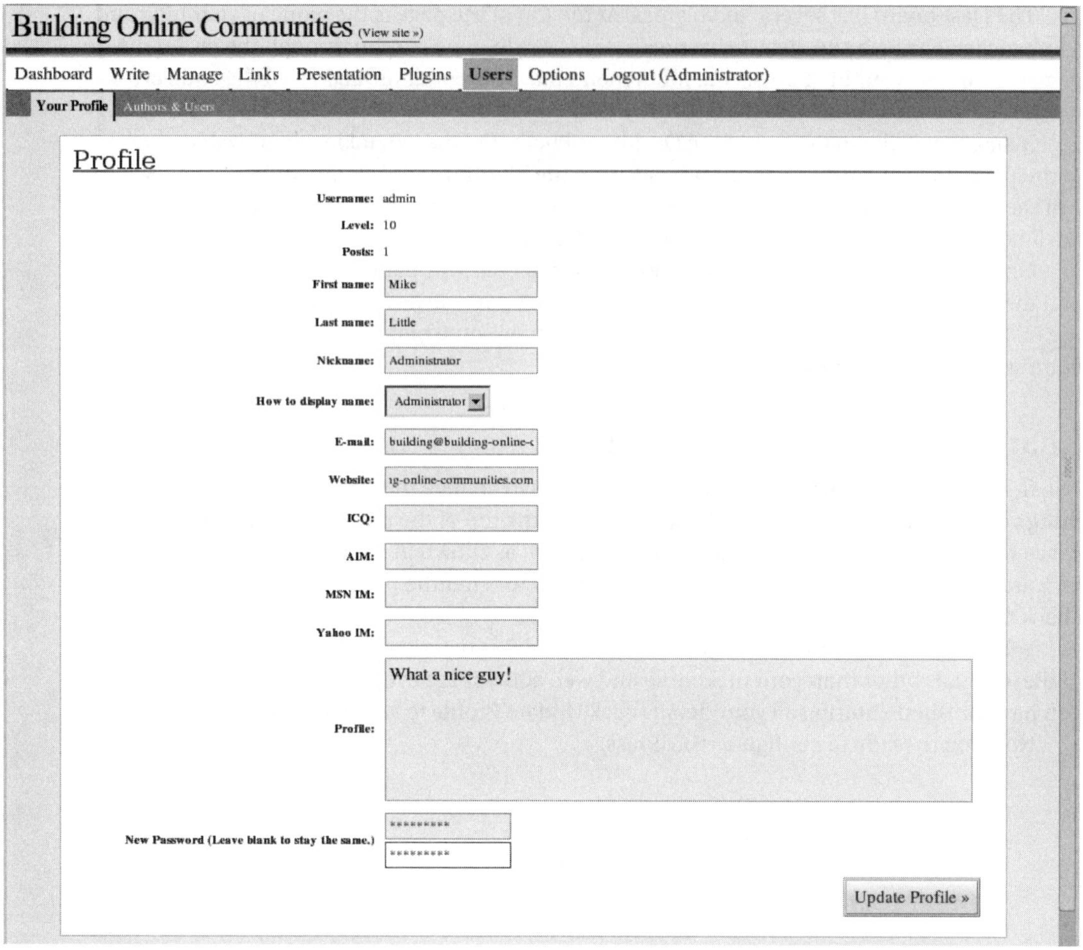

Figure 14-9. *Editing your user profile*

Configuring WordPress

WordPress offers many options and features that you can control through its Options page. These range from general settings for blog membership to important methods for preventing comment spam.

Setting General Options

I'll take you through the basic configuration of your blog next. To start, click the Options tab near the top of the page. You can see that you are editing "General Options," as shown in Figure 14-10. Within the options system, you can always check the top of the page to see where you are. The current subtab will be highlighted, and the title of the page will tell you which options you are editing.

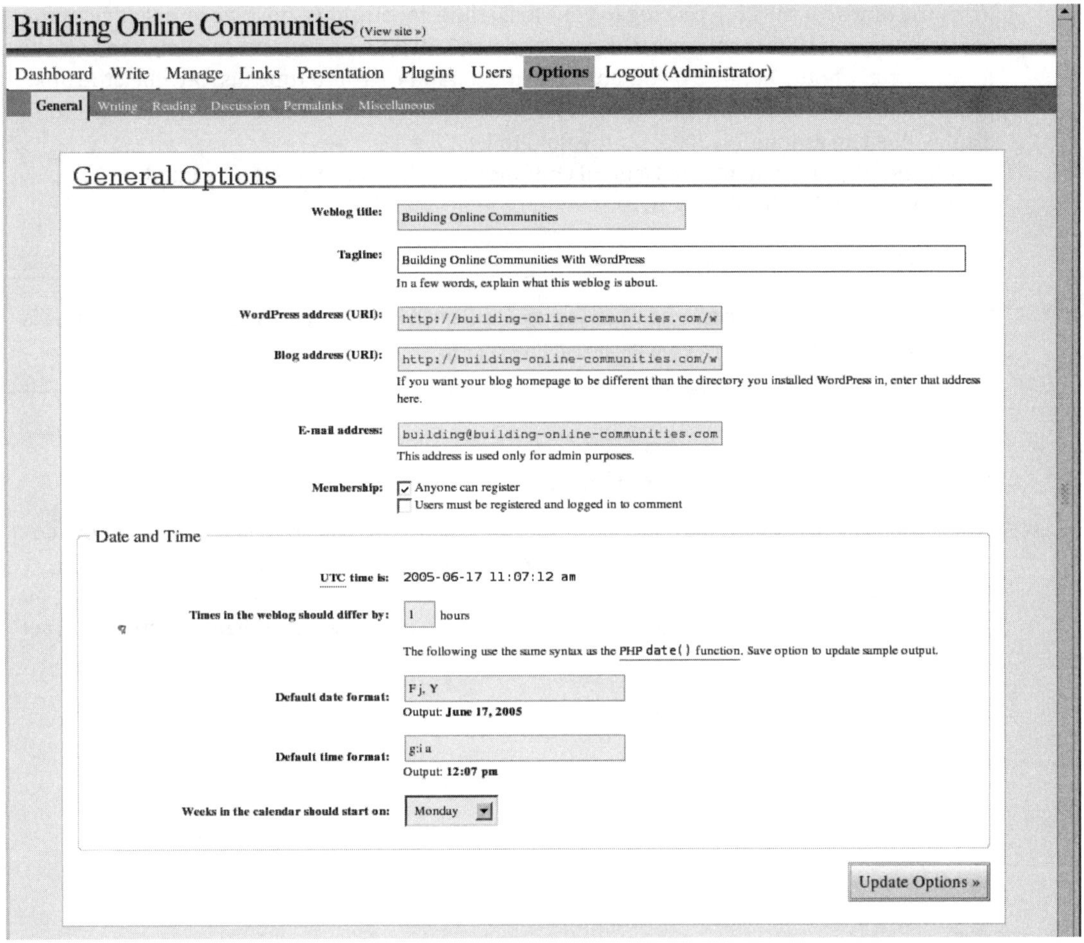

Figure 14-10. *General Options page*

Here, you can see the blog title you entered when you ran the install script, as well as the blog tag line, which is like the tag line you find under a newspaper masthead. Change the default to something appropriate for your blog. Don't worry if you can't think of something witty or impressive just now. You can always change it later.

You generally don't need to change the WordPress address and Blog address fields unless you are doing something unusual with the location of WordPress's files. Your e-mail address appears as the one you entered when you installed WordPress. If you need to change it, you can.

The next two options are about membership of your blog. If you want to run your blog as a community site, you might consider enabling these two options. The Anyone can register option causes a link to a registration form to appear on your main page. This allows new users to register themselves. By default, these newly registered users won't be able to post new stories. You need to promote them first, as described in Chapter 15.

The date and time options are self-explanatory. The software usually gets the time right based on your server's setting. You can use the setting "Times in the weblog should differ by" to set the times for the blog posting to your local time, by putting a positive or negative number in this box. If UTC is showing 9:30 p.m. and it is 1:30 p.m. on your wristwatch, then set this to –8, for eight hours behind. If you don't like the default date and time display, click the link provided to read the documentation on PHP's `date()` function. For example, if you want to display the date as June 17, 2005, set the field to F j, Y.

Finally, the last item on the General Options page allows you to set on what day of the week your calendar should begin.

■ **Note** The calendar is not displayed when you use the Default theme, but does appear when you use the Classic theme. I'll cover how to switch themes in Chapter 16.

Configuring Discussion Options

When you click the Discussion tab on the Options page, you will see a set of options related to the various discussions that can take place around your blog, as shown in Figure 14-11. The important settings on this page allow you to prevent comment spam from appearing on your blog. I'll cover comment spam in the next section and focus on the other discussion settings here.

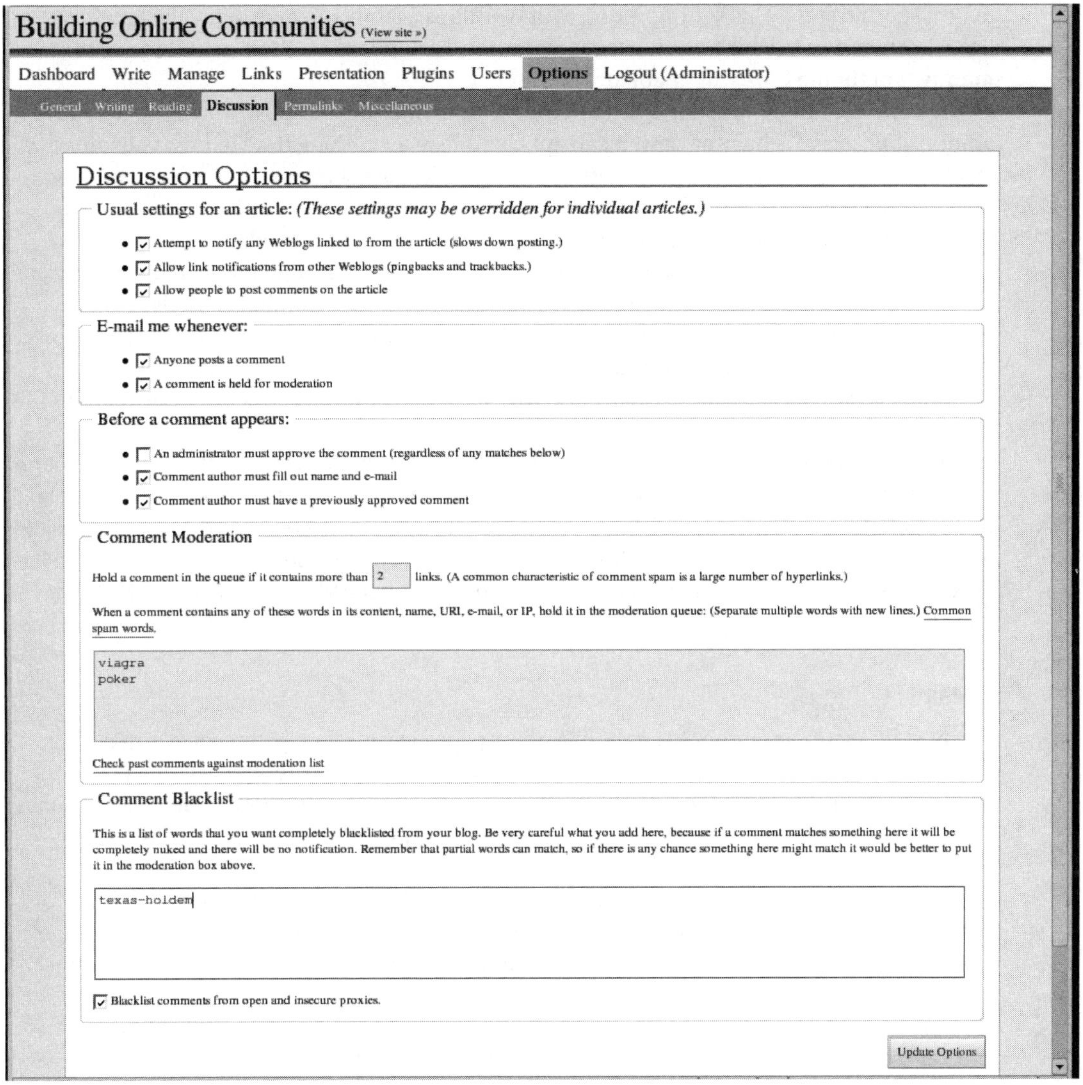

Building Online Communities (View site »)

Dashboard Write Manage Links Presentation Plugins Users Options Logout (Administrator)

General Writing Reading Discussion Permalinks Miscellaneous

Discussion Options

Usual settings for an article: *(These settings may be overridden for individual articles.)*

- ☑ Attempt to notify any Weblogs linked to from the article (slows down posting.)
- ☑ Allow link notifications from other Weblogs (pingbacks and trackbacks.)
- ☑ Allow people to post comments on the article

E-mail me whenever:

- ☑ Anyone posts a comment
- ☑ A comment is held for moderation

Before a comment appears:

- ☐ An administrator must approve the comment (regardless of any matches below)
- ☑ Comment author must fill out name and e-mail
- ☑ Comment author must have a previously approved comment

Comment Moderation

Hold a comment in the queue if it contains more than 2 links. (A common characteristic of comment spam is a large number of hyperlinks.)

When a comment contains any of these words in its content, name, URI, e-mail, or IP, hold it in the moderation queue: (Separate multiple words with new lines.) Common spam words.

viagra
poker

Check past comments against moderation list

Comment Blacklist

This is a list of words that you want completely blacklisted from your blog. Be very careful what you add here, because if a comment matches something here it will be completely nuked and there will be no notification. Remember that partial words can match, so if there is any chance something here might match it would be better to put it in the moderation box above.

texas-holdem

☑ Blacklist comments from open and insecure proxies.

Update Options

Figure 14-11. *Discussion Options page*

Pingbacks, TrackBacks, and Comments

The first setting on the Discussion Options page, "Attempt to notify any Weblogs linked to from the article (slows down posting)," specifies that when you post a story that contains links, WordPress will attempt to send a Pingback message to each of those links. It uses a little discrimination in that it pings only links it thinks are permalinks. Links that are only to domains (such as `http://www.google.com` or `http://amazon.co.uk`) are not pinged. The reasoning is that it only makes sense to Pingback a specific story, and a link to a web site homepage is not likely to be a specific story. This setting, along with WordPress's ability to automatically Pingback links you mention in your post, is a great feature and a good way to start to build your community. You should have this enabled.

A word of caution, though: if you mention a lot of links in your post, and if the network around your server is busy or slow, it can appear to take a *very* long time to post your story. In fact, the story is posted quite quickly, but the Pingback process involving a conversation with several other servers that might be equally busy can take over a minute. It might appear as though your server has stopped, but a lot is going on in the background.

The next setting, "Allow link notifications from other Weblogs (Pingbacks and TrackBacks)," is about allowing Pingbacks and TrackBacks to your posts. You should probably leave this enabled, too. Another word of caution: there have been attempts to exploit the concept of TrackBacks for spamming purposes. WordPress comes configured to handle this, but you should be aware of the issue. I'll elaborate when I cover the subject of comment spam in the next section.

The next setting turns on user comments (it is off by default). Without this setting, no one can leave a comment on your posts. If you want to build a community, you'll need to enable this option. Comments are the lifeblood of a community blog, or even one that just wishes to interact with its readers. Note that this setting governs the default setting for all new posts. It doesn't affect posts you've already created, and an individual post can override this setting. WordPress is very flexible!

E-Mail

The next two settings on the Discussion Options page govern when you receive e-mail from your WordPress blog. You can have WordPress send you an e-mail message whenever anyone posts a comment or sends a TrackBack or Pingback. And you can have WordPress send you an e-mail message whenever a comment is held for moderation. Comment moderation is covered in the next section.

Figure 14-12 shows a sample e-mail message sent when a comment has been left on your blog. In it, you can see the blog name and posting title included in the subject. The message also includes details of the comment author's name, e-mail, and URI, if supplied, and, of course, the visitor's comment.

For checking and tracing purposes, the e-mail also includes the IP address of the visitor as reported by the web server, a reverse DNS lookup, and a link to a WHOIS lookup of that IP address. These three items should give you useful information if you are the victim of comment spam or some other comment nastiness. Unfortunately, some of the spammers post remotely from innocent machines or through third-party proxies, or else spoof the IP address, rendering those pieces of information less useful.

For convenience, the e-mail also includes a link to the posting on which the comment was made. This allows you to read the comment in context of the post and other comments. It also includes a direct link to automatically delete the comment. If the e-mail is about a comment that is waiting for moderation, there will also be a link to automatically approve the comment and one to take you to the comment moderation page.

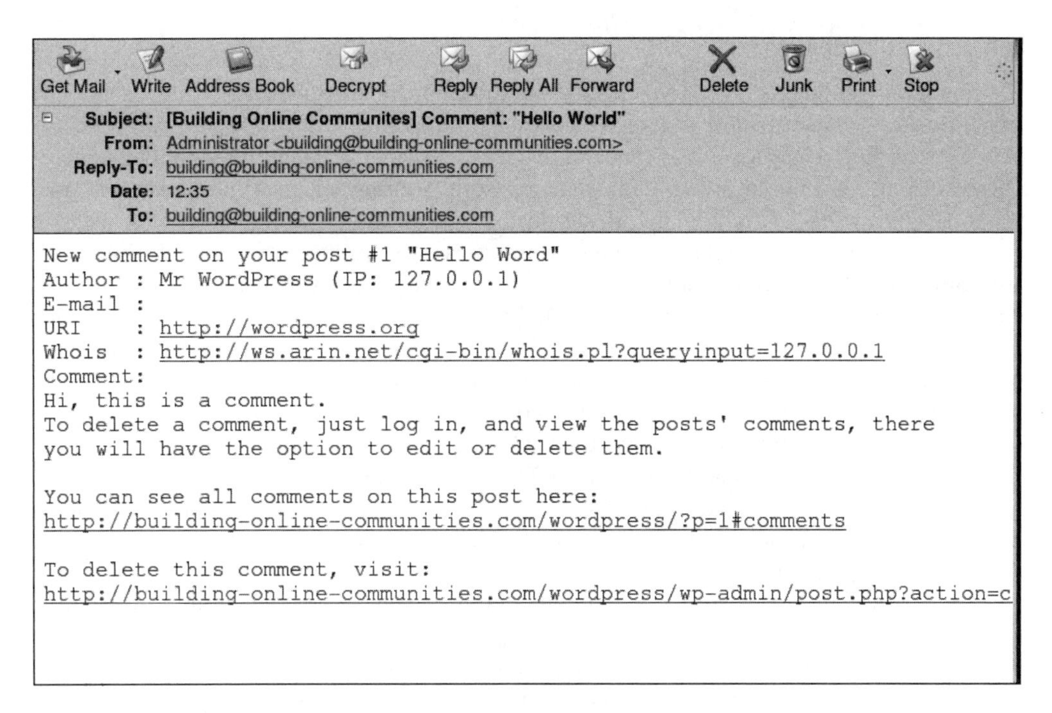

Figure 14-12. *Sample notification e-mail*

Avoiding Comment Spam

Comment spam refers to comments that are made on your blog by comment spammers for the purpose of promoting their commercial sites. They usually have one of two purposes in mind, sometimes both:

- They want to get links to their sites in as many places as possible in the hope that a lot of people will click the link.
- They want to gain higher placing in search-engine rankings by being linked to from as many places as possible.

The commercial sites the spammers link to are usually online casinos, drug-selling sites, or porn sites. Quite often, the comments link to sites that don't appear to be commercial sites, but rather seem to be offering useful information about their subject. Don't be fooled. The idea is that you and search engines won't penalize these sites because they appear to be innocent. Often, the comments with links to these sites seem innocuous, something like, "This is my first visit to your site. I thought it was great." The spammers hope that the links to these sites will remain in place and gain various advantages, particularly with search engines. At some point in the future, they will switch on the commercial pages, either as links within the text to the commercial sites or by replacing the page with a commercial one.

WordPress includes several measures to combat and thwart the spammers. These are available through the comment settings on the Discussion Options page (see Figure 14-11).

Before a Comment Appears

The first setting in this section, "An administrator must approve the comment," means that an administrator must approve every single comment (including TrackBacks and Pingbacks) before it is displayed on your site. To that end, all comments are placed in a moderation queue. This is the most effective anti-comment spam measure. Nothing gets past WordPress, because you must approve each comment before it is posted on your site.

As you can imagine, enabling comment approval is the most inconvenient setting for you and your readers. They must wait to see their comments appear, so you lose out on the immediacy of the blog-commenting system. This can have quite an effect on the ability to build and maintain a community based around your blog. You must also process these comments by hand, preferably at regular intervals in order to maintain some kind of immediacy for your community. That can be a lot of work, given that some comment spammers use automated scripts that can submit many hundreds of comments to your blog each day. This setting is really a last resort.

The next setting, "Comment author must fill out name and e-mail," simply requires that a comment author fill in the name and e-mail settings in order to post a comment. While not too exacting (you don't need to add a real e-mail address), this setting will defeat a couple of the more basic spam scripts.

The final setting in this section, "Comment author must have a previously approved comment," works in conjunction with its predecessor. If a comment author enters the same name and e-mail address as that of a previously approved comment, then WordPress will allow the comment to appear on the site immediately. Conveniently, WordPress will set a cookie in a visitor's browser that will allow it to prepopulate the username, e-mail, and URL for that visitor.

Comment Moderation

The next group of settings are more directly concerned with defeating comment spam. First, you can set a threshold for the number of links a comment can contain before it is considered to be possible spam and placed in the comment moderation queue. A common feature of one type of spam is dozens of links to sites of a dubious nature. This setting (with a default setting of 2) addresses that.

The next setting is a space for a list of trigger words. If a comment has any of these words in it (in any part of the comment), WordPress will immediately place the comment in the moderation queue. For convenience, there is a link to a centrally maintained list of common spam words. You can visit that page and copy the list there into your own list.

Comment Blacklist

The final section of the Discussion Options page is a comment blacklist. If any of the words in this list are found in a comment, that comment does not even appear in the moderation queue. Be careful which words you put in this list. If any word matches—and even partial words can match—you will not even be notified by e-mail about the comment, unlike with all of the other methods. Thus, you will not normally get chance to approve a comment that matches the blacklisted words here.

In fact, blacklisted comments (and ones that you designate as spam during moderation) are still in the database. WordPress does not currently provide any way to access them once they are marked as spam. However, at least one WordPress plug-in (`http://www.coldforged.org/paged-comment-editing-plugin/`) allows you to browse through spam comments and reclassify them.

Below the comment blacklist box is the "Blacklist comments from open and insecure proxies" check box. This setting blacklists comments that are made through a particular open proxy known for being used by spammers. Comments matching this criterion also "disappear" without notification.

Setting File Upload Options

The next set of options you will want to tweak are those involving adding images and other media to your blog. Click the Miscellaneous tab under Options to get to these options, as shown in Figure 14-13.

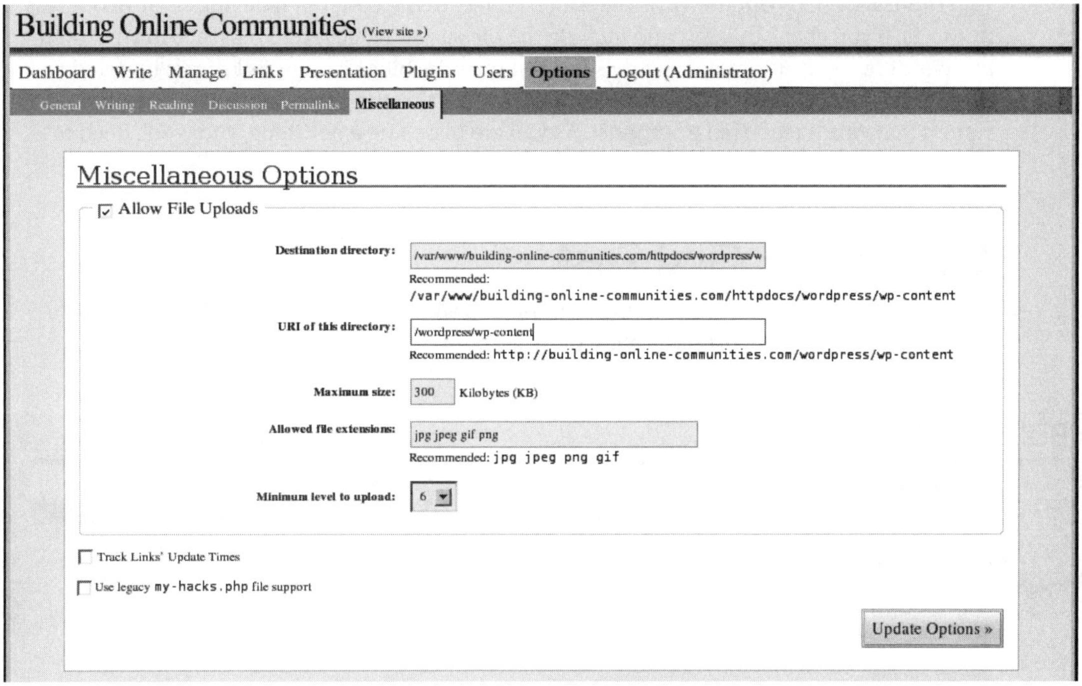

Building Online Communities (View site »)
Dashboard Write Manage Links Presentation Plugins Users Options Logout (Administrator)
General Writing Reading Discussion Permalinks Miscellaneous
Miscellaneous Options
Allow File Uploads
Destination directory: /var/www/building-online-communities.com/httpdocs/wordpress/w
Recommended: /var/www/building-online-communities.com/httpdocs/wordpress/wp-content
URI of this directory: /wordpress/wp-content
Recommended: http://building-online-communities.com/wordpress/wp-content
Maximum size: 300 Kilobytes (KB)
Allowed file extensions: jpg jpeg gif png
Recommended: jpg jpeg png gif
Minimum level to upload: 6
Track Links' Update Times
Use legacy my-hacks.php file support
Update Options »

Figure 14-13. *Miscellaneous Options page*

If you want to be able to add images and other media to your blog posts, you need to enable file uploads. WordPress usually guesses the Destination directory setting correctly. This is the full path to the `wp-content` folder on your server.

The URI of this directory setting is the web-visible URI the server will expose this folder as. WordPress sometimes gets this wrong. The URI it guesses works, but not all the time, particularly in the administration pages, so you cannot see your images in preview mode. Change this to an absolute path on the server. For example, if your blog URI is `http://example.com/myblog`, set it to `/myblog/wp-content`. You can use a folder completely outside the WordPress folder if you like. For example, you may have an existing `/images` folder you wish to use. Whichever folder you choose, it will need to be writable by the web server.

The next setting on this page allows you to specify a maximum file upload size. You may want to set this to some value appropriate to the files you will be uploading. If you are going to allow other people to post and upload files to your blog, you may want to set this to a lower value.

The Allowed file extensions setting is a space-separated list of file extensions that WordPress will allow to be uploaded. You might want to add mp3 if you are going to add MP3s to your posts, perhaps if you are podcasting.

The last setting in this section is the minimum user privilege level required before a registered user is able to upload files. If you have multiple authors on your blog, you might want to allow only certain authors to upload files. You would raise their user level to this value to allow them to do that (raising user levels is discussed in Chapter 15).

The Track Links' Update Times check box refers to the blogroll-style links that WordPress supports. If you check this box and include the file `wp-admin/update-links.php` in your theme file, WordPress will automatically track the last time the blogs in your links were updated.

Finally, the "Use legacy my-hacks.php file support" setting refers to an old pre-plug-in system that WordPress used to support. As you are installing a new blog, you won't need to turn on this setting.

Making Your First Post

You are now in a position to make your first post to your blog. Go ahead and click the Write tab. You'll see the Write Post page, shown in Figure 14-14.

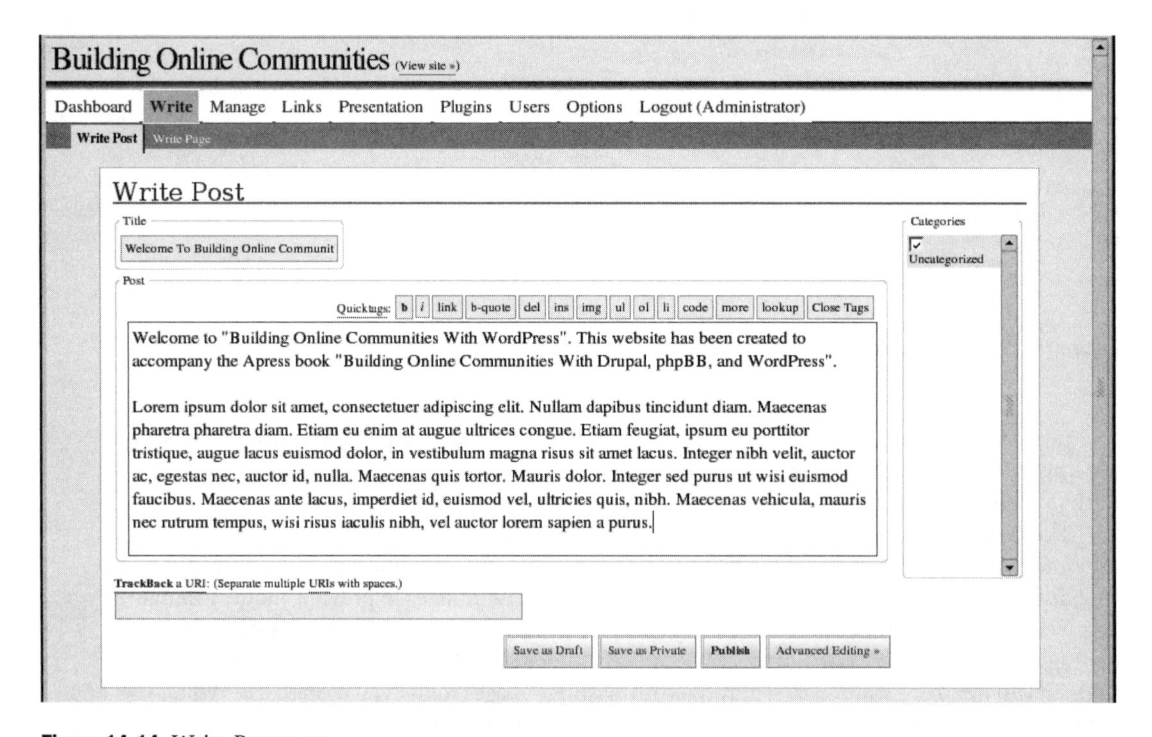

Figure 14-14. *Write Post page*

Type in a title and the content of your post. You can use the quicktag buttons just above the large edit area to format your story, to add links, and so on. I'll go into detail about the quicktags and other posting options in the next chapter. When you are happy with your story, click the Publish button. That's it, you've made your first post!

Click the *View site* link at the top of the page and admire the masterpiece you just produced! Figure 14-15 shows an example. You may notice that there is already another post on your site. That is a test post the system creates for you as part of the installation. You can safely delete that once you have created your own post.

Figure 14-15. *A first post*

Summary

This chapter took you through obtaining, installing, and configuring a simple out-of-the-box WordPress blog. It covered the requirements for WordPress and the tasks for preparing your hosting server. I introduced you to some of the basic features of WordPress. Finally, you made your first post.

In the next chapter, I will take you through the posting process in depth and introduce some of the more advanced features of WordPress. You will learn how to create pages, manage categories, and perform other tasks to start to build your community.

CHAPTER 15

Starting to Blog and Building Your Community

In this chapter, I'll take you through some simple steps to enhance your blog and build your community. First, you'll look in a little more depth at posting to your blog, using both the standard and advanced editing options. I'll show you that you don't need to have any great HTML skills to make rich content for your site. Then you'll see how to manage categories, manage comments, add multiple authors for your site, and create blog pages. During the course of this chapter, you'll install and use two plug-ins, giving you an idea of what WordPress plug-ins can help you do on your site. Finally, I'll give you some tips on improving the search engine visibility of your site, to attract more visitors.

Using Basic Post Options

In the previous chapter, you created your first post and got a glimpse of the options available for writing posts. Here, I'll describe these options in more detail. You will need to go to the Write Post page to follow along with the discussion. If you are already logged in to your blog, click the *Site Admin* link at the bottom of the sidebar. If you are not logged in, click the *Login* link in the same place. From the Dashboard page, click the *Write* link.

Marking Up Your Post with Quicktags

As you are writing your post, you can use the quicktag buttons, as shown in Figure 15-1, to add some markup to your posts. Table 15-1 shows the functions of these buttons.

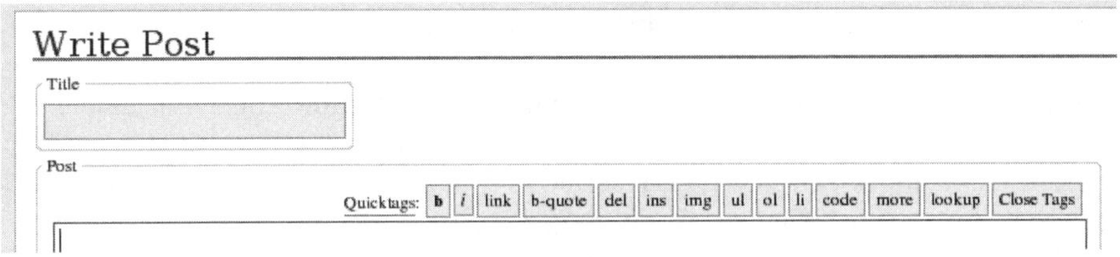

Figure 15-1. *You can use the quicktag buttons to mark up your post.*

Table 15-1. *Quicktag Functions*

Quicktag	Function
b	Adds strong tags to some text for stronger emphasis
i	Adds em tags to some text for emphasis
link	Adds a link to your post
b-quote	Adds blockquote tags to your post
del	Marks up text as deleted (usually rendered with strike-through)
ins	Marks up text as inserted. (usually rendered as underline)
img	Adds an image to your post
ul	Starts an unordered list in your post
ol	Starts an ordered list in your post
li	Adds an item to your unordered or ordered list
code	Marks up text with code tags
more	Adds a special WordPress more tag to your post
lookup	Allows you to look up a word in an online dictionary
Close Tags	Closes any open tags in your post (but you should normally close them yourself to achieve the markup you intend)

By using these quicktags, you are marking up the text of your post to describe its *meaning*. You can emphasize a word, set off a quoted block of text, type out a list of points, and so on. Unlike with a word processor, you are not directly styling your text. You will do that with the CSS of the theme you choose for the blog, as you'll learn in the next chapter.

One way to use the quicktags is to select the text in your post you want to mark up, and then click the corresponding quicktag button. For example, if you have written a sentence and want to emphasize a word or phrase, select the words and click the **b** or *i* button. This will enclose your selected words with `<strong>` or `<em>` tags, respectively. The `<em>` tag marks up a word or words as emphasized. Your browser usually represents this by rendering the words in italics. The `<strong>` tag means a stronger emphasis and is usually rendered as bold.

Another way to use quicktags is to apply them first, and then add the text you want to affect. For example, suppose you are writing a post about an article you read on another web site. You know you want to paste in a block of text as a quotation from the article, marked up with the `<blockquote>` tag. Click the b-quote quicktag button, and an opening `<blockquote>` tag will be inserted in your post. You can then paste in your quoted text, as shown in Figure 15-2. You'll see that the b-quote quicktag button has changed to /b-quote. This indicates that you have yet to close the opening `<blockquote>` tag. Click the button again, and the closing `</blockquote>` tag will be inserted.

Another quicktag worth noting is the link quicktag. Click the button, and a little dialog box pops up, asking you to "Enter the URL," as shown in Figure 15-3. Type in your URL, and then click OK. The opening anchor tag `<a>` is inserted in your post with the URL you specified. Type in the words you want to be linked (that is, the words the reader will click on). Click the button (which now says /link) again, and the closing anchor tag `</a>` will be inserted. Alternatively, if you already have the link words typed into your post, you can use a shortcut: select the words, and then click the link quicktag button. The same dialog box pops up, asking for your URL. After you enter the URL and click OK, the anchor tags for the link will be inserted around your selected words, creating the link in one step.

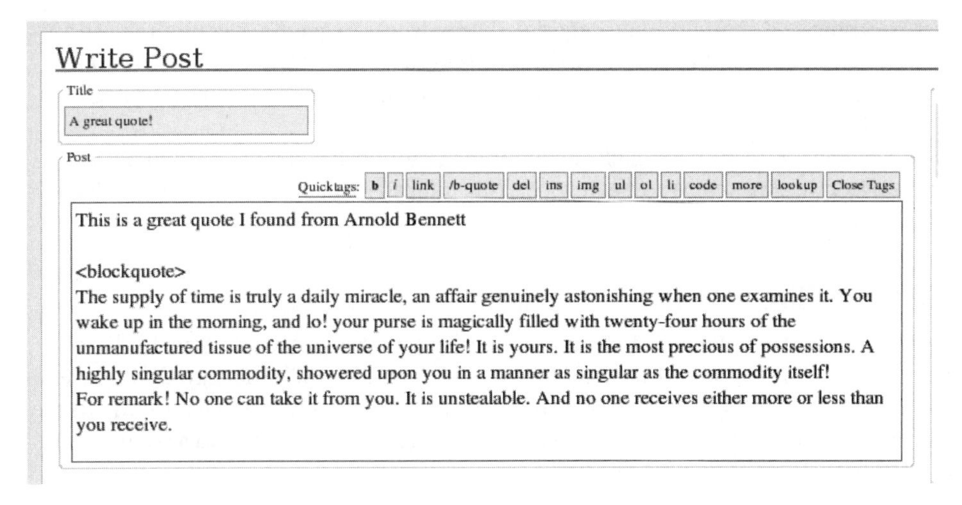

Figure 15-2. *Adding a <blockquote> tag with the b-quote quicktag button*

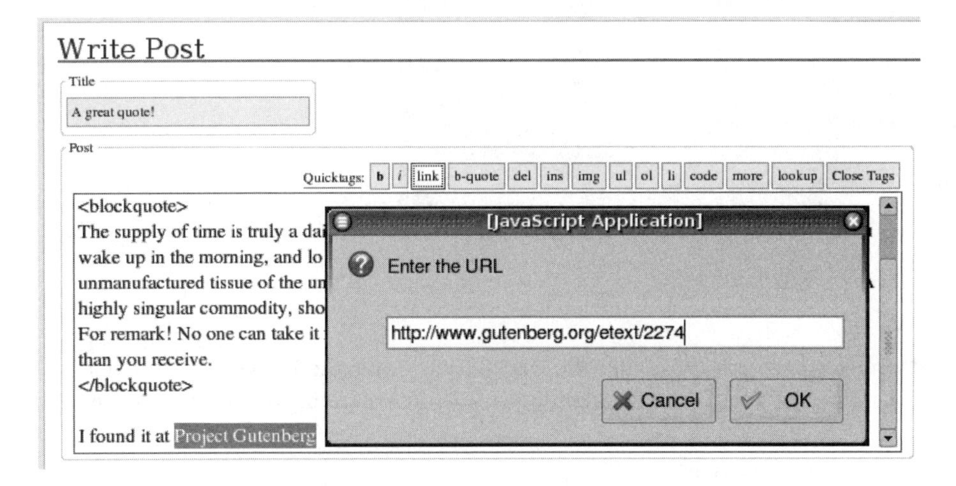

Figure 15-3. *Adding a link with the link quicktag*

■ **Note** If you have the appropriate option set on the Discussion tab of the Options page ("Attempt to notify any Weblogs linked to from the article"), any links in your post that look like permanent links to blog posts or news stories will be automatically pinged when you publish your blog post. This behavior can be overridden for individual posts by using the Advanced Editing mode, which is described later in this chapter.

Categorizing Posts

You should add one or more categories to your post. Adding categories helps your readers understand the context of the post. If your blog is diverse enough to have several distinct areas of interest, choosing well-thought-out categories allows visitors to get to the content they want quickly. For example, you could post an entry on your local action support group blog about a meeting you attended last night that introduced a new board member. You might categorize the post in both the Events and Staff categories.

To add a category to your post, click one or more of the check boxes to the right of the editing area. A tick displayed next to a category name indicates that the post will be published with that category.

Adding TrackBack URIs

As well as having links to other blogs in your post, you might also want to add TrackBacks to other posts. If the other blog supports TrackBack, a TrackBack URI will be displayed somewhere on the blog post. Often, this URI is not visible unless just that one posting and its comments are displayed, as shown in Figure 15-4. This is because TrackBacks are meant to add a comment or comment-like entry to that other blog posting.

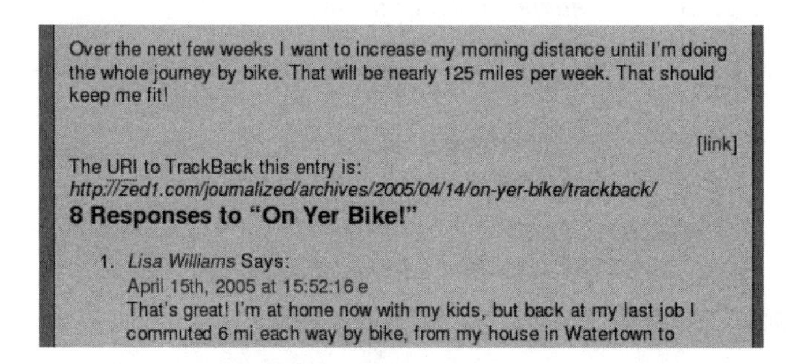

Figure 15-4. *TrackBack URI displayed*

To add a TrackBack to your post, type the TrackBack URI into the TrackBack a URI field just below the main post area. You can add multiple URIs by separating them with a space.

Publishing or Saving Your Post

Below the main editing area are several buttons that allow you to either publish or save your post: Save as Draft, Save as Private, and Publish. The default option is Publish.

Publishing a Post

If you are finished with your post, click the Publish button to publish it. The post will immediately be visible on the blog's main page. If there were any links in the body of the post, and the automatic Pingback option is on (set through the "Attempt to notify any Weblogs linked to from the article" option discussed in Chapter 14), the URIs mentioned will be notified of your post. Similarly, if you added one or more TrackBack URIs to the post, they, too, will be notified of your blog post. Finally any central update services will be notified of your post. These update services are listed in the Update Services section of the Writing Options tab.

All this notification is quite important in building your community blog and attracting visitors. Many people monitor the Update Services looking for interesting new stories to read.

If they see the notification of your story, they might just come and visit. Similarly, the authors and readers of blogs on which you comment in your posts will likely see your Pingback or TrackBack (they are often displayed as comments on the blog) and visit your site to see what you might have to say.

■ **Tip** Almost by definition, people reading other blogs on the subjects about which you write are likely to be interested in your blog. Pingback and TrackBack notifications are great ways to get those people to visit your site.

Saving a Draft Post

If you need to look up something, or perhaps just want to take a break from editing your post, you can save it as a draft. Click the Save as Draft button below the main edit area. This saves your post in the database, without publishing it for the world to see. This allows you the luxury of taking your time to put together your content. It also has the side effect of making your post safe from browser crashes and the like, just as when you save a word processor document periodically while you are working on it.

WordPress will remind you of your saved drafts on the administration pages. On the Write Post and Manage Posts pages (accessed by clicking Write and Manage on the administration pages, respectively), the list of saved drafts is presented just below the second-level tab area. On the Dashboard, the list of drafts is presented at the bottom of the page. Clicking the title of the draft opens that post in the main edit area, ready for you to continue. It also puts you into Advanced Editing mode, which I'll cover in just a moment.

Saving a Private Post

If you save a post as private, the post will be visible only to you. If you are logged in to the blog, you will see the post on the main blog page, as well as in the administration interface. No one else will see the post, even if they are logged in. Not even an administrator will see those posts through the blog or the administration pages.

You might want to use private posts as personal diary entries. Another possible use is to share a login with someone so that you both can see those posts, but no one else can view them.

Using Advanced Post Editing Options

If you click the Advanced Editing button while writing a post, you will find yourself in WordPress's Advanced Editing mode. You'll also be in this mode when you click the title of a saved draft post to edit it. Advanced Editing mode offers you more control over your post than the standard Write Post page.

Figure 15-5 shows the top of the Write Post page in Advanced Editing mode. The advanced features are added to the standard Write Post page in separate areas, so that the page remains understandable. Advanced Mode adds Discussion and Password options, an Excerpt field, plus a set of Advanced options grouped together at the foot of the page, described later in this section.

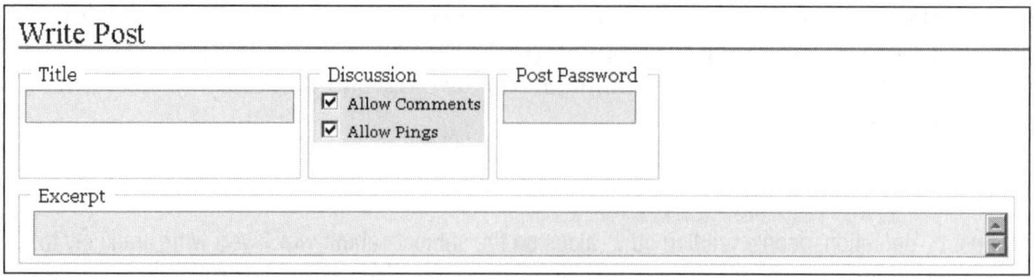

Figure 15-5. *Additional options in Advanced Editing mode*

Note In the current alpha development version of WordPress (which will either be version 1.6 or 2.0 when it is released), the advanced editing controls are available all the time. A smart, new, dynamic interface allows you to collapse these controls out of sight when you don't need them.

Allowing Comments and Pings

Just to the right of the post title is a Discussion section, with a couple of check boxes. These allow you to override the options controlling comments and pings for this individual post. The Allow Comments and Allow Pings check boxes normally reflect the blog's Discussion Options settings (discussed in Chapter 14) for the "Allow people to post comments on the article" and "Allow link notifications from other Weblogs (pingbacks and trackbacks)," respectively.

Checking or clearing one of these boxes overrides that setting for this post only; it does not affect the default setting for new posts. So, if there is a check in the box for Allow Comments, comments will be enabled for this post. Similarly, a check next to Allow Pings will allow Pingbacks and TrackBacks to be accepted by this post.

Password-Protecting Posts

To the right of the Discussion check boxes is the Post Password box. Typing a word or phrase into this field (you'll notice that the password is displayed in plain text as you type it) will password-protect this posting. This means that, on the main page of your blog, this post will not, by default, display its contents. Instead the reader is presented with the title of the post (with *Protected:* prepended) and a password-entry field. The normal comments link is also replaced with the phrase "Enter your password to view comments," as shown in Figure 15-6.

Assuming you have given the password you entered when you published the post to some other people, they can type in the password and be able to read the post. The post is then displayed normally, although the title still has *Protected:* prepended to it. Comments are also accessible at that point.

Protected: Adding Plugins
June 17th, 2005

This post is password protected. To view it please enter your password below:

Password: Submit

Posted in Hints and Tips | Enter your password to view comments

Figure 15-6. *A password-protected post*

■ **Caution** The protection of posts available through WordPress's Advanced Editing mode is quite rudimentary. The password is stored in plain text in a cookie on the reader's machine. Anyone else using that same browser will be able to read that post for the next ten days (the lifetime of the cookie). The password is even stored in plain text in the database. Please don't use this feature for anything that is really sensitive.

Adding Excerpts

The next advanced feature is the Excerpt box, where you can write your own excerpt to describe your post to people browsing feeds.

When a reader subscribes to one of the XML feeds available from your blog—RSS, Atom, or RDF—one of the pieces of information provided as part of that feed is a description, along with the title, date, and so on. This is usually an excerpt of the post content. By default, WordPress will create that excerpt for you by stripping all the tags from your post and extracting the first 250 or so characters. Often, this will be sufficient for most people's needs.

Sometimes, however, the opening sentence or two from your post isn't really a good description of what it is about. It's kind of like the difference between the blurb on the back of a paperback novel and the opening two sentences. If you want to make sure that people browsing the latest feeds will want to visit your blog and read your posts, you should write the excerpt yourself. Think of it as a targeted summary of the post that may additionally improve your site's search engine visibility, as discussed at the end of this chapter.

■ **Note** You can change the default setting so that the full contents of the post will also be sent with a feed. Click Options, then Reading to display the Reading Options page. In the Syndication Feeds section, check Full text for the "For each article, show" option. If you specify Summary for that option, only the excerpt is contained in the feed.

Using Advanced Options

More options are contained in the Advanced section at the bottom of the Write Posts page, as shown in Figure 15-7.

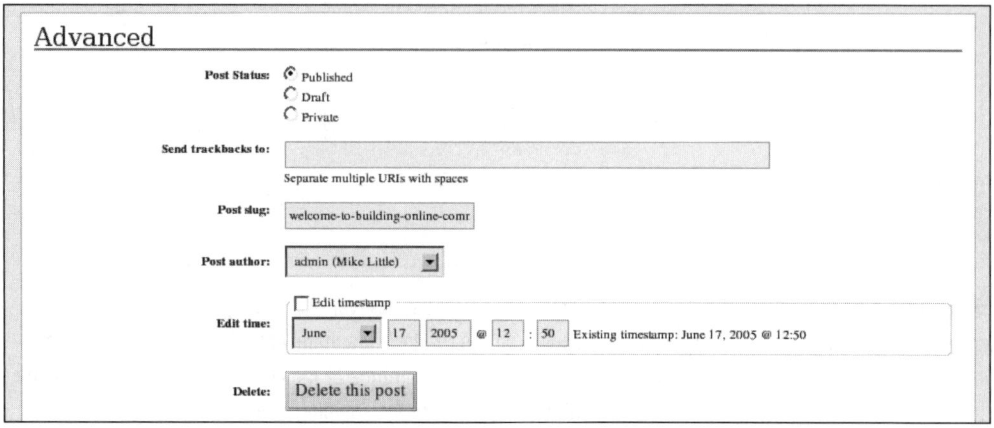

Figure 15-7. *Advanced options in Advanced Editing mode*

These options work as follows:

Post Status: Just below the standard editing controls, you will find radio buttons to set the post status. These statuses—Published, Draft, and Private—correspond to the statuses resulting from clicking the Save as Draft, Save as Private, and Publish buttons, as described earlier.

Send trackbacks to: This field corresponds to the TrackBack URI described earlier.

Post slug: This strange-sounding field is the part of the permanent URI to your post used in the search engine-friendly URLs you can configure in WordPress. See the "Improving Search Engine Visibility" section later in this chapter for more details.

Post author: This drop-down list allows you to assign the authorship of a post to another author. If you don't see this field, that's because it works only if your own user level is level 7 or greater. If you do have access to it, you can assign posts only to authors of lower levels than yourself. (See the "Assigning User Permissions" section later in this chapter for more details on user levels.)

Edit timestamp/Edit time: These options allow you to edit the published timestamp of the post. As a general rule, you probably won't want to modify this. It can, however, be used to post blog entries in the future. To use this control, fill in the date and time fields as you want, and check the Edit timestamp check box. If you are editing a post that has already been published, the box will be checked for you. The date and time will be set to the original date and time the post was published. This is so that when you're making a minor correction to the post, for example, it retains the original timestamp. If you use the date (or even time) in the permanent link URI of the post, retaining the original timestamp is more important than it might seem at first. If you were to change the date, you would also change the URI. This would make the permanent link somewhat less than permanent.

■ **Tip** If you set the Edit time control to a date and time in the future, the post won't show on the main blog page until that date and time is reached. It's great for putting together an article about, say, an announcement that you cannot publicize for a few days. Or, you might use it to post a message about a coming birthday or anniversary and have it automatically show up on the correct day. Additionally, if you know you are going to be away on a particular day, you can use this feature to post stories in advance and drip-feed them to your audience while you are gone.

Using Custom Fields

The last editable section in the Advanced Edit mode is the Custom Fields section. These are fields available to be used by various plug-ins you can add to WordPress. The use of these is always specific to the plug-ins you have installed and enabled. If you need to use any of these, the documentation for your plug-in will tell you.

Previewing Posts

The final advanced editing feature is the Post Preview section. When you are in Advanced Editing mode and click the Save and Continue Editing button, the post is saved, but you are left in edit mode with the same post still loaded. The Post Preview section displays the last saved version of your post. It will include any formatting added by you or any plug-ins you have, but does not use the style sheet of your theme. It will also display any images you have added to your post, which is the topic of the next section.

Adding Images to Your Posts

WordPress allows you to upload images to your site, and you can use this feature to add images to your post. However, a more convenient way to add images is to use the IImage Browser plug-in.

Uploading Images with WordPress

The Miscellaneous tab of the Options page holds configuration options for image file uploads. The first consideration is to ensure that the Allow File Uploads option is checked. The second consideration is the location that WordPress uses to store images you upload; the default location is usually adequate for most circumstances.

The images you upload can be referenced in your posts and pages. Assuming your user level is high enough (as discussed in the "Assigning User Permissions" section later in this chapter), to upload images, all you need to do is click *Upload* along the top of the administration pages. This takes you to a page with a file browser button and a couple of other controls. Click the Browse button, and navigate to the image that you want to upload to your blog. When you have selected an image, you can add a description of the image. You can also choose to have a thumbnail generated and specify its size. When you have specified all your options, click the Upload File button.

WordPress will tell you it has successfully uploaded the file and display the details of the image, including the name, file size, and type. It will also give you the code to display the image. You need to select the code it gives you and copy it to the clipboard. You can then paste that code into your blog post.

This way of adding images to your post is less than satisfactory. If you are in the middle of creating your post and you decide to upload an image, you need to save the post as draft, go to the upload page, upload your file, copy the code to the clipboard, click back to the Manage Posts page, click your draft post, find your place, and paste the image code into your article. If you forget to save the post as draft, you will lose what you have typed so far.

Because adding an image this way is so inconvenient, the next version of WordPress will probably have a different image upload interface. In the meantime, there is a *much* better way of handling images.

Using the IImage Browser Plug-In

WordPress allows you to install third-party plug-ins as add-ons to the software. These plug-ins can be created by anyone with an interest in changing the way WordPress works, adding extra functionality to WordPress, or even taking away functionality.

Many, many plug-ins are available for WordPress—more than 400 at the time of writing. A few good places to look for WordPress plug-ins are The WordPress Plugin DB (`http://www.wp-plugins.net/`), the Plugin Directory (`http://dev.wp-plugins.org/wiki/PluginDirectory`), and the plug-ins list on the WordPress Codex (`http://codex.wordpress.org/Plugins`).

The particular plug-in I'm going to introduce to you here is called IImage Browser, created by Martin Chlupáč. You can get it from his web site at `http://fredfred.net/skriker/index.php/iimage-browser`. This plug-in is an enhancement of the Image Browser plug-in for WordPress 1.2, created by Florian Jung (which you can find at `http://www.bistr-o-mathik.org/code/wordpress-plugins/`).

Installing and Activating the Plug-In

You need to download the latest stable version of the plug-in (1.4.2 at the time of writing) from `http://fredfred.net/skriker/index.php/iimage-browser`. Download the zip file to your computer and unzip the files. Using your FTP program, upload the `iimage-browser-plugin.php` file to your `wp-content/plugins` folder and the `iimage-browser.php` file to your `wp-admin` folder. You don't need to upload the third file, `insert_image_placement.txt`.

To activate the plug-in, go to the Plugins Management page of your blog. You will see the new plug-in listed, along with any other plug-ins you have installed. (If you do not see the new plug-in listed, make sure that you uploaded the files to the correct places.) Click the *Activate* link on the right side of the plug-in description. WordPress will highlight the line to indicate that it is activated, as shown in Figure 15-8.

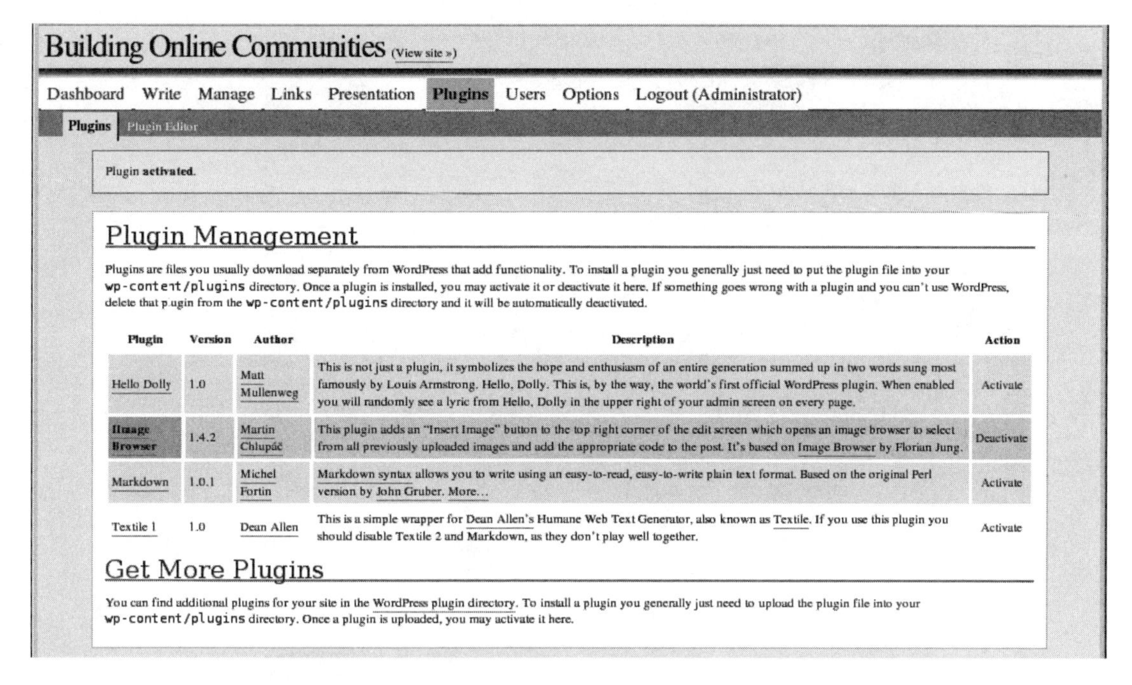

Figure 15-8. *Activating the IImage Browser plug-in*

Using the Plug-In

If you now click Write to create a new post, you will see a new link labeled *Insert Image* in the top-right corner of the Write Post page, as shown in Figure 15-9.

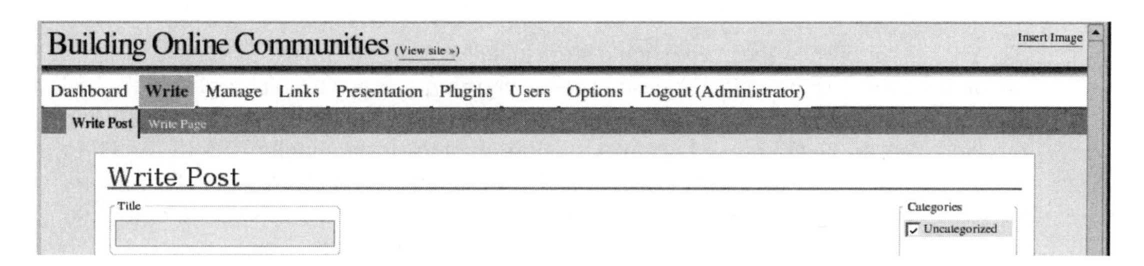

Figure 15-9. *The Insert Image link appears at the top-right corner of the page.*

Clicking the *Insert Image* link pops up a new window that displays all the images in your configured image folder. (You can instruct WordPress to use any particular folder by configuring this on the Miscellaneous tab of the Options page.) The images are paged 30 at a time. If you have more than 30 images in your image folder, the plug-in will display the first 30 in the opening page and a link (at the bottom of the window) to second and subsequent pages of images. Clicking one of the images displays a set of controls for that image, as shown in Figure 15-10.

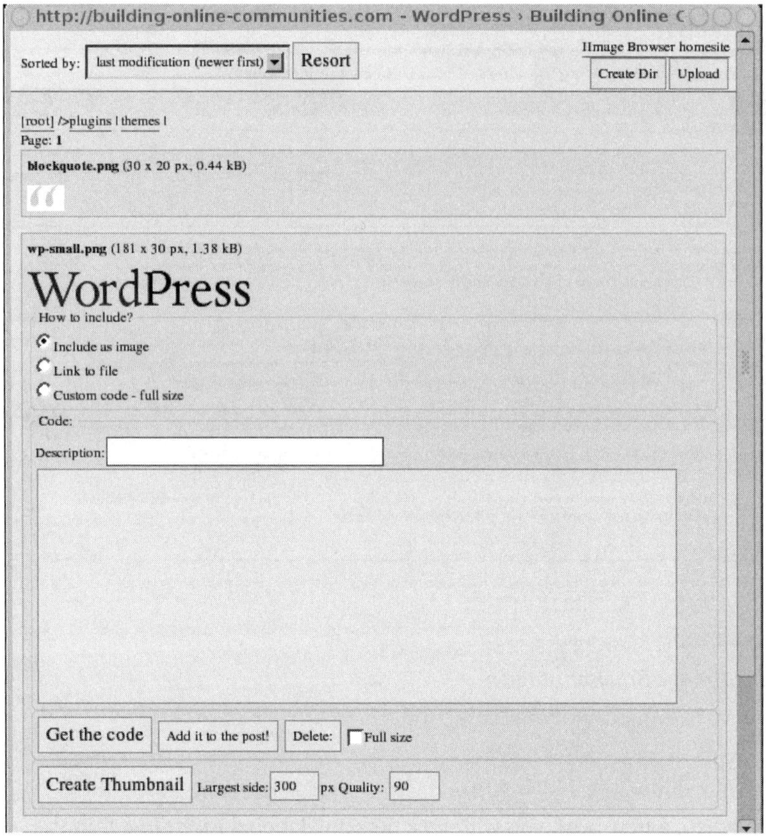

Figure 15-10. *Insert Image controls*

You can specify how the image should be included; as an in-line image, as a link to the image file, or with some custom code. The custom code option requires you to edit the plug-in file itself. To add the image, select the Include as image button, type a description in the Description box, and click the Get the code button at the bottom of the form. Finally, click the Add it to the post! button. The plug-in creates the HTML link and inserts it into the post for you, as shown in Figure 15-11. The plug-in window stays open, so you can select another image to insert. When you have finished inserting images, close the window.

The plug-in allows you to directly upload images, too. You can create folders and navigate to them when selecting images. This makes it much easier to organize your images. If your version of PHP supports it, the plug-in can also create thumbnails of your images as you upload them. It prefixes the full-size image name with an underscore (_) to recognize them. If a thumbnail is detected, you get an option to create a link to the full-size image with the thumbnail as the link. Additionally, the plug-in allows you to delete images.

You can see why the IImage Browser plug-in is a great enhancement to the default WordPress behavior and is highly recommended.

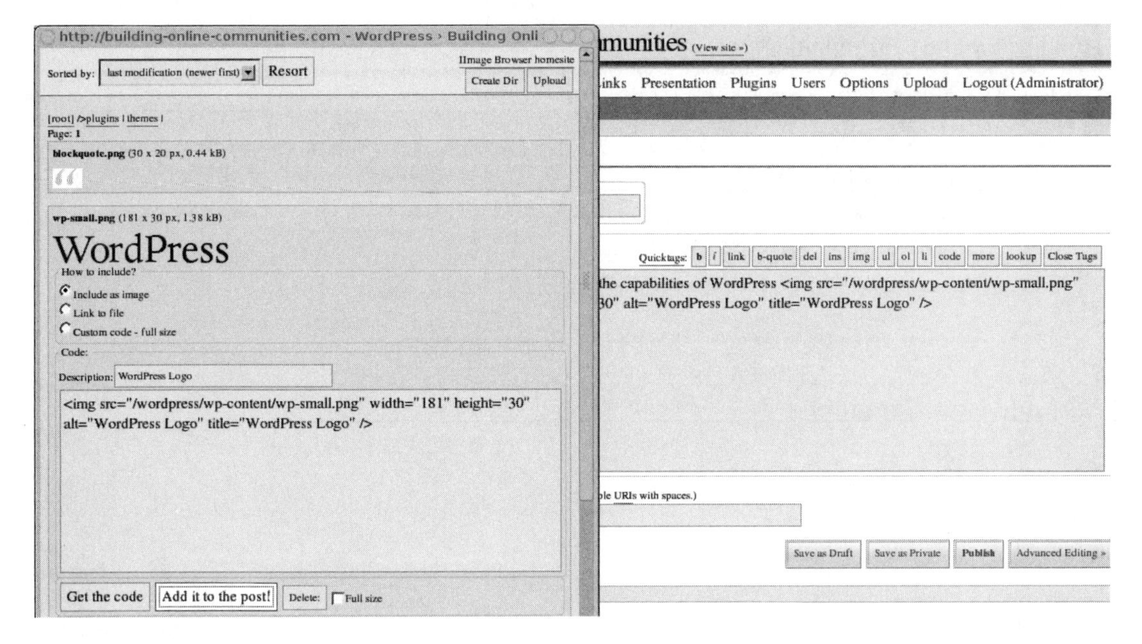

Figure 15-11. *Image code inserted into a post*

■ **Tip** An IImage Browser version in beta replaces the link in the corner with a button under the quicktag buttons. Check the `http://fredfred.net/skriker/index.php/iimage-browser` site to see when that version will be ready for release.

Managing Categories

Categories are a great way to help people understand the content on your site. They allow you to classify your posts and serve to group together posts with similar content. Categories in WordPress can also be hierarchical.

A well-thought-out set of categories will allow members of your community to find the content they want. A post generally displays which categories it is associated with. This helps your reader make a quick judgment about reading a particular article. It is worth spending some time thinking about which categories best describe the intended content of your site.

You manage categories from the Manage Categories page (no surprises there). Click Manage, then Categories, and you will be presented with a page that allows you to edit existing categories, create new ones, and delete old ones, as shown in Figure 15-12.

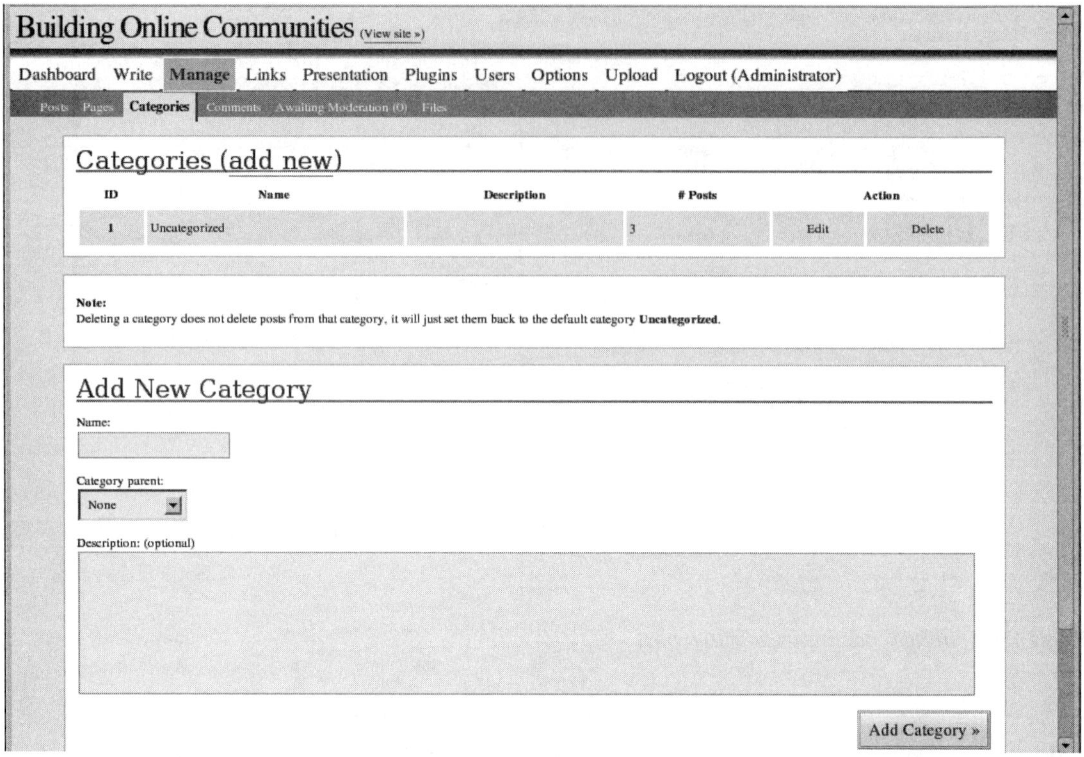

Figure 15-12. *Manage categories from this page.*

Adding a New Category

Adding a category is simple: type in the new category name into the Name field. Category names must be unique, but other than that, there are no restrictions. You should keep your category names relatively short and descriptive.

Consider how the categories are displayed on the default template. It displays the categories a post is in with the text "Posted in *x*," where *x* is the category name. Thus, category names like Hints and Tips, Technology, and Questions work well.

You can add a description to each category, too. This description can be displayed on your blog, if the theme you use supports that. For instance, the description may appear as a tool tip when you hover your mouse over a link to the category, as shown in Figure 15-13.

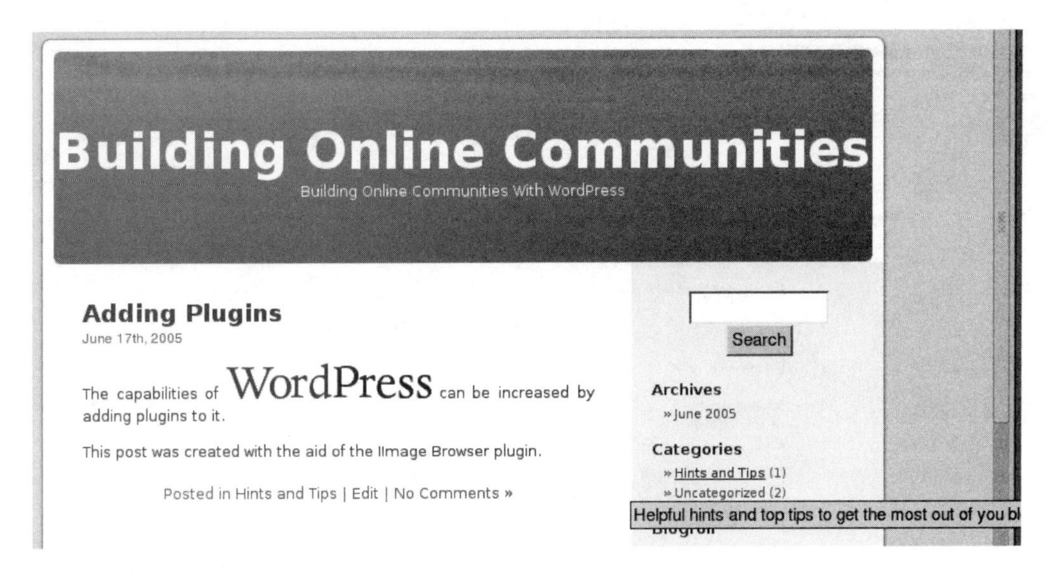

Figure 15-13. *Category descriptions can be displayed on your blog.*

Adding Subcategories

You can add new categories as subcategories of an existing one. This is very useful if your topics lend themselves to this structure. For example, a blog about programming might have a Languages category and subcategories named Object Oriented, Procedural, and Functional. The subcategories can have sub-subcategories. For example, the Object Oriented category could be further subdivided with Java, SmallTalk, and Ruby sub-subcategories, as shown in Figure 15-14.

Each of your posts can be assigned one or more categories. Most themes will display the categories for each post. Most themes also provide a list of all the categories used on your blog. Each of these different ways of listing the categories also usually includes a link to display all the posts in a category.

When you display a list of all the posts in a particular category, the posts assigned subcategories of that categories are also displayed. So, continuing with the Language category example, displaying the Object Oriented category should also display entries in the Java, SmallTalk, and Ruby subcategories.

■ **Note** If you don't have any posts assigned to a particular category, that category doesn't normally appear in the listings.

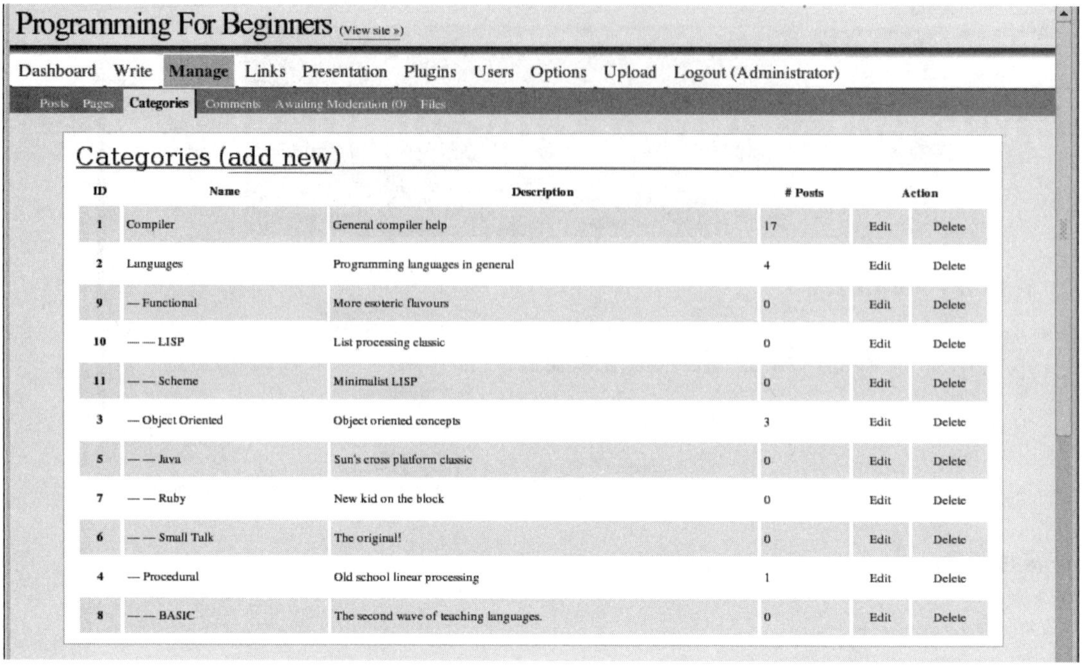

Programming For Beginners (View site »)

Dashboard Write Manage Links Presentation Plugins Users Options Upload Logout (Administrator)

Posts Pages Categories Comments Awaiting Moderation (0) Files

Categories (add new)

ID	Name	Description	# Posts	Action	
1	Compiler	General compiler help	17	Edit	Delete
2	Languages	Programming languages in general	4	Edit	Delete
9	— Functional	More esoteric flavours	0	Edit	Delete
10	— — LISP	List processing classic	0	Edit	Delete
11	— — Scheme	Minimalist LISP	0	Edit	Delete
3	— Object Oriented	Object oriented concepts	3	Edit	Delete
5	— — Java	Sun's cross platform classic	0	Edit	Delete
7	— — Ruby	New kid on the block	0	Edit	Delete
6	— — Small Talk	The original!	0	Edit	Delete
4	— Procedural	Old school linear processing	1	Edit	Delete
8	— — BASIC	The second wave of teaching languages.	0	Edit	Delete

Figure 15-14. *Hierarchical categories*

Deleting Categories

Deleting a category is as simple as clicking the *Delete* link to the right of the listing on the Manage Categories page. The link turns bright red as you hover over it to remind you that this is an irreversible change. If you do click it, a dialog box pops up to remind you of this fact and to give you a chance to cancel if you change your mind. The category will be deleted, but the posts will not be removed. They will be assigned to the default category. (Although it appears to let you try, you can't delete the default category.)

■ **Note** If you do delete a category and then change your mind, and if you had a lot of posts assigned to it, you will have a tedious job of reassigning those posts. It would be nice if someone wrote a plug-in to allow mass assignment of categories to posts.

Managing Comments

I touched on comments, comment spam, and comment notifications in Chapter 14. In this chapter, I will take you through the management of comments with WordPress. Three main pages allow you to manage comments on your blog: the Manage Comments page, the Comment Moderation page, and one mode of the Manage Posts page. Finally, the public face of your blog (with the default theme) also has a link to allow you to manage comments.

Viewing, Editing, and Deleting Comments

If you click the Manage and then Comments, you will get to the Manage Comments page. In the example shown in Figure 15-15, you can see three comments. The middle one (from Fred Flintstone) is a lighter gray than the others. This is because that comment hasn't been approved yet.

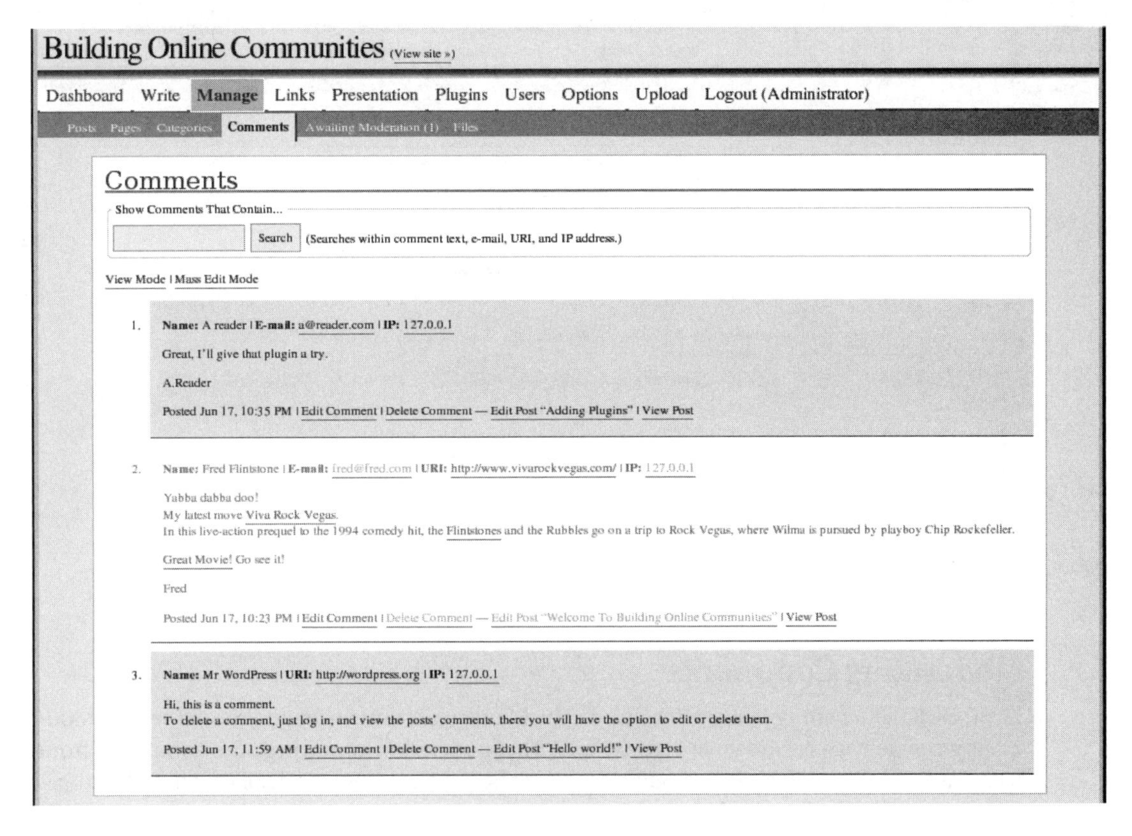

Figure 15-15. *Managing comments*

From the Manage Comments page, you can click the links associated with each comment to do the following:

- Edit a comment. Perhaps someone has used inappropriate language, or they have mistyped a URI.
- Delete a comment. When you select to delete a comment, a message pops up to give you the chance to confirm or cancel the deletion.
- Edit the post to which this is a comment. This is handy if someone points out a mistake of yours or gives some additional information worth adding to your post.
- View the post in its entirety.

The Manage Comments page also has a *Mass Edit Mode* link, which you can click to switch to a less detailed view. This displays a list of comments 20 at a time, as shown in Figure 15-16. In this mode, you can select comments en masse and delete them all in one go. This is less useful than it used to be now that comment spam detection is much improved. To exit from this mode, click the *View Mode* link.

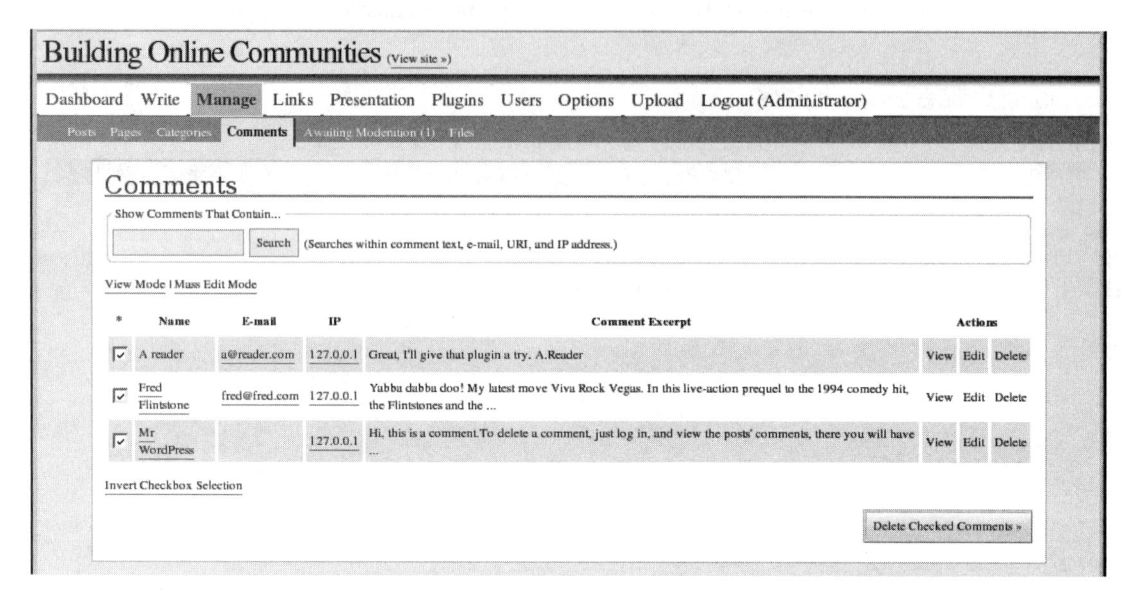

Figure 15-16. *Mass Edit mode*

Moderating Comments

If you click the *Awaiting Moderation* link on the Manage Comments page, you will see the Moderation Queue page, as shown in Figure 15-17. The moderation queue includes comments from users, as well as TrackBack and Pingback comments. Each comment is displayed in full, along with four radio buttons as follows:

- The Approve option means that the comment will be approved and appear on the blog as normal.
- The Spam option marks the comment as spam and removes it from the queue.
- The Delete option deletes the comment from the database.
- The Defer until later option (which is selected by default) makes no change to the status of the comment.

At the bottom of the list is a set of links to set the radio buttons for all the comments. This will change any that you might have already set. Finally, clicking the Moderate Comments button will perform the requested actions, and then display a summary of the actions taken (for example, "3 comments deleted, 2 comments marked as spam, 1 comment unchanged").

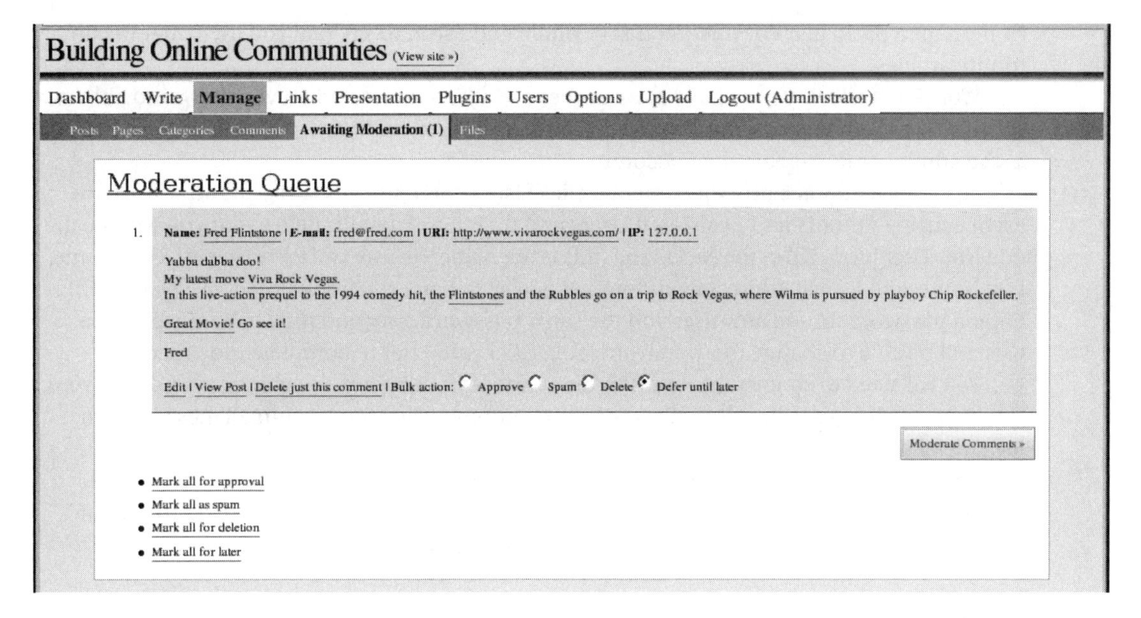

Figure 15-17. *Comment moderation queue*

■ **Note** The comments marked as spam are not deleted from the database. Furthermore, WordPress has no way to show you those comments marked as spam. The thinking behind this is that at some point, someone will create a spam analysis plug-in that could use the comments marked as spam to better detect future spam comments, much as several e-mail filters do now. So far, no one has created that plug-in. However, a good number of WordPress plug-ins are designed to help you combat comment spam with varying levels of effectiveness. Also, an article on the WordPress Codex discusses a number of methods for combating comment spam (see `http://codex.wordpress.org/Combating_Comment_Spam` for details).

Providing Comment Feeds

Comments are available to your readers as feeds. There is a feed for the most recent comments on your blog, as well the latest comments from an individual post. If you use the default theme, the link to the comment feed is provided in the footer of every page.

If you have a hot topic that generates a lot of comments, comment feeds are another great way to keep your readers involved. They can monitor the conversation with any of a number of feed readers and aggregators, without needing to remember to check your site regularly.

Adding Multiple Authors

You may want to invite other authors to contribute to your blog. Maybe you know people in your specific community (virtual or otherwise) who have interesting things to say. Maybe you want someone to share the load of keeping up with all that is happening in your field.

Or perhaps a particular commenter has so much good stuff to say that you invite her to contribute articles.

WordPress allows you to have any number of authors registered on your blog and able to contribute to your community. You can either allow the new authors to register themselves or, as the administrator, create their accounts.

To create a new account for someone click Users, then Authors & Users. You will see the list of existing Authors and Registered Users and their basic details. Below that you will see the Add New User form. Fill in the Nickname (this is the name the user will use to log in), First Name, Last Name, and E-mail Address fields for your new user. You can optionally add a web site URL. Enter a password for the new user and the same password a second time to confirm it. The user will be able to change this password later. Click Add User to complete the process.

You will need to contact the new user directly to let him know his login name and password. Unlike with self-registration, WordPress does not automatically send an e-mail message with login details.

Your new user's details will now be listed under Registered Users. Users listed there are registered on your blog, but cannot post stories. Click *Promote* to promote a user to Author status. With Author status, users can create new posts and edit their existing ones.

Allowing Self-Registering Users

If you want users to be able register themselves on your blog, there is an option on the General Options page to control this. Click Options, and on the General Options page, check the Anyone can register check box for the Membership setting. This will enable the registration page and also enable the *Register* link on the default theme. Clicking the *Register* link on the blog main page will take visitors to the registration form. They can enter a username and e-mail address. Clicking the Register button causes an e-mail to be sent to them with a randomly generated password. Figure 15-18 shows an example of a user named George registering for a blog.

■ **Note** If you are logged in to your blog, you won't see the *Register* link. It appears only for visitors who are not logged in.

When George receives his e-mail, he can click the *Login* link (one is also sent in the e-mail) and log in. He will be presented with the user profile page (discussed in the previous chapter), where he can fill in his details and change his password to something he can remember.

At this point, George can do little else. By default, WordPress does not allow newly registered users to post on the blog. As administrator, you need to give him the necessary user permissions.

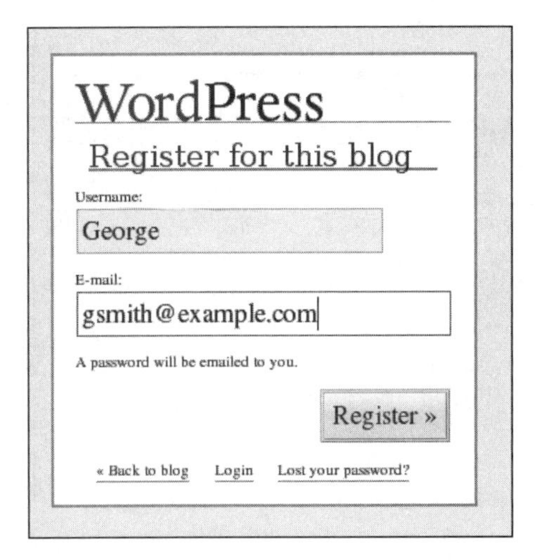

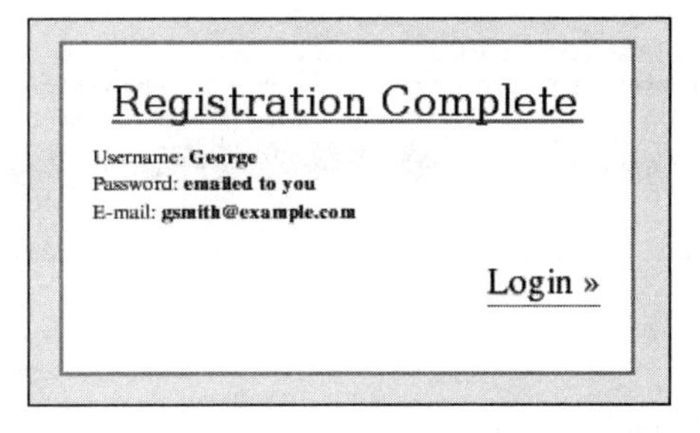

Figure 15-18. *The self-registration process*

Assigning User Permissions

Continuing with the new author George, when George registered, an e-mail message was also sent to you, as the administrator, informing you of the new registration. You need to log in to your blog and promote the new user George to allow him to post stories. Click Users along the top of the administration page, and then click Authors & Users. You will see the lists of authors and registered users, as shown in Figure 15-19. Authors are registered users who have permission to create posts. Registered users are registered but not able to create any posts.

■ **Note** If you have the "Users must be registered and logged in to comment" option turned on, those users who are registered can log in and comment, even if they haven't been promoted. You can find this setting on the General Options page in the Membership section.

Click the Promote button to promote George to level 1. He will then become an author and be listed in the Authors section (at the top of Figure 15-19). From there, you can promote him further to enable different capabilities, as listed in Table 15-2. For example, a level 2 author sees a different list of drafts than authors at other levels, as shown in Figure 15-20.

■ **Note** When authors have edit and manage privileges, they can manage the posts and links of only users with lower levels.

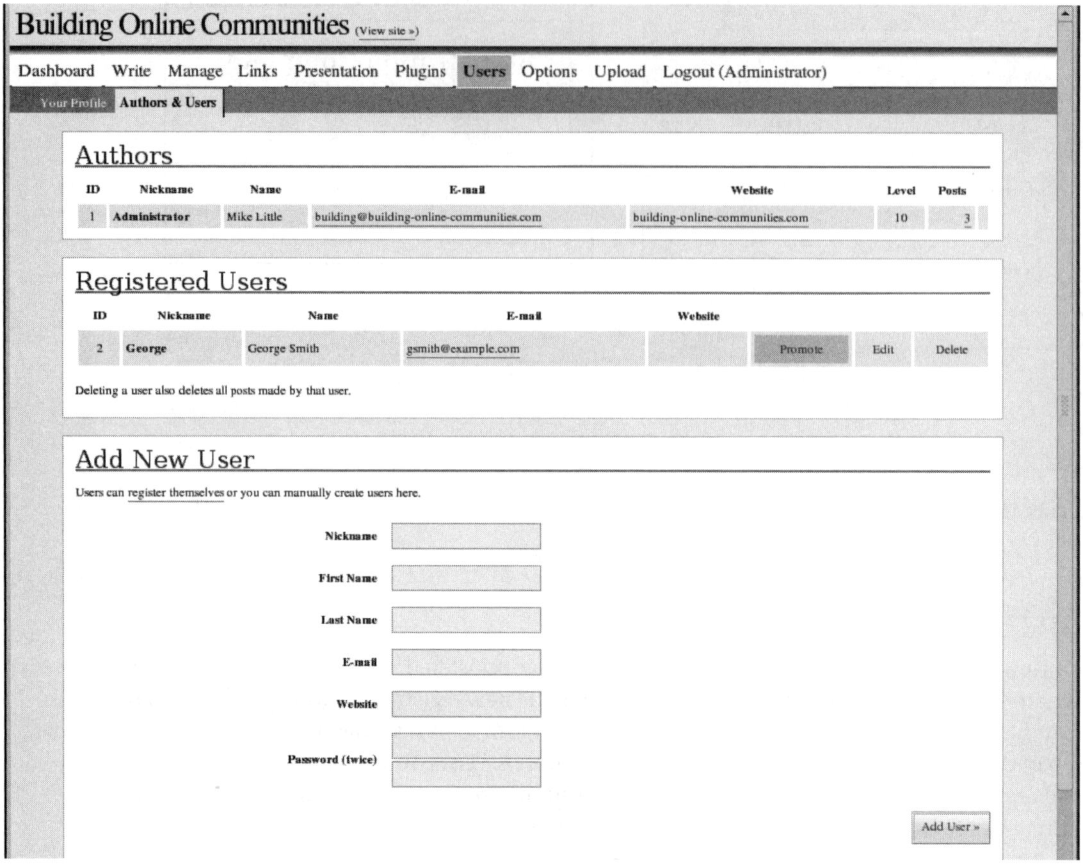

Figure 15-19. *Authors & Users page*

Figure 15-20. *Manage posts from a user level 2 perspective*

Note The next version of WordPress will have a completely overhauled user privileges system based on roles and permissions, rather than levels.

Table 15-2. *User Levels*

Level	Description
Level 1	Authors can create only drafts. They can edit their own drafts, of course. They can see comments including unmoderated ones, but cannot change them. They can delete and edit their own posts, too, even published ones. If they edit a published post, it goes back into draft mode and needs to be approved again.
Level 2	Authors can publish their own posts, as well as edit and publish the drafts of level 1 authors.
Level 3	Brings no extra privileges, other than the ability to edit and publish the posts of authors with levels 2 and 1.
Level 4	Authors can additionally manage categories and moderate comments.
Level 5	Authors can create pages, create and manage links (topics covered in the next chapter), and see and edit the details of users with lower levels.
Level 6	Authors can upload files, though this is configurable in the options. They can also change options at this level.
Level 7	By default, brings no extra privileges.
Level 8	Authors can manage the themes and plug-ins.
Level 9	Authors can manage the posts and links of level 8 users. This level brings no other extra privileges.
Level 10	The author has the same privileges as level 9, but WordPress allows only one user to be level 10.

As a level 1 author, George can create draft posts only. For some communities, this is a great feature. It allows you to have many contributing authors, but not run the risk of them publishing unacceptable posts on your blog. You can have a number of editors who can edit and approve the contributed posts for publication. If you have a wide and varied roster of contributors, this approach can really build your community.

When you have multiple authors, you can provide links to list all the posts by an individual author. Unfortunately, neither of the themes provided with WordPress has this functionality built in.

Adding Blog Pages with RSS Feeds

The IImage Browser plug-in introduced earlier in this chapter adds some great functionality to the administration interface. Now you'll install another plug-in, WordPress RSS Link List, created by Bill Rawlinson, which gives you something extra for your readers. This plug-in allows you to include RSS feeds on your blog. These aren't the RSS feeds you provide on your blog, but instead incorporate someone else's RSS feed into your blog. This is another great way to get fresh content on your blog.

The WordPress RSS Link List plug-in has two ways of working. The first is as a template function you can call in your theme template files. I'll show you how to do that in the next chapter. The other way this plug-in works is to allow you to incorporate an RSS feed in one of your posts. While this sounds like a good idea, I think it makes less sense once a post becomes old and moves off the front page of your blog. However, WordPress allows you to create pages for your blog, and this plug-in also works for pages. These are often described as "static" pages to distinguish them from normal blog posts, but as you'll see, they are far from static. Here, I'll show you how to create WordPress pages and then use this plug-in to add RSS feeds. But first, you need to install the plug-in.

Installing and Activating the RSS Link List Plug-In

Download the plug-in from the author's site at `http://rawlinson.us/blog/index.php?p=212`. It comes as a zip file. Extract it onto your local hard drive. Upload the file `lastRSS.php` to the `wpcontent` folder, and the file `rssLinkList.php` to the `wpcontent/plugins` folder.

Bill also recommends creating a new folder to allow the plug-in to cache the external RSS content. Create the folder `wpcontent/rssCache` and set the permissions so that the web server process can create and write to files in that folder. The permissions need to be the same as the `wp-content` folder. See Chapter 14 for details on setting permissions.

Go to the Plugins Management page (see Figure 15-8), as described earlier in the chapter, and activate the plug-in. That's all there is to it. There are some configuration options for this plug-in, but I'll cover those in the next chapter.

Creating a Page

WordPress pages offer a way to create more lasting content on your blog. They are often used for "About" pages, legal or copyright pages, and the like. You can also use them for more in-depth articles particular to your subject, or perhaps a comprehensive overview of a particular topic.

Internally, WordPress implements its pages as a special kind of post. The main differences from normal posts are that categories don't apply to pages, and pages are excluded from the normal chronological archive, category, and author lists. Pages can be organized hierarchically, and they can have their own templates within a theme.

To create a page, click the Write, then Write Page. The Write Page page, shown in Figure 15-21, is similar to the Write Post page. You can enter a title for the page, specify whether you want comments and pings, and password-protect the page. You can use the quicktag buttons, just as you can for a post. The Page Parent drop-down list allows you to make your page hierarchical. If you specify Main Page (no parent), the default, your page will be a top-level page. If you have already created pages, they will be in the drop-down list, so that you can specify one of them as the parent of your new page.

Below the main edit area are some more new fields:

Page Template: This allows you to select the template for this page. A WordPress theme can contain special template files that are usable for specific pages. If your currently selected theme has any templates defined, you will be able select one from the drop-down list. If your theme does not have templates, the list won't be available.

Page slug: This is similar to the post slug and is detailed in the "Improving Search Engine Visibility" section later in the chapter.

Page owner: This is a drop-down list for the page owner. If you have sufficient privileges, you can assign the ownership of a page to someone else or claim ownership of a page.

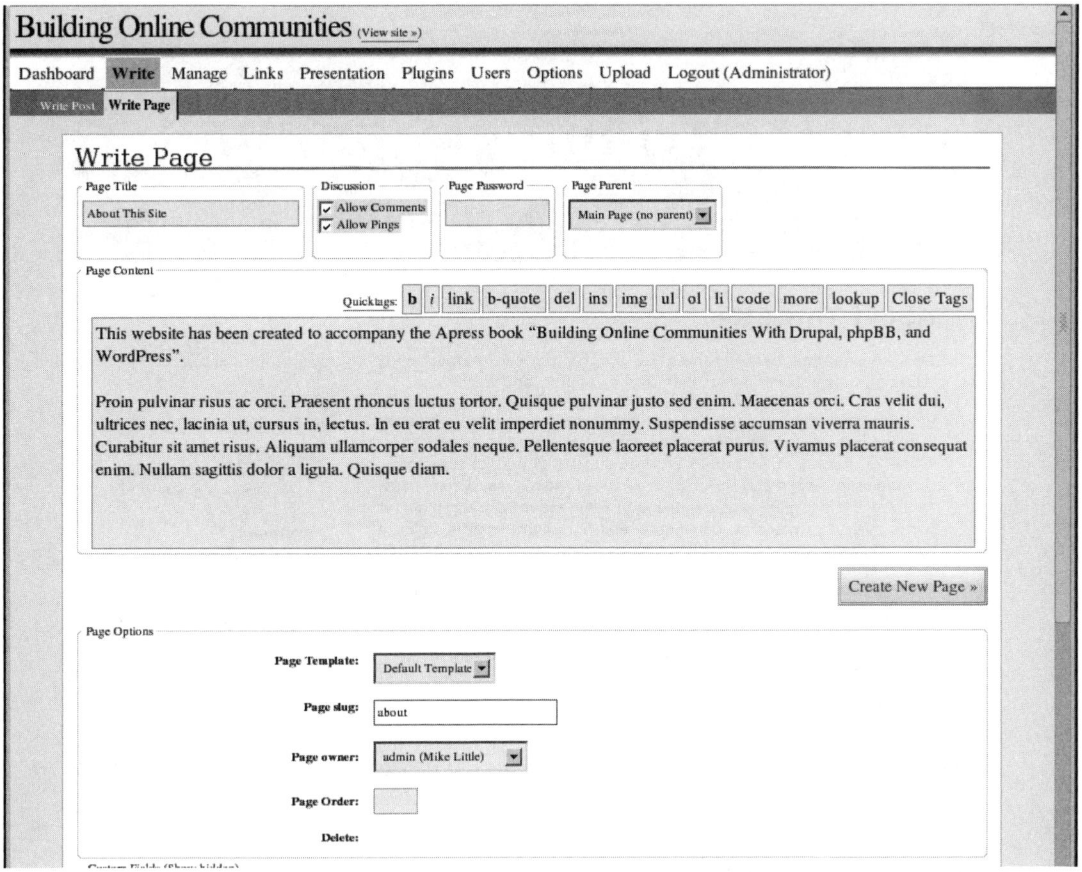

Figure 15-21. *Write Page page*

Page Order: This allows you to specify the listing order of your pages. The default theme will list all your pages on your blog. By default, it lists them in alphabetical order, preserving the hierarchy if there is one. If this is not suitable, you may specify the sort order of pages on the same level.

When you have finished setting up your page, click the Create New Page button, and your page will be created. Switch over to view your blog to see the result. In Figure 15-22, I have added some more pages to illustrate the listing in the sidebar. Compare the display of the page with the display of postings in Figure 15-13.

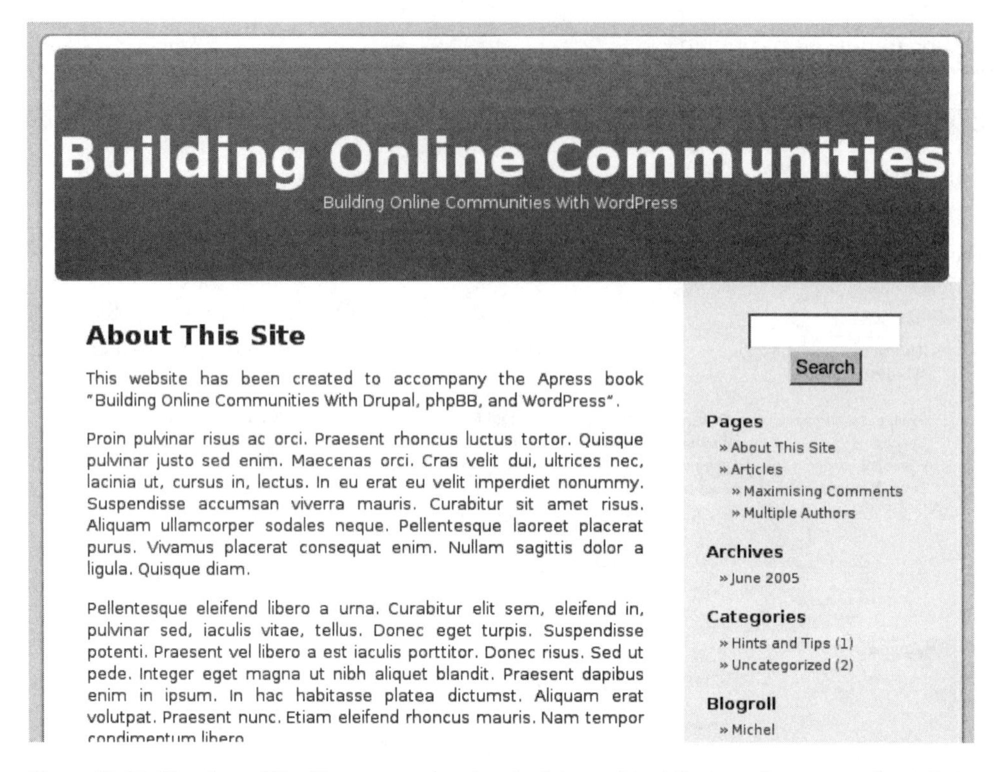

Figure 15-22. *Viewing a WordPress page (notice the hierarchical listing of pages on the right)*

Using the RSS Link List Plug-In on a Page

To use the RSS Link List plug-in on your page, you need to edit the page. Return to your administration pages and click Manage, then Pages. The Page Management page appears, as shown in Figure 15-23. From here, you can view, edit, and delete pages, as well as create new pages.

Click the *Edit* link to the right of the page you just created. You need to add in a special tag to the text of the page. This tag will invoke one of the functions in the plug-in. Insert the following text into the page.

```
You can even incorporate live RSS feeds into your pages like this one from➥
del.icio.us, the social bookmarking site:
<ul>
<!--rss:http://del.icio.us/rss/tag/community+online+blogging-->
</ul>
```

Save the page and view the page on your blog. You should get something similar to Figure 15-24. Wow! Where did that come from?

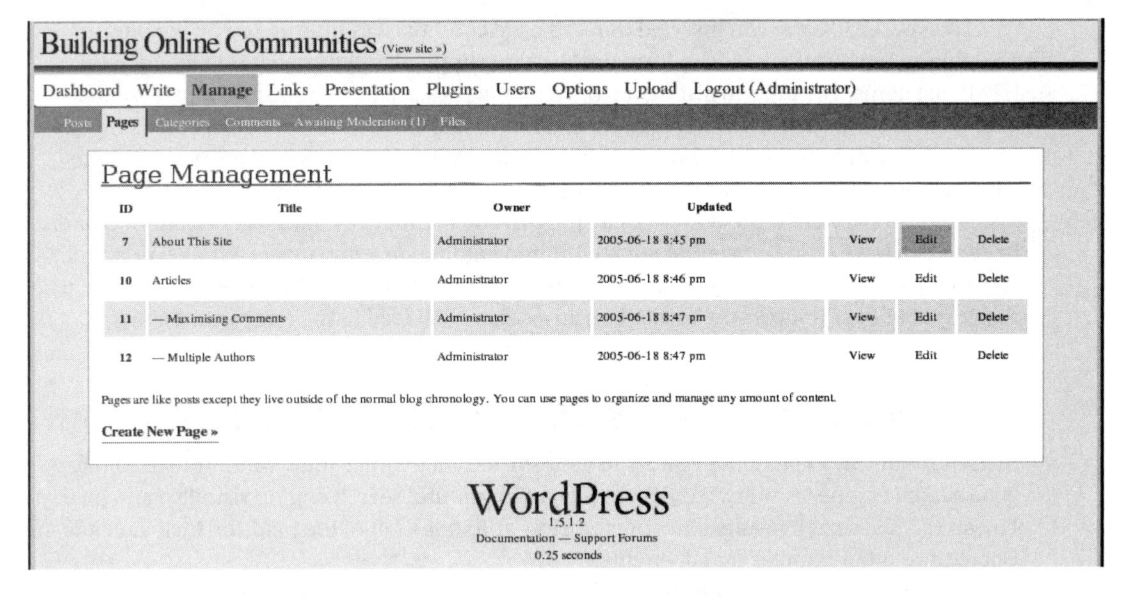

Figure 15-23. *Page Management page*

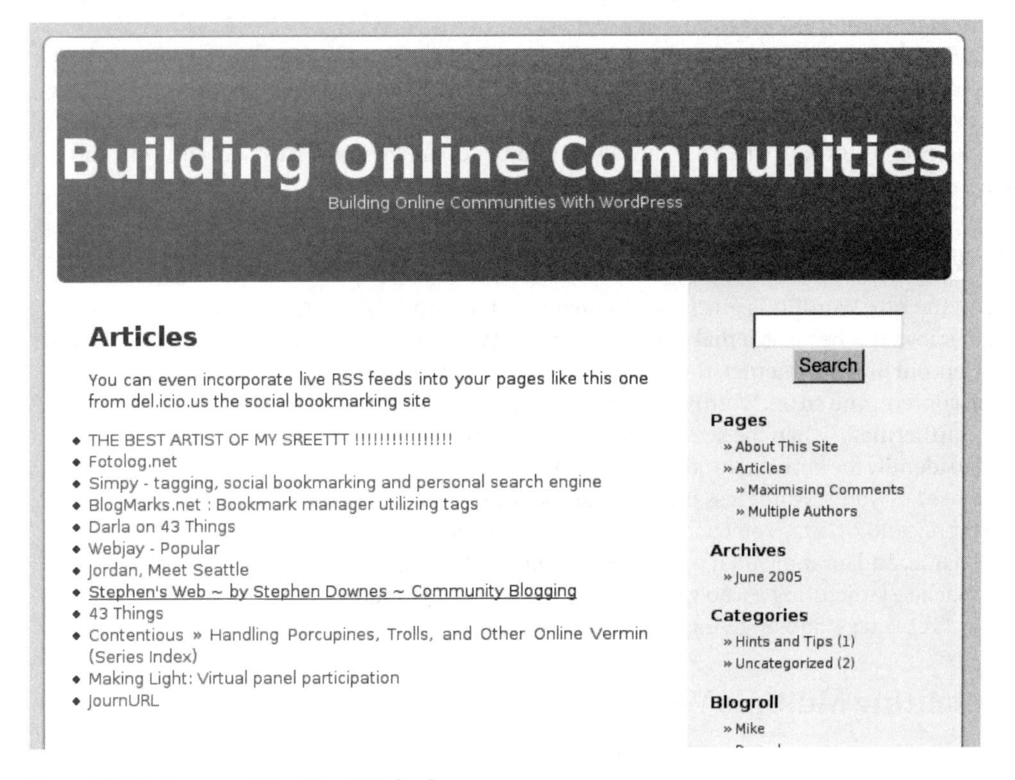

Figure 15-24. *A page with a live RSS feed*

The special RSS tag you inserted into the page contents was interpreted by the plug-in. The plug-in fetched the RSS feed from the URI you supplied and turned it into a bunch of HTML list items. The plug-in also saved the result in the `wpcontent/rssCache` folder you created earlier. It will use the saved result for a configurable amount of time before checking for new content from the feed. Without the cache, it would fetch the RSS feed *every single time* your page is requested. You would soon find yourself banned from the site if you did that.

Used appropriately, the RSS Link List plug-in could enhance your blog. Perhaps it could be used in a page describing other sources of information on your subject. Whenever people visit that page, they will see the latest news from those sources included right on the page. In the next chapter, I'll show you how to add an external RSS feed to the template of a theme.

Improving Your Site's Search Engine Visibility

An important way to get more visitors to your site and help build your community is to have good search engine visibility. WordPress is great for natural search engine visibility, and by that I mean the real search results that appear below and to the left of the paid-for-inclusion ads in Google and other popular search engines.

Getting search engine optimization for free—right out of the box—is a great bonus when you're trying to build an online community. Getting good search engine ranking—that is, getting your site higher up in the search results when people look for web sites on your subject—is essential to guiding visitors to your site.

WordPress helps you get good search engine ranking in a number of ways: by constructing structured, semantic, standards-compliant HTML; by providing multiple views of your content; and by creating search-engine-friendly permalinks. But that's not all there is to improving search engine visibility for your site. There are also a number of things that *you* can do with your content to help your site get good search engine ranking.

Providing Semantic, Standards-Compliant Content

Out of the box, WordPress gives you a semantic, standards-compliant web site. The search engines love this because it makes their job easier. When search engines send their spiders and crawlers out into the Internet, they often encounter barriers to navigating a site: JavaScript links, Flash content, and so on. WordPress blogs don't have these barriers to navigation.

Furthermore, when the search engines analyze the content of the pages they have gathered to identify the keywords and the keyword density, and determine the ranking of your pages for those keywords, WordPress makes it easy for them. WordPress uses the name of your blog in `<title>` and `<h1>` tags on each page. For category pages, the `<title>` also contains the category name, and for individual post pages, the post title is also in there. This common sense approach to structuring a web site achieves search engine optimization by publishing unique page `<title>` tags, and by giving meaning and importance to keywords.

Presenting Multiple Views

When the search engine crawls through your category pages, it gets the excerpt from your posts, rather than the full content. If you have provided brief summaries of your posts for the excerpts, as I mentioned earlier in this chapter, this gives a high keyword density on your pages. This is almost like giving your posts a second chance at being listed. The search engine sees a condensed view of your posts in each category.

Generating Search-Engine-Friendly Permalinks

WordPress allows you to generate permalinks (permanent URIs) on your blog, which appear as though each of your posts is an individual static page on your site, rather than the dynamic output of a database-driven web site. Instead of a URI to one of your stories looking like `http://example.com/?p=29`, WordPress can use something like this link:

```
http://example.com/card-games/how-to-win-at-poker/
```

Because this type of URI is already loaded with your keywords, it has an immediate advantage over the `?p=29` version. It also is more readable to your human visitors. It's easier for them to remember the link or to read it out over the phone.

To configure the structure of your permalink, from the administration pages, click Options, then Permalinks. The Edit Permalink Structure page allows you to configure the structure of your permalink URIs, as shown in Figure 15-25.

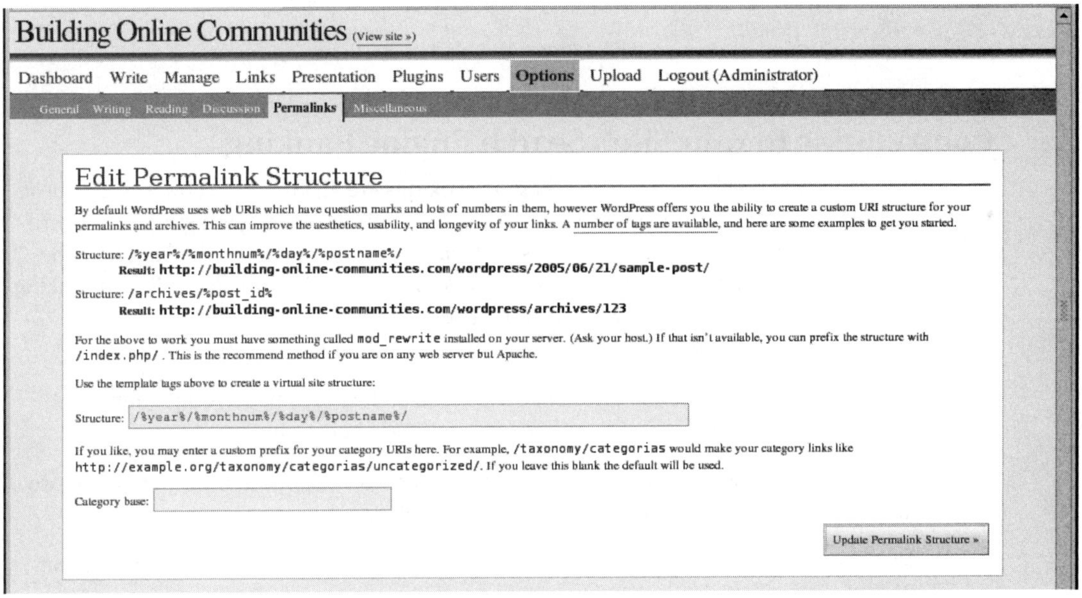

Figure 15-25. *Editing your permalink structure*

Choose a permalink structure that you feel comfortable with and that fits your blog. The suggestions made by WordPress work well, especially the following structure:

```
/%year%/%monthnum%/%day%/%postname%/
```

If your site has mostly chronological entries, this format makes lots of sense. As a bonus, these URLs truncate, too, which means that someone visiting a URL containing just the year and month will receive all posts for that month.

If your site isn't ordered chronologically and has a flat structure, then a permalink structure of `/archives/%postname%` might be more appropriate, but be sure to keep the post titles unique!

These features rely on using Apache as your web server and having a feature of Apache called `mod_rewrite` enabled on your site. If you don't have `mod_rewrite` or Apache, you can put a filename in the URL, like this:

```
/index.php/%year%/%monthnum%/%day%/%postname%/
```

and it will still work under some circumstances. You can also set up a prefix for your category links; `/topic/` is a reasonable alternative.

Figure 15-26 shows some examples of the type of URIs you can generate.

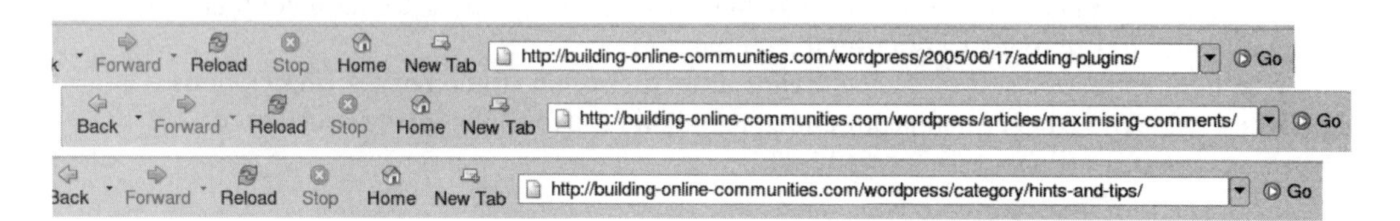

Figure 15-26. *Search-engine-friendly URIs*

Contributing to Your Site's Search Engine Ranking

The things you can do to help your search engine rankings are all about the content. The best and most important advice I can give you is to write well. By sticking to your subject and writing relatively short or medium-length articles that stay on topic, written in the language the community uses, you will not only keep your readers interested, but you also will gain ranking for the very keywords your readers will use in their searches.

Still you should bear in mind what measures are important to the search engines:

- *Keyword density* refers to the ratio of keywords to all text on a page. A high density would indicate the bad practice of *keyword stuffing* is being employed.
- *Keyword proximity* refers to how close keywords are to each other. If they are too close, that would again suggest keyword stuffing is being employed.
- *Keyword prominence* refers to how close keywords are to the start of the page, indicating a measure of the keyword's importance.
- *Inbound links* are links pointing to the page from an external web site, indicating a measure of the page's popularity.

Each search engine has its own recipe for what its administrators believe is the right mixture of the keyword and link measures. However, here are a few simple guidelines that will help you with all search engine ranking algorithms:

- Write keywords into the `<title>` tag.
- Move keywords to the start of the `<title>` tag.

- Use a different <title> tag for each page.
- Structure each page using correct HTML markup (such as <h1>, <h2>, and so on) and write keywords into those tags.
- Write keywords closer to the start of the page.

WordPress is designed to help you achieve the goal of following these guidelines, but what it can't help you with is choosing the keywords and writing compelling posts that someone seeing your web site in a search engine results list would be interested in reading. Write knowledgeably about your subject in a natural and interesting way. Otherwise, visitors may be able to find you with a search engine, but then see that you don't have anything interesting to say. Providing the content is up to you!

Summary

This chapter showed you how to write posts using WordPress's basic tools, as well as how to use advanced editing to fine-tune individual posts. You also learned how to add images to your posts, enable multiple trusted content authors to provide a collaborative effort in generating a more rewarding reading experience, create WordPress pages, and improve your site's search engine visibility. Along the way, you installed two plug-ins to ease administration and enhance the richness of your content.

The next chapter covers the exciting topic of themes—what they are and how to install a ready-made theme. Better still, I'll show you how to modify a theme to suit your blog and offer a unique personalized touch.

CHAPTER 16

Changing the Look of Your Blog

This chapter is about the reader's view of your blog. It is about what your visitors see and how they interact with your blog. That interaction, or experience, is important in ensuring your visitors get the most from your site. If the experience is positive—they find what they want, and they can interact easily and successfully—then they will want to come back. A good design will drive that experience.

It is also about the aesthetic experience, too. The look of your blog, especially the first page, must either fit the users' expectations or surprise them in a positive, pleasing way. If you and your community are discussing fan fiction for a Gothic TV horror show, they want a dark, slightly sinister, experience. If you are all about craft fun for preschool children, you'll want to present a bright, airy, fun face to your readers (but not childish, since the parents are your audience).

The face of your blog—its outward appearance—is provided by the *theme* in use on your blog. In this chapter, you'll learn how to activate themes in WordPress, find and install new themes, and modify themes. But first, let's start with the purpose of your theme.

Using Themes to Communicate with Your Audience

How do we communicate? Let me answer that question with another question. Have you ever had a phone conversation with a person speaking in a monotone voice? If so, you'll understand that it's not very engaging. You might have even found yourself overemphasizing your own parts of the dialogue just to compensate!

Compare this situation to a face-to-face discussion with multiple participants. You may have witnessed first hand the complex body language taking place throughout the conversation as people start to use their hands to convey emphasis, or move their body between passive and aggressive stances depending on their activity in the group. Now consider a lecture given by a speaker at a conference. A good presentation is enhanced by visuals, moving parts, and engaging with the audience. It's as if the speaker understands the audience.

■ **Note** Andrew Chak, in his book *Submit Now: Designing Persuasive Websites* (New Riders Press, 2002) defined visitors to web sites in three different ways of moving around the site. *Wanderers* encounter the site with no real purpose in mind, looking for something to catch their attention. *Finders* are looking for something specific or help to find it, even though they don't know exactly what they want. *Learners* are looking for some information to learn something new.

When visitors come to your site, it needs to communicate in more than text alone. WordPress doesn't hinder you in your quest to communicate with visitors. It enables you to configure your blog to add images, define an organization, and use a style for each page consistently if the whole site maintains a single theme or idea, or individually if each page has a theme of its own. A simple example is to define each category to have unique colors and images while maintaining a consistent arrangement on each page. In this chapter, I'll show you how to use WordPress themes to have your blog's appearance achieve this communication with your audience.

A WordPress theme is like a template. WordPress inserts the posts you write, the comments your readers leave, the links you create, and other information into the page *dynamically*. Themes consist of a number of PHP files and a style sheet.

Before going any further, let me assure you that you do not need to understand the internals of how a theme works or how it's managed by WordPress to use it. Adopting a theme can be as simple as uploading it to your blog and enabling it in the Themes tab of the Presentation page. On the other hand, if you want to start investigating a theme with the intention of learning from it or modifying it, you can do that, too. I will show you how to do that later in this chapter, in the "Modifying an Existing Theme" section.

Selecting an Installed Theme

WordPress comes with two built-in themes. The Default theme, based on Michael Heilemann's Kubrick theme, is shown in Figure 16-1. It is a fixed-width layout centered in the browser window.

The other built-in theme is the WordPress Classic theme produced by Dave Shea for WordPress 1.2, shown in Figure 16-2. This is a flexible theme that stretches to fill the width of the browser.

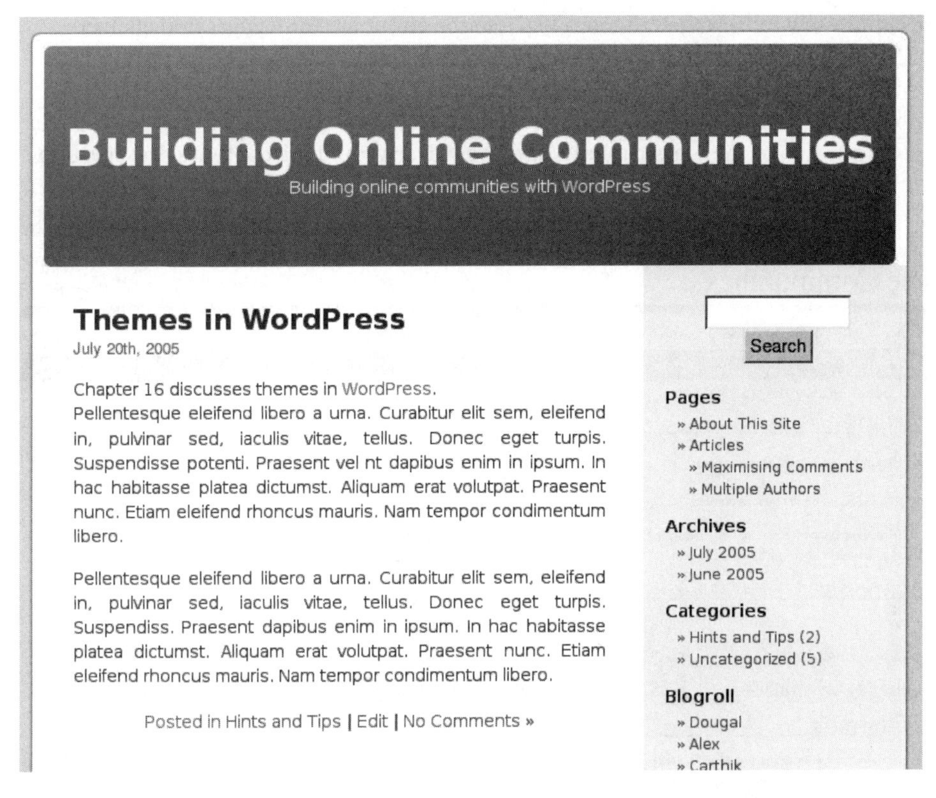

Figure 16-1. *WordPress Default theme*

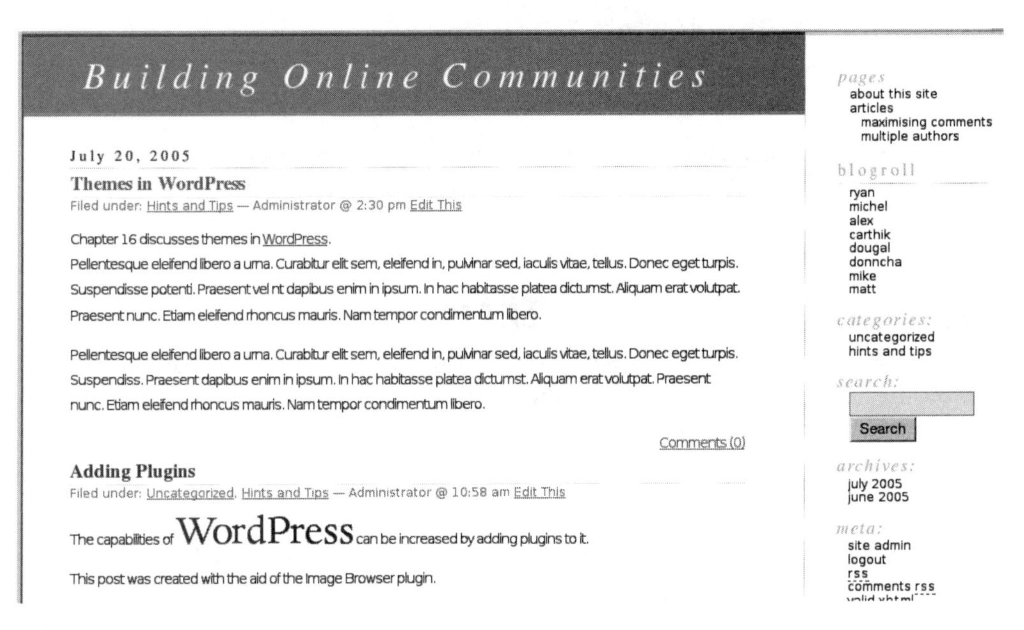

Figure 16-2. *WordPress Classic theme*

To select one of your installed themes, log in to the administration pages and click Presentation. You will be presented with the theme selection page, as shown in Figure 16-3. This page shows you all the installed themes and highlights the currently active theme. Click the Select button of the theme that you wish to use, and then click *View site* at the top of the page. Try that now to switch to the Classic theme, and you will see your blog content's presentation change (see Figure 16-2).

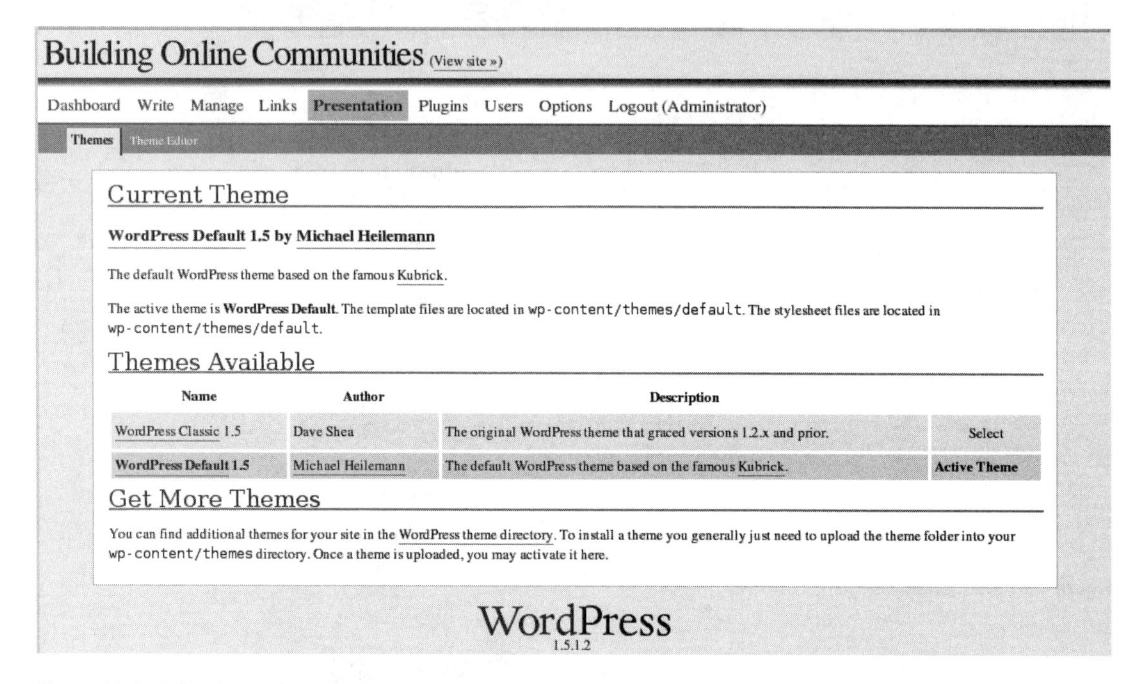

Figure 16-3. *Selecting a theme*

You can see how easy it is to completely change the style of your blog. Both of the built-in themes include a variety of information in their sidebars, such as lists of categories, links to archives, meta-information, and so on.

Adding New WordPress Themes

Adding themes to your WordPress installation is easy. You just download a theme and install it. After the theme is installed, it will be listed on the Themes tab of the Presentation page, where you can activate it, as described in the previous section.

Finding Themes

You can find lists of WordPress themes many places, including the following sites:

- The most comprehensive list at the time of writing is on WordPress' Codex at `http://codex.wordpress.org/Using_Themes/Theme_List`.

- A small selection of themes is highlighted at `http://wordpress.org/extend/themes/`.
- A large collection of themes is available at Alex King's WordPress Themes Competition site (`http://www.alexking.org/index.php?content=software/wordpress/themes.php`). That competition is over now, but all of the entries are still available for viewing and downloading.

In all, currently more than 300 themes are available for download from these sites. Most of them are free to use with no restrictions. Some might require a link back to the designer of the theme. Also, a number of designers will sell you a WordPress theme or design one to your exact specifications—for a fee, of course.

Quite a variety of different styles are available: common two-column layouts with a wide main column for posts and a second narrower column for lists, links, and so on; several three-column themes; some four-columns ones; and a small number of themes with more unusual shapes. The appearance of all these themes covers a wide range—from business-like to just plain weird!

I mentioned earlier that you should style your site to suit the main subject of your blog. Consider the theme shown in Figure 16-4, which is a Franz Ferdinand theme from Francey (`http://francey.org/linkware/15/`), a talented young college student who produces web designs for fun. This is a dark theme in a style suited to a music fan site.

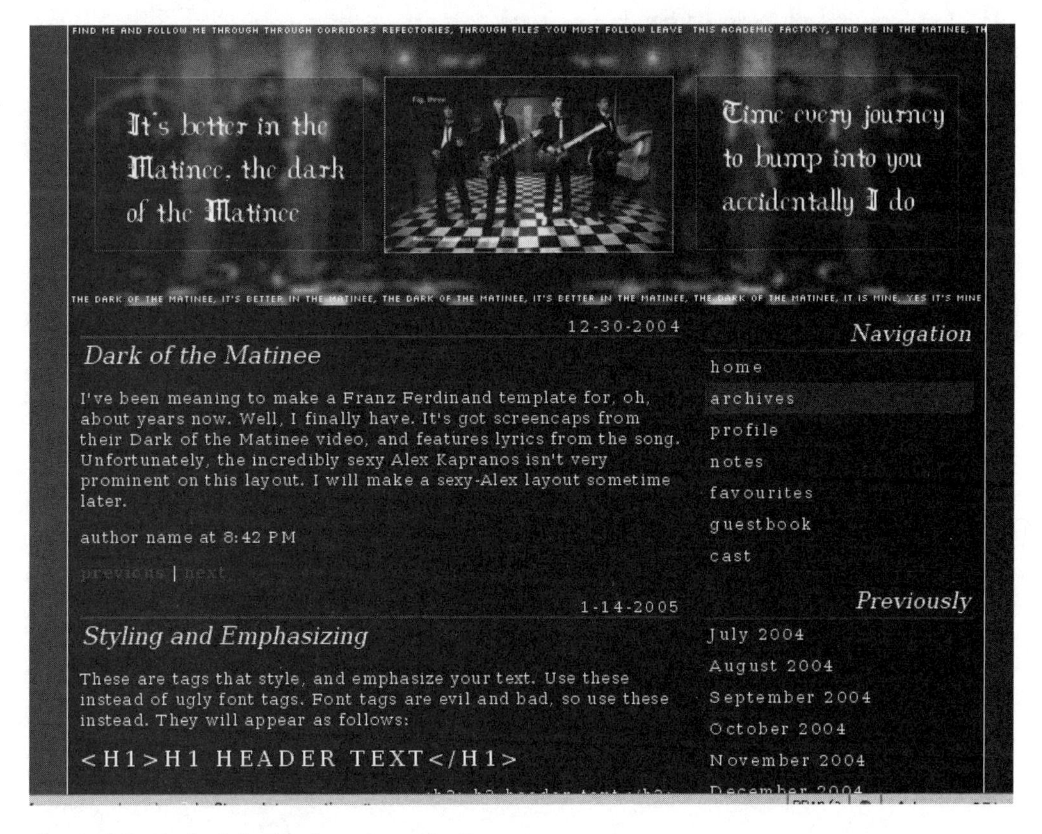

Figure 16-4. *Dark of the Matinee theme by Francey*

As another example, take a look at the Juicy theme by Joni Mueller of Web Jones Designs (`http://webjones.org/`), shown in Figure 16-5, which I spotted on Alex King's site (`http://managedtasks.com/wpthemes/blog/index.php?wptheme=Juicy`). This theme would perhaps be suited to a blog about healthy eating. Its clean, fresh look and pertinent imagery would help keep your readers focused on the subject.

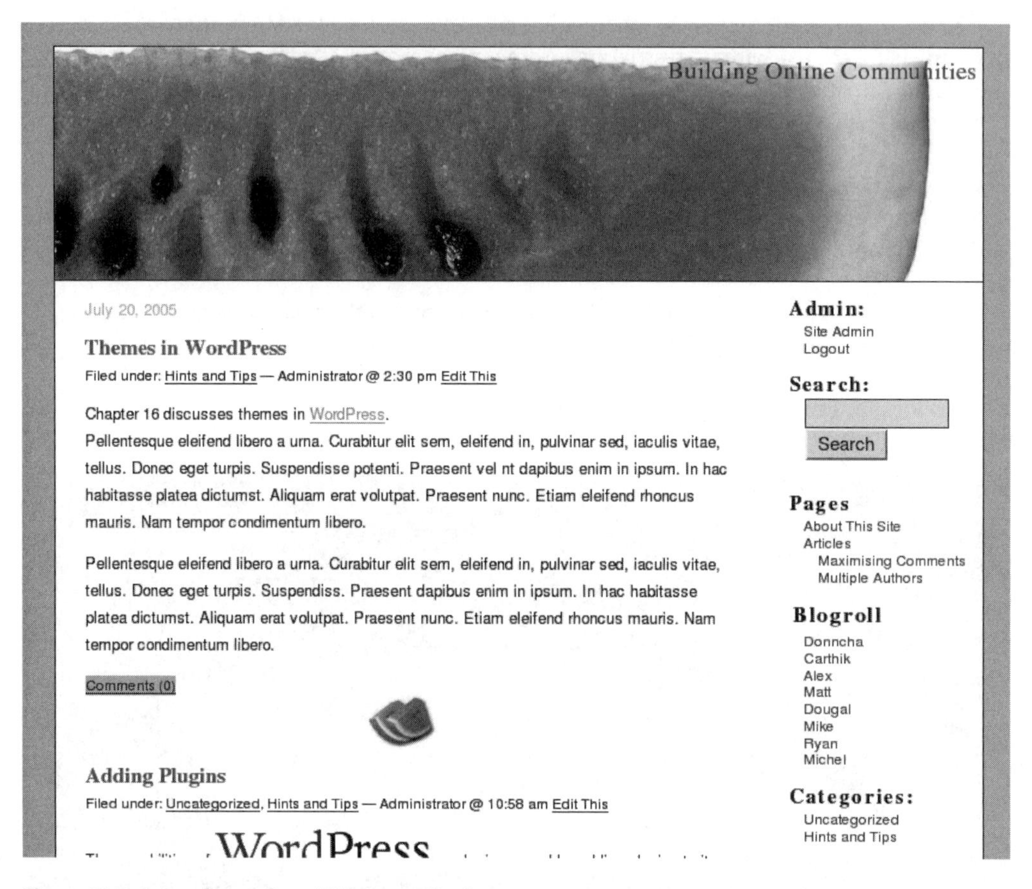

Figure 16-5. *Juicy theme from Web Jones Designs*

■ **Tip** Some designs for older versions of WordPress are available around the Web, particularly WordPress styles for version 1.2, many of which are listed at Alex King's old competition site `http://www.alexking.org/index.php?content=software/wordpress/styles.php`. These are not compatible with the current version 1.5 and need to be converted. A straightforward conversion is fairly painless, and you can find details of that process on the WordPress Codex at `http://codex.wordpress.org/Upgrade_1.2_to_1.5#Upgrading_Old_Templates_-_Easy`.

Installing Themes

Once you have chosen a theme, you need to install it. Here are the steps:

1. Find the download site and download the zip file.
2. Unzip the theme zip file to your local machine.
3. Upload the files to your server, placing them in the `wp-contents/themes` folder.
4. Go to the Presentation administration page of your blog and activate the theme (see Figure 16-3, shown earlier in this chapter).

If a theme requires a particular plug-in that you don't have installed and the theme author hasn't coded it well, you may get an error message (see Figure 16-18 later in this chapter). If this happens, activate another theme that you know does work and check the `readme.txt` file or the theme's documentation page (there should be a link to it on the Presentation admin page). The `readme` file may mention any requirements for the theme or any restrictions on usage. If you still want to use the theme, download and install any required plug-ins before activating the theme again. (Refer to Chapter 15 for instructions on installing plug-ins.)

Modifying an Existing Theme

If you cannot find a theme that matches your requirements, you could create your own, but that's not a trivial task. Rather than create a new theme from scratch, it is often quicker to take an existing theme similar to what you want and modify it, assuming the license allows that. This is the approach I describe here. First, let's look at the components of a theme.

Examining a Theme's Components

A theme consists of two or more files. At the very least, it requires a CSS style sheet named `style.css` and a PHP template named `index.php`. The style sheet must contain a specially formatted comment at the beginning of the file. This comment identifies meta-information about the theme, such as a name and description for the theme, version number, URL for the theme, and so on. Figure 16-6 shows this comment for the WordPress Default theme.

The PHP file contains the HTML and WordPress tags to display your content. This file contains what WordPress calls The Loop, which is a fairly short but important piece of PHP code that is the heart of your blog page. This code displays the title and contents of your blog posts, as well as information related to it. It also displays a count of the comments a post has and a link to the comments themselves.

All the rest of the information displayed on a typical blog page—the blog title, links in a sidebar, archive links, and so on—is peripheral to The Loop. Most of this other information is displayed by calls to template tags.

```
style.css
/*
Theme Name: WordPress Default
Theme URI: http://wordpress.org/
Description: The default WordPress theme based on the famous <a href="http://binarybonsai.com/kubrick/">Kubrick</a>.
Version: 1.5
Author: Michael Heilemann
Author URI: http://binarybonsai.com/

    Kubrick v1.5
     http://binarybonsai.com/kubrick/

    This theme was designed and built by Michael Heilemann,
    whose blog you will find at http://binarybonsai.com/

    The CSS, XHTML and design is released under GPL:
    http://www.opensource.org/licenses/gpl-license.php


    *** REGARDING IMAGES ***
    All CSS that involves the use of images, can be found in the 'index.php' file.
    This is to ease installation inside subdirectories of a server.

    Have fun, and don't be afraid to contact me if you have questions.
*/
```

Figure 16-6. *Stylesheet meta-information*

Template tags are small pieces of PHP code (typically one line of code) placed in your template. These tags do a variety of work. Here are just a few examples of what template tags can do:

- List the categories in your blog. This list includes links to make your blog display all the posts in each particular category.
- List your archives by month, by week, or individually.
- Create a calendar on your page, complete with links to stories for each day and links to move the visitor backwards and forwards through the history of your blog postings.
- Change the title of your web page based on the current story or current category.

All these template tags produce XHTML, not colors, borders, or columns. In other words, the tags make the real content of your blog, marked up semantically, with meaning. The CSS applies the look to this page, adding the colors, positioning different elements into columns, and so on. This allows you to deliver the content in a number of ways without changing the content itself.

Tip As an example of the variety of ways you can deliver the same content in very, very different ways, pay a visit to the CSS Zen Garden (`http://csszengarden.com`). This is a site put together to demonstrate the design capabilities of CSS. The site has hundreds of different themes in a vast range of styles from simple, business-like designs, to eastern-flavored works of art, through punk-styled graffiti-like pieces. But every single version of the site uses exactly the same HTML content!

WordPress goes further than many theming and skinning systems. It can automatically use special template files in appropriate circumstances if it finds them. For example, if you are displaying a single post and the file `single.php` exists in your current theme directory, WordPress will use that template. This allows you to present single posts with a different layout. Similarly, a file called `page.php` will be used to display pages. For example, you might decide to use the full width of the browser for your in-depth pages with more content and not display the sidebar.

In this section, I will take you through some adjustments to a theme. You will see how to remove elements you don't want and add extra information you do want. You will also learn how to adjust the CSS to make things appear differently, without needing to change the HTML generated from the template.

Installing and Copying the Theme

First, you need to obtain the theme that you want to modify. For the original theme to use in this chapter's example, I have chosen the c3ro mask theme by C3ro, created by Chris Carlevato (`http://c3ro.com/themes/`), shown in Figure 16-7. This is a beautiful, three-column theme with a graphical masthead and a fading background. It is a little unusual in that it has its two narrow informational columns, both on the right.

I made a couple of changes to the original theme to make it valid XHTML, as standards compliance is an important part of WordPress. The validated theme is available from the Source Code area of the Apress web site (`http://www.apress.com`), as `c3romask-xhtml.zip`. Use this as your starting point.

After you download `c3romask-xhtml.zip`, unzip it into a folder call `c3romask`. Then upload the folder and its contents to your `wp-content/themes` folder. Go to the Presentation administration page and select the c3ro mask theme to activate it. If you view your blog now, it should look like Figure 16-7.

So that you can compare the before and after versions of the theme, you will make changes to a copy of the theme. On your local machine, in the place you unzipped the original theme, rename the `c3romask` directory to `c3romask2`. (You could instead copy the directory and not rename it in order to retain the original code on your local machine for later comparison should things go drastically wrong.)

You will also need to edit the `style.css` file to change the name defined in the file. If two installed themes have the same name, even if they are in different folders, WordPress gets confused. See Listing 16-1 for the new header comment.

Listing 16-1. *New Theme Meta-Information in style.css*

```
/*
    Theme Name: c3ro mask 2
    Theme URI: http://c3ro.com/themes/
    Description: A modified version of c3ro's mask theme
    Version: 1.0
    Author: Mike Little (after c3ro http://c3ro.com/)
    Author URI: http://building-online-communities.com/wordpress/
*/
```

Upload this new folder with the modified `style.css` into `wp-contents/themes` and check the Presentation page. You should now have the c3ro mask and c3ro mask2 themes listed. Activate the c3ro mask 2 theme.

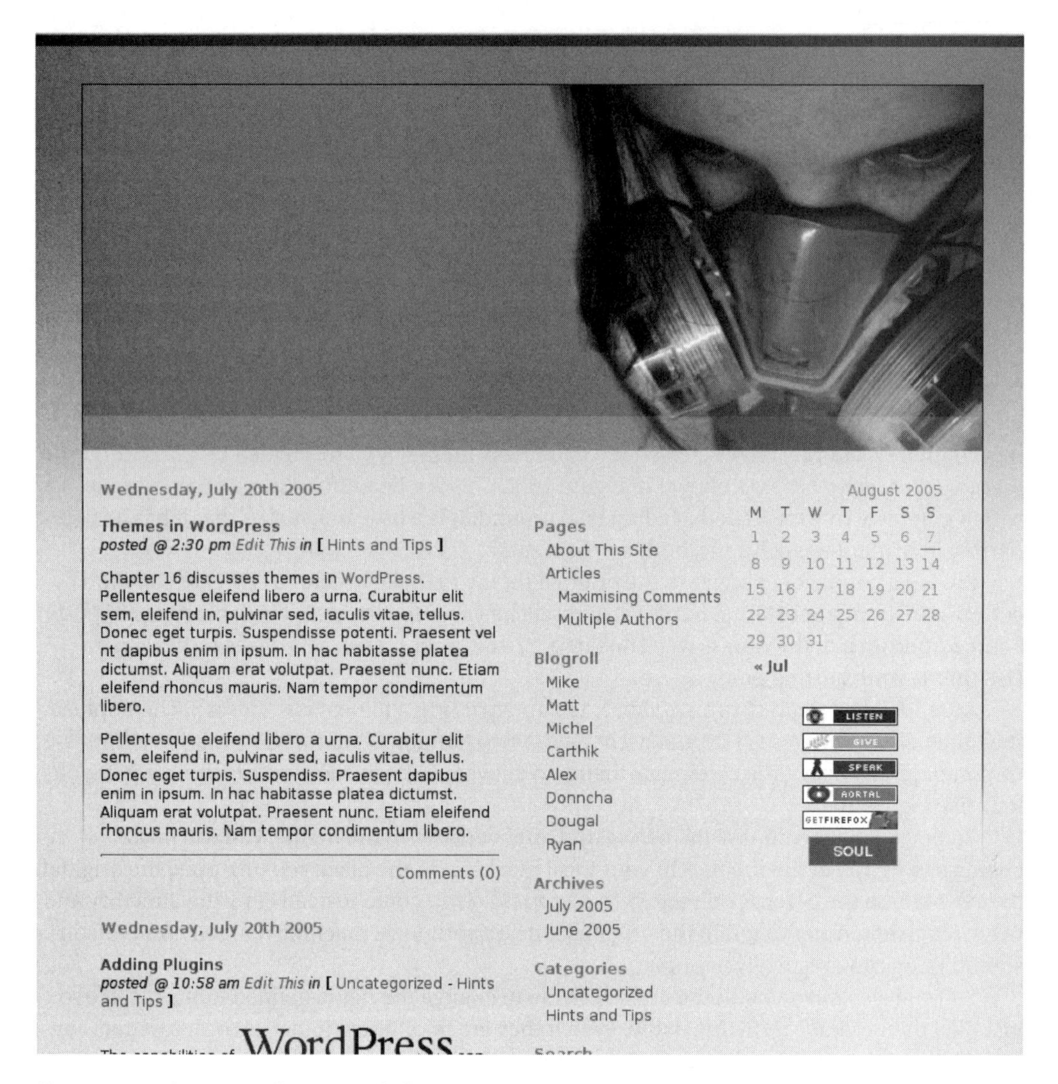

Figure 16-7. *The original c3ro mask theme*

Modifying Theme Images

To change the tone of the theme, choose a different header graphic. You can use any image or images you find to convey the appropriate impression about your blog. You could take a photo yourself or buy an image from one of the many photo agencies on the Web. For this example, I thought the group of horses shown in Figure 16-8 seemed to convey the idea of a community.

Figure 16-8. *A new base image for a theme*

To replace the header graphic in the theme, I cropped the image to match the dimensions of the original header graphic. I also overlaid the blog name onto the image. The original theme header deliberately left that area blank for the same purpose. My header image is shown in Figure 16-9.

Figure 16-9. *Cropped and modified image ready for the theme*

After you are happy with your main header image, copy it to the same name as the theme header image, overwriting the original. The theme now automatically uses your new version of the header image.

You can continue to modify the other background images that accompany the theme, again copying over the originals. I re-created them using colors from the new masthead image to blend with it. Finally, I tweaked the CSS style sheet to use the same colors from the header image for highlights and so on. See Figure 16-10 for the progress so far. You can download this version of the theme, `c3romask2-step1.zip`, from the Source Code area of the Apress web site (`http://www.apress.com`).

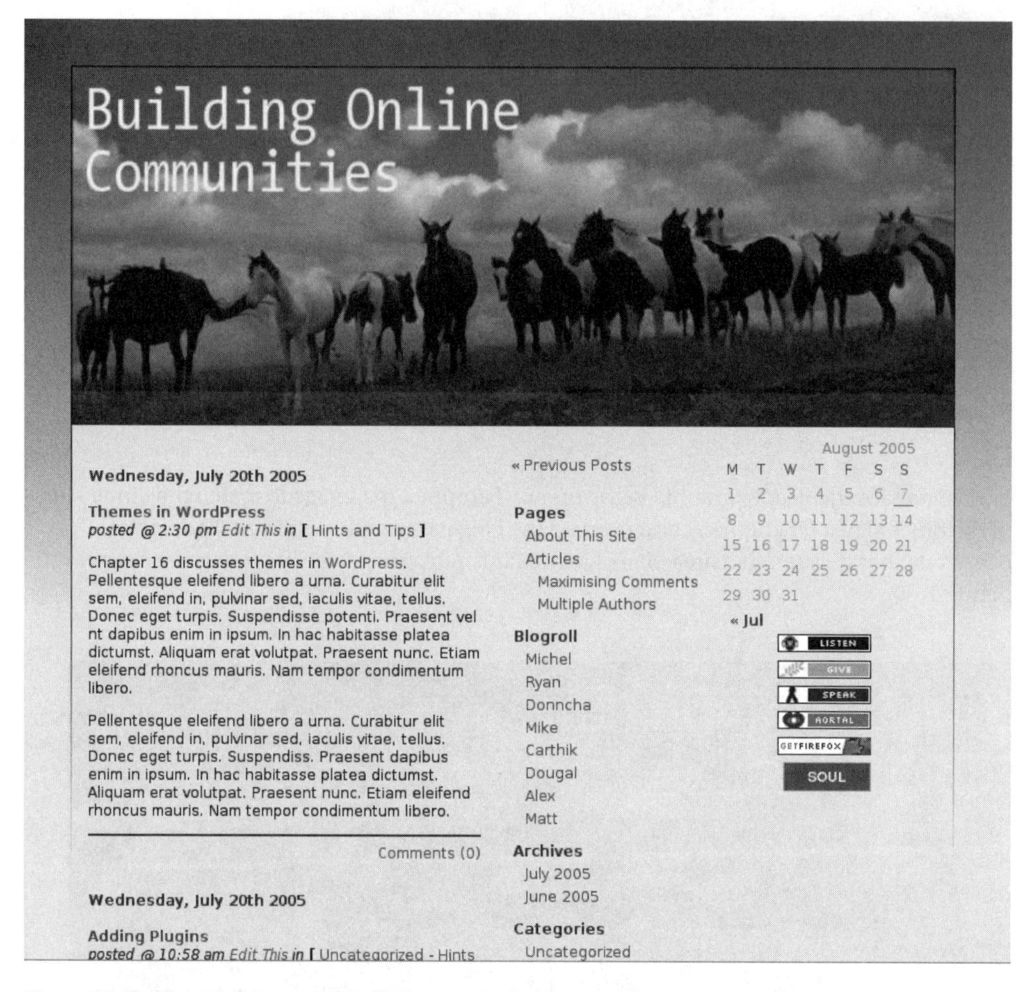

Figure 16-10. *The new theme with all images and colors in place*

Changing the Template

If you want to make modifications to your theme files, you can edit them in WordPress's Theme Editor, as long as the theme files are writable by the web server process (see the "Setting File Upload Options" section in Chapter 14). To activate the Theme Editor, go to the Presentation administration page and click the Theme Editor tab. Make sure that the theme you want to edit (c3ro mask 2 in this example) is selected in the drop-down list.

Alternatively, you can edit the theme files on your machine with your favorite editor and upload them when you are ready. In both cases, you will want to make a backup copy, in case something goes wrong.

In this example, you will remove the list of buttons underneath the calendar and add a list of news stories using the RSS Link List plug-in introduced in Chapter 15. To remove the buttons from the rightmost column, choose the Main Template `index.php` from the drop-down list of theme files on the right side of the page. When that file loads, find the section of `index.php` that begins `<div id="right">`. *Remove* the code shown in Listing 16-2.

Listing 16-2. *HTML Code to be Removed from index.php*

```
<div id="buttons">
<ul>
  <li><a class="img" href="http://www.rantradio.com/" title="listen"><img sr. . .
  <li><a class="img" href="http://www.thehungersite.com/" title="hunger"><im. . .
  <li><a class="img" href="http://www.eff.org/br/" title="speak"><img src="<. . .
  <li><a class="img" href="http://internetbrothers.com/aortal/" title="aorta. . .
  <li><a class="img" href="http://www.spreadfirefox.com/?q=affiliates&amp;id. . .
  <li>
  <form action="">
    <input style="width:75px; font:bold 11px verdana, helvetica, sans-serif;. . .
  </form>
  </li>
 </ul>
</div>
```

At this point, you are left with a section of the code that looks like Listing 16-3.

Listing 16-3. *The Remains of the Right Column Code in index.php*

```
<div id="right">
  <?php get_calendar(); ?>
</div><!-- /side -->
```

If you check the blog now after saving and/or uploading your changed file, you will find the buttons have gone!

Adding the RSS Feed

Now you will add in a call to display an RSS feed using the WordPress RSS Link List plug-in you installed in the previous chapter. In that chapter, you saw how to add a special tag to a blog post or page and have the plug-in convert that tag to a list of links driven from an external RSS feed. This time, you want the list of links to appear in the sidebar. To do this, use the template PHP function provided by the plug-in, rather than the special tag, which works only in posts or pages.

The template function provided by the plug-in is `_rssLinkList()`. This function can take a number of parameters, any of which can be provided in the call to the function. If you don't provide any parameters, the function uses a complete set of defaults, including the default RSS feed of `http://del.icio.us/rss`. For this example, you will use a different del.icio.us RSS feed, which will provide a list of WordPress tools. Also, by default, the plug-in outputs the links in *list item* markup (`<li></li>`). You will need to add unordered list tags (`<ul></ul>`), so that you can address this list in the CSS to improve its appearance. Add the code marked in bold in Listing 16-4 to the template.

Listing 16-4. *Template Function _rssLinksList Added to index.php*

```
<div id="right">
    <?php get_calendar(); ?>
    <h2><?php _e('del.icio.us Links'); ?></h2>
    <ul class="rsslinks">
      <?php _rssLinkList(array("rss_feed_url"=>
       "http://del.icio.us/rss/tag/wordpress+tools")); ?>
    </ul>
</div><!-- /side -->
```

View your blog page now, and you should see something like Figure 16-11.

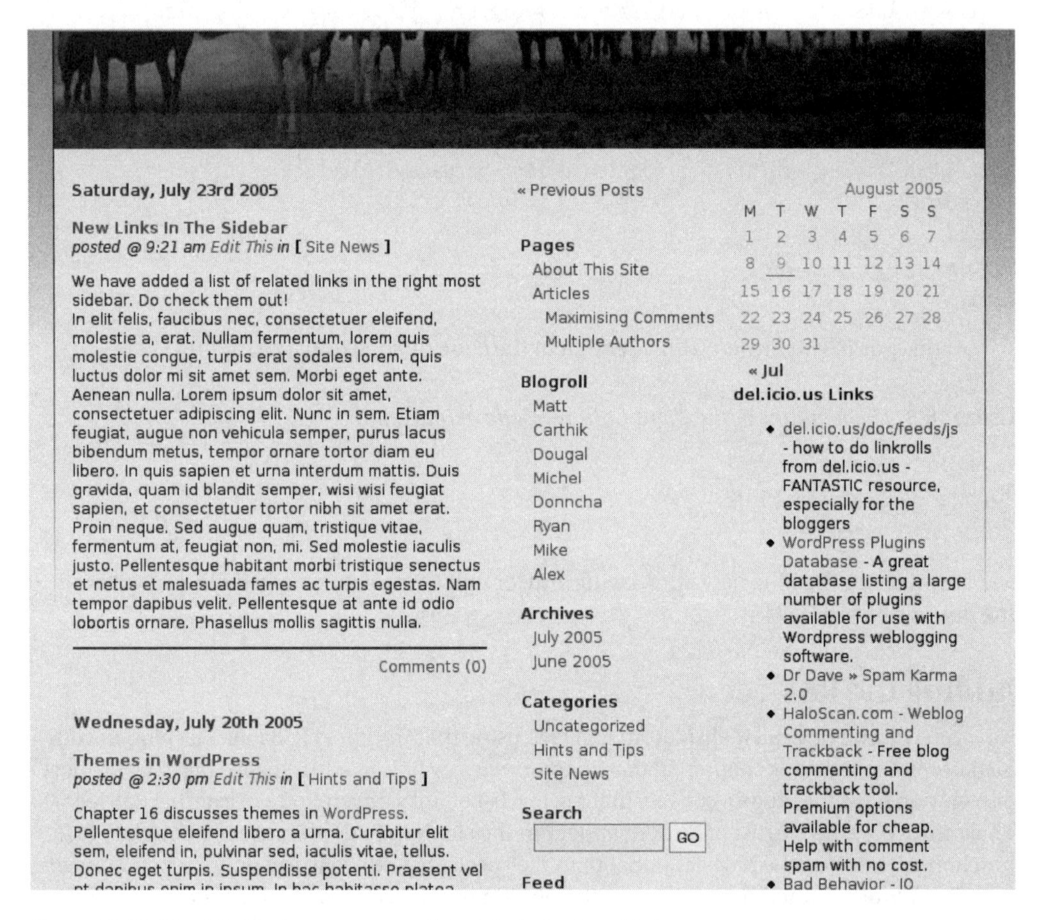

Figure 16-11. *The RSS feed appears as a list of links in the sidebar.*

Adjusting the Links

The links appear in the sidebar, but they are not quite as pretty as you might like. Let's add some style rules for the header and the list to the end of the `style.css` style sheet, as shown in Listing 16-5.

Listing 16-5. *CSS Rules for the List of Links Added to style.css*

```
#right h2 {
    margin-top: 1.2em;
}

ul.rsslinks {
    list-style-type: none;
    margin:0;
    padding-left: 10px;
}

ul.rsslinks li  {
    margin-top: 4px;
    margin-left: 1em;
    text-indent: -1em;
}
```

Also notice that some of the links have a description after them. If the RSS feed includes a description, the plug-in will display it by default. You can turn that off quite easily. Another default the plug-in provides is the number of links, which is 15. I think 10 is a more suitable number. The resultant code in the `index.php` template file looks like Listing 16-6.

Listing 16-6. *Additional Parameters to Restrict the Link List Output in index.php*

```
<ul class="rsslinks">
  <?php _rssLinkList(array("rss_feed_url"=>
   "http://del.icio.us/rss/tag/wordpress+tools",
   "show_description"=>FALSE,
   "num_items"=>10)); ?>
</ul>
```

If you check your blog page now, it should look like Figure 16-12. You will see the list looks much neater and blends in with the rest of the content.

You have now added an external resource as part of the blog. Here, I chose one that is pertinent to the readers. You could also have added a feed of related news items from another web site or a list of the latest topics from a companion forum. The possibilities are quite extensive. As long as there is a resource available in RSS format, you can add it this way.

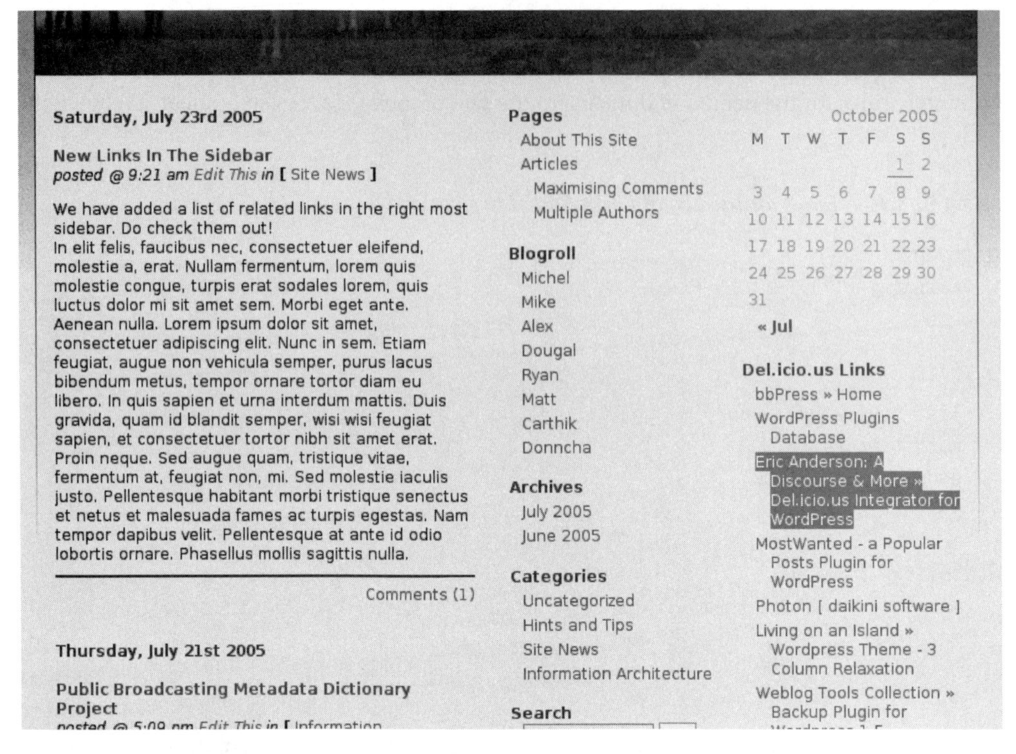

Figure 16-12. *The improved list of links*

Adding Registration and Login Links

Something missing from this template are the links to register and log in to the blog. Most WordPress blogs, being one-person blogs, don't need these links. Many themes don't even bother to include them. For a community blog, you will want to add them to your theme.

To the `index.php` template file, add the code highlighted in bold in Listing 16-7.

Listing 16-7. *WordPress Template Tags for Registration and Login Links Added to index.php*

```
    "show_description"=>FALSE,
    "num_items"=>10)); ?>
  </ul>
  <h2><?php _e('Contribute'); ?></h2>
  <ul id="contribute">
    <?php wp_register(); ?>
    <li><?php wp_loginout(); ?></li>
  </ul>
</div><!-- /side -->
```

The additions in Listing 16-7 are standard WordPress template tags. The call to `wp_register()` produces a link to the registration page, but it does so only if registration is enabled. If you are logged in, however, it produces a link to the administration pages.

The call to wp_loginout produces a link to the login page if the current visitor is not already logged in, and a logout link if the visitor is logged in.

Next, add the CSS rules from Listing 16-8 to the end of the style sheet. This will ensure the display of the links matches that of the other parts of the sidebar.

Listing 16-8. *CSS Rules for Login and Register Links Added to style.css*

```
ul#contribute {
    list-style-type: none;
    margin:0;
    padding-left: 10px;
}
ul#contribute li  {
    margin-top: 4px;
    margin-left: 1em;
    text-indent: -1em;
}
```

Figure 16-13 shows how your register and login links should appear, and Figure 16-14 shows the site admin and logout links.

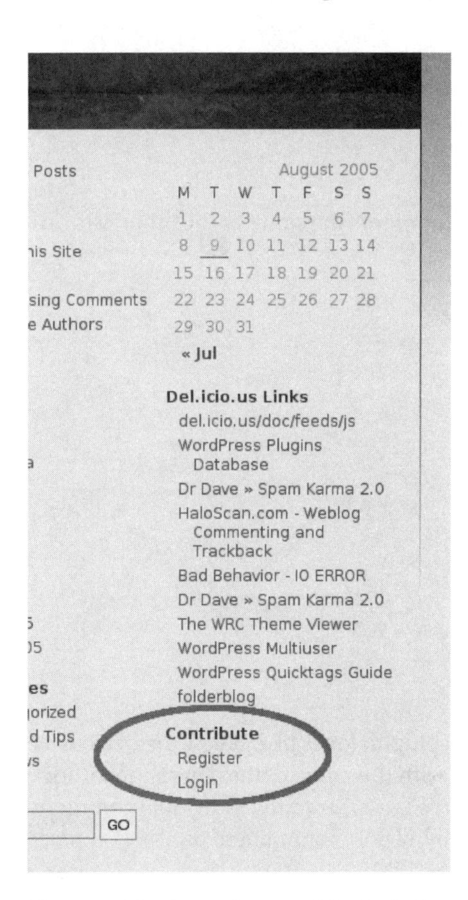

Figure 16-13. *The register and login links*

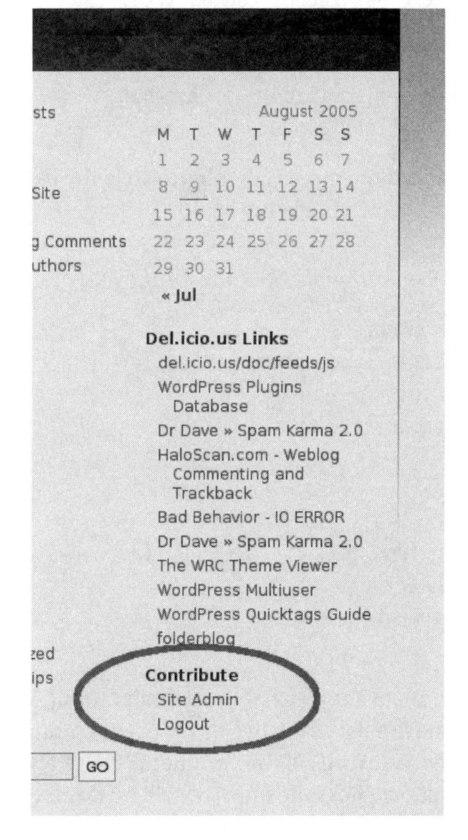

Figure 16-14. *The site admin and logout links*

Adding a Recent Comments Plug-In

Now you will install another plug-in, which will list a number of the most recent comments to the blog in the sidebar. This is great mechanism to keep your readers interested. It allows them to see which topics are still being discussed, and thus is an added incentive to keep reading those topics and to continue to get involved. Real conversation about a shared interest between your readers is the lifeblood of an active online community.

The plug-in is the Customizable Comment Listings plug-in by Scott Reilly. You can download this plug-in via Scott's site at `http://www.coffee2code.com/archives/2005/03/30/plugin-customizable-comment-listings/`.

Download, install, and activate the plug-in using the procedure covered in Chapter 15. Read through the comprehensive documentation on Scott's site.

Next, add the code shown in Listing 16-9 (from one of the examples in the plug-in's documentation) to the `index.php` template file, just before the contribute section. The single parameter `5` tells the plug-in to list only the five most recent comments.

Listing 16-9. *Code to Insert into index.php Immediately Before the Contribute Links*

```
<h2><?php _e('Recent Comments'); ?></h2>
<ul class="recentcomments">
  <?php c2c_get_recent_comments(5); ?>
</ul>

<h2><?php _e('Contribute'); ?></h2>
<ul id="contribute">
```

Now add some more CSS rules to style the list of comments the same as the other lists on that page, as shown in Listing 16-10.

Listing 16-10. *Additional CSS Rules for the End of style.css*

```
ul.recentcomments {
    list-style-type: none;
    margin:0;
    padding-left: 10px;
}

ul.recentcomments li  {
    margin-top: 4px;
    margin-left: 1em;
    text-indent: -1em;
}
```

Figure 16-15 shows what the default output of this plug-in looks like. Below the del.icio.us links, you have a list of the five most recent comments with the name of the comment author and the first few words of the comment. Those few words are a link to the individual comment itself. If a reader clicks the link, she will be taken to the blog post commented on with the page scrolled to the individual comment.

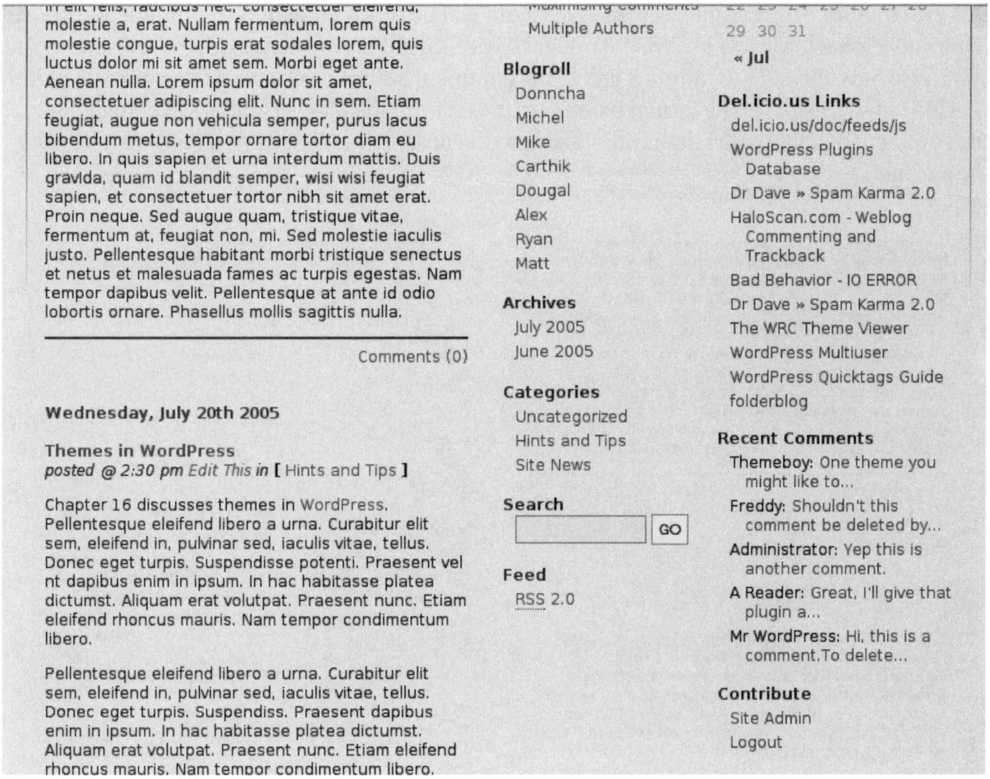

Figure 16-15. *Recent comments listed*

This is a useful addition to the blog, but it could be better. It doesn't show to which story or post the comments belong. A reader might be particularly interested in what other people have to say about a story he commented on recently. A contributor might be looking for comments on her own stories. As its name implies, the Customizable Comment Listings plug-in is flexible enough to accommodate such additions.

Let's replace the simple call to the plug-in function with the code shown in Listing 16-11. This is another example provided in the plug-in's documentation.

Listing 16-11. *New Version of the get_recent_comments Template Function in index.php*

```
<h2><?php _e('Recent Comments'); ?></h2>
<ul class="recentcomments">
  <?php c2c_get_recent_comments(5,
  "<li>%comment_author% said \"%comment_excerpt%\" in <br />%post_URL%</li>"); ?>
</ul>
```

This function looks complicated, but it has only one more parameter. It uses a very powerful format template Scott has defined. Each of the terms enclosed in percent signs (%) is substituted by some data from the list of recent comments. The substitution names are fairly self-explanatory. For example, `%comment_author%` will be replaced with the comment author's name, and `%comment_excerpt%` will be replaced with the first few words from the comment. You could also have the plug-in output a link to the comment author's web site, if the comment writer provided one. The rest of the format parameter (taken from the plug-in author's example) puts the comment details in a list item with the link to the post on a separate line. Figure 16-16 shows the output.

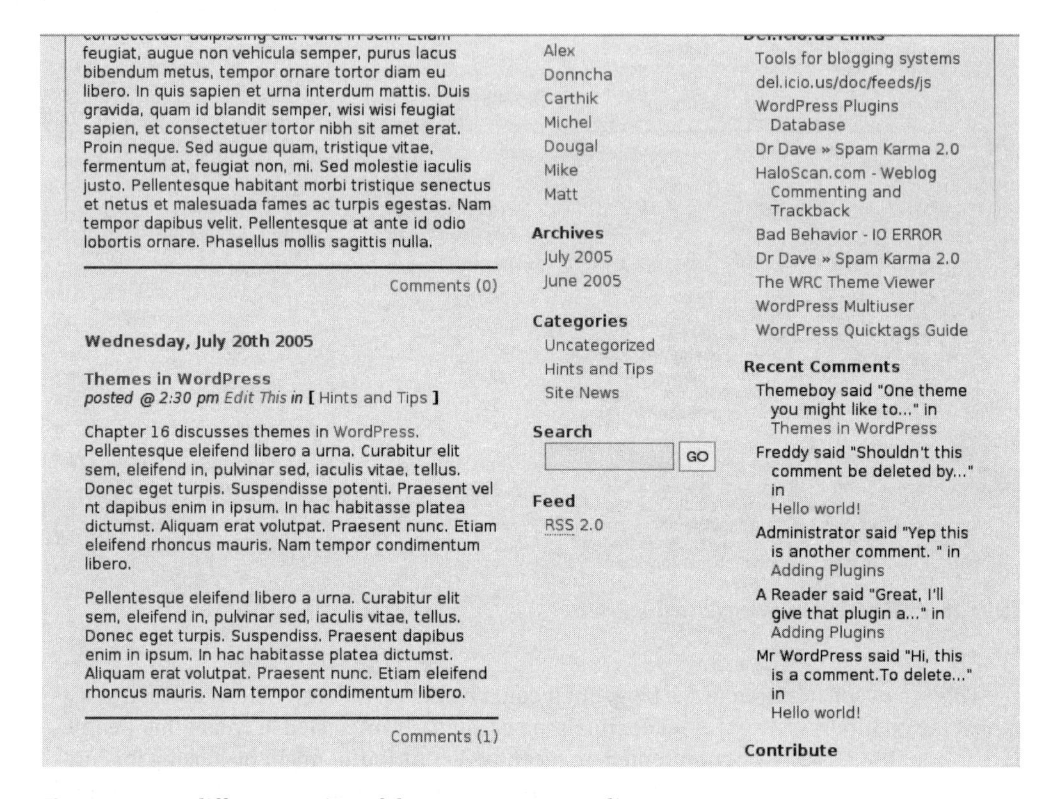

Figure 16-16. *A different version of the recent comments list*

This version gives more information, but it seems rather cluttered and the most important information—the name of the post and its link—isn't easy to discern. So, let's make one more change to this code. You will remove the comment excerpt and just link to the comment, but with the post title. Surprisingly, although this plug-in has more than 40 replaceable tags, none of them match the desired format exactly. You could have the post title as a link to the post, or the post title as a link to the top of the comment section, but none have the post title as a link to the specific comment. However, you can create this format by using two separate replaceable tags, as shown in Listing 16-12.

Listing 16-12. *Final Version of the Recent Comments Code in index.php*

```
<h2><?php _e('Recent Comments'); ?></h2>
<ul class="recentcomments">
  <?php c2c_get_recent_comments(5,
  "<li>%comment_author% on <a href=\"%comment_url%\" "
  . "title=\"%comment_excerpt%\" >%post_title%</a></li>"); ?>
</ul>
```

As you can see in Figure 16-17, the list is much less cluttered now. As a bonus, hovering over the link to the comment gives the comment excerpt as a tool tip. That's the `title` part of the code in the format parameter used in Listing 16-12.

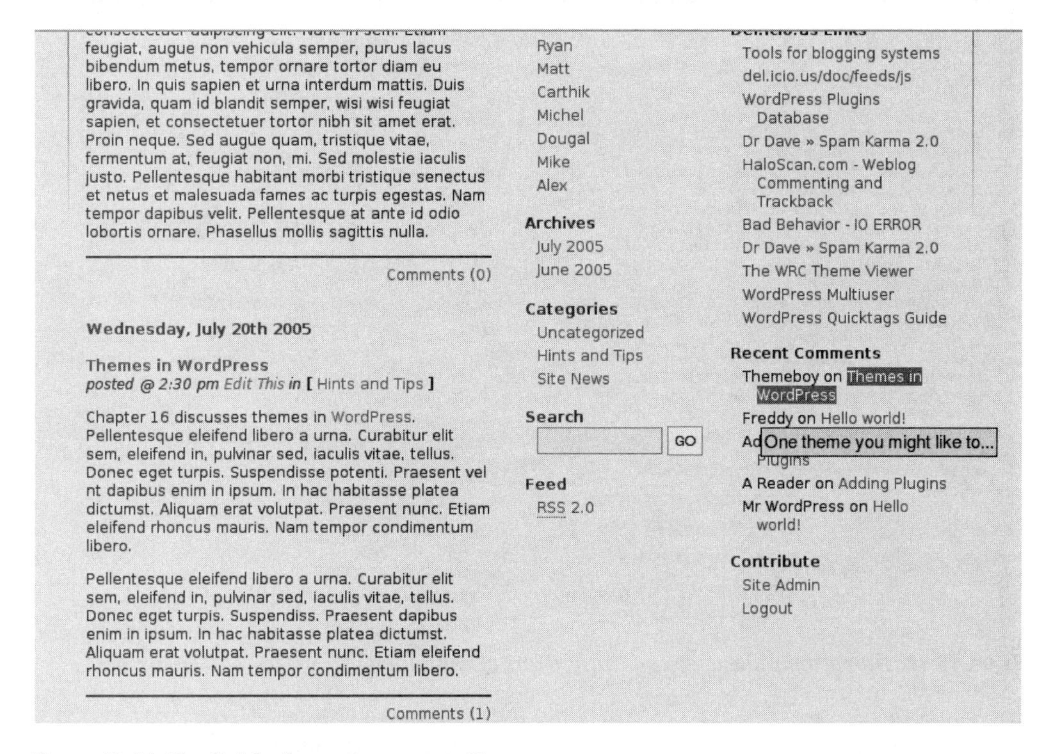

Figure 16-17. *The finished recent comment list*

Cleaning Up the Code

You have modified an existing theme, expanding it to do what you want. However, a couple areas could use some cleaning up. These involve making the PHP code safer and eliminating duplication in the CSS rules.

Safer PHP Code

I mentioned earlier that if a theme requires a plug-in and that plug-in is not present, you will get errors on your blog. Sometimes, depending on the place the error occurs, your blog page may not work at all.

Take a look at Figure 16-18. Here, I have disabled the RSS Link List plug-in. The error on the page is at exactly the place the plug-in template function is called. No more of the template code is executed, even though the rest of the page would have displayed correctly. Imagine if you had a call to a template function at the beginning of your theme template. The resultant page might contain a cryptic error message and nothing else!

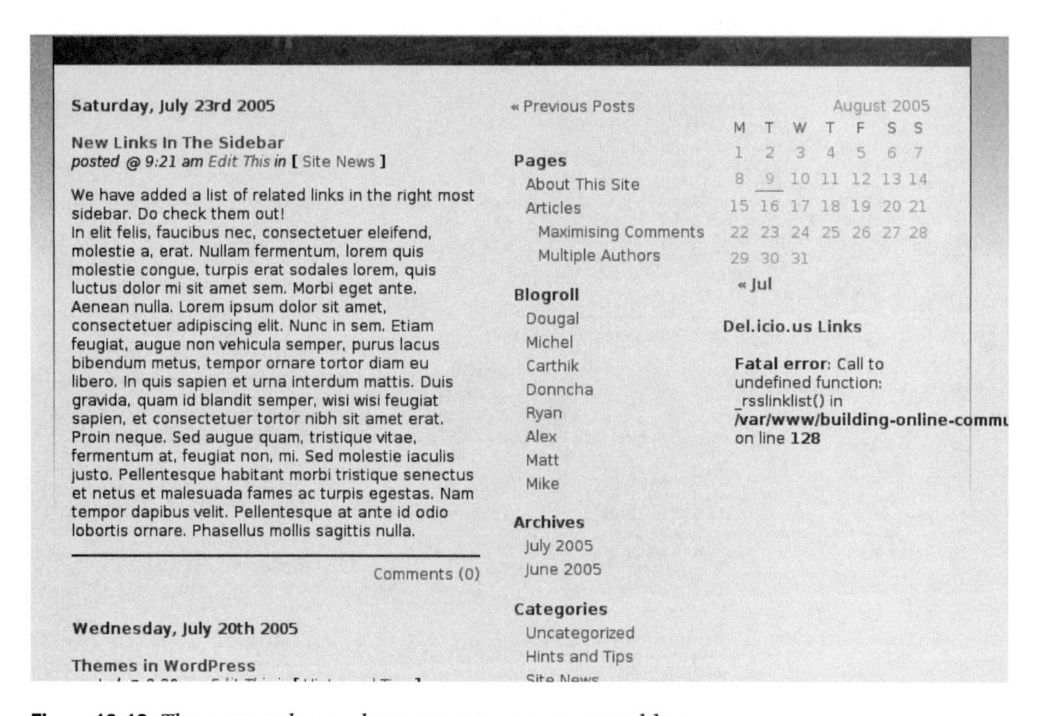

Figure 16-18. *Theme template code can cause errors on your blog.*

There is a simple solution to this problem. PHP has a special ability to test whether a function exists. This means you can test to see if the plug-in function exists before trying to call it. If it doesn't exist, you don't call it. There will be no error, and if you write your template code carefully, there won't even be a header with nothing below it. Listing 16-13 shows the new version of the code.

Listing 16-13. *Additional PHP Function in index.php to Protect Against Errors with the rssLinkList Function*

```
<div id="right">
  <?php get_calendar(); ?>
<?php if (function_exists('_rssLinkList')) : ?>
  <h2><?php _e('Del.icio.us Links'); ?></h2>
  <ul class="rsslinks">
    <?php _rssLinkList(array("rss_feed_url"=>
     "http://del.icio.us/rss/tag/wordpress+tools",
     "show_description"=>FALSE,  "num_items"=>10)); ?>
  </ul>
<?php endif; ?>
  <h2><?php _e('Recent Comments'); ?></h2>
```

The test code (highlighted in bold) uses the PHP function `function_exists` to check whether the `_rssLinkList` function exists. If it does, the code in between that line and the matching `endif` line is executed to output the HTML code and call the plug-in function. If the function does *not* exist, because the plug-in is either disabled or not installed, the code between the two highlighted lines is not executed, so you won't even get the redundant header. Figure 16-19 shows the resultant page with the plug-in still disabled.

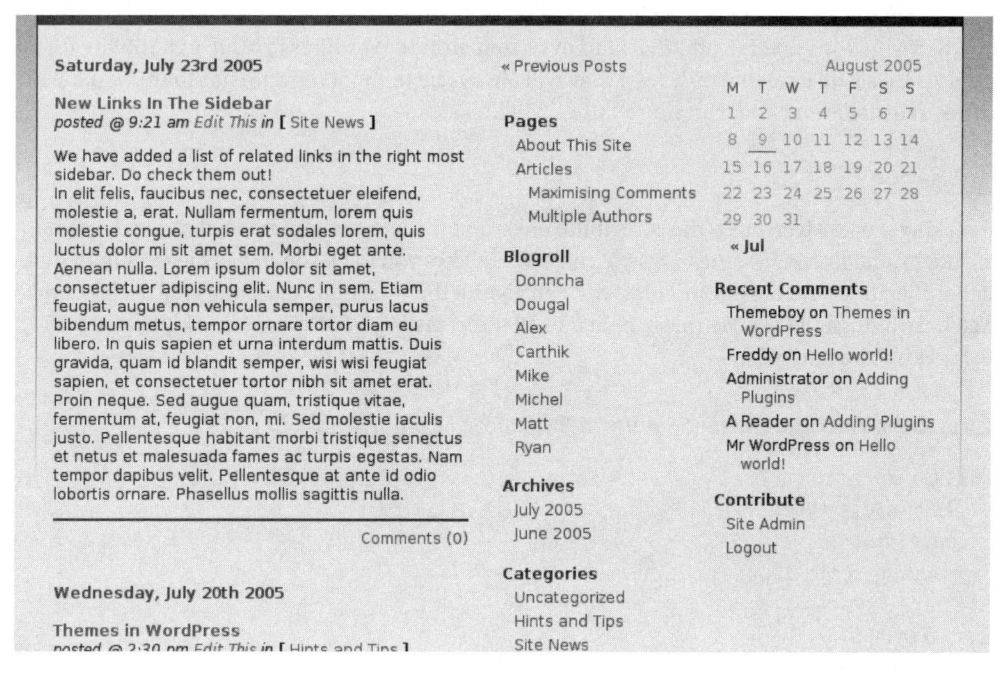

Figure 16-19. *No plug-in and no errors*

Go ahead and make a similar change to the call to the recent comments plug-in, as shown in Listing 16-14.

Listing 16-14. *Additional PHP Function in index.php to Protect Against Errors with the c2c_get_recent_comments Function*

```
<?php if (function_exists('c2c_get_recent_comments')) : ?>
  <h2><?php _e('Recent Comments'); ?></h2>
  <ul class="recentcomments">
    <?php c2c_get_recent_comments(5,
    "<li>%comment_author% on <a href=\"%comment_url%\" "
    . "title=\"%comment_excerpt%\" >%post_title%</a></li>"); ?>
  </ul>
<?php endif; ?>
  <h2><?php _e('Contribute'); ?></h2>
  <ul id="contribute">
    <?php wp_register(); ?>
```

You will be pleased to hear that there is no need to take the same kind of precautions with the special `rssLinkList` tag embedded in your posts or pages. The technology WordPress uses to process special tags is more sophisticated than simply executing PHP code. In fact, you can't execute PHP code in a post (although there are plug-ins that allow you to do this). Instead, the tags are simply ignored if the plug-in is disabled or not installed.

Also, you don't need to add this kind of testing around WordPress's built-in template functions. As these are core to WordPress, they will always be there. If they are not there, you have a broken installation, and a lot more things will break!

Cleaner CSS

In making the RSS feed links, the contribute links, and the latest comments links look the same, you have duplicated the same CSS style rules. CSS allows you to be somewhat cleverer than that. Rather than have three separate rules, you can give all three sections the same HTML class, and then have a single set of style rules applied to all three. Listing 16-15 shows the duplicated CSS that needs to be removed.

Listing 16-15. *The Duplicated CSS Rules to Be Removed from style.css*

```
ul.rsslinks {
    list-style-type: none;
    margin:0;
    padding-left: 10px;
}
ul.rsslinks li  {
    margin-top: 4px;
    margin-left: 1em;
    text-indent: -1em;
}
```

```
ul#contribute {
    list-style-type: none;
    margin:0;
    padding-left: 10px;
}
ul#contribute li  {
    margin-top: 4px;
    margin-left: 1em;
    text-indent: -1em;
}
ul.recentcomments {
    list-style-type: none;
    margin:0;
    padding-left: 10px;
}
ul.recentcomments li  {
    margin-top: 4px;
    margin-left: 1em;
    text-indent: -1em;
}
```

Listing 16-16 shows an improved version with a new class name, `rightsidelists`, which is a little more semantic and can be applied to all three sections.

Listing 16-16. *The Reduced Multiple Class CSS Rules Added to style.css*

```
ul.rightsidelists {
    list-style-type: none;
    margin:0;
    padding-left: 10px;
}
ul.rightsidelists li  {
    margin-top: 4px;
    margin-left: 1em;
    text-indent: -1em;
}
```

Using the reduced CSS rules in Listing 16-16 means applying a class attribute matching the class name to each unordered list in the right column, as in `<ul class="rightsidelists">`. This is fine for a couple of lists, but gets a little repetitive and is tedious to remember. A better solution is to use the combination of a unique identifier and an element selector, instead of a class selector, to apply rules to *all* unordered lists in the right column. This eliminates the need to remember to use the class for each one. Listing 16-17 shows the CSS rules that will apply to all unordered lists in the right column.

Listing 16-17. *The Reduced Element Selector CSS Rules in style.css*

```
#right ul {
    list-style-type: none;
    margin:0;
    padding-left: 10px;
}
#right ul li {
    margin-top: 4px;
    margin-left: 1em;
    text-indent: -1em;
}
```

You need to change the HTML in the template to remove the eliminated class names, as they're now not needed or even defined. You can see in Listing 16-18 that the class attributes have been removed from the `<ul>` tags. You can download this version of the theme from the Source Code area of the Apress web site (`http://www.apress.com`), as `c3romask2-step2.zip`.

Listing 16-18. *Leaner HTML Without Class Attributes in index.php*

```
<div id="right">
  <?php get_calendar(); ?>
  <?php if (function_exists('_rssLinkList')) : ?>
  <h2><?php _e('Del.icio.us Links'); ?></h2>
  <ul>
    <?php _rssLinkList(array("rss_feed_url"=>
     "http://del.icio.us/rss/tag/wordpress+tools",
     "show_description"=>FALSE,  "num_items"=>10)); ?>
  </ul>
  <?php endif; ?>
  <?php if (function_exists('c2c_get_recent_comments')) : ?>
  <h2><?php _e('Recent Comments'); ?></h2>
  <ul>
    <?php c2c_get_recent_comments(5,
    "<li>%comment_author% on <a href=\"%comment_url%\" "
     . "title=\"%comment_excerpt%\" >%post_title%</a></li>"); ?>
  </ul>
  <?php endif; ?>
  <h2><?php _e('Contribute'); ?></h2>
  <ul>
    <?php wp_register(); ?>

    <li><?php wp_loginout(); ?></li>
  </ul>
</div><!-- /side -->
```

You have now completed the process of customizing a theme to use different images, add new content, and display the links in a different format. You can apply this approach to modify other themes to suit your needs.

Summary

This chapter demonstrated how to change the face of your blog to make your site more appealing to your visitors. I've shown you how to add pertinent information to enhance the readers' experience of your site. All of this has been about the front page of your blog. This is important, as it is the first impression your first-time visitor gets. But you can go much further.

WordPress can do a lot more to enhance your visitors' time on your site. It can help you keep your readers engaged by presenting the right information at the right time. In the next chapter, I will show you how to change the appearance of the blog depending on the page being viewed and include different content on different pages. I will also introduce more plug-ins to enhance the readers' experience.

CHAPTER 17

■ ■ ■

Customizing Your Blog's Layout

In this chapter, I will show you how to improve your users' experience by tailoring your blog's layout to your audience. As with the previous chapters, the focus is on building your community and making it enjoyable and rewarding for people, so they will return again and again. To achieve this goal, you need to think about the users' experience as they use your site. What are your readers doing on the site? What are they trying to achieve? When you have the answers to these questions, you can help your readers by customizing your site to accommodate their interests.

Considering What Your Reader Is Doing

When users click the comments link of a story, they are taken to a new page where they are presented with the story in full and the related conversation. Almost everything else they see looks the same as the layout on the front page. That's the beauty of a template-driven system. You don't need to do anything to get the same look and feel, as well as common content across all your pages.

But sometimes presenting the same layout is not the right thing to do. You should think about what the users are doing. What are their intentions? What benefit will they get from this action? What will they want to do next? The answers to these questions depend somewhat on the nature of your site.

Having a Conversation

People love to chat. They love to have their say. In pubs and clubs, in their homes, in bus queues, and in supermarket aisles, people love to talk.

For many people, it is just as rewarding to have those conversations without the face-to-face contact, such as on the phone or on a shortwave radio. People still have conversations with pen and paper, sending letters to each other. Similarly, people love to have conversations online.

The nature of some online conversations is analogous to other types of conversations. Real-time chat in a chat room is most like a face-to-face meeting with several people. Instant messaging is like a phone conversation between two people. E-mail is like a paper-and-pen correspondence. Yet the online world gives us other ways to converse that don't have true parallels in the real world. That e-mail conversation can take place on a mailing list, where many people join in. Bulletin boards are like conversations with a lot of people, but the conversation can be in near real-time, like a chat, or time-delayed over many hours, days, or weeks, more like a mailing list.

Blog comment conversations can be similar to bulletin boards and forums in some respects, but in other ways are quite different. One big difference is that often blog conversations are lead by an article or post of substantial length.

Discussing the News

If your site is all about commenting on some type of news, like current political events, users are likely to want to read the full details of the story you posted and to contribute to the conversation about it. Their benefit is that they got to hear what their peers have to say and contribute to the conversation themselves. The ability to have a lively conversation with one's peers is a very rewarding experience.

You and your writers might post a long, thought-out opinion piece or a proposal for a new direction your group might take, and from that trigger a substantial debate with your readers. In these situations, your readers might not want any distractions from the conversation or the debate. Their main aim in visiting the page is to continue taking part in that debate.

Coming to Learn

Perhaps your blog is primarily about offering information of a tutorial nature and soliciting feedback. In this case, your visitors still want to read what you have to say and perhaps provide feedback, but they will also want to find more information and other resources about the subject. Your articles are likely to have more structure than a news-type blog post, and perhaps include images or illustrations. It may be that the piece is long enough to split into multiple pages.

Your readers might want to read more on the subject you are discussing. They might want to see a brief list of related resources, perhaps with some kind of summary or rating system.

Looking for a Review

Your blog could be specialized review site, where you discuss and review the latest science fiction books, movies, and games. Here, your main articles will probably be in-depth reviews of the latest DVD releases, complete with publicity photos, cast lists, and so on. But you may also have, for example, a news category where the nature of the stories will be different. On such a site, you might want to have links to allow your readers to purchase the products you are reviewing. If they are affiliate links, you could even earn money that way.

To encourage readers to return, you could have a voting or rating system. Or perhaps, you will just want to encourage them to leave their own reviews in the comments.

Moving to the Next Step

In all the scenarios I've mentioned, and in any others appropriate to your blog, you must try to anticipate what your visitors will want to do next. You want to help them take their next step, even if that next step is to leave your site! Here are some possibilities of what visitors will want to do next and how you can help them:

- Participate in the conversation. Have the comment form right there.
- Find what else you have been discussing. Have links to other articles in the same category.
- Buy the game you've just reviewed. Have the link there ready for them.
- Go off and do more research. Have links to other related sites right there.

It may sound strange to want to help people leave your site, but sometimes that is a good thing. Have you ever wanted to return to a site you found useful, but you forgot to bookmark it? You can't remember the URL, but you *do* remember a related site you visited on your journey to get there. You return to the related site, and try to retrace your steps. Of course, you want your site to be the one everyone wants to visit, but that isn't always the case. Being that related site that people return to find links can be just as important. Having a reputation for being *the* place to find out about other sites on your subject is one of the things that started this whole weblog business.

Changing the Layout

In this section, I'll show you how you can configure your blog to cater to different types of users. You'll see how to create different layouts for different views in your blog. Some layouts will have both sidebars, some will have one or the other, and some will have none. First, you need the elements that you will use to build your layouts.

Building Blocks

Think of a layout as building blocks or puzzle pieces that you want to fit together in certain ways. PHP allows you to split up your files in this way and include them into the original. Furthermore, WordPress encourages this kind of split in its support for theming. The themes supplied with WordPress are structured this way.

So, first you'll break down the theme files into multiple pieces. You will take each of the elements of the header, the main section, the individual sidebars, and so on, and split them into separate files. You can then choose to include those files as appropriate based on the type of page to display.

Rather than take you through splitting each file piece by piece, I will show you one such piece and leave the rest as an exercise. You will be able to download the completed version from the Source Code area of the Apress web site (`http://www.apress.com`).

The example I will take you through is splitting the rightmost column from the main file into its own file. Listing 17-1 shows the code to be moved. All of this code will go into a new file called `sidebar-b.php`. The name is not related to its position on the page, because it may not always be on the right.

Listing 17-1. *The Right Sidebar Code to Go in sidebar-b.php*

```
<div id="right">
  <?php get_calendar(); ?>
<?php if (function_exists('_rssLinkList')) : ?>
  <h2><?php _e('Del.icio.us Links'); ?></h2>
  <ul class="rightsidelists">
    <?php _rssLinkList(array("rss_feed_url"=>
     "http://del.icio.us/rss/tag/wordpress+tools",
     "show_description"=>FALSE,
     "num_items"=>10)); ?>
  </ul>
<?php endif; ?>
<?php if (function_exists('c2c_get_recent_comments')) : ?>
  <h2><?php _e('Recent Comments'); ?></h2>
  <ul  class="rightsidelists">
    <?php c2c_get_recent_comments(5,
    "<li>%comment_author% on <a href=\"%comment_url%\" "
     ."title=\"%comment_excerpt%\" >%post_title%</a></li>"); ?>
  </ul>
<?php endif; ?>
  <h2><?php _e('Contribute'); ?></h2>
  <ul class="rightsidelists">
    <?php wp_register(); ?>

    <li><?php wp_loginout(); ?></li>
  </ul>
</div><!-- /side -->
```

Once the code is in its own file, you need to insert the instruction to include that file in the main `index.php` file exactly where the code was, as shown in Listing 17-2.

Listing 17-2. *Include the New File in index.php*

```
            </div><!-- /side -->
<?php include_once('sidebar-b.php'); ?>
            <div id="footer">
```

Also adjust the CSS style names to match in both `sidebar-b.php` and `style.css`, as shown in Listings 17-3 and 17-4.

Listing 17-3. *Renamed Styles in style.css*

```
#sidebar-b {
    float: left;
    text-align: left;
    padding-left: 15px;
    width: 190px;
}
```

```
#sidebar-b h2 {
    margin-top: 1.2em;
}

ul.sidebar-b-sidelists {
    list-style-type: none;
    margin:0;
    padding-left: 10px;
}

ul.sidebar-b-sidelists li  {
    margin-top: 4px;
    margin-left: 1em;
    text-indent: -1em;
}
```

Listing 17-4. *New CSS Names in sidebar-b.php*

```
  <div id="sidebar-b">
    <?php get_calendar(); ?>
<?php if (function_exists('_rssLinkList')) : ?>
    <h2><?php _e('Del.icio.us Links'); ?></h2>
    <ul class="sidebar-b-sidelists">
      <?php _rssLinkList(array("rss_feed_url"=>

      . . .

      <li><?php wp_loginout(); ?></li>
    </ul>
  </div><!-- /sidebar-b -->
```

A quick check on the main blog page shows that everything still works. If you download the completed split-out version from the Apress web site (as file `c3rohorses-step1.zip`) and unzip it into your `wp-content/themes` directory, you will see that I have split it into quite a few files and renamed the theme to c3rohorses. The file list now looks like this:

- `comments.php`
- `footer.php`
- `header.php`
- `html-head.php`
- `index.php`
- `main-content.php`
- `search-form.php`
- `sidebar-a.php`
- `sidebar-b.php`
- `style.css`

If you examine index.php (you can use the WordPress Theme Editor, as described in Chapter 16), you will see that it has become very simple and modular. Listing 17-5 shows the whole file. It has been reduced to a mere 18 lines. Each of the main areas of the file has now been extracted to its own file.

Listing 17-5. *The Lean index.php*

```
<!DOCTYPE html PUBLIC "-//W3C//DTD XHTML 1.0 Transitional//EN"
  "http://www.w3.org/TR/xhtml1/DTD/xhtml1-transitional.dtd">
<html xmlns="http://www.w3.org/1999/xhtml">
<?php include_once('html-head.php'); ?>
<body>
<div id="wrapper">
  <?php get_header(); ?>
  <div id="container">
    <div id="pagecontent">
    <?php include_once('main-content.php'); ?>
    <?php include_once('sidebar-a.php'); ?>
    <?php include_once('sidebar-b.php'); ?>
    </div><!-- /pagecontent -->
  </div><!-- /container -->
  <?php get_footer(); ?>
</div><!-- /wrapper -->
</body>
</html>
```

Note that the header.php and footer.php files are not directly included by this file. Instead, the WordPress template functions get_header() and get_footer() have been called. These standard template tags automatically include a file called header.php and footer.php, respectively. If one of these files doesn't exist in the theme, the tags will include the corresponding files from the default theme.

This modularity now allows you to be incredibly flexible in the layout of the theme. As an example, simply commenting out any combination of the three include files in the central section allows you to change which pieces of the page are included. Figures 17-1 through 17-5 demonstrate how you can change the layout by commenting out files.

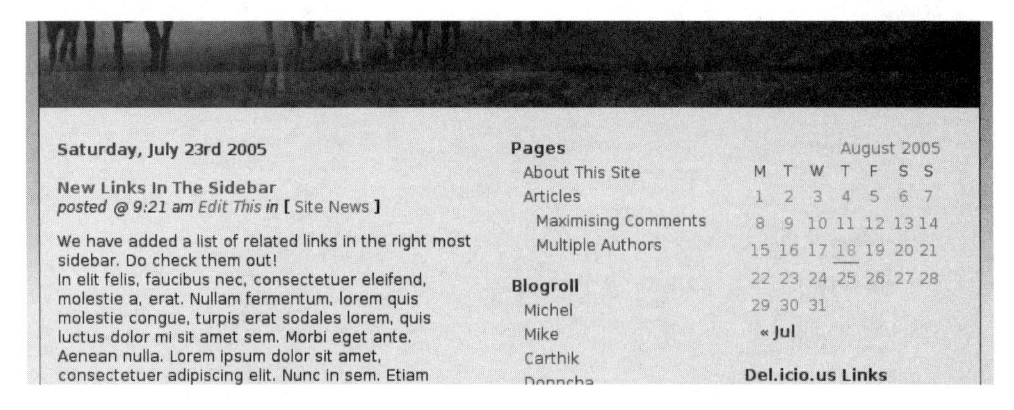

Figure 17-1. *All three files included*

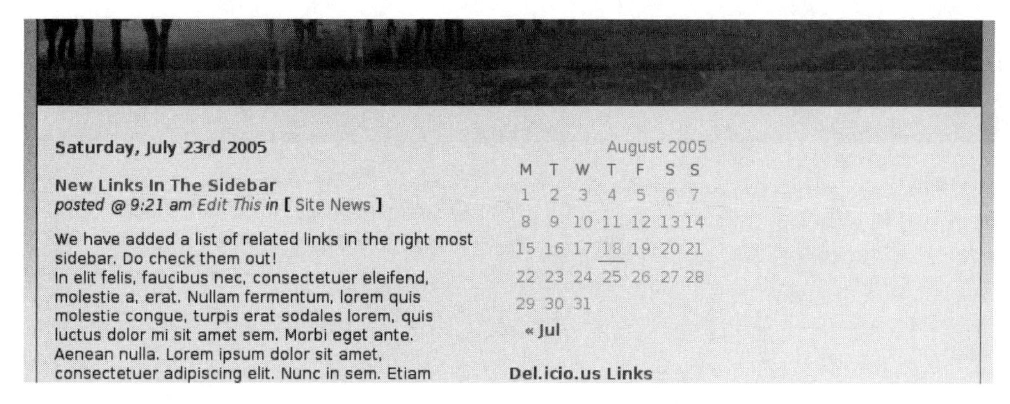

Figure 17-2. *Sidebar A commented out*

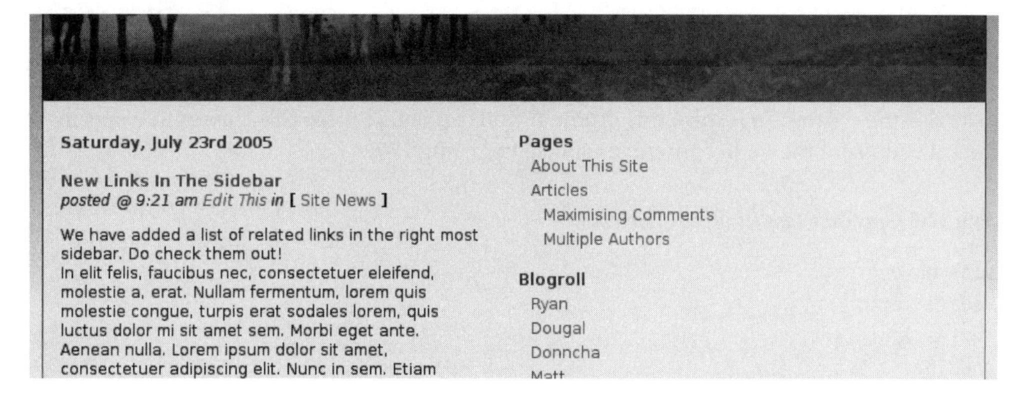

Figure 17-3. *Sidebar B commented out*

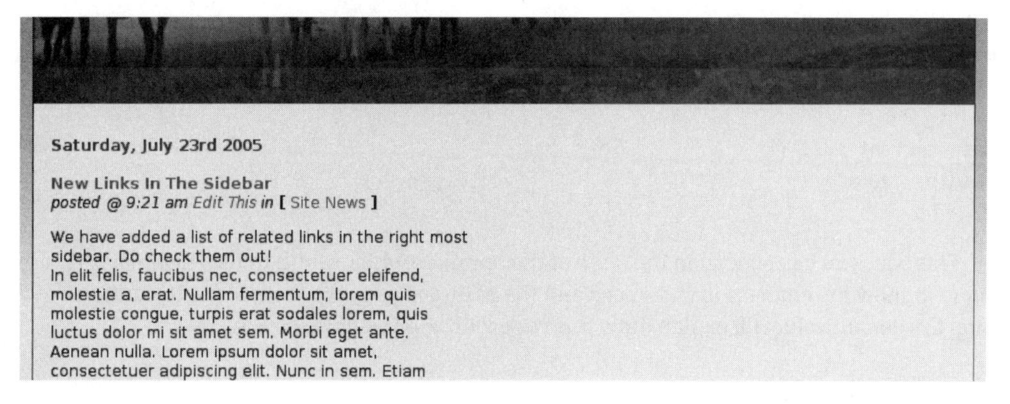

Figure 17-4. *Both sidebars commented out*

Figure 17-5. *Main content commented out*

Before moving onto building a layout from these pieces, you need to make one more change to the basic structure. You can see in Figure 17-2 that the combination of main content and sidebar B does not fill the width of the theme. Similarly, the main content with no sidebars is also too narrow. To resolve this problem, you can define three CSS classes that specify different widths for the main content, as shown in Listing 17-6.

Listing 17-6. *Special Class Rules in style.css*

```
#main-content {
  float: left;
  text-align: left;
  padding: 0 10px 0 5px;
}
.main-content-norm {
  width: 340px;
}
.main-content-wide {
  width: 530px;
}
.main-content-full {
  width: 720px;
}
```

This way, you can specify in the code of the template which width to use. Listings 17-7 and 17-8 show the changes in `index.php` and the `main-content.php` include file to continue using the default value. I'll explain how this code works in the next section.

Listing 17-7. *Setting the Class Variable in index.php*

```
<div id="pagecontent">
<?php $main_content_class = 'main-content-norm'; ?>
<?php include_once('main-content.php'); ?>
```

Listing 17-8. *Using the Class Variable in main-content.php*

```
<div id="main-content" class="<?php echo $main_content_class; ?>">
  <div id="content">
```

A Conversation Layout

Now that you have your building blocks in place, you can make some decisions about which pieces to use in appropriate circumstances. This first example demonstrates a layout to satisfy the readers who want to go straight to the conversation and join in.

A Single-Post View

WordPress has a template function that tells you if the page you are viewing contains a single post: the `is_single` function. You'll use that template function to decide to exclude the sidebars and allow the post and comments to fill the width of the template. Listing 17-9 show the modified code to make this happen.

Listing 17-9. *Testing for a Single Page in index.php*

```
    <div id="pagecontent">
<?php
    if (is_single()) {
      $main_content_class = 'main-content-full';
    }
    else
    {
      $main_content_class = 'main-content-norm';
    }

    include_once('main-content.php');

    if (!is_single()) {
      include_once('sidebar-a.php');
      include_once('sidebar-b.php');
    }
?>
    </div><!-- /pagecontent -->
```

Notice a couple of big changes here. First, all the PHP code is inside one block. You don't need to include each line of PHP inside its own `<?php ?>` tags. You can amalgamate multiple PHP lines. This works well in this case because there is no longer any HTML code mixed in.

Second, you use the WordPress template function `is_single` to test if the reader is viewing a single post. If the function returns `true`, then you set your CSS class variable to `main-content-full`. If it is not true, the `else` part of the clause is executed, setting the CSS class variable to the normal `main-content-norm`. The `main-content` building block isn't included. Then you test again whether you are viewing a single page. This time the test is negative. The exclamation mark in front of the `is_single` function negates the test. This test means, "If the page is *not* a single post, include the two sidebar building blocks." When you are viewing a single page, the main content should be full width and the sidebars will not be output. This results in the view shown in Figure 17-6.

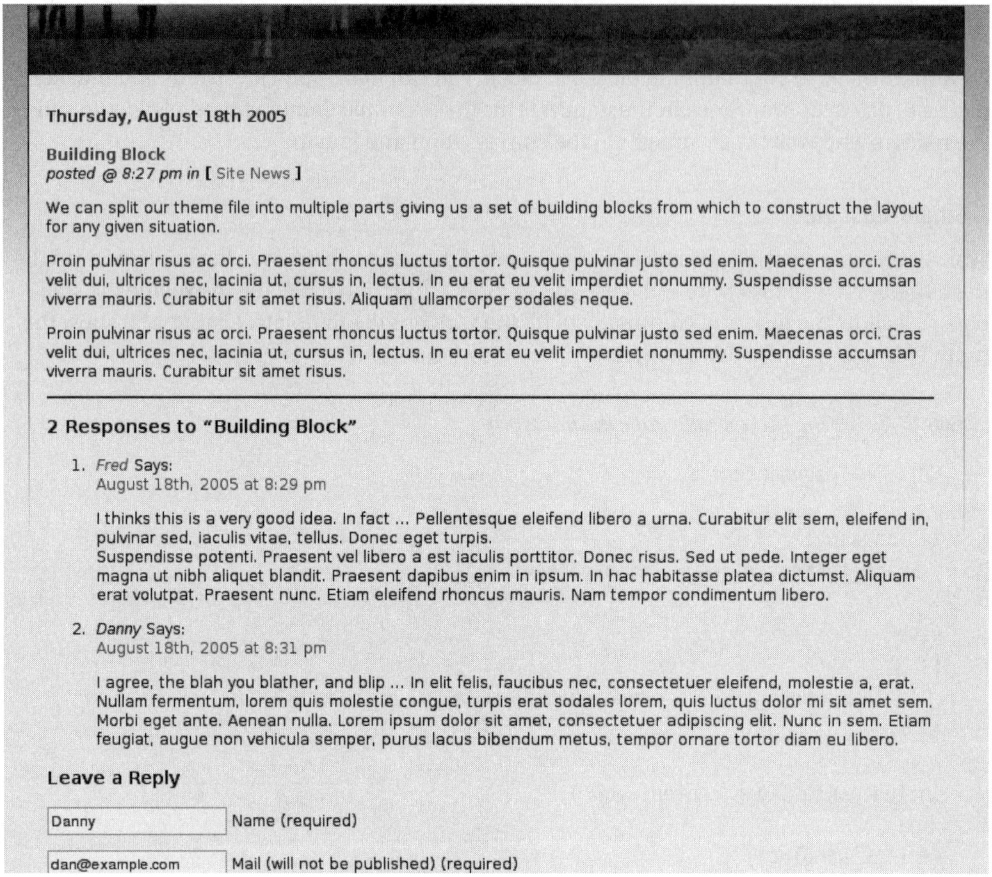

Figure 17-6. *Single-post view without sidebars*

Subscribe to Comments

For a scenario of a reader who is solely interested in your article and the discussion stemming from it, an extension can help to keep that reader involved. An appropriate plug-in is one named Subscribe to Comments, created by Mark Jaquith, originally by Jennifer at ScriptyGoddess (`http://www.scriptygoddess.com/archives/2004/06/03/wp-subscribe-to-comments/`). You can download this plug-in from `http://txfx.net/code/wordpress/subscribe-to-comments/`.

The Subscribe to Comments plug-in allows your readers to subscribe to the comments of a post. This will appeal to those readers who enjoy the conversation aspect of your blog and want to know whenever someone else has posted a comment.

To install this plug-in, download the zip file, expand the archive, and upload it to your server following the instructions in the `readme.txt` file found in the plug-in package. Put the plug-in file `subscribe-to-comments.php` in `wp-content/plugins` and the user administration file `wp-subscription-manager.php` in your main WordPress directory. Go to the plug-ins administration page and activate the plug-in. That's all you need to do.

WordPress automatically calls the plug-in when the comments are displayed. The plug-in adds a check box to the standard comment form, giving your reader the ability to sign up to be notified when follow-up comments are posted. Figure 17-7 shows this in action.

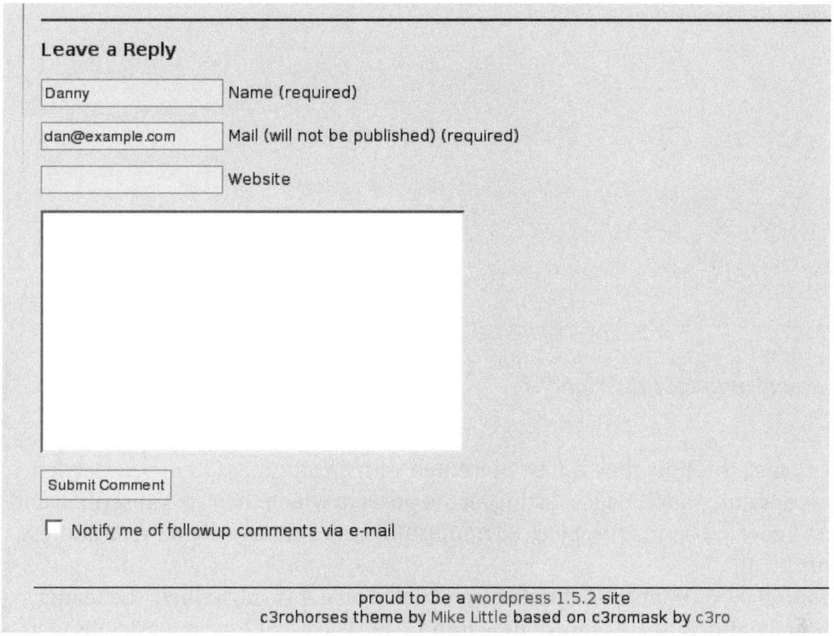

Figure 17-7. *The Subscribe to Comments plug-in in action*

By default, this plug-in allows your visitors to subscribe only when they leave their own comments. If you prefer, you can allow them to subscribe without leaving a comment. Simply add a call to the plug-in's template tag `show_manual_subscription_form` in the `comments.php` theme file (full instructions are in the `readme.html` file; see step 5 of the installation section). The resultant comment form will have a section named Subscribe Without Commenting, as shown in Figure 17-8.

Once your readers have subscribed to the comments on a story, the plug-in recognizes them (via a cookie) when they subsequently revisit the same post. This time, a *Manage your subscriptions* link is presented, as shown in Figure 17-9.

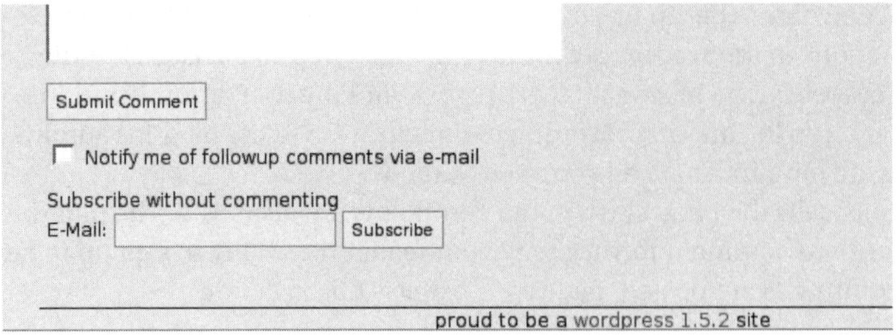

Figure 17-8. *Subscribe without commenting*

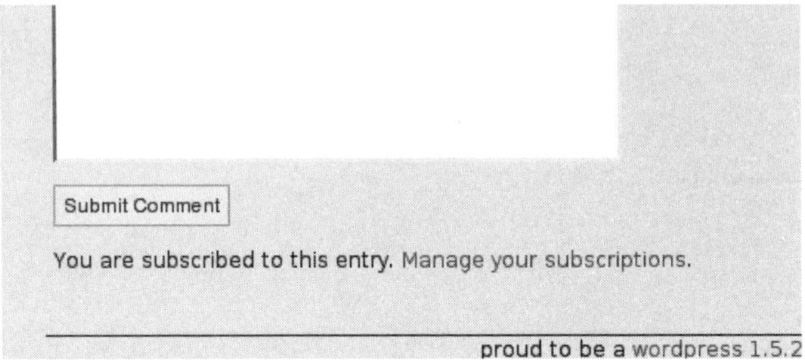

Figure 17-9. *New link to manage subscriptions*

If your visitors click this link, they will be presented with an administration page (styled like the WordPress administration pages) listing all the posts to which they are subscribed and allowing them to remove subscriptions, block all notifications, and change their e-mail address, as shown in Figure 17-10.

When someone else comments on the story to which a reader is subscribed, the reader will receive an e-mail notification, as shown in Figure 17-11. The e-mail message details who commented and what the comment was, and includes a link taking the recipient directly to the post. Another link in the e-mail message takes the recipient to the subscription management page (see Figure 17-10).

Building Online Communities Comment Subscription Manager

Return to the page you were viewing: Themes in WordPress

Subscriptions

dan@example.com is subscribed to the posts listed below. To unsubscribe to one or more posts, click the checkbox next to the title, then click "Remove Selected Subscription(s)" at the bottom of the list.

1. Themes in WordPress
2. New Links In The Sidebar

Invert Checkbox Selection

Remove Selected Subscription(s) »

Advanced Options

Block All Notifications

If you would like **dan@example.com** to be blocked from receiving any notifications from this site, click the button below. This should be reserved for cases where someone is signing you up for notifications without your consent.

Block Notifications »

Change E-mail Address

If you would like to change the e-mail address for your subscriptions, enter the new address below. You will be required to verify this request by clicking a special link sent to your current address (**dan@example.com**).

New E-mail Address:

Change E-mail Address »

Figure 17-10. *The subscription administration page*

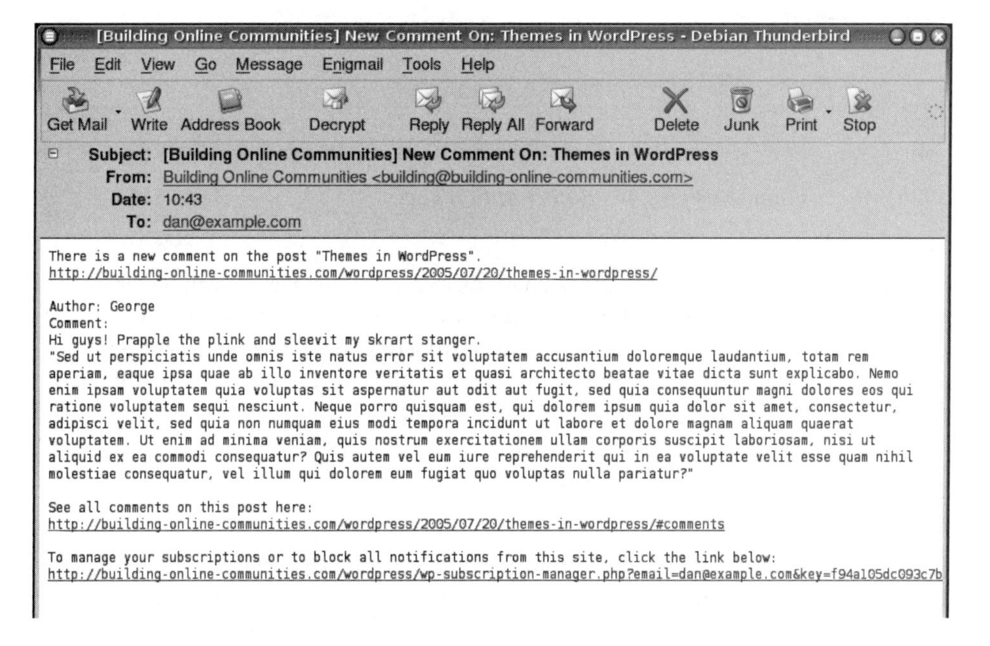

Figure 17-11. *E-mail notification of a new comment*

You can customize the styling of the subscription management page, the wording of the form controls, and the messages that different visitors see from the plug-in administration page, shown in Figure 17-12. As you can see, this plug-in is quite powerful and could provide a great addition to your blog and your visitors' experience.

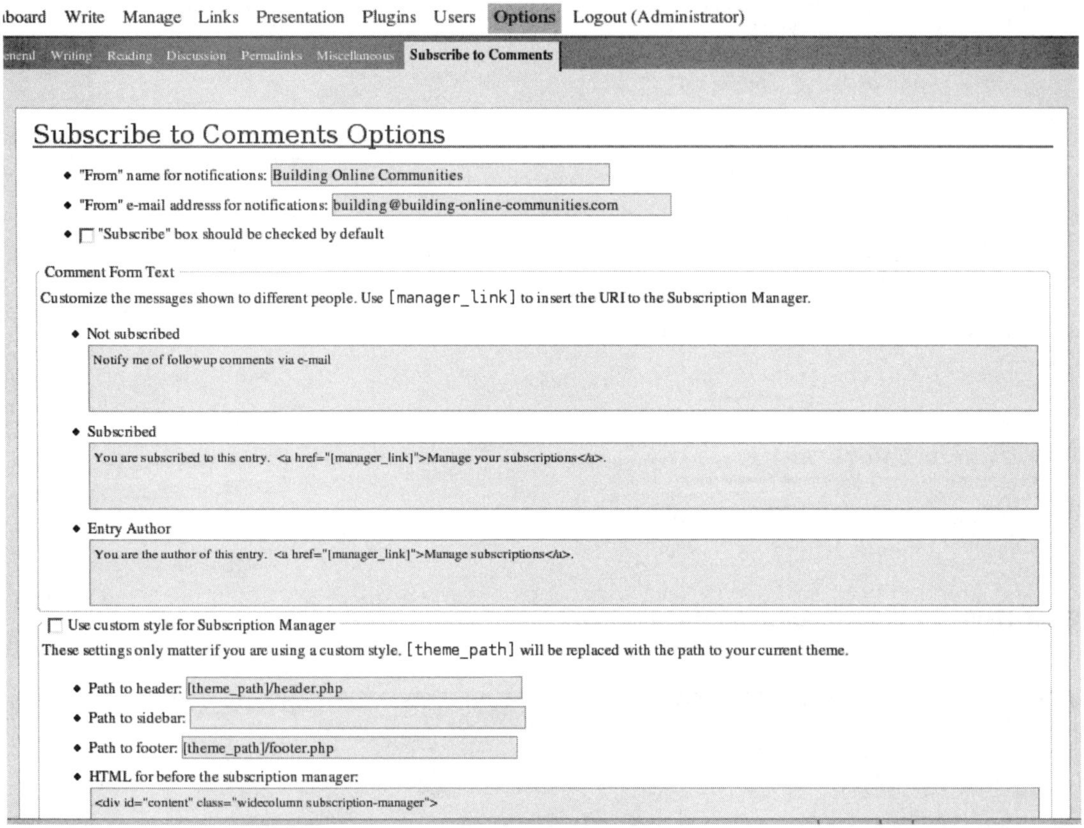

ıboard Write Manage Links Presentation Plugins Users Options Logout (Administrator)

eneral Writing Reading Discussion Permalinks Miscellaneous Subscribe to Comments

Subscribe to Comments Options

- "From" name for notifications: Building Online Communities
- "From" e-mail addresss for notifications: building@building-online-communities.com
- "Subscribe" box should be checked by default

Comment Form Text

Customize the messages shown to different people. Use [manager_link] to insert the URI to the Subscription Manager.

- Not subscribed

  Notify me of followup comments via e-mail

- Subscribed

  You are subscribed to this entry. <a href="[manager_link]">Manage your subscriptions</a>.

- Entry Author

  You are the author of this entry. <a href="[manager_link]">Manage subscriptions</a>.

Use custom style for Subscription Manager

These settings only matter if you are using a custom style. [theme_path] will be replaced with the path to your current theme.

- Path to header: [theme_path]/header.php
- Path to sidebar:
- Path to footer: [theme_path]/footer.php
- HTML for before the subscription manager:

  <div id="content" class="widecolumn subscription-manager">

Figure 17-12. *The Subscribe to Comments plug-in administration page*

A version of the theme with the changes I have described in this section can be downloaded from the Source Code area of the Apress web site (`http://www.apress.com`) as `c3rohorses-discussion-layout.zip`. This is a good starting point to developing a site with a "conversation" layout. A next step might be to customize the subscriber management page to match the rest of the site. If you read through the rest of this chapter, you may find more features you would like to incorporate on your site.

A Learning Layout

The next type of layout is one that would suit a blog that is mostly about learning. This type of layout is more likely to incorporate multiple images and other elements in a post. The post itself might span multiple pages. The layout could have links to related articles of interest to the readers. The readers might also see value in a list of related resources.

Teasers and the More Tag for Lengthy Articles

If you are writing lengthy articles on your blog, they tend to overpower the front page of your blog. While an article is new enough to still be on the front page, its length will push all the other articles a long way out of the visitors' sight. For example, I added a 700-word article as the newest post on my sample blog. This meant that a visitor would need to scroll down through four screens before the next story was visible. If you had several such articles on your front page, it could quickly become a dozen or more screens long. Having a home page of that length is a big turnoff to visitors. They feel overwhelmed by the amount of text presented and are likely to go elsewhere. WordPress has a couple of mechanisms to deal with this.

The first is a special tag you use in your post that allows you to present the first part of your article as a "teaser." The rest of the article is then available by clicking on a *more* link. To enable this feature, simply add the `<!--more-->` special tag to your post at an appropriate point in the text—the end of the first paragraph might be a good place. Figure 17-13 shows the special tag in place while editing an article.

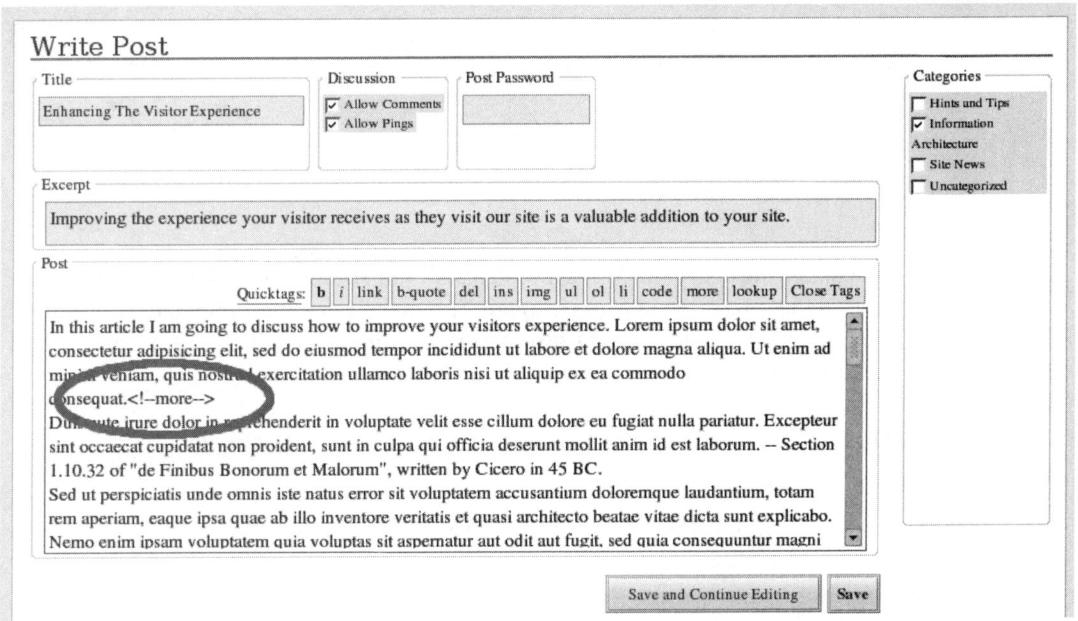

Figure 17-13. *Special more tag inserted into an article*

Note that although the `<!--more-->` tag looks like an HTML comment, it isn't. Specifically, it does not contain any spaces, which a normal HTML comment tag does include. If the `<!--more-->` tag is not exactly like this, WordPress will ignore it. To be sure to get it right, you should use the more quicktag button above the post editor (see Chapter 14 for details on the quicktag buttons).

Adding the `<!--more-->` tag to your post changes the way WordPress presents the post on the front page of your blog. WordPress will display your article up to the teaser tag. It will then add a link with, by default, the text "(more...)," as shown in Figure 17-14. This link will take your reader to the single-page view of your article. This view will have the full text of your article followed by any comments and the comment form as normal. As a nice feature for the reader, the page will be scrolled to the text following the *more* link, ready for them to continue reading.

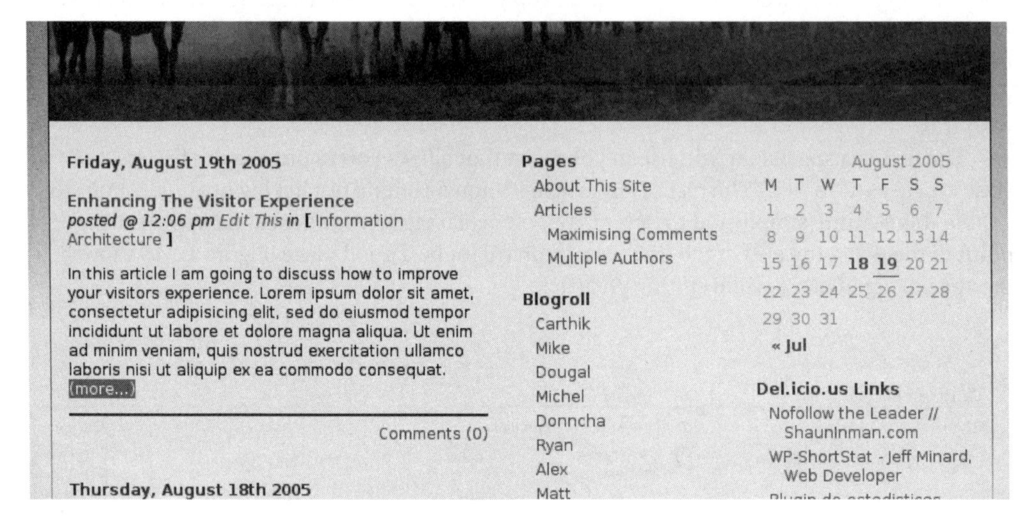

Figure 17-14. *The more link on the page*

You can change the text used for the link so it says something other than "more" by using the template tag `the_content()` in your template. This tag retrieves the content of your post and can take a parameter specifying the text to use in the link. Listing 17-10 shows an example of a different prompt.

Listing 17-10. *Alternative Teaser Prompt Passed to the_content() in main-content.php*

```
<div class="storycontent">
  <?php the_content('<br />Click to read this article...'); ?>
</div>
```

Notice that Listing 17-10 includes an XHTML break tag, `<br />`, in the text. You can add any HTML tag valid in a link. For instance, you could include an image as part of the link. The output from this example is shown in Figure 17-15.

A final point about this teaser tag is a companion tag you can use: `<!--noteaser-->`. This tag will stop WordPress from displaying the teaser part of your article on the page after the reader clicks; that is, the text before the `<!--more-->` tag will not be displayed. You can place the `<!--noteaser-->` tag anywhere in your article, but I tend to place it next to the `<!--more-->` tag to remind myself that I am using it. Whether removing the teaser introductory text makes sense depends very much on the structure of your article.

Enhancing The Visitor Experience
posted @ 12:06 pm Edit This in [Information Architecture]

In this article I am going to discuss how to improve your visitors experience. Lorem ipsum dolor sit amet, consectetur adipisicing elit, sed do eiusmod tempor incididunt ut labore et dolore magna aliqua. Ut enim ad minim veniam, quis nostrud exercitation ullamco laboris nisi ut aliquip ex ea commodo consequat.
Click to read this article...

Comments (0)

Thursday, August 18th 2005

Articles
Maximising Comments
Multiple Authors

Blogroll
Ryan
Matt
Alex
Mike
Carthik
Dougal
Donncha
Michel

1 2 3 4 5 6 7
8 9 10 11 12 13 14
15 16 17 **18** **19** 20 21
22 23 24 25 26 27 28
29 30 31
« Jul

Del.icio.us Links
Nofollow the Leader // ShaunInman.com
WP-ShortStat - Jeff Minard, Web Developer
Plugin de estadisticas para wp

Figure 17-15. *Alternate teaser link*

Multiple Pages for Articles

Another way that WordPress can help you deal with long articles is by splitting your article into multiple pages. You can do this with the `<!--nextpage-->` special tag. Each time you add the tag to your article, WordPress will know to count that as the start of the next page. Figure 17-16 shows the `<!--nextpage-->` tag added to a long article. You can use it at the same time as the `<!--more-->` and `<!--noteaser-->` tags, though it won't work if you place it *before* the `<!--more-->` tag (it doesn't make sense to do that).

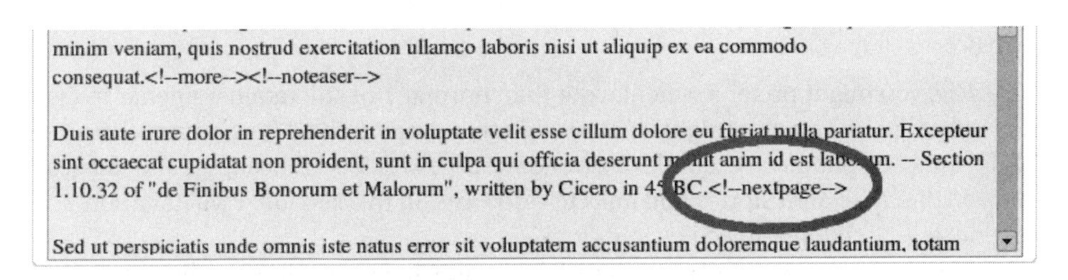

Figure 17-16. *The nextpage tag embedded in an article*

By default, WordPress produces a simple list of links to the pages at the bottom of your post or wherever the `wp_link_pages` template tag is placed in your theme. Figure 17-17 shows the default paging links that WordPress outputs. In this example, the current page is page 2. The numbers 1, 3, and 4 are links to their respective numbered pages.

As with the teaser tag output, you can customize the paging tags with WordPress. You can specify the leading word "Page:" in the default case, whether numbers or words are used, and several other parameters. In the next section, I will show you one example of how you might format the paging links.

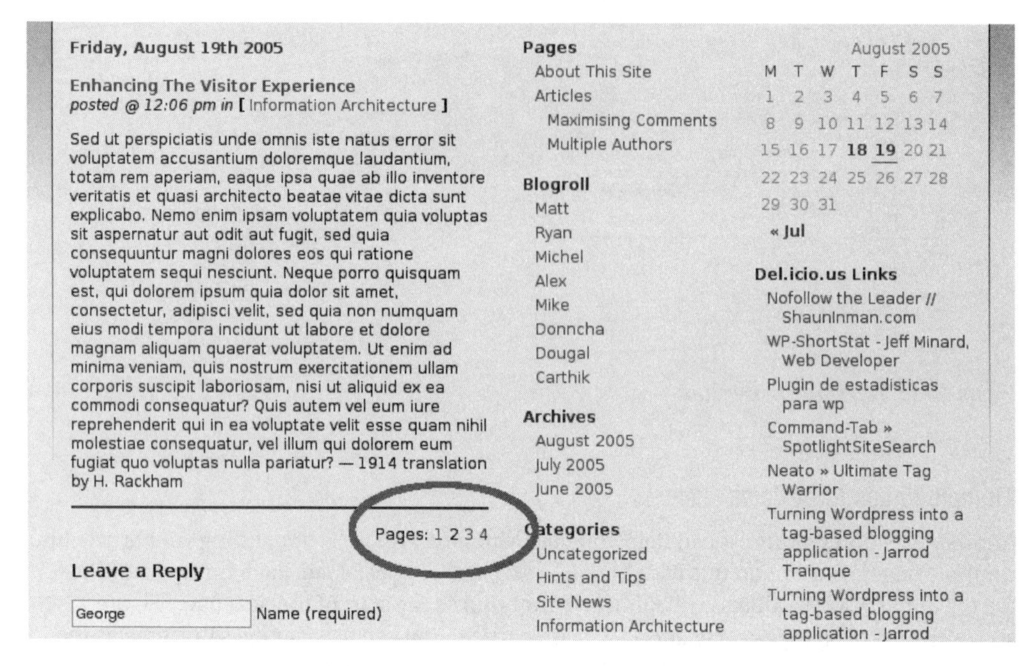

Figure 17-17. *Default paging links*

A Wider Picture

For a long article, you might prefer a wider layout than normal, but still retain a sidebar to display related information. You also might want to add more structure and formatting to the story itself. Figure 17-18 shows an example of a multiple-page article with headings and images, along with a sidebar of related stories and links to resources. In this section, I will take you through the necessary changes to achieve this look.

The first step is to change the appearance of the paging links described in the previous section. In the include file `main-content.php`, which defines The Loop that outputs the articles (see Chapter 16 for more information about The Loop), change the call to `wp_link_pages`. Add parameters to produce the *Next Page* and *Previous Page* links you can see in Figure 17-18. Listing 17-11 shows the changes in the code (highlighted in bold).

Listing 17-11. *Paging Link Code in main-content.php*

```
<div class="feedback" align="right">
  <?php wp_link_pages('before=<p>&next_or_number=next'
     .'&nextpagelink= [Next Page]&previouspagelink=[Previous Page] '); ?>
  <?php comments_popup_link(__('Comments (0)'),__('Comments (1)'),...
</div>
```

Figure 17-18. *The completed learning layout*

Next comes some style tweaking. To do something more attractive with the images, which otherwise display sequentially in the text, add two rules to allow you to float images to the left or right as you feel appropriate. Floating an image in this way allows the text to flow around the image. Add a margin to prevent the text from flowing too closely to the images. Also add two `.storycontent` rules to adjust the margins of the article paragraphs and headings to add a little more white space to the article. If text is too dense, it can be hard for your visitors to read. Listing 17-12 shows the new rules added to the style sheet.

Listing 17-12. *New Style Rules in styles.css*

```
.imageleft {
  float: left;
  margin-right: 1.5em;
  margin-bottom: 0.5em;
}

.imageright {
  float: right;
  margin-left: 1.5em;
  margin-bottom: 0.5em;
}

.storycontent p {
    margin-bottom:0.75em;
}

.storycontent h2 {
  margin-top:1.5em;
  margin-bottom:0.5em;
}
```

In order to choose which way an image floats, you just need to add the appropriate class attribute to the image tag in the article. Figure 17-19 shows the code in the article, in this case floating an image to the left.

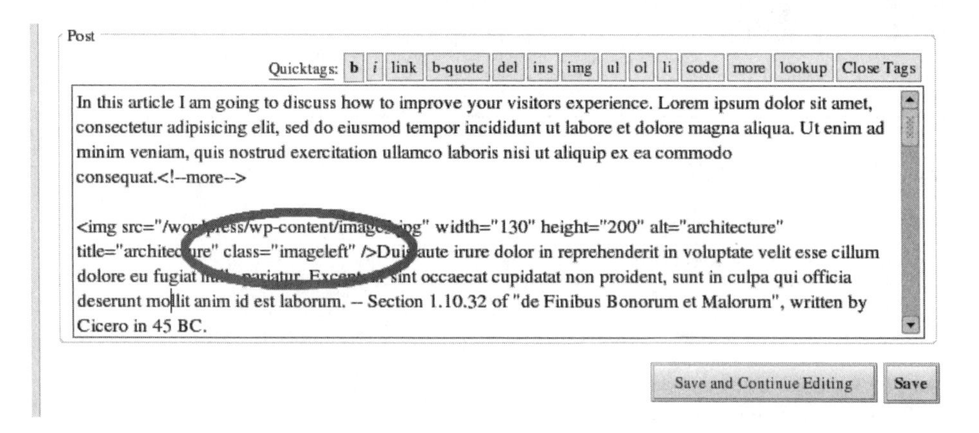

Figure 17-19. *The class in the tag will cause the image to float left.*

For the layout's one sidebar, you could add more code to one of the existing sidebar files to include the information you want. But for this example, let's add a completely new sidebar. Create a new building block `sidebar-c.php` to use in the layout by copying `sidebar-b.php`. Listing 17-13 shows `index.php`. Similar to the code for the other sidebars, you test for the blog displaying a single page and change the main content width appropriately. You then use the single-page test to choose whether to include the new sidebar or both the old ones. The result is that on single pages, the new sidebar is displayed, and on all other pages, both sidebars A and B are displayed.

Listing 17-13. *Adjusting the Layout Based on the Single-Page Test in index.php*

```
    <div id="pagecontent">
<?php
    if (is_single()) {
      $main_content_class = 'main-content-wide';
    } else {
      $main_content_class = 'main-content-norm';
    }

    include_once('main-content.php');

    if (is_single()) {
      include_once('sidebar-c.php');
    } else {
      include_once('sidebar-a.php');
      include_once('sidebar-b.php');
    }
?>
    </div><!-- /pagecontent -->
```

Sidebar C will contain almost all new content. The reader will want recent articles in the same category available as a possible next destination. Also, a list of links to external related resources is a valuable addition to the page. You can use WordPress's built-in Link Manager to collate the list of links. So, let's take a brief side trip to the Link Manager, before continuing with the new sidebar.

A Digression: Using the Link Manager

WordPress comes with a powerful Link Manager, which allows you to create lists of links as part of the content of your blog. If you remember from the history covered in Chapter 13, lists of links to other sites, or *blogrolls*, are one of the essential parts of a traditional blog.

Click the Links menu in the administration pages to start managing your links. WordPress comes with a small list of links already built in. These link to some of the members of the WordPress team and are in the Blogroll category.

Link Manager categories are separate from your post categories, but it can be a good idea to keep them pretty much in sync. Figure 17-20 shows the link categories in my sample blog. Apart from category 1, Blogroll, all the categories match the post categories in name and number. Because you cannot control the number a new category is given when you create it, it is a good idea to create both sets of categories at the same time. This will allow you to do some clever things in your theme code, as I will show you shortly.

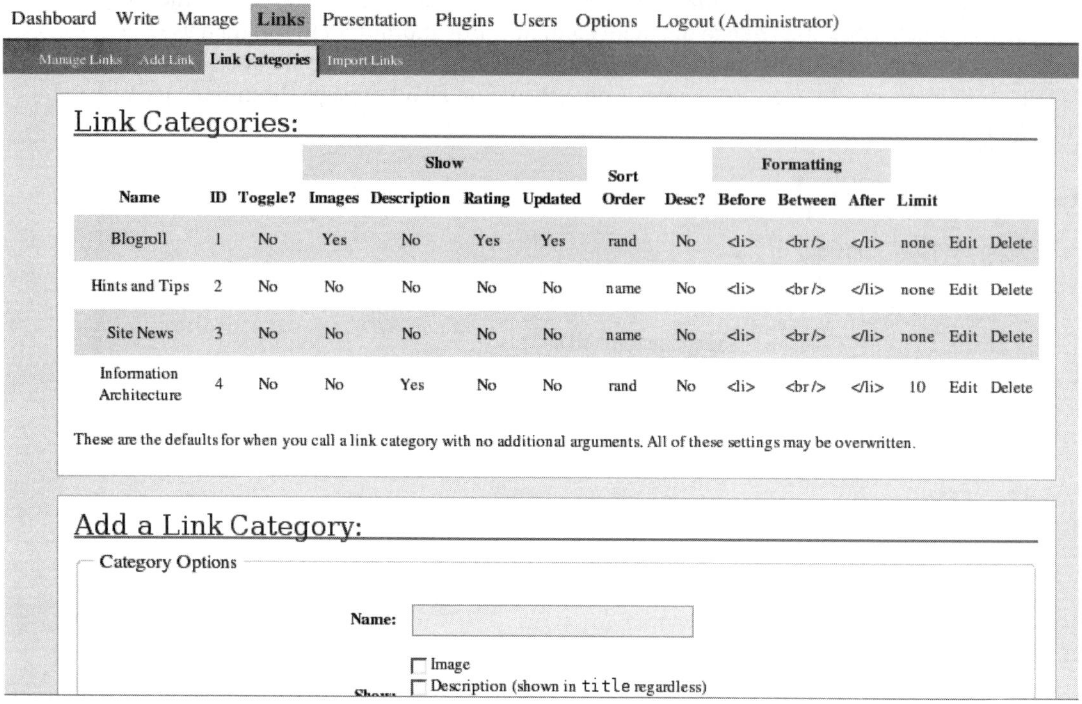

Dashboard Write Manage **Links** Presentation Plugins Users Options Logout (Administrator)

Manage Links Add Link **Link Categories** Import Links

Link Categories:

			Show				Sort		Formatting					
Name	**ID**	**Toggle?**	**Images**	**Description**	**Rating**	**Updated**	**Order**	**Desc?**	**Before**	**Between**	**After**	**Limit**		
Blogroll	1	No	Yes	No	Yes	Yes	rand	No	<li>	 	</li>	none	Edit	Delete
Hints and Tips	2	No	No	No	No	No	name	No	<li>	 	</li>	none	Edit	Delete
Site News	3	No	No	No	No	No	name	No	<li>	 	</li>	none	Edit	Delete
Information Architecture	4	No	No	Yes	No	No	rand	No	<li>	 	</li>	10	Edit	Delete

These are the defaults for when you call a link category with no additional arguments. All of these settings may be overwritten.

Add a Link Category:

Category Options

Name:

Image

Description (shown in `title` regardless)

Figure 17-20. *Link categories*

Once you have created your link categories, you can start adding links and assigning them to the categories. Figure 17-21 demonstrates adding a new link. You can supply the URI, a name for the link, a brief description, and assign a category. If the link is to someone you know, you can designate an XFN relationship. Further down the page, you can also assign an image to the link, specify an RSS feed associated with the link, assign a rating, and even add substantial notes to the link.

■Note XFN, for XHTML Friends Network, is a simple way to represent human relationships using hyperlinks. See `http://gmpg.org/xfn/` for more information.

Figure 17-22 shows a small selection of links in the list management page. You can see one of the original blogroll links and several added to the Information Architecture category. (Not all of the sites listed are *really* about information architecture; they are purely for illustration.)

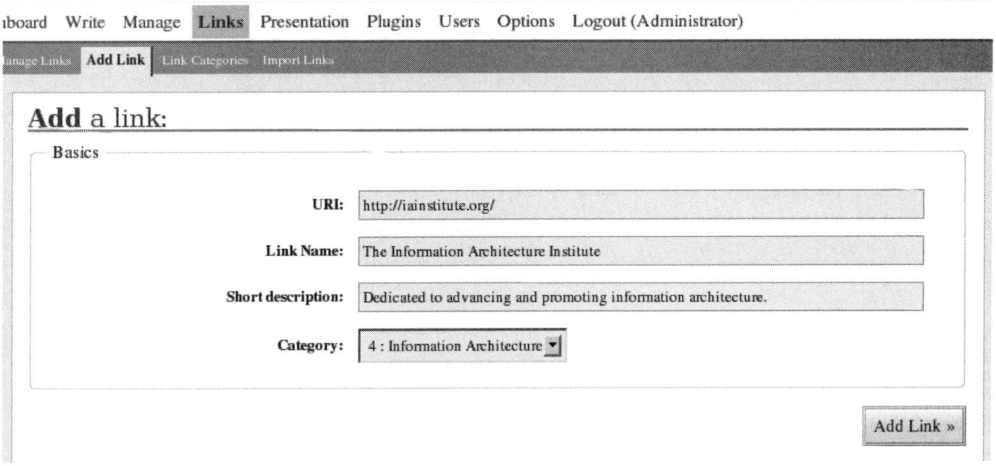

Figure 17-21. *Creating a link*

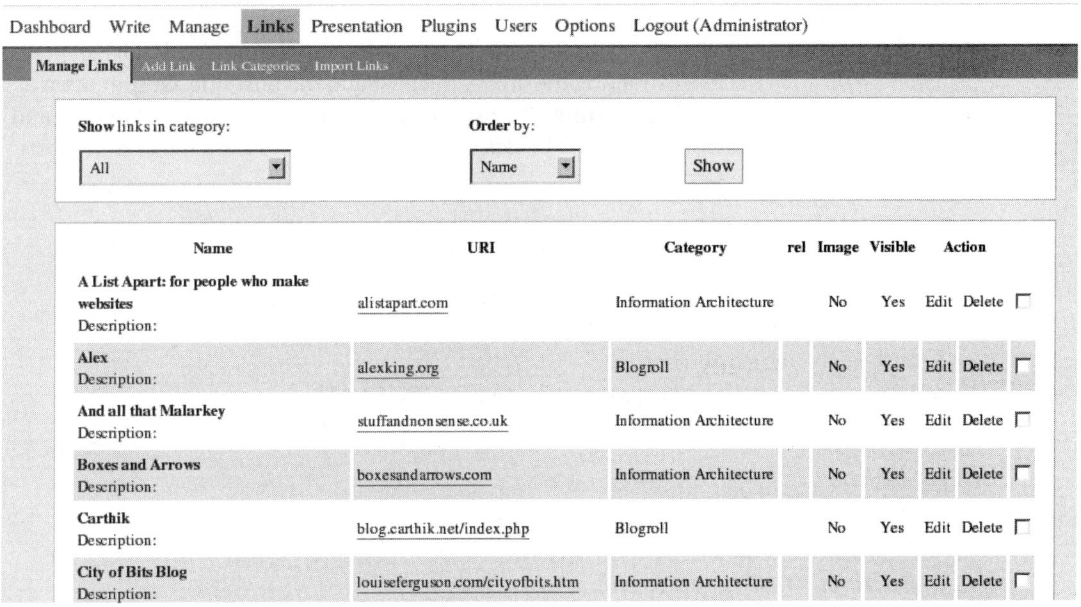

Figure 17-22. *A partial list of links*

A New Sidebar: Tying It All Together

Now that you have a list of links in the same category as the article in this example, you can see how it all fits together. In the new sidebar code, you first need to find the category of the current article. A standard template tag helps you with that: `get_the_category` returns a list of the category IDs for the current post. Save the first category ID in a variable, `$cat`. For this example, you deal with only the first category from the list. I have set my sample blog to use only single categories per post. Listing 17-14 shows this first step.

■ **Note** It is quite natural to have multiple categories per post. The code would need to be more sophisticated to handle that situation. It may be easier to use a plug-in like Related Posts by Mark Ghosh (`http://weblogtoolscollection.com/archives/2004/06/08/contextual-related-posts-in-wordpress/`).

Listing 17-14. *Saving the First Category from the Post in sidebar-c.php*

```
<?php
    $categories = get_the_category();
    $cat = $categories[0]->cat_ID;
?>
```

Once you have the category ID, you can use it with another standard template function `get_posts`. Not surprisingly, this function will get a list of posts. If you pass in the category ID from the last step, via the variable, the function will return a list of posts in the given category. Add an extra parameter to limit the number of posts returned. Once you have that list of posts, you can loop through the list, extracting the link to the post and the post title. Output them as an HTML link in an unordered list. Listing 17-15 shows the completed code with a header and a class style specified or the list. Note that because it uses the category from the current post, this list will also be in the same category.

Listing 17-15. *Generating the List of Posts in sidebar-c.php*

```
<?php
    $categories = get_the_category();
    $cat = $categories[0]->cat_ID;
    $posts = get_posts('numberposts=10&category=' . $cat);
?>

  <div id="sidebar-b">
    <h2><?php _e('Other articles'); ?></h2>
    <ul class="sidebar-b-sidelists">
    <?php foreach($posts as $post) : ?>
      <li><a href="<?php the_permalink(); ?>">
          <?php the_title(); ?></a></li>
    <?php endforeach; ?>
    </ul>
```

Next, add a list of links in the same category to the sidebar, using the WordPress template tag `wp_get_links`.

Listing 17-16 shows the complete code for `sidebar-c.php`. As with the `get_posts call`, if you pass the variable containing the current category as a parameter to the function, the function will output a list of links from that category.

Listing 17-16. *Complete sidebar-c.php*

```
<?php
    $categories = get_the_category();
    $cat = $categories[0]->cat_ID;
    $posts = get_posts('numberposts=10&category=' . $cat);
?>

  <div id="sidebar-b">
    <h2><?php _e('Other articles'); ?></h2>
    <ul class="sidebar-b-sidelists">
    <?php foreach($posts as $post) : ?>
      <li><a href="<?php the_permalink(); ?>"><?php the_title(); ?></a></li>
    <?php endforeach; ?>
    </ul>

    <h2><?php _e('Resources'); ?></h2>
    <ul class="sidebar-b-sidelists">
    <?php wp_get_links($cat); ?>
    </ul>

    <h2><?php _e('Contribute'); ?></h2>
    <ul class="sidebar-b-sidelists">
      <?php wp_register(); ?>
      <li><?php wp_loginout(); ?></li>
    </ul>
  </div><!-- /sidebar-b -->
```

Although this function can take a long list of parameters specifying how many links are displayed, what information from each link is output, and so on, it is easier to use the Link Categories tab of the Links page, shown in Figure 17-23, to control the output. The values and options you set there are used by `wp_get_links`.

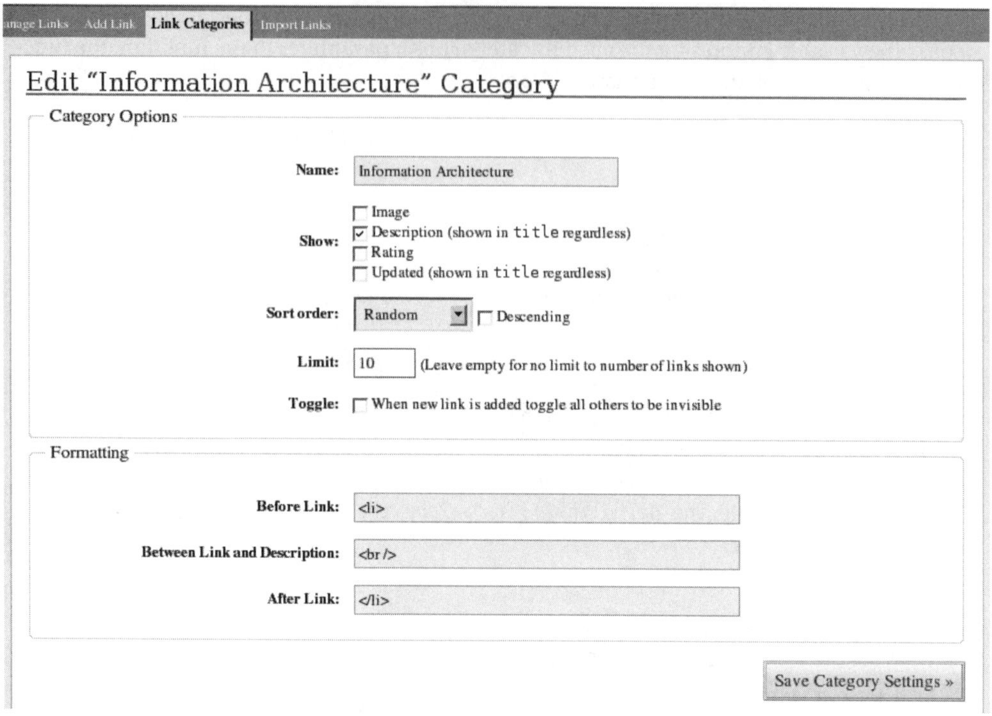

Figure 17-23. *Link category administration*

A Limited Main Page Sidebar

The last change for this layout is related to the main page. Now that you have added a list of links in another category, a problem has emerged on the main blog page. Sidebar A uses the template tag `get_links_list`. This tag outputs a header and a list of links for each of the link categories you have created in Link Manager. This is great for normal use and when you have a small list of links in each category. However, in a learning scenario, you may want links for each category to show up only on a page showing an article in that category. On the front page, or any page that uses sidebar A, you want only the default Blogroll category to be displayed. Listing 17-17 shows the simple change to `sidebar-a.php` to accomplish this.

Listing 17-17. *Only List Category 1 in sidebar-a.php*

```
<li><h2><?php _e('Blogroll'); ?></h2>
  <ul>
    <?php wp_get_links(1); ?>
  </ul>
</li>
```

Although the changes for the learning layout have been relatively complicated, the results are worth the effort. You can apply these same techniques to a real-world blog. Take another look at Figure 17-18. It shows that WordPress can be used to power a site that is much more sophisticated than a simple blog. You can download the completed version of the theme from the Apress web site as c3rohorses-learning-layout.zip.

Other Layouts

You can do a lot more with WordPress. Here are some suggestions for other layouts:

- For a review site, you might include affiliate links on your articles or sidebars. Plug-ins are available to help you manage those links. One example is AdRotator by Angsuman Chakraborty (http://blog.taragana.com/index.php/archive/wordpress-plugin-adrotator-rotate-your-ads-including-adsense-dynamically/).
- For a site that has a number of authors producing articles, you can use plug-ins that allow you to list posts just by a particular author. For example, Customizable Post Listings (http://www.coffee2code.com/archives/2004/08/27/plugin-customizable-post-listings/) is another useful plug-in by Scott Reilly, who wrote the Customizable Comment Listings plug-in introduced in Chapter 16. It might make sense to use the excerpt on your main page instead of the whole content or the post teaser.
- You can also find plug-ins that will allow your readers to vote on each article, giving your authors valuable feedback about what does and doesn't work. Chris J. Davies has a great voting plug-in, available from http://www.chrisjdavis.org/2004/11/30/new-plugin/.
- Numerous photo and gallery plug-ins are available, too. Examples include IImage Gallery by Martin Chlupáč (http://fredfred.net/skriker/index.php/iimage-gallery) and FAlbum by Elijah Cornell (http://www.randombyte.net/blog/projects/falbum/), which uses photos stored on Flickr. A model-building or car-customizing community site could get immense value from these.

If you are prepared to put a little thought into what your community wants and a little effort into giving it to them, WordPress can become the backbone of an online community. Aim to give the most to your community, and in turn, you will get the most back from it. Listen to your readers and your contributors, too. Don't jump at everything they ask, but consider their complaints, their praise, and their suggestions with equal value.

Summary

In this chapter, you've seen how you can tailor WordPress to better fit the needs of your community readers. I have given you some ideas about how to anticipate your readers' expectations and how to help them get a better experience from your site. These things are essential if you are to have a successful online community site and keep your visitors coming back for more.

In the next chapter, I will cover some essential maintenance practices that will keep your blog running smoothly for years.

CHAPTER 18

Maintaining Your Blog

You need to do some regular housekeeping if you are to maintain a working, active community web site. Some of those housekeeping tasks are standard things you should do for any kind of web site: making backups, checking your links, and so on. Some things are WordPress-specific, and some of them are specific to maintaining your readers' interest.

None of these maintenance tasks are particularly daunting, and most of them should occupy no more than a few hours a week. Your biggest maintenance time should be spent "feeding" your blog: responding to comments, writing new posts, and adding links. In this chapter, I will show you how to look after your blog, beginning with the most important maintenance task: backing up your database.

Backing Up and Restoring Your Database

"Why should I make a backup?" you may ask yourself. The answer can be found by imagining having to ask yourself "Why didn't I make a backup?" when it all goes wrong. You never want to be in the situation where you regret not making a backup.

The procrastinator in us will put off generating a backup countless times until it's too late. And that's just the one backup, not an ongoing weekly regime.

Those of you who have been on the receiving end of a disk crash, a software update that went wrong, or even an Internet service provider going out of business will have learned the hard way, by having your whole cyber-existence wiped out seemingly at the touch of a button. Never again will you let yourself be placed in such a disastrous situation. It has happened to me more than once. Now I think hard about a disaster recovery plan even before I start on a new project. Even as I write this chapter, I find myself pressing Ctrl+S to save the document at the end of each line.

The primary considerations of a good backup strategy are that a backup should be easy to do, should rely as little on human interaction as possible (hence making it easy), and should be performed regularly. Oh, and of course, because there isn't much point in generating a lot of backups without being able to restore them when something does go wrong, a good backup strategy is only as good as its recovery plan.

You have a few choices when deciding how to back up WordPress databases. You can use phpMyAdmin or the MySQL Administrator application, which you may have used to create the databases. You can use the command-line interface to MySQL if you have remote access to your server. Finally, you can use the WordPress backup plug-in from Skippy.net, which is the approach I'll describe here.

■ **Note** Instructions for backing up WordPress databases using graphical interfaces such as phpMyAdmin, MySQL Administrator, and the command-line interface to MySQL are available on the WordPress Codex at `http://codex.wordpress.org/Backing_Up_Your_Database`.

Making Backups with the WP-DB Backup Plug-In

The WP-DB Backup plug-in provides an easy-to-use interface for backing up your database tables. With just a few clicks, you can back up all of your WordPress tables.

Installing and Activating the Plug-In

Point your web browser at `http://www.skippy.net/blog/category/wordpress/plugins/wp-db-backup/` and download the WP-DB Backup plug-in from Skippy.net. At the time of writing, it's currently at version 1.7 and mature in development.

Unpack the zipped file to your local drive. It contains four files. Depending on your primary language, you'll probably be interested in only two of them: `wp-db-backup.php` and `wp-dp-backup.txt`. The former is the plug-in, and the latter contains the documentation for the plug-in. The other two files are for language localization.

Installation and configuration are simple. All you need to do is create a directory, upload the plug-in, and then activate it.

On the web server, navigate to the `wp-content` folder. Create a directory here named `backup` and make it writable by the web server process. This normally involves setting the properties by right-clicking the directory in the FTP window, or by providing the instruction `chmod g+w backup` at the shell command line. If configured to store the generated backups on the web site, this directory is where the plug-in will store them, which is why it needs to be writable by the web server. However, by default, the plug-in will expect you to download the backups to your own local machine and not use this folder. Using a `backup` folder is the most secure way to handle your backups and is the approach I recommend.

Next, you need to upload the `wp-db-backup.php` file to the `wp-content/plugins` folder. Finally, go to the administration pages, click Plugins, scroll down until you reach the WordPress Database Backup plug-in, and click *Activate* in the right column.

That's it! The plug-in is installed, configured, and activated.

Backing Up WordPress Tables

Navigate to WordPress's Manage page, where you'll notice a new tab labeled Backup. Select this tab, and you'll be presented with a page like the one shown in Figure 18-1.

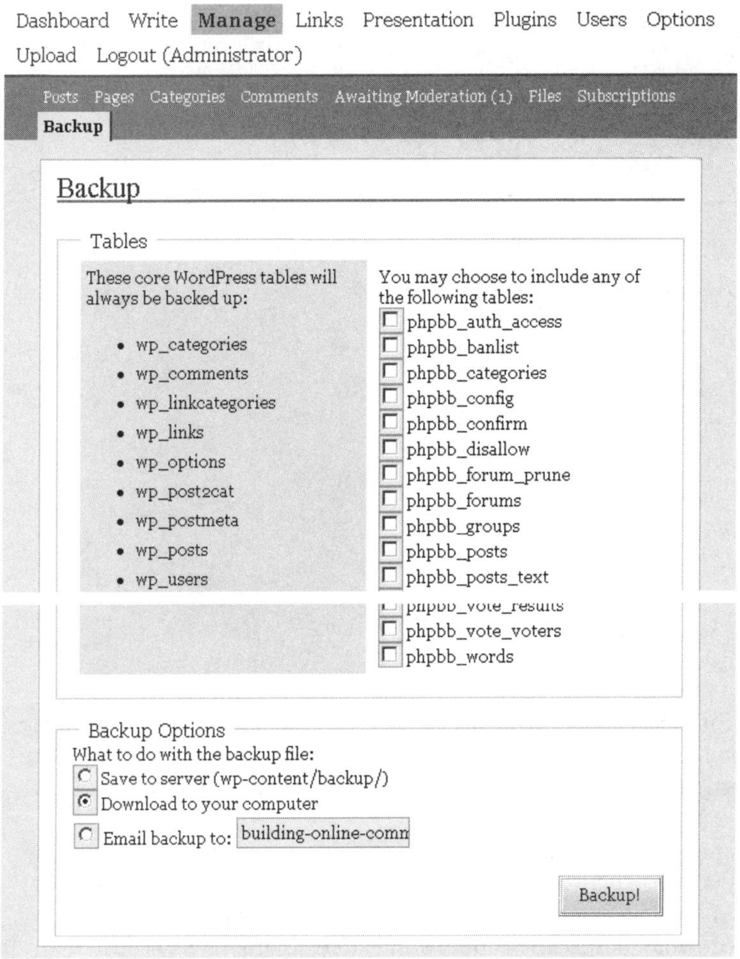

Dashboard Write Manage Links Presentation Plugins Users Options
Upload Logout (Administrator)

Posts Pages Categories Comments Awaiting Moderation (1) Files Subscriptions
Backup

Backup

Tables

These core WordPress tables will always be backed up:

- wp_categories
- wp_comments
- wp_linkcategories
- wp_links
- wp_options
- wp_post2cat
- wp_postmeta
- wp_posts
- wp_users

You may choose to include any of the following tables:

- phpbb_auth_access
- phpbb_banlist
- phpbb_categories
- phpbb_config
- phpbb_confirm
- phpbb_disallow
- phpbb_forum_prune
- phpbb_forums
- phpbb_groups
- phpbb_posts
- phpbb_posts_text
- phpbb_vote_results
- phpbb_vote_voters
- phpbb_words

Backup Options
What to do with the backup file:
Save to server (wp-content/backup/)
Download to your computer
Email backup to: building-online-comm

Backup!

Figure 18-1. *The standard WP DB-Backup page*

WP-DB Backup lists all the tables it can find in the database. Here, you can see it lists both the WordPress tables and the phpBB tables that happened to be installed in the same database. The plug-in automatically selects all the standard WordPress tables and provides check boxes to allow you to include any other tables with the backup.

For now, leave the default backup option to download to your computer selected and click the Backup! button. If all goes well (and there's no reason why it shouldn't), you should see the Backup Progress page, as shown in Figure 18-2.

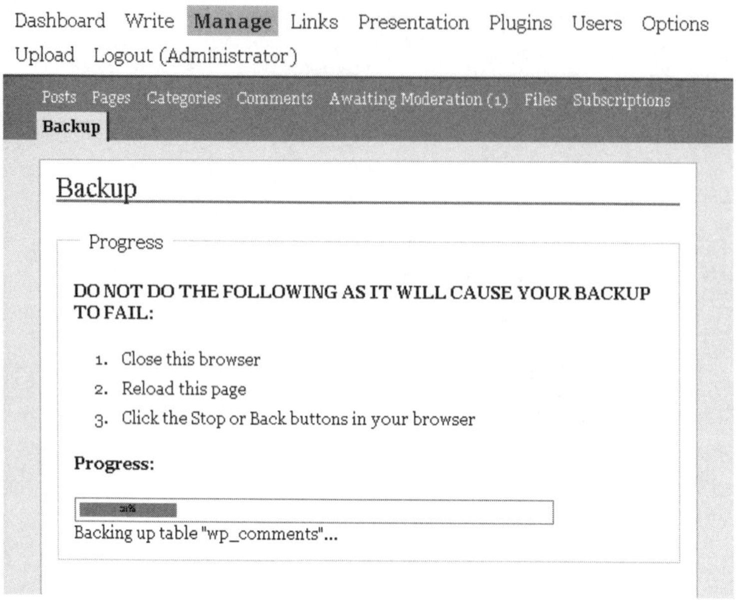

Dashboard Write Manage Links Presentation Plugins Users Options
Upload Logout (Administrator)

Posts Pages Categories Comments Awaiting Moderation (1) Files Subscriptions
Backup

Backup

Progress

DO NOT DO THE FOLLOWING AS IT WILL CAUSE YOUR BACKUP TO FAIL:

1. Close this browser
2. Reload this page
3. Click the Stop or Back buttons in your browser

Progress:

Backing up table "wp_comments"...

Figure 18-2. *The WP DB-Backup progress page*

The progress bar indicates how far along the backup is. Please do follow the instructions on this page, which tell you not to touch anything, as the backup will fail otherwise. Note that until you have a lot of information on your blog to back up, the procedure will likely take only a few seconds.

The file that is generated and automatically downloaded is a compressed file containing a single `.sql` file of MySQL instructions. The size of the `.sql` file depends on the amount of information stored on your blog. Once you have a few hundred blog posts and a few thousand comments, the download file can become quite large. Thankfully, because it is text, it compresses to a manageable size for downloading, storing on your web server, or possibly being e-mailed to you. Given that there are e-mail providers giving away 2GB of storage space for free these days, you could even set up an account purely to receive and store your blog backups.

■ **Note** Usually, backup experts advise against storing backups in compressed form, mainly because if any part of the file becomes corrupt, the whole archive is rendered unusable. However, the use of compression in this instance is appropriate, considering if any part of the single MySQL instruction file contained in the compressed gzip file becomes corrupt, the whole archive should be discarded anyway. This is because of the overwhelmingly large proportion of database instructions compared with database information (your blog data). If one instruction is wrong, recovery is likely to fail catastrophically.

Take notice of the security warning contained in the documentation for Skippy.net's WordPress database backup plug-in and don't store your backups on the server for any length of time. This is because the backup files contain sensitive information about your blog. Don't let them be seen by unscrupulous people. Keep your backup files not only safe, but secure.

Using the WP-Cron Plug-In for Regular Unattended Backups

Recall the core directives of a good backup strategy: backups must be easy to do, rely as little on human interaction as possible, and be performed regularly. The WP-DB Backup plug-in certainly makes backups easy. Now I'm going to introduce to you another useful plug-in from the same author that will take care of the other two backup strategy requirements.

This next plug-in is WP-Cron, which takes its name from the UNIX command that executes jobs at a specific time and or date, either once or at regular intervals. You can download WP-Cron from Skippy.net's web site at `http://www.skippy.net/blog/category/wordpress/plugins/wp-cron/`. By itself, the WP-Cron plug-in doesn't do much, but when combined with WP-DB Backup, it enables unattended backups of your WordPress database.

■ Tip WordPress Codex "strongly recommends" blog administrators to back up their databases at regular intervals and before upgrades. You should take this advice!

Unattended—how does that work? The WP-Cron plug-in doesn't install anything on the web server, or configure a cron job that the underlying operating system (such as Linux or Windows Server 2003) runs. In fact, a lot of hosting providers wouldn't allow you to do that. Instead, this plug-in relies entirely on someone or something visiting your site, which is a fairly safe bet these days, with the number of search engine crawlers, TrackBacks, and Pingbacks interoperating with your site—however unpopular it may be! Any time a page on your site is requested, it triggers the plug-in. If a preconfigured interval has elapsed, the task will be executed. In this case, at approximately the same time every day, an unattended backup will be generated and e-mailed to you.

Download the WP-Cron plug-in from Skippy.net's web site at `http://www.skippy.net/blog/category/wordpress/plugins/wp-cron/`. By now, you know how to install a WordPress plug-in: unpack the zipped file to your local drive, upload the single file `wp-cron.php` to the `wp-content/plugins` folder, and then go to the Plugins page and activate the WP-Cron plug-in.

You now need to configure unattended backups, because they're not enabled by default. Thankfully, this is no more complex than specifying an e-mail address for your backup archive file delivery.

Return to the Manage page and again choose the tab labeled Backup. Scroll down the page, and you'll notice an extra section at the foot of the page, as shown in Figure 18-3. As with the attended backup (the one requiring you to click the Backup! button), you can also archive non-WordPress database tables that are present in the same database. To configure unattended backups, select the Daily check box, enter your chosen archiving e-mail address, and click the Submit button.

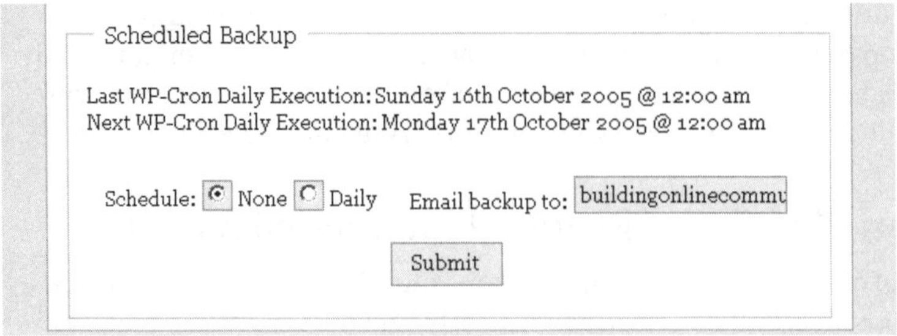

Figure 18-3. *The WP-Cron extension adds a Scheduled Backup section to the WP-DB Backup page.*

So, with a couple of great plug-ins and a few clicks, you've managed to accomplish your goal of achieving the magical triumvirate of a good backup strategy: easy to do, with little human interaction, and performed regularly. Give yourself a pat on the back(up)!

Restoring Your Database

Okay, so you're here because something catastrophic has gone wrong and you need to restore your backup. Or you could be moving your blog to a different hosting provider. Or perhaps you are one of those people who like to prepare for the worst. In any case, you're interested in the process of restoring your database from a backup.

■ **Caution** Please understand that even if you've been generating backups, you won't be able to retrieve the information lost since the last backup.

First, let's take a look at the recipe for restoring databases. At the top of the list is an archive file generated by any of the methods: the WP-DB Backup plug-in, the graphical user interfaces of either phpMyAdmin or MySQL Administrator, or from the command line. Without the archive file, you can't achieve much.

■ **Note** If you came here looking for help with a damaged database but haven't performed a backup, then you should consider searching through and perhaps posting to the WordPress support forums at `http://wordpress.org/support/`.

Although Skippy.net's WP-DB Backup plug-in makes it easy for you to generate backups and automate unattended backups, there is no companion restore plug-in or option. This is because there doesn't need to be. Restoring is a simple process of applying the generated archive file to the database, which you can do using the phpMyAdmin interface.

Tip If you're moving your WordPress blog to a new hosting provider, you'll need to first create the database as you did in Chapter 14. To make things easy for yourself, name the database exactly as in your previous installation.

Navigate your web browser to the phpMyAdmin page for your database. It should look similar to Figure 18-4, which shows the WordPress tables.

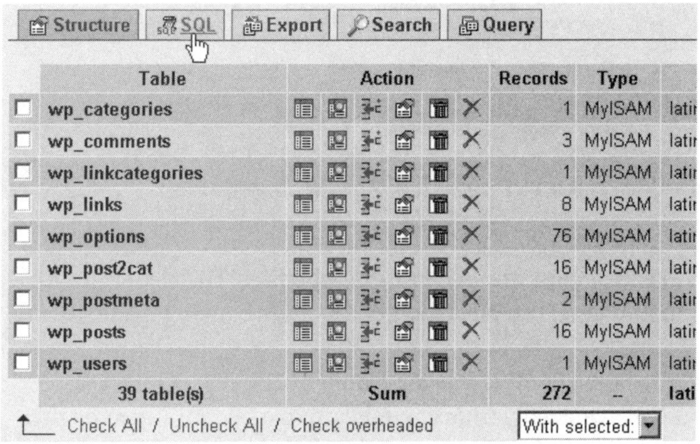

Structure | SQL | Export | Search | Query

	Table	Action	Records	Type	
☐	wp_categories		1	MyISAM	lati
☐	wp_comments		3	MyISAM	lati
☐	wp_linkcategories		1	MyISAM	lati
☐	wp_links		8	MyISAM	lati
☐	wp_options		76	MyISAM	lati
☐	wp_post2cat		16	MyISAM	lati
☐	wp_postmeta		2	MyISAM	lati
☐	wp_posts		16	MyISAM	lati
☐	wp_users		1	MyISAM	lati
	39 table(s)	Sum	272	--	lati

Check All / Uncheck All / Check overheaded   With selected:

Figure 18-4. *The WordPress database tables in phpMyAdmin*

Choose the SQL tab at the top of the page, and you will see a page like the one shown in Figure 18-5. Here, you can enter a query in the large text area in the top part of the page or choose a text file to upload by clicking the Choose button next to the Location of the textfile box. Notice that there is a maximum file size indicated, which is 8MB in the example shown in Figure 18-5. Your limit may differ from this, but the general rule is that uploading files of around 3MB and above usually proves unsuccessful. In this event, you're forced to cut segments from the text file to paste into the text area of the SQL tab, one piece at a time, until the whole file has been completed.

Note Prior to populating the WordPress databases with your backup, you'll need to ensure that all the current information in there is removed by using the `DROP TABLE` command in MySQL. The process used by the WP-DB Backup plug-in does this for you when restoring the backup.

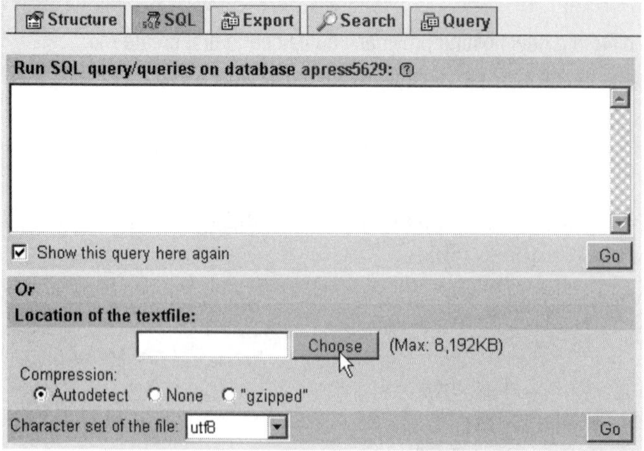

Figure 18-5. *Restoring WordPress database backup using phpMyAdmin*

Note that the file upload method can accept gzipped compressed files. This is perfect if you've followed my recommendation and used the WP-DB Backup plug-in, which generates such a compressed file type.

To restore your backup, upload the latest archive file generated by the WP-DB Backup plug-in and click the Go button. You will eventually (this can take up to a few minutes) be presented with a page containing a message similar to the one in Figure 18-6, indicating that the upload was successful.

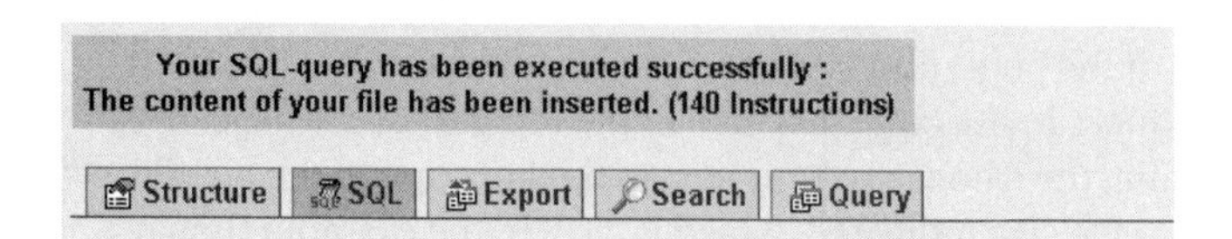
Your SQL-query has been executed successfully :
The content of your file has been inserted. (140 Instructions)
Structure
SQL
Export
Search
Query

Figure 18-6. *Successful WordPress database restore using phpMyAdmin*

Check your blog site now to determine that all is well. Sometimes, a faulty theme can display a blank page at this stage. If so, swap out the theme to the Default theme (see Chapter 16) to see if that solves the problem. If that fails to resolve the situation, you may need to resort to reapplying a new set of WordPress files, but that is a rare event.

Monitoring Storage Space and Bandwidth

To keep your WordPress blog healthy, you need to be conscious of any limits imposed by your hosting company, because your blog is dynamic—it grows whenever people add comments or when you write new articles. The following are three limits you need to consider.

- The storage space used by WordPress, your images, your download files, and so on
- The space taken by your database holding your posts, comments, links, and so on (this is sometimes counted separately from your main storage)
- The bandwidth used each month by your visitors accessing your pages

Monitoring Your Storage Space

The storage space used by your files is usually more than adequate in current hosting packages, unless you have an exceptionally large number of images or files. Many hosting companies' cheapest packages allow from 500MB of storage to as much as 4GB. Some offer considerably less. I would steer clear of those.

As a rough guide to how much space you might need, WordPress itself, including the built-in themes and perhaps a couple more themes, is unlikely to be more than 2MB. But if you have a lot of images, photographs, product images, maps, charts, and so on, this amount can soon increase. My main web site uses just over 150MB for around 1,800 images, 70% of which are high-resolution photographs. If you were to store high-quality MP3 music files, then 350 such files might use up 1GB. If you stored lower-quality speech files, 350 of them might take only 400MB.

The space taken by your database is significantly less. For example, my main blog with 1,100 posts and 58,000 comments uses just 21MB of storage space.

You will need to monitor your storage space usage regularly. The way you check exactly how much space you are using is different from one hosting company to another. Generally, you can expect your administration pages, or control panel, to have an option to calculate the space you have used. How often you should check depends on how quickly your blog grows. That growth rate is something you will need to judge for yourself. Start by checking once a week and make a judgment after a month or two. If you are allocated, say, 1GB, and after a month, you've used 10MB, then you don't really need to check too often. A monthly check should be enough to give you plenty of warning before you start to run out. If, after a couple of months, you've used 400MB, you will need to monitor it more closely, perhaps on a weekly basis.

If you do find yourself running low on space, or at least heading that way, you have several options. If you have a lot of high-resolution images, you should consider replacing the older ones with lower-resolution versions, if that won't detract from the value of your old posts. Similarly, if your community blog is a support site for your software and you offer downloads, you could consider removing the older versions. But make sure any old posts that link to them are updated. You don't want to leave bad links in your old posts. I'll show you how to check for bad links later in this chapter, in the "Checking Your Links" section.

With regard to your database, there isn't really a lot you can do to reduce its size. The bulk of your database is your content: your posts and pages, your visitors' comments, and your links. You don't want to get rid of any of that because it is the lifeblood of your blog. However, the spam comments can go, as described next.

Cleaning Comment Spam

If you recall from Chapter 15, I mentioned that WordPress doesn't give you any way to access comments marked as spam. For that, you need a third-party plug-in. Chris J. Davis's Spam Nuker is one such plug-in.

Download the Spam Nuker plug-in from `http://www.chrisjdavis.org/2005/03/05/spam-nuker-151/`. Install this as a plug-in on your blog and activate it. Go to WordPress's Manage page, and you will see an extra tab labeled Spam. Click the Spam tab, and you will be presented with a page like the one shown in Figure 18-7. The tab includes the number of spam comments in its title. In the example, a rather excessive 39,000 spam comments were found. Note that the e-mail and URI in the figure have been intentionally blurred.

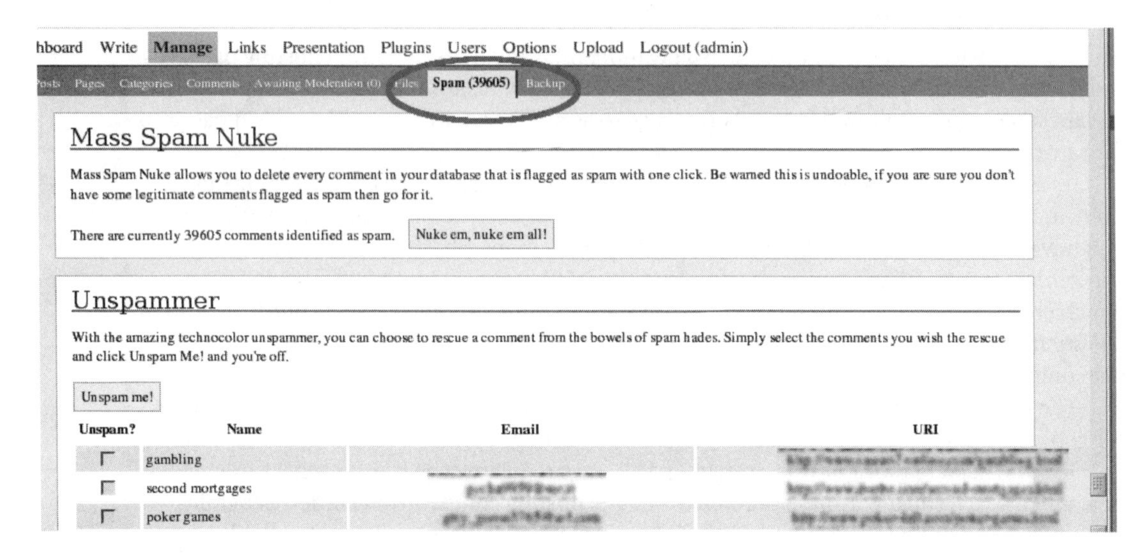

Figure 18-7. *Spam Nuker management page*

The plug-in has two functions:

Mass Spam Nuke: This allows you to remove all the comments marked as spam with a single click. Simply click the Nuke em, nuke em all! button. However, as the page cautions, this step is *irreversible* (database backup not withstanding). You might want to look at the other function first.

Unspammer: This allows you to change the status of a comment marked as spam. Depending on how you detect and mark comments as spam, you may end up with some false positives—some comments marked as spam that should not be. This function allows you to correct that and rescue those comments. Look down the list of comments. The name, e-mail, URI, IP address, and a count of duplicates are provided to help you decide the status of a comment. If you find any comments that should not be marked as spam, click the check box to the left of the comment. When you have finished with the list, click the Unspam me! button at the bottom of the page. The comments you marked will be changed to be ordinary comments, disappear from the spam list, and appear on your site as normal comments.

When you are sure you have rescued all the legitimate comments, go ahead and click the Nuke em button. All of your spam comments will be removed from the database, saving you valuable space.

Monitoring Bandwidth

Bandwidth usage is another limit your hosting service will specify. Strictly speaking, *bandwidth* is the wrong term to use. Hosting companies usually restrict your monthly data transfer allowance; that is, they monitor how much data is transferred from your account each month. Unfortunately, the term *bandwidth* is so commonly used for this allowance that it has become the way to describe it.

If you exceed the allowed bandwidth, several things may happen:

- The hosting company may shut down your site until the end of the month.
- The hosting company may allow your site to go over the limit but charge you for the excess (often an excessive amount).
- The hosting company may force you to upgrade your account to one with more bandwidth allowance.

Most control panels provided by your hosting company have some way to monitor your bandwidth usage. Figure 18-8 shows one such example from the Plesk control panel (`http://www.sw-soft.com/en/products/plesk/`).

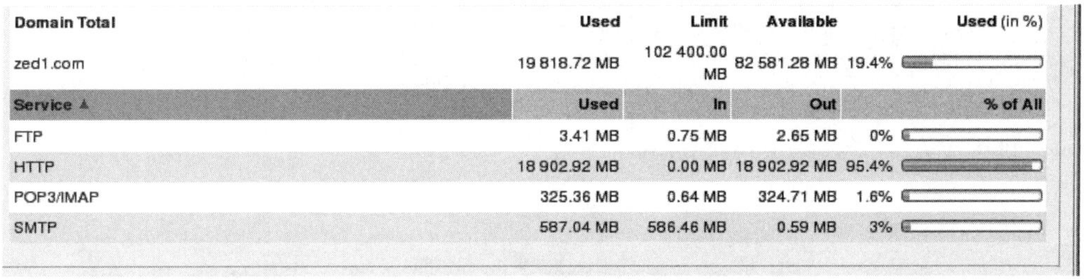

Domain Total	Used	Limit	Available	Used (in %)
zed1.com	19 818.72 MB	102 400.00 MB	82 581.28 MB	19.4%

Service ▲	Used	In	Out	% of All
FTP	3.41 MB	0.75 MB	2.65 MB	0%
HTTP	18 902.92 MB	0.00 MB	18 902.92 MB	95.4%
POP3/IMAP	325.36 MB	0.64 MB	324.71 MB	1.6%
SMTP	587.04 MB	586.46 MB	0.59 MB	3%

Figure 18-8. *Plesk traffic report*

If your hosting service provides traffic statistics derived from your web server logs, those can be another way to monitor your traffic. Figure 18-9 shows a typical monthly chart from the Webalizer package (`http://www.mrunix.net/webalizer/`). From a chart like this, you can get a good idea of the growth of your traffic and look for trends that look like you might be exceeding your bandwidth allowance.

Figure 18-10 shows another statistics report from the Webalizer package. This particular report shows the URLs that use the most bandwidth. In this example, you see that the third page in the list has managed to generate almost 1.3% of the traffic, despite having only 791 hits. Compare that to the first page in the list, which has of 22,000 hits for 7.4% of the traffic. In other words, that third file is using a disproportionate amount of bandwidth allowance. I investigated that post on my blog and saw that it has more than 530 comments, making it a huge, 400KB page. I can choose to address this issue in some way, perhaps by trimming the comments that are over a year old. Many statistics package provide reports like this that allow you to delve into the aggregated data from your server's web logs.

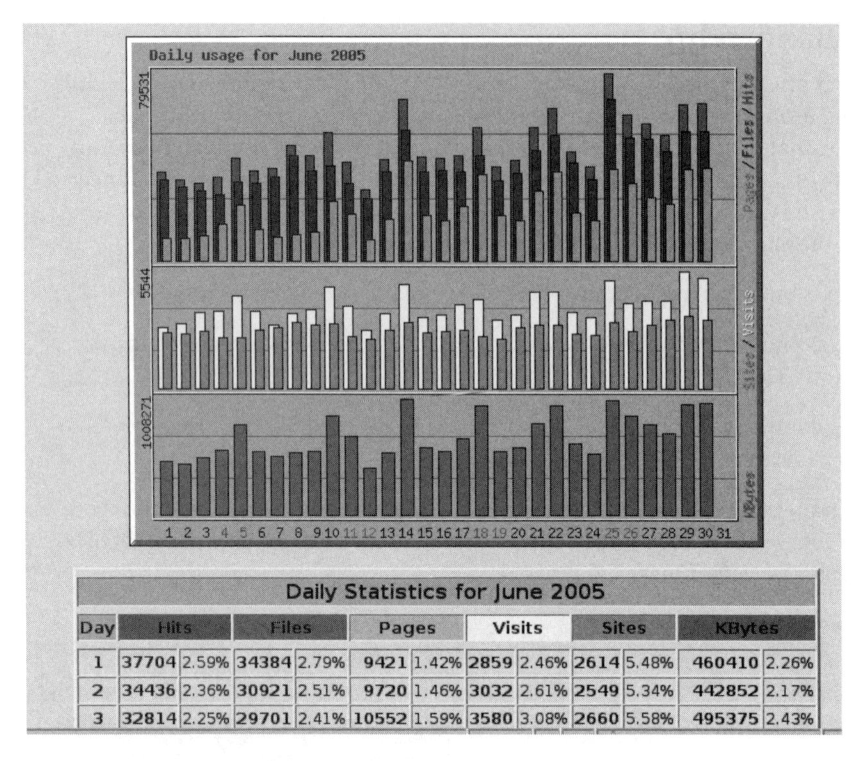

Daily Statistics for June 2005												
Day	Hits		Files		Pages		Visits		Sites		KBytes	
1	37704	2.59%	34384	2.79%	9421	1.42%	2859	2.46%	2614	5.48%	460410	2.26%
2	34436	2.36%	30921	2.51%	9720	1.46%	3032	2.61%	2549	5.34%	442852	2.17%
3	32814	2.25%	29701	2.41%	10552	1.59%	3580	3.08%	2660	5.58%	495375	2.43%

Figure 18-9. *Webalizer monthly summary*

Top 10 of 10889 Total URLs By KBytes					
#	Hits		KBytes		URL
1	22355	1.53%	1511278	7.42%	/journalized/
2	8035	0.55%	713140	3.50%	/journalized/archives/2002/10/20/ntl-proxy-servers/
3	791	0.05%	262595	1.29%	/journalized/archives/2003/06/03/chester-bennington-hospitalisedhospitalized/
4	187	0.01%	183005	0.90%	/images/joy-of-work.rm
5	5526	0.38%	171575	0.84%	/
6	24938	1.71%	164492	0.81%	/journalized/wp-content/themes/journalized/themes/sand/layout.css
7	25330	1.74%	163525	0.80%	/journalized/wp-content/themes/journalized/themes/newyear2003/layout.css
8	26130	1.79%	156100	0.77%	/journalized/wp-content/themes/journalized/themes/halloween/layout.css
9	27677	1.90%	149195	0.73%	/journalized/wp-content/themes/journalized/style.css
10	25171	1.73%	144530	0.71%	/journalized/wp-content/themes/journalized/themes/winter/layout.css

Figure 18-10. *Another view of Webalizer statistics*

One way to reduce your bandwidth usage is to reduce the size of your pages. A properly constructed, valid, XHTML web page will be smaller in size than one written in the old-school style using font tags, tables, and spacer images for layout. Using CSS for styling and layout reduces the size of your web page so that it downloads quicker and reduces your bandwidth usage. It will most likely render more quickly in your readers' browsers, too, which is an added bonus.

WordPress strives to conform to the XHTML standard, but even though the code delivered by WordPress may be minimal, it still doesn't prevent you from writing pages and posts using the old-school style of web page writing, though it does encourage you to separate presentation and content by the appropriate use of CSS. In the previous chapter, I illustrated how to remove the sidebar of calendars, del.icio.us links, and login/register controls. Doing so not only makes the page cleaner for a single-post-entry context, but also reduces the page weight—considerably, if your sidebars contain a lot of information, such as a long list of pages, posts, categories, and so on. The example in Chapter 17 would work well if your most weighty pages are individual posts, like two of the top three URLs in Figure 18-10.

Checking Your Links

Another regular routine task you should undertake is to check the links on your site. Nothing is quite so frustrating to a user than to click a link referenced in a blog post, only to find the page has disappeared. Inevitably, people do move their web sites to new URLs, or they rearrange their site so that old links to pages no longer work. Sometimes, they abandon their sites altogether. You cannot control what other people do with the pages you link to, but you can at least make sure your readers are not disappointed too often.

What you can control is your own links. You should make sure that your own links you make to, for example, past stories still work. Another source of broken links is the list of links you have in your blogroll, resources list, and so on, managed by WordPress's Link Manager (described in Chapter 17). Finally, readers sometimes leave links in their comments, which can go out-of-date. You could check each of those links by hand: clicking each in your browser and checking that the link still works. Unfortunately, that gets tedious after about the first five! Luckily, a number of solutions to this problem are available, in the form of both online services and desktop tools.

Using Online Link Checking Services

A number of web sites provide online link checking services. They work by reading your web page after you provide the URL, and checking each of the links they find on your page. One such tool is Link Valet from the Web Design Group (`http://valet.htmlhelp.com/link/`). Figure 18-11 shows a portion of a typical report page.

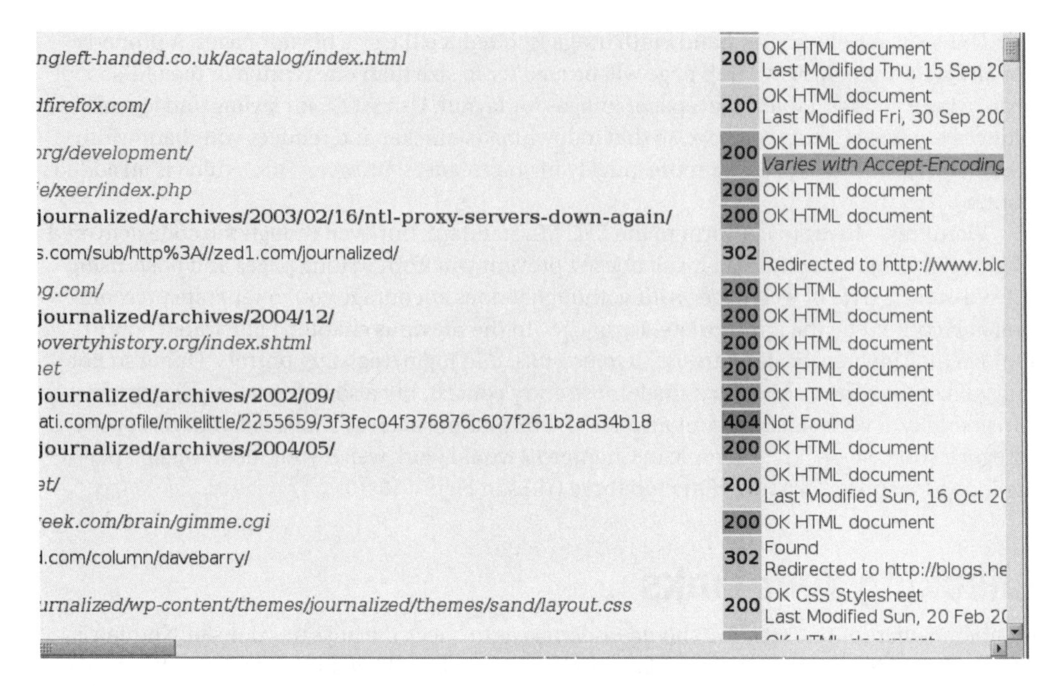

Figure 18-11. *Link Valet report page*

As you can see, the report lists each link on the submitted page, along with a status indicating the link's health: status 200 is OK, status 302 is also OK, and status 404 means that the page you linked is reported as not found. Link Valet highlights these in red as an indicator for you to do something about it: either to correct the inaccurate link or generate the page it's attempting to link to.

Another similar service is Link Checker from SiteOwner.com (`http://siteowner.bcentral.com/system/linkcheck.asp`). This service reports only links with errors. You don't need to wade through screens full of good links to find the broken ones.

The problem with services like these is that you need to submit every single page on your site to check for bad links. As you start to accumulate more and more posts on your site, this quickly becomes an unworkable solution. Recognizing this, most of the online services offer a more sophisticated service, whereby their software automatically loads the pages on your own site (by following links), and checks the links on each of those pages. Although this is a much better way of doing things, even automated checking of the links on every page of a large site can take a considerable time—as much as a few hours. These services generally e-mail you the results or a link to the results in a private area on their server. Not surprisingly, all the services I have seen charge a fee for this more sophisticated checking. They often offer other services, too, like checking your HTML for validity, checking your site for accessibility, and so on. Shop around to find the deal that suits you best.

Using Desktop Link Checking Tools

An alternative to online link checking services is desktop link checking tools. One such tool I came across is an extension for the Firefox web browser. If you are using this browser, you can install the LinkChecker extension (`http://www.kevinfreitas.net/extensions/linkchecker/`), by Kevin A. Freitas. This extension allows you to check the links on any page you are viewing.

After you install the extension into Firefox from Kevin's site, you will have a new command in the Tools menu: Check Page Links, as shown in Figure 18-12. Click this command, and the extension will check the links in the page one at a time. As it checks each link, it will highlight it to indicate its status. The colors used are green for a good link, red for broken links, yellow for redirected or forbidden links, and gray for skipped links.

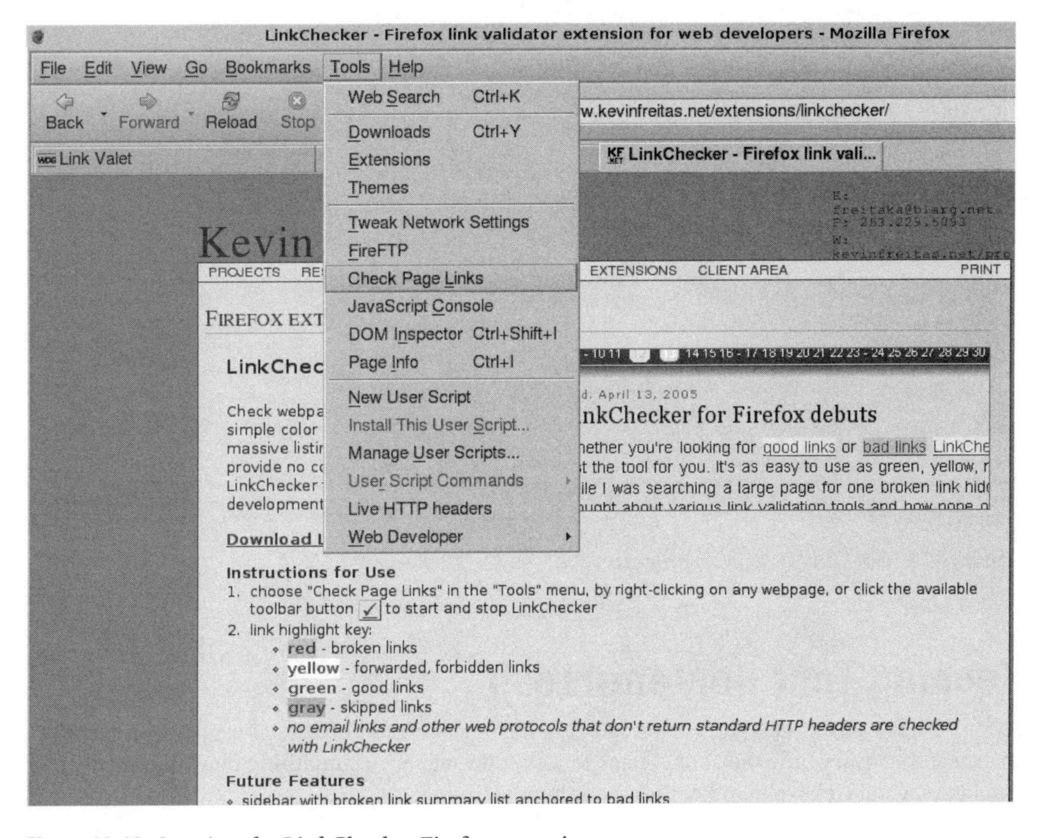

Figure 18-12. *Starting the LinkChecker Firefox extension*

The extension also shows its progress in the Firefox status bar. Figure 18-13 shows this in action. Notice that even the image header of the blog is highlighted, as it is a link to the main page.

An advantage of the LinkChecker Firefox extension is that it is cross-platform. It will run on any computer that Firefox runs on. The disadvantage of it is that, like the simple online services, it checks only one page at a time. For a more sophisticated solution, you need to look at stand-alone programs for your desktop. A number are available, of varying functionality and quality. A good place to start looking is in Google's directory, at `http://directory.google.com/Top/Computers/Software/Internet/Site_Management/Link_Management/`.

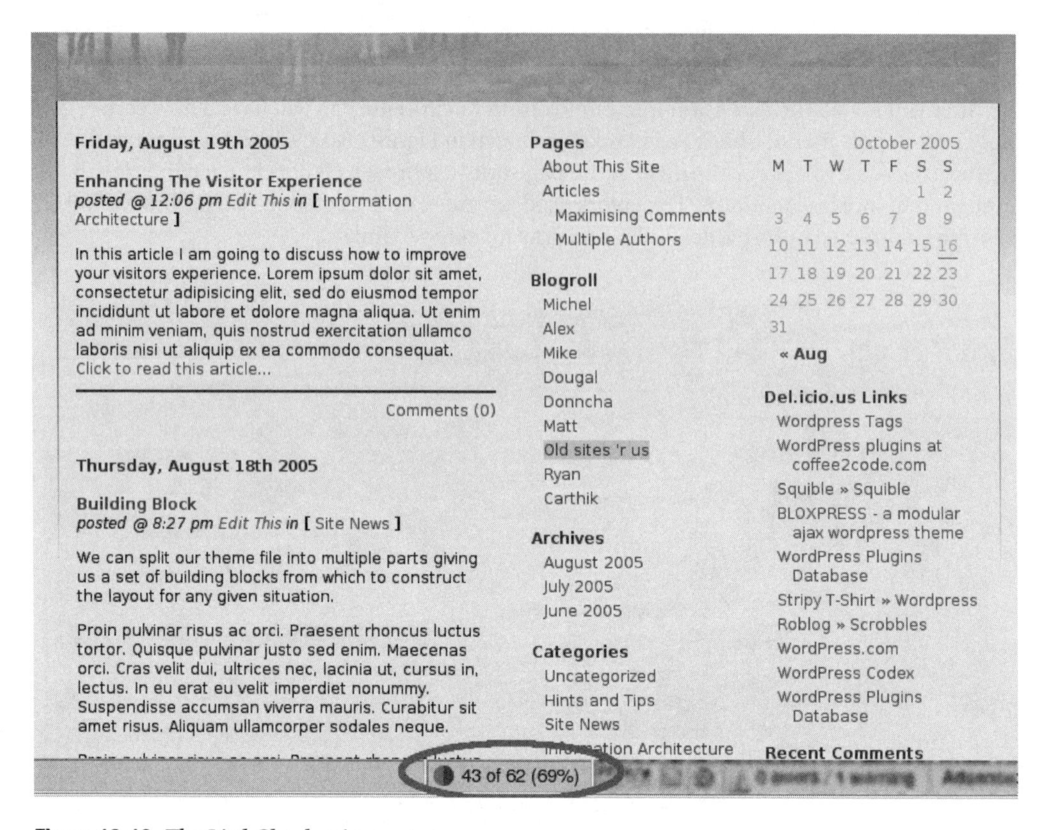

Figure 18-13. *The LinkChecker in progress*

Keeping Your Content Fresh

Along with search engines such as Google ranking fresh content highly, your readers will come to expect that every time they come back to visit, they will have something new to read. You can take several steps to help keep your content fresh.

Adding New Posts Regularly

One of the important things you can do to keep your community active is to add new posts regularly. Try to get into the habit of posting regularly. It often doesn't matter how often you post, as long as it is on a regular basis. If you can update once a week, or perhaps every four days, that sets a good pace.

Resist the temptation to post as often as possible. At first, you will probably be able to sustain that pace, but as soon as it becomes too much work—and it will unless it is your full-time job—you will start skipping days. As soon as you do that, you start to disappoint your readers, who will have come to expect very frequent new posts.

If you think of a lot of things to say ahead of schedule, save them in draft form for the time when you don't have anything new to say. If you are stuck for something new to say, it is worth checking that your static pages are still up-to-date. For example, does the About page still summarize what your site is about. If you have a policy page, does it still state your site policy? If you do update any of these pages, make a post about that update, inviting feedback.

Seeking New Readers

Submit your site to related directories and special-interest sites. Politely invite people to your site. Don't spam those other sites; show respect for their owners, who are likely trying to build their own readership. Always consider reciprocal links to sites that contain links to your site.

Keep abreast of new sites in your subject area. If new ones appear, visit them regularly to see if they offer potential to gain you new visitors. Comment on their stories, and post your own stories about the things they are discussing. Don't forget to use WordPress's Pingback and TrackBack capabilities to create an automatic relationship between the stories. Visitors from the other sites will come to read the stories on your site.

Keeping Your Site Interesting

Track your subject matter around the Web. Keep up-to-date with the changes in the field. It may be that over time, the slant of your blog will change as people's interests change or as your chosen field develops. Be sure to update old articles as appropriate.

For instance, maybe you wrote a speculative piece last year and now some of the things you speculated about have come to fruition. Write a new piece referencing the old article and either blow your own trumpet about how you guessed right, or comment on how things turned out if you got it wrong. It doesn't actually matter whether you were right or wrong; if you write interestingly about your subject, people will still read your post and comment on it.

Encouraging Contributors

If you can encourage some of your readers to contribute stories or articles, that is a great way to get more content for your blog. If you do have guest authors, make sure you come to an agreement over copyright and publishing rights. If they are writing explicitly for you, make sure to allow them to quote or reproduce their articles on their own sites.

It can also be worth investigating republishing third-party articles (with appropriate permissions, of course) as another source of new content. Many authors out there will be glad to have a platform for their writings.

Maintaining Security

The best way to maintain your blog's security is to keep up-to-date with WordPress releases. You can check the postings listed in the Dashboard on your administration pages. Any new releases, especially security fixes, will be noted there. If there are any new releases, the announcement usually details the steps you need to take to update your blog. Invariably with WordPress, the process is very simple.

It is also a good idea to check the home sites of any plug-ins and themes you have installed. Perhaps once a month is often enough. Again, any new releases or security fixes will be noted there.

Summary

This chapter covered how to back up and restore your blog. I've given you tips on how to keep your blog healthy and functioning. I've also given you some ideas on how to feed your blog—how to keep it fresh and interesting for your readers.

My intention in these six chapters about WordPress was to show you how you can use it to build an active and lively community centered on your interests. WordPress is a great tool for self-publishing. It's easy to shape to suit you and your readers.

If you aren't already up and running with WordPress, your next step should be to find a hosting service and go for it! Pick a subject you are passionate about, install WordPress, and start blogging!

Index

D

E

H

I

J

K

L

M

U

X